NO MORE SEPARATE SPHERES!

NEXT WAVE: WOMEN'S STUDIES BEYOND THE DISCIPLINES

A series edited by Inderpal Grewal, Caren Kaplan, & Robyn Wiegman

NO MORE

★ ★ ★ **A NEXT WAVE AMERICAN STUDIES READER**

SEPARATE SPHERES!

EDITED BY CATHY N. DAVIDSON AND JESSAMYN HATCHER

Duke University Press ★ *Durham and London* ★ 2002

© 2002 DUKE UNIVERSITY PRESS
All rights reserved
Printed in the United States of
America on acid-free paper ∞
Designed by Amy Ruth Buchanan
Typeset in Carter & Cone Galliard
by Tseng Information Systems, Inc.
Library of Congress Cataloging-in-
Publication Data appear on the last
printed page of this book.

For our teachers and our students

CONTENTS

Preface

CATHY N. DAVIDSON AND JESSAMYN HATCHER

By bringing together several essays from the influential "No More Separate Spheres!" special issue of *American Literature,* plus a number of classic essays and three new pieces commissioned especially for this volume, we have created a book intended as a core text in undergraduate and graduate courses on American literature, women's literature, feminist theory, or the public sphere. For undergraduates, *No More Separate Spheres!* is an introduction to a range of feminist criticism, beginning with our introduction that spells out relationships between women and men, femininity and masculinity, feminism, gender, sex, public and private culture, and the ideology of the separate spheres. Because individual essays treat a range of American authors—including Catharine Maria Sedgwick, Nathaniel Hawthorne, Herman Melville, Harriet Beecher Stowe, Catharine Beecher, Sarah Josepha Hale, Ralph Waldo Emerson, Frederick Douglass, Booker T. Washington, María Ampara Ruiz de Burton, Pauline Hopkins, W. E. B. Du Bois, Sarah Orne Jewett, Gwendolyn Brooks, Cynthia Kadohata, Chang-rae Lee, and Samuel Delany—this could also serve as a "case book" in an American literature survey course. For graduate students, *No More Separate Spheres!* exemplifies many different ways that gender can be approached and incorporated into literary interpretations and, conversely, shows how using gender as an explanatory rubric reveals new insights into texts, authors, literary history, and theory. For all—scholars or students—this book is designed to show how other factors (notably race, sexuality, class, nationalism, and affect) are essential to the gendered reading of American culture.

This book is a collaborative effort in every way, and one equally rooted in our lives as teachers and scholars. We have brought to this book our experiences team-teaching an undergraduate survey course, "American Literature, 1865–1915," in which we raised key issues about the multiple factors that go into literary interpretation and cultural analysis. Beginning in 1999, we also began meeting almost weekly to discuss our ideas about gender in this cultural moment and to decide which essays to include in our book in an order that would help students to grapple with foundational ideas in gender criticism. As we worked back and forth between our experiences as teachers and our own scholarly work, we also evolved ideas about what fundamental (and often unspoken) discussions had to be included in our introduction (1) to make this accessible to undergraduate and graduate students and, equally important, (2) clarify assumptions often hidden within divisive discussions of gender, feminism, postfeminism, and antifeminism (terms often conflated in the most heated of debates). We are convinced that our own dialogue, as well as our ongoing dialogues with our students, has led to a volume that will be the beginning of many discussions of "next wave" feminism. For that reason, we are especially grateful and honored to be among the first books included in the Next Wave series from Duke University Press edited by Inderpal Grewal, Caren Kaplan, and Robyn Wiegman.

This book is also a product of a cross-generational conversation that we have mined with gusto and delight. Since Cathy Davidson came into the profession at a formative time when feminist literary criticism was at its heyday and since Jessamyn Hatcher came through undergraduate and graduate school at a moment of intense feminist response and rebuttal to 1970s feminism, our conversations have been increasingly rich and exciting as we both reach toward new models of analysis that move beyond either the binary "separate spheres" paradigm or the sometimes dismissive critique of that model. Basically, this volume asks the reader to look for more creative, constructive, and exciting ways to discuss gender. To that end, we have profited from Davidson's historical materialist leanings and Hatcher's historical and ethnographic work on psychoanalysis in early twentieth-century America. We share a conviction that political criticism (and this book is avowedly political) must be rooted in the historical as well as in the psychological, and that it is crucial to understand that "identity" is always both individual and collective, a psychology enacted and performed within a specific historical time and place, and is socially situated and politically constituted. Much of the logic of "separate spheres" criticism (as we explain in the introduction) assumes different relationships between individual and collective identities—the personal and the political—without making explicit a theory of those relationships or how identity travels from the specific account to the generalization. In scholarly or casual generalizations about gender ("women want *x*" or "it's a guy thing"), we constantly ask what those statements really mean about living, individual women or men from diverse backgrounds, social circumstances, or generations.

Over the course of the two years that we have shaped this book and written the introduction, we have often found ourselves reflecting not only on our subject but also on the larger question of why so many political movements devolve from landmark (if simplistic) revolutions in consciousness (such as the canon debates that have altered forever what "American literature" is) to vehement (and often disrespectful) repudiations of those revolutions that lend new energy to next-generation criticism but often recapitulate in negative or reverse form the oversimplifications of the revolutionary forebears. Too often, and sadly, the process of critique by next-generation critics then leads to a rear-guard action by former revolutionaries who suddenly find themselves cast as (or eagerly cast themselves as) conservatives. It is an all-too-familiar social narrative: "I was once a radical, but now I have grown up and found my way." It is also one that is always warmly embraced (and exaggerated) by the culture as *the* paradigmatic story of social maturation, a perfect way of trivializing both youthful social action and those who dare to "keep the faith" into maturity. If that is true, then why bother? We present these diverse essays on gender to suggest that there can be other models than this dispiriting cultural narrative of immature social progressiveness and mature conservatism.

We write this preface in an increasingly conservative era of attacks against affirmative action, diversity, and reproductive freedom; diminished government support of a host of social programs and academic programs; fundamental changes to the structure and funding of public education, welfare, and self-help programs; laws that require mandatory imprisonment (including joining only Somalia among the world's nations that treat juvenile offenders as adults eligible for life imprisonment without parole); unlegislated ownership of handguns, and increases in military spending, including a renewal of effort to fund the scientifically untenable "Star Wars" programs of the Reagan era. Given external forces that would turn back the clock to the time *before* the gay activism of the 1980s, the feminist work of the 1970s, the antiwar efforts of the late 1960s, or the great civil rights advocacy of the late 1950s and 1960s, it becomes even more necessary to think beyond internecine models of feminist critique to larger antifeminist forces beyond.

As we have learned from preliminary studies of hiring practices at the University of California in the wake of Proposition 209 (which makes affirmative action or other forms of "preferential hiring" by race or gender illegal), women of all races as well as men of color are hurt by reactionary politics. Not surprising, then, are the results of surveys that reveal that the number of white women faculty who have been hired by the University of California system since Proposition 209 has decreased appreciably. The 1998 introduction to the original "No More Separate Spheres!" special issue of *American Literature* predicted exactly this result. We quote those predictions in full:

> Race was used, divisively, as the focus of the anti-affirmative action campaign for another reason. . . . By focusing on race, the campaign diverts attention from the issue of gender, de-emphasizing that white women, as a group, have been the largest beneficiaries of affirmative action. Indeed, opponents of affirmative action deploy rhetoric that encourages white women to think of themselves not as "women" but as "non-blacks" in order to elicit their vote against affirmative action— even though an end to affirmative action stands, potentially, to hurt them, as women, as much as it will hurt any other group. This is a 1990s version of the hideous divide-and-conquer tactic that has often been used to pit poor whites against African Americans. One could argue that if women had a more solid sense of themselves as a separate, identifiable political category, then this racially divisive tactic could not work. What, one should ask, has happened to feminist politics here?

Writing in spring 2001, as these predictions have come to pass, we reaffirm that divisive attempts to discover some "one true feminism" are as short-sighted as they are morally and socially objectionable. If it were simply a contest between one versus another repressed group, gender or other forms of progressive critique would be just as silly as reactionaries say it is. What we are aiming at is an expansive and appreciative way to assess literary and cultural texts that helps us understand ourselves—as individuals, as members of overlapping groups with multiple affiliations, and as citizens or noncitizens living within the borders of the world's most powerful and dominant nation. Each of those conditions changes the circumstances of the other, and *that* is the complex social reality that literature helps us to understand.

Many different cultures have a version of the Moses story—a tale of the great leader whose single-minded monomania is necessary to lead a straggly and doubtful band through the desert to the promised land but who dies (or is killed) before entering that land himself (rarely, herself). It is curious to ponder the reasons or need for this recurring and ambivalent myth of change and settlement. What we would suggest is that settling the land, sorting out the competing interests of a diverse populace, and coming up with equitable laws for supporting those different interests requires a very different temperament and way of seeing than does inspiring the masses to walk through an implausibly parted Red Sea. The ideology of unity against odds may be useful when you are in the middle of the desert; it can, however, be confining when you are trying to establish an equitable, just, and representative society. That is, admittedly, an awfully grandiose paradigm for explaining the difference between feminists of the 1970s and early 1980s who worked for astonishing changes in American social values, cultural norms, and literary evaluations and those later feminists, including scholars of color and queer theorists, who insistently challenged those earlier leaders with a range of diverse interests around race, sexuality, class, imperialism, and the transnational. Our point in drawing on such an outlandish example is simply to underline that we have here a pattern the world has seen many, many times before. Major social change often requires single-minded leaders who are willing to dispense with ambiguity or uncertainty to forge some new path or, stated negatively, who are unable to see anything beyond their own particular view and vision. It is a rare path-breaker who settles comfortably in the real, messy, contradictory, and yet plausible society that must be negotiated in the land beyond the dream.

The introduction spells out many of the assumptions hidden within the metaphor of the "separate spheres." The essays in this volume exemplify different forms of criticism that work within, without, or around those polarized spheres. We are grateful to all of our contributors for being part of this energizing discussion. We also appreciate the generous assistance, critical insights, and editorial suggestions offered by Margaret Barry, Alice Kaplan, Ada Norris, and our editor, Ken Wissoker, at Duke University Press. In creating this book together, we have enjoyed a fantastically enriching conversation, opening up myriad possibilities for our own scholarship and teaching.

We have each gained an increasing appreciation for both those who have gone before us and those who will come after, and thus we dedicate this volume, with deepest appreciation, to our teachers and to our students, with hope and gratitude for their contribution and inspiration.

Note

The essays included in this volume by Judith Fetterley, Marjorie Pryse, José F. Aranda Jr., Amy Kaplan, You-me Park and Gayle Wald, and Lauren Berlant originally appeared in the "No More Separate Spheres!" special issue of *American Literature* 70 (Sept. 1998), edited by Cathy N. Davidson. This volume earned the award for the "Best Special Issue of 1998" by the Council of Editors of Learned Journals and has influenced a number of articles and books that have come later. We have also included in this volume two essays from earlier issues of *American Literature*—Elizabeth Renker's "Herman Melville, Wife Beating, and the Written Page," *American Literature* 66 (March 1994): 124–50; and Siobhan Somerville's "Passing through the Closet in Pauline E. Hopkins's Contending Forces," *American Literature* 69 (March 1997): 139–64. Maurice Wallace's landmark essay "Constructing the Black Masculine: Frederick Douglass, Booker T. Washington, the Sublimits of African American Autobiography" originally appeared in *Subjects and Citizens: Nation, Race, and Gender from Oroonoko to Anita Hill*, ed. Michael Moon and Cathy N. Davidson (Durham, NC: Duke University Press, 1995), 245–70. In addition, we are pleased to include Linda K. Kerber's classic essay "Separate Spheres, Female Worlds, Woman's Place: The Rhetoric of Women's History," which first appeared in the *Journal of American History* 75 (June 1988): 9–39. Essays commissioned especially for this volume include Dana D. Nelson's "Representative/Democracy: Presidents, Democratic Management, and the Unfinished Business of Male Sentimentalism"; Ryan Schneider's "Fathers, Sons, Sentimentality, and the Color Line: The Not-Quite-Separate Spheres of W. E. B. Du Bois and Ralph Waldo Emerson"; and Christopher Newfield and Melissa Solomon's "'Few of Our Seeds Ever Came Up at All': A Dialogue on Hawthorne, Delany, and the Work of Affect in Visionary Utopias." The order of the essays has been changed to help this book serve in the undergraduate and graduate classroom. Also new are the preface, introduction, and bibliography.

Introduction

CATHY N. DAVIDSON AND JESSAMYN HATCHER

The term *separate spheres* in our title is a metaphor that has been used by scholars to describe a historically constituted ideology of gender relations that holds that men and women occupy distinct social, affective, and occupational realms. According to this separate spheres metaphor, there is a public sphere inhabited by men and a private sphere that is the domain of women. Scholars have searched for and found evidence of gender relations organized along these lines at various moments in the history of Western culture, but like to argue that the separate spheres ideology took on renewed power and urgency in nineteenth-century America. They insist that not only was nineteenth-century American society organized around the model of the separate spheres but also that the female sphere of sentiment, home, and hearth suddenly became a source of great national value, pride, and inspiration.

How these scholars prize this bifurcated social structure and the purported ascendancy of domesticity and sentimentalism in the nineteenth century varies widely. For some, the nineteenth century's appreciation of the female sphere meant a decline in the original Puritanical (and male) values that lead to the colonization of America, a revolution against England, and the creation of a new nation.[1] For others, the literature, ideas, and social activities of women in the nineteenth century were a high point in the history of women precisely because the values of the "feminine" social sphere had national cultural importance. Scholars working in this latter tradition, for instance, have generated landmark histories of literary production, women's friendship, the novel as a genre, and women's reading groups, to name only a few.[2] Whether assessing the contributions positively or negatively, together these scholars have created a composite portrait of a nineteenth-century United States where women were installed in female, domestic, sentimental, collective private spaces (basically, the world of the home), and men in the individualistic, public sphere of commerce, politics, and reason.

We have mapped out these scholarly traditions because the purpose of this volume is to dismantle them.[3] We have brought together thirteen essays that differently complicate the separate spheres model and question its underlying assumptions. Some of the essays contest the division between public and private life, showing how those two states are intimately inter-twined and mutually constitutive. Others are skeptical of a bifurcation of "men" and "women" that also implies qualities of "masculinity" and "femi-ninity"—as if such complex human qualities were unique, separable, and de-finable. Others refute the notion that "gender" means "women," or that any discussion about women or gender is necessarily "feminist" (whatever that means). Others argue that the term *woman* in the separate spheres debate actually describes only white, middle-class, Northeastern, and putatively heterosexual women. Still others suggest that the neat model of the sepa-rate spheres attributed to the nineteenth century really describes unspoken assumptions (some would say prejudices) held by contemporary critics who analyze the public sphere as if it were inhabited only by men. By bringing these essays together, we seek to find ways to describe American literature and life that acknowledge the complex factors contributing to gender roles, everyday life, political forms, and creative expression in American society and American literature over the last two hundred years.

Thus the challenges our contributors issue to the separate spheres rubric are methodological, historical, and political. Building on the insights of black feminist criticism, queer theory, and post-Habermasian studies of the interdependence of the private and public spheres, the essays suggest that the explanatory power of the separate spheres model ultimately resides in a concept of "woman" that is historically circumscribed and narrowly de-fined.[4] Yet, as each of the essays makes clear, the contributors are less in-vested in critiquing the separate spheres model per se than they are in explor-ing what thinking past this pervasive way of reading the nineteenth century can let us freshly see and know.

Many of the essays collected below disrupt the fixity of the separate spheres model by introducing the importance of other variables the construct has been symptomatically unable to address—crucially race, sexuality, class, nation, empire, affect, region, and occupation. And many of the essays place these variables, texts, and authors into productive contact and conversation with each other in a way that the congealed binary logic of the separate spheres has worked to cordon off from one another. Our intention is that *No More Separate Spheres!* will yield both new readings and histories of nineteenth-century America and fresh critical tools for its continued exploration.

A Brief History of the Separate Spheres Debate

Because our own work depends on the contributions of earlier feminist scholars, it is worth attending to the history of the separate spheres debate with care. The flagship piece in our volume is Linda K. Kerber's important 1988 historiographic "Separate Spheres, Female Worlds, Woman's Place: The Rhetoric of Women's History," which details the ascendancy of the separate spheres as an explanatory model over the past several decades. Kerber suggests that the separate spheres metaphor has a complex history intertwined with the history of twentieth-century academic feminism.

According to Kerber, the renewed energy invested in this model derived largely from the 1945 republication of Alexis de Tocqueville's classic *Democracy in America* (1840), a survey of distinctive features of American culture, including the situation of women, based on Tocqueville's visit to the country in the 1830s. "In no country has such constant care been taken as in America to trace two clearly distinct lines of actions for the two sexes," Tocqueville observed, "and to make them keep pace with the other, but in two pathways that are always different." In the post–World War II era, *Democracy in America* became, as Kerber notes, "among the few—perhaps the only—classic texts read by students of American history that seriously examined the situation of women in American society. When historians—whether inspired by Simone de Beauvoir or Eleanor Flexner or Betty Friedan—began again to study women's history, they could point to Tocqueville for evidence that at least one classic Great Author had conceded the significance of their subject."

From the outset, then, the separate spheres paradigm gave scholars interested in women's history not only a potent organizing metaphor but also a source within the dominant culture for legitimizing their interest. Moreover, it seems likely that Toqueville's separate spheres discourse might have had special appeal in the post–World War II era and may have been less convincing as a way to describe what actually happened in the nineteenth century than as an explanation for what was happening, ideologically, in the American 1950s as white, middle-class women (who had the vote, could hold elected office, and had worked in factories and boardrooms during the war) were being encouraged to return to their domestic roles as wives of returning GIs. One could even say that a generation of women historians who felt marginalized by the neglect of women's history used the separate spheres metaphor to write about neglected women of a previous century.

Significantly, the major feminist historians of the 1960s and the early 1970s began by using the separate spheres paradigm as a tool for depicting the legal, institutional, occupational, and affective *limitations* placed on women. Contributions from such critics as Barbara Welter, Aileen S. Kraditor, and Gerda Lerner anatomized what Welter termed "The Cult of True Womanhood," arguing that relegation of women to the domestic sphere subordinated and devalued them. It wasn't until another decade—in the late 1970s and into the 1980s—that numerous critics such as Nina Baym, Carroll Smith-Rosenberg, and many others (including two of our contributors, Judith Fetterley and Marjorie Pryse) began to turn the metaphor from something negative into something potentially positive. These critics argued that women's culture—charged by female bonding, spirituality, political commitment, and sometimes homoeroticism (if never quite lesbian sexuality)—was separate from men's and, through marginality, had found a source of female cultural power and productivity worthy of celebration. As Kerber explains, given these different evaluations, "The language of the separate spheres was vulnerable to sloppy use"; when scholars used the metaphor of separate spheres, they "often interchangeably" referred to "an ideology *imposed on* women, a culture *created by* women, a set of boundaries *to be observed by* women."[5]

The Limits of the Metaphor

For all the different ways of understanding the separate spheres, the arguments also share some basic assumptions. Chief among these is the assumption that the term *women* is transparent. There is an assumption that *gender* means *women,* that *feminism* means *women,* and that what a woman is needs no definition or qualification. In separate spheres discourse, *woman* is distinct from and even opposite to *man;* nothing else counts. By this logic, *woman* is the one universal or stable category, and other attributes are transient or irrelevant. When applied to literature, the criticism that is produced by those holding to a separate spheres model requires that gender is the most or, sometimes only, significant subject for discussion, whether focusing on the gender of the author, the characters, or the reader. No other personal conditions of identity or material conditions of authorship are relevant except as they support the separate spheres model. For example, Harriet Jacobs, a poor, African American woman—who spent years hiding in her grandmother's nine-by-seven-by-three-foot attic crawl -space to avoid sexual exploitation by a white slaveholder—is a "woman" in the same definitive way as Catharine Beecher, a Long Island daughter from the privileged Beecher family, is a "woman."[6]

Obviously, for every generalization about women that might be relevant to both Harriet Jacobs and Catharine Beecher, there are many more that miss one or the other. Black feminist critics were the first to powerfully deconstruct the racialized nature of the "woman" about whom separate spheres arguments were being made. In 1982, Gloria T. Hull, Patricia Bell Scott, and Barbara Smith published the now-classic *All the Women Are White, All the Blacks are Men, But Some of Us Are Brave,* a collection of essays whose provocative title itself undermines the many discussions of "women" or "African Americans" of the 1970s that left black women out of the explanation, description, or theories.

Many other critiques have followed, deconstructing the heteronormative biases, class assumptions, and nationalist positionings of separate spheres criticism. Although some separate spheres critics accept these important adjustments in the paradigm, others have insisted that these critiques are no longer "feminist." Because most separate spheres criticism rests on the assumption that "woman" is a *universal* gender signifier, attention to other factors is thought to compromise the status of "woman" as explanation and diminishes the feminist impact of the argument.[7]

By contrast, the contributors to *No More Separate Spheres!* argue that we have run the gamut of what the separate spheres model can tell us about nineteenth-century America and beyond. They are not, by any means, saying that gender is irrelevant to an understanding of American literature or human identity. Questions of gender remain crucial to American literary study. Rather they are saying that many other factors complicate the binary model of men versus women. In fact, these contributors would insist that if we want to understand operations of gender, we *must* understand other factors contributing to identity and literary creativity.

Most of the essayists in *No More Separate Spheres!* insist that it is nearly impossible to find any experience that can be solely ascribed to the condition of being a "woman." For example, You-me Park and Gayle Wald, in "Native Daughters in the Promised Land," reconsider the domesticity prized by separate spheres critics as a calm, intimate, loving, nearly sacred female space removed from the bustle of consumer capitalism. Park and Wald examine the condition of "domestics"—female laborers (either white working-class women or women of color) whose invisible toil allowed the nineteenth-century "female world of love and ritual" to flourish so "effortlessly." They ask why isn't the female domestic housekeeper, working for minimal wages, every bit as much a woman as the virtuous believer in the salutary power of a genteel domesticity beyond the marketplace? Park and Wald, like many of the authors in this book, insist that gendered criticism must be attuned to other factors of race, class, and occupation.

Another salient feature of post–separate spheres criticism is that it does not assume that women (or members of any identity group) were virtuous simply because they lacked the status, power, and position attained by middle-class white men. Being excluded from full citizenship by the U.S. Constitution does not, in and of itself, make one good. Too much separate spheres criticism carries an unexamined weight of sanctimony, as if powerlessness *equals* virtue. It does not. Power is not uniformly distributed, and neither is virtue. The same nineteenth-century middle-class woman unfairly excluded from the world of public politics might well be a tyrant to the slave or indentured servant who cleans her home and tends her children. Post–separate spheres criticism asks us to attend to those shifting dynamics of power and privilege. It insists that gender is a significant contributor to human identity, but that it does not encompass, stand in for, obviate, or trump all other factors. Nor does "being a woman" exculpate women in situations where their words, actions, or prejudices are harmful to others.

In fact, post–separate spheres criticism is more generally circumspect about awarding virtue or assigning blame, realizing that both literature and human nature are too complex for a rating on a kind of meritorious hit parade. Similarly, post–separate spheres critics insist that literary criticism should not be hagiography—especially because hagiography almost inevitably results in fudging the historical record or covering up the occasional warts so that the writer can seem perfect. This new, posthagiographic model is important because, between separate spheres criticism of the 1970s and 1980s and the postseparatist essays in this volume, came a backlash against white feminist literary criticism that could be even more sanctimonious in its diligent fault-finding than had been the earlier attempts to valorize the nineteenth-century women authors who had long been neglected or under-appreciated. As narrow as some of the first-generation separate spheres critics may now seem to have been in their uncritical appreciation of women writers, there is something extremely suspect in those who condemn the prejudices of nineteenth-century white women so that we can return to a literary history dominated by white men. Richard Brodhead, Walter Benn Michaels, and other critics who gleefully point out the sins of the fore-mothers or of nineteenth-century men of color to return us to a "gender-neutral" or "color-blind" form of literary analysis are simply part of a swinging pendulum that gets us, precisely, back to where we began.[8] It adds little new knowledge or interest to our understanding of either the nineteenth-century world or our own. More to the point, this moralistic form of criticism assumes that finding a failing in an author means that we should not read that author. Post–separate spheres criticism is a lot more curious and less condemnatory. It also supports reading other kinds of cultural texts, including tracts, advice books, letters, diaries, newspapers, and other ephemeral forms that can shed light on curious concatenations of social attitudes and identity formations. It can move with dexterity between elite and popular culture or between radical and reactionary works because such comparisons often yield a wealth of historical insights. It is a criticism with fewer rules and more interest in how such rules are constructed and what is or is not included within these rules. Post–separate spheres criticism also has a certain self-reflexive modesty about itself and assumes that the present era has as many blind spots as past eras, and it is the job of the next generation of critics to uncover those, too.

As the late scholar Lora Romero argues in her landmark work *Home Fronts: Domesticity and Its Critics in the Antebellum United States,* "Study of nineteenth-century culture seems to have consistently organized itself around binarisms (dominant/marginal, conservative/countercultural, unconscious/self-reflexive, active/passive)."[9] Romero follows Michel Foucault in noting that these dyadic models see both power and resistance as so constant, centralized, and static that they can be separated from the immediate social situations they pervade. However, we are arguing that—whether evaluating nineteenth-century American culture *or* the contemporary analysis of that culture—it is often hard to mark precisely where power ends and resistance begins. How can we even begin to assess a "sentimental power" that both derives in compensatory fashion from political exclusion and, at the same time, is based on forms of privilege (of race and class, for example) that derive from exactly the same political system that excludes women (of all races) from voting? Post–separate spheres criticism focuses on those intertwining relations and wants us to understand how complicated, confused, and even contradictory they are.

The essays in this volume tend to define both power and subjectivity as mobile and uneven in their development and inconsistent in their deployment. As Romero insists, not every text or every author is going to be equally perceptive, persuasive, or progressive on every issue of concern to readers and critics (whether in the nineteenth century or the present). One text need not address "the entire range of relationships, extending from the sexual to the international realm." As Romero wisely concludes, by understanding these limitations in how power operates (and how fully any one person can resist power), we can also "temper our disappointment when we realize that authors have not done the impossible; that is, discovered the one key for the liberation of all humankind."[10]

A positive outcome of a post-Foucauldian understanding of the complicated interconnections between dominance and resistance may well be what Eve Kosofsky Sedgwick has termed "reparative criticism," a criticism that concerns itself less with the policing of literature for its failings than an appreciation of the daunting complexities of the attempt to represent, with the linguistic tools available to any author, the most freighted and fraught social, political, and psychological problems of one's day.[11] Sedgwick's reparative criticism is one of the best antidotes we know to the despair of the Foucauldian regime of literary hypercriticalism. We are seeking a post-Foucauldian model of criticism based on the complexity and interdependence of power and resistance, coupled with an awareness that aesthetic expression is never monolithic and unambiguous. This model allows for the critique (even quite pointed at times) of one aspect of a text or a writer without the trashing of everything that writer is and represents. Pointing out someone else's faults does not make one, de facto, a revolutionary. There is an easy self-congratulation that comes from one critic decrying the political myopia of a preceding critic—and then doing nothing at all to further the political aims that the first critic was trying (however imperfectly) to promote. Post–separate spheres criticism is more fluid in its evaluation of how power operates and is coopted and therefore tends to be both less hyperbolic in its appreciations and more temperate in its condemnations (neither of which makes it any less politically engaged or motivated).

The Canon Debates

Part 1 of this volume focuses on issues of the canon. By *canon*, we mean a body of texts that has been sanctioned as definitive or praised as classic. Canonical texts—such as Thoreau's *Walden*, Hawthorne's *The Scarlet Letter*, or Melville's *Moby Dick*—make up the standard syllabus of the American literature classroom as well as the typical focus of literary criticism. A discussion of the process of canonization—how texts come to be taught and how that syllabus changes from decade to decade—necessarily is both an aesthetic and a political discussion.

The essays that make up part 1 depict how interwined recent efforts to make the canon more inclusive are with separate spheres paradigms. Through their anatomizations of the politics and sentiments underpinning the refurbished canon, the essayists in this section reveal the deep structures of longing and loss undergirding separate spheres logic. For example, the essays in part 1 implicitly and explicitly acknowledge that feminist literary critics of the 1970s and early 1980s may well have adopted the separate spheres model out of a similar sense of frustration with women's exclusion from the literary canon. Indeed, we suggest that part of what has made the metaphor of the separate spheres not only compelling and resilient but also ultimately unconvincing lies in the fact that it is compensatory in two ways that are mutually sustaining. On the one hand, the gender binary has allowed the literary historian to focus exclusively on women writers who have been excluded from the standard histories; on the other hand, it roots its logic of exclusivity in an explanation of nineteenth-century binary gender relations. That is, the metaphor allows the literary historian both to model the nineteenth century's binary view of gender and to practice it.

Certainly the view of literary history that prevailed in the decades before the explosion of feminist criticism in the late 1970s was remarkably, monolithically masculinist. F. O. Matthiessens's landmark volume *American Renaissance* (1941),[12] perhaps more than any other, had argued that the nineteenth-century American writing that counted (whether judged by aesthetic principles or liberal democratic ideas of nationalism) was written by five "Renaissance" writers: Emerson, Thoreau, Melville, Hawthorne, and Whitman (not even Emily Dickinson made the grade). The New Critics of the next decades solidified the interest in these writers by concentrating on close, textual analysis of a few selected works deemed to be "masterpieces," mostly by Mattheissen's pantheon of writers.

In 1977, Ann Douglas's massive study *The Feminization of American Culture* worked once again to entrench the separatist model of literary history, although her take on the feminization of nineteenth-century American culture was more dystopic than utopic. Douglas argued that Puritanism represented the hard-edged, masculine side of American culture, whereas by the last decades of the eighteenth century a more polite, feminine, weaker (both philosophically and aesthetically) version of American culture prevailed, ultimately devolving into the sentimental strain in American literature.

Douglas's thesis of devolution helped spur a range of supporting and contravening studies of the separate spheres, most notably by Nina Baym in her encyclopedic *Woman's Fiction: A Guide to Novels by and about Women in America, 1820–1870* (1978), a book that argued for and identified an interesting body of nineteenth-century women's writing. In her now-classic essay "Melodramas of Beset Manhood: How Theories of American Fiction Exclude Women Authors" (1981), Baym also contested the notion that a canon was comprised of "masterpieces."[13] As its wry title suggests, this essay looks at the various jealousies and anxieties that, in the nineteenth century as in the twentieth, led to the privileging of a canon of white male writers.

This combative strain in the feminist literary analysis of canon formation culminated in Jane Tompkins's *Sensational Designs: The Cultural Work of American Fiction, 1790–1860* (1985),[14] which both supports and contradicts the separatist view of the nineteenth century by showing how a classic text of "woman's fiction," such as Harriet Beecher Stowe's *Uncle Tom's Cabin,* performed its own version of political work through its sentimental, spiritual agenda, and how authors such as Charles Brockden Brown enacted their own version of the sentimental. Finally, Tompkins turns Nathaniel Hawthorne's complaint against the "d——d mob of scribbling women" on its head by arguing that, rather than being the great artist victimized by all those women producing bestsellers, Hawthorne originally gained his status through a confraternity of male influence and privilege.

Baym's and Tompkins's valuations were two of myriad contributions by scholars who worked to make visible a women's tradition in American literature. Scholars supported these theoretical treatments with archival work, finding, editing, and reprinting dozens of forgotten titles to make nineteenth-century American women's writing available to contemporary readers. Series at Beacon Press, the Feminist Press, Oxford University Press (notably the Schomburg Library of Nineteenth-Century Black Women Writers), and Rutgers University Press—to name just a few, changed the canon of American literature.[15]

As this history shows, the paradigm is shared, albeit in an unlikely co-incidence between Tocqueville and mid–twentieth-century feminist liter-ary scholars. Because of this lineage, the separate spheres paradigm has come to seem as if hardwired to feminist recovery projects. In this way, the femi-nist work that changed the face of literary criticism, American studies, and the larger academy as it changed what counted as "American literature" can seem inextricably linked to separate spheres thinking. To recognize the his-toricity of the weld between separate spheres paradigms and feminist contri-butions to reshaping the American literary canon is helpful in several ways. To begin with, it adds to our understanding, at least in part, of why let-ting go of the separate spheres construct can feel so difficult. Projects like *No More Separate Spheres!*—clearly dependent on the contributions and re-covery projects of earlier feminist scholars—can seem at best to suffer from ingratitude or grandiosity and, at worst, amnesia. But exploring this history also puts us in a position to ask how deep or how necessary the accord really is between the separate spheres construct and the feminist transformation of the literary canon. To argue that, enabled by a particular set of histori-cal circumstances, the separate spheres paradigm proved useful to scholars seeking to redress the systematic exclusion of women from the canon of American literature is not the same as arguing that the shape of the refur-bished canon depends, whether theoretically or ontologically, on the logic of the separate spheres. By extension, as we've been arguing in this introduc-tion thus far, it's worth asking how necessary the separate spheres model, and, moreover, the particular ways of thinking about gender it promotes, is to our work as feminists.

The essays by Linda Kerber, Judith Fetterley, José F. Aranda Jr., Eliza-beth Renker, and Marjorie Pryse collected in part 1 of *No More Separate Spheres!* examine the issues constellating around separate spheres and can-onicity in depth and from a variety of points of view. We have gathered these five essays because, in different ways, they not only talk about the process of canonization but also contest the uniformity of this process, including the vaunted categories of "women's fiction" or "canonical author." As these essays differently attest, none of those terms is simple. Each essay helps us think through the politics and meanings of recovery as well as what is lost by the heroic narrative of "recovery." Each finds still other ways that the "separate spheres" is not only faulty as metaphor but greatly compromised (and maybe even chimerical) as fact.

These essays speak for themselves. However, we wish to look at one of these essays precisely because of the brushfire of attention caused when first published in *American Literature* in 1994, a reaction that went all the way to the *New York Times Magazine*.[16] Elizabeth Renker pairs the most canonical of American writers—Herman Melville—with what, by now, is a canonical subject of feminist criticism (wife abuse), and ties both of these to Melville's frustrations as a noncommercial writer. Her argument that Melville's inability to find a public for his work—that is, melodramas of beset manhood—is partly what motivated his alleged physical violence. Even more notably, Melville's own anguish as a writer must be read backward from his illustrious, canonical status. By that we mean that "being canonical" is an estate not to which one is born but to which one arrives after time. The canonical status of the hallowed author can too often obscure the painful path of the living writer. Impressively, at the same time that Renker documents this disparity—between the living writer and the canonical author—she points out the hidden labor of women that undergirds the famously "womanless" writings. In short, on every level, this essay gives us pause as we understand the rhythms and privileges of canonicity as well as the material conditions of gender roles and relationships.

The Case against Domesticity

Part 2, "Domesticity Undone: Case Studies," revisits and remaps one of separate spheres criticism's most favored terrains: the world of the home. The contributors to this section demonstrate, through a series of case studies, how domesticity is saturated by and dependent on a range of factors, terms, and agents imagined to lie outside its domain. Showing, for instance, the links between domesticity and imperialism; domesticity and the labor of women of color; and domesticity, race, and sexuality, the essays in this section puncture the logic of separate spheres that constructs domesticity as feminine, private, white, and apolitical. Factors fantasized to be in opposition to one another, these essays show, are in fact welded together.

In this way, the "domestic sphere" becomes one of the most productive sites for revealing its own limitations.

Like much separate spheres criticism, the work clustering around domesticity has tended to suffer from a myopic focus on the lives and domesticities of white middle-class women. As such, studies that have grown out of this tradition have been most useful to explain the conditions and everyday lives of a narrowly circumscribed group of Americans. The four essays collected in the second section—Amy Kaplan's "Manifest Domesticity," Siobhan Somerville's "Passing through the Closet in Pauline E. Hopkins's *Contending Forces*," Maurice Wallace's "Constructing the Black Masculine," and You-me Park and Gayle Wald's "Native Daughters in the Promised Land"— each revisit scenes of domesticity. But by pressurizing the paradigm of the separate spheres they radically multiply and revise both the meanings of "domesticity" and what we can learn from their continued exploration.

No longer guided by separate spheres discourse, Kaplan, Somerville, Wallace, and Park and Wald demonstrate that domesticity has as much to tell us about the constitution and operation of race, class, sexuality, nation, empire, and citizenship as it does about gender. Thus, these essays, along with other contributions to the volume, make a powerful argument for the necessity of evolving histories and methodologies that can begin to account for the ways these historical fields are constituted through and against one another. Strikingly, in "Constructing the Black Masculine," Wallace demonstrates the particular salience of paradigms developed by Hortense Spillers and other black feminist critics to understand the operations of "domesticity" under a slave world where motherhood is determinative because fatherhood is absent. He looks in particular at the autobiographies of two famous black men born into slavery, Frederick Douglass and Booker T. Washington, who were the "bastard sons of enslaved black mothers and obscure white fathers/masters" to show how the "nuclear relations" of the vaunted family celebrated in the nineteenth-century "cult of domesticity" matter far "less in slavocracy than the bourgeois imperatives of ownership, dominance, commodity, and (re)production." Wallace's psychoanalytic theorization of the slave domesticity and the central Oedipal panic it necessarily induces in black men not only amplifies the history of domesticity but also exposes the conditions of stability, affluence, comfort, autonomy, and patrilineage that silently support the nineteenth-century middle-class white woman's celebration of hearth and home.

As all of the contributors to part 2 argue, one of the most serious limitations of a separate spheres model is its tendency to block such alternate historical accounts. It also tends to ignore material, political, and social conditions, concealing the operations of capitalism, imperialism, or (as Wallace demonstrates so powerfully) slavery that are necessary support both financially and ideologically for the American nineteenth-century middle-class home. Moreover, contrary to the fear that expanding categories of analysis will eclipse our ability to attend to gender, these essays show that any understanding of the operations of gender in the nineteenth-century United States and beyond *depend* on our continued exploration of other co-terminous and co-constitutive realms. As Park and Wald write, "Instead of producing analyses that make visible the interconnectedness of terms like race and gender, the binary of public-private initiates a process in which these terms eventually annul one another. . . . Our goal . . . is to make these categories more historically responsible and responsive to the needs of subjects who have been marginalized by the separate spheres model."

Public Sentiment

Within the rigid logic of the separate spheres, the originary organizing binary of male/female on which the concept is grounded aligns and affiliates with any number of other dualities: woman/man, femininity/masculinity, emotion/reason, sentiment/logic, domesticity/politics, private/public, and so on. As we have discussed above, reading the nineteenth century through these inflexible binaries has often worked to obscure the centrality of other historically constituted fields and terms to the social relations, conditions, institutions, and quotidian lives structuring and populating the nineteenth century. In addition, we suggest, the separate spheres model has narrowed the possibility that terms and fields occupying "opposite" sides of these binaries will come into contact and conversation with one another: That is, separate spheres logic creates a structural disincentive for thinking about nation in relationship to home, politics in relationship to privacy, femininity in relationship to reason, and so on. The essays collected in the third section of this volume, "Public Sentiment," strive to dislodge this tendency.

In particular, contributors Lauren Berlant, Dana Nelson, Ryan Schneider, and Christopher Newfield and Melissa Solomon ask us to rethink the historical locations and cultural work of sentiment. Interrogating the separate spheres logic that yokes feeling exclusively and often putatively to femininity, these essayists chart sentimentality's centrality to the constitution and operations of a range of cultural productions and agents often imagined to be outside sentiment's purview. Representative democracy, national identity, masculinity, public intellectualism, and utopian liberation projects, although frequently fantasized to inhabit a realm safely outside the scope of sentiment, are, as the essayists teach us, critically saturated by it. Dedicated to theorizing sentiment's changing meanings across time, the essays in this section also demonstrate that whether used by its practitioners or its critics, "sentimentality" is a complex cultural phenomenon whose affective power can be politically persuasive, manipulative, or obfuscatory.

In different ways, the essays in part 3 have already moved beyond the separate spheres. In the process, they give us a taste of how exciting criticism can look in a post–separate spheres era. Pairing texts that are "normally" not read alongside each other (the Articles of Confederation and a popular biography by Mason Weems, *Uncle Tom's Cabin* with *The Bridges of Madison County,* Emerson and Du Bois, Hawthorne and Delany), these essays show that if we can move past separate spheres blinders, texts that seemingly have nothing to do with one another suddenly talk to each other in new ways. By bringing together popular and high culture, nineteenth- and twentieth-century authors, male and female, black and white, new relations among texts become apparent. As the final essay (which takes an experimental form) dramatizes, new conversations continue to enact new ways of structuring the academic essay. This, too, seems necessary as part of the process of piercing the separate spheres.

What we have in these essays is an unpunitive criticism that acknowledges and appreciates the complicated and sometimes even vexed interrelationship between identity factors and politics. They do not assume that sharing certain identity characteristics necessitates a shared political view or a consistent one. They explore contradictions within and around politics as well as the excrescence of nationalist fervor or sentimental affect above and beyond what can be simply explained by political affiliation or by gender. They show not only how the categories are confused but also writers themselves in the process of working in, around, through, and beyond those categories.

Pedagogical Aims

Many contemporary teachers might recall a moment in a course dealing with gender when one of the bright women in the class put up her hand and said, "I'm not a feminist, but . . ." We suggest that at least part of that daunt-ing denial and affirmation stems from the residue of a notion of feminism tethered to "separate spheres." Separate spheres feminism, we suggest, has the potential to foster anxiety for students who—at least in part thanks to the gains made by women's movements—grew up in a world where spheres could be characterized by a fluidity seemingly at odds with generalizations about women's or men's worlds, behavior, character, aptitude, or other at-tributes. However, at the same time that experience might be fluid (i.e., mothers who are full-time CEOs), the rhetoric most readily available often remains as static and bifurcated as the separate spheres. (Classroom mo-ments in which a student says, "Women are more emotional and nurturing than men" are as common as the moments when a student says, "I'm not a feminist but . . ."). What is helpful about the separate spheres debate—and the literature that tackles these issues—is that it offers a different model for discussing feminism, one that attends to fluidity, contradiction, and uneven developments.

As such, we are particularly interested in the ways the essays collected herein might serve as one foundation for new approaches to teaching nine-teenth-century American literature alongside its feminist historiography. In the imaginative labor of transforming *No More Separate Spheres!* from a spe-cial issue of *American Literature* into its present form, we've conceived of the collection as a kind of rapturous textbook accompanying an ideal survey course. If there is one feature we want students to take away from *No More Separate Spheres!,* it is a sense of the complexity of the categories of analy-sis we choose, the way those categories change historically, and the way the categories themselves are only crude maps to more complex subjects. In this introduction and the essays that follow, the treatment of gender serves as a crucially important case study illustrating these points.

No one critic can ever do justice to all categories of analysis or identity, nor can any one literary work. (What we are longing for when we ask them to do so is part of the subject of this book.) Neither, of course, can one col-lection. But by convening one group of important scholars and asking for their various points of view on the question of the separate spheres, we hope to set in motion conversations that will honor the subject's complexity.

It is in this spirit we conclude with ten interrelated points crucial to cur-rent discussions of gender that have lead us to our admonitory title, *No More Separate Spheres!:*

(1) Gender is a vital and interesting category of analysis. Whether in literary interpretation or in critiques of modernity or the public sphere, ignoring the role of gender diminishes the argument.

(2) Because gender remains significant, it is important to historicize what we mean by "gender." Moreover, it is important to historicize its significance: how and why it gained interpretive salience—and why it's important to restate its importance again and again.

(3) Gender is a variable and limited category that does not exist by, for, in, or of itself. It changes over time; it is shaped and changed by other factors; and, in turn, it shapes other conditions of existence ("representative democracy," "the professional managerial class," "the flaneur," "the individual autonomous subject," and so forth).

(4) Insisting on gender as the sole factor motivating critical analysis has too often led to devaluing other factors. Gender, race, class, and sexuality are mutually constitutive.

(5) *Gender* does not mean "woman." Men have one, too. And not only that—as queer theory has shown, masculinity and femininity don't map onto male and female bodies in predictable ways.

(6) Gender does not entail intrinsic, universal, or necessary affective qualities (such as sentiment). It is suspect to generalize about which behaviors, emotions, actions, or beliefs are synonymous with or even characteristic of all women or all men.

(7) Being concerned with gender does not make one a feminist. Being vitally concerned with race, sexuality, or class does not prevent one from being a feminist.

(8) The definition of *feminism* is neither transparent nor universal. Terms such as *feminist, antifeminist, sexist,* or *misogynist* require definition and explanation.

(9) Adding other categories to the discussion of gender in no way diminishes its political impact. Leaving out gender as a category of analysis limits political impact.

(10) If using the metaphor of the "separate spheres" requires ignoring points 1–9, then it is time we gave it up. It has outlasted its usefulness.

Notes

1 See, for instance, Ann Douglas's classic work, *The Feminization of American Culture* (New York: Knopf, 1977).

2 A few examples of this vast body of work include Carroll Smith-Rosenberg, "The Female World of Love and Ritual: Relations between Women in Nineteenth-Century American," *Signs* 1 (autumn 1975): 1–29; Barbara Sicherman, "Sense and Sensibility: A Case Study of Women's Reading in Late-Victorian America," in *Reading in America: Literary and Social History,* ed. Cathy N. Davidson (Baltimore, Md.: Johns Hopkins University Press, 1989), 201–25; Nancy Cott, *The Bonds of Womenhood: "Woman's Sphere" in New England, 1780–1835* (New Haven, Conn.: Yale University Press); Mary Kelley, *Private Woman, Public Stage: Literary Domesticity in Nineteeth-Century America* (New York: Oxford University Press, 1984).

3 We by no means want to suggest that we are alone in this project: Criticism with the aim of dismantling the separate spheres itself has a long and interesting history. See, for instance, Linda K. Kerber, Nancy F. Cott, Robert Gross, Lynn Hunt, Carroll Smith-Rosenberg, and Christine M. Stansell, "Beyond Roles, Beyond Spheres: Thinking about Gender in the Early Republic," *William and Mary Quarterly* 46 (July 1989): 565–85. For recent discussions that complicate the separate spheres model, see Leonard Tennenhouse and Philip Gould, eds., "America the Feminine," a special issue of *differences: A Journal of Feminist Cultural Studies* 11, no. 3 (1999/2000) and Karen Kilcup, ed., *Soft Canons: American Women Writers and Masculine Tradition* (Iowa City: University of Iowa Press, 1999).

4 Salient critiques of the separate spheres model from black feminist critics include the now-classic collection edited by Gloria T. Hull, Patricia Bell Scott, and Barbara Smith, *All the Women Are White, All the Blacks Are Men, But Some of Us Are Brave* (Old Westbury, N.Y.: Feminist Press, 1982). For more recent contributions to this extensive body of work, see Houston Baker Jr., *Workings of the Spirit: The Poetics of Afro-American Women's Writing* (Chicago: University of Chicago Press, 1991); Hazel V. Carby, *Reconstructing Womanhood: The Emergence of the Afro-American Woman Novelist* (New York: Oxford University Press, 1987); Patricia Hill Collins, *Black Feminist Thought: Knowledge, Consciousness, and the Politics of Empowerment* (New York: Routledge, 1990); Ann duCille, *The Coupling Convention: Sex, Text, and Tradition in Black Women's Fiction* (New York: Oxford University Press, 1993); Henry Louis Gates Jr., ed., *Reading Black, Reading Feminist: A Critical Anthology* (New York: Meridian, 1990); Karla F. C. Holloway, *Moorings and Metaphors: Figures of Culture and Gender in Black Women's Literature* (New Brunswick, N.J.: Rutgers University Press, 1992); bell hooks, *Feminist Theory: Thinking Feminist, Thinking Black* (Boston: South End Press, 1989); Deborah E. McDowell, *"The Changing Same": Black Women's Literature, Criticism, and Theory* (Bloomington: Indiana University Press, 1995); Claudia Tate, *Domestic Allegories*

of Political Desire: The Black Heroine's Text at the Turn of the Century (New York: Oxford University Press, 1992); and Hortense J. Spillers, ed., *Comparative American Identities: Race, Sex, and Nationality in the Modern Text* (New York: Routledge, 1991). For contributions from the field of queer theory see, for example, Michael Moon, *A Small Boy and Others: Imitation and Initiation in American Culture from Henry James to Andy Warhol* (Durham, N.C.: Duke University Press, 1997); Eve Kosofsky Sedgwick, *Between Men: English Literature and Male Homosocial Desire* (New York: Columbia University Press, 1985), and *Epistemology of the Closet* (Berkeley and Los Angeles: University of California Press, 1990); Michael Warner, ed., *Fear of a Queer Planet: Queer Politics and Social Theory* (Minneapolis: University of Minnesota Press, 1993); and Lauren Berlant, *The Queen of America Goes to Washington City: Essays on Sex and Citizenship* (Durham, N.C.: Duke University Press, 1997). For an elegant example of a post-Habermasian critique, see Nancy Fraser's work, including "Rethinking the Public Sphere: A Contribution to the Critique of Actually Existing Democracy," in *The Phantom Public Sphere*, ed. Bruce Robbins (Minneapolis: University of Minnesota Press, 1993), 1–32.

5 Barbara Welter, "The Cult of True Womanhood: 1820–1860," *American Quarterly* 18 (summer 1966): 151–74. Aileen S. Kraditor, ed., *Up from the Pedestal: Selected Writings in the History of American Feminism* (Chicago: Quadrangle Books, 1968). Gerda Lerner, "The Lady and the Mill Girl: Changes in the Status of Women in the Age of Jackson," *Midcontinent American Studies Journal* 10 (spring 1969): 5–15. Nina Baym, *Woman's Fiction: A Guide to Novels by and about Women in America, 1820–1870* (Ithaca, N.Y.: Cornell University Press, 1982). Smith-Rosenberg, "The Female World of Love and Ritual." Judith Fetterley, *The Resisting Reader: A Feminist Approach to American Fiction* (Bloomington: Indiana University Press, 1978). Judith Fetterley and Marjorie Pryse, *American Women Regionalists, 1850–1910: A Norton Anthology* (New York: Norton, 1991). Although one of the clichés of feminist literary criticism of the 1970s and 1980s is that it is only about white women, this is often inaccurate. Pryse, for example, has written extensively on African American women writers. For example, see the volume she edited with Hortense Spillers, *Conjuring: Black Women, Fiction, and Literary Tradition* (Bloomington: Indiana University Press, 1985).

6 Harriet Ann Jacobs, *Incidents in the Life of a Slave Girl*, ed. Nellie Y. McKay and Frances Smith Foster (New York: Norton, 2001). Kathryn Kish Sklar, *Catherine Beecher: A Study in American Domesticity* (New Haven, Conn.: Yale University Press, 1973).

7 For a provocative discussion of this turn in the argument, see Susan Lurie, *Unsettled Subjects: Restoring Feminist Politics to Poststructuralist Critique* (Durham, N.C.: Duke University Press, 1997).

8 Walter Benn Michaels, *The Gold Standard and the Logic of Naturalism: American Literature at the Turn of the Century* (Berkeley and Los Angeles: University of California Press, 1987). Richard Brodhead, *Cultures of Letters: Scenes of Read-*

ing and Writing in Nineteenth Century America (Chicago: University of Chicago Press, 1993). Three other important books that generalize about "American" culture while paying little or no attention to women (of all races) are Eric Lott, *Love and Theft: Blackface Minstrelsy and the American Working Class* (New York: Oxford University Press, 1993); Eric Sundquist, *To Wake the Nations: Race and the Making of American Literature* (Cambridge: Harvard University Press, 1993); and Michael Warner, *The Letters of the Republic: Publication and the Public Sphere in Eighteenth-Century America* (Cambridge: Harvard University Press, 1990).

9 Lora Romero, *Home Fronts: Domesticity and Its Critics in the Antebellum United States* (Durham, N.C.: Duke University Press, 1997), 5.

10 Ibid., 4–5.

11 See Sedgwick's introduction to *Novel Gazing: Queer Readings in Fiction* (Durham, N.C.: Duke University Press, 1997).

12 F. O. Matthiesen, *The American Renaissance* (London: Oxford University Press, 1941).

13 Nina Baym, "Melodramas of Beset Manhood: How Theories of American Fiction Exclude Women Authors," *American Quarterly* 33 (summer 1981): 123–39.

14 Jane Tompkins, *Sensational Designs: The Cultural Work of American Fiction, 1790–1860* (New York: Oxford University Press, 1985).

15 It would be coy not to acknowledge here the place of Cathy N. Davidson's own *Revolution and the Word: The Rise of the Novel in America* (New York: Oxford University Press, 1986) and her Early American Women Writers series at Oxford University Press in this history. Although *Revolution and the Word* was written explicitly to complicate the gendered account of American literature by arguing that both women and men wrote and read sentimental fiction and both women and men wrote and read other forms (picaresque, political, gothic, and so on) as well, it also sought to analyze once-admired and popular texts that had long ago dropped off the literary map. The Early American Women Writers series made several of those texts available again and helped make *Charlotte Temple* and *The Coquette* academic bestsellers.

16 Philip Weiss, "Herman-Neutics," *New York Times Magazine,* 15 December 1996, 60–65, 70–72.

★ ★ ★ **PART I**

CANONS

Separate Spheres, Female Worlds, Woman's Place:

The Rhetoric of Women's History

LINDA K. KERBER

In no country has such constant care been taken as in America to trace two clearly
distinct lines of action for the two sexes and to make them keep pace one with the
other, but in two pathways that are always different.
—Alexis de Tocqueville, 1835

The Sphere of Woman and Man as moral beings [is] the same.
—Angelina Grimké, 1838

Too much has already been said and written about woman's sphere.
—Lucy Stone, 1855

A century and a half after the publication of Alexis de Tocqueville's account of his visit to the United States, a mode of behavior that he may have
been the first systematic social critic to identify has undergone extraordinary waves of analysis and attack. In four brief chapters in the third book of
the second volume of *Democracy in America,* published in 1840, Tocqueville
addressed the situation of women. His observations display Tocqueville's
habitual charm, his fearlessness in making broad generalizations, his mastery of language. When *Democracy in America* was rediscovered and widely
reprinted in the years after World War II, his chapters were among the few—
perhaps the only—classic texts read by students of American history that
seriously examined the situation of women in American society. When historians—whether inspired by Simone de Beauvoir or Eleanor Flexner or
Betty Friedan—began again to study women's history, they could point to

Tocqueville for evidence that at least one classic, Great Author had conceded the significance of their subject.

Tocqueville restricted his observations on women to a section entitled "Influence of Democracy on Manners Properly So Called." He alluded to the separation of male and female spheres in the course of his contrasting and impressionistic portraits of young middle-class American women. The breakdown of aristocratic government, he argued, had important implications for family life in that patriarchal authority was impaired, leaving young women with a high degree of independence, which encouraged a high degree of self-confidence. Yet when one of those same young women married, Tocqueville reported, "The inexorable opinion of the public carefully circumscribes [her] within the narrow circle of domestic interests and duties and forbids her to step beyond it." In this sentence he provided the physical image (the circle) and the interpretation (that it was a limiting boundary on choices) that would continue to characterize the metaphor. He ended by contrasting American women with European feminists who, he thought, wished to erase the boundaries between the spheres of women and of men, thus "degrading" both. Tocqueville concluded with what he thought was a compliment: "As for myself, I do not hesitate to avow that although the women of the United States are confined within the narrow circle of domestic life, and their situation is in some respects one of extreme dependence, I have nowhere seen women occupying a loftier position; and if I were asked, to what the singular prosperity and growing strength of the [American] people ought mainly to be attributed, I should reply: To the superiority of their women."[1]

When, more than a hundred years later, another generation began to search for explanations of women's lives, no concept seemed more promising than Tocqueville's. He had urged that the "circle of domestic life" be searched for the distinguishing characteristics of American women, and once we looked, the separation of spheres seemed everywhere underfoot, from crocheted pillows reading "Woman's Place Is in the Home" to justifications for the exclusion of women from higher education, to arguments against birth control and abortion. Women were said to live in a distinct "world," engaged in nurturant activities, focused on children, husbands, and family dependents.

The metaphor of the "sphere" was the figure of speech, the trope, on which historians came to rely when they described women's part in American culture. Exploring the traditions of historical discourse, historians found that notions of women's sphere permeated the language; they in turn used the metaphor in their own descriptions. Thus the relationship between the name—sphere—and the perception of what it named was reciprocal; widespread usage in the nineteenth century directed the choices made by twentieth-century historians about what to study and how to tell the stories that they reconstructed. The trope had an effect on readers as well, predisposing them to find arguments that made use of familiar language persuasive. "Common sense," writes Clifford Geertz, "is not what the mind cleared of cant spontaneously apprehends; it is what the mind filled with presuppositions . . . concludes." One of our culture's presuppositions has been that men and women live in separate spheres. The power of presupposition may have been at work in the formulations of Erik H. Erikson, which gave the trope of separate spheres a psychological foundation. In 1964, reporting on play patterns of children, Erikson observed that little girls used blocks to construct bounded, interior spaces, while little boys used blocks to construct exterior scenes. He concluded that the differences between "Inner and Outer Space" "correspond to the male and female principles in body construction," to psychological identity, and to social behavior. For their part, historians were not immune to tropic pressures; the metaphor of separate spheres helped historians select what to study and how to report what they found.[2]

Writing in the mid-1960s, three historians substantially reinforced the centrality of the metaphor of separate spheres. Barbara Welter, Aileen S. Kraditor, and Gerda Lerner, all influenced to some degree by Betty Friedan and all writing in the climate created by the popular success of *The Feminine Mystique,* argued that American women's history had to be understood not only by way of events but through a prism of ideology as well. Between the historians and the reality of women's lives impinged a pervasive descriptive language that imposed a "complex of virtues . . . by which a woman judged herself and was judged by . . . society."[3]

Welter's 1966 essay was a frank attempt to do for the nineteenth century what Friedan had done for the twentieth. Retrieving sources resembling Friedan's—women's fiction and popular prescriptive literature—and reading them freshly, Welter identified a nineteenth-century stereotype, which she called the "Cult of True Womanhood" and for which she said a synonym might be "mystique." Among the cardinal virtues Welter found associated with women was domesticity (the others were piety, purity, and submissiveness); home was referred to as women's "proper sphere." She quoted a woman's revealing defense of that choice of sphere: "St. Paul knew what was best for women when he advised them to be domestic. There is composure at home; there is something sedative in the duties which home involves. It affords security not only from the world, but from delusions and errors of every kind." And Welter concluded that American women of the nineteenth century, saddled with a stereotype so encouraging and yet so constraining, experiencing "guilt and confusion in the midst of opportunity," had been as much bemused by ideology as Friedan's (and Welter's) troubled contemporaries.[4] Unlike Tocqueville's, Welter's judgment of the separate sphere was a negative one. Separation denigrated women, kept them subordinate. The choice of the word "cult" was pejorative. Welter's essay—thoughtful, subtle, witty—was much cited and often reprinted; the phrase "cult of true womanhood" became an essential part of the vocabulary of women's history.

Less than two years later, Kraditor published *Up from the Pedestal,* still a striking anthology of documents. Considering what Kraditor called "the primitive state of historiography" in 1968, her introduction was pathbreaking. In it she identified what she called "the question of 'spheres'" as central to an understanding of American feminism. She contrasted "autonomy" with "women's proper sphere": "Strictly speaking," she wrote, "men have never had a 'proper *sphere,*' since their sphere has been the world and all its activities." She proposed that the separation of spheres was somehow linked to the Industrial Revolution, which "broadened the distinctions between men's and women's occupations and certainly provoked new thinking about the significance and permanence of their respective 'spheres.'" And she noted the persistent description of home as refuge in antifeminist literature, a refuge that had somehow become vulnerable long before Christopher Lasch coined the phrase "haven in a heartless world."[5]

Three years later, Lerner used the social history of women as a base for hypotheses about general political and economic questions in an important essay, "The Lady and the Mill Girl." Introducing class into the analysis and extending the link to the Industrial Revolution, Lerner argued that "American industrialization, which occurred in an underdeveloped economy with a shortage of labor, depended on the labor of women and children" and that one "result of industrialization was in increasing differences in life styles between women of different classes. . . . As class distinctions sharpened, social attitudes toward women became polarized." Welter's "cult of true womanhood" was interpreted by Lerner as a *vehicle* by which middle-class women elevated their own status. "It is no accident," Lerner wrote in 1969, "that the slogan 'woman's place is in the home' took on a certain aggressiveness and shrillness precisely at the time when increasing numbers of poorer women *left* their homes to become factory workers."[6]

The careful reader of Kraditor and Lerner could hardly fail to notice that their description of women's sphere as separate from and subordinate to that of men was congruent with Marxist argument. For Lerner and Kraditor, the metaphor of sphere related not only to Tocqueville but to Friedrich Engels's conceptualization of a dichotomy between public and private modes of life. Tracing the development of gender relations, Engels had argued that the "world-historical defeat of the female sex" had been accompanied by a shift in control of space: "The man took command in the home also." Engels gave classic expression to the concept of a public/private split, a split in which the most important psychic locus was the home, understood to be a woman's place, but ultimately controlled by man. "With . . . the single monogamous family . . . household management lost its public character. . . . It became a *private service.*"[7]

Rhetorically, Engels identified a psychological and legal shift (from matrilocality to patrilocality) and gave it a physical context: the nuclear family's home. (Perhaps because this cultural shift had been accomplished long before his own time and had already come to seem the common sense of the matter, Engels did not feel the need to make explicit or defend the equivalencies he identified.) His strategy was to link private-home-woman and then to speak in synecdoche; any part of the triad could stand for any other part. He did so despite his explicit statement that the home was also a locus of men's behavior; indeed for Engels and for Karl Marx, the home is the locus of struggle between the sexes.

Awareness of the socially constructed division between public and private, often expressed through the image of sphere, gave energy to much Marxist-feminist writing in the late 1960s and early 1970s. "The contemporary family," wrote Juliet Mitchell, "can be seen as a triptych of sexual, reproductive and socializatory functions (the woman's world) embraced by production (the man's world) — precisely a structure which in the final instance is determined by the economy. The exclusion of women from production . . . is the root cause of the contemporary *social* definition of women as *natural* beings." At the end of her powerfully argued *Woman's Estate,* Mitchell reiterated that the central problem for women was their relegation to the home during their child-bearing years, "the period of adult psychic and political formation." Bourgeois and working-class women alike were deprived of the opportunity to learn from any but the most limited experience. "The spider's web is dense as well as intricate . . . come into my parlour and be a true woman," Mitchell concludes. "In the home the social function and the psychic identity of women as a group is found."[8]

The great power of the Marxist interpretation was that it not only described a separation of spheres but also offered an explanation of the way in which that separation served the interests of the dominant classes. Separate spheres were due neither to cultural accident nor to biological determinism. They were social constructions, camouflaging social and economic service, a service whose benefits were unequally shared.

The idea of separate spheres, as enunciated by Welter, Kraditor, Lerner, and Mitchell, took on a life of its own. Women's historians of the mid-1960s had inherited a subject that had been, with only few conspicuous exceptions, descriptive and anecdotal. Books like Alice Morse Earle's *Home Life in Colonial Days* loomed large.[9] When earlier historians of women had turned to politics, a Whiggish progressivism had infused much of their work, suggesting that the central theme in women's history was an inexorable march toward suffrage. The concepts of separate spheres and of a public/private dichotomy offered ways of addressing women's history that employed social and cultural, as well as political, material. Historians who did not think of themselves as Marxists were nevertheless deeply indebted to Marxist analysis. Social theory enabled women's historians to introduce categories, hypotheticals, and analytical devices by which they could escape the confines of accounts of "great ladies" or of "the progress of women." Still—whether handled by Erikson, who grounded the separation of spheres in what he took to be permanent psychological verities; Welter, who grounded it in culture; or socialist feminists (including Lerner and Kraditor), who grounded it in property relations—in the early 1970s separation was generally associated with subordination, deteriorating status, and the victimization of women by men.[10]

In 1975 Carroll Smith-Rosenberg offered a striking reinterpretation of the possibilities of separation in her pathbreaking essay "The Female World of Love and Ritual." Several years later she recalled: "I began with a question. How can we understand the nature of the emotionally intense and erotic friendships between eighteenth- and nineteenth-century married women and society's benign approval of such relationships?" Smith-Rosenberg maintained that separation could make possible psychologically sustaining and strengthening relationships among women. Victorians did not make rigid distinctions, as we do, between heterosexuality and homosexuality. A culture of separate spheres was not simply an ancestral culture differing from our own primarily in the extent of industrialization; it was, Smith-Rosenberg argued, a *dramatically* different culture in which boundaries were differently marked, anxieties differently expressed. Nineteenth-century women had available sources of psychological support that had eroded in our own day. Smith-Rosenberg's work implied that there had existed a distinctive women's culture, in which women assisted each other in childbirth, nurtured each other's children, and shared emotional and often erotic ties stronger than those with their husbands.[11]

Other work of the 1970s filled in details of the distinctive women's culture that Smith-Rosenberg had identified. In "Female Support Networks and Political Activism," Blanche Wiesen Cook focused on four women who had significant political careers in the late nineteenth and early twentieth centuries. Cook dealt with the probability of homosexual relationships among some of her subjects, arguing that politically activist women were sustained by complex and powerful friendships with other women. She maintained that such friendships were part of the history historians sought to trace and that, instead of ignoring them as irrelevant, historians should address them frankly, understanding that the "sisterhood" of which so many women spoke included female friendships that ran the gamut from acquaintance to long-sustained sexual relationships. Kathryn Kish Sklar's biography of Catharine Beecher analyzed the woman who did most to define the ingredients of the traditional women's sphere: domesticity, nurture, and education. Beecher took the position that women's sphere did not encompass politics, notably in exchanges with Angelina Grimké. Significantly, Beecher addressed extensively the elements of the physical location of the women's sphere, not only in abstractions like "the classroom" or "the home" but also in explicit and original physical plans for *The American Woman's Home*.[12]

In *The Bonds of Womanhood*, Nancy F. Cott explored the way in which "the doctrine of woman's sphere" actually was practiced in early-nineteenth-century New England. Cott found in middle-class women's diaries and letters a distinctive "orientation toward gender" that derived from shared patterns of work. She found in those writings an understanding of domesticity that placed it in direct opposition to ongoing "social and economic transformation" and that emphasized the complexity of the role of motherhood.

Organized church groups became one of the few institutional contexts in which women could "connect purposefully" to the community, and such groups, in turn, set a "pattern of reliance on female friendships for emotional expression and security."

Cott ended by proposing that the feminist political movement of the nineteenth century had grown out of the separation of spheres and taken its distinctive shape and interests *from* that separation. For Cott the "ideology of woman's sphere formed a necessary stage in . . . softening the hierarchical relationship of marriage." Although the idea of women's sphere was not necessarily protofeminist, domesticity and feminism were linked by "women's perception of 'womanhood'" as an all-sufficient definition and of sisterhood as implicit in it. That *consciousness,* Cott argued, was a necessary precondition for feminism, even though in opening up certain avenues to women because of their sex it barricaded all others.[13]

Like others before her, Cott sought an economic base for the social transformation she discerned. E. P. Thompson had argued that the crucial psychological change of the early stages of the Industrial Revolution was a shift from the task orientation of traditional artisan work patterns to the time discipline associated with modernity. Cott added the thought that married women's work became less like men's work in the early nineteenth century, as men's work was subjected to modern time discipline while women's work remained task oriented. Work patterns reinforced women's sense that their lives were defined differently from men's. Domesticity could even embody "a protest against that advance of exploitation and pecuniary values . . . by upholding a 'separate sphere' of comfort and compensation. . . . The literature of domesticity . . . enlisted women in their domestic roles to absorb, palliate, and even to redeem the strain of social and economic transformation."[14]

Perhaps the historian to use the concept of separate spheres most energetically was Carl N. Degler, whose book *At Odds: Women and the Family in America from the Revolution to the Present* was published in 1980. For Degler, the definition of separate spheres was an important nineteenth-century development that accompanied and made possible the replacement of patriarchal family relationships by companionate ones. Drawing on the work of Daniel Scott Smith, he suggested that women's political autonomy in the public world had been preceded by a form of sexual autonomy, or at least assertiveness, in the private world, and he pointed to the declining birth rate in the nineteenth century as evidence that women were able to exercise a growing degree of control in their sexual relations. Domesticity offered advantages as well as disadvantages to women, smoothing the way to popular acceptance of extrafamilial activities by women. "Separate spheres" deflected conflict; the very language anticipated negotiation. The metaphor of separate spheres helped Degler establish order among issues as disparate as abortion, suffrage, literacy, and friendship. Reference to the omnipresent ideology became a useful guide, enabling the historian to anticipate which changes Americans could be expected to support (for example, the entry of women into the teaching profession) and which they would resist (for example, suffrage, because it could not be accommodated to the concept of separate spheres). *At Odds,* a wide-ranging, fluent, and thoughtful survey of women's history and family history may well represent the high-water mark of reliance on separate spheres as an organizing device.[15]

The first stage of the development of the metaphor—in the late 1960s and early 1970s—was marked by an effort to identify separate spheres as a theme central to women's historical experience, locating the ideology in the context of antebellum American society. The second stage—in the later 1970s—encompassed an effort to refine the definition and identify complexities, introducing the liberating possibilities of a "women's culture." By 1980 historians had devised a prism through which to view the diaries, letters, and organization records that had been freshly discovered and whose analytical potential was freshly appreciated.

But the language of separate spheres was vulnerable to sloppy use. Above all, it was loosely metaphorical. Those who spoke of "cult" did not, after all, mean a voluntary organization based on commitment to explicit ideological or theological tenets; by "sphere" they did not mean a three-dimensional surface, all points of which are equidistant from a fixed point. When they used the metaphor of separate spheres, historians referred, often interchangeably, to an ideology *imposed on* women, a culture *created by* women, a set of boundaries *expected to be observed* by women. Moreover, the metaphor helped historians avoid thinking about race; virtually all discussion of the subject until very recently has focused on the experience of white women, mostly of the middle class.[16]

In response to this problem, *Feminist Studies* published an exchange in which five historians—Lerner, Smith-Rosenberg, Temma Kaplan, Mari Jo Buhle, and Ellen DuBois—discussed the problems of usage inherent in the terms "women's sphere" and "women's culture." The *Feminist Studies* symposium of 1980 conveniently marks the opening of a third stage, in which historians have sought to embed women's experience in the main course of human development and to unpack the metaphor of "separate spheres." In this stage, historians have undertaken a conscious criticism of their own rhetorical constructions. The comments of the symposium contributors showed that the word "cult" had virtually dropped out of professional historians' usage, although its challenge—that we allocate how much was prescribed for women and how much created by women—remained. DuBois warned that pride in the possibilities of a distinct women's culture might blind historians to the facts of women's oppression. Her respondents tended to caution against conflating the terms "women's sphere," which they took to express a limiting ideology, and "women's culture," a term which embraced creativity in the domestic arts, distinctive forms of labor, and particular patterns of social relationships.[17] The need to break out of the restrictive dualism of an oppressive term (women's sphere) and a liberating term (women's culture) has propelled what I think is a third stage in the development of the metaphor of separate spheres. Taking an interactive view of social processes, historians now seek to show how women's allegedly "separate sphere" was affected by what men did, and how activities defined by women in their own sphere influenced and even set constraints and limitations on what men might choose to do—how, in short, that sphere was socially constructed both *for* and *by* women.

The first major characteristic of the third stage of understanding is the application of the concept to the entire chronology of human experience, rather than to the discussion of antebellum society where, perhaps by accident, perhaps thanks to Tocqueville, historians first encountered it. A great deal of recent work has made it clear that the separation of spheres was not limited to a single generation or a single civilization.

Surveys of the history of political thought have shown that the habit of contrasting the "worlds" of men and of women, the allocation of the public sector to men and the private sector (still under men's control) to women is older than Western civilization. In *The Creation of Patriarchy,* Lerner locates the crucial moment in a prehistoric shift from hunting and gathering societies to agricultural ones and an accompanying intertribal "exchange of women" in the Neolithic period. "Women themselves became a resource, acquired by men much as the land was acquired by men. . . . *It was only after men had learned how to enslave the women of groups who could be defined as strangers, that they learned how to enslave men of those groups and, later, subordinates from within their own societies.*"[18]

The distinction between the private and the public was deeply embedded in classical Greek thought. As Hannah Arendt lucidly explained, the Greeks distinguished between the private realm, defined by the "limitation[s] imposed upon us by the needs of biological life," which preclude choice, and the public realm of action and choice. Women, "who with their bodies guarantee the physical survival of the species," were understood to live wholly on the private sector; in Greece they were confined to the large family household and did not mingle, promiscuously, with people on the streets. They were understood to lack the civic virtue that enabled men to function as independent moral beings. Men were advantaged; they lived in *both* the private and the public mode; men realized themselves most fully in the activities of the *polis*. For Aristotle, "the *sophrosyne* (strength of character) of a man and of a woman, or the courage and justice of a man and of a woman are not . . . the same; the courage of a man is shown in commanding, of a woman in obeying." In the ancient formulation, the separate world of women was located securely in a larger patriarchal social context. Classical assumptions about the appropriate relationship between men and women have been attacked only sporadically until recent times. Except for social writers, Western political theorists have treated women in what Susan Moller Okin has called a "functionalist" mode, which assumes that women cannot be dissociated from their function in the family.[19]

When Europeans ventured to the New World, they brought with them the long-standing Western assumptions about women's separate world. Colonial American culture made firm distinctions about what was appropriate for each sex to do and took for granted the subordination of women. Whether viewed skeptically or sympathetically, English colonists in North America appear to have done little questioning of inherited role definitions. From northern New England to the Carolinas there stretched a society in which a woman was defined by her family life and acted in response to relatives' and neighbors' claims on her. The Christian faith of the immigrants ratified both distinctive roles and a subordinate status for women. "Of all the Orders which are unequals," wrote the Congregational minister Samuel Willard, "[husband and wife] do come nearest to an Equality, and in several respects they stand upon even ground. . . . Nevertheless, God hath also made an imparity between them, in the Order prescribed in His Word, and for that reason there is a Subordination, and they are ranked among unequals."

Recent studies of witchcraft have suggested that women at risk for accusation included those who pressed at the boundaries of expected women's behavior, intentionally or unintentionally. One of the major factors in the colonists' perception of Indians as uncivilized was the Indians' tendency to define gender relations differently than did Europeans. Europeans were particularly dismayed when Indian women played roles that were not subordinate or when Indian societies did not display a separation of spheres as Europeans understood them. (For example, Europeans found matrilocality indecipherable.)[20]

As the American Revolution began to impinge on white middle-class women, what Mary Beth Norton has called the "circle of domestic concerns" bounded their lives: the choice of husband (an especially important decision in a virtually divorceless society), the nurture of children, the management or service of the household. The revolution shook old assumptions about women's place and suggested new possibilities; guerrilla war made few concessions to alleged frailty, and many women, whether Loyalist or Patriot, were involuntarily given an accelerated course in politics and independence. By the end of the war, the domestic roles of women could no longer be taken for granted; such roles now required defensive ideological articulation. Thus emerged the antebellum prescriptive literature we have come to know.[21]

As I have argued elsewhere, the ideology of republican womanhood was an effort to bring the older version of the separation of spheres into rough conformity with the new politics that valued autonomy and individualism. Issues of sexual asymmetry dominated public discourse to an unprecedented extent as people tried to define a place for women in postrevolutionary society. Even as Americans enlarged the scope, resonance, and power of republicanism they simultaneously discounted and weakened the force of patriarchy. They recoded the values of women's sphere, validating women's moral influence on their husbands and lovers, ascribing world-historical importance to women's maternal role, and claiming for women a nature less sexual and more self-controlled than the nature of men. The ideology of republican womanhood recognized that women's choices and women's work did serve large social and political purposes, and that recognition was enough to draw the traditional women's "sphere" somewhat closer to men's "world." But to use the language of domesticity was also to make a conservative political choice among alternative options, rejecting the frankly feminist option, articulated by Mary Wollstonecraft in England and Etta

Palm in France, that claimed for women direct connection with republican political life. Indeed, I believe that the American Revolution was kept from spinning on an outwardly expansive and radical track in part by the general refusal to entertain proposals for redefining the relationship between women and the Republic. By contrast, major changes in women's political life were associated with the radical stages of the French Revolution, and erasure of those changes was associated with the retreat from radicalism.[22]

The second major characteristic of the current stage of understanding is that we are giving more attention to questions about the social relations of the sexes and treating the language of separate spheres itself as a rhetorical construction that responded to changing social and economic reality. Tocqueville's visit occurred at the end of more than a half century during which one variant of the separation of spheres and the patriarchal culture in which it was embedded had been undermined by commercial, political, and industrial revolutions. Adam Smith had given voice to the great commercial transformation, the founders at Philadelphia had articulated the political one, and new technology embodied the industrial one. In each realm the world maintained itself by the spinning gyroscope of successive decision and choice. Political rules, like economic ones, had been written anew. In a world from which familiar boundaries had been erased, new relationships had to be defined, new turf had to be measured, and in Thomas L. Haskell's phrase, new "spheres of competition" had to be freshly aligned. In a system of laissez-faire, which relied on the dynamic force of self-interest in commerce and in politics, the "sphere of competition" was everywhere. In a Tocquevillean world of equality, where all the old barriers had been removed, little was left that was not vulnerable. Marvin Meyers discerned many years ago that Tocqueville's American Man was characteristically anxious, as well he might be in a world in which so little seemed reliably fixed.[23]

The capitalist revolution also had deeply unsettling implications for women. As patriarchy eroded, social reality involved unattached individuals, freely negotiating with each other in an expansive market. The patriarchal variant of separate spheres was not congruent with capitalist social relations; capitalism required that men's and women's economic relations be renegotiated. A capitalist system tended to undermine an older scheme of property relations that, by keeping a woman's property under the control of the men to whom she was entrusted, could also keep it out of the marketplace, for example, when dower property was shielded from seizure for debt.

Capitalism had the potential to enhance the position of women by loosening patriarchal control of property and removing factors that shielded property from the pressures of the marketplace. The revised understanding of the relationship between women and the marketplace was embodied in the married women's property acts, devised state by state in the middle decades of the nineteenth century. Such statutes gave married women the right to hold and manipulate their own earnings and property. The statutes created a vast new group of property-holding but unenfranchised citizens; married women's property acts unintentionally but inexorably created an internally contradictory situation that was ultimately resolved by granting the vote—and with it, service on juries and the opportunity to hold public office. The franchise acknowledged women's connection to the political community as the law of property had acknowledged their entry into the marketplace. As the patriarchal corporate economy broke down, the traditional version of the separate sphere was destabilized. One plausible way to read nineteenth-century defenses of separate spheres, not least among them Tocqueville's, is to single out the theme of breakdown; the noise we hear about separate spheres may be the shattering of an old order and the realignment of its fragments.[24]

But the old order, like the parson's one-horse shay, took a long time breaking down. Patched up and reconstructed, it continued to rattle along for a long time. The first wave of married women's property acts did not seem to usher in a new era; they protected only property given or willed to women, expressing fathers' distrust of irresponsible sons-in-law. In protecting gift property from seizure for debts contracted by husbands, married women's property acts were debtor relief acts that directly benefited men. The new property acts expressed a relationship between men—as well as a revised relationship among men, women, and the marketplace. Only at the stage of revision—1855 in Michigan, 1860 in New York, later elsewhere— did the new statutes specifically protect married women's earnings and their right to manage their own property. Not until 1911 did Michigan law permit a married woman to define the full use of her own earnings; until then her husband had the right to decide whether or not a woman could work for wages.[25]

Thus the older property relations between husbands and wives persisted long after limited elements of those relations had been modified by statute. Studying nineteenth-century Michigan women's correspondence, Marilyn Ferris Motz has argued for the continuing instrumental usefulness of the separate female sphere as "a system of human relations" that provided a "cushion" against a legal system whose rules privileged the authority of husbands and fathers over married women's property relations during a lengthy transitional period. Because the early versions of married women's property acts protected only inherited and gift property, they created a paradox in which a woman exercised much more control over property she inherited from her parents than over property she had helped build—on a farm or in a family business—in the course of her marriage. In such a legal context, Motz argues, there was good economic reason for women to work energetically to establish and maintain networks of female kin. "Women attempted to balance their lack of authority within the nuclear family with the collective moral, social, and financial pressure of their kin networks," Motz observes, ". . . from whom [they] could inherit and to whom [they] could turn for alternative support." In an era when alimony was rare, women who wished to divorce their husbands leaned on female kin for support. A woman who faced early death in childbirth counted on her sisters to protect her children from mistreatment by possible future stepmothers. Young widows turned to their female kin to sustain them and their children; elderly widows counted on their daughters and daughters-in-law to nurse them in reciprocity for earlier care. Motz draws an analogy between the social dynamics that sustained the separate sphere of middle-class nineteenth-century Michigan women and the patterns of service and reciprocity traced by Carol B. Stack among twentieth-century working-class women. She argues forcefully that the "women's culture" and "women's values" of the separate sphere rested on long-term economic and psychological self-interest.[26]

In Motz's Michigan, as in Cott's New England, the work patterns of men deviated ever farther from those of women, perhaps reinforcing the need to maintain the boundaries of the separate women's sphere. But as Tamara K. Hareven observed in 1976, members of families might be drawn into capitalist ways at different rates. When women worked in factories and taught in schools, their work was modernized and forced into the new timebound, clock-measured matrix to which E. P. Thompson has given classical formulation. For the first time in history, substantial numbers of women could earn substantial amounts of cash. In a careful reading of the letters of Lowell mill women, Thomas Dublin criticizes the older assumption that mill women remained embedded in the traditional family economy. "Work in the mills," he writes, "functioned for women rather like migration did for young men. . . . the mills offered individual self-support." Perhaps the clearest expression of that position comes in a letter written by a father on a farm to a foster daughter in the mills: "You now feel & enjoy independence trusting to your own ability to procure whatever you want, leaning on no one no one depending on you."[27]

How are we to find our way through the confusions of local idiosyncrasy, sometimes providing dependence, sometimes independence? Two important books, published in the early 1980s, both community studies built on demographic and quantitative research in documents revealing economic relationships, offer complex but carefully nuanced analyses. Together they testify to the dramatic force of capitalist pressures on women's sphere.

In antebellum Petersburg, Virginia, the language of domesticity and the deferential separation of spheres escaped explicit public challenge. But Suzanne Lebsock can unambivalently conclude from her intensive analysis of public records that "women in Petersburg experienced increasing autonomy, autonomy in the sense of freedom from utter dependence on particular men. Relatively speaking, fewer women were married, more women found work for wages, and more married women acquired separate estates." The changes occurred largely without the assistance of a politically oriented discourse. Separate estates—a legal device that deflected coverture and assured married women control over property—provided a shelter against family bankruptcy and an apolitical response to repeated economic panics. "It stands to reason," Lebsock writes, "that an ideology that tried to fix the boundaries of women's sphere should have become pervasive and urgent just as women began to exercise a few choices. . . . As women acquired new degrees of power and autonomy in the private sphere, they were confronted with new forms of subordination in the public sphere."[28]

The character of the women's sphere of the mid-nineteenth century as distinctive social construction is elaborately developed and richly argued in Mary P. Ryan's important study of Oneida County, New York, *Cradle of the Middle Class*. Stressing the connections between public and private realms, Ryan begins by describing the patriarchal assumptions of the traditional early modern domestic economy. In her reading, many aspects of patriarchy broke down in the early nineteenth century, under blows from an increasingly commercial economy that made unentailed estates and liquid inheritance advantageous to heirs. Instead of the language of separate spheres, Ryan speaks of the changing interests of families as a whole. Ryan interprets the retreat to the private conjugal family as a way of mobilizing private resources for upward social mobility. Over a half century, from 1810 to 1855, the number of children per family dropped sharply, from 5.8 to 3.6, permitting more attention to each child. At the same time, the language of domesticity, which emphasized the role of mothers in raising children, was congruent with increased psychological investment in child nurture and education and, most important, with keeping *sons* out of the workforce in order to extend their education and improve their chances for upward mobility. One major surprise is Ryan's finding that as boys were kept out of the workforce, middle-class women and daughters were increasingly apt to work for pay—for example, by keeping boarders or serving as domestics. Women's energy was used "to maintain or advance the status of men in their families."[29]

In Ryan's account, women's "separate sphere" was deeply paradoxical. The concept clearly served the interests of men with whom women lived. Yet women also claimed it for their own, defining their own interests as inextricably linked to the upward mobility of their families, repressing claims for their own autonomy. When women went to work for pay, they entered a severely segregated workforce (the white-collar jobs of clerks were still reserved for their sons and brothers). The diaries of their friendships show them circulating in a world of women. The logic of their situation drove a very few to political feminism, but for most, the "female world of love and ritual" and the ideology of domesticity that purported to explain it remained powerful and persuasive.

Black families were not immune to the ideology of separate spheres, and recent work by James Oliver Horton and Lois E. Horton, Dorothy Sterling, Jacqueline Jones, and Deborah Gray White has been particularly shrewd in tracing their ambivalent responses to it.[30] The American ideology was to some limited extent congruent with African traditions of matrilocality, of women's clear responsibilities for child support and child raising, and of a sex-linked division for child support and child raising, and of a sex-linked division of labor. Enslaved men lacked the economic power that white men exercised over their families; the nuances of relationships between slave men and women are debated by historians. It is clear that directly after the Civil War, prescriptive literature addressed to recently freed slaves, people living in hovels with dirt floors, counseled delicacy among women and a clear division of their work from men's work, implicitly promising that adoption of the ideology would ensure elevation to the middle class.[31]

The ideology of separate spheres could be both instrumental and prescriptive; its double character has made it difficult for historians to work with. In the first mode, it was an ideology women found useful and emotionally sustaining, a familiar link between the older patriarchal culture and the new bourgeois experience. This aspect could be particularly welcome as a hedge against secularization; religious women of virtually all persuasions sustained a pattern of separateness both in their religious activism and in their own religiosity.[32] It could also, as Gerda Lerner discerned, protect the interests of one class of women in a time of change. But in its prescriptive mode, the ideology of separate spheres required constant attention if it were to be maintained.

In *Beyond Separate Spheres,* Rosalind Rosenberg has located the beginnings of modern studies of sex differences in the Progressive Era. Two generations of brilliant social scientists, among them Helen Thompson, Jessie Taft, W. I. Thomas, Franz Boas, and Elsie Clews Parsons, established the foundation for a "fundamental shift that took place in the way women viewed themselves and their place in society." By the early twentieth century at least some psychologists, sociologists, and anthropologists were coming to understand that many sex differences were the result of socialization, not biology. Finally it became possible to imagine a culture that was not divided into separate spheres. Our own ideas about sex differences still rely heavily on their work.[33]

Yet the real world took its time catching up with what academics believed they knew. Quite as much energy, male and female, has gone to maintain boundaries as to break them down. One result of the traditional assumption that what women have done is trivial is that historians have severely underestimated the extent of the energy—psychological, political, and legal—thus expended. Writing of rural communities in the nineteenth-century Midwest, John Mack Faragher describes the dynamics of the process: "The regulation of the sexual division of labor was achieved through the perpetuation of a hierarchical and male-dominant family structure, linked to a public world from which women were excluded. . . . Men were free to pursue the work of the public world precisely because the inequitable division of labor at home made them the beneficiaries of women's and children's labor."[34]

Examples of the energy put into maintaining boundaries abound. Thus Mary Kelley's *Private Woman, Public Stage* is in part an extended accounting of the price paid in pain and anguish by the first generation of professional women writers who sought to break their traditional intellectual isolation, and the "deprivation and devastation of spirit," the "subversion of intellect," to which the tradition of separate spheres had consigned them. Degler and Kraditor have emphasized the energy that antisuffragists dedicated to maintaining the boundaries of the separate spheres as they knew them. Cindy Sondik Aron's important study of the continuing negotiation of manners and reciprocal obligations in the mid-nineteenth-century civil service, the first large-scale labor force that was genuinely mixed in gender, shows that the ideology of separate spheres—like all ideology—is not frozen in time but is in a constant state of refinement until it fits reality so badly that a paradigm shift in conceptualization is unavoidable. Margaret W. Rossiter's *Women Scientists in America* provides, among many other things, a case study in the strategies of boundary maintenance and renegotiation. As women scientists successfully met the traditional markers of professional accomplishment, the standards themselves were redefined so as to enclose a sector of the population that was male.[35]

Feminist historians of the Progressive Era have been particularly sensitive to the force of opposition that women met when they sought public influence. The years 1870–1920 may be the high-water mark of women's public influence: through voluntary organizations, lobbying, trade unions, professional education, and professional activity. But women also met unprecedented hostility and resistance that seems disproportionate, even in the no-holds-barred political arena: When she opposed U.S. intervention in World War I, Jane Addams was attacked as "'a silly, vain, impertinent old maid' who had better leave the fighting to the men." Barbara Sicherman asks, "Why did the Anti-Saloon League replace the WCTU as the leading temperance organization? Why were women's organizations especially subject to red-baiting in the 1920s?" We might add other examples from the 1920s and later: the extraordinary bitterness of the American Medical Association's campaign against the modest recommendations of the Sheppard-Towner Act; the bitterly vindictive, personal attacks on Eleanor Roosevelt throughout her life; the marginalization and isolation of political women like Oveta Culp Hobby in the 1950s; the rich resources of advertising used in the 1920s to redefine the housewife and again in the 1950s to sustain that definition. The evidence that the woman's sphere is a social construction lies in part in the hard and constant work required to build and repair its boundaries.[36]

In the last decade historians of working women have made it abundantly clear that the phrase "separate spheres" is a metaphor for complex power relations in social and economic contexts. Capitalist social relations from the late eighteenth century until now have balanced precariously on the fictions that women "help" rather than work, that their true "place" is in the home, that when they venture "out" of the home they are best suited to doing work that replicates housework. Such work is "unskilled," interruptible, nurturing, and appropriately rewarded primarily by love and secondarily by a segregated marketplace that consistently values women's work less than men's. The point is not only that the marketplace is segregated by gender; it is also that the segregation has been constantly under negotiation and constantly reaffirmed. That these broad patterns are worldwide and cross-cultural was made clear in a special issue of *Signs* in 1977.[37]

The particulars of the American experience have been the target of sustained investigation by social historians who have developed a powerful feminist critique of Marxism for its conflation of the situation and interests of working-class men and working-class women. In *Out to Work,* published in 1982, Alice Kessler-Harris offered an important history of women's labor force participation. For Kessler-Harris, the dynamics of the marketplace and the ideology of separate spheres were interdependent, together defining a gender-segregated workplace, while forcing working-class women to live with the depressing ironies inherent in their situation as physically exhausted workers who were regarded as not really at work. Mary H. Blewett's studies of the work culture of shoemakers in preindustrial New England reveal that women were assigned the single task of binding the uppers of the shoes, a task housewives did in their kitchens, isolated from the shop, in a setting that denied them access to other aspects of the craft or to the collective experience of working with colleagues. Thus the industrial work culture of the nineteenth century inherited, writes Blewett, "gender categories [that] made it difficult for male artisans to regard women as fellow workers, include them in the ideology and politics based on their work culture, or see in the experience of working women what awaited all workers under industrialization."[38]

In the late nineteenth century, groups as disparate as the carpet weavers organized by the Knights of Labor, studied by Susan Levine; women socialists, studied by Mari Jo Buhle; and the Women's Trade Union League, studied by Nancy Schrom Dye and Robin Jacoby were torn in various ways by simultaneous commitments to "equal rights" in the public sector, to a future in which women would "return" to their "natural" sphere of the home and to an ugly reality in which working women labored in the public sector by day and returned to domestic chores by night. The result was to make the segregation of women in unskilled jobs a permanent feature of the American industrial scene. The boundaries of gender segregation were maintained by enormous efforts undertaken by elite owners of factories, middle-class managers, and unionized male workers. Judith McGaw has recently pressed the ironies further, arguing that the "unskilled" character of women's industrial work was itself a fiction that ensured a steady supply of cheap labor. The fiction devalued women's work because it was unmechanized, obscuring the extent to which unmechanized work could require a degree of skill too high for machines to replicate, and the fact that unmechanized work fulfilled functions essential to factory production.[39]

The dynamics have persisted. Sheila Tobias established male trade unionists' insistence on the exclusion of Rosie the Riveter from post–World War II factories, denying women who had joined the skilled work force during the war not only the jobs promised to returning veterans but their own earned seniority and thrusting a generation of working women into a pink-collar ghetto. Ruth Milkman has shown in convincing detail how even during World War II, unions and management cooperated to ensure that the work Rosie did was defined and redefined as women's work even if it involved skills and physical capacities previously understood to be male. Myra H. Strober has been demonstrating how in our own time, the new computer technology was quickly and emphatically assigned a gendered identity.[40]

Historians of working women have thus had especially good reason to understand that the language of separate spheres has been a language enabling contemporaries to explain to themselves the social situation—with all its ironies and contradictions—in which they understood themselves to be living. "Separate spheres" was a trope that hid its instrumentality even from those who employed it; in that sense it was deeply ambiguous. In the ambiguity, perhaps, lay its appeal.[41]

A third major characteristic of recent work, one whose potential is at last being vigorously tapped, is the use of "sphere" in a literal sense. Historians are paying considerable attention to the physical spaces to which women were assigned, those in which they lived, and those they chose for themselves. Stressing the interplay between the metaphorical and the literal, historians in the 1980s were on their way toward a resolution of the paradoxes of women's politics/women's culture with which the symposiasts of *Feminist Studies* wrestled. Historians are finding it worthwhile to treat "sphere" not only as metaphor but also as descriptor, to use it to refer to domain in the most obvious and explicit sense.

In adopting that approach historians have learned much from anthropologists, who have long understood the need to scrutinize separate men's and women's spaces. Men's places were often clearly defined; menstruating women were often excluded from them. Men's space normally included the central community meeting place and the fields; that is, as Lucienne Roubin writes, the village government "tends to juxtapose and to fuse male space with public space." Women's space, by definition, is what is left: sleeping enclosures, gardens. In the mid-1970s historians found *Woman, Culture, and Society,* an anthology edited by anthropologists Michelle Zimbalist Rosaldo and Louise Lamphere, deeply resonant for its analyses of the significance of women's behavior in domestic settings.[42]

As we have seen, historians who examined sex roles were likely to link physical separation with social subordination. That was particularly true for historians of early America: As Lyle Koehler observed, "Puritan society was organized in a way that explicitly affirmed the belief in sex segregation as a reminder of men's and women's different destinies." In a 1978 essay, Mary Maples Dunn reversed the argument. In a brilliant examination of the way control of physical space could affect public behavior, Dunn argued that the spiritual equality that Quaker theology offered women was confirmed and authenticated by the device of separate women's meetings. Women's meetings enabled women to control their own agenda, to allocate their own funds, and to exercise disciplinary control over their members, especially by validating marriages. Those roles were reinforced by Quaker women's control over their physical space, in meetinghouses with sliding partitions in the center that provided "women and men with separate spaces for the conduct of their separate business." Women of no other denomination claimed such control over their space and their recordkeeping, and Dunn suggests that the elements of physical control were central to women's more autonomous spiritual role in the Quaker community.[43]

In 1979, Estelle Freedman published an important essay, "Separatism as Strategy: Female Institution Building and American Feminism, 1870–1930." In it she sought to overcome the simplifications of the traditional male-public/female-private hierarchy by a construction that bridged the two categories: the "public female sphere." By that she referred to the "'female institution building' which emerged from the middle-class women's culture of the nineteenth century." She had in mind women's clubs (like

Sorosis, which was initiated when the New York Press Club excluded women journalists in 1868); women's colleges; women's settlement houses, most notably Hull House; women's political organizations; women's trade unions; even the women's buildings at the International Centennial Exposition in 1876 and the World's Columbian Exposition in 1892. In each case, the refusal to merge their groups into male-dominated institutions gave women not only crucial practical and political experience but also a place where they could rest the levers with which they hoped to effect social change. The space that Freedman ended by recommending to women was in part metaphorical: Women needed their own networks, and they needed to nurture their own culture. Embedded in her essay, however, was also the observation that feminists had been most successful when they had commanded actual physical space of their own, which they could define and control.[44]

If we imagine Freedman as staking out an empty shelf in the bookcase of women's history in 1979, we could now say that the shelf is crowded with books and articles that illustrate her point. New studies of the history of domesticity have understood domesticity to be an ideology whose objective correlative is the physical space of the household. The "material feminist" reformers of Dolores Hayden's *The Grand Domestic Revolution,* who flourished between 1870 and 1930, sought to reappropriate that space and to redesign it to socialize domestic work. Central kitchens, cooked food delivery, professionalized home cleaning, and other efforts to reconstruct women's work within the domestic sphere severely challenged the traditional social order. Such inventions were squelched. Powerful interest groups countered them with home mortgage policies that privileged male-headed households, highway construction that encouraged diffuse suburban development, and urban design that stressed single-family homes lacking central services. Hayden's book was followed by detailed histories by Susan Strasser and Ruth Schwartz Cowan, which tracked the development of housework and household technology. Cowan argued that the definition of the home as women's sphere was accompanied by a change in household technology with the result that men—excused from chopping wood for fire, pounding meal, and other household tasks—found the home a place of leisure, a "haven in a heartless world," while it retained its character as a place of labor for women. The work of Faye E. Dudden on household service shows that women's domestic space was pervaded by class considerations; the home was a theater, in which the mistress of the house claimed her space and assigned to the servant the space she might occupy.[45]

The philosophy and ideology of other institutions are increasingly understood to be embedded in their arrangement of physical space. Helen Lefkowitz Horowitz has traced the complex relationships between the visions that women's college founders had for their institutions and the architecture that they commissioned. In her work, even intellectual history is understood to be deeply affected by its physical context. And a rich outpouring of work on the women of the Hull House community has made it increasingly clear that having control of the physical institution of Hull House—which at its height included thirteen large structures spaced over two square blocks—provided an institutional base permitting women reformers, in Kathryn Kish Sklar's words, to "enter realms of reality dominated by men, where, for better or for worse, they competed with men for control over the distribution of social resources." Hull House was many things, not least among them a physical space in which the divorced Florence Kelley could find housing, community, and child care while she went to law school. Hull House's communal dining room was an innovative solution to the practical problems of self-maintenance for single professional women, a vigorous testimony to the advice of the material feminists whose work was chronicled by Hayden.[46]

Hull House was also a physical space in which women whose closest relationships were with other women could live comfortably in a world that increasingly scorned their relationships and their values. In this aspect of its services, the walls of Hull House were of enormous significance in marking an enclosure within which women could define the terms of their most private relationships and defend themselves against social criticism. In her memoir of her early days at Hull House, Kelley emphasized the significance of crossing the threshold into Hull House—a threshold no less metaphorical because it was also literal. Jane Addams was reticent about the psychological service Hull House performed for its residents; in *Twenty Years at Hull House* she reprinted, with apology, her classic essay on "The Subjective Necessity for Social Settlements" and then turned almost exclusively to an account of what the residents did for their neighbors. Only occasionally— "the fine old house responded kindly to repairs"—did her sense of the house as having a life of its own slip through her careful prose.[47]

The residents of Hull House understood that a city was not a single, unified entity. It was not merely that a city was *perceived* differently by each observer; the single city was many cities, selectively constructed. They would have understood Christine Stansell's coinage "City of Women," a phrase evoking her vision of public space as inhabited on different terms by men and by women, "a city of women with its own economic relations and cultural forms, a female city concealed within the larger metropolis." The first major publication project of Hull House, after all, was *Hull-House Maps and Papers,* an innovative study in social geography that plotted the neighborhood around Hull House to make it plain that the Chicago appearing on the usual maps was not the Chicago Hull House residents knew. In remapping their neighborhood, they located the philosophical construction that was Hull House squarely in physical space. Moreover, the residents understood that the experience of the city varied with gender, that working girls were particularly vulnerable in its public spaces. One of the earliest Hull House projects was a small but significant effort to claim city space for single women by establishing a cooperative residence for working girls. By establishing the Jane Club, Hull House residents announced their recognition that the physical spaces of the city were inhospitable to single women and suggested a practical model for redrawing that space.[48]

In *City of Women,* Stansell has given voice to a sweeping reformulation of social relations in urban places; the story she tells is of antebellum New York, but its point of view and its understanding of how geography can serve social analysis are of formidably broad applicability. The city of women has its own political economy, its own patterns of sociability, its own uses of the streets. It varies by class: The world of working-class women has not been the same as the world of middle-class women, but neither has it been the same as the world of working-class men.

In Stansell's work, in Joanne Meyerowitz's study of the construction of space for working women in Progressive Era Chicago, and in work by Mary Ryan on the nineteenth-century urban creation of formal public spheres, one assigned to women, the other to men, whose boundaries shifted and overlapped, our understanding of the "separate sphere" is becoming both simpler and more complex.[49] It is simpler because the separate women's sphere can be understood to denote the physical space in which women lived, but more complex because even that apparently simple physical space was complexly structured by an ideology of gender, as well as by class and race. Courtrooms in which women appear singly as plaintiffs, defendants, or witnesses are male spaces; streets on which women are afraid to walk are male spaces; universities that women enter only at male invitation are male spaces. When Susan B. Anthony led a delegation of woman's rights activists to disrupt the public ceremonies celebrating the centennial of the Declaration of Independence in Philadelphia, they challenged both male control of public space and an anthropocentric interpretation of American rights and values. When the delegation of women marched to the other side of Carpenters' Hall, there to hear Anthony declaim her own centennial address, which called for the impeachment of all officers of government because they had been false to the values of the declaration (notably, "no taxation without representation"), they both asserted their own claim to public space and implicitly rejected a politics based on the separation of spheres.[50]

Tocqueville had discerned "two clearly distinct lines of action" for the two sexes. Actually he was reporting the discourse of separate spheres, which in his day was increasing in shrillness, perhaps to cover the renegotiation of gender relations then underway. But the task of the historiographer is to comment on historians more than to evaluate actual phenomena, and from the historiographer's perspective "separate spheres" was at least in part a strategy that enabled historians to move the history of women out of the realm of the trivial and anecdotal into the realm of analytic social history. Making it possible to proceed past Mary R. Beard's generalization that women have been a force in history, the concept of separate spheres proposed a dynamic by which that force was manifest.[51]

But if our predecessors were constrained by dualisms—home versus market, public versus private, household versus state—we need no longer be so constrained. In an important essay written late in her tragically abbreviated life, Michelle Zimbalist Rosaldo, who had made her reputation exploring the contrasts between the public and the private, nature and culture, argued forcefully that it was time to move on to more complex analyses. "The most serious deficiency of a model based upon two opposed spheres," she wrote, "appears . . . in its alliance with the dualisms of the past, dichotomies which teach that women must be understood not in terms of relationship—with other women and with men—but of difference and apartness." Approaches that attempt to locate "women's 'problem' in a domain apart . . . fail to help us understand how men and women both participate in and help to reproduce the institutional forms that may oppress, liberate, join or divide them."[52] To continue to use the language of separate spheres is to deny the reciprocity between gender and society, and to impose a static model on dynamic relationships.

As we discuss the concept of separate spheres, we are tiptoeing on the boundary between politics and ideology, between sociology and rhetoric. We have entered the realm of hermeneutics; our task—insofar as it involves the analysis and demystification of a series of binary opposites—is essentially one of deconstruction. What are we to make of this polarity between the household and the world, an opposition as fundamental as the opposition between the raw and the cooked, the day and the night, the sun and the moon? We do not yet fully understand why feminists of every generation—the 1830s, the 1880s, the 1960s—have needed to define their enemy in this distinctively geographical way. Why speak of worlds, of spheres, or of realms at all? What is it in our culture that has made feminists think of themselves, in Mary Wollstonecraft's words, "as immurted in their households, groping in the dark?"[53]

The metaphor remains resonant because it retains some superficial vitality. For all our vaunted modernity, for all that men's "spheres" and women's "spheres" now overlap, vast areas of our experience and our consciousness do not overlap. The boundaries may be fuzzier, but our private spaces and our public spaces are still in many important senses gendered. The reconstruction of gender relations, and of the spaces that men and women may claim, is one of the most compelling contemporary social tasks. It is related to major social questions: the feminization of poverty, equal access to education and the professions, relations of power and abuses of power in the public sector and in the family. On a wider stage, the reconstruction of gender relations is related to major issues of power, for we live in a world in which authority has traditionally validated itself by its distance from the feminine and from what is understood to be effeminate.[54]

Little is left of Tocqueville except what he left to implication: that political systems and systems of gender relations are reciprocal social constructions. The purpose of constant analysis of language is to ensure that we give power no place to hide.[55] But the remnants of "separate spheres" that still persist are symptoms, not cause, of a particular and historically located gender system. One day we will understand the idea of separate spheres as primarily a trope, employed by people in the past to characterize power relations for which they had no other words and that they could not acknowledge because they could not name, and by historians in our own times as they groped for a device that might dispel the confusion of anecdote and impose narrative and analytical order on the anarchy of inherited evidence, the better to comprehend the world in which we live.

Notes

I am deeply grateful for the good counsel provided on earlier versions of this essay by Dorothy Ross, Tom Haskell, Barbara Sicherman, Alice Kessler-Harris, Mary Ryan, Bruce Gronbeck, Drew Faust, Cindy Aron, Joan Jacobs Brumberg, Evelyn Brooks, Allan Megill, Gerda Lerner, Susan Armeny, and the members of the Transformation Project of the Philadelphia Center for Early American Studies, all of whom tried valiantly to keep me from error and surely did not fully succeed.

1   Alexis de Tocqueville, *Democracy in America,* 2 vols. (New York: Knopf, 1945) 2: bk. 3, ch. 9–12, esp. 201, 211, 214. Just as Edward Pessen has taught us to distrust Tocqueville's observations on social mobility, it is now long past time to dispose of Tocqueville's observations on the condition of American women. Edward Pessen, "The Egalitarian Myth and the American Social Reality: Wealth, Mobility, and Equality in the 'Era of the Common Man,'" *American Historical Review* 76 (Oct. 1971): 989–1034. George Wilson Pierson's careful list of Tocqueville's encounters with Americans includes few women and none as primary informants. George Wilson Pierson, *Tocqueville and Beaumont in America* (New York: Oxford University Press, 1938), 782–86. Tocqueville's women are stereotypes. Tocqueville claims, for example, "American women never manage the outward concerns of the family or conduct a business or take a part in political life, nor are they, on the other hand, ever compelled to perform the rough labor of the fields or to make any of those laborious efforts which demand the exertion of physical strength." Tocqueville, *Democracy in America,* 2: 212. In *Democracy* we meet no adult single women, no widows. We learn nothing of women's relations with each other or of the revolutions in child nurture, women's education, and women's organizational life occurring at the very time of Tocqueville's visit. Although his companion Beaumont wrote a whole novel about the situation of a white woman who loves a black man, Tocqueville made no comment about women who sought to cross the barrier between the races. Gustave Auguste de Beaumont de la Bonninière, *Marie; or, Slavery in the United States: A Novel of Jacksonian America,* trans. Barbara Chapman (Stanford, Calif.: Stanford University Press, 1958).

2   Clifford Geertz, *Local Knowledge: Further Essays in Interpretive Anthropology* (New York, 1983), 84. Erik H. Erikson, "Inner and Outer Space: Reflections on Womanhood," in *The Woman in America,* ed. Robert Jay Lifton (Boston: Houghton Mifflin, 1965), 1–26. These papers, originally read at a 1963 conference, include Alice S. Rossi, "Equality between the Sexes: An Immodest Proposal," ibid., 98–143, and offer important evidence of the state of academic thinking about sex roles in the early 1960s.

3   Barbara Welter, "The Cult of True Womanhood: 1820–1860," *American Quarterly,* 18 (summer 1966): 151–74, esp. 152; Betty Friedan, *The Feminine Mystique* (New York: Norton, 1963).

4 Welter, "Cult of True Womanhood," 162, 174.

5 Aileen S. Kraditor, ed., *Up from the Pedestal: Selected Writings in the History of American Feminism* (Chicago: Quadrangle Books, 1968), 9, 14, 10; Christopher Lasch, *Haven in a Heartless World: The Family Besieged* (New York: Norton, 1977).

6 Gerda Lerner, "The Lady and the Mill Girl: Changes in the Status of Women in the Age of Jackson," *Midcontinent American Studies Journal* 10 (spring 1969): 5–15, esp. 10–12. Lerner also observed that Friedan's "feminine mystique" is the continuation of the old myth of woman's proper sphere. With no reference to Lerner, Neil McKendrick made much the same argument for England: The literature of separate spheres was an effort of middle-class women to maintain the difference between themselves and working-class women. McKendrick also noted men's resentment of the new purchasing power of working women; the language of separate spheres expressed their view of the new earnings "as a threat to male authority, a temptation to female luxury and indulgence, and an incitement of female independence." Neil McKendrick, "Home Demand and Economic Growth: A New View of the Role of Women and Children in the Industrial Revolution," in *Historical Perspectives: Studies in English Thought and Society in Honour of J. H. Plumb,* ed. Neil McKendrick (London: Europa, 1974), 152–210, esp. 164–67.

7 Friedrich Engels, *The Origin of the Family, Private Property and the State,* ed. Eleanor Burke Leacock (New York: International Publishers, 1972), 120, 137.

8 Juliet Mitchell, *Woman's Estate* (New York: Pantheon, 1971), 148, 182. See also Karen Sacks, "Engels Revisited: Women, the Organization of Production, and Private Property," in *Woman, Culture, and Society,* ed. Michelle Zimbalist Rosaldo and Louise Lamphere (Stanford, Calif.: Stanford University Press, 1974), 207–22; and Elizabeth Fox-Genovese, "Placing Women's History in History," *New Left Review* (May–June 1982): 5–29.

9 Alice Morse Earle, *Home Life in Colonial Days* (New York: Macmillan, 1898).

10 See Barbara Sicherman et al., *Recent United States Scholarship on the History of Women* (Washington, D.C.: American Historical Association, 1980).

11 Carroll Smith-Rosenberg, "The Female World of Love and Ritual: Relations between Women in Nineteenth-Century America," *Signs* 1 (autumn 1975): 1–29. Her later observations appeared in Carroll Smith-Rosenberg, "Politics and Culture in Women's History: A Symposium," *Feminist Studies* 6 (spring 1980): 55–64, esp. 60. See also her collected essays, Carroll Smith-Rosenberg, *Disorderly Conduct: Visions of Gender in Victorian America* (New York: Oxford University Press, 1985).

12 Blanche Wiesen Cook, "Female Support Networks and Political Activism: Lillian Wald, Chrystal Eastman, Emma Goldman," *Chrysalis* 3 (1977), 43–61; Kathryn Kish Sklar, *Catharine Beecher: A Study in American Domesticity* (New Haven, Conn.: Yale University Press, 1973). In Catharine E. Beecher, *A Treatise on Do-*

mestic Economy (Boston: T. H. Webb, 1842), 26–36, Beecher quoted Tocqueville at length and with admiration.

13 Nancy F. Cott, *The Bonds of Womanhood: "Woman's Sphere" in New England, 1780–1835* (New Haven, Conn.: Yale University Press, 1977), 200, 125, 70, 173, 197, 200, 205.

14 E. P. Thompson, "Time, Work-Discipline, and Industrial Capitalism," *Past and Present* (Dec. 1967), 56–97; Cott, *Bonds of Womanhood,* 58, 68–70. In 1964, David M. Potter had observed, "The profound differences between the patterns of men's work and women's work are seldom understood by most men, and perhaps even by most women." He noted that middle-class women's lives remained task-oriented deep into the twentieth century. David M. Potter, "American Women and the American Character," in *History and American Society: Essays of David M. Potter,* ed. Don E. Fehrenbacher (New York: Oxford University Press, 1973), 277–303, esp. 287.

15 Carl N. Degler, *At Odds: Women and the Family in America from the Revolution to the Present* (New York: Oxford University Press, 1980), 9, 298. See also ibid., 26–29, 50–54, 189, 283–98, 302–8, 317, 429. Daniel Scott Smith, "Family Limitation, Sexual Control, and Domestic Feminism in Victorian America," in *Clio's Consciousness Raised,* ed. Mary S. Hartman and Lois W. Banner (New York: Octagon, 1974), 119–36.

16 Note, however, Elizabeth Fox-Genovese, *Within the Plantation Household: Black and White Women of the Old South* (Chapel Hill: University of North Carolina Press, 1988), which addresses with subtlety the intersection of the spheres of slaveholding and enslaved women; and see Deborah Gray White, *Ar'n't I a Woman? Female Slaves in the Plantation South* (New York: Norton, 1985); and Jacqueline Jones, *Labor of Love, Labor of Sorrow: Black Women, Work, and the Family from Slavery to the Present* (New York: Basic Books, 1985).

17 Ellen DuBois, Mari Jo Buhle, Temma Kaplan, Gerda Lerner, and Carroll Smith-Rosenberg, "Politics and Culture in Women's History: A Symposium," *Feminist Studies* 6 (spring 1980): 26–64.

18 Gerda Lerner, *The Creation of Patriarchy* (New York: Oxford University Press, 1986), 212–13. Emphasis added. "For nearly four thousand years women have shaped their lives and acted under the umbrella of patriarchy," Lerner continues. "The dominated exchange submission for protection, unpaid labor for maintenance. . . . It was a rational choice for women, under conditions of public powerlessness and economic dependency, to choose strong protectors for themselves and their children." Ibid., 217–18. See also ibid., 27–28.

19 Hannah Arendt, *The Human Condition* (Chicago: University of Chicago Press, 1958), 22–78, esp. 24, 72. Aristotle, *Politics,* trans. Benjamin Jowett (New York: Modern Library, 1943), 77 (1260a). I am grateful to Judith F. Hallett for this reference. Susan Moller Okin, *Women in Western Political Thought* (Princeton, N.J.: Princeton University Press, 1979), 9–11, 233. Jean Bethke Elshtain, *Public Man,*

Private Woman: Women in Social and Political Thought (Princeton, N.J.: Princeton University Press, 1981), builds on a similar dichotomy, although Elshtain ends by decrying contemporary feminists for permitting the intrusion of politics into the private sector. See also Ruth H. Bloch, "Untangling the Roots of Modern Sex Roles: A Survey of Four Centuries of Change," *Signs* 4 (winter 1978), 237–52.

20 Samuel Willard, *A Complete Body of Divinity in Two Hundred and Fifty Expository Lectures* (Boston, 1726), 609–12, quoted in Laurel Thatcher Ulrich, "Vertuous Women Found: New England Ministerial Literature, 1688–1735," *American Quarterly*, 28 (spring 1976): 20–40, esp. 30. For skeptical views, see Lyle Koehler, *A Search for Power: The "Weaker Sex" in Seventeenth-Century New England* (Urbana: University of Illinois Press, 1980). Ulrich describes a social order in which men's and women's life roles were sharply distinct, overlapping, however, in the role of "deputy husband," which enabled women to act in the public sector if authorized by husbands and fathers. See Laurel Thatcher Ulrich, *Good Wives: Image and Reality in the Lives of Women in Northern New England, 1650–1750* (New York: Random House, 1982). Even Ulrich, however, represents a drastic revision of the generalizations about early American life made in the 1950s. See Daniel J. Boorstin, *The Americans: The Colonial Experience* (New York: Random House, 1958), 186–87. For the boundaries of witchcraft, see John Putnam Demos, *Entertaining Satan: Witchcraft and the Culture of Early New England* (New York: Oxford University Press, 1982), 281–83 (the maps of relationships between alleged witches and their accusers); and Carol F. Karlsen, *The Devil in the Shape of a Woman: Witchcraft in Colonial New England* (New York: Vintage, 1987). On European attitudes toward sex roles in Indian societies, see James Axtell, *The Invasion Within: The Contest of Cultures in Colonial North America* (New York: Oxford University Press, 1985). For an example of Europeans who observed intensely, but rarely understood, Indian culture, see Paul Le Jeune, *Relation of What Occurred in New France in the Year 1633*, in *The Jesuit Relations and Allied Documents,* ed. Reuben Gold Thwaites. 73 vols. (Cleveland, Ohio: Burrows Bros., 1896–1901), 5–6. William Penn was a major exception to this rule. See, for example, "Letter to the Free Society of Traders," Aug. 16, 1683, in *William Penn and the Founding of Pennsylvania, 1680–1684: A Documentary History,* ed. Jean R. Soderlund (Philadelphia: University of Pennsylvania Press, 1983), 308–19.

21 Mary Beth Norton, *Liberty's Daughters: The Revolutionary Experience of American Women, 1750–1800* (Boston: Little, Brown, 1980), 298. Norton found reference to women's sphere in the late colonial period. Samuel Quincy wrote to Robert Treat Paine in 1756, fearing that women want "to obtain the other's Sphere of Action, & become Men," but hoped "they will again return to the wonted Paths of true Politeness, & shine most in the proper Sphere of domestick Life." Ibid., 8. See also Linda K. Kerber, "Daughters of Columbia: Educating Women for the Republic, 1787–1805," in *The Hofstadter Aegis: A Memorial,* ed. Stanley Elkins and Eric McKitrick (New York: Knopf, 1974), 36–59.

22 Linda K. Kerber, *Women of the Republic: Intellect and Ideology in Revolutionary America* (Chapel Hill: University of North Carolina Press, 1980), 185–231. See also Linda K. Kerber, "The Republican Mother: Women and the Enlightenment —An American Perspective," *American Quarterly* 28 (summer 1976): 187–205. For France, see Darline Gay Levy, Harriet Branson Applewhite, and Mary Durham Johnson, *Women in Revolutionary Paris, 1789–1795: Selected Documents Translated with Notes and Commentary* (Urbana: University of Illinois Press, 1979). On sexuality, see Nancy F. Cott, "Passionlessness: An Interpretation of Victorian Sexual Ideology, 1790–1850," *Signs* 4 (winter 1978): 219–36. For the implications of republican ideology for the relations between women and men, see Jan Lewis, "The Republican Wife: Virtue and Seduction in the Early Republic," *William and Mary Quarterly* 44 (Oct. 1987): 689–721.

23 Marvin Meyers, *The Jacksonian Persuasion: Politics and Belief* (Stanford, Calif.: Stanford University Press, 1957), 45. Thomas L. Haskell used the phrase in a letter to me in May 1984.

24 On fathers in commercial settings willing real estate to daughters, see Toby L. Ditz, *Property and Kinship: Inheritance in Early Connecticut, 1750–1820* (Princeton, N.J.: Princeton University Press, 1986). For the anomalies of the impact of capitalism on the status of women, see Elizabeth Fox-Genovese and Eugene D. Genovese, *Fruits of Merchant Capital: Slavery and Bourgeois Property in the Rise and Expansion of Capitalism* (New York: Oxford University Press, 1983), esp. 299–336. For a succinct review of these developments, see Norma Basch, "Equity vs. Equality: Emerging Concepts of Women's Political Status in the Age of Jackson," *Journal of the Early Republic* 3 (fall 1983): 297–318, esp. 305.

25 Basch, "Equity vs. Equality." See also Norma Basch, *In the Eyes of the Law: Women, Marriage, and Property in Nineteenth-Century New York* (Ithaca, N.Y.: Cornell University Press, 1982); and Suzanne O. Lebsock, "Radical Reconstruction and the Property Rights of Southern Women," *Journal of Southern History* 43 (May 1977): 195–216.

26 Marilyn Ferris Motz, *True Sisterhood: Michigan Women and Their Kin, 1820–1920* (Albany: State University of New York Press, 1983), 29, 33–35, 121–25, 155–56, 168; Carol B. Stack, *All Our Kin: Strategies for Survival in a Black Community* (New York: Harper and Row, 1974).

27 Tamara K. Hareven, "Modernization and Family History: Perspectives on Social Change," *Signs* 2 (autumn 1976): 190–206; McKendrick, "Home Demand and Economic Growth," 164–67; Thomas Dublin, ed., *From Farm to Factory: Women's Letters, 1830–1860* (New York: Columbia University Press, 1981), 22–23, 166. Class, race, ethnicity, location, and time all affected the psychological impact of work outside the home. Leslie Woodcock Tentler found that factory women in early twentieth-century Boston, New York, Philadelphia, and Chicago not only continued to think of themselves as embedded in the family economy but

also found in the workplace other young women who reinforced this traditional understanding. Leslie Woodcock Tentler, *Wage-Earning Women: Industrial Work and Family Life in the United States, 1900–1930* (New York: Oxford University Press, 1979). See also Jacquelyn Dowd Hall, et al., *Like a Family: The Making of a Southern Cotton Mill World* (Chapel Hill: University of North Carolina Press, 1987).

28 Suzanne Lebsock, *The Free Women of Petersburg: Status and Culture in a Southern Town, 1784–1860* (New York: Norton, 1984), xv, 234.

29 Mary P. Ryan, *Cradle of the Middle Class: The Family in Oneida County, New York, 1790–1865* (Cambridge: Cambridge University Press, 1981), esp. 56, 185.

30 James Oliver Horton and Lois E. Horton, *Black Bostonians: Family Life and Community Struggle in the Antebellum North* (New York: Holmes and Meier, 1979); Dorothy Sterling, ed., *We Are Your Sisters: Black Women in the Nineteenth Century* (New York: Norton, 1984); Jones, *Labor of Love, Labor of Sorrow;* White, *Ar'n't I A Woman?* I am indebted to the interpretations of Evelyn Brooks, "The Problem of Race in Women's History," in *Coming to Terms: Feminism/Theory/Politics,* ed. Elizabeth Weed (New York: Routledge, 1989).

31 Sterling, *We Are Your Sisters,* 319–20.

32 Hareven's point that the rate of modernization may be different for men and women even within the same family applied to secularization as well. Nineteenth-century American Protestant women sustained a pattern of separateness in their religious activism and in their own religiosity. See Barbara Welter, *Dimity Convictions: The American Woman in the Nineteenth Century* (Athens: Ohio University Press, 1976), 83–102; and Joan Jacobs Brumberg, "Zenanas and Girlless Villages: The Ethnology of American Evangelical Women, 1870–1910," *Journal of American History* 69 (Sept. 1982): 347–71.

33 Rosalind Rosenberg, *Beyond Separate Spheres: Intellectual Roots of Modern Feminism* (New Haven, Conn.: Yale University Press, 1982), xiv.

34 John Mack Faragher, "History from the Inside-Out: Writing the History of Women in Rural America," *American Quarterly* 33 (winter 1981): 537–57, esp. 550. Faragher proceeded to write a history that demonstrated the gendered nature of community formation and the uneven allocation of work and power. See John Mack Faragher, *Sugar Creek: Life on the Illinois Prairie* (New Haven, Conn.: Yale University Press, 1986).

35 Mary Kelley, *Private Woman, Public Stage: Literary Domesticity in Nineteenth-Century America* (New York: Oxford University Press, 1984), 187, 100; Cindy Sondik Aron, *Ladies and Gentlemen of the Civil Service: Middle-Class Workers in Victorian America* (New York: Oxford University Press, 1987); Margaret W. Rossiter, *Women Scientists in America: Struggles and Strategies to 1940* (Baltimore, Md.: Johns Hopkins University Press, 1982). Carl Degler pointed to the paradox that woman suffrage met severe resistance while other barriers to suffrage—prop-

erty and race requirements for men—were being removed. He suggested that the resistance was in part due to the psychological investment that many women, as well as men, had in the status quo. Degler, *At Odds,* 340–61.

36 Barbara Sicherman, "Separate Spheres as Historical Paradigm: Limiting Metaphor or Useful Construct?" comment delivered at the annual meeting of the Organization of American Historians, Los Angeles, April 1984 (in Barbara Sicherman's possession); Cynthia Harrison, *On Account of Sex: The Politics of Women's Issues, 1945–1968* (Berkeley and Los Angeles: University of California Press, 1988). Elaine Tyler May, *Homeward Bound: American Families in the Cold War Era* (New York: Basic Books, 1988).

37 "Women and National Development: The Complexities of Change," *Signs,* 3 (autumn 1977), 1–338.

38 Alice Kessler-Harris, *Out to Work: A History of Wage-Earning Women in the United States* (New York: Oxford University Press, 1982). The argument is developed forcefully in Alice Kessler-Harris, "The Just Price, the Free Market and the Value of Women," paper delivered at the Seventh Berkshire Conference on the History of Women, Wellesley, Mass., June 1987 (in Alice Kessler-Harris's possession). Mary H. Blewett, "The Sexual Division of Labor and the Artisan Tradition in Early Industrial Capitalism: The Case of New England Shoemaking, 1780–1860," in *"To Toil the Livelong Day": America's Women At Work, 1780–1980,* ed. Carol Groneman and Mary Beth Norton (Ithaca, N.Y.: Cornell University Press, 1987), 35–46, esp. 36.

39 Susan Levine, *Labor's True Woman: Carpet Weavers, Industrialization, and Labor Reform in the Gilded Age* (Philadelphia: Temple University Press, 1984), 10, 148; Mari Jo Buhle, *Women and American Socialism, 1870–1920* (Urbana: University of Illinois Press, 1981); Nancy Schrom Dye, *As Equals and As Sisters: Feminism, the Labor Movement, and the Women's Trade Union League of New York* (Columbia: University of Missouri Press, 1980); Robin Miller Jacoby, "The Women's Trade Union League and American Feminism," *Feminist Studies* 3 (fall 1975): 126–40; Judith A. McGaw, *Most Wonderful Machine: Mechanization and Social Change in Berkshire Paper Making, 1801–1885* (Princeton, N.J.: Princeton University Press, 1987), 335–74. Judith A. McGaw, "No Passive Victims, No Separate Spheres: A Feminist Perspective on Technology's History," in *In Context: History and the History of Technology—Essays in Honor of Mel Kranzberg,* ed. Stephen Cutliffe and Robert W. Post (Bethlehem, Pa.: Lehigh University Press, 1988), argues that a transformation of housework *preceded* the Industrial Revolution and made many of its characteristics possible.

40 Sheila Tobias and Ruth Milkman, *Gender at Work: The Dynamics of Job Segregation by Sex during World War II* (Urbana: University of Illinois Press, 1987); Myra Strober and Carolyn L. Arnold, "Integrated Circuits/Segregated Labor: Women in Computer-Related Occupations and High-Tech Industries," in *Computer Chips and Paper Clips: Technology and Women's Employment,* ed. Heidi Hart-

mann, Robert E. Kraut, and Louise Tilly (Washington, D.C.: National Academy Press, 1986), 136–82. For important studies of the "tipping" of an occupation from male to female, see Myra H. Strober, "Toward a General Theory of Occupational Sex Segregation: The Case of Public School Teaching," in *Sex Segregation in the Workplace: Trends, Explanations, Remedies,* ed. Barbara F. Reskin (Washington, D.C.: National Academy Press, 1984), 144–56; and Myra H. Strober and David Tyack, "Why Do Women Teach and Men Manage? A Report on Research on Schools," *Signs* 5 (1980): 494–503.

41 "When we seek to make sense of such problematical topics as human nature, culture, society, and history, we never say precisely what we wish to say or mean precisely what we say," warns Hayden White. "Our discourse always tends to slip away from our data towards the structures of consciousness with which we are trying to grasp them . . . the data always resist the coherency of the image which we are trying to fashion of them." Hayden White, *Tropics of Discourse: Essays in Cultural Criticism* (Baltimore, Md.: Johns Hopkins University Press, 1978), 1.

42 Lucienne Roubin, "Male Space and Female Space within the Provençal Community," in *Rural Society in France: Selections from the* Annales: Economies, Sociétés, Civilisations, ed. Robert Forster and Orest Ranum, trans. Elborg Forster and Patricia M. Ranum (Baltimore, Md.: Johns Hopkins University Press, 1977), 152–80, esp. 155. See also Michelle Zimbalist Rosaldo, "Women, Culture, and Society: A Theoretical Overview," in *Women, Culture, and Society,* ed. Michelle Zimbalist Rosaldo and Louise Lamphere (Stanford, Calif.: Stanford University Press, 1974), 17–42; Sherry B. Ortner, "Is Female to Male As Nature Is to Culture?" ibid., 67–87; and Louise Lamphere, "Strategies, Cooperation, and Conflict in Domestic Groups," ibid., 97–112. Also important is Rayna R. Reiter, ed., *Toward an Anthropology of Women* (New York: Monthly Review Press, 1975), especially Reiter's own essay, "Men and Women in the South of France: Public and Private Domains," ibid., 252–82 (her description of the "sexual geography" of a village).

43 Koehler, *Search for Power,* 41; Mary Maples Dunn, "Saints and Sisters: Congregational and Quaker Women in the Early Colonial Period," in *Women in American Religion,* ed. Janet Wilson James (Philadelphia: University of Pennsylvania Press, 1980), 27–46, esp. 45; originally published in *American Quarterly* 30 (winter 1978): 582–601, esp. 600. About the most clearly bounded women's religious social space—the convent—we know little. In the colonial period there was a convent in Montreal, but we have no studies of its internal dynamics, though we know that some American women captives chose to stay there rather than be repatriated. See Axtell, *Invasion Within,* 302–27. On the general problem, see Elizabeth Kolmer, "Catholic Women Religious and Women's History: A Survey of the Literature," in *Women in American Religion,* ed. James, 127–39.

44 Estelle Freedman, "Separatism as Strategy: Female Institution Building and American Feminism, 1870–1930," *Feminist Studies* 5 (fall 1979): 512–29, esp. 513.

45 Dolores Hayden, *The Grand Domestic Revolution: A History of Feminist Designs for American Homes, Neighborhoods and Cities* (Cambridge: Harvard University Press, 1981); Susan Strasser, *Never Done: A History of American Housework* (New York: Pantheon, 1982); Ruth Schwartz Cowan, *More Work for Mother: The Ironies of Household Technology from the Open Hearth to the Microwave* (New York: Basic Books, 1983); Faye E. Dudden, *Serving Women: Household Service in Nineteenth-Century America* (Middletown, Conn.: Wesleyan University Press, 1983).

46 Helen Lefkowitz Horowitz, *Alma Mater: Design and Experience in the Women's Colleges from Their Nineteenth-Century Beginning to the 1930s* (New York: Knopf, 1984); Kathryn Kish Sklar, "Hull House in the 1890s: A Community of Women Reformers," *Signs* 10 (summer 1985): 658–77, esp. 659.

47 Florence Kelley, "I Go to Work," *Survey* (1 June 1927): 271–74, 301; Jane Addams, *Twenty Years at Hull House, with Autobiographical Notes* (New York: Macmillan, 1910), 93.

48 Christine Stansell, *City of Women: Sex and Class in New York, 1789–1860* (Urbana: University of Illinois Press, 1986), xi; Residents of Hull House, *Hull-House Maps and Papers* (New York: Thomas Y. Crowell, 1895). For the Jane Club, see Mary Kenny's reminiscence in Allen F. Davis and Mary Lynn McCree, eds., *Eighty Years at Hull-House* (Chicago: Quadrangle Books, 1969), 34–35.

49 Joanne J. Meyerowitz, *Women Adrift: Independent Wage Earners in Chicago, 1880–1930* (Chicago: University of Chicago Press, 1988); Mary P. Ryan, *Women in Public: Between Banners and Ballots, 1825–1880* (Baltimore, Md.: Johns Hopkins University Press, 1990).

50 Elizabeth Cady Stanton, Susan B. Anthony, and Matilda Joslyn Gage, eds., *History of Woman Suffrage,* 6 vols. (Rochester, N.Y.: S. B. Anthony, 1881–1922), 3: 3–56.

51 Tocqueville, *Democracy in America,* 2: 212; Mary R. Beard, *Woman as Force in History: A Study of Traditions and Realities* (New York: Macmillan, 1946).

52 M. Z. Rosaldo, "The Use and Abuse of Anthropology: Reflections on Feminism and Cross-Cultural Understanding," *Signs* 5 (spring 1980): 389–417, esp. 409, 417. See also the important essay, Joan Kelly, "The Doubled Vision of Feminist Theory: A Postscript to the 'Woman and Power' Conference," *Feminist Studies* 5 (spring 1979): 216–27. "Woman's place is not a separate sphere or domain of existence but a position within social existence generally." Ibid., 221. Jeanne Boydston is a historian who understands this point. See Jeanne Boydston, "To Earn Her Daily Bread: Housework and Antebellum Working-Class Subsistence," *Radical History Review* 35 (1986): 7–25; and Jeanne Boydston, "Home and Work: The Industrialization of Housework in the Northeastern United States from the Colonial Period to the Civil War" (Ph.D. diss., Yale University, 1984).

53 Mary Wollstonecraft, *A Vindication of the Rights of Woman,* ed. Miriam Brody Kramnick (Harmondsworth, Eng.: Penguin Books, 1975), 87.

54 On gender in Nazi ideology, see Renate Bridenthal, Atina Grossman, and Marion

A. Kaplan, *When Biology Became Destiny: Women in Weimar and Nazi Germany* (New York: Monthly Review Press, 1984). On gendered language and birth images in contemporary strategic analysis, see Carol Cohn, "Sex and Death in the Rational World of Defense Intellectuals," *Signs* 12 (summer 1987): 687–718.

55 The reciprocal relationship of political and gender systems is developed far more explicitly throughout Charles Louis de Secondat, Baron de Montesquieu, *Persian Letters,* trans. C. J. Betts (Harmondsworth, Eng.: Penguin Books, 1973), esp. 270–81; and Baron de Montesquieu, *The Spirit of the Laws,* trans. Thomas Nugent (New York: Hafner Publication Co., 1949), 94–108. For a brilliant analysis, see Joan W. Scott, "Gender: A Useful Category of Historical Analysis," *American Historical Review* 91 (Dec. 1986): 1053–75. And see Michael J. Shapiro, "The Political Responsibilities of the Scholar," in *The Rhetoric of the Human Science: Language and Argument in Scholarship and Public Affairs,* ed. John Nelson, Allan Megill, and Donald N. McCloskey (Madison: University of Wisconsin Press, 1988), 380.

"My Sister! My Sister!":

The Rhetoric of Catharine Sedgwick's

Hope Leslie

JUDITH FETTERLEY

Hope Leslie is arguably one of the most under-analyzed texts of nineteenth-century American literature. While sales figures from the Rutgers University Press American Women Writers series indicate its extensive use in classrooms across the country, and perhaps its interest for the general reader as well, scholarly and professional readings of the text have not developed proportionately.[1] This lag gains further resonance if we recognize that in little over a decade Catharine Sedgwick wrote five major novels—a fictional output equaled only by Cooper. Responding, like Cooper, to the call for a distinctively American literature, she rivaled him in her own day as the writer who could answer Sydney Smith's sneering question, "Who in the four quarters of the globe reads an American book?" by putting America on the literary map. Moreover, like her contemporary Lydia Huntley Sigourney, she created a space for the woman writer to participate in creating an American literature and hence in constructing the new Republic. While Nina Baym claims that if Sigourney "had not existed, it would have been necessary to invent her," Catharine Sedgwick could never have been made up, for she exceeds the imagination that did, in fact, as Baym goes on to point out, invent Sigourney as the "epitome of the specifically *female* author in her range of allowed achievements and required inadequacies."[2] In a certain sense, Catharine Sedgwick is too good to make up, and if she could not have been invented in her own day, neither has she been successfully reinvented in our own.

An essay seeking to explain this phenomenon would, I believe, work against efforts to "reinvent" Catharine Sedgwick, for it would inevitably address the conversations surrounding the construction and reconstruction of nineteenth-century American literary history more than Sedgwick's own texts. In an earlier essay on American women writers and the politics of recovery, I argued that "those of us interested in nineteenth-century American women writers may need to find ways to revitalize modes of criticism no longer fashionable because these modes may represent stages in the process of literary evaluation that we cannot do without," and I referred specifically to the techniques of close reading associated with the New Criticism of the 1950s and 1960s.[3] While those techniques were designed to establish and justify the canonization of a limited set of texts, I believe it is possible to disengage the methodology of New Criticism from its ideology and to use that methodology to serve very different political ends. Indeed, in recovering and reading women's texts from the last century, I think it is not only possible but desirable to use the master's tools to dismantle the master's house. For if a primary effect of New Critical methodology was to accord value to the objects of its attention—to find them worthy of intensive, sustained analysis, to assign them, in a word, the status of the analyzable—then to apply this methodology to texts that the ideology of New Criticism rejected as unworthy has a potentially radical effect. I would argue further that it is essential to undertake this activity at this moment in the construction of American literary history to prevent the possibility that a text such as *Hope Leslie* will be "re-vanished" on the grounds that there was really nothing to say about it anyway. It is in the effort to prevent such a disappearance that I offer the following unabashedly close reading.

I offer this essay as well as a way of reading texts by nineteenth-century American women that balances the polarity between the hagiography characteristic of the first phase of recovery, a hagiography directly proportional to the misogyny informing previous treatment of these writers and texts, and the critique associated with the second phase, a critique that implicates these writers and their texts in a variety of nineteenth-century racist, classist, and imperialist projects.[4] Like other late-twentieth-century readers of these texts, themselves recovering from the intensity associated with the alternating phases of celebration and critique, I want to move beyond the binary opposition of these impulses by proposing that what is admirable about *Hope Leslie* cannot be separated from what is problematic, and that, moreover, it is this very entanglement that makes the text worth recovering in the first place. In proposing this approach, I am also writing against what has been a primary model for the work of recovery, namely, the assumption that these works can be best understood in terms of a dominant text and a subtext—a conventional surface text that covers and contains a radical subtext (or vice versa, depending on the reader's politics). While such a model may indeed be useful for reading certain works, it tends to produce a false sense of coherence and to rationalize too readily what are clearly incompatible stories. My own approach, based on rhetorical analysis and informed by Joan Scott's work on French feminists, relies more on the concept of paradox than on coherence. Given Scott's analysis of the importance of coherence to the legitimation of ideological/political systems such as the French and American republics, and given her understanding of the role played by the production of "sexual difference" in achieving such coherence in the face of women's actual exclusion from the categories of individual and citizen, we may well conclude that those texts that have "only paradoxes to offer" are the ones we should most work to recover.[5]

Pre-text

Sedgwick opens *Hope Leslie* in England with the words of William Fletcher the elder, who represents all that is "old"—loyalty, obedience, sovereignty, authority, law:

> Take good heed that the boy be taught unquestioning and unqualified loyalty to his sovereign—the Alpha and Omega of political duty. . . . One inquiry should suffice for a loyal subject. "What is established?" and that being well ascertained, the line of duty is so plain, that he who runs may read. . . . Liberty, what is it! Daughter of disloyalty and mother of all misrule—who, from the hour that she tempted our first parents to forfeit paradise, hath ever worked mischief to our race.[6]

Fletcher's admonitions construct a "pre-text" that enables Sedgwick to propose her own theory for the origins of America. In contrast to the efforts of some of her contemporaries who gendered the nation's origins in intensely masculine terms—heroic forefathers battling a howling wilderness and warring against savage enemies—and equated republican America with manliness, Sedgwick offers a different vision of the relation of gender to the new nation. A good rhetorician, Fletcher places his most powerful argument last, convinced that by gendering "Liberty" feminine he will have created a natural and hence insuperable barrier to his nephew's identification with the concept. In the context of Sedgwick's text, however, Fletcher's strategy serves to associate the gendering of America, whether as feminine or masculine, with a specific set of political interests understood as emphatically un-American. Thus, for Sedgwick, America begins with the history of men like the younger William Fletcher who refuse to accept the gendering of "liberty" and are therefore immune to the gender terrorism of being labeled "women." Though her initial emphasis is on those men willing to pass as "women," Sedgwick's real agenda is the construction of a rhetoric that will enable women in America to become "men."

The pre-text of *Hope Leslie* provides Sedgwick with a pretext for beginning her work as well. Through the story of Alice Fletcher, forcibly prevented from joining her lover in passage to America, returned to her father's home against her will, and ordered to marry a man of her father's choosing, Sedgwick represents the fate of biological women in a country where they have no chance of becoming "men." Though William Fletcher the younger is no seducer, Alice's attempted elopement to America evokes the history of Charlotte Temple. In *Hope Leslie,* Sedgwick defines *Charlotte Temple,* one of the most popular stories in America, even in 1827, as essentially un-American, a story of the old country, for whether dragged off by a seducer or dragged home by a father, women in stories like *Charlotte Temple* are subject to patriarchal control. Committed to the structures of heterosexual romantic love, both Charlotte and Alice seek America for the wrong reasons. In preventing Alice from reaching America, Sedgwick in effect reverses and undoes the story of Charlotte Temple, clearing the ground for a new and different story based on a different understanding of America. Moreover, Sedgwick embeds *Charlotte Temple* in the text of *Hope Leslie* through the story of Rosa and Sir Philip, and, as Christopher Castiglia has observed, when she concludes her own novel with an explosion that blows up both seduced and seducer, we recognize her desire to annihilate romantic love with its plot of "seduced and abandoned" as a basis for the story of America.[7]

Romantic love stands between women and the possibility of becoming "men" in part because it reifies the separation of public and private by gender, thus supporting a model of the civic in which events in the private sphere cannot or need not have any effect on the public sphere. In challenging this model, Sedgwick not only goes beyond the postulates of Enlightenment liberal feminism that did not, for the most part, challenge the division between public and private but only argued for women's larger inclusion in the public sphere; she also rewrites her own family history. As

Mary Kelley has noted in her introduction to *The Power of Her Sympathy,* Sedgwick's father, whom she admired, even adored, assumed that service to one's country required putting aside the claims of the domestic and the private, even when doing so led to the depression, illness, and death of his wife.[8] According to Kelley, in the autobiographical memoir Sedgwick began when she was in her sixties, she articulates, however indirectly, the cost to women like her mother of her father's definition of citizenship, one that led him to serve twelve years in Congress and to be absent from home for long periods of time despite the evident distress this caused his wife. Much earlier, however, in *Hope Leslie,* Sedgwick had argued that there can be no meaningful understanding of public good separate from a recognition of its "private" cost, that in fact the true America cannot be built by men and women like her father and mother. Rather, the construction of America falls to the decidedly antiromantic Hope Leslie and to her "brother" Everell, whose understanding of citizenship makes no distinction between the public and private. When Everell rejects Governor Winthrop's argument for refusing to release Magawisca—namely, that "private feelings must yield to the public good"—he does so because he recognizes that in such formulations one person's private needs are in fact recast as public good (234).[9]

Republican Sisterhood

When the younger William Fletcher arrives in Boston, he almost immediately finds it necessary to move further west to achieve the condition of liberty for which he left the mother country. When the new so quickly becomes the old, when here becomes there, "America" emerges as a future possibility, perhaps an ever-receding one, but certainly one not yet realized in colonial Boston or the early republic of the United States. In this context the ahistoricity of Hope Leslie, a republican heroine two hundred years before her time who still occupies a space of future possibility in relation to "the girls of today," becomes legible as well. And if "America" is essentially a future possibility, then fiction provides an appropriate space for its construction through an imaginative act that might move the present toward that desired future. In *Women of the Republic,* Linda Kerber argues persuasively that in the years between 1790 and 1820 American women "were left to invent their own political character" and that they did so primarily by devoting their political imagination and energy to the construction of Republican motherhood.[10] Writing some few years after the end of the period Kerber analyzes,

Sedgwick proposes in *Hope Leslie* a different and more radical model for the inclusion of women in the American republic, a model I call "Republican sisterhood." While Republican motherhood brought women into the public and political sphere by focusing on a woman's role as the mother of sons and hence a producer of the nation's future citizens, *Hope Leslie* emphasizes the figure left out of this picture, the daughter, and holds out the hope that a daughter need not be a mother. Indeed, if Republican motherhood left the daughter out of the picture, absorbing her into the figure of the mother by conceiving of her as merely a mother in the making, *Hope Leslie* reverses the image, imagining the disappearance of the mother through her absorption into the daughter. Equally significant, the removal of the mother allows the son to be reconfigured as brother and substitutes the relation of brother and sister for the iconography of mother and son. In *Hope Leslie,* then, the daughter imagined primarily as a sister occupies the center of the picture, and because she inhabits the same subject position as her brother—in contrast to the Republican mother, whose subject position differs significantly from that of her son—she offers a different basis and hence an alternative model for women's inclusion in the American republic.

Sedgwick begins the text proper of her novel with Hope Leslie writing a very long letter to her absent "brother," Everell Fletcher. Because letters in *Hope Leslie* figure as the site where one's "true" identity is revealed (for example, when we read Sir Philip's letters we discover who he "really" is), introducing Hope Leslie through letters authenticates her character, giving the reader grounds for believing that she really is what she appears to be. Moreover, if letters provide evidence of one's "true" identity, they by necessity provide evidence of identity itself. By writing, Hope reveals not only who she *really* is but that she really *is;* she establishes her ability to construct a coherent and functioning "I" and hence her possession of the kind of literacy that matters for citizenship—the literacy of subjectivity that makes her capable of writing her own version of "history." Further, with this epistolary opening the narrative voice is displaced by a character's voice, signaling from the outset the degree to which character voice and narrative voice are one and the same. In this text, then, whose pre-text includes not only the removal of Hope's biological mother but also that of her potential surrogate mother, Mrs. Fletcher, the attack on Republican motherhood implicit in the violence of Mrs. Fletcher's removal extends even to narrative strategy, for in *Hope Leslie* there will be no "mother" voice to cover and contain the daughter.

Though the logic of Republican sisterhood requires the prior existence of the brother as ground for the claims of the sister, Sedgwick's narrative imaginatively inverts this priority to create a subliminal argument more radical still than the one she makes explicitly. This opening scene presents Everell as removed: Hope writes to him on the anniversary of his "recovery" from his first removal because he is once again removed, this time to England. Thus Sedgwick positions Hope as the original American, Eve preceding Adam in the garden.[11] Though this American Eve clearly needs her Adam/Everell, this need is not the need of romantic love, of opposites attracting and completing each other; rather, it is the need to discover someone just like her, someone who will identify with and be identical to her, who will mirror and support her. Though Hope possesses the literacy of subjectivity without Everell, her ability to construct him as identical to her plays a considerable part in her ability to construct herself through writing. Reporting her testimony to the magistrates on the question of Nelema's escape, Hope writes, "What I would fain call courage, Mr. Pynchon thought necessary to rebuke as presumption:—'Thou art somewhat forward, maiden,' he said, 'in giving thy opinion; but thou must know, that we regard it but as the whistle of a bird; withdraw, and leave judgment to thy elders'" (109). Clearly speech can be equivalent to silence, depending on who listens; and just as clearly Hope's literacy—her ability to write her own history, in which defending Nelema is understood as courage, not presumption—depends on Everell's sympathetic ear.

Sedgwick's argument for the inclusion of women as equal partners in the American republic, whether now or in the future, depends on the rhetoric of identity between brother and sister, a key component of Enlightenment liberal feminism. Thus Sedgwick carefully positions Everell as Hope's brother—his father should have been hers, her mother should have been his, they are raised together, and Hope signs her letter "sister," addressing him as "brother." Moreover, Sedgwick's initial description of Everell could easily describe Hope as well: "His smooth brow and bright curling hair, bore the stamp of the morning of life; hope and confidence and gladness beamed in the falcon glance of his keen blue eye; and love and frolic played about his lips. . . . His quick elastic step truly expressed the untamed spirit of childhood" (22). We hardly need the word *hope* here to recognize the identity of this boy to the girl who bounds from the litter carrying her to Bethel and dashes forward to be reunited with her sister.

When, in the second half of the text, Sedgwick reintroduces her characters to each other on Everell's return from England, she is even more careful to employ the rhetoric of sameness. She describes Hope as "open, fearless, and gay," with a face that reflects her "sportive, joyous, and kindly" feelings. Physically, Hope has the "elastic step and ductile grace which belongs to all agile animals"; intellectually, she has "permitted her mind to expand beyond the contracted boundaries of sectarian faith" (122, 123). In Everell, we find "a youth in manhood's earliest prime, with a frank, intelligent, and benevolent countenance over which . . . joy and anxiety flitted with rapid vicissitude" (124). Later we hear of his "unsubdued gaiety," his "unconstrained freedom," and the charm of his "ease, simplicity, and frankness" (136). Thus Hope is open and Everell frank; Everell is intelligent and Hope has an expanded mind; Hope is filled with kindly feelings and Everell is benevolent — the list could be expanded, but the point is clear.

Though Sedgwick creates an escape hatch that will allow her to conform at the eleventh hour to the conventions of the novel and specifically of the historical romance, the relationship between Hope and Everell is decidedly antiromantic. Moreover, Everell's "universal" desirability — all the girls adore him — leads one to suspect that he functions less as an object of love than as the sign of a desired state of being, a desired subjectivity. He is what girls want to be more than to have, the brother as mirror and ground for what the American sister can also become, the point of comparison that enables women in America to imagine themselves as "men."

What Then Is the American, This New Person?

Writing to Everell, Hope describes how she managed, despite the initial resistance of her "father" and aunt, to become one of a party of men venturing to climb a nearby mountain: "I urged, that our new country developes faculties that young ladies, in England, were unconscious of possessing" (98). In this carefully crafted comment, Sedgwick indicates the difference America makes: Young women in England possess the same faculties as young women in America, but England keeps women unconscious and therefore undeveloped. America allows a woman like Hope Leslie to recognize in herself the same faculties developed and promoted in her "brother" — namely, those quintessential American virtues of independence, self-reliance, and self-determination. America develops in women the ability to think critically and hence to challenge established authority.

Hope insists not only on the physical freedom to climb mountains and visit graveyards alone at night; she insists on intellectual freedom as well, having learned from the arguments of those around her to doubt all dogma and to let her mind expand "like the bird that spreads his wings and soars above the limits" (123). Perhaps most crucially, America develops in women that "reverence of self" that Judith Sargent Murray claimed was essential for the success of the new Republic in her essay of 1784, "Desultory Thoughts upon the Utility of Encouraging a Degree of Self-Complacency, Especially in Female Bosoms." Proposing that she "would early impress under proper regulations, a reverence of self . . . , that dignity, which is ever attendant upon self-approbation, arising from the genuine source of innate rectitude," Murray further suggests that such reverence for self would cure the "depression of soul" that she, like Mary Wollstonecraft, saw as afflicting many women "all their life long."[12]

Though Sedgwick gives Murray's concept a far more radical cast, Hope Leslie is clearly characterized by a "reverence of self . . . arising from the genuine source of innate rectitude." As Aunt Grafton puts it, "It's what everybody knows, who knows Hope, that she never did a wrong thing" (177)—and her hopefulness can be directly linked to her self-approbation. Moreover, Hope's reverence for self leads her to a decided lack of reverence for established authority, simply because it is established. Though rebuked for her "levity" and irreverence in suggesting to Mr. Holioke that they name the mountain they have just climbed after him, she observes that "the good man has never since spoken of his name-sake, without calling it '*Mount Holioke*,'" an observation designed to indicate to Everell that she has taken the measure of such men (101).

Hope's lack of reverence for authority manifests itself more seriously, however, in her willingness to challenge decisions on matters pertaining to the state and the "public good." Despite the disapproval of authority, Hope speaks out in defense of Nelema and when she fails to be heard takes matters into her own hands, releasing the prisoner and effecting her escape. Similarly, Hope agrees to participate in Everell's plan to free Magawisca, thereby risking her freedom and even her life by putting herself in the way of Sir Philip Gardiner and his plot. Indeed, Hope's courage in choosing to challenge the authority of the state becomes more pronounced when we recognize the degree to which the state perceives itself to be in danger and is willing to mobilize against such danger, whether real or apparent.

References to treason and sedition, to plots against the state, appear with considerable frequency in *Hope Leslie,* a story that takes place against the background of the English civil war with its monitory icon of a beheaded king. Within the text we have the multiply treacherous Sir Philip, the imprisoned Thomas Morton, instances of treachery within and among Indian tribes and between Indians and whites, and the threat of a possible conspiracy among the Indians to annihilate the English settlers. Though Sedgwick minimizes the reality of the last threat by portraying the Indian tribes as weak, dispirited, and internally divided, Hope's decision to free Magawisca suggests that she is indeed willing to take treason as her text to realize the possibility of America.[13] Thus the model of citizenship Sedgwick proposes as necessary to actualize the rhetorical premise of the equality of brother and sister requires acts of civil disobedience that may be labeled treason. Founded in the original treason of defying gender terrorism, the true and gender-neutral America may require continued acts of treason for its ultimate realization.

Sedgwick refrains, however, from making this claim an overt part of her text, for Magawisca's release in fact provokes no reprisal. Though Governor Winthrop does occasional duty as a patriarchal heavy, "impatient to put jesses on this wild bird of yours, while she is on our perch" by marrying her to William Hubbard, future author of the infamous portrayal of the slaughter of the Pequods whom Sedgwick quotes in her text, he also figures as the reconstructed father, reborn during the passage to America because he is willing to embrace the identity of "mother" and "daughter" in the pursuit of America (155). Thus we are led to believe that Winthrop too secretly desires Magawisca's release and approves of, even identifies with, Hope's act. In *Hope Leslie,* then, Sedgwick accomplishes nothing less than the deployment of biological woman as the representative American. Witty, smart, compassionate, gutsy, Hope Leslie is a lover of self and a challenger of arbitrary authority who, while insisting on her physical and intellectual freedom, is willing to take extreme risks for what she believes. She is a remarkably "American" figure, yet one whom we will not see again in American fiction for a long time. And despite the treasonous implications of her text, Sedgwick manages to keep Hope out of jail, both literally and figuratively. Yet we might well be justified in asking at what cost Sedgwick has produced this amazingly hopeful story. I turn now to a complex answer to this question, one that will, not surprisingly, present a far more complicated and less hopeful story.

Slippage and Modulation

Hope Leslie is clearly meant to be hopeful, yet whether by design or slip its title acknowledges the existence of a different tonality and a text that might as accurately be named *Hope-lessly*. As Dana Nelson observes in her own analysis, "tension and ambivalence mark the [text]," and "*Hope Leslie* is finally equivocal."[14] While Nelson locates this ambivalence partly in Sedgwick's investment in "Anglo-America's historical inheritance" and partly in the uneven developments of critique ("cultural hegemony is pervasive, and enlightenment not always foolproof"),[15] reading Sedgwick as both radical and conservative, I wish to argue that contradictions are an inevitable element of Sedgwick's project and that one cannot separate *Hope Leslie* from *Hope-lessly*. Slippages occur in the hope-ful text that operate as a kind of modulation, enabling us to move from one tonal register to another and to recognize that they are both part of the same composition. Writing to Everell, Hope remarks, "As you already know, Everell, therefore it is no confession, I love to have my own way" (114). Though this phrase can seem a gender-neutral assertion of independence, a version of that "universal" American quality celebrated, for example, in Thoreau's "different drummer," in this context it has overtones of the willful, the self-indulgent, and the personal that can make it seem gender-specific, not indeed the locution of a "brother." Later, when Hope insists on remaining alone overnight on the island where Digby, the former family servant now himself modulated into the independent supervisor of the governor's garden, resides, he situates her desire to have her own way in the context of America: "Why this having our own way, is what every body likes; it's the privilege we came to this wilderness world for" (225). Yet he also subtly undercuts the legitimacy of Hope's insistence by suggesting the potential irresponsibility of her willfulness: "I always said, Miss Hope, it was a pure mercy you chose the right way, for you always had yours" (225). Moreover, as events unfold, it becomes clear that Hope does not always choose the right way and that her insistence on having her own way places others as well as herself in danger. "Having my own way" becomes similarly gendered still later when Hope has recourse to methods of manipulation that can easily be labeled "feminine." To persuade Barnaby to let her visit Magawisca even though she does not have the authorizing pass, she bursts into tears, knowing that Barnaby will be unable to refuse "this little kindness" to "one who had been an angel of mercy to his habitation" (308).

Sedgwick similarly problematizes Hope's "reverence of self." In one of the novel's strangest scenes, she acknowledges certain anxieties on the subject of Hope's self-love, anxieties perhaps aggravated by her refusal to create a narrative voice that would itself put "jesses" on her character through narrative distance. Hope escapes being raped by the drunken sailors she encounters on her flight from Oneco by impersonating a Catholic saint; and while she justifies her act by claiming that the woman who became a saint "might not have been a great deal better than myself" (271), the excessiveness of her claim reminds readers that, where women are concerned, it may be hard to distinguish between an appropriate reverence for self and an inappropriate willingness to let the self be reverenced, for in a historical context in which self-love is specifically proscribed for women and in which women are socially constructed as selfless, self-love may seem, and even be, narcissistic. Thus while Sedgwick does present the rhetoric of "sister equals brother" as fixed and absolute, providing the theoretical ground for a gender-neutral America, she also, like Scott's French feminists who argue both "for the identity of all individuals and the difference of women,"[16] allows gender to function as a powerful field of force, destablizing the rhetoric of equality and suggesting significant distinctions between sisters and brothers. If we return to the scene in question for a moment, we can move still closer to an understanding of the rhetorical complexity of *Hope Leslie,* for the very mechanism Sedgwick uses to restabilize her rhetoric of equality points to and opens up the central rhetorical fissure of the text.

When Esther rebukes Hope for taking her rescue out of the hands of providence and into her own, and for supporting superstition even to save her own life, Everell turns "disappointed away," recognizing only the difference between Esther and Hope (272). Implicitly asserting his identification with Hope, his response returns her reverence of self to the gender-neutral context of American self-reliance. In this scene, however, Esther becomes the scapegoat, attracting all the negative energy that might otherwise be directed at Hope. Indeed, throughout the text Hope is compared explicitly and implicitly to various "sisters" and, with the exception of Magawisca, always to her advantage. Primary among these sisters are, of course, the "English" twins, Rosa and Esther. Both are women who accept male authority and see their own position as subordinate, who regard romance and religion as the main concerns of women, and who accept the separation of public and private, which entails their own confinement to the latter. Though superficially Rosa appears the opposite of the severe, chaste, and religious Esther, their equal susceptibility to romantic love, with its attendant addiction to masculine authority and consequent lack of self-reverence, links them and distinguishes them from Hope.

But what are we to make of a text in which the logic of the sister-sister relationship is so different from the logic of the sister-brother relationship? What are we to make of a text that seeks to establish equality between brother and sister while insisting on distinctions among sisters, thus presumably arguing that only some sisters get to be equal to brothers, only some women get to be sisters? What are we to make of a text that is so hard on "sisters," in which Rosa commits suicide, Jennet is blown up, and Esther is exiled? This question becomes particularly acute and particularly painful when we turn our attention to the real sisters in the text. But it is only when we turn our attention to these figures that we can begin to grasp the complexity of *Hope Leslie* and to comprehend the extent of Sedgwick's "hopelessness."

"My sister! My sister!"

Perhaps no scene in *Hope Leslie* is so troubling as the one in which Hope is temporarily reunited with her long-lost sister, Mary/Faith/White Bird. (This sister, we might note, has another name, the Indian words translated as White Bird, that even Sedgwick recognizes cannot be uttered within her text.) This scene becomes less strange, however, if we read it as the moment when "Hope Leslie" encounters "Hope-lessly," when Sedgwick confronts the contradictory impulses of her text and her own rhetorical dilemma. In this scene, we see a different Hope, one who is revolted by rather than respectful of difference, one who cannot imagine that her sister has made choices or even that she has any life at all. Hope seems desperate to recover her sister, yet her efforts place that sister in actual danger; she is obsessed with keeping her sister, yet she loses her by resorting to cheap tricks. Although we may understand why Hope views her sister as lost, we are less able to see why she should care so much, since she has been separated from this sister for years and has lived quite hopefully without her. Nor can we readily understand why she finds her sister's Indianness sickening and disgusting, since up to this point Hope's interactions with Indians have fallen within the liberal humanist and unitarian position of respect, recognition of essential sameness, and, in the case of Nelema, one might argue, even covert identification. Here, as elsewhere, Sedgwick's narrative voice doubles Hope's perspective, for Hope too constructs Mary as simply not there, without language or memory: her face "pale and spiritless was only redeemed from absolute vacancy by an expression of gentleness and modesty" (229). Though one might expect Sedgwick to recognize the implications of the word *vacant*, echoing as it does the phrase *vacuum domicilium* used by the English to justify their appropriation of Native American lands (126), like Hope she seems suddenly to be confronted with a difference so profound that she can only represent the fact that she cannot represent it.[17] But the difference of this scene, its strangeness and excessiveness, as well as its obvious contradictions—Hope wants to keep her sister but goes about it in a way guaranteed to lose her—forces us to confront extraordinary embedded questions: Why does Hope wish to recover her sister, why is she unsuccessful, and why is the experience of loss and failure so traumatic, placing her in both literal and spiritual danger? Answers to these questions become clearer if we raise another query: Who is the sister whom Hope has really lost and seeks to recover?

When Hope first encounters Magawisca, disguised as a stranger selling moccasins who shows her a "necklace of hair and gold entwined together," she exclaims, "My sister! my sister!" (183). As Sandra Zagarell has observed, Sedgwick carefully constructs the relation of Hope and Magawisca as that of "metaphoric sisters. Their first meeting takes place in the Boston cemetery in which their mothers are buried. . . . In Winthrop, Magawisca and Hope share a symbolic Puritan father, . . . and they are literal sisters-in-law."[18] Moreover, when Hope finally meets Magawisca she is in effect recovering her "brother's" lost "sister." In this context we might be justified in reading Mary's "vacantness" as a sign that she represents a space actually occupied by someone else; she is not there because she is in fact not the "true" sister. If we imagine this sister to be Magawisca, then indeed we can begin to understand Hope's hopelessness.

In her preface, Sedgwick identifies Magawisca as the figure who represents her own creativity; in imagining Magawisca she allowed herself to move from the "actual" to the "possible." Given that in this text America itself is conceived as the possible, we might reasonably assume that for Sedgwick the fate of America is inextricably linked to the fate of Magawisca. Rhetorically speaking, Magawisca's function in the text is clear; she makes the argument, articulated by Sedgwick in her preface, "that the elements of virtue and intellect are not withheld from any branch of the human family" and "that the difference of character among the various races of the earth, arises mainly from difference of condition" (6). In other words, she makes the argument that "red equals white," just as Hope makes the argument that "sister equals brother." Moreover, Magawisca realizes the more radical implications of Sedgwick's rhetoric, for having "obtained an ascendancy over her father's mind by her extraordinary gifts and superior knowledge," she has acquired substantial political power in the world of the fathers, effectively displacing her brother in her father's affection and, more significantly, in his council (326). In a word, she is the daughter understood as son.

Presumably, when Magawisca returns to Boston, Hope has the opportunity to recover this sister as well as her birth sister, but ultimately Magawisca is as lost to her as Mary. We must then ask the final and most painful question: Why can't Hope keep this sister; why, like Rachel seeking her lost children, must she continue to lament, "Oh, my sister! my sister!" (188)?

Interlude

At the end of *Hope Leslie* both Hope and Everell beg Magawisca to remain in Boston and become "American," and to the degree that Sedgwick's rhetorical model has constructed her as same and equal this plea seems eminently reasonable. During Magawisca's trial, Sir Philip has been noticeably unsuccessful in his effort to render her as "other," since she so clearly possesses those virtues understood as "universal" and particularly those understood as universal to women (note, for example, the reference to "the modesty of her sex" [282]). Yet from the outset Sedgwick has also constructed Magawisca under the mark of difference. Though introduced as one "beautiful even to an European eye," in contrast to Everell, who "bore the stamp of the morning of life; hope and confidence and gladness," Magawisca's expression is one of "thoughtfulness, and deep dejection . . . , the legible record of her birth and wrongs" (22, 23). Indeed, it is Magawisca's difference as much as her sameness that makes her attractive to Everell. In describing the interaction of Everell and Magawisca to her absent husband, Mrs. Fletcher describes a relationship that we might now identify as ideally multicultural:

> The boy doth greatly affect the company of the Pequod girl, Magawisca. If, in his studies, he meets with any trait of heroism, (and with such, truly, her mind doth seem naturally to assimilate) he straightway calleth for her and rendereth it into English, in which she hath made

such marvellous progress, that I am sometimes startled with the beautiful forms in which she clothes her simple thoughts. She, in her turn, doth take much delight in describing to him the customs of her people, and relating their traditionary tales, which are like pictures, captivating to a youthful imagination. (31–32)

Similar enough to inhabit the same world, Magawisca and Everell are yet different enough to provide opportunities for each other's growth. Indeed, one could argue that Everell's and Hope's "expanded" minds depend on Magawisca's difference, for they could not present themselves as open, tolerant, and unprejudiced if there were no differences to overcome. Yet Sedgwick's rhetorical model has no way of recognizing difference as an argument for equality. If Magawisca were to agree at the end to remain in "America," she would not in fact be able to retain those differences of race, religion, and culture that actually constitute her value. For if one argues for citizenship by invoking the rhetoric of equality, how can one at the same time promote a respect for difference? In thus confronting the limitations of her rhetorical model, Sedgwick indicates that political situations are actually far more complex than the rhetorical models designed to address them. We might recognize the persistence of this problem today in the language of affirmative action, for the phrase "women and minorities," by making women white and minorities male, excludes minority women. Since in the rhetoric of liberalism white men are understood as grounding all claims for equality, those who cannot be equated with them by either race or gender have no basis for their claims. One could make the affirmative action phrase inclusive by specifying "white women and minorities" or "women and minority males," but only at the cost of rhetorical power and the risk of being meaningless.

In this context we might acknowledge Sedgwick's courage in seeking to accomplish the rhetorically difficult and culturally unimaginable move of equating the racialized woman with the white man. Though her primary energy is clearly devoted to the equation of white women with white men, the relationship of Magawisca and Everell actually precedes that of Hope and Everell and constitutes an unprecedented and unduplicated moment in American literary history. That such an extraordinary equation should ultimately prove unstable and the strategy for accomplishing it unworkable is hardly surprising. Indeed, I have already indicated the inherent incompatibility of the value of difference with the rhetoric of equality. If we consider as well the issue of rhetorical power, we will find a further source of difficulty, for the rhetorical power of the equation of sister and brother finds its ground in the nonnegotiable privilege of the brother. To argue for the equation of sister with brother so as to make gender the sole and hence potentially insignificant variable requires from the outset a certain occlusion of race and class privilege. In making this argument, Sedgwick inevitably commits herself to a construction of the sister and brother as equally privileged except in the area of gender. Like Everell, Hope is rich, white, literate, and the beloved child of a member of the ruling elite. If we return for a moment to our first encounter with her, we may discover that her understanding of the privilege attendant on difference is as powerful as her recognition of the privilege to be gained from similarity.

We first see Hope exercising her American sense of independence, which is also her feminine insistence on having her own way, when, over the protests of the Indian men who are carrying her, she leaps from the litter, giving each a tap on his ear "for," as she puts it, "your sulkiness" (70). That Hope's motive for exercising the privilege of race is her overwhelming desire to be reunited with her sister who has in fact just then "gone native" only underscores the extraordinary complexity of this text. Placing the problematic of the sister-sister relationship at the heart of a text designed to propose optimistically and even breezily the nonproblematic equation of brother and sister requires Sedgwick to critique the very rhetoric that structures her text. For a rhetoric designed to bring privileged white women into citizenship may not do much for their differently raced (or classed) sisters. To put it slightly differently, as long as the rhetoric of equality begins from the ground of the "brother," there will be no place in America for "my sister! my sister!"

Hopelessly

We might, however, be advisedly suspicious of an argument that explains Hope's loss solely in terms of the limitations of a rhetorical model, for hopelessness seems an excessive response to rhetorical frustration. To understand the text of *Hope-lessly,* we must look more closely at the relationship of Magawisca and Everell and at the reasons for the instability of this particular equation. In so doing we may discover not only an additional rhetorical complexity; we may also uncover the more profound emotional and political causes of this complexity and instability, for such an investigation leads inevitably to a recognition of the difference between the sister-sister relationship and the brother-sister equation.

Though Sedgwick clearly constructs *Hope Leslie* as an alternate history of relations between whites and Native Americans with Magawisca as an alternative to the image of both the savage savage (she is noble) and the noble savage (she is "white"), nothing in her text suggests that Sedgwick can imagine a future for Magawisca within America. Indeed, as we have noted, while Everell is introduced in terms of future possibility ("the morning of life"), Magawisca is consistently described by images that suggest the "evening" of life—something fading, disappearing. In her final exchange with Everell and Hope, Magawisca herself points to the impossibility, and perhaps even the speciousness of their hopes: "It cannot be—it cannot be. . . . The Indian and the white man can no more mingle, and become one, than day and night" (330). Although we surely would not fault Sedgwick for failing to imagine what no one of her time seemed capable of imagining—that is, how there could be a nation within a nation, persons who could be at once Indians and Americans—we might well fault her for participating in the "cult of the Vanishing American," that "elegiac mode" so common to the literature of the period that by asserting the inevitability of Indian removal naturalizes as it deplores it. Sedgwick's text could be said to accomplish what Lora Romero has called "the historical sleight-of-hand crucial to the topos of the doomed aboriginal: it represents the disappearance of the native as not just natural but as having already happened."[19] Though Sedgwick acknowledges at various points within *Hope Leslie* the actual motive behind the removal of native Americans (the desire for their land), and though she herself may well have protested the Indian Removal Act of 1830, she does not choose to use her text as an opportunity to challenge American complacency and complicity in removal or to propose that the failure to solve the conundrum of difference lies more in a lack of commitment than in the limitations of rhetorical models or a failure of imagination. Given the extent of Sedgwick's investment in Magawisca, we might well ask why she is willing to let her go. Or, to put it somewhat differently, we might ask whether or not Magawisca's removal serves interests still more powerful than those that would be served by her inclusion.

In the scene that begins a sequence of events that by their strangeness, their difference bring all the problems of the text to the surface, Digby makes an observation that seems to come out of nowhere: "Time was," says

Digby, speaking to Everell, "when I viewed you as good as mated with Magawisca"; and Everell himself acknowledges, "I might have loved her" (214). Digby continues, however, by observing that it was just as well that Magawisca had "disappeared" before Hope's arrival at Bethel, "for I believe it would have broken [her] heart, to have been put in that kind of eclipse by Miss Leslie's coming between you and her," and he concludes by saying, "Now all is as it should be" (214). Digby's sense of resolution is, of course, premature, as it precipitates Hope's announcement of Everell and Esther's "engagement." In her haste to give Everell away to someone else, we might read an acknowledgment of Hope's discomfort with Digby's model of "natural" succession; indeed, we might read her response as evidence of her sense of the "unnaturalness" of her displacement of Magawisca and of the violence required to bring about the "should be" of her possession of Everell. While, as I have argued, the text of *Hope Leslie* is decidedly antiromantic, it may be more than just the conventions of the novel that brings about the intrusion of romance at this point in the text. Indeed, it may be that romance here serves to identify the heart of the problem in the relationship of sister to sister. For if Hope and Magawisca are constructed as rivals for the possession of Everell, then the relationship of sister to sister becomes antagonistic to that of sister to brother. And if this is so, we might expect to see as much effort directed to disrupting as to constructing the equation between sister and sister. In this context, we can better understand the relentless construction of difference between Hope and her sisters—Rosa, Esther, and Jennet—for this cumulative construction of difference supports the key distinction between Magawisca and Hope, which is muddled by the presentation of Magawisca as the red who equals white yet is clearly essential to removing Magawisca from competition with Hope.

To return, then, to the question of why Hope is unsuccessful in recovering her sister, we might say that the answer lies in the fact that as much as she wishes to recover her she equally wishes to remove her. And if we reconsider what Hope sees when she looks at her sister, we may understand more fully why she might desire her removal. In Mary's "vacantness" Hope confronts the terror of nonidentity—that absence of and from self she hopes to escape through identification with her brother—to which her identification with her sister inevitably leads. And in Mary's "degradation" Hope confronts the reality of her position as a woman, whether white or red, in the American republic of then and now. In this context, Sedgwick's assumption of the insignificance of gender, so essential to the hopeful part of *Hope Leslie,* turns into a fantasy designed to obscure the actual fact of women's radical inequality. References to the degraded condition of women break through the text in figures like Mrs. Fletcher, Madam Winthrop, Rosa, Esther, and even Magawisca, for in this context Magawisca's "redness" can be read less as a sign of race and more as a sign of gender. The rhetoric of sibling equality, then, works differently for sister and sister than for brother and sister; indeed, the one destabilizes the other as it threatens to reinforce the actual inequality of sister and brother by underscoring the significance of gender. For sisterhood, however powerful it may become, begins with the recognition of mutual misery, perhaps the reason that Hope flees the weeping Rosa. If equation with the brother represents for the sister a securing of identity and an accession to power, and if equation with the sister represents a potential threat to these possibilities, then we can appreciate the value of the construction of difference between sisters, for such difference provides the sole protection against the disintegration of identity embodied in sister Mary, "gone native."

Yet we must finally return to the implications of Sedgwick's decision to racialize the figure I have been calling the "real" sister. If we assume that her primary goal was to equate Hope and Everell and secondarily to equate Magawisca and Everell, and that these two equations would result in a third, that of Hope and Magawisca, we must ask what went wrong. The answer to this question lies not simply in the limitations of a rhetorical model that cannot at once argue for equality through sameness and promote a recognition of the value of cultural difference as an alternative basis for equality. Nor does it lie simply in the fact that the claim for the insignificance of gender is compromised by the equation of sister with sister. Rather, it also lies in the fact that Sedgwick ultimately had to confront her fear that her case for the equality of white women would be undermined if she made the same case for racially other women, that her argument for gender would be hopelessly compromised by the issue of race. Unable to imagine how she could both be and have her brother if she must also serve as the ground for her sister's equation with the brother, indeed if she must share him with her sister, Hope chooses to lose her sister.[20] In *Hope Leslie*, then, racial passing comes to seem as impossible and incomprehensible as gender passing seems obvious and simple, and the opportunity to become "men" is reserved for white women. And since the text imaginatively presents racial passing as more possible than gender passing—sister Mary becomes Indian, Magawisca could be white, but Rosa is unconvincingly male—we might argue that the construction of racial difference implicit in Hope's losing her sister is in fact essential to the argument for gender equality. If such be the case, then the rhetoric of *Hope Leslie* is hopelessly at odds with itself.[21]

Removal?

Hope Leslie provides powerful evidence of the anxiety that accompanies an argument for the equality of white middle-class "American" women. When Sir Philip visits Magawisca in jail and is accidentally locked up in a cell with Thomas Morton, he experiences a terror out of proportion to either his situation or his character. We might therefore be justified in reading this terror symptomatically—somebody is afraid of being caught, imprisoned, and driven mad as the consequence of challenging the state. In *Declarations of Independence,* Bardes and Gossett acknowledge "the repeated concern with prisons and imprisonment found in Sedgwick's novels," and suggest that this pattern derives from Sedgwick's recognition that those who challenge authority, particularly women, may well end up in prison.[22] Indeed, within the text of *Hope Leslie* we find a representation of the woman whose claim to equality met with banishment and death, not indulgence and acceptance. This figure serves to remind us of the radical nature of *Hope Leslie*'s rhetoric of gender equality and of the potential danger in making such a claim. I refer, of course, to the figure of Anne Hutchinson, who makes her appearance almost immediately in the America of *Hope Leslie*. When Mr. Fletcher haltingly tries to tell his wife that the two children of his beloved Alice have arrived in Boston, she is "perplexed by his embarrassment," and immediately inquires, "Has poor deluded Mrs. Hutchinson again presumed to disturb the peace of God's people?" (19). That Hope Leslie's arrival in America should be marked by a reference to Anne Hutchinson seems hardly accidental. Although, according to Amy Lang, the view of Anne Hutchinson as "prompted to dissent by her resentment of the lowly status assigned women in New England" is "doubtful on a number of counts," what is clear, as Lang further observes, is that she came to be seen as the embodiment of the radical possibilities for women of the American experiment, the transformation attendant on that North Atlantic passage.[23] In this light, her fate came to be understood as representing the danger attendant on the argument for gender equality because it exposed the lengths to which male authority would go to protect its own interest.

This reading of Anne Hutchinson was, of course, particularly true for the early nineteenth century, and to find Hutchinson so immediately on the threshold of our text suggests that she provides a powerful interpretive frame for what follows, just as she does later for Hawthorne. Her significance is further underscored by the prominence in *Hope Leslie* of Governor Winthrop, historically the architect of her persecution, and by the fact that the trial of Magawisca corresponds with the date of Anne Hutchinson's death. Since the supporters of Hutchinson refused to take part in the expedition against the Pequods, we might be justified in reading the trial of Magawisca as a coded representation of the trial of Anne Hutchinson. But what, then, would we make of this "fact"?

For one thing, as previously suggested, the presence of Anne Hutchinson signals the radical nature of Sedgwick's argument for gender equality and identifies the dangers of taking up such an argument. For another, the displacement of the figure of Anne Hutchinson from Hope Leslie to Magawisca suggests that Sedgwick determined to handle this danger by removal, creating a text that potentially argues for the equality of race but ultimately abandons that potential to participate in the ideology of removal, the "inevitable" and "natural" disappearance of the Indian. That such a move serves the purpose of making the argument for gender equality look less radical by comparison seems clear. However, that the price Sedgwick pays for this strategy may be so extreme as to call into question the value of her entire rhetorical enterprise seems equally clear, for the identities of Catharine Sedgwick, Hope Leslie, Magawisca, and Anne Hutchinson are hopelessly entangled in this text, and to exclude Magawisca from the rhetoric of equality leaves a text as disfigured and disarmed as Magawisca herself. Yet the power of *Hope Leslie* lies in this very entanglement, and Sedgwick's most radical act may be to propose that a text so disfigured and disarmed is the only meaningful, whole text possible for an author willing to risk engagement with the actual mess of America in the effort to realize its potential. Textually speaking, Sedgwick refuses a model of separation and removal, insisting instead on a single text whose contradictions, compromises, and complicities she thrusts on us, exposed and raw.

Notes

1 Paperback sales for *Hope Leslie* from the date of publication by Rutgers University Press (June 1987) to December 1997 are listed at 17,182. In the same series, comparable texts and figures include Fanny Fern's *Ruth Hall* (June 1986) at 17,775;

Maria Cummins's *The Lamplighter* (October 1988) at 2,906; and Caroline Kirkland's *A New Home, Who'll Follow?* (April 1990) at 3,547.

2 Nina Baym, "Reinventing Lydia Sigourney," *American Literature* 62 (Sept. 1990): 385.

3 Judith Fetterley, "Nineteenth-Century American Women Writers and the Politics of Recovery," *American Literary History* 6 (fall 1994): 605.

4 For an analysis of these two phases of recovery, see June Howard, "Unraveling Regions, Unsettling Periods: Sarah Orne Jewett and American Literary History," *American Literature* 68 (June 1996): 365–84. For examples of what I am calling the hagiographic phase as applied to *Hope Leslie*, see Christopher Castiglia, "In Praise of Extra-vagant Women: *Hope Leslie* and the Captivity Romance," *Legacy* 6 (fall 1989): 3–16; and Sandra Zagarell, "Expanding 'America': Lydia Sigourney's *Sketch of Connecticut*, Catharine Sedgwick's *Hope Leslie*," *Tulsa Studies in Women's Literature* 6 (fall 1987): 225–45. For readings of nineteenth-century American women and their texts as "complicit," see Richard Brodhead, *Cultures of Letters* (Chicago: University of Chicago Press, 1993); Lori Merish, "'The Hand of Refined Taste' in the Frontier Landscape: Caroline Kirkland's *A New Home, Who'll Follow?* and the Feminization of American Consumerism," *American Quarterly* 45 (Dec. 1993): 485–523; and more recently, Rosemarie Garland Thomson, "Benevolent Maternalism and Physically Disabled Figures: Dilemmas of Female Embodiment in Stowe, Davis, and Phelps," *American Literature* 68 (Sept. 1996): 555–86.

5 See Joan Wallach Scott, *Only Paradoxes to Offer: French Feminists and the Rights of Man* (Cambridge: Harvard University Press, 1996), 1–18.

6 Catharine Maria Sedgwick, *Hope Leslie; or, Early Times in the Massachusetts* ([1827] New Brunswick, N.J.: Rutgers University Press, 1987), 7–8. All future references are to this edition and will be cited parenthetically in the text.

7 Castiglia, "Extra-vagant Women," 9–10.

8 *The Power of Her Sympathy: The Autobiography and Journal of Catharine Maria Sedgwick*, ed. Mary Kelley (Boston: Massachusetts Historical Association, 1993), 12–15.

9 Sedgwick identifies the public nature of "private" space at various points within her text. For example, the Indian guests of Governor Winthrop refuse their placement at a side table during a family dinner, aware that this apparently private act has major implications for public policy.

10 Linda K. Kerber, *Women of the Republic* (Chapel Hill: University of North Carolina Press, 1980), 269. See especially Kerber's introduction, 7–12.

11 In arguing for the existence in the 1820s of "an admittedly short-lived female alternative" to the male construction of the genre of frontier fiction, Leland Person proposes as one of its components "an alternative, female, frontier fantasy — a pact between Indians and women, an Eden from which Adam rather than Eve has been excluded" ("The American Eve: Miscegenation and a Feminist Fron-

tier Fiction," *American Quarterly* 37 [winter 1985]: 670). While I share Person's recognition of Sedgwick's manipulation of the Edenic myth, I do not see her as seeking to exclude Adam/Everell since he is so essential to the larger rhetorical strategy of her text. Indeed, it is his necessary inclusion that finally disrupts "the pact between Indians and women."

12 *Selected Writings of Judith Sargent Murray,* ed. Sharon M. Harris (New York: Oxford University Press, 1995), 48.

13 The phrase "treason as her text" is intended to evoke the title and content of Lillian Robinson's "Treason in Our Text: Feminist Challenges to the Literary Canon," *Tulsa Studies in Women's Literature* 2 (spring 1983): 83–98.

14 Dana D. Nelson, "Sympathy as Strategy in Sedgwick's *Hope Leslie*," in *The Culture of Sentiment,* ed. Shirley Samuels (New York: Oxford University Press, 1992), 200, 202.

15 Ibid., 202, 199.

16 Scott, "Only Paradoxes," 11.

17 Though one might argue, as would Nina Baym, that Hope's reaction stems from her belief that Christianity is the only true faith and that she cannot bear to think of her sister as other than Christian, in the graveyard scene in which Hope and Magawisca meet to arrange for Hope to see her sister, Sedgwick actually distances herself from Hope's position. While Hope is relieved to discover that her sister is at least a Catholic, "for," as the narrator observes, "she thought that any Christian faith was better than none," Sedgwick does not indicate that this is her position, and indeed she gives Magawisca the last word in the exchange (189). See Nina Baym, *American Women Writers and the Work of History, 1790–1860* (New Brunswick, N.J.: Rutgers University Press, 1995), 156–62, and chap. 2.

18 Zagarell, "Expanding 'America,'" 237–38.

19 Lora Romero, "Vanishing Americans: Gender, Empire, and New Historicism," *American Literature* 63 (Sept. 1991): 385.

20 Though I am focusing here on the rhetorical interests at stake, one might argue that Sedgwick's text is haunted by the economic interests at stake as well. In a footnote to the text of Sedgwick's *Autobiography,* Mary Kelley points out that the socioeconomic standing of Sedgwick's maternal grandparents was achieved by the profit they made from their management of the Stockbridge Indian School. If this is the case, then Sedgwick's own socioeconomic standing, essential to her career as author, indirectly derived from the act of Indian removal. See Kelley, *Autobiography,* 46.

21 In "Catharine Sedgwick's 'Recital' of the Pequot War" (*American Literature* 66 [Dec. 1994]: 641–62), Philip Gould arrives at a similar analysis of Sedgwick's rhetorical dilemma, though from a rather different if not necessarily oppositional understanding of her purpose. Arguing that Sedgwick's primary agenda in *Hope Leslie* is to redefine Republican manhood as savagery and to replace this definition of virtue with one that reflects feminine values, he suggests that this gen-

der agenda is subverted by her equal desire to humanize and defend the Pequot through an appeal to the very rhetoric of manhood she is seeking to displace. Therefore she presents them as people who "admirably chose to live free or die" and valorizes them "within the culturally sanctioned terms of masculine republican heroism." Thus he concludes that Sedgwick's text "demonstrates the difficulty of carrying on simultaneous revisions of gender and race." For Gould's discussion of this issue, see 651–52.

22 Barbara Bardes and Suzanne Gossett, *Declarations of Independence* (New Brunswick, N.J.: Rutgers University Press, 1990), 35.

23 Amy Schrager Lang, *Prophetic Woman: Anne Hutchinson and the Problem of Dissent in the Literature of New England* (Berkeley and Los Angeles: University of California Press, 1987), 41, 42.

Herman Melville, Wife Beating, and the Written Page

ELIZABETH RENKER

In 1975 the *Proceedings of the Massachusetts Historical Society* published an article bringing to light some newly discovered letters, dated May 1867, that suggest Herman Melville physically and emotionally abused his wife. One letter reveals that Elizabeth Shaw Melville's minister proposed a feigned kidnapping to get her out of the house and away from her husband.[1] In 1981 twelve commentators responded to this discovery in a monograph published by the Melville Society. Several of them believed the new information to be crucial to Melville studies, while others dismissed its importance. Beyond this monograph, which I will discuss in detail presently—and despite its aim to put the new evidence "quickly . . . in the widest possible scholarly and critical perspectives" (*EWW*, v)—the discovery has received astonishingly little sustained attention.[2]

In the pages that follow I will present and review the indications in the historical record that Herman Melville physically and emotionally abused Elizabeth Shaw Melville.[3] I will then argue that his wife abuse is one crucial element in a network that also includes his tortured relation to writing and his simultaneous dependence on and resentment of the Melville women whose labor he needed to produce his texts. Finally, I will consider the implications of my analysis for understanding the position of woman in Herman's notoriously "womanless" fiction. My argument thus intends both to call specific and corrective attention, as a biographical and historical issue, to the wife beating that scholars have either silenced or failed to confront and to explore the implications of such a revelation for our understanding of Herman's writing.

The 1867 letters, one written by Elizabeth's half-brother Samuel S. Shaw and one by Elizabeth herself, were both found in the papers of Henry Whitney Bellows, the minister of the All Souls Unitarian Church in New York City from 1839 to 1882. Elizabeth and Herman were members of this church and rented a pew there beginning in 1849 (Kring, introduction, *EWW,* 1, 5–6). Samuel's letter is a response to what was apparently Bellows's suggestion that the Shaws arrange to "kidnap" Elizabeth with her covert participation. Although Samuel rejects the kidnapping plan, he stresses the necessity of getting his sister out of the house in response to unspecified "ill treat[ment]."[4] He cites Elizabeth's "belief in the insanity of her husband" and complains of "the present lamentable state of things"; he also refers to Herman and Elizabeth's domestic situation as "a cause of anxiety to all of us for years past," reporting that even "the Melvilles also, though not till quite recently, have expressed a willingness to lend their assistance" (6 May 1867, Kring and Carey, 13–15). The second letter, from Elizabeth herself, thanks Bellows for his interest and writes—apparently indicating that she has decided not to leave—"whatever further trial may be before me, I shall feel that your counsel is a strong help to sustain, more perhaps than any other earthly counsel could. . . . I lay to heart your encouraging words, and pray for submission and faith to *realize* the sustaining power of the Master's love, and to approach his Table in the very spirit of his last command" (20 May 1867, Kring and Carey, 15; emphasis in original). In her work on wife beating and battered women's resistance, Linda Gordon argues that marital violence has often been aimed at forcing a wife to stay when she threatens to leave;[5] this makes one think hard about the circumstances surrounding Elizabeth's decision, and about the "further trial" she envisioned.

Samuel's letter explains that Elizabeth would have acted to extricate herself from the domestic situation "long ago if not for imaginary and groundless apprehensions of the censure of the world upon her conduct." He reports that she has "a most exaggerated dread" of how "the eyes of the world" would look upon her "case" (6 May 1867, Kring and Carey, 14). Ensuring the credibility of the "case" clearly concerns both Elizabeth and Samuel. Samuel's rejection of the kidnapping scheme, and in fact of any scheme to make Elizabeth look as if she has not herself decided to leave Herman, is predicated on such concerns:

> But if *we* are to seem to be the real putters asunder of man and wife and she is merely to acquiesce I do not think it could be managed better

than by having her at our house and by keeping her there and carefully preventing her husband from seeing her, and telling him and everybody that we had made up our minds not to let her return.

But this might embarrass our subsequent relations with Mr. Melville and really injure my sisters case because if he should commence legal proceedings it would throw suspicion over her motives in acquiescing in a separation.

It may well be said Here is a case of mischief making where the wifes relations have created all the trouble. "She says *now* that her husband ill treated her so that she could not live with him but why did she not say so before. She goes to Boston and by dint of argument and remonstrances and bad advice of all sorts is at last persuaded into thinking herself a much injured woman." &c &c &c

And her very patience and fortitude will be turned into arguments against her belief in the insanity of her husband. (6 May 1867, Kring and Carey, 14; emphasis in original)

The hypothetical resistance to Elizabeth's charges that Samuel imagines suggests that it was not uncommon for such charges brought by wives to meet these kinds of suspicion. Samuel's experience as a lawyer presumably informs his assessment of the situation (Kring and Carey, 11). In fact, women who brought wife beating charges to court in the nineteenth century met with little success.[6] In addition, white, native-born women—like Elizabeth Shaw Melville—appear to have been less likely than black and immigrant women to complain to police about wife beating, which may indicate that they were more likely to fear the stigma of dealing with police and courts.[7] Elizabeth apparently dreaded publicizing her "trial." Furthermore, the intervention of family and friends—like Samuel, the Shaws, and even "the Melvilles"—was the primary informal means for the regulation of wife beating in the period and was far more effective than any formal means.[8]

The grievances abused women did bring against their husbands were often indirect indications rather than direct charges of physical violence. Typically they charged abusive men with related offenses that were clearer and more actionable violations of prevailing norms, including intemperance, bad language, and nonsupport, rather than with physical abuse as such. The temperance movement in particular insisted on the implicit connection between intemperance and wife abuse. In fact, "drinking" became a code word for male violence by about 1850.[9] According to Gordon, "indirect" accusations of the kinds listed above gave women a clearer claim on the community's protection than did their often-unsuccessful charges of wife beating per se. Only after 1930 did the women in her study begin to complain directly rather than indirectly about physical abuse.[10] Samuel and Elizabeth's oblique language about Herman's "ill treat[ment]" and "insanity," combined with indications that he drank heavily,[11] assumes ominous overtones in conjunction with all the other available evidence.

The additional evidence is largely anecdotal. Its primary source is Eleanor Melville Metcalf, Herman's oldest grandchild, the daughter of his youngest daughter, Frances (1855–1938). Eleanor was nine years old when Herman died (1891). In addition to her own memories of her grandfather, she reports having learned about him and about the family history primarily from her grandmother Elizabeth (1822–1906), from her parents, Frances and Henry B. Thomas, and from her great-uncle Samuel Shaw;[12] thus she presumably knew a great deal indeed about the Melvilles' domestic circle.

It was Eleanor's cooperation with Raymond M. Weaver, who contacted her in 1919, that made possible Weaver's groundbreaking *Herman Melville: Mariner and Mystic* (1921); her subsequent cooperation with the scholars who followed him fueled the Melville Revival of the 1920s. In Eleanor's *Herman Melville: Cycle and Epicycle* (1953), she mentions "such men as Harry Murray, Charles Olson, Francis Matthiessen, and many others, [who] come to the house seeking Melville."[13] She granted Weaver complete access to what he describes as "all the surviving records of her grandfather: Melville manuscripts, letters, journals, annotated books, photographs, and a variety of other material," including the "undiscovered" manuscript of *Billy Budd*.[14] The word *surviving* here is especially weighty, since many family letters and records had been destroyed, by Herman himself and by others.[15] Reports that family papers were deliberately burned by Herman and his descendants have horrified and enticed Melville scholars for generations.

Anecdotal evidence of Herman's wife abuse at last emerged in print in the 1981 Melville Society monograph obliquely entitled *The Endless, Winding Way in Melville: New Charts by Kring and Carey,* edited by Donald Yannella and Hershel Parker, with an introduction by Walter D. Kring. The monograph reprinted Kring and Jonathan S. Carey's 1975 article announcing the discovery and presented responses to it by Paul Metcalf, William Braswell, Leon Howard, Elizabeth S. Foster, Edward H. Rosenberry, Tyrus Hillway, Joyce D. and Frederick J. Kennedy, G. Thomas Tanselle, Edwin Haviland Miller, Edwin S. Shneidman, and Robert Milder. In his comments Paul Metcalf, Eleanor's son and Herman's great-grandson, reports having been told by Charles Olson that Herman came home drunk on brandy, beat Elizabeth up, and threw her down the stairs. Although Olson never revealed his source, the record indicates that Eleanor did tell others that Herman struck his wife. Paul Metcalf is right to point out both that this story has not been verified and that it is possible that worse may be true.[16] Paul has further suggested that his mother's central involvement in the Melville Revival caused what he believes to have been her nervous breakdown at the time, as she was "forced to wrestle with a new conception of her grandfather" as "the 'beast' was now becoming a 'Great Man.'"[17] Frances herself remarked of Herman as late as 1928, "I don't know him in the new light."[18] Olson claimed that Eleanor and all the Melville women hated Herman, who said of his own mother late in life, "She hated me."[19]

Braswell reports more family oral history, for which Weaver was the source: When Herman took a voyage to the Holy Land after completing *The Confidence-Man*, "some members of the family hoped he would get lost and never return" (*EWW*, 19). This story is presumably the kind that Eleanor is reputed to have told Weaver with the expectation that he would suppress it.[20] Clare Spark points out that Eleanor objected to Jay Leyda's inclusion in *The Melville Log* of letters indicating that Herman's father Allan died a "Maniac!"[21] When Paul Metcalf began to take a serious interest in Herman in the 1950s, he quickly found himself on the verge of what he calls the "forbidden territory" of Herman and Elizabeth's marital difficulties: "It became clear that she [his mother Eleanor] was privy to information—dirt, as we would call it—that she had no intention of sharing with me—being convinced (and from her point of view, rightly so) that I would probably misuse it." His mother suppressed family "dirt" to "defend at all costs" the good names of Herman and Elizabeth, and "her method was to suppress any information that might be subject to derogatory interpretation" (*EWW*, 21). As Paul notes in a letter to Clare Spark, Eleanor wanted Paul to be proud of Herman's literary accomplishments, but his drinking and wife abuse were not to be discussed.[22] Walker Cowen's *Melville's Marginalia* points to a corollary suppression. Cowen notes the frequency of misogynous markings and annotations among Herman's marginalia and suggests that many of these markings were deliberately erased. He believes that Herman's daughters or granddaughters, or perhaps Elizabeth herself, "attempted to remove the traces of embarrassing marginalia."[23]

While Eleanor would not tell Paul any "derogatory" stories, he believes that she passed such information along to *"responsible* ears" (*EWW*, 21; emphasis in original). Henry A. Murray is widely reputed to have known the "dirt"; perhaps Howard P. Vincent and Charles Olson knew as well. Harrison Hayford notes that "it was the general belief all during my Melville lifetime that he [Murray] had Melville materials and knowledge which he was withholding for inclusion in his biography."[24] Both Murray and Vincent denied having been privy to any such information (*EWW*, 21). Spark reports that Murray admitted in a 1987 interview with her that he was in possession of "family secrets" about Herman and that he intended to divulge them before his death.[25] In his correspondence with Jay Leyda in 1947, Harrison Hayford complained, "It just makes me think what a general fuck-up the whole Melville business has been, including Murray who in my calendar qualified as one of the criminals of the century to have sat on this stuff all these years. . . . Scholars for nearly a generation now have stewed around in ignorance that he could have enlightened." In his recent gloss on this letter, Hayford completely retracts his description of Murray as "one of the criminals of the century" and remarks that "it might take a like psychologist [as was Murray][26] to explain why I myself have published so little of what I 'know'—not that I am sitting on primary documents, which I've never done,"[27] certainly a cryptic and provocative allusion in the middle of a discourse on the "secrets" Murray withheld. Paul Metcalf believes that the "secret" in Murray's possession may have been the secret of Herman's wife abuse.[28] Murray died in June 1988; if he did divulge any such secrets, they have not yet been made public.[29] Forrest G. Robinson's 1992 biography of Murray reveals that his surviving unfinished manuscript of the Herman Melville biography, more than one thousand pages long, identifies Herman's "disastrous" marriage as "the incommunicable grief, the ever-gnawing pain that he, apostle of chivalry, could neverr [*sic*] confess to anyone." Robinson believes that Murray was unable to complete and publish the biography because of the extent to which he was "brought up short by what he learned of his subject, especially of his failures in later life as a husband and father."[30]

Edwin S. Shneidman suggests that when the Melvilles' eldest son, Malcolm, committed suicide in September 1867 by shooting himself in the head—four months after the kidnapping plan was discussed—he was perhaps wielding the weapon that was meant to be used "if his father, whether in an intoxicated or crazy state, ever again physically abused his mother" (*EWW*, 38). Shneidman argues that Herman, himself a rejected child, in turn became a rejecting father and "battered his own children psychologically"; he coins the term "dementia domesticus" for Herman, to describe a tortured individual "who shared his deepest self in his written works, who behaved within normal limits before most of the public world, but who at home was something of a tyrant."[31] Edwin Haviland Miller concludes from the available evidence that Herman was a heavy drinker and that he was verbally abusive toward Elizabeth and the children with the intention to humiliate. He too mentions the family tale about Herman throwing Elizabeth down the stairs but does not discuss the possibility of a pattern of physical abuse as well as verbal abuse. He does, however, see Malcolm's suicide as an act of hostility toward his father for a lack of attention and affection.[32]

The Melvilles' second child and other son, Stanwix, suffered from a mysterious deafness after Malcolm's death, which Paul Metcalf and Miller read as a hysterical deafness in response to both Malcolm's gunshot and arguments at home. In later years Herman suffered from a "sudden & severe" illness during one of Stanwix's temporary visits, which disappeared when Stanwix left.[33] Indeed, the picture of the four Melville children is a tragic one: the eldest, Malcolm, dead by his own hand; Stanwix, "possessed with a demon of *restlessness*," according to his mother,[34] and dead at thirty-five; Elizabeth, an invalid crippled with arthritis to the extent that a doctor once suggested that her fingers be straightened "*by force*";[35] and Frances, the only child to marry, who late in life would not hear the name of her father spoken.[36] After meeting Frances, Murray reported that it was a terrible experience for her even to recall her father; he diagnosed Herman's attitude in the home as one of "ritualized, emphasized, exaggerated aggression."[37]

Paul Metcalf, Braswell, Miller, Shneidman, and others who responded to the new letters in the ways I've been describing took them quite seriously. Joyce D. and Frederick J. Kennedy hailed them as an "unprecedented event in Melville scholarship," although "tantalizingly insufficient and inconclusive regarding the bizarre details that they hint at" (*EWW*, 30). Braswell concluded that Elizabeth "must have suffered a very great deal for her brother to write to Dr. Bellows as he did" (*EWW*, 20). Others, however, were more inclined to dismiss the discovery, in some cases by apologizing for Herman and blaming Elizabeth instead. Edward H. Rosenberry called the new letters an "unfortunate discovery" except in its indication that the Melvilles' marriage survived "a moment of truth"; other than that, Rosenberry says, they "tell us nothing we did not know about Herman's moodiness and emotional perversity ('insanity'), or about Lizzie's imperfect understanding of the tormented artist in her husband" (*EWW*, 26). Tyrus Hillway reminds us that "on the whole she [Elizabeth] could not have been an easy person to live with," reporting the Gansevoorts' opinion that she was "disorganized" and "a poor housekeeper" (*EWW*, 29–30). While family history presents Elizabeth this way—Eleanor reported that Elizabeth's "gifts as a practical housekeeper were never of the highest order" and that the daughter Frances was the "one practical household manager" in the family[38]—to invoke Elizabeth's poor housekeeping as if it mitigated the seriousness of Herman's abuse is disturbing logic indeed. Gordon reports that men accused of wife beating "usually countered that their wives were poor housekeepers and neglectful mothers, making themselves the aggrieved parties."[39] That such charges should be made against Elizabeth to effect Herman's exoneration, whether by her own contemporaries or by Melville scholars, is thus all the more unsettling.

The scholar's desire to exonerate Herman is no doubt rooted in the perspective Shneidman describes in the introduction to his essay on Malcolm's suicide: "I wish to begin on solid ground, by making at least one statement with which everyone will agree: Herman Melville is the hero of the Melville Society."[40] While Shneidman goes on to explain that such admiration should not preclude considerations of Herman's "all too-human characteristics,"[41] the apology with which he begins his essay indicates the immense power of Herman Melville's image as hero among Melville scholars. This powerful image may help explain why the terrible issue I here attempt to bring to wider attention has gone largely uninvestigated. Paul Metcalf's remark on Herman's "reputation" is pertinent: "By making him into a monument they tame him."[42]

This "monumental" image, as Metcalf himself suggests, is predicated on blindness to or suppression of evidence of Herman's wife abuse. But this willful blindness in the service of reputation-making has not only "tamed" Herman Melville: It is also part of a greater blindness to the absolute priority of Herman's domestic relations for understanding his writing. As my introduction suggests, his wife abuse is one crucial element in a network that also includes his agonized relation to writing and his dependence on the women in his household to produce those agonizing texts.

Herman's tortured relation to his writing is well known. His account in *Pierre* (1852) of Pierre's excruciating process of composition has traditionally and correctly been read as an autobiographical sketch. Accounts written by Elizabeth Shaw Melville; her father, Lemuel Shaw; Herman's mother, Maria Gansevoort Melville; his sister Augusta; Nathaniel Hawthorne; and others confirm the correspondences.[43] Robert Milder points out that family crises seem to have occurred for the Melvilles during or immediately after Herman's periods of intense writing: in 1852, when finishing *Pierre;* in 1856, when finishing *The Confidence-Man* and brooding about debts; and again in 1859–60, when reconciling himself to failure as a lecturer and writing his first volume of poems. By 1867, the time of the letters in question, Herman had become not only a failed novelist but also a failed poet (*EWW,* 41, 43).

Herman chronically associated writing with maddening forms of blockage. He conceived of his fiction-writing enterprise as part of what he called in "Hawthorne and His Mosses" the "great Art of Telling the Truth,"[44] but as early as 1849 he lamented that an author could never be frank with his readers under any conceivable circumstances.[45] The paradox "Hawthorne and His Mosses" presents is that the art of telling the truth requires speaking "craftily," since "it were all but madness for any good man, in his own proper character, to utter, or even hint" of the things we feel "to be so terrifically true" ("Mosses," 244). A few years later Herman again figured authorship as a frustrated attempt at truth-telling in the newly embittered tone of *Pierre,* in which the hero's desire to tell the truth ultimately produces both failure as a novelist and self-destruction.

Herman described his books, in a well-known phrase, as "botches"[46]—books that were neither the kind that would sell nor "what I feel most moved to write," but an unsuccessful combination of the two. He associated popular books with apparent meanings suited to the superficial skimmer of pages, and unpopular books with deep truths suited to "men who dive," thought-divers who come up with bloodshot eyes.[47] "So far as I am individually concerned, & independent of my pocket, it is my earnest desire to write those sort of books which are said to 'fail,'"[48] he wrote in 1849, but even those books, he lamented, had to be written secretly, to disguise and manage the truth, as Solomon did, to suit the limitations of the audience.[49] But the problem he blamed on the limitations of his readers ("What a madness & anguish it is, that an author can never—under no conceivable circumstances—be at all frank with his readers")[50] displaced what was more profoundly a frustration with his own writing as such. It would be "madness" to speak the things that are terrifically true, but it was also "madness" that he could not do so. Placing those two propositions side by side does not leave much room for writing in a calm, cool, silent, grass-growing mood—precisely the frame of mind that he himself said could never be his.[51]

Physically, too, writing was a struggle for Herman: his handwriting was illegible; he found spelling impossible; and, among other ailments, he suffered from eye, back, and head trouble that made the activity painful. In 1849 he complained to Evert Duyckinck of the "vile small print unendurable to my eyes which are tender as young sparrows."[52] Having set out on a journey in 1856 to escape the strains of authorship under which he seemed to be breaking down, he reported to his brother Allan from Liverpool, "Concerning my enjoyment of the thing, it is rather solitary business, poking about the world without a companion. Still, my health is benefited. My hip & back are better, & also my head."[53] The operative association for Herman (and his family) between his writing and both insanity and physical suffering is emblematized by two symbolic acts: first, his attempt to sell Arrowhead, his home in Pittsfield, Massachusetts, to the Insane Asylum Commission; second, his donation of funds given to him for the publication of *Clarel* to the New-York Society for the Relief of the Ruptured and Crippled.[54]

The physical engagement with the written page that threatened Herman in such a profoundly physical sense was in fact a violent one: He disfigured the surface of his writing paper, filling up every available white space with writing, as well as with cross-outs, revisions, carets, circles, and other manipulations. He cut pages apart and pinned passages together; he wrote on both sides of the page; he turned the paper upside-down and wrote some more (see figure 1).[55] His consuming relation to the written page in general also informed his relation to the written character in particular. He typically abbreviated his written marks, condensing words, eliding or combining characters, even fusing strokes of the pen that are conventionally formed as discrete units (for example, at the end of one letter and the beginning of another). When Herman was writing at white heat, his hand became increasingly rough and more and more abbreviated and elided.[56] As a writer, and especially as one whose writing was characterized by a particular set of compositional practices, the material thing confronting Herman as he struggled with "the angel—Art" was a page, blank or in various stages of inscription.[57]

These frustrations with his writing illuminate a series of textual effects that associate women with blank pages and textual production. We can see

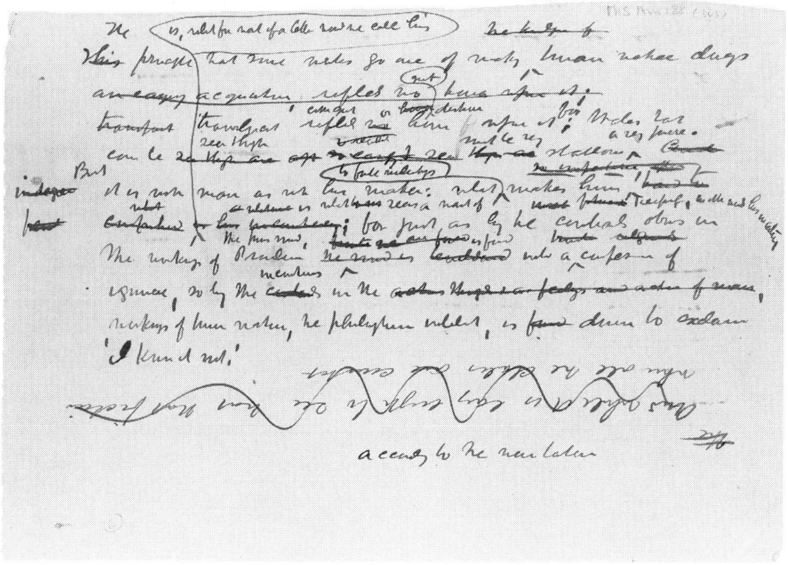

FIGURE I Manuscript fragment from chapter 14 of Herman Melville's *The Confidence-Man*, with revisions and upside-down passage. By permission of the Houghton Library, Harvard University [bMS Am188(365)]. The complicated uses to which Herman put this single sheet (and others) are traced in the Manuscript Fragments appendix to *The Confidence-Man*. In the case from which the pictured fragment derives, Herman first copied a passage in ink onto an unused full leaf from a nonextant earlier draft. After copying this passage into its next form, he struck the passage through with a wavy line. He cut narrow scraps from the middle and foot of the leaf; both surviving scraps are inscribed on both sides. He also turned the "new" page upside down for more writing, as pictured (416, 420, 431, 436–37).

this association in his first known published sketches, "Fragments from a Writing Desk," which appeared in the *Democratic Press, and Lansingburgh Advertiser* in May 1839.[58] The title of these sketches itself emphasizes the material fact of the "fragments" as inscribed pieces of paper. I suspect too that the pseudonymous initials "L. A. V." under which Herman submitted and published the tale cryptically encode not the name of a person, but rather the name of the paper in which they appeared (*Lansingburgh Ad*v*ertiser*). The first sketch sets out, in epistolary form, to describe to someone identified only as "M—" the types of female beauty found in Lansingburgh:

> I feel my powers of delineation inadequate to the task; but, nevertheless I will try my hand at the matter, although like an unskilful limner, I am fearful I shall but scandalize the charms I endeavor to copy.
>
> Come to my aid, ye guardian spirits of the Fair! Guide my awkward hand, and preserve from mutilation the features ye hover over and protect! Pour down whole floods of sparkling champaigne, my dear M—, until your brain grows giddy with emotion.[59]

The narrator sets out to "delineate" the women's "loveliest faces" ("Fragments," 193) and, at the same time, acknowledges that his "awkward" writing hand threatens them with mutilation. The lovely faces that the narrator's hand threatens and simultaneously seeks to preserve are embodiments of his writing paper. Thus the "fragment" represents the women's faces in terms it has already appropriated for itself as a material object. The narrator implores "M—": "Lay down I beseech you that odious black-lettered volume [in your lap] and let not its musty and withered leaves sully the virgin purity and whiteness of the sheet which is the vehicle of so much good sense, sterling thought, and chaste and elegant sentiment" ("Fragments," 191). The qualities of "the sheet" of paper—virgin purity, whiteness, chasteness, and elegance—are qualities then transferred to the women whom the written surface of the paper sets out to delineate. He describes them with terms including *purity, fair, chaste,* and *elegant.* Thus the writing hand and the mutilating hand are the same hand, and this hand takes as its objects both pieces of paper and the faces of women.

In the second sketch, the association between the faces the narrator describes and his own written page continues. He receives a mysterious billet-doux from a romantic admirer and is led to a secretive house for a rendezvous with the unknown woman. He encounters her "habited in a flowing robe of the purest white" ("Fragments," 203). He gazes at her silent face, tormented by desire, then flees when he realizes, "Great God, she was dumb! DUMB AND DEAF!" ("Fragments," 204; emphasis in original). The virgin whiteness thematized in these sketches under the sign of the female is metonymically the whiteness of paper and is ultimately figured as a blankness or dumbness that terrifies the narrator/writer. The "virgin purity and whiteness of the sheet" with which the narrator opens the first sketch becomes the woman in a white robe that he confronts in the second. A similar metonymy associates the woman he flings from him at the conclusion of sketch 2—"I flung her from me, even though she clung to my vesture, and with a wild cry of agony I burst from the apartment!" ("Fragments," 204)—with the "ancient Lexicon" he flings from him in the first sentence of that same sketch— "'Confusion seize the Greek!' exclaimed I, as wrathfully rising from my chair, I flung my ancient Lexicon across the room, and seizing my hat and cane, and throwing on my cloak, I sallied out" ("Fragments," 197). The violence directed at a book with which the sketch opens is converted into the violence directed at a woman with which it closes, reinforcing the association between pages and women and presenting both as objects to be "flung" from him.

The nature of the particular threat investing the dumb face becomes clear when we consider that the "Fragments" present themselves, above all, as a debut. Thus the narrator announces to "M—," his mentor, that he is ready to enter society, having conquered his "hang-dog modesty" and at last developed "a good opinion" of himself ("Fragments," 191, 192). The thematized textuality of the sketches (the letter of announcement, the faces/pages, the Lexicon, the billet-doux) contextualizes this debut in terms explicitly linked to writing. In such a context the final confrontation with the blank face of the "dumb" woman assumes especially threatening overtones for the new writer confronting the white page. As he gazes into the woman's dumb face, he meets "the gaze of this glorious being with a look as ardent, as burning, as steadfast as her own" ("Fragments," 203), confronting a face like his own but incapable of speech: "I cried 'Speak! Tell me, thou cruel! Does thy heart send forth vital fluid like my own? Am I loved,—even wildly, madly, as I love?'" ("Fragments," 204). Herman was to write later, in "Hawthorne and His Mosses," that fine authors are portrait painters whose texts "almost always" sketch their own portraits ("Mosses," 249); the narrator/writer's confrontation with the dumb face in "Fragments" is one that threatens to requite him only with its power of blankness. Indeed, even the woman's first appearance leaves him "mute" ("Fragments," 203). In the confrontation with the dumb white face that concludes sketch 2, then, the writing debut of sketch 1 ultimately gives way to a terrifying scene of writing anxiety.

The hand's power of preservation and mutilation in sketch 1 is associated with the address to the figure called "M—," the closest this early text comes to naming the pseudonymous author. Melville family letters routinely abbreviate the name "Melville" with the letter "M."[60] "Fragments" was presumably written in early 1839, when Herman was living at home with his mother, his four sisters, his elder brother Gansevoort (who had become mysteriously bedridden), and his nine-year-old brother;[61] later that year he would go to sea for the first time, leaving behind (temporarily) the home that Leon Howard's biography persistently characterizes as "adjusted to an entirely feminine regime" and thus a chronic obstacle to Herman's writing.[62]

Herman's metonymic chain associating writing with misery, women with misery, and women with writing is both most notable and most notably symptomatic of the effects I'm describing in "The Paradise of Bachelors and the Tartarus of Maids" (1855), in which the "Tartarus of Maids" is a paper mill staffed by pale girls who incarnate the blank paper the mill produces. As the narrator beholds Blood River, the menstrual flow that powers the mill, he remarks that it's "so strange that red waters should turn out pale chee—paper, I mean," substituting blank paper for the pale cheeks of the girls, a metonymy that drives the sketch.[63] The production of paper is further linked to the female body in this tale in its oft-noted associations with copulation, gestation, and birth.[64] Thus a "nurse formerly," presumably a midwife, who has left her profession because "business is poor in these parts," handles instead "piles of moist, warm sheets, which continually were being delivered into the woman's waiting hands" ("Tartarus," 333). By 1853–54, when the tale was composed, Herman was the only man in a household composed of women and children: his wife, Elizabeth; their three children; his mother, Maria; and his three unmarried sisters, Helen Maria, Augusta, and Frances Priscilla.[65] Thus, as several critics have pointed out, the Melville household itself seemed both to be generating children and to be staffed by virginal operatives.[66]

Criticism of the tale is largely divided over whether it is a biological allegory or an indictment of the machine age.[67] The distance that critics—and perhaps Herman as well, in writing allegorically—want to sustain between the biological and industrial elements of the story, and between the character of the narrator and Herman himself, needs to be collapsed. Q. D. Leavis, for example, correctly points out a link by noting that woman's toil produces Herman's children as well as his writing paper, thus drawing the biological and industrial elements of the story into relation.[68] What has not to date been grasped is that the biological and the industrial "levels" of the story are inextricably parts of a single scenario, by which I mean that the women who labored over Herman's children were the same women who produced his writing paper.

Thus the two "dimensions" of the tale that have been most compelling to critics converge in the Melvilles' domestic sphere, where Herman struggled to produce writing while the women of the household acted as laborers in the tormenting processes of both textual production and domestic economy, including childbearing and rearing. The Melvilles' domestic sphere—populated by women and children—is the site of Herman's textual production, and its "girls" are his factory operatives. The fact that Herman's model for the sketch was his visit to a local paper mill in the Berkshires[69] to buy paper for his own writing merely reinforces the association between the factory "girls" and the women who assisted him with his writing at home. Judith A. McGaw's historical study of nineteenth-century paper-making in the Berkshires points out that the tale is a "deliberate alteration of what he [Herman] must have observed," since the mill Herman visited was not staffed exclusively by female workers, and they did not operate the heavy machinery. McGaw points out that, while his description of the mill and the machines is "essentially accurate," he excluded all the male workers and their jobs.[70] It is of course crucial that Herman eliminate the male factory operatives—but not the male boss—from his vision of production, since both the biological subtext and the operations of production in the Melville home called for female laborers.[71]

In confronting the miserable blankness of the paper the mill endlessly produces, the narrator imagines what will become of the sheets. "All sorts of writings would be writ on those now vacant things—sermons, lawyers' briefs, physicians' prescriptions, love-letters, marriage certificates, bills of divorce, registers of births, death-warrants, and so on, without end" ("Tartarus," 333). The endless production of paper simultaneously raises the specter of writing "without end"; thus the relentless production of blank paper associated with the girls challenges the narrator's own ability to produce. The endless papers he catalogs are not literary texts but "domestic" matters: births, illnesses, marriages, deaths. The narrator is, of course, a "seedsman" whose seeds are disseminated in paper envelopes, but these seeds—while no doubt "intentionally" part of the sexual allegory—are more crucially a figure for Herman's own writing.[72]

As he stands watching the machinery, the narrator reflects: "A fascination fastened on me. I stood spell-bound and wandering in my soul. Before my eyes—there, passing in slow procession along the wheeling cylinders, I seemed to see, glued to the pallid incipience of the pulp, the yet more pallid faces of all the pallid girls I had eyed that heavy day. Slowly, mournfully, beseechingly, yet unresistingly, they gleamed along, their agony dimly outlined on the imperfect paper, like the print of the tormented face on the handkerchief of Saint Veronica" ("Tartarus," 333–34). The paper pulp passing before the narrator is first associated in its "pallor" with the faces of the pallid girls, reinforcing the dominant association in the tale between girls and paper. Yet the girls' "agony dimly outlined" on the paper unwittingly changes gender in the final clause, as the "pallid faces" of the girls are replaced by "the print of the tormented face on the handkerchief of Saint Veronica," a now explicitly male face (Christ's) in which the narrator's own face begins to emerge. Now the "agony" and "torment" that the tale is concerned to attribute to the girls begins to participate in an intimately related story, the story of Herman's tormented confrontation with his own writing.[73]

The configurations of this activity for him were deeply associated with the circumstances of production in what Evert A. Duyckinck called "the daughter-full house."[74] By the time of the composition of *Mardi* (1849), Herman's third novel, his wife and his sisters had become his copyists and were necessary to his process of production. Elizabeth had writing duties to fulfill, and her letters describe making plans for the rest of her day around her "copying."[75] Augusta in particular was exhaustless in copying manuscript.[76] Their writing duties were stressful for the Melville women. On 3 August 1851 Elizabeth wrote to her stepmother, "I cannot write any more—it makes me terribly nervous—I don't know as you can read this I have scribbled it so."[77] By the time Herman turned to poetry, his daughters Frances (Fanny) and Elizabeth (Bessie) were also put to work in the service of his writing. Eleanor recounted that Frances recalled with derision "the rhythm with which her father would recite, while pacing the floor, certain verses he had written, looking for approbation, she thought, from his wife and daughters." Herman also awakened one of his daughters at two in the morning to read proof of *Clarel*.[78] In 1879 Elizabeth complained that she was sick and "hardly able to guide my pencil"; in the same letter, she described Bessie's "poor hands," crippled with arthritis and consequently bound up in splints.[79] Assessed in their broader context, it's hard not to see the particularities of these illnesses as responses to enforced literary duties. Eleanor reports that Herman's sisters "were all a little afraid of him," that his daughters "developed resentments against him," and that Elizabeth was "emotionally unequal" to life with Herman.[80]

We also know that, at least on occasion, Elizabeth was sworn to secrecy[81] about Herman's writing projects and about his health and was in fact afraid to speak or write about either of these subjects. In 1860 she says of his poetry, "It has been such a profound secret between Herman and myself for so long." In a letter of 1869 (two years after the domestic crisis with which I opened this essay), she begged, "If you see Herman, please do not tell him that I said he was *not well*" (emphasis in original). In a letter of 1875, she writes, "pray do not mention to any one that he is writing poetry—you know how such things spread and he would be very angry if he knew I had spoken of it."[82] The link between Elizabeth's misery and enforced silence and Herman's writing emerges starkly in a letter of 1876 declining a visit from Herman's cousin Catherine Lansing. Enclosed inside Elizabeth's letter explaining that she and Herman were too busy reading proof to entertain a visitor was a second letter that reads as follows:

> Dear Kate, I have written you a note that Herman could see, as he wished, but want you to know how painful it is for me to write it, and also to have to give the real cause—The fact is, that Herman, poor fellow, is in such a frightfully nervous state, & particularly now with such an added strain on his mind, that I am actually *afraid* to have any one here for fear that he will be upset entirely, & not be able to go on with the printing. . . . If ever this dreadful *incubus* of a *book* (I call it so because it has undermined all our happiness) gets off Herman's shoulders I do hope he may be in better mental health—but at present I have reason to feel the gravest concern & anxiety about it—to put it in mild phrase—please do not speak of it—you know how such things are exaggerated—& I will tell you more when I see you—which I hope will be before long—you know how I enjoy your visits—And I count on your affection for us, not to say your good sense, to take this as you should & in no wise feel hurt at it—Rather pity & pray for yr ever affectionate Cousin Lizzie.[83]

Elizabeth was clearly afraid of her husband, who apparently scrutinized her correspondence and commanded her secrecy. Since, as I have argued, Herman's simultaneous dependence on and resentment of Elizabeth and the other Melville women constitutes the secret "madness & anguish" of his writing, it is not at all coincidental that Herman's only "domestic" fiction, *Pierre,* is also the only one of his texts that explicitly presents the production of writing in excruciating and destructive terms.

The women produced fair copies from which they omitted punctuation, at Herman's direction, so he could add it himself.[84] In a letter to her step-mother of 5 May 1848, Elizabeth wrote:

> I should write you a longer letter but I am very busy today copying and cannot spare the time so you must excuse it and all mistakes. I tore my sheet in two by mistake thinking it was my copying (for we only write on one side of the page) and if there is no punctuation marks you must make them yourself for when I copy I do not punctuate at all but leave it for a final revision for Herman. I have got so used to write without I cannot always think of it.[85]

If we imagine Herman scrutinizing his fair copies and running down his sheets of paper with quick, pointed gestures of the hand and arm—called "punctuation" because marking points resembles puncturing—we can also see that the physical act of punctuation marking that he reserved for himself speaks to a particularly aggressive relation to his paper. Herman's meta-phoric association between writing and violence emerges in a letter of 1849, after the disappointing reception of *Mardi:* "Hereafter I shall no more stab at a book (in print, I mean) than I would stab at a man.—. . . Had I not written & published 'Mardi,' in all likelihood, I would not be as wise as I am now, or may be. For that thing was stabbed *at* (I do not say *through*)—& therefore, I am the wiser for it.—But a bit of note paper is not large enough for this sort of writing—so no more of it."[86] Here Herman analogizes "stab-bing" at a book with "stabbing" at a man, suggesting that the acts are (at least) metaphorically equivalent. Furthermore, while at one level his figura-tion of *Mardi* as a text that can be stabbed *at* but not *through* suggests that it was philosophically too thick to be demolished by its critics, at another level his language suggests a constitutive inability to penetrate the surface of the text, for himself as well as for other aggressors: a blocked "striking through" that returns in Ahab's frenzied cry to "strike through the mask!" of the dead, blind wall of the white whale.

The mask that Ahab wants to strike through is made of "pasteboard," the binder's board made of pasted layers of paper[87] whose resonance for the author is starkly literal. "Striking through" the pasteboard mask carries a profoundly material connotation for Melville's own relentless striking through and crossing out and rewriting in an effort to find a satisfactory relation to his own white page. The pasteboard mask that can't be struck through, the text that can't be stabbed through, and the fair copies that he must himself punctuate are dramas of composition in which paper acts as a material site of blockage, frustrating the author's desire to penetrate and so to transcend material conditions. Thus in the letter cited above, "a bit of note paper is not large enough for this sort of writing": Its material dimensions are figured as that which frustrates the author's aspirations to write beyond them, a spatial metaphor for a meta/physical problem.

The material dimensions of his writing frustrations are, I have been arguing, constitutive of the terms of Melville's fiction. The network of relations I've described allows us to see that "striking through" is a materially loaded gesture for Herman Melville in terms of his violent frustration with the pages over which he labored and with the laboring women in his household. In *Mardi*, the only woman on board the *Parki* is the pilfering Annatoo, whose presence threatens the world of her male shipmates: she takes apart the ship's instruments and drops its log overboard. But Annatoo meets an early death. During a terrible storm, "the two shrouds flew madly into the air, and one of the great blocks at their ends, striking Annatoo upon the forehead," pitches her out of the ship and into the whirlpool.[88] "Striking" Annatoo out of the ship, and striking women out of the fiction whose relative womanlessness has been oft remarked, would thus constitute attempts to remove the sites of blockage—although they were not the only ones—that Herman Melville struggled with throughout his writing life.

Notes

1 Walter D. Kring and Jonathan S. Carey, "Two Discoveries Concerning Herman Melville," *Proceedings of the Massachusetts Historical Society* 87 (1975): 137–41, rpt. in *The Endless, Winding Way in Melville: New Charts by Kring and Carey*, ed. Donald Yannella and Hershel Parker, intro. Walter D. Kring (Glassboro, N.J.: Melville Society, 1981), 11–15. Kring and Carey's reprinted article is hereafter cited parenthetically as "Kring and Carey" by the page numbers from the reprinted text (11–15). The Yannella and Parker volume is cited parenthetically as *EWW*,

and Kring's introduction to that volume is cited parenthetically as Kring, intro., *EWW*.

2 In addition to Kring and Carey, who first brought the letters to light, and Yannella and Parker, who solicited responses to them for the monograph on the subject, Parker discusses the letters in his Historical Supplement to *Clarel: A Poem and Pilgrimage in the Holy Land,* by Herman Melville, ed. Harrison Hayford, Alma A. MacDougall, Hershel Parker, and G. Thomas Tanselle (Evanston, Ill.: Northwestern University Press/Newberry Library, 1991), 649–50; Parker also includes the proposed separation of Elizabeth from Herman in his 1990 "Melville Chronology" based on *The New Melville Log,* in his *Reading* Billy Budd (Evanston, Ill.: Northwestern University Press, 1990), 186. Other scholars who allude to the Kring and Carey discovery include David Leverenz, who writes that Herman "probably beat" his wife (*Manhood and the American Renaissance* [Ithaca, N.Y.: Cornell University Press, 1989], 179); Philip Young (*The Private Melville* [University Park: Pennsylvania State University Press, 1993], 153, 157); William H. Shurr ("Melville's Poems: The Late Agenda," in *A Companion to Melville Studies,* ed. John Bryant [New York: Greenwood, 1986], 365); John Bryant (introduction, *A Companion to Melville Studies,* xxiii); Hennig Cohen, whose 1991 postscript to *Selected Poems of Herman Melville* ([1964] New York: Fordham University Press, 1991) notes "the recent discoveries regarding his [Herman's] estrangement from his wife" (xvii); and Michael Paul Rogin (*Subversive Genealogy: The Politics and Art of Herman Melville* [(1979) Berkeley and Los Angeles: University of California Press, 1985], 259). When this article was first published, the Northwestern-Newberry edition of Herman Melville's *Correspondence,* ed. Lynn Horth, had just appeared (Evanston, Ill.: Northwestern University Press/Newberry Library, 1993). Horth reprints the two letters discovered by Kring and Carey in an appendix entitled "Two Letters Concerning Melville" (857–60). Thus Melville scholars are once again challenged to assess this information.

3 To avoid confusion as well as sexism in my discussions of family history, I will refer to Herman and Elizabeth by their first names throughout this essay.

4 I have not been able to determine how the particular term *ill-treatment* functioned rhetorically in the mid–nineteenth century, or if it was a euphemism for beating. Additional research in the area of wife abuse may demonstrate the cultural codes through which such behavior was discussed. Linda Gordon points out that late-nineteenth-century social workers who did not "see" wife beating often used the term *quick-tempered* to describe husbands who engaged in such behavior. See Linda Gordon, *Heroes of Their Own Lives: The Politics and History of Family Violence: Boston, 1880–1960* (New York: Viking, 1988), 264.

5 Gordon, *Heroes of Their Own Lives,* 271.

6 Ibid., 259.

7 Elizabeth Pleck, "Wife Beating in Nineteenth-Century America," *Victimology: An International Journal* 4 (1979): 65; Gordon, *Heroes of Their Own Lives,* 273.

8 Pleck, "Wife Beating," 67–68, 71.

9 See Gordon, *Heroes of Their Own Lives*, 254; Pleck, "Wife Beating," 64–65; and Barbara Leslie Epstein, *The Politics of Domesticity: Women, Evangelism, and Temperance in Nineteenth-Century America* (Middletown, Conn.: Wesleyan University Press, 1981), 106, 109. According to Pleck, by the late nineteenth century wife beating was prohibited by statute in eight states (Massachusetts, Tennessee, Nebraska, Georgia, Maryland, New Mexico, Delaware, and Arkansas). All but the Massachusetts statute, which predated the others, were passed between 1853 and 1903. Wife beating was also prohibited by judicial decision in five states (New York, Texas, Delaware, Alabama, and Kentucky; Pleck records Delaware on both lists). The absence of a specific statutory prohibition does not necessarily imply that wife beating was legal, since, for example, wife beaters were arrested for assault and battery in Maryland before it passed an explicit wife beating statute in 1882. But criminal penalties for those wife beaters who were convicted varied widely, sometimes amounting only to a fine. And many women who did bring complaints against their husbands then withdrew them or pleaded for their husbands' release lest they and their families be left without support ("Wife Beating," 61, 63, 65, 67).

10 Gordon, *Heroes of Their Own Lives*, 258–59.

11 Herman's letters frequently speak orgiastically of alcohol. Eleanor Melville Metcalf reports that in his desperation it became a "solace" to him. Edwin Haviland Miller reports that the family maintained "a conspiracy of silence" about the fact that "Herman at times leaned heavily on the bottle," especially after 1852. See Eleanor Melville Metcalf, *Herman Melville: Cycle and Epicycle* (Cambridge: Harvard University Press, 1953), 215, and Edwin Haviland Miller, *Melville* (New York: George Braziller, 1975), 321.

12 E. Metcalf, family tree (paste-down endpaper and free endpaper), in *Herman Melville*, xv.

13 E. Metcalf, *Herman Melville*, 293, xvi.

14 Raymond M. Weaver, *Herman Melville: Mariner and Mystic* (New York: George H. Doran, 1921), [acknowledgments, vii]. On the history of the *Billy Budd* manuscript, see Parker, *Reading* Billy Budd, 43–50.

15 E. Metcalf, *Herman Melville*, xvi; and Jay Leyda, *The Melville Log: A Documentary Life of Herman Melville 1819–1891*, 2 vols. (New York: Harcourt, Brace, 1951), 1:xiiiff.

16 See the remarks of Paul Metcalf and William Braswell in *EWW*, 19, 21–22. When it assists clarity I will refer to Paul Metcalf and Eleanor Melville Metcalf by their first names hereafter in the text.

17 Paul Metcalf to Clare Spark, 20 June 1989, in *Enter Isabel: The Herman Melville Correspondence of Clare Spark and Paul Metcalf*, ed. Paul Metcalf (Albuquerque: University of New Mexico Press, 1991), 79–80.

18 Quoted by E. Metcalf, *Herman Melville*, 292.

19 P. Metcalf to Spark, 15 March 1988, in *Enter Isabel*, 19; Weaver, *Herman Melville*, 62.

20 Spark quoted by P. Metcalf, in *Enter Isabel*, 33.

21 Spark to P. Metcalf, 18 May 1989, in *Enter Isabel*, 77.

22 P. Metcalf to Spark, 3 September 1988, in *Enter Isabel*, 46.

23 Walker Cowen, introduction, *Melville's Marginalia*, 2 vols. (New York: Garland, 1987), 1:x–xlv, xxii. Many of the erasures, he concludes, "reveal that Melville spent a lifetime thinking about women in spite of the rather limited use he made of them in his fiction." He goes on to suggest that the "misogynous nature of the markings" indicates that Herman was "too much bothered by the subject to trust himself to write about it" (xix). The erasures note "unpleasant aspects of women in general"; others "censure wives in particular and criticize family life from the point of view of one held captive by, but alienated from the family circle" (xx). See also Miller's comments in *EWW*, 46, on this issue.

24 Harrison Hayford, "The Melville Society: A Retrospective," *Melville Society Extracts* 88 (1992): 6.

25 Spark quoted by P. Metcalf, *Enter Isabel*, 8.

26 Murray was the cofounder of the Harvard Psychological Clinic and author of *Explorations in Personality* (Forrest G. Robinson, preface, *Love's Story Told: A Life of Henry A. Murray* [Cambridge: Harvard University Press, 1992], vii).

27 The letter from Hayford to Leyda was quoted by Spark in her 6 April 1990 letter to Hayford, and in turn quoted by Hayford in his discussion of Spark's work and P. Metcalf's in *Enter Isabel* ("The Melville Society," 5). For his 16 April 1990 gloss on the correspondence with Leyda, see "The Melville Society," 5–6. Hayford concludes his article with the words, "We 'Melville Society types,' as Clare Spark called us in that foreboding book *Enter Isabel,* are under scrutiny, our own ways and works becoming historical data" ("The Melville Society," 6).

28 P. Metcalf to Spark, 22 February 1988, in *Enter Isabel*, 14–15.

29 On the date of Murray's death, see Robinson, *Love's Story Told*, 370.

30 Murray quoted by Robinson, *Love's Story Told,* 240–41; ibid., 239, 240. Robinson refers without elaboration to Herman as a "sometimes violent husband and father" (134). He also identifies Herman's "fractious discontent with marriage" as one of the multiple sites of Murray's "personal identification" with Herman, an identification that was consuming for Murray (134). Murray's vigorous whipping sessions with his love "slave" Christiana Morgan (*slave* is their term) were understood by both of them as an integral part of Murray's work on the Melville biography. "Thou shalt be my slave until I have finished Melville to your utter satisfaction," Murray ordered Morgan. Robinson goes on: "In the months that followed there was much of Melville and, in return, much of the bruising sex that they both now craved" (257–58).

31 Edwin S. Shneidman, "Some Psychological Reflections on the Death of Malcolm Melville," *Suicide and Life-Threatening Behavior* 6 (1976): 233; *EWW*, 40.

32 *EWW,* 36–37; Miller, *Melville,* 319ff. Miller's 1975 biography calls forceful attention to Herman's enduring attraction to bachelorhood and male clubs in the context of his hostility toward marriage and family responsibilities and his demeaning strictness toward Elizabeth and the children.

33 Paul Metcalf, *Genoa: A Telling of Wonders* (Highlands, N.C.: Jonathan Williams,
1965), 75; Miller, 321–23.

34 Elizabeth to Catherine Gansevoort, 26 May 1873 (quoted by E. Metcalf, *Herman
Melville,* 228; emphasis in original).

35 E. Metcalf, *Herman Melville,* 215; Miller, *Melville,* 345 (emphasis in original).

36 My sketch of the children is indebted to Spark as quoted by P. Metcalf in *Enter
Isabel,* 59. Others who have read the tragedy of the Melville children in terms
of their father's influence on them include P. Metcalf and Shneidman. In *Genoa,*
Metcalf writes:

> And there were the children:
> Mackey,
> Stanny,
> Bessie,
> & Fanny,
>
> hovering at the edge of the storm, the vortex, and
>
> killed, crippled or withered, according to the order of birth, to how
> near in time (the father's space) they came
>
> to the eye of it.
> (73)

Shneidman's case study of Malcolm's suicide cites this passage, which is indeed
an especially apt one (238).

37 Quoted by Shneidman, "Some Psychological Reflections," 237.

38 E. Metcalf, *Herman Melville,* 98, 133.

39 Gordon, *Heroes of Their Own Lives,* 260.

40 Shneidman, "Some Psychological Reflections," 231.

41 Ibid., 232.

42 P. Metcalf to Spark, 16 October 1989, in *Enter Isabel,* 89.

43 Maria, for example, wrote to her brother Peter Gansevoort, "The constant In-
door confinement with little intermission to which Herman's occupation as author compels him, does not agree with him. This constant working of the brain,
& excitement of the imagination, is wearing Herman out" (20 April 1853; quoted
by E. Metcalf, *Herman Melville,* 147). Lemuel Shaw wrote to his son Samuel, "I
suppose you have been informed by some of the family, how very ill Herman has
been. It is manifest to me from Elizabeth's letters that she has felt great anxiety
about him. When he is deeply engaged on one of his literary works, he confines
himself to his study many hours in the day, with little or no exercise, & this espe-

cially in writing for a great many days together. He probably thus overworks himself & brings on severe nervous affections" (1 September 1856; quoted by E. Metcalf, *Herman Melville*, 159). Augusta wrote, "We all feel that it is of the utmost importance that something should be done to prevent the necessity of Herman's writing as he has been obliged to for several years past. Were he to return to the sedentary life which that of an author writing for his support necessitates, he would risk the loss of all the benefit to his health which he has gained by his tour, & possibly become a confirmed invalid" (7 April 1856; quoted by Miller, *Melville*, 293).

44 Herman Melville, "Hawthorne and His Mosses," in *The Piazza Tales, and Other Prose Pieces, 1839–1860,* ed. Harrison Hayford, Alma A. MacDougall, G. Thomas Tanselle, et al. (Evanston, Ill.: Northwestern University Press/Newberry Library, 1987), 244; hereafter parenthetically cited as "Mosses." Although this essay takes Hawthorne as its subject, its focus on the problems facing the American genius clearly refers to Herman himself, who was in the process of composing *Moby-Dick* at the time (Merton M. Sealts Jr., historical note to *The Piazza Tales,* 459).

45 To Evert A. Duyckinck, 3 March 1849, and to Duyckinck, 2 and 14 December 1849, in *The Letters of Herman Melville,* ed. Merrell R. Davis and William H. Gilman (New Haven, Conn.: Yale University Press, 1960), 80, 96. (At the time of this article's composition, the Northwestern-Newberry edition of the correspondence had not yet been published; hence I cite the Davis and Gilman edition throughout.)

46 "What I feel most moved to write, that is banned,—it will not pay. Yet, altogether, write the *other* way I cannot. So the product is a final hash, and all my books are botches" (to Nathaniel Hawthorne, 1? June 1851, in *Letters,* 128; emphasis in original).

47 "I love all men who *dive.* Any fish can swim near the surface, but it takes a great whale to go down stairs five miles or more," he wrote to Duyckinck in a discussion of Emerson (to Evert A. Duyckinck, 3 March 1849, in *Letters,* 79; emphasis in original).

48 To Lemuel Shaw, 6 October 1849, in *Letters,* 92.

49 "It seems to me now that Solomon was the truest man who ever spoke, and yet that he a little *managed* the truth with a view to popular conservatism; or else there have been many corruptions and interpolations of the text" (to Nathaniel Hawthorne, 1? June 1851, in *Letters,* 130; emphasis in original).

50 To Evert A. Duyckinck, 2 and 14 December 1849, in *Letters,* 96.

51 To Nathaniel Hawthorne, 1? June 1851, in *Letters,* 128.

52 To Evert A. Duyckinck, 24 February 1849, in *Letters,* 77.

53 To Allan Melville, 10, 13, 14 November 1856, in *Letters,* 184; *Letters,* 181 n.9.

54 On Herman's attempt to sell Arrowhead, see Leyda, *The Melville Log,* 2:506, which reprints an item from the *Berkshire County Eagle* (31 August 1855). The story of the publication of *Clarel* is the following: Melville's uncle, Peter Gan-

sevoort, provided $1200 to publish *Clarel* in August 1875. After Peter's death, Peter's daughter, Catherine Gansevoort Lansing, gave Melville another $100 to cover additional publication expenses that the original gift had not covered. Apparently Melville agonized over this additional gift, alternately accepting it and returning it and then accepting it again over the course of almost a year. Melville accepted the $100 in August 1876; thought better of it in September and donated it to the organization mentioned; accepted another $100 from Catherine in January 1877; revoked it by letter in March; and finally returned the money in June, apparently ending the exchange. (To Peter Gansevoort, 26 August 1875, in *Letters,* 243–44, and 244 n.6; and to Catherine Gansevoort Lansing, 25 July 1876, 246; 2 August 1876, 247; 13 September 1876, 250; 4 January 1877, 254; and 7 March 1877, 254–55; see also 255 n.1, all in *Letters.*)

55 For some examples of these practices, see the Manuscript Fragments appendix to *The Confidence-Man: His Masquerade,* by Herman Melville, ed. Harrison Hayford, Hershel Parker, and G. Thomas Tanselle (Evanston, Ill.: Northwestern University Press/Newberry Library, 1984), 401–99; hereafter referred to as *The Confidence-Man.*

56 He characteristically omitted certain letters of the alphabet singly or in groups, and abbreviated certain words ("recvd" for "received" and "Mondy Eveng" for "Monday Evening," for example). These "condensed words" are not always consistent, and Davis and Gilman speculate that they are in some cases deliberate abbreviations, but in others are more likely irregularities produced by Melville's "haste or carelessness or enthusiasm" in the formation of letters. See Davis and Gilman's introduction to their edition of the *Letters,* especially "Melville's Hand," xxi–xxv. On the difficulties of reading Melville's handwriting in general, see John Bryant, "Melville's L-Word: First Intentions and Final Readings in *Typee,*" *New England Quarterly* 63 (1990): 120–31, and the textual notes to Davis and Gilman's *Letters,* 321–85.

57 The quoted phrase is from Melville's poem "Art" (reprinted from *Timoleon* [1891] in Howard P. Vincent, *Collected Poems of Herman Melville* [Chicago: Hendricks House, 1947], 231). My assessment of the material configurations of the scene of writing for Herman Melville is indebted to Michael Fried's explorations of the materiality of writing and the facial quality of the page in the work of Stephen Crane, Joseph Conrad, and Frank Norris. See "Almayer's Face: On 'Impressionism' in Conrad, Crane, and Norris," *Critical Inquiry* 17 (1990): 193–236 and *Realism, Writing, Disfiguration: On Thomas Eakins and Stephen Crane* (Chicago: University of Chicago Press, 1986).

58 Harrison Hayford, Alma A. MacDougall, G. Thomas Tanselle, et al., "Notes on Individual Prose Pieces," in *The Piazza Tales,* 622.

59 Herman Melville, "Fragments from a Writing Desk," in *The Piazza Tales,* 191–204, 194; hereafter cited parenthetically as "Fragments."

60 See, for examples, letters quoted by E. Metcalf, *Herman Melville,* 7 and 171; and

Weaver, *Herman Melville*, 266. Miller also reads this "M" as a sign for "Melville" (47).

61 Of Maria and Allan Melville's eight children, four sons and four daughters, the three older sons—Gansevoort (b. 1815), Herman (b. 1819), and Allan (b. 1823)—all struggled to earn a living in the wake of their father's death in 1832, in various short-lived and unsuccessful ventures away from home. In late 1838 Herman had returned home to Lansingburgh after a brief attempt at teaching in a rural school. The family was in deep financial trouble; the Melvilles had moved from Albany to Lansingburgh in May 1838 because of their serious financial difficulties. Eleanor Melville Metcalf writes that despite the economic crisis of this period, "She [Maria] felt it necessary to keep a servant she could not pay, her wages being half the rent. The day had not come when she was to be 'energetic about the farm' in Pittsfield, and when her daughters would all lend a hand with the housework" (*Herman Melville*, 19). On 5 June Herman embarked on his first sea voyage, from New York to Liverpool. See Leon Howard, *Herman Melville: A Biography* (Berkeley and Los Angeles: University of California Press, 1951), 7–14; E. Metcalf, *Herman Melville*, 15–21; Leyda, *The Melville Log*, 1:82–86; Hayford, et. al., "Notes on Individual Prose Pieces," in *The Piazza Tales*, 622–23.

62 Howard, *Herman Melville*, 93. The domestic arena that figures in such negative prominence for Howard includes both the household in which Herman grew up, presided over by his mother Maria, and the household in which he produced most of his writing, after his marriage in 1847, in which he was surrounded by wife and children in addition to mother and sisters. Thus, in the former case, Howard notes that Herman fled to New York City to write *Typee* since "writing could hardly have been easy in a household adjusted to an almost entirely feminine regime" (93); in 1846 Tom Melville, Herman's youngest brother, at age sixteen "had begun to show signs of manly restlessness in his feminine environment" and thus had determined to sail the South Seas before the mast (98); during the composition of *Omoo*, his sister Augusta was preparing to be a bridesmaid, "and the Melville household turned busily to dressmaking. The atmosphere was hardly productive of easy literary composition" (99). In the latter case, during the early stages of the composition of *Moby-Dick*, Herman and Allan were sharing a household in New York City, "and a household consisting of a widow, two wives, three babies, and four spinsters would provide an impossible environment for a writer who was just hitting his stride" (153).

63 Herman Melville, "The Paradise of Bachelors and the Tartarus of Maids," in *The Piazza Tales*, 316–35, 329; hereafter cited parenthetically as "Tartarus."

64 For an early example of this reading, see E. H. Eby, "Herman Melville's 'Tartarus of Maids,'" *Modern Language Quarterly* 1 (1940): 95–100; see also Lea Bertani Vozar Newman's summary of the critical history of the tale in *A Reader's Guide to the Short Stories of Herman Melville* (Boston: G. K. Hall, 1986), 283–305.

65 See Hayford et al., "Notes on Individual Prose Pieces," in *The Piazza Tales*, 709;

Weaver, *Herman Melville*, 303; Newman, *A Reader's Guide*, 287. Herman's other sister, Catherine (Kate), married John Hoadley in September 1853; in that same month Helen Maria became engaged to George Griggs. Augusta and Frances Priscilla remained single (see E. Metcalf, *Herman Melville*, 150; family tree, pastedown endpaper and free endpaper).

66 Miller, *Melville*, 260; Newton Arvin, *Herman Melville* ([1950] New York: Viking, 1957), 238; Newman, *A Reader's Guide*, 287.

67 See Newman, *A Reader's Guide*, 283–305.

68 Q. D. Leavis, "Melville: The 1853–6 Phase," in *New Perspectives on Melville*, ed. Faith Pullin (Kent, Ohio: Kent State University Press, 1978), 205–6.

69 This was probably the Carson mill in Dalton. See Hayford, et al., "Notes on Individual Prose Pieces," in *The Piazza Tales*, 710.

70 Judith A. McGaw, *Most Wonderful Machine: Mechanization and Social Change in Berkshire Paper Making, 1801–1885* (Princeton, N.J.: Princeton University Press, 1987), 335 n.1.

71 Although McGaw's assessment is enormously useful, I disagree with her conclusions about why Herman changed what he would have observed at the mill. She argues that he meant the tale as a critique of the period's "well-known female textile mill employees as well as of the more general exploitation of women in industrializing America." She offers as further evidence the narrator's route in the story, which, she argues, is based on the route from Pittsfield to North Adams, a textile manufacturing center, rather than on the route from Pittsfield to Dalton, where the paper mill was located. Thus, her argument holds, he eliminated men from among the factory operatives at the paper mill in order to invoke textile mills and "women's employment generally" (*Most Wonderful Machine*, 335 n.1).

72 Herman also figures writing as seed in "Hawthorne and His Mosses," in which Hawthorne's writing is metaphorically seminal: "But already I feel that this Hawthorne has dropped germinous seeds into my soul. He expands and deepens down, the more I contemplate him; and further, and further, shoots his strong New-England roots into the hot soil of my Southern soul" ("Mosses," 250).

73 I explore the subject of Herman Melville and the scene of writing further in *Strike through the Mask: Herman Melville and the Scene of Writing* (Baltimore, Md.: Johns Hopkins University Press, 1996).

74 Duyckinck to his wife Margaret, 7 August 1851 (quoted by E. Metcalf, *Herman Melville*, 115).

75 See, for example, the letter quoted by Weaver, *Herman Melville*, 280–82.

76 Weaver, *Herman Melville*, 272.

77 Elizabeth to her stepmother, Hope Savage Shaw, whom she addressed as "mother," 3 August 1851, quoted by Weaver, *Herman Melville*, 311.

78 E. Metcalf, *Herman Melville*, 76–77; 215.

79 Elizabeth Shaw Melville to Catherine Gansevoort Lansing, 7 March 1879, extracted in *Family Correspondence of Herman Melville, 1830–1904, In the Gansevoort-*

Lansing Collection, ed. Victor Hugo Paltsits (Brooklyn, N.Y.: Haskell House, 1976), 57–58. See also Miller, *Melville,* 345, 320.

80   E. Metcalf, *Herman Melville,* 26, 215, 55.

81   Miller notes that Herman forced Elizabeth to be secretive and that to live with him she "had to accept his abuse, the anger which he projected on her, and to lie and to apologize in order to salve the feelings of relatives" (*Melville,* 320).

82   E. Metcalf, *Herman Melville,* 213, 230, 185.

83   2 February 1876; quoted by E. Metcalf, *Herman Melville,* 237; emphasis in original.

84   See Harrison Hayford, Hershel Parker, and G. Thomas Tanselle, textual record in *Mardi and a Voyage Thither,* by Herman Melville (Evanston, Ill.: Northwestern University Press/Newberry Library, 1970), 686; and Hayford et al., notes to *The Piazza Tales,* 652.

85   Elizabeth to her stepmother, 5 May 1848, quoted by Harrison Hayford, Hershel Parker, and G. Thomas Tanselle, Historical Note to *Moby-Dick or the Whale,* by Herman Melville (Evanston, Ill.: Northwestern University Press/Newberry Library, 1988), 619. See also Weaver, *Herman Melville,* 271–72.

86   To Evert A. Duyckinck, 2 and 14 December 1849, in *Letters,* 96; emphasis in original.

87   Pasteboard covers for books had become the rule by the late eighteenth century in America, replacing the wooden boards used prior to this time. See Hannah Dustin French, "Early American Bookbinding by Hand," in *Bookbinding in America: Three Essays,* ed. Hellmut Lehmann-Haupt (New York: Bowker, 1967), 14, 50, 95.

88   Melville, *Mardi and A Voyage Thither,* 117.

Contradictory Impulses:

María Amparo Ruiz de Burton, Resistance

Theory, and the Politics of Chicano/a Studies

JOSÉ F. ARANDA JR.

It has been neither an Alexander nor a Napoleon, desirous of conquest in order to extend his dominions or add to his glory, who has inspired the proud Anglo-Saxon race in its desire, its frenzy to usurp and gain control of that which rightfully belongs to its neighbors; rather it has been the nation itself [the Colossus of the North] which, possessed of that roving spirit that moved the barbarous hordes of a former age in a far remote north, has swept away whatever has stood in the way of its aggrandizement.
—José María Tornel y Mendívil, *Relations between Texas, the United States of America and the Mexican Republic* (1837)

In the passage above, Tornel y Mendívil, Mexican Secretary of War during the Texas revolt from Mexico, deploys "nation" in a manner that recalls Benedict Anderson's "imagined communities."[1] Strikingly, for Tornel y Mendívil, "nation" is a distinctly New World phenomenon, easily distinguishable from the empire-building of Alexander or Napoleon, yet vastly more powerful, more difficult to hold accountable. Because of his sophisticated understanding of Anglo America in 1837, Tornel y Mendívil is an important precursor of writers, such as María Amparo Ruiz de Burton, who emerged in the wake of the Mexican American War of 1846 to produce a literary culture fully aware of and engaged with the major discourses of the United States. Tornel y Mendívil's image of the United States as the Colossus of the North becomes more nuanced and contradictory in the writings of the various people of Mexican descent who begin to make sense of their evolving identities under the alienating colonial enterprise known as Manifest Destiny. For the generation of Mexicanos that witnessed the handing over of the Southwest to the United States—themselves a product of Spanish and Mexican colonialisms—never did the future seem more unpredictable: Full of opportunity, yes, but it was unclear for whom.

Though separated by some thirty-five years, Ruiz de Burton's first novel, *Who Would Have Thought It?* (1872), and Tornel y Mendívil's history consider Mexico's decline as a reflection of the explosive ascendancy of the United States in the nineteenth century. Both authors employ a rhetorical strategy that positions the United States, its civil institutions, and its political structures through allusions to Greek and Roman empire-building. Both argue that there are racial differences between Anglo Saxons and the sons and daughters of Spain. Most important, both construct an imagined intervention in the cycle of Anglo American dominance in the hemisphere. While each imagined intervention is grounded in its own historical and cultural moment and is therefore unique, taken together these texts signal the immense discursive attention paid to Manifest Destiny by its intended targets. From 1803 on, the Louisiana Purchase made actual what had been potential since 1776: that the United States would grow into a colonial power, threatening the status quo in Latin America, until it alone controlled the hemisphere.

This essay examines María Amparo Ruiz de Burton's imagined intervention in the U.S. colonization of North America and delineates her contradictory responses to the post-1848 realities of the Treaty of Guadalupe Hidalgo. Because of Ruiz de Burton's status as a recovered author, no textual analysis can proceed without some attention to biography. While this approach may seem reasonable, even logical, the relationship between textuality and biography must be negotiated cautiously to avoid a reductive privileging of one over the other, as Jesse Alemán has pointed out.[2] And yet, because of the difficulties inherent in archival research on minorities and women in the United States, biographical and textual analyses inevitably feed off one another until all possible resources have been exhausted. Thus, the task of this essay is to present a Ruiz de Burton that, given current biographical information, best approximates the complexities and idiosyncrasies of her text. This essay also attempts to make sense of the historic contradictions brought to light by Ruiz de Burton's life and writings. Though these contradictions have much to say about a Mexican American past, they are equally important for the future of Chicano/a literary and historical studies. Indeed, her emergent status as Mexican American, her land-grant claims in the United States and Mexico, and her frequent critiques of Anglo and

Mexican governance together challenge the usefulness of resistance theory when applied to writers who preceded the Chicano Movement.

On the other hand, Ruiz de Burton's importance to any interrogation of Chicano/a Studies cannot be claimed solely on the basis of her life and writings. The claim must take into account the cultural moment that reproduced her works and reinvented her as an author. It is vital to acknowledge that Ruiz de Burton's literary resurrection began quietly within a cooperative scholarly venture known as Recovering the United States Hispanic Literary Heritage Project.[3] Begun in 1990 and backed by such diverse foundations and corporations as the National Endowment for the Humanities, the Andrew W. Mellon Foundation, the AT&T Foundation, and the Ford Foundation, the project is directed by Nicolás Kanellos and housed at the University of Houston. The Recovery Project has as its mission the location, preservation, and publication of literary texts by Hispanic writers from the colonial period to 1960. The broader intention of the Project is the narration of the lives of people of Hispanic descent since the sixteenth century, using such sources as histories, diaries, memoirs, prose, poetry, fiction, and newspapers. Native Americans and *mestizos* loom large in this history, and scores of scholars have been funded to carry out research on forgotten or lost authors, texts, and manuscripts.

Yet the Recovery Project is not without its critics, and the case of Ruiz de Burton serves as an object lesson in the complexities and contradictions in reconstructing literary history. In recovering the nineteenth century for Chicano/a Studies, the Recovery Project has inadvertently reactivated a long-standing debate about the heterogeneity of Mexican American culture and history and its relation to left-activist politics, and questioned anew the idea that Mexican Americans have always been proletarian in character. To date, treatment of recovered texts has mapped out an uneasy alliance between the traditional working-class paradigms of Chicano/a Studies and the liberal, bourgeois leanings of the individuals who wrote after 1848. Early attempts to identify a writer like Ruiz de Burton as "subaltern" were premature, I argue, because Chicano/a Studies has yet to conceptualize adequately the inclusion of writers and texts that uphold racial and colonialist discourses that contradict the ethos of the Chicano movement.[4]

This essay makes the case for moving scholarship beyond counternationalist arguments that conceive Chicano/a culture and history in strict opposition to U.S. and Western cultures by insisting on the need to formulate histories and analyses that place some people of Mexican descent at the center of discourses more typically associated with Anglo America. Future nuanced studies will increasingly demonstrate that nineteenth-century Mexican American participation in hegemonic discourses reflected two opposing forces: strategic refusals to shed a previous "majority" status, and the process by which the elite communities of Mexican descent were nevertheless deprived of their civil rights, property, and upper-class status and over time incorporated into "minority" communities largely populated by mestizo, working-class individuals. Thus my essay renarrates American literary history from the vantage point of a reformulated Chicano/a Studies. In this new literary history, Mexican Americans, far from being always marginalized, have had a historic role in the cultural and literary production of the United States since 1848. Finally, the republication of Ruiz de Burton's writings not only opens a window onto the ethnic successes and conflicts of a Mexican American past but also holds up a mirror for our times. As more and more Chicanos/as enter the middle class and gain access to the structures of U.S. power and authority, Ruiz de Burton's life provides a cautionary tale about the need to make public one's communal past, especially when it's compromised, especially when the enemy is also "us."

In the growing critical industry being built around the reemergence of Ruiz de Burton, many have followed the lead of her recoverers, Rosaura Sánchez and Beatrice Pita, in locating a "resistance" narrative in her life and writings and historicizing her biography as a "subaltern." While some elements of her published writings support these identities, her life reveals an individual willing to wage a rhetorical war on her conquerors but also anxious to reassume the privileges of a colonialist. Consider the following letter to her fellow compatriot and member of the Californio elite M. G. Vallejo:

> I feel . . . a true hatred and contempt (as a good Mexican) for this certain "Manifest Destiny." Of all the wicked phrases invented by stupid people, there is not one more odious for me than that, the most offensive, the most insulting; it raises the blood in my temples when I hear of it, and I see it instantly in photographs, all that the Yankees have done to make us, the Mexicans, suffer: the robbery of Texas, the war, the robbery of California, the death of Maximilian. If I were to believe in "Manifest Destiny," I would cease to believe in justice or Divine wisdom. No friend of mine, this Manifest Destiny is nothing more than "Manifest Yankee trash."[5]

As this letter shows, María Amparo Ruiz de Burton could simultaneously decry the effects of Manifest Destiny on Mexico and lament the death of Maximilian, an Austrian imperialist who crowned himself emperor of Mexico. Unless we take the position that Ruiz de Burton was naive about the nature of colonialism in the Americas—which is hard to imagine given the content of her two novels—or that her pronouncements on colonialism are suspect because of a certain ambivalence toward the United States (after all, she married an Anglo hero of the Mexican American War), then we have to admit that she represents a group of elite individuals who resisted their social and class demotion after 1848 but nevertheless had more in common with their conquerors than they were willing to acknowledge.

We have in the figure of María Amparo Ruiz de Burton a complex person and writer who easily exploded stereotypes in her own day and continues to do so today. And yet—and here's the idea that needs to be entertained—she is not a Dolores Huerta of the United Farm Workers Union or a Gloria Anzaldúa of the borderlands in nineteenth-century clothes. As much as we, Chicano/a scholars and our allies, would like to read Ruiz de Burton as a prototypical Chicana feminist, resistance fighter, in-your-face Abraham Lincoln basher, and go-to-hell Supreme Court critic, she was none of these. Discovering who she actually was necessitates an exciting venture into biography, history, and literature. My conclusions may be discomforting to some, but I believe the more complicated portrait that emerges from my research compensates us for what might feel like a loss. More importantly, the biography I reconstruct enables us to read *Who Would Have Thought It?* for all its complexities, which is especially crucial now that the novel's entry into Chicano/a literary canon is prompting a full-scale reevaluation of the assumptions that underlie Chicano/a Studies.

María Amparo Ruiz de Burton was born on 3 July 1832 (or perhaps 1833) in Loreto, Baja California, to an aristocratic family.[6] Her paternal grandfather, Don José Manuel Ruiz, was once "commander of the Mexican northern frontier in Baja California and later (1822–25) Governor of Baja California" (8). The Ruizes were a military family that eventually amassed ranch lands in Baja California. Yet "in a largely barren peninsula with a very small population, the Ruiz family undoubtedly could boast more about its prestige and political recognition than about its economic power" (8–9). They were related by blood and marriage to some of the most prominent families in Alta California, which included los Carillo, los Vallejos, los Guerra y Noriegas, los Alvarados, los Pachecos, los Castros, los Picos, and los Estradas.

The family's entry into Alta California was precipitated by the Mexican American War. Captain Henry S. Burton was ordered into Baja California to quell an armed uprising. Successful in his mission, Captain Burton apparently met and fell in love with María Amparo Ruiz during this occupation, and she returned his love. At the signing of the Treaty of Guadalupe Hidalgo in 1848, it was made clear that Baja California was to remain in the possession of Mexico. Prior to the treaty's signing, occupying U.S. officials had promised local residents transport to Alta California on two refugee ships. Some of these refugees later returned to Baja California, but others remained in the San Francisco area with full U.S. citizenship. María Amparo Ruiz was among these. It is not clear why, if these 480 Baja Californians were "refugees," they would choose to go to newly conquered U.S. territories rather than the interior of Mexico. Yet whether with the promise of U.S. citizenship or not, it is certain that María Amparo Ruiz left Baja California to marry Captain Burton. Their courtship and marriage have a folkloric quality, as Sánchez and Pita observe.

After her marriage in 1849, María Amparo Ruiz de Burton, about twelve years younger than her spouse, made a life for herself in a rapidly changing U.S. territory. The discovery of gold at Sutter's Mill in 1849 accelerated not only internal immigration from Anglo America but also California's petition for statehood and entry into the Union. During this period abolitionists and anti-abolitionists were debating the expansion of slavery into the newly acquired western territories. The Missouri Compromise of 1850 settled the issue of slavery for a decade, basically by ensuring an equal number of slave and nonslave states. This compromise eventually collapsed under the paralyzing polarization between advocates of slavery and states' rights on the one hand and supporters of abolition and federalism on the other.

After being posted to San Diego, the Burtons purchased land from Pío Pico's Jamul land grant. The Jamul Ranch was a source of legal trouble for Ruiz de Burton until 1889 because Pico's title was rejected by the infamous Land Commission.[7] In 1869 Captain Burton died of malaria contracted in Florida during the Civil War.[8] The Civil War had, in fact, forced the entire family to go East. In their introduction to *Who Would Have Thought It?*, Sánchez and Pita write that Ruiz de Burton lived in various places on the East Coast, including Rhode Island; New York; Washington, D.C.; Delaware; and Virginia.[9] Ruiz de Burton returned to San Diego in 1870 with her children, Nellie and Harry, taking up residence again at the Jamul Ranch, which she had left in the care of her brother and mother. From then on, Ruiz de Burton devoted herself to securing the family's livelihood. She was involved in "the large scale cultivation of castor beans and . . . the building of a water reservoir at Jamul . . . [and in] establishing a Cement Company to exploit the Jamul limestone deposits that her husband had first used in 1856 to make lime" (13).

In addition to taking on these family responsibilities, Ruiz de Burton began a literary career in the 1870s. In 1872 she published *Who Would Have Thought It?*, a satirical novel clearly based on her experiences and observations of New England society and culture. The novel was published by J. B. Lippincott of Philadelphia, the firm responsible for the incredible explosion of book buying that occurred soon after the Civil War.[10] Lippincott's publication of Ruiz de Burton's first novel testifies to her access to the sources of Anglo cultural authority. In 1876 she published a comedy in five acts based on Miguel de Cervantes's *Don Quixote de la Mancha* with J. H. Carmany and Co. in San Francisco. It is no doubt significant that she chose a Spanish writer during a period that idolized Shakespeare in everything from the theater to vaudeville acts. The year 1885 saw the publication of *The Squatter and the Don,* a novel partly based on her own legal trials with the Jamul Ranch. Finally, among the numerous letters and papers held by the Bancroft Collection at Berkeley is a biography of Ruiz de Burton's grandfather, Don José Manuel Ruiz (1878).[11]

María Amparo Ruiz de Burton died in 1895 in Chicago with many projects still afloat, shortly after returning from Mexico City, where she had been unsuccessful in maintaining her claim on an "Ensenada tract of land in Baja California which she tried for many years to have recognized as her own" (13). According to Sánchez and Pita, Ruiz de Burton identified herself as Mexican in this dispute with U.S. investors seeking "to colonize the Baja California area" (14). Historian Lisbeth Haas elaborates on this episode: "In 1871 [Ruiz de Burton] won her claim to the Rancho Ensenada de Todos Santos from the Mexican courts, but Mexico's 1883 Law of Colonization later enabled part of this rancho to be claimed by the international land developing firm of George Sisson and Luis Huller. She continued to fight, however, and finally won claim to most of that land, only to see her title reversed in 1889 by the Supreme Court of Mexico."[12] Like many of her Californio peers, Ruiz de Burton died in poverty. Her children, Nellie and

Harry, eventually married and settled in the San Diego area.[13] Sánchez and Pita mention that Harry continued to be involved in the operation of the cement company.

Up to this point, I have primarily been summarizing the biography provided by Sánchez and Pita in their introduction to *The Squatter and the Don*. Sánchez and Pita read Ruiz de Burton's biography in terms of established critiques of patriarchy, capitalism, eighteenth–century liberal ideology, Western colonialism, and U.S. imperialism. This is to say that Ruiz de Burton's biography lends itself to the kind of analysis currently deployed by resistance theorists and postcolonial critics. Her editors see Ruiz de Burton as part of a collectivity they identify as "subaltern," arguing that Californios represent a conquered people, conquered as much by capitalist ideology as by the U.S. military, a collectivity held to a subordinated legal status for reasons of race, class, and political and economic expediency.[14] This subordination is especially outrageous given the provisions of the Treaty of Guadalupe Hidalgo, which granted Mexican nationals the rights of citizenship and property if they remained in the newly conquered territories.

While I agree that these critiques are supported by Ruiz de Burton's writings, her biography indicates that she saw herself as part of a white, educated elite—aristocratic in its origins and with a history in Alta California as colonizers—not as colonized. Further, even Sánchez and Pita argue that the central story told in *The Squatter and the Don* is not about the illegal dispossession of lands held by Californios but about corporate monopoly and political corruption: "It is this monopolistic power and the government-monopoly collusion, not the capitalist system *per se,* that Ruiz de Burton's novel attacks. This anti-monopolistic stance is simultaneously also a defense of entrepreneurial competitive capitalism" (29). In short, Ruiz de Burton did not see herself exclusively in agrarian, feudal terms. The economic ventures cited by Sánchez and Pita, from cattle raising to a cement plant, indicate her inclination toward capitalism.

Haas interprets Ruiz de Burton's life in a slightly different manner. In a section entitled "Gender Stories of Conquest," Haas compares Ruiz de Burton's career with that of Apolinara Lorenzano, who, unlike Ruiz de Burton, did not belong to the aristocratic, educated class:

> The lives of Ruiz Burton and Lorenzano illustrate the social differences among Californio landowners and the potential meaning of those differences in the American period. Ruiz Burton was from a colonial mili-

tary elite family and married an American in 1849. . . . Lorenzano, in contrast, represents the relatively poor landowners of the colonial and Mexican periods who worked with their hands or labored for others. (81)

These two stories represent more than just tales of personal loss; they introduce the effects of conquests on women landowners and the multiple ways Californianas defended their land by acting on a long tradition of women exercising their property rights. . . . Women's sense of entitlement rested, in part, on the fact that Spanish and Mexican law gave them the right to control their property and wealth and to litigate on questions related to their person, their families, and their holdings. . . . During the Mexican period Californianas continued to have greater privileges, benefiting from the land politics that enabled a significant number of them, but very few Indian women, to own land and preside over the family economy on the ranchos. . . . Californianas' sense of entitlement to property and to a place in public memory derived from social practices unfamiliar to many Anglo-Americans. (81, 81, 83, 85)

Consequently, Californianas and Indian women had particular burdens as they negotiated more than one gender system in the American period. They were vulnerable as women in U.S. society, where women were not accorded equal status in law or custom, and they were vulnerable to the anti-Mexican prejudices of Anglo-American migrants. Ruiz Burton was aware of these vulnerabilities when she set her elite California characters apart from the world of business and landownership and asserted Californios' European lineage, despite the contradiction of such a portrayal with the actual order of the time.[15]

Haas refers here to characters in *The Squatter and the Don*. Her assertion that Ruiz de Burton was well aware of the vulnerabilities entailed by her status as a U.S. citizen is echoed by Sánchez and Pita, who observe of *The Squatter and the Don* that the "identity the novel constructs of the Californio is itself class-based (aristocracy), but collective rather than individual ('We, the conquered'), regional ('native Spaniards' or 'Spanish Californians' and 'Mexican'), religious (Catholic), political ('the conquered natives' or 'the enemy') and racial ('my race')" (39). Given the general agreement here, what is the difference between Sánchez and Pita's and Haas's biographical readings? In fact, Sánchez is particularly adept in elaborating the class differences among Californianas in her book *Telling Identities*.[16]

The difference lies, I argue, in what is being privileged. Sánchez and Pita construct Ruiz de Burton's biography, as they construct her literary career, as emblematic of "the counter-history of the sub-altern, the conquered Californio population" (5). In contrast, Haas privileges the class differences between women like Ruiz de Burton and Apolinara Lorenzano before and after 1848. The Ruiz de Burton who emerges from Haas's metanarrative is an individual in a position to secure for herself and her family certain advantages because of her marriage to Henry S. Burton, her white skin, and her aristocratic class background. Haas offers no moral judgment about Ruiz de Burton's character, ethnic loyalties, or the opportunities that life presented her; she was who she was.

This brings me back to my original question: Who was María Amparo Ruiz de Burton? In answer I offer two new glimpses into her life. In following up Haas's contention that Ruiz de Burton socialized with Abraham Lincoln, I discovered in the collected works of Lincoln this record of a meeting between them:

To Simon Cameron

Hon. Sec. of War   Executive Mansion
My dear Sir: June 1. 1861

Mrs. Capt. Burton is very desirous that her husband may be made a Colonel. I do not know him personally; but if it can be done without injustice to other officers of the Regular Army, I would like for her to be obliged.

Yours truly   A. Lincoln.[17]

Readers of *Who Would Have Thought It?* will recognize this meeting's resemblance to the fictional meeting between Julian Norval and Abraham Lincoln, as well as to Miss Lavinia's attempt to gain an audience with officials on Capitol Hill who might free Isaac Sprig from a Confederate prison camp. In itself Lincoln's memo is an interesting footnote for literary criticism. It ties Ruiz de Burton's satirical treatment of Washington, D.C., and Lincoln to her presence in the nation's capitol during the Civil War. But this is a secondary matter. What is really interesting is the person, Mrs. Capt. Burton, who successfully negotiates her spouse's promotion with the president of the United States. Lincoln admits that he does not even know the captain.

He makes his recommendation on the strength of his faith in María Amparo Ruiz de Burton. Simon Cameron is asked to accede to the president's request for her sake, not Capt. Burton's. Six months later the Senate formally approved the promotion. Lincoln's memo demonstrates that Ruiz de Burton was formidable in person and that she was at the center of U.S. history. Given Lincoln's mythic stature both in mainstream history and popular culture, is it not amazing to learn that Ruiz de Burton had her own history with the president? Where in this meeting is her liminality, her marginality, her lack of historical agency? We must keep in mind, however, that her personal empowerment is not representative of the Californios in 1861.

Some five years after this meeting Ruiz de Burton was once again at the center of history, but with a decidedly different cast of players. On 27 November 1865, Bvt. Brigadier-General Burton took command of Regiment Headquarters, Fort Monroe, Virginia.[18] This was an important duty because he was in charge of the nation's most notorious prisoner of war at the time, the ex–Confederate president Jefferson Davis. At Fort Monroe, Ruiz de Burton, presumably with her children, made her home. One of the differences General Burton brought to his command was his conciliatory treatment of Jefferson Davis. In fact, General Burton made it possible, despite some political risk to himself, for Davis's wife, Varina, to join her husband in a respectable manner. Varina Davis's gratitude for the general's gentlemanly treatment of her spouse is recorded in a letter to William Preston Johnston, a former aide-de-camp to Davis, a family friend, and the son of Confederate General Albert Sidney Johnston. Ruiz de Burton appears in an interesting light in this letter:

> Mr Davis is not so strong as he was during the last few weeks—I am afraid his health is permanently injured. He is always calm and quiet. Since Genl Burton came into position here, he has been very civil and kind to me and to him. His wife is a sympathetic warm-hearted talented Mexican woman who is very angry with the Yankees about Mexican affairs, and we get together quietly and abuse them—though to say truth since Miles' departure all here are kind to us, and considerate.[19]

Reading this letter makes one speculate about those "quiet conversations." It is clear that Ruiz de Burton's anger against the Yankees is nationalistic.[20] But how curious it is that Varina Davis identifies Ruiz de Burton as Mexican. Is this a racialized identification or a regional one? Is it the identity that Ruiz de Burton herself claimed? If so, what does this mean for her position as the General's wife? General Burton was a "veteran of both the Seminole and Mexican wars [and] had also been a professor at West Point."[21] He had been deeply involved in U.S. territorial acquisitions and the displacement of Native Americans. And how did the fact that Jefferson Davis was the ex-president of the Confederacy and a champion of states' rights and slavery affect Ruiz de Burton's relationship with Varina Davis? Finally, what, if anything, does this letter suggest about Ruiz de Burton's own politics with regard to race, class, nationhood, and U.S. foreign policy?

Taken together, these two biographical glimpses are provocative and highly suggestive, but not conclusive. Abraham Lincoln, the Yankee president, is persuaded by Ruiz de Burton to advance her husband's career; Varina Davis, the ex–Confederate First Lady, takes comfort in the enmity toward the Union that Ruiz de Burton shares with her. Varina Davis's letter suggests an odd collusion between the vanquished South and defeated Mexico. This collaboration is all the more curious given the moral support Abraham Lincoln and Benito Juárez gave one another during their respective wars. There's a complexity here that defies easy explanation. Friends and foes, loyalties and histories are all set loose from their traditional moorings. The only conclusion one can venture is that a fuller and more nuanced biography of Ruiz de Burton waits to be written. Her novels reveal that she was a complex woman. Historicizing her complexity will be a cautious affair for years to come. If Chicano/a Studies does indeed come to accept Ruiz de Burton as a subaltern, it will have to be conceded that she is so sophisticated a one as to require a major redefinition of subaltern status.[22]

Having read Ruiz de Burton as a complex, aristocratic, educated, and elitist white European creole, how do we now read her writings, especially *Who Would Have Thought It?*, the first and more complex of her two novels? I argue that her rendering of Mexico should be central to any study of the novel's cultural politics. Furthermore, I argue that Ruiz de Burton's imagined intervention in the U.S. domination of North America is constrained by the same cultural and historical forces that allow her to negotiate her newly emerging status as a Mexican American within Anglo society. What this means is that even as she imagines her intervention, it is already circumscribed rhetorically, militarily, and ideologically by Anglo American hegemony. While there are no utopias in Ruiz de Burton's text, political idealism fuels her narrative. This is no doubt a contradictory stance on her part, but it nevertheless reflects the forces acting on her as writer and citizen. In this regard, her first novel, like her biography, provides a powerful means of assessing the social and political transformations felt so acutely by all people of Mexican descent in the United States—perhaps even more acutely by Ruiz de Burton because of her access to the hegemonic discourses of her time.

Ruiz de Burton's imagined intervention takes the form of a satire that unmasks several of the most beloved myths of the United States in the nineteenth century.[23] The novel's title, *Who Would Have Thought It?*, is a phrase used several times to underscore the surprising nature of the affairs that have sullied the pristine image of the nation.[24] With the intent of demystifying the United States and its cultural institutions, Ruiz de Burton's satire debunks the claims to moral righteousness of Protestant clergymen and their argument that the United States is a Christian nation destined for greatness. She pits the rhetoric of politicians against their avarice, cowardice, and duplicity. Political representation in her novel is a farce played out at the expense of the illiterate and the working class. She lashes out equally at constitutionally sanctioned notions of inequality that bar women from elected office and at social norms that infantilize and deny women's potential. She depicts the hypocrisy of white abolitionists who hold racist views of blacks while championing their cause and savagely ridicules the pretense of respectability and republican patriotism associated with Anglo American women who fiercely attempt to embody the reigning "cult of domesticity."[25]

The vehicles for this satire are two plots that become so entangled that one resolves the other. The first plot is essentially a romance centered on Lola Medina, a young girl rescued by an Anglo geologist in California in 1857. Her benefactor, Dr. James Norval, a cross between Ralph Waldo Emerson and Melville's principled Starbuck, promises Lola's dying mother, a Mexican national who had been kidnapped and held captive by Sonoran Indians in 1846 and made a mistress to their chief, that he will look after Lola, adopt her, and raise her in the Catholic faith if her father is not found.[26] As part of her dowry, Doña María Theresa de Medina bequeaths to Lola and Dr. Norval a treasure in gold and diamonds she has accumulated in her wanderings with the tribe. Dr. Norval accepts charge of Lola only if Doña Theresa understands that he will see to it that Lola receives the bulk of her mother's inheritance when she comes of age. Dr. Norval returns to New England with Lola, where he is greeted by his wife's hostility and racism toward Lola, who is at first thought to be black because of her dark skin.

Lola's dark color fades in time because it was only a dye applied by her Indian captors to avoid her recapture by Mexican whites.

At home with the Norvals, Lola suffers a multitude of indignities and slights because of Mrs. Norval's racism and prejudice against Mexicans and Catholics and her growing jealously of Lola's beauty, which is slowly revealed as the dye wears off. Mrs. Norval is particularly antagonistic to Lola because of her son Julian's interest in the girl. Mrs. Norval fears, quite correctly, that Julian will fall in love with Lola precisely because his father encouraged him to study in Europe to develop tolerance for the unfamiliar. Unbeknownst to Lola, Dr. Norval, and Julian, Mrs. Norval has from the beginning plotted with the unscrupulous Rev. Hackwell to keep Doña Theresa's treasure and to put an end to Julian's plan to marry Lola.

Intertwined with this romance plot are the effects of the Civil War on this New England family. These historical elements serve to heighten the symbolic significance of the romance plot.[27] The intrigues of Mrs. Norval and Rev. Hackwell, as Sánchez and Pita note, parallel the national narrative being written in Washington, a narrative that excuses the suspension of constitutional rights, such as the right to habeas corpus and to free speech, as well as the illegal conscription of men into the army, as necessary to the defense of the Union. To further dramatize the relationship between the domestic drama and the national crisis, Ruiz de Burton has Dr. Norval choose self-exile through an expedition to Egypt rather than face increasing hostility from members of Congress who view his reluctance to engage the South militarily as an act of cowardice and betrayal. Julian Norval becomes an officer in the Union army to defend the country, but he abhors war. Julian's principled defense of his country is sorely tested when he eventually becomes a victim of character assassination in Washington, despite having been wounded twice in battle. His attempts to clear his name disillusion him about the possibility of justice and due process in the United States as long as politicians, including Lincoln, pander to the masses for political advantage.

Given this plot, it should be evident that Ruiz de Burton satisfies many of our current expectations of "resistance literature." As Sánchez and Pita point out:

> *Who Would Have Thought It?* satirizes American politics, an emerging consumerism, and dominant representations of the nation itself, often through a mocking of divisive political discourses and practices of the

period set against the backdrop of idealized constructs of domesticity and nationhood. (xv–xvi)

Class, gender and race, here interconnected, reveal cultural constraints on women and their consent to norms that subordinate them significantly, the novel shows, as much in Mexico as in the United States; the novel also counters stereotypical notions of Mexicans with a construction of upper-class Latino/as as white, a perhaps defensive—though not defensible—move on Ruiz de Burton's part, in view of the fact that Congressional records of the period refer to Mexicans in the Southwest as a "mongrel race." (xix–xx)

[With regard to the Civil War,] Ruiz de Burton's novel deconstructs notions of a unified "imagined community" on which the nation predicated itself (a national identity only fully constituted as a mass phenomenon after the Civil War) [Foner, 1980, 53]. This is achieved by the narrative's focusing not only on political divisions within the North but on divisions between the political system and the mass population, "the public." . . . [In the course of the novel, slavery becomes] a metaphor for disempowerment and disenfranchisement. It is the meaninglessness of "citizenship," the fragmentation of the union and with it any illusions of national identity, as well as the glaring discrepancies in the social contract, ably concealed by ideological discourses, that most concern the novel. (xliii)

It is evident from these passages that Sánchez and Pita believe they have recovered a major "resistance" novel. But then the unexpected occurs.

As briefly noted above, Ruiz de Burton conceives of her protagonist and narrator as white, European, and educated. Sánchez and Pita declare, "In spite of its acerbic critique, Ruiz de Burton's novel is not at all populist" (xlix). This is an important observation because in contemporary Chicano/a criticism a working-class ideology is central to the construction of Chicanismo in the late 1960s and early 1970s. Ruiz de Burton's patrician stance is as threatening to a "resistance" labeling of *Who Would Have Thought It?* as her implicitly racist attitudes toward Native Americans and African Americans in the novel. Sánchez and Pita continue: "On the contrary, [the novel] favors an elitist standard, that of an intellectual 'aristocracy,' that is, of an enlightened professional class, a perspective akin to that of the Liberals of 1872 who supported rule by the 'best men' [Foner, 1990, 214]" (xlix). Ruiz de Burton's editors contend that the writer's position aligns her with an "'American intelligentsia' who saw abroad the mass uprising of the Paris Commune [1871] as a harbinger of things to come in the U.S. and was particularly upset with the likes of the Democratic machine of 'Boss' William M. Tweed" (li).

Ruiz de Burton's liberal politics achieve their most complicated rendering in *Who Would Have Thought It?* when the plot shifts to Mexico during its own turbulent 1860s. One of the New England characters, Isaac Sprig, brother of Mrs. Norval, travels to Mexico City to make his fortune after barely surviving a Confederate prisoner of war camp. The change in setting provides Ruiz de Burton the opportunity to ruminate about Mexico's crisis in the 1860s: the presence of an invading French army and the Austrian Maximilian, sent by Napoleon III to be emperor of Mexico. But rather than focusing on how to expel the invading French, Ruiz de Burton's narrative occupies itself with Mexican nationals, supporters of Benito Juárez's government in exile, contemplating the political viability of monarchy's return to Mexico in the figure of Maximilian. Their discussion is driven by a shared perception that Mexico's attempts since its war of independence in 1821 to emulate U.S. democracy have resulted in a series of civil wars, depopulation of the country, destruction of commerce and lands, and the terrible defeat at the hands of "norteamericanos."[28] In short, electoral politics have left Mexico weak and defenseless against armed invasion, its sovereignty mortgaged to foreign nations. Maximilian's aristocratic pedigree at least ensures a claim on behalf of the Spanish Bourbons, an ethnic tie these men consider the minimum requirement for recognition of Mexico as an extension of Spain and therefore European.

Sánchez and Pita are judicious scholars; out of a three hundred-page novel they focus on a section of five pages in all its complexity and potential for controversy because it deals with Mexican history and politics. What they find disturbing is that Ruiz de Burton's upper-class Mexican characters "support a liberal economic policy" (lvi) that would welcome the Austrian Archduke Maximilian as emperor of Mexico in a constitutional monarchy. Ruiz de Burton reenacts this political crisis in Mexico to reproduce the debates "between pro-capitalist, anti-clerical Liberal and pro-monarchy, pro-oligarchy conservatives (church and landowners)" (liii). As Sánchez and Pita observe, Ruiz de Burton seemingly sides with those who concluded during the long war with the French that a republican form of government was not in Mexico's best interests:

We have a situation, then, in which the novel, on the one hand, advocates support for individual political freedom and equality for women, but, on the other, is ambivalent in its judgment of democracy as mass politics. . . . Whether Ruiz de Burton herself favored a liberal monarchy is not clear nor really at issue. What is clear is that by 1872, having lived in the United States for about 25 years—about two-thirds of her life—she had a highly developed sense of self as a Latina in opposition to Anglo-dominant society. What particularly concerned her was, on the one hand, the perceived misrepresentations of the U.S. as regards its democratic and egalitarian principles, and, on the other, the subordinate status of Mexicans, especially Californios in the United States, and U.S. imperialist policies toward Mexico. (liii–lvi)

One can see that, having chosen to discuss the episode in Mexico, the Chicana editors go to great lengths to remind their audience of Ruiz de Burton's resistant character. They seem to feel an anxiety about Ruiz de Burton that is difficult to allay. Sánchez and Pita finally admit that the novel's critique of the United States is "circular in its argument, for its critique of the U.S. government, as has been noted, revolves precisely around the transgression of guarantees protected by the Constitution and Congress. In many cases it is the government's failure to follow its own precepts that is criticized. . . . [Ruiz de Burton's] perspective is reformist and ultimately in good measure elitist" (lvii).

The predicament in which Sánchez and Pita find themselves when evaluating Ruiz de Burton's political affiliations is an institutional problem of Chicano/a Studies. It derives from the way canonical status has been conferred on writers of Mexican descent.[29] Sánchez and Pita make it clear that the Mexican episode is "very insightful in its reconstruction of [the political debates in Mexico during the French invasion] and in its constructed distinction between economic and political liberalism and democracy" (liii). I agree, and I think we can use it to arrive at a more nuanced understanding of Ruiz de Burton's politics in 1872. I believe Ruiz de Burton's figuring of a new monarchy for Mexico frames the critiques she launches against the United States and the New England culture she associates with American Manifest Destiny. For her, what's at issue is not colonialism per se, or even which European group becomes the majority, but whether or not a certain genteel, educated, white middle class can become the moral authority of the country. The final form of government, representative or monarchical, is the least of her concerns.[30] I would argue she was ultimately a Pan Americanist open to any form of government that would guarantee intellectuals a leading role and provide for a system of checks and balances that would undermine populist movements and discourage political corruption and nepotism. Her imagined intervention aims towards a universalist position on nationalism, citizenship, and democracy. In this regard, she echoes the politics of the Spanish-language newspaper *El Nuevo Mundo* and its Californio readership, who subscribed to a politics of universal democracy that they perceived was in keeping with U.S. culture and ideology.[31]

The question remains, why would such a position appeal to Ruiz de Burton's sensibility as an irreparably dispossessed Californiana? I would argue that Ruiz de Burton had a stake in this brand of political idealism. It is precisely because Spanish-Mexican colonialism had failed her that Ruiz de Burton ends her novel with a marriage between Lola Medina and Julian Norval that suggests a union between two colonial enterprises. Here Mexican colonialism and its material wealth are merged with U.S. colonialism and its promises of representative democracy. The fictional marriage imagines a parallel movement in the geopolitical governance of North America, implicitly placing individuals like Ruiz de Burton at the center of this new nationalism. Thus in 1872 she is cautiously optimistic about the role that upper-class Hispanics will play in the reformation of the United States—despite the loss of Texas to Anglos in 1836, despite the loss of the northern Mexican territories in 1848, despite the second-class citizenship of Mexicans already apparent by the 1850s, and despite the stereotypical views of Mexicans held by many Anglos, some of which still have currency in today's political arena.

Given these problems, how could Ruiz de Burton be optimistic? The answer lies in the much larger issue the novel hints at in its portrayal of the United States as the Colossus of the North. In the Mexican episode, one of the Mexican characters laments his nation's loss of prestige:

> Of course the ideas of this continent are different from those of Europe, but we all know that such would not be the case if the influence of the United States did not prevail with such despotic sway over the minds of the leading men of the Hispano-American republics. If it were not for this terrible, this *fatal* influence—*which will eventually destroy us*—the Mexicans, instead of seeing anything objectionable in the proposed change, would be proud to hail a prince who, after all,

has some sort of a claim to this land, and who will cut us loose from the leading strings of the United States. (198)

Sánchez and Pita read this section as an attack on U.S. imperialism, a force more terrible and problematic than the occupation army of the French (lv). Although I do not dismiss this reading, I would argue in addition that the passage concedes the degree to which the United States has become a model of nationhood, capitalism, and democracy in Latin America. It was the U.S. model of democracy that was clearly implied in the Mexican Constitution in 1824 and reaffirmed in that of 1857. In this passage Ruiz de Burton reinvents the image of the United States as the Colossus of the North—an image already well established by 1837, as Tornel y Mendívil's history demonstrates. Her reinvention confirms that during the nineteenth century there were political forces in Mexico that saw themselves as participating in the tradition of liberal ideology that had made the United States a success.[32]

This reinvention also dramatizes the quandary in which Mexican intellectuals found themselves when a liberal ideology failed to take hold in Mexico. It should have worked, but it didn't. As Tornel y Mendívil wrote in 1837:

> Too late have we come to know the restless and enterprising neighbor who set himself up as our mentor, holding up his institutions for us to copy them, institutions which transplanted to our soil could not but produce constant anarchy, and which, by draining our resources, perverting our character, and weakening our vigor, have left us powerless against the attacks and the invasions of this modern Rome. . . . Thus we have chosen to live in perpetual contradiction, in an anomalous state. How costly have been to us the gifts of these new Greeks![33]

Tornel y Mendívil makes clear that the loss of Texas in 1836 had two causes: the United States' unbridled lust for territory and the Mexican ruling class's naive adoration of Anglo American institutions of governance. In his allusions to the *Iliad*, Tornel y Mendívil invariably consigns Mexico to the fate of Troy. Because of its hubris, Mexico will fall to the United States as Troy fell to the Greeks. Tornel y Mendívil cites the unwillingness of both Troy and Mexico to acknowledge that they have invited the enemy inside the gates. The choice of obvious gifts over prudence has left Mexico open to further Anglo American incursions and colonization. Even more disturbing, American-style liberal ideology has bankrupted belief in the earlier colonial

traditions of Spain. With its old mechanisms of governance through custom and law soundly deconstructed, Mexico is now caught in an endless
cycle of trying to fend off the enemy by becoming like the enemy. Yet each
step toward the enemy, such as the Mexican policies that ratified land grants
to Anglo Americans like Stephen F. Austin Sr., produces the unintended
result of U.S. annexation—a loss of Mexican sovereignty. In this competition between the colonizing nations of North America, the United States
emerges as the victor because it—the nation—promotes a rhetoric of conquest that anticipates the rise of the modern state in Western culture. By
contrast, Mexico's defense of its feudal, colonial past delays the nation's engagement with modernity, thereby forever creating doubt about its own
independence from Europe in 1821. Hence, by 1837 Mexico found itself "in
perpetual contradiction, in an anomalous state."[34]

Tornel y Mendívil's analysis of U.S. domination in North America contextualizes the "endgame" that *Who Would Have Thought It?* attempts to
transcend.[35] Ruiz de Burton's novel seeks to wrest from the United States
the rhetoric of conquest, offering in its place a subtle reminder of Mexico's
eighteenth-century Enlightenment credentials. That the novel cannot offer
a better resolution is, of course, not the fault of Ruiz de Burton. Significantly, Mexico's liberal ideology was severely shaken after the French crisis,
which prepared the way for Porfirio Díaz's seizure of the government in
1877. Díaz, for many reasons, will reinscribe Mexico as Troy and the United
States as gift-bearing Greeks. His dictatorship set up the political forces that
culminated in the Mexican Revolution of 1910. Ruiz de Burton's treatment
of Mexico prefigures not only Díaz's rise to power but liberal ideology's
ultimate collapse at the hands of peasant revolutionaries.

Who Would Have Thought It? will have a major impact on Chicano/a and
American Studies because it documents the participation of Mexican Americans in discourses of politics, literature, and aesthetics that have heretofore
been believed to be the exclusive province of Anglo and African American writers during the nineteenth century. Ruiz de Burton's perspective on
a variety of issues confronting the nation—from slavery to sexuality—is
different from those of Anglos and African Americans because she brings
to her writing a different colonial tradition. Her observations and judgments about New England society and U.S. politics are informed by the
memory of her former status as a Mexican citizen. Few nineteenth-century
American writers share this history. Whereas many writers have to con-

struct an imaginary distance from their subjects, Ruiz de Burton could rely on her memories of a Spanish-Mexican past to alienate her from the culture and society that now dominate her worldview. This alienation casts her critique of the United States in terms that are not instantly recognizable. She stands rhetorically outside the histories and discourses that usually construct her subject matter. Because she can avoid submission to those histories and discourses, Ruiz de Burton can write from a perspective analogous to those of ex-slaves or Anglo American women, but with the advantage of having once belonged to a different colonial enterprise. For this reason alone, *Who Would Have Thought It?* will revise significantly what we think of nineteenth-century America.

Who Would Have Thought It? will also help clarify the role of postcolonial theory in Chicano/a criticism. The recent adoption of postcolonial criticism by Chicano/a Studies overlaps institutionally with its past applications of poststructural theory as a vehicle for developing and sustaining anti-imperialist, anticolonialist, "resistance" strategies of reading Chicano/a texts. The overt intent of this adoption was a desire to counteract the historic marginalization and erasure of peoples of Mexican descent in the United States. Unfortunately, the incorporation of postcolonialism into Chicano/a Studies has been awkward because of institutional forces that consistently reduce the field of analysis to only U.S. colonialism. What is sometimes mentioned but quickly dismissed as a nontopic is a Spanish-Mexican colonial past. Chicano/a scholars consistently cite the Mexican American War of 1846 and the 1848 Treaty of Guadalupe Hidalgo as geopolitical and psychic ruptures that made possible the internal colonization of 100,000 Mexican citizens. While this assessment is irrefutable, what is lost on most Chicano/a scholars is the prior colonialist status of these same citizens. Who were these individuals? What historical subjectivity did they have prior to 1846? Were they all mestizos? Were they all people of color? How did the Mexican Constitution of 1824 figure them as citizens, given that it was modeled on the U.S. Constitution? Finally, were Anglo Americans the only colonialists, the only imperialists in nineteenth-century "America"?

I argue that *Who Would Have Thought It?* complicates scholarly attempts to theorize all of Chicano/a literature as "resistance" or "postcolonial." The novel demands instead close attention to the multiple, and sometimes competing, colonial histories of peoples from Texas to California.[36] The novel is only superficially about a Spanish-Mexican girl adopted by a New England family a decade before the Civil War. Its true subject, as Sánchez and Pita argue, is a critique, sometimes ambivalent, of the United States' colonial enterprise in North America, a critique, I would emphasize, directed specifically at the United States' failure to live up to eighteenth-century Anglo American ideals with respect to the "rights of man," property, and the role of government. Although the novel's recovery has been framed by its recent discoverers within an ethnic studies praxis that privileges resistance to white Anglo-Saxon hegemony, its narrative takes up questions of nationhood, citizenship, civilization, race, and gender in ways that invariably concede the power of the United States as a hegemonic force in the hemisphere. By arguing for the perfectibility of a United States-style democracy, Ruiz de Burton indicts Spanish and Mexican colonialisms for failing to secure North America for their white, educated, European elite. What emerges in the course of the novel is a wistful attitude toward the Mexican-Spanish colonial past and an anxiety about the future of the Americas. Will the Americas succeed where Europe has failed? Will the Americas produce a just society? And will the educated elite be at the helm of such an enterprise? Such questions are raised but left unanswered by *Who Would Have Thought It?*

In closing, I would like to return to the construction of María Amparo Ruiz de Burton as a subaltern and her biography as an unproblematized counterimperialist history. I prefer not to identify her as a subaltern, although I find intriguing José David Saldívar's recent argument that Ruiz de Burton should be considered a "subaltern supplementary subject" because she is "not a subaltern subject in the traditional Gramscian subordinate-class sense."[37] Saldívar's construction of her as a "subaltern mediator" works only if one ignores her colonialist history as a monarchist and her characterization of herself as a daughter of the Enlightenment, and only if one discounts the rhetorical strategies in her novels that affirm a colonialism that would return both her and her community to a position of material and social power over people of color and the working class.[38] I am more comfortable historicizing Ruiz de Burton and her Californio peers as products of competing colonial enterprises in Alta California. The critiques and contradictions that surface in such people's writings about U.S. colonialism do so not from newly subordinated subject positions but from enraged and embittered equals who in losing the material trappings of elite society resort to words to set the record straight on the Colossus of the North. Precisely because Ruiz de Burton learns to prefer her former identity as a Mexican colonialist—despite all its compromises and failures—we come to understand the subtle dimensions of two colonialisms and the ways they do and do not overlap.

Finally, I prefer to think that *Who Would Have Thought It?* is Ruiz de Burton's exploration of the two colonial legacies in North America that until 1848 were openly in competition with one another. The novel dramatizes, contrary to nineteenth-century popular belief, that the United States has failed to live up to its democratic ideals and therefore risks forfeiting its moral authority in the Americas. For Ruiz de Burton, what is often wrong with the United States is not its ideals but those who fail to practice them. Such leaders need only to be reformed to set the nation back on a moral path. Despite good reasons to see the United States negatively, Ruiz de Burton wants her readers to understand that she has a stake in reforming U.S. democracy. This seems incredible given our current political and cultural environment—post–Prop 187, post–Hopwood decision, and now post–Prop 209. In 1872, however, Ruiz de Burton's contradictory impulse was to hold fast to the notion that she had a role to play in the latest colonial enterprise to invade North America.

Notes

A significant amount of the research and thinking for this paper was the result of my participation in a 1996 NEH summer seminar "Integrating Curricula through Southwestern Studies," at Southwest Texas State University, San Marcos, Texas. I thank the director, Mark Busby, for his leadership; the historians David Weber and Dan Flores for their expertise and guidance; and my colleagues in the seminar for their companionship. A special thanks goes to Jaime Mejía, assistant professor of Chicano Literature at Southwest Texas State University, for our provocative conversations, his extremely helpful editing, and his friendship.

1 José María Tornel y Mendívil, *Relations between Texas, the United States of America and the Mexican Republic* (Mexico: Impreso por I. Cumplido, 1837); reprinted in *The Mexican Side of the Texan Revolution,* ed. and trans. Carlos E. Castañeda (Austin, Tex.: Graphic Ideas, 1970), 295; cf. Benedict Anderson, *Imagined Communities: Reflections on the Origin and Spread of Nationalism* (London: Verso, 1983).

2 I am grateful to Jesse Alemán for making this point after our joint panel on Ruiz de Burton at the Fourth Conference of Recovering the U.S. Hispanic Literary Heritage Project, "Interpreting and Contextualizing the Recovered Text," University of Houston, November 1996.

3 My work on Ruiz de Burton follows the intellectual and historical lead of re-

covery scholars like Genaro M. Padilla in *My History, Not Yours: The Formation of Mexican American Autobiography* (Madison: University of Wisconsin Press, 1993), Rosaura Sánchez in *Telling Identities: The Californio Testimonios* (Minneapolis: University of Minnesota Press, 1995), and Tey Diana Rebolledo in *Women Singing in the Snow: A Cultural Analysis of Chicana Literature* (Tucson: University of Arizona Press, 1995).

4   For more on this debate, see Manuel M. Martín Rodríguez, "Textual and Land Reclamations: The Critical Reception of Early Chicana/o Literature," in *Recovering the U.S. Hispanic Literary Heritage,* vol. 2, ed. Erlinda Gonzales-Berry and Chuck Tatum (Houston, Tex.: Arte Público Press, 1996), 40–58.

5   María Amparo Ruiz de Burton, letter to M. G. Vallejo, 15 February 1869, in Frederick Bryant Oden, "The Maid of Monterey: The Life of María Amparo Ruiz de Burton, 1832–1895" (master's thesis, University of California, San Diego, 1992), 77. This letter and all others quoted in this article were translated from the Spanish by Oden. On 10 April 1864, Maximilian, archduke of Austria, accepted the petition of Mexican conservatives opposed to the presidency of Benito Juárez to be emperor of Mexico. After two years of war, Juárez regained control of Mexico. Maximilian was tried and executed on 19 March 1867. M. G. Vallejo was a prominent Californio and a lifelong friend of Ruiz de Burton.

6   This biographical information is taken from Rosaura Sánchez and Beatrice Pita's introduction to María Amparo Ruiz de Burton's *The Squatter and the Don* (Houston, Tex.: Arte Público Press, 1992), 8–14. Parenthetical page references in this section are to this introduction.

7   Sánchez and Pita write: "The Mexican land grant title for Jamul Ranch was finally validated in 1875, but by then the land was heavily mortgaged; Ruiz de Burton then petitioned for a homestead and finally in 1887 secured title to part of the Jamul Ranch—986.6 acres. Even this title, however, would be challenged in court by lien-holders and only in 1889 did the California Supreme Court rule that her homestead petition was valid" (introduction to *The Squatter and the Don,* 13).

8   For a summary of Captain Burton's military career, see *Biographical Register of the Officers and Graduates of the U.S. Military Academy,* ed. Bvt. Major General George W. Cullum (Boston: Houghton, Mifflin, 1891), 744–45.

9   Rosaura Sánchez and Beatrice Pita, introduction to *Who Would Have Thought It?* (Houston, Tex.: Arte Público Press, 1995), vii–ix.

10 See John Tebbel, *A History of Book Publishing in the United States,* 2 vols. (New York: R. R. Bowker, 1972), 1:374–77; 2:284–87.

11 For a description of this biography, see Sánchez, *Telling Identities,* 59. The Huntington Library archives also hold over a hundred letters by Ruiz de Burton. Amelia María de la Cruz Montes is currently editing and translating these. I thank her for her comments on this essay and, of course, for her invaluable research.

12 Lisbeth Haas, *Conquests and Historical Identities in California, 1769-1936* (Berkeley and Los Angeles: University of California Press, 1995), 79.

13 See Kathleen Crawford, "María Amparo Ruiz Burton: The General's Lady," *Journal of San Diego History* 30 (summer 1984): 207–8.

14 For a summary of this argument, see the introductions by Sánchez and Pita to *Who Would Have Thought It?* and *The Squatter and The Don*. For a more extensive treatment of the Californios as subalterns, see Sánchez's *Telling Identities*.

15 See Haas, *Conquests and Historical Identities*, 81–86.

16 See Sánchez's analysis of class throughout *Telling Identities*.

17 Abraham Lincoln, letter to Simon Cameron, 1 June 1861, in *The Collected Works of Abraham Lincoln*, 9 vols., ed. Roy P. Basler (New Brunswick, N.J.: Rutgers University Press, 1953), 4:392.

18 There are many accounts of the imprisonment of Jefferson Davis. I suggest starting with Hudson Strode, *Jefferson Davis, Tragic Hero: The Last Twenty-Five Years, 1864–1889* (New York: Harcourt, Brace, and World, 1964). Fort Monroe figures as one of the Civil War settings in *Who Would Have Thought It?*

19 Varina Davis to William Preston Johnston, in "Notes and Documents," ed. Arthur Marvin Shaw, *Journal of Southern History* 16 (Feb. 1950): 75–76. The Miles mentioned was the former commandant of Fort Monroe, who took a personal delight in showing disrespect for Davis; see Strode, *Jefferson Davis, Tragic Hero*, 280–81.

20 Amelia María de la Cruz Montes's research on Ruiz de Burton's letters at the Huntington Library adds an interesting twist to this anger. In the paper she delivered at the Fourth Conference of Recovering the U.S. Hispanic Literary Heritage Project ("Es necesario mirar bien: María Amparo Ruiz de Burton as a Precursor to Chicana(o) Literature in the American Landscape"), de la Cruz Montes read letters from Ruiz de Burton to M. G. Vallejo. These letters make clear that Ruiz de Burton felt she was living among the enemy during her time out East. And yet this feeling did not prevent her from making associations with prominent Anglo Americans. Kathleen Crawford notes that the Burtons attended Lincoln's inaugural ball, and that Ruiz de Burton became a friend of the First Lady soon after. Further research is needed to confirm this friendship, as well as to investigate the suggestion that Abraham Lincoln might have known Ruiz de Burton well before their documented meeting.

21 See *Who Was Who in the Civil War*, ed. Stewart Sifakis (New York: Facts on File Publications, 1987), 94.

22 We can see here how problematic the use of the term *subaltern* is when the historical context is enlarged to consider other groups that meet two essential criteria: that they were conquered by a Western European nationalist group and that the conquered had themselves been colonialists. Under these conditions, French Canadians could be counted as subalterns because of British colonialism, and — even more distressing — we would have to agree that Dutch Afrikaaners qualify as subalterns under British colonialism. This is an untenable use of the concept and of postcolonialism.

23 For a more developed summary of *Who Would Have Thought It?*—its plots, themes, and historical contexts—see Sánchez and Pita's introduction to the novel. Throughout this section of my essay, roman numeral page numbers indicate quotations from this introduction.

24 Strange as this title is, Ruiz de Burton was not the first to use it. A play written by John Day in 1608 was called *Law-Trickes, or who would have thought it*. It is unclear whether Ruiz de Burton knew this English play; if she did, it would be yet another indication of her command of Western literature and discourses. It's possible she was drawn to the title by her own focus on law and justice in the novel.

25 For more on the intersections of gender, race, and nation, see Anne E. Goldman, "'Who ever heard of a blue-eyed Mexican?': Satire and Sentimentality in María Amparo Ruiz de Burton's *Who Would Have Thought It?*" in *Recovering the U.S. Hispanic Literary Heritage,* ed. Erlinda Gonzales-Berry and Chuck Tatum (Houston, Tex.: Arte Público Press, 1996), 2:59–78.

26 The year of Do na Theresa de Medina's captivity coincides with the outbreak of war between the United States and Mexico. This is undoubtedly a very deliberate use of irony to mark the disruption of regional power that enabled Native American groups to take action against Mexican settlers. Dr. Norval's rescue of Lola Medina figures here as poetic justice, since it was his nation that made Mexican citizens vulnerable to native retaliation in the first place.

27 This kind of dual plot is of course quite familiar in Western literature, ranging from *War and Peace* to *Gone with the Wind*. Ruiz de Burton alludes to William Makepeace Thackeray, and *Who Would Have Thought It?* resembles Thackeray's *Vanity Fair* in many respects.

28 Ruiz de Burton expressed her view of Mexico's situation directly in an 1869 letter to M. G. Vallejo: "I agree with you that Mexico is 'completely wretched' . . . but I do not believe it is 'dying.' . . . It is *very sick,* yes, and in its hours of delirium, it may commit suicide, but if it does not kill itself, *it will live*! . . . do you know what class of suicide is most risky to commit? The worst, the ugliest, is to hang oneself, to hang oneself with the rope that your 'sister republic' [the United States] has given you, which cord, *Manifest Destiny,* with its own hand does us the honor of braiding, the same hand. . . . How glorious for the Mexicans who adore, prostrated in the dust, the Colossus of the North! . . . the Latin race has decayed in such a way that it can only live by leaning on the Anglo Saxon" (in Oden, "Maid of Monterey," 79).

29 Ruiz de Burton's second novel, *The Squatter and the Don* (1885), a humorless indictment of the illegal dispossessions of Mexican landowners in California after Reconstruction, though recovered simultaneously with *Who Would Have Thought It?*, was published first. I venture to guess that the later novel was published first because its "resistance" character is less ambiguous, although the text also significantly undermines this characterization. For more on the institutional

problem of reading recovered texts within traditional Chicano/a Studies, see John M. González, "Romancing Hegemony: Constructing Racialized Citizenship in María Amparo Ruiz de Burton's *The Squatter and the Don*," in *Recovering the U.S. Hispanic Literary Heritage,* ed. Gonzales-Berry and Tatum, 2:23–39.

30 Throughout this scene there is a definite displacement of the elected president, Benito Juárez. Juárez's indigenous roots and dark skin may very well be behind this displacement.

31 For this connection, I am beholden to Nancy Hernández's research in her conference paper "The Lynching of Mexican American Identities." Hernández writes: "The writers involved in *El Nuevo Mundo* were firm believers in the universal ideals of democracy, freedom and separation from monarchy. These writers were firmly convinced that all people in the Americas could get along because they all wanted one thing—freedom from the crown. It made perfect sense to the writers of *El Nuevo Mundo* that the Americas would become one land full of people who held the same ideals" (paper delivered at the Fourth Conference of Recovering the U.S. Hispanic Literary Heritage Project, "Interpreting and Contextualizing the Recovered Text," University of Houston, November 1996).

32 Rodrigo Lazo's research on nineteenth-century Cuban exiles in New York suggests a similar pattern of collusion with U.S. institutions of colonialism. In his paper "A Man of Action: Cirilo Villaverde as American Revolutionary Journalist," delivered at the Fourth Conference of the Recovering U.S. Hispanic Literary Heritage Project, Lazo notes that certain Cuban exiles, in their desire to rid themselves of Spain, were actively promoting the idea of a U.S. annexation and colonization of Cuba.

33 Tornel y Mendívil, *Relations between Texas, the United States of America and the Mexican Republic,* 296–97.

34 I have greatly condensed Tornel y Mendívil's argument for the sake of space. His analysis of Mexico's problems has its roots in the colonial practices of Spain since 1492. The practice of allowing Anglo colonists into northern territories was begun by Spain, which in the 1780s feared the encroachments of France and England more than it feared the United States. The Trojan horse allusion also has relevance for Spanish, English, and French colonial practices, which favored a policy of acculturating Native Americans to European customs, traditions, and especially technologies as a means of conquering them. Finally, by Ruiz de Burton's generation the perception of U.S. influence in the New World had been enlarged to encompass all of Latin America. For more on this topic, see David Weber's *The Spanish Frontier in North America,* in particular "Improvisations and Retreats: The Empire Lost" and "Frontiers and Frontier Peoples Transformed" (New Haven, Conn.: Yale University Press, 1992).

35 Ruiz de Burton's letter to M. G. Vallejo on 26 August 1867 clearly demonstrates what's at stake in this "endgame": "With Maximilian died our nationality. There perished the last hope of Mexico . . . and now the Yankees only wait for the hour

to bury it forever, and to trample well the land above and defeat every disagreeable vestige afterwards. . . . In this era of illustration, strength commands, and we have to submit. How much the world has progressed under the impulse of *practical* republicans! Before, judgments were made in the name 'of the king,' and today in the name of 'liberty' . . . the politicians have made great progress. . . . Certainly it was worth the pain" (in Oden, "The Maid of Monterey," 78).

36 The current dominance of postcolonial theory within Chicano/a studies is not a problem in itself, but postcolonial theory must take into account the historical record that shows people of Mexican descent to have been sometimes colonized and sometimes colonizers; pains must be taken to differentiate past struggles from current geopolitical issues that negatively affect Chicano/a communities in the United States. For an example of how Chicano/a Studies and postcolonialism are currently being negotiated, see Rafael Pérez-Torres, *Movements in Chicano Poetry: Against Myths, Against Margins* (New York: Cambridge University Press, 1995).

37 This is not to say that I object to the subaltern thesis altogether. I believe it can be applied to certain nineteenth-century Mexican American figures. For example, the life and writings of Lucy Eldine Gonzales Parsons would make a wonderful case study of the applicability of this concept. She appears in history as an anarchist, socialist, union activist, speech writer, and biographer. Rodolfo Acuña refers to her as a "charter member of the Chicago Working Women's Union" and a "founding member of the Industrial Workers of the World." Possibly of Mexican, Native American, and African descent, she was born 1853 in Johnson County, Texas; see Rodolfo Acuña, *Occupied America: A History of Chicanos,* 3d ed. (New York: Harper and Row, 1988), 151; see also Carolyn Asbaugh, *Lucy Parsons: American Revolutionary* (Chicago: Herr, 1976).

38 See José David Saldívar, *Border Matters: Remapping American Cultural Studies* (Berkeley and Los Angeles: University of California Press, 1997), 170.

Sex, Class, and "Category Crisis":

Reading Jewett's Transitivity

MARJORIE PRYSE

A century after the publication of *The Country of the Pointed Firs* (1896), Sarah Orne Jewett continues to attract critics while eluding their classificatory schemes, since her fiction does not fit traditional literary categories: She was unable to sustain plot in the traditional sense, as she herself acknowledged, and her attempts at novels[1] have been considered less significant and less successful than her other work; she wrote sketches instead of short stories, and both *Deephaven* and *The Country of the Pointed Firs* are often treated as collections of sketches rather than as sustained narratives with their own form;[2] and her rural, female, unmarried or widowed, poor, and often elderly fictional characters live well outside the centers of power and urban social hierarchies common in fiction by her realist contemporaries. Since the early 1980s feminist critics have contributed to a revaluation of Jewett and her work; indeed, feminist perspectives have allowed readers to understand Jewett's fiction and its regionalism as a deliberately minor literary mode that avoids reliance on sexist, racist, or classist stereotypes in the depiction of character and, in the process, creates an alternative narrative space that shifts the reader's perceptions to the margins of cultural influence.[3]

However, a critique of Jewett's work has emerged in the 1990s, building in part on Amy Kaplan's reading of *The Country of the Pointed Firs,* which associates the ability of Jewett's urban narrator to move in and out of rural life with "literary tourism."[4] This type of analysis appears to reflect new critical and theoretical directions in American literary studies but often relies more on the politics of critical reception than on careful rereadings of Jewett's texts. Some of the new interpretations fault feminist criticism for failing to historicize racism, classism, and imperialism in Jewett's fiction, and for overestimating her transformative cultural vision, but these readings reduce Jewett's complexity and destabilize the power of her work for cultural analysis, especially of gender relations. I am interested in reading Jewett again in light of these recent critical developments because I see her work as continuing to imagine regionalism as an alternative cultural vision—a vision Philip Fisher describes, before proceeding to discredit it, as "the counterelement to central myths within American studies."[5] I am also interested in examining the question of Jewett's critical reception in the 1990s as symptomatic of the way "new" directions in theory do not necessarily offer socially progressive alternatives. Rather, decentering gender as a framework for analysis can serve conservative interests by once again relegating a writer like Jewett to the margins of literary history. On the grounds that instead of critiquing emerging nationalism and imperialism at the turn of the twentieth century her work is instead complicit in consolidating these trends, her radical representation of gender relations and its implications for understanding cultural and political power can be discounted.

Jewett's resistance to traditional categories produces a salutary crisis for critics. To object to simplistic categorical or reductionist readings of Jewett is to argue for blurring old and creating new categories of analysis, or at least for understanding the way new categories transform old ones. Thus when we are trying to understand a body of work as resistant to classification as Jewett's, we learn fluidity in our own critical frameworks. In this essay I begin by examining the curious and recent reaction to Jewett and to feminist criticism of her work as a way of reading what I will characterize— in analyses of "An Autumn Holiday," "Martha's Lady," and other works— as Jewett's transitivity. Critics who fault Jewett for racism and classism have attempted to "overwrite" feminist criticism of her work[6] but subsequently find their own arguments outmoded by analytical frameworks that straddle intersections of class and sexuality. Feminist criticism—and indeed the very articulation of the politics of criticism—is transformed by such frameworks. Since emerging readers in a universe of critical theory are likely to argue that their own new categories have been "always already" on the horizon, and since the power of their critical lenses may add both new categories and compelling new readings, complicating our own reductive approaches to

Jewett may help us to move toward the very transitivity her work demonstrates — and without which we cannot follow her.

When Henry James damned *The Country of the Pointed Firs* by terming it Jewett's "beautiful little quantum of achievement,"[7] he relegated Jewett to the category of "minor literature," a place she continued to occupy until revisionary criticism of her work appeared in the 1980s. According to Louis Renza, minor literature, as a category, can interrupt the production of major literature and thereby resist becoming culturally representative. Thus, "minor literature" appears to have the potential for occupying a newly privileged critical status. Renza writes, "To this end, it enacts a passive-aggressive strategy that promotes parts over the whole and in this way exists in the process of becoming 'the third linguistic world,' a literature that de facto sabotages whatever social or systematic code happens to control the means of major literary production at the moment."[8] Invoking Deleuze and Guattari's understanding of minor literature,[9] Renza proposes to evaluate the extent to which Jewett may be read as a "minority writer" producing a resistant "minor" literature, a project that might seem to be a strategy for elevating her critical status.

However, while Renza suggests that this "nineteenth-century American, regionalist, and woman writer" might have produced resistant literature, he concludes that we should not view Jewett as a "minority" writer because her works "manifest the desire to reterritorialize their incipient politically minor or 'collective' minority context" (32, 35). In other words, while Jewett did write "minor literature," she should not be viewed as a writer whose work "sabotages" the social codes because she creates regional characters only to "reterritorialize" or recolonize them. Renza both raises and rejects the possibility of Jewett as literary saboteur, arguing finally that while "minor literature originates in the comparative binary context of major and minor literature," Jewett "outlines a nondialectical category of minor literature," one "accidentally located in the 'district' of regionalist, feminist, pastoral, and sketchy modes of literary production" (167). It is only "accidentally" that Jewett occupies a category of literary production with potentially radical content, and therefore, for Renza, her work cannot be said to occupy the "third linguistic world." While Renza is arguably the first nonfeminist critic to consider Jewett resistant to the hegemonic visions of "major" American literature, he nevertheless continues the pattern established by

Henry James of raising the question of Jewett's cultural significance only to ascribe "little" value to her achievement. Indeed, Renza goes beyond James by suggesting that Jewett deliberately contains her own potential power. In Renza's reading Jewett was determined to remain "minor," like the young protagonist of her sketch "A White Heron," despite what he describes as efforts to understand her work "as a scene of minor or major feminist *righting*" (emphasis in original, 97).

Renza's attempt to deconstruct both Jewett and feminist criticism of Jewett anticipated by a decade more recent critiques that have ironically done more than feminist criticism to bring Jewett into critical and theoretical focus. Although these critiques have suggested some intriguing new directions for understanding Jewett's work, they have once again curiously emphasized the limitations of her ideological vision, an argument that circumscribes Jewett's value. Echoing Renza, some recent critics have argued that Jewett "reterritorializes" her rural Maine communities with her racist, classist, and imperialist attitudes.[10] In the most intense of the recent critical attacks on Jewett to date, Elizabeth Ammons repudiates her own earlier writing about *The Country of the Pointed Firs* to argue that when Jewett's readers "eat the word(s) and swallow the house" in the Bowden reunion scene, "what we commemorate . . . is white imperialism."[11] In what she admits is a "disconcerting" interpretation of the reunion, Ammons describes "the subtle but clear protofascist implications of all those white people marching around in military formation ritualistically affirming their racial purity, global dominance, and white ethnic superiority and solidarity." Thus, for Ammons, "there is no escaping that the communion at the end of *The Country of the Pointed Firs* is about colonialism."[12] Sandra Zagarell, whose interest in exploring what she calls Jewett's "hierarchical racialized thinking" involves an attempt to complicate her own earlier view of *Pointed Firs* as a "narrative of community,"[13] concurs, arguing that while "Jewett would never have employed . . . crude, derogatory racial categories," *Pointed Firs* nevertheless "does echo the more genteel advocacy of racial exclusion articulated by members of Jewett's Boston circle."[14]

Discussion of Jewett's ideas about race preceded the 1990s interest in her "racialized thinking." As early as 1957, Ferman Bishop found references to the belief that the population around Berwick possessed "inherent worth" because of their supposed Norman lineage; he claims that "those more especially singled out for approbation were certain members of the local aristocracy, who presumably enjoyed a less adulterated Norman inheritance than their lesser brethren."[15] Bishop's argument seems an uncanny precursor of 1990s charges, like those by Ammons and Zagarell, of Jewett's imperialism and implicit racism.[16] However, the differences between Bishop's claim for Jewett's Nordicism and Ammons's assertions of Jewett's racism derive from the political stakes in the 1990s revaluation of Jewett's work, which were not present during the 1950s when Jewett and her fiction remained safely marginalized.[17]

In 1957 Bishop could raise the question of Jewett's "aristocratic emphasis upon the racial inequalities of mankind" while also acknowledging "her admiration for Whittier and Harriet Beecher Stowe," early-nineteenth-century abolitionists; and although he mentions Jewett's reference to Negroes in "A War Debt" (1895), he does not find it necessary to analyze Jewett's representation of Caesar in *The Tory Lover* (1901) and the few other African Americans in her fiction, or the French-speaking Mrs. Captain Tolland in "The Foreigner" (1900), or the characters in Jewett's Irish stories, all of whom might allow a closer examination of race in Jewett's texts. When Bishop explains Jewett's interest in a "theory of 'race'" after the 1880s by suggesting that "the time-spirit must have done its work,"[18] he may be alluding to attitudes that would culminate in *Plessy v. Ferguson* (1896). We might be able to infer Jewett's critique of such attitudes from her representations of the Irish, which Jack Morgan and Louis Renza describe as "a kind of specific cultural-historical work. Not least, [the stories] serve to undo the 'Paddy' stereotype."[19] Although Morgan and Renza consider Jewett's treatment of the Irish "ethnographically problematical," they comment that Jewett's stories represent "the first serious treatment of the Irish in America by an important literary figure and a prescient engagement with what today we would term the issue of multiculturalism." They end by invoking Jewett's "respect for Irish cultural otherness."[20] Writing within a context informed by the attitudes toward civil rights that emerged in the years following *Brown v. Board of Education* (1954), Bishop could assert his own awakening interest in issues and representations of race. Nevertheless, despite his contention that "after all allowance has been made, [Jewett] must still be counted a consistent adherent to the ideas of nordicism,"[21] he does not equate Jewett's pride in what she believed was her Anglo-Norman and French heritage with white supremacy.[22]

In contrast to Bishop, Susan Gillman does associate Jewett with white supremacy of the most egregious kind when she writes in 1994 of the reunion scene from *The Country of the Pointed Firs:* "The Bowden family might as well be one of the many fraternal organizations—among them the Knights of Columbus and the Ku Klux Klan—that flourished during this period of growing U.S. interest in expansion overseas."[23] If the Bowden family "might as well be" the Ku Klux Klan, then Jewett's fiction does promote white supremacy. It may appear that by discrediting feminist interpretations of Jewett we can correct inadequacies in feminism itself. Following on the complaints by African American and other theorists that the participants in second-wave U.S. feminism were primarily white and middle class, both feminism and projects of early feminist criticism can be discredited as racist and classist.[24] However, if Jewett were truly complicit in promoting white supremacy, most readers in the 1990s would not be interested in reading, much less writing about her work. Ironically, demonstrating Jewett's racism and imperialism can become a move to exonerate critics from similar charges while allowing them to continue to write about Jewett and thereby to suggest the importance of reconsidering her work.

Gillman, for example, makes a symptomatic gesture toward feminism that suggests her uneasiness in collocating the Bowden family and the Ku Klux Klan and that helps explicate the politics of 1990s critiques of Jewett. She argues that because the Bowden clan is "predominantly female," they can "supplant" a Klan vision with "a road of their own, or what amounts to a feminist nationalism" that allows the "Bowden militarism to partially undercut itself" (113–14). She finds evidence in the feast's abrupt end that "the whole reunion episode contains its own critique" and that "Jewett's feminism locates a place where she can be critical of the culture within which she speaks" (114). But what kind of nationalism is a "feminist nationalism," and is it a better or a worse kind? And since Gillman argues that recent work by "revisionist feminists" (115) "has tended to construct an essentialized rather than historicized conception of woman" (103), how does she herself escape essentialism in her description of the "predominantly female" (and therefore implicitly "feminist") Bowden "clan"? Gillman's argument itself appears to "supplant" feminist criticism of Jewett by focusing on her fiction's nationalism and racism, yet it ends by invoking a concept of feminism that disavows "a specifically female world of love and ritual" to admit both literary readings of regionalism and "celebratory" feminist critics "back into the fold of their dialogue with the dominant culture" (115). A gendered critique of that culture, her essay implies, becomes "celebratory" or what Zagarell terms "informed appreciation."[25] For Gillman, only a critique that subsumes feminism into a critique of nationalism will allow for a "fully historicized" reading of Jewett.

The difficulty with this position lies in the fact that subsuming a feminist critique, or terming it merely "celebratory," may lead readers to wonder why feminists have tried to make a "major" issue of Jewett's marginalization, and why we should bother to read Jewett if she only "partially undercuts" the racism and nationalism her fiction contains. Judith Fetterley cites Richard Brodhead as a critic who "explicitly positions himself in opposition to feminist efforts to recuperate as resistant writers like Sarah Orne Jewett and chooses instead to present nineteenth-century American women writers from Warner to Stowe to Alcott to Jewett as simply complicit in a variety of cultural projects designed to consolidate their own race and class privilege."[26] The operative word here is "simply," for Brodhead's claims about class in Jewett, like Ammons's, Zagarell's, and Gillman's assertions about imperialism and racism, seem to result from the premise that a writer's analysis of race, class, and empire can be readily determined without thoroughly historicized close readings of texts in all their contextual complexity. Brodhead, however, as Fetterley observes, uses "class and race as categories of analysis that cancel rather than complicate attention to gender," thereby understanding white women writers "as sites of race and class privilege" and making it impossible to argue "that recovering their texts is an act of enfranchising the disenfranchised."[27] For Brodhead and Ammons in particular, Jewett's race and class enroll her in social and cultural categories that render any analysis of her resistance to those categories suspect.

In her 1994 collection *New Essays on "The Country of the Pointed Firs,"* June Howard occupies the position of mediator, attempting to resolve the apparent contradiction between feminist criticism of the novel and recent critiques that would supplant it. Howard underscores the existence of "two separate bodies of literary criticism" on Jewett, urges her readers not to be misled "into thinking that the literary culture they describe was so thoroughly segregated," and offers her collection of essays as a "dialogue rather than a consensus," one that will "combine the insights of feminist readings of Jewett with the new analysis of regionalism that has emerged in the past few years."[28] In a more recent acknowledgment of the critical controversy, Howard addresses what she describes as a binary opposition between two critical approaches to Jewett's work, the "historicizing" and the "feminist."[29] Kaplan, Brodhead, and three contributors to Howard's collection

(Ammons, Zagarell, and Gillman) fall into the "historicizing" category.[30] Howard characterizes the conflict as "the opposition between celebration and critique" (370), as "the strongly opposed current views of Jewett as an empathetic artist of local life or as a literary tourist" (377), and as a "hermeneutic of restoration" set against "a complementary hermeneutic of suspicion" (378). As a result of specifying her "disagreements with [Brodhead's] account of Jewett" (370) and presenting her reading of Jewett's 1878 story, "A Late Supper," Howard concludes that neither the historicizing view nor "the celebratory" view is adequate to understanding Jewett, ending as she began by admonishing critics to avoid what she calls "interpretation by classification" (365).

As a closer analysis of the classification of Jewett's fiction reveals, rather than consolidating categories her work asks us to "leap the fence" of classificatory systems (as her narrator does in "An Autumn Holiday," which I will discuss later). What has created the apparent oppositionality within recent Jewett criticism may indeed be, as Howard notes, the critics' tendency toward "interpretation by classification." Jewett's work creates what Marjorie Garber has termed a "category crisis"—or rather, the critical controversy her work has elicited in the 1990s reflects the extent to which many critics continue to endorse restrictive boundaries contained in modern understandings of social structures and literary hierarchies.[31] The real crisis lies not in Jewett's fiction but in the critics' inability to fully incorporate Jewett's strategies into their reading practices. Destabilizing gender as a framework for analysis masquerades as a critical strategy, but it reinforces gender as a cultural binary and, as Brodhead does, implicates women—especially nineteenth-century American women writers—in establishing and maintaining the terms of their own oppression.

Although the sex-gender classifications of the critics Howard sets in opposition to one another may appear to deflect the relationship between current critical controversy and gender because several in the "historicizing" group are women, Howard's categories in fact reinforce a gender binary. The category of "feminist" criticism is clearly figured as "feminine," while the "historicizing" category is "masculine." For example, in Howard's narrative of regionalism's complicity in the "drive towards national unification" ("UR," 368), the (masculine) "historicizing" interpretations correct the (feminine) "limited horizons" (367) of "celebratory" interpretations of women's friendships.[32] In this implicitly gendered critical binary, "the historicizing view *distances* Jewett, looking back and finding difference;

the celebratory view *embraces* her, finding similarity" (emphases mine, 380). Surely it is time to recognize that feminist criticism of the 1990s has become historicized, that gender remains a necessary component of any historical analysis of literary and cultural texts, and that to be sufficiently explanatory, critical arguments must center gender as well as other categories of analysis—race, class, imperialism, and, as I will suggest, sexuality. Because her work does not fit readily into any category, whether of traditional literary history or of a newly "historicized" model, Jewett creates a crisis in American literary criticism.

In the second and third sections of this essay, I will demonstrate that a much more complex reading of Jewett emerges when we locate her within a historical moment in which the very categories of analysis fascinating to late-twentieth-century critics began to be consolidated in modernism. What would perhaps have troubled Jewett most about the reductionism of critics who insist on viewing her "simply" as a site of race and class privilege is that Jewett herself, writing during the transition to modernism, reflects a concern with categories—especially, as I will suggest, those of sex and class—even though much of her work appears to resist the very concept of category. We can thus make a case for Jewett as a resisting minor(ity) writer: Although her fiction may not fully anticipate the critical concerns of the 1990s, it does shift the reader's focus away from social and cultural categories to the fluid, permeable movement *across* and *between* borders. This movement may be understood most clearly in Jewett's analysis of sexuality and the way sex and class interact to limit women's freedom. Despite efforts by Jewett's critics and biographers to "locate" her, she will not be confined within any category that 1990s critics attempt to impose on her work in the name of historicism.[33]

Eve Sedgwick uses the term *transitivity* to describe what she calls "inversion models" of homosexuality that "locate gay people—either biologically or culturally—at the threshold between genders."[34] *Transitivity* also describes Jewett's own liminality and her resistance to being confined, whether as the narrator in "An Autumn Holiday" explaining her unexpected visit to someone she knows far from the village ("It was too pleasant to stay in the house, and I haven't had a long walk for some time before");[35] as a storyteller whose lack of plot defies genre, if not form; or as an artist whose writing was inextricable from her love for women[36] and who resisted being confined by her culture's construction of gender. *Transitivity* also offers a term for the kind of reading practice Jewett's work invites, one that encourages us to avoid substituting one category for another and also to be less reductive, more attuned to the borders across and between the categories we construct as critics, whether we understand these categories to be literary modes (realism, local color, regionalism), subject positions (race, class, gender), or narrative forms (story, sketch, novel).

In a letter to Willa Cather in 1908, Jewett comments on Cather's story "On the Gull's Road." While she praises the story's "feeling," she suggests to Cather that the dying woman's lover, whom Cather made a man, might have been more convincing as a woman. Sexuality, for Jewett, was not a fixed category. The letter suggests Jewett's own awareness, as a reader, of the way Cather's insistence on a heterosexual frame limits her story's potential power:

> The lover is as well done as he could be when a woman writes in the man's character,—it must always, I believe, be something of a masquerade. I think it is safer to write about him as you did about the others, and not try to be he! And you could almost have done it as yourself—a woman could love her in that same protecting way—a woman could even care enough to wish to take her away from such a life, by some means or other.[37]

Whether we understand Jewett to be describing a "long-lived, intimate, loving friendship between two women"[38] or the kind of same-sex relationship that sexologists at the turn of the century were calling "sexual inversion," her advice to Cather resists pathologizing same-sex love and holds out the possibility of sexual indeterminacy as a source for creativity.

Jewett's resistance to rigid sexual categories in this letter emerged from the context within which both Jewett and Cather were writing, as women who formed primary emotional and relational bonds with other women at the turn of the century. According to Lillian Faderman, as women gained freedom in the United States, people began to fear that "the distinction between the sexes would be obliterated." This cultural anxiety fostered a belief that women who sought equality with men were "inverts" and thus "Love between women was metamorphosed into a freakishness."[39] For Faderman, the medical interest in homosexuality had political motivation: "love between women had been encouraged or tolerated for centuries—but now that women had the possibility of economic independence, such love became potentially threatening to the social order" (240). "The sexologists thus created a third sex, which, they said, was characterized by a neurotic desire to reject what had hitherto been women's accepted role" (248).

The central force in the emergence of the turn-of-the-century patholo-gizing of same-sex love was not Freud, although Freud did contribute to the new visibility of homosexuality in his 1905 essays,[40] but Havelock Ellis, whose *Sexual Inversion* appeared in 1897.[41] Paul Robinson claims that Ellis's larger work, *Studies in the Psychology of Sex,* the first six volumes of which were published between 1897 and 1910, "established the basic moral cate-gories for nearly all subsequent sexual theorizing."[42] For Robinson, "sexual modernism represented a reaction against Victorianism" (2), a reaction that moved beyond morality to the construction of new categories. In a curious way, then, modernism both expanded our understanding of sexuality by ex-ploring homosexuality and women's sexuality in general and confined our understanding by categorizing it. Modernism, Faderman argues, gave us sexual categories women had not been aware of before—and then patholo-gized them. Love between women "became a condition for which women were advised to visit a doctor and have both a physical and mental exami-nation" (252). Robinson offers evidence that supports Faderman's concern, noting that Ellis "argued that the prime objective of the Women's Move-ment ought to be not equality with men but official recognition of the dis-tinctive needs that resulted from woman's physical and psychological con-stitution" (35).

The dates of Ellis's and Freud's contributions to turn-of-the-century sexology might be said to indicate that Jewett had already accomplished her major work before modernist categories of sexuality were constructed. However, as Josephine Donovan has convincingly argued, Jewett's *A Coun-try Doctor* (1884) suggests that she was aware of the work of the German physicians (especially Richard von Krafft-Ebing) "who had been publish-ing their theories about female inverts since 1869."[43] Donovan's article cites several passages in *A Country Doctor* that provide evidence that Jewett had read Krafft-Ebing's *Psychopathia Sexualis,* published in Europe in 1882, the year Jewett and Annie Fields made their first European trip. Donovan cites the manuscript obituary that Jewett wrote for her father, Theodore Herman Jewett, in which Jewett identifies him as a specialist in "obstetrics and dis-eases of women and children" (26) and notes that Dr. Leslie in *A Country Doctor,* Dr. Jewett's analog, "has an extensive medical library, subscribes to the latest medical journals, and rejects European medical opinion. . . . Nan herself occasionally reads these works but generally with similar disregard" (26). Donovan concludes: "It seems likely that Dr. Jewett would have been aware of the sexologists' theories and that he and Sarah may have discussed them. Her own proclivities could have readily identified her with this 'new type' of woman that European theorists were condemning as a pathological freak" (26). Jewett and her father, Donovan argues, like Dr. Leslie and Nan in *A Country Doctor,* rejected those theories. Jewett's fiction supports Donovan's conclusion.[44]

In her depiction of the transvestite Captain Dan'el Gunn in her 1880 story "An Autumn Holiday," Jewett seems to anticipate the work of both Josephine Donovan and Marjorie Garber. "Category crisis" is Garber's term for "a failure of definitional distinction, a borderline that becomes permeable, that permits of border crossings from one (apparently distinct) category to another: black/white, Jew/Christian, noble/bourgeois, master/servant, master/slave."[45] Garber notes that "category crises can and do mark displacements from the axis of *class* as well as from *race* onto the axis of gender," and she reads transvestism in particular as "the disruptive element that intervenes, not just a category crisis of male and female, but the crisis of category itself" (17). She argues that the transvestite challenges binary thinking about gender, "putting into question the categories of 'female' and 'male,' whether they are considered essential or constructed, biological or cultural" (10), and often takes shape "as the creation of what looks like a third term. . . . But what is crucial here . . . is that the 'third term' is *not* a *term.* Much less is it a *sex.* . . . The 'third' is a mode of articulation, a way of describing a space of possibility" (11). For Garber, the "third" is something "that challenges the possibility of harmonious and stable binary symmetry" (12), that "puts in question identities previously conceived as stable, unchallengeable, grounded, and 'known'" (13): "The transvestite figure in a text . . . that does not seem, thematically, to be primarily concerned with gender difference or blurred gender indicates a *category crisis elsewhere,* an irresolvable conflict . . . that displaces the resulting discomfort onto a figure that already inhabits, indeed incarnates, the margin" (17).

One of Jewett's fascinations includes her challenge to binary thinking, in which the "third" not only articulates a "space of possibility" but appears to realize its potential. Jewett's "An Autumn Holiday" begins with the narrator springing over stone walls and "shaky pasture fences" and expressing her delight in the new, the unexplored, even the transgressive:

I am very fond of walking between the roads. One grows so familiar with the highways themselves. But once leap the fence and there are a hundred roads that you can take, each with its own scenery and entertainment. Every walk of this kind proves itself a tour of exploration and discovery, and the fields of my own town, which I think I know so well, are always new fields. (*CB*, 141)

As the sketch opens, Jewett's sense of discovery appears to invoke Thoreau more readily than to merit an application of Marjorie Garber—until she arrives at the home of Miss Polly Marsh. Polly Marsh tells the story of Captain Dan'el Gunn who "got sun-struck" during his time in the militia "and at last he seemed to get it into his head that he was his own sister Patience that died some five or six years before: she was single too, and she always lived with him" (153). When he starts wearing his sister's clothes, people begin to call him "Miss Dan'el Gunn," and Polly reports that "the neighbors got used to his ways, and, land! I never thought nothing of it after the first week or two" (155).

Polly describes Dan'el's unexpected entrance into church meeting one afternoon:

> But to see him come up the aisle! He'd fixed himself nice as he could, poor creatur; he'd raked out Miss Patience's old Navarino bonnet with green ribbons and a willow feather, and set it on right over his cap, and he had her bead bag on his arm, and her turkey-tail fan that he'd got out of the best room; and he come with little short steps up to the pew: and I s'posed he'd set by the door; but no, he made to go by us, up into the corner where she used to set, and took her place, and spread his dress out nice, and got his handkerchief out o' his bag, just's he'd seen her do. He took off his bonnet all of a sudden, as if he'd forgot it, and put it under the seat, like he did his hat—that was the only thing he did that any woman wouldn't have done—and the crown of his cap was bent some. I thought die I should. (158)

The narrator asks, "What did they say in church when the captain came in?" and Polly tells how "a good many of them laughed," but "[a]fter the first fun of it was over, most of the folks felt bad. . . . I see some tears in some o' the old folks' eyes: they hated to see him so broke in his mind, you know" (159–60). For the townspeople, Gunn is a man "broke in his mind," not someone deliberately challenging categories of sex and gender; yet Polly ends with "the greatest" story—the afternoon he was "setting at home" when the Deacon stopped in to see the captain's nephew Jacob about a fence but stayed to tea at the captain's urging: "And when he went away, says he to [cousin] Statiry, in a dreadful knowing way, 'Which of us do you consider the deacon come to see?' You see the deacon was a widower" (162). "The greatest" moment, for Polly, is the one in which "Miss Dan'el Gunn" thinks (s)he might elicit a proposal; indeed, marriage, while perhaps a laughing matter for Polly in this situation, would be the mark of success for the transvestite, what a woman "ought" to want.

Telling the story about the captain therefore reveals Polly's own displaced discomfort about gender. When she describes his appearance at meeting, Polly says, "He hadn't offered to go anywhere of an afternoon for a long time," then adds, "I s'pose he thought women ought to be stayers at home according to Scripture" (157). And when (s)he decides next week to attend the Female Missionary Society meeting dressed in sister Patience's clothes, Polly reports that the ladies "treated him so handsome, and tried to make him enjoy himself," although again she wonders "if some of 'em would have put themselves out much if it had been some poor flighty old woman" (161). Jewett suggests that Polly can accommodate a potential disruption of gender norms—although the transvestite provokes her to contrast the power of the cross-dressing man with the powerlessness of actual women. Captain Gunn's transvestism does not trouble the community—but it does "trouble" the category-ridden reader by adding sexuality to Jewett's interest in gender.

It also problematizes an analysis of the class difference between the narrator of "An Autumn Holiday" and Polly. The narrator's father is a country doctor; Polly is a country nurse who without medical training has become "one of the most useful women in the world" and has spent the winter taking care of the narrator during a "very painful illness." Like the narrator, she is also a storyteller: "There was no end either to her stories or her kindness" (148). Thus when the narrator arrives at Polly Marsh's house and describes it as "low and long and unpainted" and its hollyhocks as "bowed down despairingly" in a day that otherwise "brought no thought of winter" (145, 139), she is establishing contrasts between nurse and doctor, oral storyteller and writer-narrator, that we read as class markers. The figure of the transvestite in the sketch destabilizes these markers by bringing into focus other forms of gender transgression that end by linking Polly and the narrator.

"An Autumn Holiday" appears, like much of Jewett's work, to lack form, as if the sketch's arrival at the figure of the transvestite is a roundabout effect of the narrator's "tour of exploration and discovery" and her unexpected visit with Polly Marsh. When the narrator arrives, Polly has just had a very pleasant encounter with the narrator's doctor-father, and, demonstrating "an evident consciousness of the underlying compliment and the doctor's good opinion" (147), she and her sister Mrs. Snow are happy to stop their spinning and gossip with the narrator. After a fashion reminiscent of the narrator's own roundabout walk, Polly eventually recalls the man for whom "a cousin o' my father's" kept house and whom she visited for a season when she was growing up. Mrs. Snow then encourages her sister to tell the narrator the story of Captain Dan'el Gunn: "Do tell her about him, Polly; she'll like to hear" (152). The question the story raises at this point is how Mrs. Snow knows that our narrator would "like to hear" the story about the transvestite. If the narrator had a reputation for enjoying the quaint, the queer, the "local-color," and if the women believed that her "autumn holiday" provided her merely with an opportunity to collect material for her sketch-book, it seems unlikely that they would welcome her so warmly, or that they would trust her to withhold judgment when Polly tells her story; for despite the fact that Polly reports laughing at the transvestite, the narrator does not laugh on hearing the story and seems to realize that Polly is not really telling it for her entertainment. The figure of the transvestite in the sketch calls our attention to another dynamic that leads the narrator to refer to the women as "my friends" (146).

Once Polly begins to tell her story, the narrator rarely speaks and then only to ask questions that encourage her to continue. When the story ends, so does the narrator's visit. However, when the women see the doctor returning along the road and Polly hurries out to stop him, Mrs. Snow confides to the narrator that the captain's nephew had "offered to Polly that summer she was over there, and she never could see why she didn't have him" (162). The story about the transvestite's deviance displaces Polly Marsh's own, for she has remained an unmarried woman—even, Mrs. Snow hints, a marriage resister: "Polly wasn't one to marry for what she could get if she didn't like the man," though "there was plenty that would have said yes, and thank you too, sir, to Jacob Gunn" (162). Although it is Mrs. Snow who finally tells this story about Polly, the intimacy and trust the story conveys suggest that, in Garber's terms, Polly's sharing the story about the transvestite "displaces the resulting discomfort onto a figure that already inhabits, indeed incarnates, the margin" (17)—the marginal-because-unmarried woman. Read symptomatically, Polly's story about the captain displaces the queerness of resistance to marriage—which, she recognizes in telling the story, gives her common ground with the narrator. The recognition conferred by the doctor's "good opinion" and the narrator's unexpected visit, the implied connections between Jewett's unmarried narrator and Polly Marsh, and the women's shared approach to storytelling in which one observation can "link it in my thoughts with something I saw once" somewhere else (143) allow the sketch itself to "leap the fence."

"An Autumn Holiday" is a hybrid even in Jewett's canon, neither quasi-autobiographical diary entry nor short story but a "third" form in which transgressive status and narrative strategies link country nurse and former patient to disrupt class boundaries. As the narrator rides home with her doctor-father, the sketch's final sentence suggests that the narrator gives Polly's story, and Polly's situation, a great deal of thought: "It was a much longer way home around by the road than by the way I had come across the fields" (162). In Garber's understanding of "category crisis," the transvestite in "An Autumn Holiday" shows Polly something about the way men and women are accorded differential power that she might not otherwise have seen, thereby allowing the story to critique both gender (despite the community's way of explaining the captain's transvestism by claiming he was "broke in his mind") and class, as the unmarried "queer" status of Polly Marsh finds common ground with the fence-crossing doctor's daughter from town, who can afford to spin sketches rather than yarn.

Although transvestism does not recur in Jewett's work (except as a joke in "Hollowell's Pretty Sister"),[46] Jewett does not portray gender as a binary construction. Rather, Jewett's characters inhabit the "third" space of possibility in which gender is a category many of them resist. Indeed, as feminist critics have observed since the 1970s, Jewett's major fiction deliberately blurs gender distinctions.[47] In *The Country of the Pointed Firs* Jewett creates a world where men and women behave in ways that do not necessarily conform to categories of masculine and feminine and where gender does not determine power valences in the community. Jewett imagines a society constructed not on an imbalance of power between men and women but on a recognition of the values of a prepatriarchal and preindustrial world symbolized most clearly by Mrs. Todd, whose stature in the community of Dunnet Landing derives from her skills as a healer and herbalist who, like Polly Marsh, maintains cordial professional relations with the medical doctor.

Among the 1990s critics hostile to feminist interpretations of Jewett, Richard Brodhead is perhaps the most scathing in his rejection of what he calls the feminist critics' "rescue plan" for Jewett.[48] Brodhead wants us to move beyond, in his terms, "the feminist rehabilitation of regionalism" to read Jewett in the context of "a nineteenth-century leisure-class culture" whose primary relation to rural life is that of the vacationer. When the narrator of *The Country of the Pointed Firs* travels to Dunnet landing, Brodhead writes, "she is an urbanite, a native of the world of 'anxious living'—the world of stressful modernity and its social arrangements" (145). She has financial resources that the Dunnet Landing residents do not share: "She can command someone else's home as a second home for her leisure, and does so with a confident exercise of her rights" (146).

Brodhead's argument is provocative in reminding us to examine class distinctions in Jewett, yet it may benefit from the same kind of historicizing he recommends for her. Brodhead accurately depicts Jewett's narrator as belonging to a different world—a different socioeconomic class—than Mrs. Todd; what he fails to give Jewett credit for, however, is her resistance to such categories as "urban world" and "social class," and her fiction's struggle to remain always on the borders that create barriers within such categories. Amy Kaplan reminds us that tourism began as an industry at the end of the nineteenth century; and Jewett herself, in her preface to the 1893 edition of *Deephaven,* describes Kate Lancaster and Helen Denis as "pioneers" of an urban life that "had made necessary a reflex current that set countryward in summer."[49] Yet Kate and Helen's summer in Deephaven, like the narrator's extended visits to Dunnet Landing in *The Country of the Pointed Firs,* complicates a construction of the tourist as urbanite vacationer; Kaplan's and Brodhead's readings do not distinguish between those outsiders to rural life who come to gawk and those whose perspective alters to take in the lives of rural people, a distinction Judith Fetterley and I have elsewhere characterized as the difference between "local color" and regionalist fiction: "Because regional narrators identify with rather than distance themselves from the material of their stories, regionalist texts allow the reader to view the regional speaker as subject and not as object and to include empathic feeling as an aspect of critical response . . . [by] shifting the center of perception."[50] In "An Autumn Holiday," when the narrator withholds laughter and listens empathically, she is modeling for her readers an expansive critical response. The dramatic moment in the fiction, which allows us to reread the sketch and its transvestite character, occurs at the end, when Mrs. Snow tells the narrator the story of Polly Marsh's refusal to marry and we can then understand the basis for the cross-class relationship.

In *The Country of the Pointed Firs* Mrs. Todd's economic situation blurs rather than reifies class distinctions. Mrs. Todd diversifies her occupations to earn her living: She gathers and sells herbs and herb products, provides a form of psychotherapy to many patients who come to her for herbal healing, and takes in lodgers, such as Jewett's narrator. Mrs. Todd's employment thus follows the pattern for rural New England women throughout the nineteenth century. Providing lodging, in particular, was one source of income for women, one that remained located within the household even after industrialization had removed most production from the home.[51] Taking in summer lodgers makes it possible for Mrs. Todd to continue her more important work, and when Jewett's narrator describes the "two dollars and twenty-seven cents" she has collected one day during Mrs. Todd's absence, she calls herself Mrs. Todd's "business partner" (*CPF,* 6). Mrs. Todd regrets the narrator's decision to move her own "literary employments" (7) to the schoolhouse. "Well, dear," Mrs. Todd tells her, "I've took great advantage o' your bein' here. I ain't had such a season for years, but I have never had nobody I could so trust. All you lack is a few qualities, but with time you'd gain judgment an' experience, an' be very able in the business. I'd stand right here an' say it to anybody" (7).

Yet the "business" Mrs. Todd alludes to here involves more than the narrator's ability to mind the store; it also includes her potential as a good listener, which forms the heart of Mrs. Todd's "psychotherapy" practice. The text makes clear that Mrs. Todd does more than dispense herbal remedies. As the narrator observes, Mrs. Todd's remedies often require "whispered directions" and "an air of secrecy and importance" because "it may not have been only the common ails of humanity with which she tried to cope; it seemed sometimes as if love and hate and jealousy and adverse winds at sea might also find their proper remedies among the curious wild-looking plants in Mrs. Todd's garden" (4). The "plot" of *The Country of the Pointed Firs* goes beyond its portrait of the narrator's development from an isolated urbanite to a person capable of human connection; it also demonstrates the narrator's implicit apprenticeship to Mrs. Todd. Mrs. Todd helps the narrator acquire the "few qualities" that allow her to "gain judgment an' experience"—but within the context of the narrator's "literary employments"; she becomes not an herb-dispensing healer but rather a narrator who views border-crossing between urban and rural worlds as psychically healing—

both for her readers and the residents of Dunnet Landing, about whom Captain Littlepage says,

> In the old days, a good part o' the best men here knew a hundred ports and something of the way folks lived in them. They saw the world for themselves, and like's not their wives and children saw it with them. They may not have had the best of knowledge to carry with 'em sight-seein' but they were some acquainted with foreign lands an' their laws, an' could see outside the battle for town clerk here in Dunnet; they got some sense o' proportion. (20)

In the relationship between Jewett's narrator and Mrs. Todd, which Jewett continues to explore in her late stories "The Queen's Twin" and "The Foreigner," she suggests that empathic exchange characterized by careful listening is a method of border-crossing.

Brodhead attempts to locate Jewett as an elite member of the world of early modernism, arguing that as "a virtual native of the social world that sponsored nineteenth-century high culture," she was complicit in that culture's acceptance of social and artistic stratification (*CL,* 174). Yet although Jewett certainly did publish in the "high culture" journals of the period, Charles Johanningsmeier has identified what he refers to as her "lost" newspaper writings and has discovered that Jewett reached millions of readers, including readers at every rural post stop, with the stories she sold to syndicated newspapers—hardly the act of someone interested only in "high culture."[52] The complexity of Jewett's resistance to social stratification and to the categories of sexual modernism reveals itself most clearly in those fictions in which she represents cross-class relationships between women directly, neither as a transvestite effect, as in "An Autumn Holiday," nor as the result of an economic exchange, as in *The Country of the Pointed Firs.*

In one of her most subtle fictions, "Miss Tempy's Watchers," for example, Jewett dramatizes the process of careful listening and comfort one character offers another—and situates this action in the liminal region of the richer woman's anxieties about death and the poorer woman's sensitivity to her companion's distress. Jewett's drama "takes place" on the class border that separates the characters and allows the dead woman, Miss Tempy, to intervene, using her own death as the crisis that precipitates the moment of connection between the living women, fulfilling Miss Tempy's hope that "the richer woman might better understand the burdens of the poorer" (*CPF,* 243). "Miss Tempy's Watchers" combines Jewett's belief in empathic listening as the highest form of human action with her dramatization of a cross-class relationship in formation.

In Jewett's fiction, a crisis often precipitates connections between people, usually women; it is not disruptive, in the postmodern use of that word, but rather facilitative. Nevertheless, as "An Autumn Holiday" suggests, sharing queerness disrupts class boundaries. We see this most clearly in those fictions—like "Miss Tempy's Watchers," *Deephaven, The Country of the Pointed Firs,* and especially the late story "Martha's Lady" (1899)—in which Jewett's portraits of close, even romantic (some have argued lesbian) relationships between women sometimes cross class borders. *Deephaven,* for example, presents Helen Denis and Kate Lancaster as young women of, respectively, the middle and upper classes, who discover that Kate's deceased Aunt Katharine had inspired devotion in her poor but proud neighbor, the Widow Jim. Yet only in "Martha's Lady" does Jewett foreground rather than mute class differences. The question "Martha's Lady" raises is whether the hinted sexual disruption displaces class and thereby flags an unexamined classism, or whether Jewett uses the class difference between the women to contain anxieties about same-sex relationships that, despite her letter to Cather, could not be openly represented in fiction. In my analysis of "Martha's Lady," I suggest that even by asking the question this way we confine our readings of Jewett to precisely those modernist categories that her fiction not only resists but also critiques.

The most extensive critical discussions of "Martha's Lady" have treated it as a portrait of a romantic, even a lesbian, friendship.[53] Yet from the perspective of class analysis, the story is one of Jewett's most disturbing because of its portrait of the maid, Martha. While Helena is described as a "beauty" and a "light-hearted girl" of "good breeding," Martha has a "tall, ungainly shape" and possesses a "simple brain" that is "slow enough in its processes and recognitions" that her employer, Harriet Pyne, calls her as "clumsy as a calf" (*CPF,* 257, 261). Yet after Martha meets Harriet's niece Helena, who establishes "friendly relations" with her, Martha's eyes become "as affectionate as a dog's, and there was a new look of hopefulness on her face; this dreaded guest was a friend after all, and not a foe come from proud Boston to confound her ignorance and patient efforts" (260). Read as a story about class relations, "Martha's Lady" appears to reinforce the separation of the beautiful, rich, generous, kind, and imaginative upper-class Helena and the unattractive, poor, dull, insecure, and slow-to-learn maid Martha; to make matters worse, the story's action shows Martha learning her job as maid and looking "almost pretty and quite as young as she was" under the influence of her increasing love and devotion to serving Helena (263). As Jewett writes, "All for love's sake she had been learning to do many things" (265). Helena becomes Martha's fairy godmother—until she leaves to get married. Forty years then separate the friends. At the end of the story Helena returns dressed in black, apparently widowed, and the two women discover that, despite their aging, their feelings for each other remain the same. For Martha, Helena has simply returned; for Helena, the moment marks her recognition of Martha's feelings: "Oh, Martha, have you remembered like this, all these long years!" (277).

Glenda Hobbs notes that "Martha's Lady" "is one of the few Jewett stories to focus on women before they reach old age."[54] Thus, as she does in *Deephaven*, Jewett chooses to begin her story just prior to the time in young women's lives when they are expected to marry. Yet as Judith Fetterley notes in "Reading *Deephaven* as a Lesbian Text," this moment creates "lesbian anxieties":

> Though Kate obviously loves Helen enough to select her as the special friend with whom she wishes to spend her summer, Helen is telling the story, and the story she tells is the story of her love for Kate. Indeed, the very qualities that Helen identifies as making Kate so lovable— her class and family status, her tact, her sociability—equally identify Kate as pre-eminently marriageable. Moreover, while Helen, by writing *Deephaven*, can be imagined as beginning a career that will displace marriage, no such alternative interest seems present for Kate. Thus Kate figures in the text as heterosexual, and thus *Deephaven* presents a classic lesbian experience: a lesbian woman in love with a heterosexual woman who is willing to take time off before getting married to play, but only to play, with an alternative. The shadow of eventual separation hangs over Helen's summer, providing sufficient cause in itself for her pervasive depression.[55]

If we apply Fetterley's lesbian argument to "Martha's Lady," Helena's class position becomes a liability. Precisely because she possesses, like Kate Lancaster, class and family status (for which her tact, beauty, and sociability become metonymic), she is "eminently marriageable" and, in Victorian society, therefore "heterosexual." Helena's class position, like Kate's in *Deephaven*, prevents her from imagining, much less choosing, a rural retreat and a life with Martha; Helena's construction as an upper-class hetero-sexual woman means that she cannot conceive Martha. Martha, on the other hand, is presented as having a choice. She can either work for Harriet and love Helena at a distance or follow the footsteps of her aunt, who formerly worked for Harriet Pyne "but lately married a thriving farm and its pros-perous owner" (260). Jewett's phrasing here is quite deliberate: Martha can marry a house or she can marry a farm, and at least marrying the house offers her an opportunity to love. Helena has no choice but to marry a diplomat. In a world in which fathers and husbands define women's class position, class barriers between women eliminate for most of them the possibility of same-sex love and commitment. Not having her aunt's reason to remain unmarried—Miss Pyne, the youngest in her family, "had been the dutiful companion of her father and mother in their last years, all her elder brothers and sisters having married and gone" (256)—Helena really has no socio-economically viable choice *but* to marry, just as Martha has no choice but to keep her position if she does not wish to marry a farm. As Martha tells Helena, she is the sole support of her mother and younger brothers: "We're dreadful hard pushed" (266). In "Martha's Lady," it is class that separates the two women and prevents the fictional realization of their relationship; how-ever, Jewett seems to be suggesting that it is *only* women's lack of economic independence and therefore lack of economic choice that does so.

Thus, rather than using female friendship to obscure class issues, Jewett is calling attention to the pathology of class—not of sexual object choice—as the reason for the forty-year deferral of Martha and Helena's final kiss. This story provides us with an excellent example of how the categories with which we read can obscure other categories in (or other readings of) texts. Reading the story through the lens of sexuality—as a lesbian text—mutes the category of class and, hence, the class differences between Martha and Helena. However, reading the story as a conservative and even sentimental treatment of class displaces Jewett's lesbian critique. Jewett's unwieldy and uncomfortable interweaving of sex and class creates a "category crisis" for the critic. Forced to choose between reading the story as about sex *or* about class, we become the category-ridden readers Jewett will not accommodate and wishes to challenge. Jewett presents class not as a quasi-essentialist bar-rier to lesbian love but as a socioeconomic identity that constructs a woman as either marriageable (and therefore heterosexual) or not (and therefore boylike, as Martha becomes when she climbs a tree to pick cherries for Helena).

Jewett made it clear at the turn of the twentieth century, even before the cultural consolidation of modernism, that categories undermine women's agency. What allowed both Jewett and Annie Fields, her companion for more than twenty years, to realize their commitment to one another was not an option Jewett imagined as possible for most women in her historical moment. Jewett had to care for her aging and ill mother with her sister Mary but inherited enough money to support herself; Fields was safely widowed and therefore controlled her own money. "Martha's Lady" suggests that it is precisely class-based economic differences that prevent most women from enjoying the kind of "Boston marriage" that she and Fields were able to afford. Without question, Jewett's class position gave her different choices than were available to her contemporaries, such as Mary E. Wilkins Freeman, to cite just one writer whose need to support herself with her work restricted her choice of subject matter in much of her fiction. However, to move from a recognition of Jewett's class privilege to associating her, as Brodhead does, with the values of "high culture" creates a symptomatic gap in interpretation: It elides the passage Jewett takes through gender as the site where sexual identity and class position converge to limit women's choices.

Jewett suggests in "Martha's Lady" that Helena's forty years of marriage (her world traveling as the wife of a diplomat and the births, deaths, and marriages of her children) were worth writing home about, but that she has been, as Harriet tells Martha, "a good deal changed. . . . She has had a great deal of trouble, poor girl" (274). As Jewett writes Helena's life, these years become a parenthesis to the moment she wants to get to, when Martha and Helena both have lived beyond the years in which women are constructed as heterosexual and marriageable. That they both do so—and that Martha has "remembered . . . all these long years!"—articulates much more than the possibility of lesbian love. At the end of the story, Jewett, through Helena, portrays the high cost of the social construction of woman-as-marriageable-heterosexual. Helena's cousin Harriet clarifies the price when she attends Helena's wedding "but not without some protest in her heart against the uncertainties of married life." In Harriet's view, "Helena was so equal to a happy independence and even to the assistance of other lives grown strangely dependent upon her quick sympathies and instinctive decisions, that it was hard to let her sink her personality in the affairs of another" (268).

In "Martha's Lady," Jewett suggests that lesbianism is not a medical condition but an economic one. The pathologizing of same-sex love at the end of the nineteenth century supported the privilege of the emerging professional class of white male doctors with medical specialties who practiced in urban centers—the kind of privilege and professional practice Dr. Leslie, in *A Country Doctor,* explicitly rejects as a career path for himself. His rural practice and his concomitant encouragement of Nan Prince's desire to become, like him, a "country doctor," reinforce Jewett's view that it is the modern economy that is pathological for women, not sexual object choice or the choice to either heal or write as a vocation. Jewett's own class position made her "equal to a happy independence," and she used that position to move freely across the border between rural and urban life, between the premodern and the modern, between a moment in which women still retained a certain agency and autonomy (represented best in Almira Todd) and their modern struggle "against the wind" of the new society represented in *A Country Doctor.* Only in Nan Prince—whose mixed class origins allow her to move between rural patients and upper-class relatives and patrons—does Jewett make her own position explicit: Nan hopes Dr. Leslie will not consider her decision to become a doctor (and a "country doctor" at that, a metonym for the way Jewett conflates social movement across class borders and geographical movement across regions) "a freak of which she would soon tire" (*CD,* 130). Jewett knows she is violating increasingly rigid gender conventions when she writes about Nan, "She had the feeling of a reformer, a radical, and even of a political agitator, as she tried to face her stormy future" (173, 174). By choosing regionalism as her mode, Jewett also used her own class privilege and her experience moving in and out of Boston's literary world to keep open a discursive space for writing that resists modern categorization of "high" and "low"—for what Garber calls a "third" term. Establishing regionalism as such a "third" term calls into question the literary categories of local color and realism, both of which have long been used to devalue regionalist texts and their place in the classroom.[56]

New readings of Jewett's work that attempt to bypass her analysis of gender demonstrate the same myopia that afflicts the upper-class citizens of Dunport in *A Country Doctor,* who are disappointed in their conservative hope that George Gerry's arrival on the scene will serve as "the most powerful argument for their side of the debate" over Nan Prince's future, despite her refusal to marry (*CD,* 286). Like Brodhead, these citizens refuse to take into account Nan Prince's (and Jewett's) compelling critique of gender as a binary social construct. The citizens of Dunport, and some of the "new (Jewett) critics" of the 1990s, have not yet learned to read gender as the site where sexual identity and class position come together to limit women's choices. Jewett's description of Nan Prince reveals her own resistance to the modernist categories of sex, class, and especially gender: "It must be confessed that every one who had known her well had discovered sooner or later the untamed wildnesses which seemed like the tangles which one often sees in field-corners, though a most orderly crop is taking up the best part of the room between the fences" (*CD,* 269–70). Choosing to remain in the field-corners of American regionalist fiction, Jewett was willing to present the tangles of class and the "untamed wildnesses" of lesbian sexuality for an audience that might have preferred a more "orderly crop," and even for critics who read Jewett as complicit in the very process of categorizing sex and class that her work moves through gender to critique. That she managed to insert such "tangles" while "a most orderly crop [was] taking up the best part of the room between the fences" makes it possible to read her work for its resistance to the urban, upper-class, and "high culture" world to which she became a regular visitor from her home in Maine. More than a tourist in Boston, Jewett occupied her "Fields-corner" (Annie's home, 148 Charles Street) but always returned to South Berwick. Transitivity much more than tourism serves as our figure for understanding Jewett's border-crossing almost a century before such practices might be theorized by literary critics, although they have long been fully understood by readers who have loved Jewett beyond the boundaries of academic discourse.

Notes

I delivered a shorter version of this paper as the keynote address at "Sarah Orne Jewett and Her Contemporaries: The Centennial Conference" at Westbrook College in Portland, Maine, 21–23 June 1996. I am indebted to conference participants for comments, as well as to Sarah Way Sherman, whose incisive reading of the conference draft has helped me think further about Jewett's relation to gender and particularly to class. Sherman's own new introduction to *The Country of the Pointed Firs* has just appeared (Hanover, N.H.: Published for University of New Hampshire by University Press of New England, 1997). I also thank Judith Fetterley for her (always) careful and critical reading.

1 Sarah Orne Jewett, *A Country Doctor* (New York: Grosset and Dunlap, 1884) and *The Tory Lover* (Boston: Houghton Mifflin, 1901). Subsequent references to *A Country Doctor* are to this edition and are cited parenthetically in the essay by page number and, when necessary, by the abbreviation *CD*.

2 For example, when Willa Cather edited Jewett's *The Country of the Pointed Firs*

and wrote a preface that, as Paula Blanchard describes it, "has become a classic of Jewett criticism" (*Sarah Orne Jewett: Her World and Her Work* [Reading, Mass.: Addison-Wesley, 1994], 360), she incorporated three of the later Dunnet Landing sketches into Jewett's 1896 text, apparently not perceiving the original as complete in itself. For fuller discussion of Cather's role in editing Jewett, see Marjorie Pryse, introduction to *"The Country of the Pointed Firs" and Other Stories* by Sarah Orne Jewett (New York: Norton, 1981), vi–vii; Blanchard, *Sarah Orne Jewett,* 360–61; and June Howard, "Sarah Orne Jewett and the Traffic in Words," in *New Essays on "The Country of The Pointed Firs,"* ed. June Howard (New York: Cambridge University Press, 1994), 20–21.

3 See Elizabeth Ammons, "Going in Circles: The Female Geography of Jewett's *Country of the Pointed Firs,*" *Studies in the Literary Imagination* 16 (fall 1983): 83–92; Pryse, introduction to *Pointed Firs;* Josephine Donovan, *Sarah Orne Jewett* (New York: Frederick Ungar, 1980); Judith Fetterley, "'Not in the Least American': Nineteenth-Century Literary Regionalism," *College English* 56 (Dec. 1994): 877–95; Judith Fetterley and Marjorie Pryse, introduction to *American Women Regionalists 1850–1910,* ed. Judith Fetterley and Marjorie Pryse (New York: Norton, 1992), xi–xx; Marcia McClintock Folsom, "'Tact is a Kind of Mind-Reading': Empathic Style in Sarah Orne Jewett's *The Country of the Pointed Firs,*" in *Critical Essays on Sarah Orne Jewett,* ed. Gwen L. Nagel (Boston: G. K. Hall, 1984), 76–89; Marilyn Mobley, *Folk Roots and Mythic Wings in Sarah Orne Jewett and Toni Morrison* (Baton Rouge: Louisiana State University Press, 1991); Sarah Way Sherman, *Sarah Orne Jewett: An American Persephone* (Hanover, N.H.: Published for University of New Hampshire by University Press of New England, 1989); and Cecilia Tichi, "Women Writers and the New Woman," in *Columbia Literary History of the United States,* ed. Emory Elliott (New York: Columbia University Press, 1988), 589–606.

4 Amy Kaplan, "Nation, Region, and Empire," in *The Columbia History of the American Novel,* ed. Emory Elliott (New York: Columbia University Press, 1991), 252.

5 Philip Fisher, "American Literary and Cultural Studies since the Civil War," in *Redrawing the Boundaries: The Transformation of English and American Literary Studies,* ed. Stephen Greenblatt and Giles Gunn (New York: Modern Language Association, 1992), 232.

6 See Susan Gillman, "Regionalism and Nationalism in Jewett's *The Country of the Pointed Firs,*" in *New Essays,* ed. Howard, 101–17; Sandra Zagarell, "Country's Portrayal of Community and the Exclusion of Difference," in *New Essays,* ed. Howard, 39–60; Richard Brodhead, *Culture of Letters: Scenes of Reading and Writing in Nineteenth-Century America* (Chicago: University of Chicago Press, 1993); Kaplan, "Nation, Region, and Empire"; and Elizabeth Ammons, "Material Culture, Empire, and Jewett's *Country of the Pointed Firs,*" in *New Essays,* ed. Howard, 81–99.

7 Henry James, "Mr. and Mrs. James T. Fields," *Atlantic Monthly*, July 1915, 30.

8 Louis Renza, *"A White Heron" and the Question of Minor Literature* (Madison: University of Wisconsin Press, 1984), 33. Further quotations from this source are cited parenthetically in the text.

9 Gilles Deleuze and Félix Guattari, *Kafka: Pour une littérature mineure* (Paris: Editions de Minuit, 1975).

10 See Gillman, "Regionalism and Nationalism," 101–17; Zagarell, *"Country*'s Portrayal," 39–60; Brodhead, *Culture of Letters;* and Kaplan, "Nation, Region, and Empire."

11 Ammons, "Material Culture, Empire, and Jewett's *Country*," 91–92. "Going in Circles" is the earlier essay (see note 3).

12 Ibid., 97.

13 Sandra Zagarell, "Narrative of Community: The Identification of a Genre," *Signs* 13 (spring 1988): 498–527.

14 Zagarell, *"Country*'s Portrayal," 47.

15 Ferman Bishop, "Sarah Orne Jewett's Ideas of Race," *New England Quarterly* 30 (June 1957): 249.

16 In *"Country*'s Portrayal," Zagarell writes that she is "much indebted" to Bishop's article (57).

17 It is important to acknowledge several scholars and biographers who did take an interest in Jewett during the 1950s and 1960s and without whose work Jewett scholarship would be much impoverished. See in particular Perry D. Westbrook, *Acres of Flint: Writers of Rural New England 1870-1900* (Washington, D.C.: Scarecrow Press, 1951); John Eldridge Frost, *Sarah Orne Jewett* (Kittery Point, Maine: Gundalow Club, 1960); and Richard Cary, *Sarah Orne Jewett* (New York: Twayne, 1962). Before publishing their books, Westbrook and Frost had written dissertations on Jewett, Westbrook for Columbia University (1951) and Frost for New York University (1953). During this period, F. O. Matthiessen's 1929 biography of Jewett was also reprinted (*Sarah Orne Jewett* [Gloucester, Mass.: Peter Smith, 1965]). See also Gwen L. Nagel and James Nagel, whose bibliographical work in *Sarah Orne Jewett: A Reference Guide* (Boston: G. K. Hall, 1978), makes it possible to trace Jewett's slow emergence from the margins of literary history.

18 Bishop, "Ideas of Race," 244.

19 Jack Morgan and Louis A. Renza, introduction to *The Irish Stories of Sarah Orne Jewett* (Carbondale: Southern Illinois University Press, 1996), xxi.

20 Ibid., xix, xliii.

21 Bishop, "Ideas of Race," 249.

22 In an essay Bishop published two years later, he complicates his earlier argument by noting that at the end of Jewett's *The Story of the Normans* (1887), a volume of history Jewett was commissioned to write for young people, she "tempered her observations with criticism" of the Normans ("The Sense of the Past in Sarah Orne Jewett," in *Appreciation of Sarah Orne Jewett*, ed. Richard Cary [Waterville,

Maine: Colby College Press, 1973], 139; reprinted from *University of Wichita Bulletin,* University Studies no. 41 (1959).

23 Gillman, "Regionalism and Nationalism," 113. Further quotations from this article are cited parenthetically in the text by page number.

24 By invoking this view of the "inadequacies" of feminism, I mean neither to subscribe to it nor refute it. By now, this view of "second wave" feminism has become a cliché, often unexamined. Although across the body of their work African American feminist critics and theorists (Audre Lorde, Barbara Smith, bell hooks, and others) have critiqued racism in the (white) women's movement, some white women from the 1970s and early 1980s have done significant work to expand feminist analysis well beyond the cliché. One of the earliest was Adrienne Rich, in "Disloyal to Civilization: Feminism, Racism, Gynophobia," in *On Lies, Secrets, and Silence: Selected Prose, 1966–1978* (New York: Norton, 1979), 275–310. Other white feminists who have invoked racism (and its extensions into classism and imperialism) as a focus for feminism include Charlotte Bunch, Minnie Bruce Pratt, and Robin Morgan.

25 Zagarell, "*Country*'s Portrayal," 56.

26 Judith Fetterley, "Commentary: Nineteenth-Century American Women Writers and the Politics of Recovery," *American Literary History* 6 (fall 1994): 608.

27 Ibid., 609–10.

28 Howard, introduction to *New Essays,* 15, 23.

29 June Howard, "Unraveling Regions, Unsettling Periods: Sarah Orne Jewett and American Literary History," *American Literature* 68 (June 1996): 369. Further quotations from this article will be cited parenthetically by page number in the text and, when necessary, by the abbreviation "UR."

30 Michael Davitt Bell's essay is the only one in Howard's collection that terms the feminist readings "new," examines *The Country of the Pointed Firs* as a book that avoids the "rigid bifurcation" of American realism, and argues for moving beyond gendered readings of Jewett when they "reimpose these bifurcations on *The Country of the Pointed Firs,* even in the interest of finding in it an *inversion* of realist values" ("Gender and American Realism in *The Country of the Pointed Firs,*" 77.)

31 Marjorie Garber, *Vested Interests: Cross Dressing and Cultural Anxiety* (New York: HarperCollins, 1992), 16.

32 See also Howard's discussion of visiting and friendship between women in her introduction to *New Essays,* 6–8.

33 Jewett's biographers have either ignored Jewett's sexuality, attempted to deflect attention from her possible lesbianism, or argued that she was not a lesbian. Margaret Roman describes the "lifelong relationship of support and comfort" that Jewett and Annie Fields enjoyed and writes that "neither Fields nor Jewett took on a specific male or female role in their association" (*Sarah Orne Jewett: Reconstructing Gender* [Tuscaloosa: University of Alabama Press, 1992], 145); Elizabeth

Silverthorne argues that "attempts have been made to interpret [the relation-ship between Jewett and Fields] in terms of late-twentieth-century ideology," which has "led to confusion and controversy, since it modifies and extends the dictionary definition of lesbianism" even though "it is doubtful that Sarah or her friends knew the term 'lesbian' at all" (*Sarah Orne Jewett: A Writer's Life* [Wood-stock, N.Y.: Overlook Press, 1993], 105–6); and Paula Blanchard concludes that Jewett "was not, in the strictest sense of the term," a lesbian because Jewett's love for other women "belongs in a category hardly imaginable to the modern sensi-bility, that of romantic friendship" (*Sarah Orne Jewett,* 54). For critics more will-ing to consider Jewett's (sexual) love for women and its influence on her work, see Josephine Donovan, "The Unpublished Love Poetry of Sarah Orne Jewett," *Frontiers: A Journal of Women Studies* 4 (Jan. 1980): 26–31; Lillian Faderman, "Boston Marriage" and "The Contributions of the Sexologists," in *Surpassing the Love of Men: Romantic Friendship and Love between Women from the Renaissance to the Present* (New York: William Morrow, 1981); Judith Fetterley, "Reading *Deep-haven* as a Lesbian Text," in *Sexual Practice/Textual Theory: Lesbian Cultural Criti-cism,* ed. Susan J. Wolfe and Julia Penelope (Cambridge, Mass.: Basil Blackwell, 1993), 164–83; and Marjorie Pryse, "Archives of Female Friendship and the 'Way' Jewett Wrote," *New England Quarterly* 66 (March 1993): 47–66. See also Sher-man, *Sarah Orne Jewett,* especially 78–84.

34 Eve Kosofsky Sedgwick, *Epistemology of the Closet* (Berkeley and Los Angeles: University of California Press, 1990), 88.

35 Sarah Orne Jewett, "An Autumn Holiday," in *Country By-Ways* (Boston: Hough-ton Mifflin, 1881), 147. Further references are to this edition and will be cited parenthetically in the essay by page number and, when necessary, by the abbre-viation *CB*.

36 See Pryse, "Archives of Female Friendship."

37 *Letters of Sarah Orne Jewett,* ed. Annie Fields (Boston: Houghton Mifflin, 1911), 246–47.

38 Carroll Smith-Rosenberg, "The Female World of Love and Ritual: Relations between Women in Nineteenth-Century America," in her *Disorderly Conduct: Visions of Gender in Victorian America* (New York: Oxford University Press, 1985), 53.

39 Faderman, *Surpassing the Love,* 239–40. Further references to this source will be cited parenthetically by page number in the text.

40 Sigmund Freud, *Three Essays on the Theory of Sexuality,* trans. James Strachey ([1905] New York: Basic Books, 1962).

41 Havelock Ellis, *Sexual Inversion* (London: Wilson and Macmillan, 1897).

42 Paul Robinson, *The Modernization of Sex* (New York: Harper and Row, 1976), 3. Further references to this source will be cited parenthetically by page number in the text.

43 Josephine Donovan, "Nan Prince and the Golden Apples," *Colby Library Quarterly* 22 (March 1986): 26. Further references to this article will be cited parenthetically in the text.

44 When Faderman wrote that Jewett's 1908 letter to Cather "must have made Cather blush—but Jewett probably would not have known what she was blushing about" (*Surpassing the Love*, 202), she was not taking into account Donovan's research, which suggests that Jewett knew very well what she was talking about.

45 Garber, *Vested Interests*, 16. Further references to this source will be cited parenthetically by page number.

46 Mrs. Fosdick in *The Country of the Pointed Firs* also tells a story about going to sea with her family at the age of eight and having to wear her brother's clothes because her mother had forgotten to bring the basket in which hers were packed. Until they reach their first port she wears trousers, which represent for her "quite a spell o' freedom"; when her mother makes her a new skirt and she feels the hem at her heels, she feels "as if youth was past and gone" (61). Further references to *"The Country of the Pointed Firs" and Other Stories* will be to the 1981 edition (New York: Norton) and will be cited parenthetically by page number and, when necessary, by the abbreviation *CPF*.

47 See Ammons, "Going in Circles"; Donovan, "Nan Prince," "The Unpublished Love Poetry," and "Jewett and Swedenborg," *American Literature* 65 (Dec. 1993): 731–50; Folsom, "'A Kind of Mind-Reading'"; Mobley, *Folk Roots and Mythic Wings;* Pryse, introduction to *Pointed Firs*, v–xx; and Sherman, *Sarah Orne Jewett*.

48 Brodhead, *Cultures of Letters*, 143. Further quotations from this source are cited parenthetically by page number and, when necessary, by the abbreviation *CL*.

49 Sarah Orne Jewett, preface to *Deephaven and Other Stories* (New Haven, Conn.: College and University Press, 1966), 31.

50 Fetterley and Pryse, introduction to *American Women Regionalists*, xvii–xviii; see also our discussion in that volume of "The Circus at Denby," 186–87. See also Fetterley, "'Not in the Least American,'" especially 887; and Pryse, "'Distilling Essences': Regionalism and 'Women's Culture,'" *American Literary Realism* 25 (winter 1993): 1–15, and "Reading Regionalism and the 'Difference' It Makes," in *Regionalism Reconsidered: New Approaches to the Field*, ed. David Jordan (New York: Garland, 1994), 47–63.

51 See Christine Stansell's description of this economic shift, which took place earlier in New York City, in *City of Women: Sex and Class in New York 1789–1860* (Urbana: University of Illinois Press, 1986), esp. 11–18.

52 Charles Johanningsmeier, "Sarah Orne Jewett and Mary E. Wilkins (Freeman): Two Shrewd Businesswomen in Search of New Markets," *New England Quarterly* 70 (March 1997): 57–82. See also Johanningsmeier, *Fiction and the American Literary Marketplace: The Role of Newspaper Syndicates, 1860–1900* (Cambridge: Cambridge University Press, 1996).

53 In 1980 Glenda Hobbs interpreted the friendship as "passionate, but not neces-

sarily erotic" ("Pure and Passionate: Female Friendship in Sarah Orne Jewett's 'Martha's Lady,'" *Studies in Short Fiction* 17 [winter 1980]: 21–29; reprinted in *Critical Essays,* ed. Gwen L. Nagel, 103). In 1981 Lillian Faderman described the relationship between upper-class Helena Vernon and her cousin Harriet's maid Martha as "what would be called lesbian love in our times" (*Surpassing the Love,* 203); and Susan Koppelman includes the story in her anthology of lesbian fiction, *Two Friends* (New York: Meridian-Penguin, 1994), 124–40.

54 Hobbs, "Pure and Passionate," 99.

55 Fetterley, "Reading *Deephaven,*" 167.

56 In addition, as Chris Gallagher has commented, *regionalism* is an oppositional term in the triads "realism, regionalism, and naturalism" and Amy Kaplan's "Nation, Region, and Empire" that foregrounds "category crisis." Gallagher has noted that while "empire" in Kaplan's triad seems to foreground "nation" and "region" as domestic concepts, this move obscures the way "reading regionalism" (see Pryse, "Reading Regionalism") works against a domestic U.S. agenda. In unpublished working notes (here quoted with permission), Gallagher elaborates:

> Regionalist texts, of course, are not often—if ever—*about* U.S. external imperialism, but . . . they do often invoke the colonizing gesture in an attempt to resist and ultimately to reject it. They also seek to represent the marginalized stories—of women, of people of color, of lower-class people—in ways that not only avoid appropriating, but resist appropriative gestures themselves, thus countering U.S. exceptionalism by foregrounding U.S. *internal* imperialism. In these ways, the category and practice of "regionalism" can contribute to the study of empire, as a project which itself puts into question the binary between "region" and "empire."

★ ★ ★ **PART II**

DOMESTICITY UNDONE: CASE STUDIES

Manifest Domesticity

AMY KAPLAN

The "cult of domesticity," the ideology of "separate spheres," and the "culture of sentiment" have together provided a productive paradigm for understanding the work of white women writers in creating a middle-class American culture in the nineteenth century. Most studies of this paradigm have revealed the permeability of the border that separates the spheres, demonstrating that the private feminized space of the home both infused and bolstered the public male arena of the market, and that the sentimental values attached to maternal influence were used to sanction women's entry into the wider civic realm from which those same values theoretically excluded them. More recently, scholars have argued that the extension of female sympathy across social divides could violently reinforce the very racial and class hierarchies that sentimentality claims to dissolve.[1]

This deconstruction of separate spheres, however, leaves another structural opposition intact: the domestic in intimate opposition to the foreign. In this context *domestic* has a double meaning that not only links the familial household to the nation but also imagines both in opposition to everything outside the geographic and conceptual border of the home. The earliest meaning of *foreign,* according to the *Oxford English Dictionary,* is "out of doors" or "at a distance from home." Contemporary English speakers refer to national concerns as domestic in explicit or implicit contrast with the foreign. The notion of domestic policy makes sense only in opposition to foreign policy, and uncoupled from the foreign, national issues are never labeled domestic. The idea of foreign policy depends on the sense of the nation as a domestic space imbued with a sense of at-homeness, in contrast to an external world perceived as alien and threatening. Reciprocally, a sense of the foreign is necessary to erect the boundaries that enclose the nation as home.

Reconceptualizing domesticity in this way might shift the cognitive geography of nineteenth-century separate spheres. When we contrast the domestic sphere with the market or political realm, men and women inhabit a divided social terrain, but when we oppose the domestic to the foreign, men and women become national allies against the alien, and the determining division is not gender but racial demarcations of otherness. Thus another part of the cultural work of domesticity might be to unite men and women in a national domain and to generate notions of the foreign against which the nation can be imagined as home. The border between the domestic and foreign, however, also deconstructs when we think of domesticity not as a static condition but as the process of domestication, which entails conquering and taming the wild, the natural, and the alien. Domestic in this sense is related to the imperial project of civilizing, and the conditions of domesticity often become markers that distinguish civilization from savagery. Through the process of domestication, the home contains within itself those wild or foreign elements that must be tamed; domesticity not only monitors the borders between the civilized and the savage but also regulates traces of the savage within itself.[2]

If domesticity plays a key role in imagining the nation as home, then women, positioned at the center of the home, play a major role in defining the contours of the nation and its shifting borders with the foreign. Those feminist critics and historians whose work has been fundamental in charting the paradigm of separate spheres, however, have for the most part overlooked the relationship of domesticity to nationalism and imperialism. Their work is worth revisiting here because their language, echoing that of their sources, inadvertently exposes these connections, which scholars have just recently begun to pursue. Jane Tompkins, for example, lauds Catharine Beecher's *Treatise on Domestic Economy* as "the prerequisite of world conquest" and claims of a later version that "the imperialistic drive behind the encyclopedism and determined practicality of this household manual . . . is a blueprint for colonizing the world in the name of the 'family state' under the leadership of Christian women."[3] As her title indicates, Mary P. Ryan's *Empire of the Mother: American Writing about Domesticity, 1830–1860* employs empire as a metaphor framing her analysis; yet she never links this pervasive imperial metaphor to the contemporaneous geopolitical movement of imperial expansion or to the discourse of Manifest Destiny. This blind spot, I believe, stems from the way that the ideology of separate spheres has shaped scholarship; until recently it has been assumed that nationalism and foreign policy lay outside the concern and participation of women. Isolating the empire of the mother from other imperial endeavors, however, runs two risks: First, it may reproduce in women's studies the insularity of an American Studies that imagines the nation as a fixed, monolithic, and self-enclosed geographic and cultural whole; second, the legacy of separate spheres that sees women as morally superior to men can lead to the current moralistic strain in feminist criticism, which has shifted from celebrating the liberatory qualities of white women's writing to condemning their racism. In this essay I try instead to understand the vexed and contradictory relations between race and domesticity as an issue not solely of individual morality nor simply internal to the nation but as structural to the institutional and discursive processes of national expansion and empire-building.[4]

My essay poses the question of how the ideology of separate spheres in antebellum America contributed to creating an American empire by imagining the nation as a home at a time when its geopolitical borders were expanding rapidly through violent confrontations with Indians, Mexicans, and European empires. Scholars have overlooked the fact that the development of domestic discourse in America is contemporaneous with the discourse of Manifest Destiny. If we juxtapose the spatial representations of these discourses, they seem to embody the most extreme form of separate spheres: The home as a bounded and rigidly ordered interior space is opposed to the boundless and undifferentiated space of an infinitely expanding nation. Yet these spatial and gendered configurations are linked in complex ways that are dependent on racialized notions of the foreign. According to the ideology of separate spheres, domesticity can be viewed as an anchor, a feminine counterforce to the male activity of territorial conquest. I argue, to the contrary, that domesticity is more mobile and less stabilizing; it travels in contradictory circuits both to expand and contract the boundaries of home and nation and to produce shifting conceptions of the foreign. This form of traveling domesticity can be analyzed in the writings of Catharine Beecher and Sara Josepha Hale, whose work, despite their ideological differences as public figures, reveals how the internal logic of domesticity relies on, abets, and reproduces the contradictions of nationalist expansion in the 1840s and 1850s. An analysis of Beecher's *A Treatise on Domestic Economy* demonstrates that the language of empire both suffuses and destabilizes the rhetoric of separate spheres, while an analysis of Hale's work uncovers the shared racial underpinnings of domestic and imperialist discourse through which the separateness of gendered spheres reinforces the effort to separate the races by turning blacks into foreigners. The essay concludes with suggestions about how understanding the imperial reach of domestic discourse might remap the way we read women's novels of the 1850s by interpreting their narratives of domesticity and female subjectivity as inseparable from narratives of empire and nation building.

Domesticity dominated middle-class women's writing and culture from the 1830s through the 1850s, a time when national boundaries were in violent flux; during this period the United States doubled its national territory, completed a campaign of Indian removal, fought its first prolonged foreign war, wrested the Spanish borderlands from Mexico, and annexed Texas, Oregon, and California. As Thomas Hietala has shown, this convulsive expansion was less a confident celebration of Manifest Destiny than a response to crises of confidence about national unity, the expansion of slavery, and the racial identity of citizenship—crises that territorial expansion exacerbated.[5] Furthermore, these movements evoked profound questions about the conceptual border between the domestic and the foreign. In the 1831 Supreme Court decision *Cherokee Nation v. the State of Georgia,* for example, Indians were declared members of "domestic dependent nations," neither foreign nationals nor United States citizens.[6] This designation makes the domestic an ambiguous third realm between the national and the foreign, as it places the foreign inside the geographic boundaries of the nation. The uneasy relation between the domestic and the foreign can also be seen in the debates over the annexation of new territory. In the middle of the Mexican War President Polk insisted that slavery was "purely a domestic question" and not a "foreign question" at all, but the expansion he advocated undermined that distinction and threatened domestic unity by raising the question of slavery's extension into previously foreign lands.[7] In debates about the annexation of Texas and later Mexico, both sides represented the new territories as women to be married to the United States; Sam Houston, for example, wrote of Texas presenting itself "to the United States as a bride adorned for her espousals"; and President Taylor accused annexationists after the Mexican War of trying to "drag California into the Union before her wedding garment has yet been cast about her person."[8] These visions of imperial expansion as marital union carried within them the specter of marriage as racial amalgamation. While popular fiction about the Mexican War portrayed brave American men rescuing and marrying Mexican women of Spanish descent, political debate over the annexation of Mexico hinged on what was agreed to be the impossibility of incorporating a foreign people marked by their racial intermixing into a domestic nation imagined as Anglo-Saxon.[9] One of the major contradictions of imperialist expansion was that while it strove to nationalize and domesticate foreign territories and peoples, annexation incorporated nonwhite foreign subjects in a way perceived to undermine the nation as a domestic space.

My point here is not to survey foreign policy but to suggest how deeply the language of domesticity suffused the debates about national expansion. Rather than stabilizing the representation of the nation as home, this rhetoric heightened the fraught and contingent nature of the boundary between the domestic and the foreign, a boundary that breaks down around questions of the racial identity of the nation as home. If we begin to rethink woman's sphere in this context, we have to ask how the discourse of domesticity negotiates the borders of an increasingly expanding empire and a divided nation. Domestic discourse both redresses and reenacts the contradictions of empire through its own double movement to expand female influence beyond the home and the nation while simultaneously contracting woman's sphere to police domestic boundaries against the threat of foreignness both within and without.

At this time of heightened national expansion, proponents of a "woman's sphere" applied the language of empire to both the home and women's emotional lives. "Hers is the empire of the affections," wrote Sarah Josepha Hale, influential editor of *Godey's Lady's Book,* who opposed the women's rights movement as "the attempt to take woman away from her empire of home."[10] To educational reformer Horace Mann, "the empire of the Home" was "the most important of all empires, the pivot of all empires and emperors."[11] Writers who counseled women to renounce politics and economics, "to leave the rude commerce of camps and the soul hardening struggling of political power to the harsher spirit of men," urged them in highly political rhetoric to take up a more spiritual calling, "the domain of the moral affections and the empire of the heart."[12] Catharine Beecher gives this calling a nationalist cast in *A Treatise on Domestic Economy* when, for example, she uses Queen Victoria as a foil to elevate the American "mother and housekeeper in a large family," who is "the sovereign of an empire demanding as varied cares, and involving more difficult duties, than are exacted of her, who wears the crown and professedly regulates the interests of the greatest nation on earth, [yet] finds abundant leisure for theaters, balls, horse races, and every gay leisure."[13] This imperial trope might be interpreted as a compensatory and defensive effort to glorify the shrunken realm of female agency, in a paradox of what Mary Ryan calls "imperial isolation," whereby the mother gains her symbolic sovereignty at the cost of withdrawal from the outside world.[14] For these writers, however, metaphor has a material efficacy in the world. The representation of the home as an empire exists in tension with the notion of woman's sphere as a contracted space because it is in the nature of empires to extend their rule over new domains while fortifying their borders against external invasion and internal insurrection. If, on the one hand, domesticity draws strict boundaries between the home and the world of men, on the other, it becomes the engine of national expansion, the site from which the nation reaches beyond itself through the emanation of woman's moral influence.

The paradox of what might be called "imperial domesticity" is that by withdrawing from direct agency in the male arena of commerce and politics, woman's sphere can be represented by both women and men as a more potent agent for national expansion. The outward reach of domesticity in turn enables the interior functioning of the home. In her introduction to *A Treatise on Domestic Economy,* Beecher inextricably links women's work at home to the unfolding of America's global mission of "exhibiting to the world the beneficent influences of Christianity, when carried into every social, civil, and political institution" (12). Women's maternal responsibility for molding the character of men and children has global repercussions: "To American women, more than to any others on earth, is committed the exalted privilege of extending over the world those blessed influences, that are to renovate degraded man, and 'clothe all climes with beauty'" (14). Beecher ends her introduction with an extended architectural metaphor in which women's agency at home is predicated on the global expansion of the nation:

> The builders of a temple are of equal importance, whether they labor on the foundations, or toil upon the dome. Thus also with those labors that are to be made effectual in the regeneration of the Earth. The woman who is rearing a family of children; the woman who labors in the schoolroom, the woman who, in her retired chamber, earns with her needle, the mite to contribute for the intellectual and moral ele-

vation of her country; even the humble domestic, whose example and influence may be molding and forming young minds, while her faithful services sustain a prosperous domestic state;—each and all may be cheered by the consciousness that they are agents in accomplishing the greatest work that ever was committed to human responsibility. It is the building of a glorious temple, whose base shall be coextensive with the bounds of the earth, whose summit shall pierce the skies, whose splendor shall beam on all lands, and those who hew the lowliest stone, as much as those who carve the highest capital, will be equally honored when its top-stone shall be laid, with new rejoicing of the morning stars, and shoutings of the sons of God. (14)

One political effect of this metaphor is to unify women of different social classes in a shared project of construction while sustaining class hierarchy among women.[15] This image of social unity both depends on and underwrites a vision of national expansion, as women's varied labors come together to embrace the entire world. As the passage moves down the social scale, from mother to teacher to spinster, the geographic reach extends outward from home to schoolroom to country, until the "humble domestic" returns back to the "prosperous domestic state," a phrase that casts the nation in familial terms. Women's work at home here performs two interdependent forms of national labor; it forges the bonds of internal unity while impelling the nation outward to encompass the globe. This outward expansion in turn enables the internal cohesiveness of woman's separate sphere by making women agents in constructing an infinitely expanding edifice.

Beecher thus introduces her detailed manual on the regulation of the home as a highly ordered space by fusing the boundedness of the home with the boundlessness of the nation. Her 1841 introduction bears a remarkable resemblance to the rhetoric of Manifest Destiny, particularly to this passage by one of its foremost proponents, John L. O'Sullivan:

The far-reaching, the boundless future will be the era of American greatness. In its magnificent domain of space and time, the nation of many nations is destined to manifest to mankind the excellence of divine principles; to establish on earth the noblest temple ever dedicated to the worship of the most high—the Sacred and the True. Its floor shall be a hemisphere—its roof the firmament of the star-studded heavens, and its congregation an Union of many Republics, comprising hundreds of happy millions, calling, owning no man master, but governed by God's natural and moral law of equality.[16]

While these passages exemplify the stereotype of separate spheres (one describes work in the home and the other the work of nation building), both use a common architectural metaphor from the Bible to build a temple co-extensive with the globe. O'Sullivan's grammatical subject is the American nation, which is the implied medium in Beecher's text for channeling women's work at home to a Christianized world. The construction of an edifice ordinarily entails walling off the inside from the outside, but in both these cases there is a paradoxical effect whereby the distinction between inside and outside is obliterated by the expansion of the home/nation/temple to encompass the globe. The rhetorics of Manifest Destiny and domesticity share a vocabulary that turns imperial conquest into spiritual regeneration to efface internal conflict or external resistance in visions of geopolitical domination as global harmony.

Although imperial domesticity ultimately imagines a home co-extensive with the entire world, it also continually projects a map of unregenerate outlying foreign terrain that both gives coherence to its boundaries and justifies its domesticating mission. When in 1869 Catharine Beecher revised her *Treatise* with her sister, Harriet Beecher Stowe, as *The American Woman's Home,* they downplayed the earlier role of domesticity in harmonizing class differences while enhancing domesticity's outward reach. The book ends by advocating the establishment of Christian neighborhoods settled primarily by women as a way of putting into practice domesticity's expansive potential to Christianize and Americanize immigrants both in Northeastern cities and "all over the West and South, while along the Pacific coast, China and Japan are sending their pagan millions to share our favored soil, climate, and government." No longer a leveling factor among classes within America, domesticity could be extended to those conceived of as foreign both within and beyond American national borders: "Ere long colonies from these prosperous and Christian communities would go forth to shine as 'lights of the world' in all the now darkened nations. Thus the Christian family and Christian neighborhood would become the grand ministry as they were designed to be, in training our whole race for heaven."[17] While Beecher and Stowe emphasize domesticity's service to "darkened nations," the existence of "pagans" as potential converts performs a reciprocal service in the extension of domesticity to single American women. Such Christian neighborhoods would allow unmarried women without children to leave their work in "factories, offices and shops" or their idleness in "refined leisure" to live domestic lives on their own, in some cases by adopting native children. Domesticity's imperial reach posits a way of extending woman's sphere to include not only the heathen but also the unmarried Euro-American woman who can be freed from biological reproduction to rule her own empire of the mother.

If writers about domesticity encouraged the extension of female influence outward to domesticate the foreign, their writings also evoked anxiety about the opposing trajectory that brings foreignness into the home. Analyzing the widespread colonial trope that compares colonized people to children, Ann Stoler and Karen Sánchez-Eppler have both shown how this metaphor can work not only to infantilize the colonized but also to portray white children as young savages in need of civilizing.[18] This metaphor at once extends domesticity outward to the tutelage of heathens while focusing it inward to regulate the threat of foreignness within the boundaries of the home. For Beecher, this internal savagery appears to threaten the physical health of the mother. Throughout the *Treatise,* the vision of the sovereign mother with imperial responsibilities is countered by descriptions of the ailing invalid mother. This contrast can be seen in the titles of the first two chapters, "Peculiar Responsibilities of American Women" and "Difficulties Peculiar to American Women." The latter focuses on the pervasive invalidism that makes American women physically and emotionally unequal to their global responsibilities. In contrast to the ebullient temple building of the first chapter, Beecher ends the second with a quotation from Tocqueville describing a fragile frontier home centered on a lethargic and vulnerable mother whose

> children cluster about her, full of health, turbulence and energy; they are true children of the wilderness; their mother watches them from time to time, with mingled melancholy and joy. To look at their strength, and her languor one might imagine that the life she had given them exhausted her own; and still she regrets not what they cost her. The house, inhabited by these emigrants, has no internal partition or loft. In the one chamber of which it consists, the whole family is gathered for the night. The dwelling itself is a little world; an ark of civilization amid an ocean of foliage. A hundred steps beyond it, the primeval forest spreads its shade and solitude resumes its sway. (24)

The mother's health appears drained not by the external hardships inflicted by the environment but by her intimate tie to her own "children of the wilderness," who violate the border between home and primeval forest. This boundary is partially reinforced by the image of the home as an "ark of civilization" whose internal order should protect its inhabitants from the sea of chaos that surrounds them. Yet the undifferentiated inner space, which lacks "internal partition," replicates rather than defends against the boundlessness of the wilderness. The rest of the treatise, with its detailed attention to the systematic organization of the household, works to "partition" the home in a way that distinguishes it from the external wilderness.[19]

The infirmity of American mothers is a pervasive concern throughout the *Treatise,* yet its physical cause is difficult to locate in Beecher's text. Poor health afflicts middle-class women in Northeastern cities as much as women on the frontier, according to Beecher, and she sees both cases resulting from a geographic and social mobility in which "everything is moving and changing" (16). This movement affects women's health most directly, claims Beecher, by depriving them of reliable domestic servants. With "trained" servants constantly moving up and out, middle-class women must resort to hiring "ignorant" and "poverty-stricken foreigners," with whom they are said in *American Woman's Home* to have a "missionary" relationship (332). Though Beecher does not label these foreigners as the direct cause of illness, their presence disrupts the orderly "system and regularity" of housekeeping, leading American women to be "disheartened, discouraged, and ruined in health" (18). Throughout her *Treatise* Beecher turns the absence of good servants—at first a cause of infirmity—into a remedy; their lack gives middle-class women the opportunity to perform regular domestic labor that will revive their health. By implication, their self-regulated work will also keep "poverty-stricken foreigners" out of their homes. Curiously, then, the mother's ill health stems from the unruly subjects of her domestic empire—children and servants—who bring uncivilized wilderness and undomesticated foreignness into the home. The fear of disease and of the invalidism that characterizes the American woman also serves as a metaphor for anxiety about foreignness within. The mother's domestic empire is at risk of contagion from the very subjects she must domesticate and civilize, her wilderness children and foreign servants, who ultimately infect both the home and the body of the mother.[20]

This reading of Beecher suggests new ways of understanding the intricate means by which domestic discourse generates and relies on images of the foreign. On the one hand, domesticity's "habits of system and order" appear to anchor the home as a stable center in a fluctuating social world with expanding national borders; on the other, domesticity must be spatially and conceptually mobile to travel to the nation's far-flung frontiers. Beecher's use of Tocqueville's ark metaphor suggests both the rootlessness and the self-enclosed mobility necessary for middle-class domesticity to redefine the meaning of habitation to make Euro-Americans feel at home in terrain in which *they* are initially the foreigners. Domesticity inverts this relationship to create a home by rendering prior inhabitants alien and undomesticated and by implicitly nativizing newcomers. The empire of the mother thus shares the logic of the American empire; both follow a double compulsion to conquer and domesticate the foreign, thus incorporating and controlling a threatening foreignness within the borders of the home and the nation.

The imperial scope of domesticity was central to the work of Sarah Josepha Hale throughout her half-century editorship of the influential *Godey's Lady's Book,* as well as to her fiction and history writing. Hale has been viewed by some scholars as advocating a woman's sphere more thoroughly separate from male political concerns than Beecher did.[21] This withdrawal seems confirmed by the refusal of *Godey's* even to mention the Civil War throughout its duration, much less take sides. Yet when Hale conflates the progress of women with the nation's Manifest Destiny in her history writing, other scholars have judged her as inconsistently moving out of woman's sphere into the male political realm.[22] Hale's conception of separate spheres, I will argue, is predicated on the imperial expansion of the nation. Although her writing as editor, essayist, and novelist focused on the interior spaces of the home, with ample advice on housekeeping, clothing, manners, and emotions, she gave equal and related attention to the expansion of female influence through her advocacy of female medical missionaries abroad and the colonization of Africa by former black slaves. Even though Hale seems to avoid the issue of slavery and race relations in her silence about the Civil War, in the 1850s her conception of domesticity takes on a decidedly racial cast, exposing the intimate link between the separateness of gendered spheres and the effort to keep the races apart in separate national spheres.

In 1846, at the beginning of the Mexican War, Hale launched a campaign on the pages of *Godey's Lady's Book* to declare Thanksgiving Day a national holiday, a campaign she avidly pursued until Lincoln made the holiday official in 1863.[23] This effort typified the way in which Hale's map of woman's sphere overlaid national and domestic spaces; *Godey's* published detailed instructions and recipes for preparing the Thanksgiving feast, while it encouraged women readers to agitate for a nationwide holiday as a ritual of national expansion and unification. The power of Thanksgiving Day stemmed from its center in the domestic sphere; Hale imagined millions of families seated around the holiday table at the same time, thereby unifying the vast and shifting space of the national domain through simultaneity in time. This domestic ritual, she wrote in 1852, would unite "our great nation, by its states and families from the St. John to the Rio Grande, from the Atlantic to the Pacific."[24] If the celebration of Thanksgiving unites individual families across regions and brings them together in an imagined collective space, Thanksgiving's continental scope endows each individual family gathering with national meaning. Furthermore, the Thanksgiving story commemorating the founding of New England—which in Hale's version makes no mention of Indians—could create a common history by nationalizing a regional myth of origins and imposing it on the territories most recently wrested from Indians and Mexicans. Hale's campaign to transform Thanksgiving from a regional to a national holiday grew even fiercer with the approach of the Civil War. In 1859 she wrote, "If every state would join in Union Thanksgiving on the 24th of this month, would it not be a renewed pledge of love and loyalty to the Constitution of the United States?"[25] Thanksgiving Day, she hoped, could avert civil war. As a national holiday celebrated primarily in the home, Thanksgiving traverses broad geographic circuits to write a national history of origins, to colonize the western territories, and to unite North and South.

The domestic ritual of Thanksgiving could expand and unify national borders only by also fortifying those borders against foreignness; for Hale, the nation's borders not only defined its geographical limits but also set apart nonwhites within the national domain. In Hale's fiction of the 1850s, Thanksgiving polices the domestic sphere by making black people, both free and enslaved, foreign to the domestic nation and denying them a home within America's expanding borders. In 1852 Hale reissued her novel *Northwood,* which had launched her career in 1827, with a highly publicized chapter about a New Hampshire Thanksgiving dinner showcasing the values of the American republic to a skeptical British visitor. For the 1852 version Hale changed the subtitle from "A Tale of New England" to "Life North and South" to highlight the new material on slavery she had added.²⁶ Pro-Union yet against abolition, Hale advocated African colonization as the only means of preserving domestic unity by sending all blacks to settle in Africa and Christianize its inhabitants. Colonization in the 1850s had a two-pronged ideology, both to expel blacks to a separate national sphere and to expand U.S. power through the civilizing process; black Christian settlers would thereby become both outcasts from and agents for the American empire.²⁷

Hale's 1852 *Northwood* ends with an appeal to use Thanksgiving Day as an occasion to collect money at all American churches "for the purpose of educating and colonizing free people of color and emancipated slaves" (408). This annual collection would contribute to "peaceful emancipation" as "every obstacle to the real freedom of America would be melted before the gushing streams of sympathy and charity" (408). While "sympathy," a sentiment associated with woman's sphere, seems to extend to black slaves, the goal of sympathy in this passage is not to free them but to emancipate white America from their presence. Thanksgiving for Hale thus celebrates national coherence around the domestic sphere while simultaneously rendering blacks within America foreign to the nation.

For Hale, colonization would not simply expel black people from American nationality but would also transform American slavery into a civilizing and domesticating mission. One of her Northern characters explains to the British visitor that "the destiny of America is to instruct the world, which we shall do, with the aid of our Anglo-Saxon brothers over the water. . . . Great Britain has enough to do at home and in the East Indies to last her another century. We have this country and Africa to settle and civilize" (167). When his listener is puzzled by the reference to Africa, he explains, "That is the greatest mission of our Republic, to train here the black man for his duties as a Christian, then free him and send him to Africa, there to plant Free States and organize Christian civilization" (168). The colonization of Africa becomes the goal of slavery by making it part of the civilizing mission of global imperialism. Colonization thus not only banishes blacks from the domestic union but, as the final sentence of *Northwood* proclaims, it proves that "the mission of American slavery is to Christianize Africa" (408).

In 1852 Hale published the novel *Liberia*, which begins where *Northwood* ends, with the settlement of Liberia by freed black slaves.²⁸ Seen by scholars as a retort to *Uncle Tom's Cabin, Liberia* can also be read as the untold story of Stowe's novel, beginning where she ends, with former black slaves immigrating to Africa.[29] Although the subtitle, "Mr. Peyton's Experiment," places colonization under the aegis of white males, the narrative turns colonization into a project emanating from woman's sphere in at least two directions. In its outward trajectory, the settlement of Liberia appears as an expansion of feminized domestic values. Yet domesticity is not only exported to civilize native Africans; the framing of the novel also makes African colonization necessary to the establishment of domesticity within America as exclusively white. While Hale writes that the purpose of the novel is to "show the advantages Liberia offers to the African," in so doing it construes all black people as foreign to American nationality by asserting that they must remain homeless within the United States. At the same time, Hale paints a picture of American imperialism as the embodiment of the feminine values of domesticity: "What other nation can point to a colony planted from such pure motives of charity; nurtured by the counsels and exertions of its most noble and self-denying statesmen and philanthropists; and sustained, from its feeble commencement up to a period of self-reliance and independence, from pure love of justice and humanity" (iv). In this passage America is figured as a mother raising her baby, Africa, to maturity; the vocabulary of "purity," "charity," "self-denial," and "love" represents colonization as an expansion of the values of woman's separate sphere.

The narrative opens with a threat to American domesticity on two fronts. The last male of a distinguished Virginia family is on his deathbed, helpless to defend his plantation from a rumored slave insurrection; the women of the family, led by his wife, "Virginia," rally with the loyal slaves to defend their home from an insurrection that never occurs. Thus the novel opens with separate spheres gone awry, with the man of the family abed at home and white women and black slaves acting as protectors and soldiers. While the ensuing plot to settle Liberia overtly rewards those slaves for their loyalty by giving them freedom and a homeland, it also serves to reinstate separate spheres and reestablish American domesticity as white.

When the narrative shifts to Africa, colonization has the effect not only of driving black slaves out of American nationhood but also of Americanizing Africa through domesticity. A key figure in the settlement is the slave Keziah, who has nursed the white plantation owners. She is the most responsive to Peyton's proposal for colonization because of her desire both to be free and to Christianize the natives. Her future husband, Polydore, more recently arrived from Africa and thus less "civilized," is afraid to return there because of his memory of native brutality and superstition. This couple represents two faces of enslaved Africans central to the white imagination of colonization: the degenerate heathen represented by the man and the redeemed Christian represented by the woman. Keziah, however, can only become a fully domesticated woman at a geographic remove from American domesticity. When Keziah protects the plantation in Virginia, her maternal impulse is described as that of a wild animal—a "fierce lioness." Only in Africa can she become the domestic center of the new settlement, where she establishes a home that resembles Beecher's Christian neighborhood. Keziah builds a private home with fence and garden, and civilizes her husband while expanding her domestic sphere to adopt native children and open a Christian school.

Keziah's domestication of herself and her surroundings in Africa can be seen as a part of the movement in the novel noted by Susan Ryan, in which the freed black characters are represented as recognizably American only at the safe distance of Africa.[30] Once banished from the domestic sphere of the American nation, they can reproduce themselves for readers as Americans in a foreign terrain. The novel not only narrates the founding of Liberia as a story of colonization, but Hale's storytelling also colonizes Liberia as an imitation of America, replete with images of an open frontier, the *Mayflower,* and the planting of the American flag. A double narrative movement at once contracts American borders to exclude blacks from domestic space and simultaneously expands U.S. borders by re-creating that domestic space in Africa. The novel thus ends with a quotation that compares the Liberian settlers to the Pilgrims and represents them as part of a global expansion of the American nation:

> I do not doubt but that the whole continent of Africa will be regenerated, and I believe the Republic of Liberia will be the great instrument, in the hands of God, in working out this regeneration. The colony of Liberia has succeeded better than the colony of Plymouth did for the same period of time. And yet, in that little company which was wafted across the mighty ocean in the *May Flower,* we see the germs of this already colossal nation, whose feet are in the tropics, while her head reposes upon the snows of Canada. Her right hand she stretches over the Atlantic, feeding the millions of the Old World, and beckoning them to her shores, as a refuge from famine and oppression; and, at the same

time, she stretches forth her left hand to the islands of the Pacific, and to the old empires of the East. (303)

African slaves are brought to America to become Christianized and domesticated, but they cannot complete this potential transformation until they return to Africa.

Hale's writing makes race central to woman's sphere not only by excluding nonwhites from domestic nationalism but also by seeing the capacity for domesticity as an innate, defining characteristic of the Anglo-Saxon race. Reginald Horsman has shown how by the 1840s the meaning of Anglo-Saxonism in political thought had shifted from a historical understanding of the development of republican institutions to an essentialist definition of a single race that possesses an innate and unique capacity for self-government.[31] His analysis, however, limits this racial formation to the male sphere of politics. Hale's *Woman's Record* (1853), a massive compendium of the history of women from Eve to the present, establishes woman's sphere as central to the racial discourse of Anglo-Saxonism; to her, the empire of the mother spawns the Anglo-Saxon nation and propels its natural inclination toward global power.[32] In her introduction to the fourth part of her volume on the present era, Hale represents America as manifesting the universal progress of women that culminates in the Anglo-Saxon race. To explain the Anglo-Saxon "mastery of the mind over Europe and Asia," she argues that

> if we trace out the causes of this superiority, they would center in the moral influence, which true religion confers on the female sex. . . . There is still a more wonderful example of this uplifting power of the educated female mind. It is only seventy-five years since the Anglo-Saxons in the New World became a nation, then numbering about three million souls. Now this people form the great American republic, with a population of twenty three millions; and the destiny of the world will soon be in their keeping! Religion is free; and the soul which woman always influences where God is worshipped in spirit and truth, is untrammeled by code, or creed, or caste. . . . The result before the world—a miracle of advancement, American mothers train their sons to be men. (564)

Hale here articulates the imperial logic of what has been called "republican motherhood," which ultimately posits the expansion of maternal influence beyond the nation's borders.[33] The Manifest Destiny of the nation unfolds logically from the imperial reach of woman's influence emanating from her separate domestic sphere. Domesticity makes manifest the destiny of the Anglo-Saxon race, while Manifest Destiny becomes in turn the condition for Anglo-Saxon domesticity. For Hale domesticity has two effects on national expansion: It imagines the nation as a home delimited by race and propels the nation outward through the imperial reach of female influence.

Advocating domesticity's expansive mode, *Woman's Record* includes only those nonwhite women whom Hale understood to be contributing to the spread of Christianity to colonized peoples. In the third volume, Hale designates as the most distinguished woman from 1500 to 1830 a white American missionary to Burma, Ann Judson (152). The Fourth Era of *Woman's Record* focuses predominantly on American women as the apex of historical development. In contrast to the aristocratic accomplishments of English women, "in all that contributes to popular education and pure religious sentiment among the masses, the women of America are in advance of all others on the globe. To prove this we need only examine the list of American female missionaries, teachers, editors and authors of works instructive and educational, contained in this 'Record'" (564). While Anglo-Saxon men marched outward to conquer new lands, women had a complementary outward reach from within the domestic sphere.

For Hale, African colonization can be seen as part of the broader global expansion of woman's sphere. In 1853 Hale printed in *Godey's Lady's Book* "An Appeal to the American Christians on Behalf of the Ladies' Medical Missionary Society," in which she argued for the special need for women physicians abroad because they would have unique access to foreign women's bodies and souls.[34] Her argument for the training of female medical missionaries both enlarges the field of white women's agency and feminizes the force of imperial power. She sees female medical missionaries as not only curing disease but also raising the status of women abroad: "All heathen people have a high reverence for medical knowledge. Should they find Christian ladies accomplished in this science, would it not greatly raise the sex in the estimation of those nations, where one of the most serious impediments to moral improvement is the degradation and ignorance to which their females have been for centuries consigned?" (185). Though superior to heathen women in status, American women would accomplish their goal by imagining gender as a common ground, which would give them special access to women abroad. As women they could be more effective imperialists, penetrating those interior feminine colonial spaces, symbolized by the harem, that remain inaccessible to male missionaries:

> Vaccination is difficult of introduction among the people of the east, though suffering dreadfully from the ravages of small-pox. The American mission at Siam writes that thousands of children were, last year, swept away by this disease in the country around them. Female physicians could win their way among these poor children much easier than doctors of the other sex. Surely the ability of American women to learn and practice vaccination will not be questioned, when the more difficult art of inoculation was discovered by the women of Turkey, and introduced into Europe by an English woman! Inoculation is one of the greatest triumphs of remedial skill over a sure loathsome and deadly disease which the annals of Medical Art record. Its discovery belongs to women. I name it here to show that they are gifted with genius for the profession, and only need to be educated to excel in the preventive department.
>
> Let pious, intelligent women be fitly prepared, and what a mission-field for doing good would be opened! In India, China, Turkey, and all over the heathen world, they would, in their character of physicians, find access to the homes and harems where women dwell, and where the good seed sown would bear an hundredfold, because it would take root in the bosom of the sufferer, and in the heart of childhood. (185)

In this passage the connections among women circulate in many directions, but Hale charts a kind of evolutionary narrative that places American women at the apex of development. Though inoculation was discovered by Turkish women, it can only return to Turkey to save Turkish children through the agency of English women transporting knowledge to Americans, who can then go to Turkey as missionaries and save women who cannot save themselves or their children. While Hale is advocating that unmarried women be trained as missionaries, the needs of heathen women allow female missionaries to conquer their own domestic empire without reproducing biologically. Instead, American women are metaphorically cast as men in a cross-racial union, as they sow seeds in the bosom of heathen women who will bear Christian children. Through the sentiment of female influence, women physicians will transform heathen harems into Christian homes.

My reading of Hale suggests that the concept of female influence so central to domestic discourse and at the heart of the sentimental ethos is underwritten by and abets the imperial expansion of the nation. While the empire of the mother advocated retreat from the world-conquering enterprises of men, this renunciation promised a more thorough kind of world conquest. The empire of the mother shared with the American empire a logical structure and a key contradiction: Both sought to encompass the world outside their borders; yet this same outward movement contributed to and relied on the contraction of the domestic sphere to exclude persons conceived of as racially foreign within those expanding national boundaries.

Understanding the imperial reach of domesticity and its relation to the foreign should help remap the critical terrain on which women's domestic fiction has been constructed. We can chart the broader international and national contexts in which unfold narratives of female development that at first glance seem anchored in local domestic spaces. We can see how such narratives imagine domestic locations in complex negotiation with the foreign. To take a few well-known examples from the 1850s, Susan Warner's *The Wide Wide World* sends its heroine to Scotland, while the world of Maria Cummins's *The Lamplighter* encompasses India, Cuba, the American West, and Brazil. In E. D. E. N. Southworth's *The Hidden Hand*, the resolution of multiple domestic plots in Virginia relies on the participation of the male characters in the Mexican War, while the geographic coordinates of *Uncle Tom's Cabin* extend not only to Africa at the end but also to Haiti and Canada throughout.[35] Such a remapping would involve more than just seeing the geographic settings anew; it would turn inward to the privileged space of the domestic novel—the interiority of the female subject—to find traces of foreignness that must be domesticated or expunged. How does this struggle with foreignness within "woman's sphere" shape the interiority of female subjectivity, the empire of the affections and the heart? While critics such as Gillian Brown, Richard Brodhead, and Nancy Armstrong have taught us how domestic novels represent women as model bourgeois subjects,[36] my remapping would explore how domestic novels produce the racialized national subjectivity of the white middle-class woman in contested international spaces.

Many domestic novels open at physical thresholds, such as windows or doorways, that problematize the relation between interior and exterior; the home and the female self appear fragile and threatened from within and without by foreign forces. These novels then explore the breakdown of the boundaries between internal and external spaces, between the domestic and the foreign, as they struggle to renegotiate and stabilize these domains. This negotiation often takes place not only within the home but also within the heroine. The narrative of female self-discipline that is so central to the domestic novel might be viewed as a kind of civilizing process in which the woman plays the role of both civilizer and savage. Gerty in *The Lamplighter,* for example, like Capitola in *The Hidden Hand,* first appears as an uncivilized street urchin, a heathen unaware of Christianity whose anger is viewed as a "dark infirmity" and whose unruly nature is in need of domesticating. We later learn that she was born in Brazil to the daughter of a ship captain, who was killed by malaria, the "inhospitable southern disease, which takes the stranger for its victim."[37] To become the sovereign mother of her own domestic empire, Gerty must become her own first colonial subject and purge herself of both her origin in a diseased uncivilized terrain and the female anger identified with that "dark" realm. This split between the colonizer and the colonized, seen here within one female character, appears in *Uncle Tom's Cabin* racially externalized onto Eva and Topsy.[38]

My point is that where the domestic novel appears most turned inward to the private sphere of female interiority, we often find subjectivity scripted by narratives of nation and empire. Even at the heart of *The Wide, Wide World,* a novel usually understood as thoroughly closeted in interior space, where the heroine disciplines herself through reading and prayer, her favorite book is the popular biography of George Washington, the father of the nation. Her own journey to live with her Scottish relatives can be seen as a feminized reenactment of the American revolution against the British empire. Similarly, in *The Hidden Hand,* the most inner recess of woman's sphere is conjoined with the male sphere of imperial conquest. While the American men in the novel are invading Mexico, in Virginia, a bandit, significantly named "Black Donald," invades the heroine's chamber and threatens to rape her. To protect the sanctity of her home and her own chastity, Capitola performs a founding national narrative of conquest. She drops the rapist through a trap door in her bedroom into a deep pit dug by the original owner to trick the Indian inhabitants into selling their land. The domestic heroine thus reenacts the originating gesture of imperial appropriation to protect the borders of her domestic empire and the inviolability of the female self.

Feminist criticism of *Uncle Tom's Cabin* has firmly established that the empire of the mother in Stowe's novel extends beyond the home to the national arena of antislavery politics. This expansive movement of female influence, I have been arguing, has an international dimension that helps separate gendered spheres coalesce in the imperial expansion of the nation by redrawing domestic borders against the foreign. In light of my reading of Hale's *Liberia*, we might remap the critical terrain of Stowe's novel to ask how its delineation of domestic space, as both familial and national, relies on and propels the colonization of Africa by the novel's free black characters. Rather than just focusing on their expulsion at the end of the novel, we might locate, in Toni Morrison's terms, "the "Africanist presence" throughout the text.[39] Africa appears as both an imperial outpost and a natural embodiment of woman's sphere, a kind of feminized utopia, that is strategically posed as an alternative to Haiti, which hovers as a menacing image of black revolutionary agency. The idea of African colonization does not simply emerge at the end as a racist failure of Stowe's political imagination; rather, colonization underwrites the racial politics of the domestic imagination. The "Africanist presence" throughout *Uncle Tom's Cabin* is intimately bound to the expansionist logic of domesticity itself. In the writing of Stowe and her contemporary proponents of woman's sphere, "Manifest Domesticity" turns an imperial nation into a home by producing and colonizing specters of the foreign that lurk inside and outside its ever shifting borders.

Notes

I wish to thank the organizers of the conference "Nineteenth-Century American Women Writers in the Twenty-First Century" (Hartford, Conn., May 1996) for inviting me to present my first formulation of the ideas in this essay. Special thanks to Susan Gillman, Carla Kaplan, Dana D. Nelson, and Priscilla Wald for their helpful and encouraging readings at crucial stages.

1 Influential studies of this paradigm by historians and literary critics include Barbara Welter, "The Cult of True Womanhood: 1820–1860," *American Quarterly* 18 (summer 1966): 151–74; Kathryn Kish Sklar, *Catharine Beecher: A Study in American Domesticity* (New Haven, Conn.: Yale University Press, 1973); Nancy Cott, *The Bonds of Womanhood: "Woman's Sphere" in New England, 1780–1835* (New Haven, Conn.: Yale University Press, 1977); Ann Douglas, *The Feminization of American Culture* (New York: Knopf, 1977); Nina Baym, *Woman's Fiction: A Guide to Novels by and about Women in America, 1820–1870* (Ithaca, N.Y.: Cornell University Press, 1978); Mary P. Ryan, *Cradle of the Middle Class: The Family in Oneida County, New York, 1790–1865* (Cambridge: Cambridge University Press, 1981), and *Empire of the Mother: American Writing about Domesticity, 1830–1860*

(New York: Institute for Research in History and Haworth Press, 1982); Mary Kelley, *Private Woman, Public Stage: Literary Domesticity in Nineteenth-Century America* (New York: Oxford University Press, 1984); Jane Tompkins, *Sensational Designs: The Cultural Work of American Fiction, 1790–1860* (New York: Oxford University Press, 1985); Gillian Brown, *Domestic Individualism: Imagining Self in Nineteenth-Century America* (Berkeley and Los Angeles: University of California Press, 1990); and the essays in *The Culture of Sentiment: Race, Gender, and Sentimentality in Nineteenth-Century America*, ed. Shirley Samuels (New York: Oxford University Press, 1992). See also the useful review essay by Linda K. Kerber, "Separate Spheres, Female Worlds, Woman's Place: The Rhetoric of Women's History," *Journal of American History* (June 1988): 9–39 (reprinted in this volume).

2 On the etymology of the word *domestic* and its relation to colonialism, see Karen Hansen, ed., *African Encounters with Domesticity* (New Brunswick, N.J.: Rutgers University Press, 1992), 2–23; and Anne McClintock, *Imperial Leather: Race, Gender, and Sexuality in the Colonial Conquest* (New York: Routledge, 1995), 31–36. On the uses of domesticity in the colonial context, see Vicente L. Rafael, "Colonial Domesticity: White Women and United States Rule in the Philippines," *American Literature* 67 (Dec. 1995): 639–66.

3 Tompkins, *Sensational Designs*, 143, 144. Despite Tompkins's well-known debate with Ann Douglas, both critics rely on imperial rhetoric. While Tompkins applauds the imperialist impulse of sentimentalism, Douglas derides sentimental writers for a rapacious reach that extends as far as the "colonization of heaven" and the "domestication of death" (240–72).

4 Even recent revisionist studies that situate woman's sphere in relation to racial and class hierarchies often overlook the international context in which these divisions evolve. In the important essays in *Culture of Sentiment*, for example, many of the racialized configurations of domesticity under discussion rely on a foreign or imperial dimension that remains unanalyzed. To take a few examples, Laura Wexler's analysis of Hampton Institute makes no mention of its founding by influential missionaries to Hawaii ("Tender Violence: Literary Eavesdropping, Domestic Fiction, and Educational Reform," 9–38); Karen Halttunen's analysis of a murder trial revolves around the uncertain identity of a white woman's foreign Spanish or Cuban lover ("'Domestic Differences': Competing Narratives of Womanhood in the Murder Trial of Lucretia Chapman," 39–57); Lynn Wardley ties domesticity's obsession with detail to West African fetishism ("Relic, Fetish, Femmage: The Aesthetics of Sentiment in the Work of Stowe," 203–20). Several essays note comparisons of slavery to the oriental harem, including Carolyn Karcher on Lydia Maria Child's antislavery fiction ("Rape, Murder, and Revenge in Slavery's Pleasant Homes: Lydia Maria Child's Antislavery Fiction and the Limits of Genre," 58–72) and Joy Kasson's analysis of Hirams's *The Greek Slave* ("Narratives of the Female Body: *The Greek Slave*," 172–90). The only essay

to treat the imperial dimensions of domesticity is Lora Romero's "Vanishing Americans: Gender, Empire, and New Historicism" (115–27).

5 Thomas R. Hietala, *Manifest Design: Anxious Aggrandizement in Late Jacksonian America* (Ithaca, N.Y.: Cornell University Press, 1985).

6 *Cherokee Nation v. the State of Georgia,* in *Major Problems in American Foreign Policy: Documents and Essays,* ed. Thomas G. Paterson, 2 vols. (Lexington, Mass.: Heath, 1989), 1:202.

7 Quoted in Walter La Feber, *The American Age: United States Foreign Policy at Home and Abroad* (New York: Norton, 1989), 112.

8 Quoted in George B. Forgie, *Patricide in the House Divided: A Psychological Interpretation of Lincoln and His Age* (New York: Norton, 1979), 107–8.

9 On popular fiction of the Mexican War, see Robert W. Johannsen, *To the Halls of the Montezumas: The Mexican War in the American Imagination* (New York: Oxford University Press, 1984), 175–204.

10 Sarah Josepha Hale, "Editor's Table," *Godey's Lady's Book,* January 1852, 88.

11 Quoted in Ryan, *Empire of the Mother,* 112.

12 From "The Social Condition of Woman," *North American Review,* April 1836, 513; quoted in Annette Kolodny, *The Land before Her: Fantasy and Experience of the American Frontiers, 1630–1860* (Chapel Hill: University of North Carolina Press, 1984), 166.

13 Catharine Beecher, *A Treatise on Domestic Economy* (Boston: Marsh, Capen, Lyon, and Webb, 1841), 144. Subsequent references to this work are cited parenthetically in the text.

14 Ryan, *Empire of the Mother,* 97–114.

15 Kathryn Kish Sklar is one of the few scholars to consider Beecher's domestic ideology in relation to nation building. She analyzes the *Treatise* as appealing to gender as a common national denominator, and as using domesticity as a means to promote national unity to counterbalance mobility and conflicts based on class and region. Sklar fails to see, however, that this vision of gender as a tool for national unity is predicated on the nation's imperial role (*Catharine Beecher*). Jenine Abboushi Dallal analyzes the imperial dimensions of Beecher's domestic ideology by contrasting it with the domestic rhetoric of Melville's imperial adventure narratives in "The Beauty of Imperialism: Emerson, Melville, Flaubert, and Al-Shidyac" (Ph.D. diss., Harvard University, 1996), chap. 2.

16 John L. O'Sullivan, "The Great Nation of Futurity," in *Major Problems in American Foreign Policy,* ed. Thomas G. Paterson, 1:241.

17 Catharine Beecher and Harriet Beecher Stowe, *The American Woman's Home* (Hartford, Conn.: J. B. Ford, 1869), 458–59.

18 Karen Sánchez-Eppler, "Raising Empires like Children: Race, Nation, and Religious Education," *American Literary History* 8 (fall 1996): 399–425; Ann Stoler, *Race and the Education of Desire: Foucault's "History of Sexuality" and the Colonial Order of Things* (Durham, N.C.: Duke University Press, 1995), 137–64.

19 Although the cleanliness and orderliness of the home promise to make American women healthier, Beecher also blames a lack of outdoor exercise for American women's frailty, suggesting that the problematic space outside the home—the foreign—can both cause and cure those "difficulties peculiar to American women."

20 This generalized anxiety about contamination of the domestic sphere by children may stem from the circulation of stories by missionaries who expressed fear of their children being raised by native servants or too closely identifying with native culture. Such stories circulated both in popular mission tracts and in middle-class women's magazines, such as *Godey's* and *Mother's Magazine;* see, for example, Stoler, *Race and the Education of Desire;* and Patricia Grimshaw, *Paths of Duty: American Missionary Wives in Nineteenth-Century Hawaii* (Honolulu: University of Hawaii Press, 1989), 154–78. The licentiousness of men was also seen as a threat to women's health within the home. For example, in "Life on the Rio Grande" (*Godey's Lady's Book,* April 1847), a piece celebrating the opening of public schools in Galveston, Texas, Sarah Josepha Hale quotes a military officer who warns that "liberty is ever degenerating into license, and man is prone to abandon his sentiments and follow his passions. It is woman's high mission, her prerogative and duty, to counsel, to sustain—as to control him" (177). On the borderlands, women have the role of civilizing savagery in their own homes, where men's passions appear as the foreign force to be colonized.

In general, domesticity is seen as an ideology that develops in middle-class urban centers (and, as Sklar shows, in contrast to European values) and is then exported to the frontier and empire, where it meets challenges and must adapt. It remains to be studied how domestic discourse might develop out of the confrontation with foreign cultures in what has been called the "contact zone" of frontier and empire.

21 Sklar, *Catharine Beecher,* 163; Douglas, *Feminization of American Culture,* 51–54.

22 Nina Baym, "Onward Christian Women: Sarah J. Hale's History of the World," *New England Quarterly* 63 (June 1990): 249–70.

23 Sarah J. Hale, "Editor's Table," *Godey's Lady's Book,* January 1847, 53.

24 Sarah J. Hale, *Godey's Lady's Book,* November 1852, 303.

25 Ruth E. Finley, *The Lady of Godey's, Sarah Josepha Hale* (Philadelphia: Lippincott, 1931), 199.

26 Sarah J. Hale, *Northwood; or, Life North and South: Showing the True Character of Both* (New York: H. Long and Brother, 1852). See Hale's 1852 preface, "A Word with the Reader," on revisions of the 1827 edition. Further references to *Northwood* will be cited parenthetically in the text.

27 On the white ideological framework of African colonization, see George Fredrickson, *The Black Image in the White Mind: The Debate on Afro-American Character and Destiny, 1817–1914* (New York: Harper and Row, 1971), 6–22, 110–17;

Susan M. Ryan, "Errand into Africa: Colonization and Nation Building in Sarah J. Hale's *Liberia,*" *New England Quarterly* 68 (Dec. 1995): 558–83.

28 Sarah J. Hale, *Liberia; or Mr. Peyton's Experiment* ([1853] Upper Saddle River, N.J.: Gregg Press, 1968).

29 On *Liberia* as a conservative rebuff to Stowe, see Thomas F. Gossett, *"Uncle Tom's Cabin" and American Culture* (Dallas, Tex.: Southern Methodist University Press, 1985), 235–36.

30 Ryan, "Errand into Africa," 572.

31 Reginald Horsman, *Race and Manifest Destiny: The Origins of American Racial Anglo-Saxonism* (Cambridge: Harvard University Press, 1981), 62–81.

32 Sarah J. Hale, *Woman's Record* (New York: Harper and Brothers, 1853).

33 Linda K. Kerber, *Women of the Republic: Intellect and Ideology in Revolutionary America* (Chapel Hill: University of North Carolina Press, 1980).

34 Sarah J. Hale, "An Appeal to the American Christians on Behalf of the Ladies' Medical Missionary Society," *Godey's Lady's Book,* March 1852, 185–88.

35 Susan Warner, *The Wide Wide World* ([1850] New York: Feminist Press, 1987); Maria Susanna Cummins, *The Lamplighter* ([1854] New Brunswick, N.J.: Rutgers University Press, 1988); E. D. E. N. Southworth, *The Hidden Hand; or, Capitola the Madcap* ([1859] New Brunswick, N.J.: Rutgers University Press, 1988); Harriet Beecher Stowe, *Uncle Tom's Cabin* ([1852] New York: Viking Penguin, 1981).

36 Nancy Armstrong, *Desire and Domestic Fiction: A Political History of the Novel* (New York: Oxford University Press, 1987); Brown, *Domestic Individualism;* Richard Brodhead, "Sparing the Rod: Discipline and Fiction in Antebellum America," in *The New American Studies: Essays from "Representations,"* ed. Philip Fisher (Berkeley and Los Angeles: University of California Press, 1991).

37 Cummins, *The Lamplighter,* 63, 321. On the male characters' involvement in imperial enterprises in India in *The Lamplighter,* see Susan Castellanos, "Masculine Sentimentalism and the Project of Nation-Building" (paper presented at the conference "Nineteenth-Century Women Writers in the Twenty-First Century," Hartford, Conn., May 1996).

38 On this split, see Elizabeth Young, "Topsy-Turvy: Civil War and *Uncle Tom's Cabin,*" chap. 1 of *Disarming the Nation: Women's Writing and the American Civil War* (Chicago: University of Chicago Press, 1999).

39 Toni Morrison, *Playing in the Dark: Whiteness and the Literary Imagination* (Cambridge: Harvard University Press, 1992), 6.

Passing through the Closet in
Pauline E. Hopkins's *Contending Forces*

SIOBHAN SOMERVILLE

In 1903, Cornelia Condict, a white subscriber to the *Colored American Magazine,* wrote to complain that "without exception [the serial stories] have been of love between colored and whites. Does that mean that your novelists can imagine no love beautiful and sublime within the range of the colored race, for each other?"[1] Condict's criticism was directed specifically toward Pauline E. Hopkins, the primary writer of fiction for the magazine at that time.[2] Condict complained that "the stories of these tragic mixed loves will not commend themselves to your white readers and will not elevate the colored readers."[3] In a response published with Condict's letter, Hopkins boldly countered these criticisms:

> My stories are definitely planned to show the obstacles persistently placed in our paths by a dominant race to subjugate us spiritually. Marriage is made illegal between the races and yet the mulattoes increase. Thus the shadow of corruption falls on the blacks and on the whites, without whose aid the mulattoes would not exist. And then the hue and cry goes abroad of the immorality of the Negro and the disgrace that the mulattoes are to this nation. Amalgamation is an institution designed by God for some wise purpose, and mixed bloods have always exercised a great influence on the progress of human affairs.[4]

Defending her stories, Hopkins used Condict's letter to her own advantage: "I am glad to receive this criticism for it shows more clearly than ever that white people don't understand *what pleases Negroes.*[5] Refusing to accommodate the racist preferences of her white reader, Hopkins located a powerful political project within her fiction—the right of African Americans to claim and represent their own desires.

Hopkins's insistence on claiming African American desire, which included the possibility of interracial desire, was part of her larger attempt to refuse the racialized boundaries that Jim Crow and antimiscegenation legislation increasingly imposed and naturalized during the 1890s and 1900s. It is important to point out, however, that Hopkins's response to Condict also resonated within dominant cultural understandings of race that, although not necessarily segregationist, were nevertheless invested in racial hierarchies.[6] For one might argue that in her association of "amalgamation" and "mixed bloods" with "progress," Hopkins participated in evolutionary narratives that posited lighter complexions as indicators of progress toward civilization. Ironically, Hopkins's response to Condict might be read as a suggestion that what "please[d] Negroes" was not "love beautiful and sublime within the range of the colored race," but interracial (hetero)sexuality. This inference would, of course, reinforce cultural myths that African Americans universally desired interracial sex, a myth that was used to justify not only segregation but also systematic racial violence.

Hopkins's fiction does not focus exclusively on interracial romance: She explores intraracial desire, for instance, in *Contending Forces* and *Of One Blood*. Reclaiming interracial desire, however, was important for her project of refusing a separation of "black" and "white" worlds. Hopkins's interest in exploring the mulatta figure and interracial desire in her fiction has been criticized more recently as a reflection of her conservatism and class privilege,[7] but, as Hazel Carby has suggested, it is useful to look at these recurring themes as literary devices within Hopkins's own historical context. Noting the increased prevalence of mulatto figures in American literature of the late nineteenth century, Carby suggests that "the figure of the mulatto should be understood and analyzed as a narrative device of mediation." She notes the historical context of this use of the mulatto figure:

> After the failure of Reconstruction, social conventions dictated an increasing and more absolute distance between black and white as institutionalized in the Jim Crow laws. In response, the mulatto figure in literature became a more frequently used literary convention for an exploration and expression of what was increasingly socially proscribed.

. . . The mulatta figure allowed for movement between two worlds, white and black, and acted as a literary displacement of the actual increasing separation of the races.[8]

Carby's comments are useful for understanding the function of the mulatto figure and of interracial romance within Hopkins's fiction. Rather than advocating interracial sexuality, as Condict concluded, Hopkins's narratives of interracial romance function as literary vehicles for exploring historically specific structures of racialization, sexuality, and power.

During the period in which Hopkins wrote fiction, interracial heterosexuality was policed through a variety of cultural practices, ranging from letters like Condict's to antimiscegenation statutes to the violent terrors of lynching and rape. While there can be no doubt that the "the color line" ubiquitously and often violently enforced prohibitions against interracial sexuality, it was not the only barrier to desire at work within American culture at the turn of the century. The period also saw the increased bifurcation of the population into "deviant" or "normal" based on newly emergent models of homosexuality and heterosexuality. As historians of sexuality have argued, although sexual acts between two people of the same sex had been punishable during earlier periods through legal and religious sanctions, these sexual practices did not necessarily define individuals as homosexual per se.[9] Only in the late nineteenth century did an understanding of sexuality emerge in which sexual acts and desires became constitutive of identity. Homosexuality as the condition, and therefore identity, of particular bodies is thus a production of that specific historical moment.[10]

In studies of African American literature, questions of sexuality, and particularly homosexuality, have recently begun to be addressed and explored in relation to African American cultural production in the 1920s. A number of critics, writers, and filmmakers have suggested that the presence of a significant number of gay and lesbian writers and visual artists shaped the literary and artistic movement that we generally call the Harlem Renaissance.[11] Indeed, it is not difficult to list writers central to the movement who had same-sex lovers or who were identified as gay: Langston Hughes, Carl Van Vechten, Countee Cullen, Alain Locke, Wallace Thurman, Bruce Nugent, Claude McKay. As Henry Louis Gates Jr. has recently written, the Harlem Renaissance "was surely as gay as it was black, not that it was exclusively either of these."[12]

But while questions of sexuality have begun to take a central place in scholarship on African American literary and artistic production in the 1920s, there exists little work on how discourses of homo- and heterosexuality might have played a part in African American literature and culture projects before the Harlem Renaissance. Drawing on the work of black feminist critics who have provided useful accounts of the ways in which gender and race were mutually imbricated in late-nineteenth- and early-twentieth-century writings by African American women, this article seeks to understand some of the ways in which these "new" discourses of sexuality shaped and were shaped by literary representations by African American writers, in particular, Pauline Hopkins. As critics such as Hazel Carby, Claudia Tate, and Ann duCille have shown, African American women writers embarked on a crucial project of dismantling sexualized stereotypes and redefining the meanings of black womanhood at the turn of the century. If definitions of black womanhood were being contested and renegotiated in this period, it seems likely that emerging notions of a lesbian sexual identity raised important questions for these writers. What role did shifting models of sexuality play in Hopkins's attempt to re-articulate cultural understandings of African American womanhood?

To clarify, I am not attempting to claim that Hopkins herself was a lesbian or that she wrote "lesbian" novels. Instead, I want to ask how questions of sexuality shaped the work of writers for whom we lack biographical information or who for other reasons are not easily classifiable as "homosexual," "heterosexual," "gay," "lesbian," or "queer." As Deborah McDowell has implicitly demonstrated in her insightful discussion of Nella Larsen's *Passing,* one need not rely on biographical evidence to show that questions about gender, homoeroticism, and homosexuality are not only relevant but often necessary for understanding cultural representations of race and racial difference.[13]

My approach places *Contending Forces* within the historical context not only of racial segregation but also of concurrent shifts in models of sexual identity. As I will show, questions about lesbian identity were present in Hopkins's texts and shaped the strategies she used to write about female characters and their relationships with one another. In her exploration of African American women's political and sexual desires, Hopkins confronted, consciously or unconsciously, the increasing cultural visibility and pathologization of lesbians and homosexuality. The often unstable division between homosexuality and heterosexuality inscribes itself thematically and narratively in Hopkins's exploration of the barriers to desire structured by the color line.

The Contending Forces of "Sappho"

Hopkins's first and only nonserialized novel, *Contending Forces,* contains two parts: a brief antebellum story and a narrative about life within an urban middle-class African American community in the 1890s.[14] The first section of the novel, set in the 1790s, introduces the Montforts, a slaveholding family in Bermuda. Responding to pressure from British abolitionists to outlaw slavery in its colonies, including Bermuda, the Montforts move to a plantation in North Carolina to continue agricultural production within a legal slave economy. The opening four chapters outline the history of the Montforts and end with the family's apparent destruction. White vigilantes bring ruin on the family by suggesting that Grace Montfort, who upholds ideals traditionally associated with nineteenth-century notions of true womanhood, has African American ancestry. The Montfort history ends with the white vigilantes' violent murder of Charles, the beating and suicide of Grace, and the separation of their two orphaned sons, Charles and Jesse. Hopkins never reveals whether the rumor about Grace's racial identity is true; instead, she shows the destructive power of racialized constructions.

The second part of the novel is set approximately one hundred years later, in Boston in 1896. The story centers on a boarding house run by "Ma" Smith and her two adult children, Dora and Will, and follows a melodramatic tale within the city's middle-class African American community. The central action begins with the entrance of a newcomer, Sappho Clark, a stenographer who takes a room in the Smith boarding house.

In her depiction of Sappho, Hopkins simultaneously borrows from and counters the conventions of the nineteenth-century novel of passing.[15] In the conventional novel of passing, the light-complexioned protagonist attempts to gain economic and social advancement by fleeing her or his African American family and community and passing for white in an anonymous landscape. As a literary genre, the passing narrative offers a space in which to explore contradictory and coexisting beliefs about race. The mobility of the passing figure "proves" that the supposed boundary between "black" and "white" bodies is not universally visible; passing is possible precisely because of the dominant culture's denial that African Americans may look "white." On the other hand, while the passing novel seems to subvert the stability of racial categories, it does so within a framework of individualism and often reinforces the cultural biases that posit hierarchies of white over black.

As constructed in the late nineteenth and early twentieth centuries (and perhaps more recently), passing involved immense losses (of family, of community—indeed of one's own history), great risks (the potential for blackmail, physical violence, and even death), and often betrayal in exchange for the privileges attached to white identity. These licenses and threats structure novels of racial passing. As the passing figure seeks to author his or her own narrative, he or she risks the possibility of any number of people from the past stepping forward to announce their version of his or her "true" identity. In most passing narratives, the protagonist's exposure is threatened not only by her or his body but also by proximity to another body, often the mother's. This body is simultaneously the site of nostalgic desire for reunion and disavowal of the past.

Frequently the central character in the late-nineteenth-century novel of passing is the tragic mulatta. In her study of the mulatto figure in American fiction, Judith Berzon notes how generic conventions were tied to the gender of the protagonist:

> In most novels with mulatto characters, the male mixed-blood characters are brave, honest, intelligent, and rebellious. . . . Few male mixed-blood characters are tragic mulattoes in the traditional sense. . . . There are almost no male suicides, whereas there are quite a few suicides by female mulatto characters. While there are some female characters who are race leaders, . . . there are not many such women in mulatto fiction.[16]

Berzon's broad mapping of narrative conventions attached to the gender of the mulatto/a figure is useful. In her study of gender and ethnicity in the American novel, Mary Dearborn adds that "the tragic mulatto, *usually a woman* . . . is divided between her white and black blood. The tragic mulatto trajectory demands that the mulatto woman desire a white lover and either die (often in white-authored versions) or return to the black community."[17] It is not surprising, then, that a certain amount of erotic tension and narrative curiosity surrounds this figure. As Werner Sollors has pointed out, "In nineteenth-century American culture the figure of the Quadroon and the Octoroon was such a taboo: puzzling, strangely attractive, forbidden (and, perhaps, attractive *because* forbidden)."[18] The figure of the mulatto characteristically symbolizes both psychic and social conflict. Positioned as a vehicle for narrative conflict and tension, the mulatta figure's movement between worlds also eroticizes her.

In *Contending Forces,* the figure of Sappho recalls the novel of passing and its conventional protagonist. She enters the story as a mysterious stranger, offering little information about her past or family. Physically she resembles the classically beautiful tragic mulatta who passes for white: "Tall and fair, with hair of a golden cast, aquiline nose, rosebud mouth, soft brown eyes veiled by long, dark lashes" (107). Significantly, although she is "a combination of 'queen rose and lily in one'" (107), Sappho refuses to pass as white. Late in the novel, however, it is revealed that she does "pass" in a different way: She has adopted the name "Sappho Clark" to escape her past as Mabelle Beaubean. Her secret is that she was raped by her white uncle and gave birth to a child as a result. Hopkins builds the narrative around Sappho's silence and the gradual discovery of her past. The novel thus positions the reader to expect, even to desire, the eventual exposure of her secrets.

A number of critics have remarked on the significance of the choice of the name "Sappho," suggesting that Hopkins's invocation of the ancient Greek poet resonates both with the feminist symbolism of this figure and the fragmentary nature of knowledge about her life and writing.[19] In a discussion of *Contending Forces* that generally criticizes Hopkins's focus on middle-class femininity, Houston Baker suggests that Hopkins's choice of the name is ironic: it "does not refer textually to anomalous sexual proclivities, but only, one assumes, to a classical mastery of the word. Ironically, such mastery for a mulatto woman in nineteenth-century Boston does not yield an island poet, but a clerk typist."[20] In his reading of the allusion and his focus on poetic "mastery," Baker too quickly dismisses the sexual significance of Hopkins's choice. What Baker refers to as "anomalous sexual proclivities," that is, the ancient Sappho's sexual attachments to other women, may indeed be relevant to Hopkins's portrayal of her heroine. In fact, it is remarkable that critical discussions of Hopkins have tended to avoid the name's obvious cultural associations with lesbian desire.[21]

During the nineteenth century, two competing narratives circulated around the figure of Sappho of Lesbos. On the one hand, she was considered a courtesan and a dangerous model of female licentiousness; on the other, she was seen as a desexualized figure, a bodiless model of "Greek Love." [22] In 1871, in an article published in the *Atlantic Monthly*, Thomas Wentworth Higginson was moved to defend Sappho—"the most eminent poetess of the world"—from scholars who had called her "a corrupt woman, and her school at Lesbos a nursery of sins." [23] He instead drew parallels between the ancient Sappho's "maiden lovers" and Boston's literary women of the mid-nineteenth century. Higginson compared Sappho specifically to Margaret Fuller and her "ardent attachments" to other women, which he characterized as passionate but nonsexual. [24]

Toward the end of the nineteenth century a different sexualized narrative increasingly circulated around the figure of Sappho, who became enmeshed in emerging understandings of female homosexuality (or "inversion"). Sappho, in fact, came to symbolize this "new" sexuality in women, as evidenced by the terms used to label it by literary and medical men alike: "sapphism" and "lesbianism." [25] This association was so strong that sexologist Havelock Ellis could proclaim, "Above all, Sappho, the greatest of women poets . . . has left a name which is permanently associated with homosexuality." [26]

A flurry of scholarly activity surrounded Sappho after new papyrus manuscripts of some of her poems were discovered in 1879 and 1898. [27] These texts, surviving on remnants of mummy wrappings, were excavated from ancient remains in Egypt. [28] Hopkins was undoubtedly aware of this renewed interest, and perhaps read new studies by Henry Thornton Wharton or John Addington Symonds. These studies compared Sappho and her circle of women on Lesbos with contemporary movements to advance the status of women: "While mixing freely with male society, they were highly educated, and accustomed to express their sentiments to an extent unknown elsewhere in history—until, indeed, the present time." [29] Viewing Sappho and her circle through the genteel women of his own day, Symonds noted that they "formed clubs for the cultivation of poetry and music." [30]

For Hopkins, the figure of Sappho may have suggested not only codes of gentility and a model of an intellectual and artistic woman but also a potential link to a specifically African past. [31] In the December 1905 issue of *Voice of the Negro*, a journal to which Hopkins contributed a number of articles in 1904 and 1905, the African American journalist John E. Bruce published an article entitled "Some Famous Negroes." The first to be listed was "Sappho the colored poetess of Mitylene, isle of Lesbos." [32] Bruce's evidence for Sappho's racial identity was both historical and mythological, and, at best, twice removed, since he cited Alexander Pope's English translation of Ovid's Latin poem, in which Sappho is indeed described as "brown," even "glossy jet" like the "Ethiopian dame."[33] Bruce's claim was, of course, speculative, but it was also an attempt to reclaim a history of African culture denied through colonialism and slavery. If Sappho's identity presented an epistemological gap, Bruce's attempt to claim her as African was no more problematic than assuming, as most critics had, that she was "white." Although Bruce's article appeared after the publication of *Contending Forces,* it is possible that Hopkins, like Bruce, may have discussed or read about the speculation that Sappho had African origins.

The figure of Sappho, like her poetry, represented fragmentation and contradiction. She symbolized seemingly irreconcilable notions of womanhood, associated as she was with prostitution, lesbianism, and chastity. Her cultural location—at times Egyptian, at times Greek—remained ambiguous. For Hopkins, this ambiguity reinforced the mystery that structured *Contending Forces:* Who is Sappho Clark? What is her past? Why is she alone? Before Hopkins describes Sappho Clark, she prepares her reader to expect that these questions have something to do with her sexuality. Hopkins introduces Sappho through Dora's fascinated description of her, to which Dora's brother Will responds, "I'll bet you a new pair of Easter gloves that she's a rank old maid with false teeth, bald head, hair on her upper lip—" (96). Expressing his sexual anxiety about this unknown woman and his sister's fascination with her, Will invokes specifically masculine characteristics ("bald head, hair on her upper lip") to evoke a stereotype of grotesque female sexuality, a "rank old maid."

Much to Will's surprise, when Sappho finally arrives, she appears beautiful beyond belief. Will is not the only character attracted to Sappho. Hopkins describes the deep physical and emotional desire between Dora and Sappho:

> After that evening the two girls were much together. Sappho's beauty appealed strongly to Dora's artistic nature; but hidden beneath the classic outlines of the face, the graceful symmetry of the form, and the dainty coloring of the skin, Dora's shrewd common sense and womanly intuition discovered a character of sterling worth—bold, strong and ennobling; while into Sappho's lonely self-suppressed life the energetic little Yankee girl swept like a healthful, strengthening breeze. Care was forgotten; there was new joy in living. (114)

Hopkins portrays Dora's and Sappho's attachment as one of mutual and transforming desire.

Yet Hopkins's attitude toward the possibility of the two women's mutual desire is contradictory, as might be expected given the uneven historical emergence of lesbian identity at the turn of the century. She seems to oscillate between a certain unselfconsciousness about representations of female attachments and an acknowledgment of their potential for transgression. The status of erotic relationships between women in the nineteenth-century United States has been the subject of vigorous debate among feminist literary critics and historians. Much of this scholarship has accepted Carroll Smith-Rosenberg's notion of "romantic friendship," in which passionate attachments between women were seen as acceptable and not incompatible with heterosexual marriage.[34] In a discussion of turn-of-the-century literary representations of lesbians, for instance, Lillian Faderman has suggested that passionate relationships between women were not pathologized. According to Faderman, "Popular magazine fiction, well into the twentieth century, could depict female-female love relationships with an openness that later became . . . impossible."[35] Recently this model has been challenged by scholars who have argued for a more complex understanding of erotic relationships between women before the twentieth century. In an insightful article on the representation of same-sex desire between women in popular fiction in the mid-nineteenth century, Marylynne Diggs has identified "the emergence throughout the nineteenth century of a specific sexual identification built upon the pathologizing of erotic and exclusive relationships between women."[36]

Hopkins's depiction of the relationship between Dora and Sappho illustrates this struggle over the definition and representation of women's erotic attachments as she oscillates between models of romantic friendship and lesbian pathology. Although Hopkins does not explicitly name lesbian desire, she does acknowledge that intimacy between two women is potentially dangerous, if not tragic. Dora herself at first treads cautiously in her friendship with Sappho: "She did not, as a rule, care much for girl friendships, holding that a close intimacy between two of the same sex was more than likely to end disastrously for one or the other" (97–98). This remarkably direct indictment of same-sex desire suggests that Hopkins clearly acknowledged the existence of sexual relationships between women and the growing tendency to pathologize them. She nevertheless appears to raise the specter of lesbian desire only to deny it as a characterization of Dora and Sappho's relationship. In spite of her professed reluctance to engage in "girl friendships," Dora cannot resist her attraction to the new lodger: "Sappho Clark seemed to fill a long-felt want in her life, and she had from the first a perfect trust in the beautiful girl" (98). Further, as a means of short-circuiting the inevitable "disastrous ending" of the narrative of desire between Sappho and Dora, Hopkins temporarily allows its expression—albeit only in a carefully controlled space set apart from the main narrative, a space of both containment and transgression not coincidentally resembling "the closet."

Sappho and the Closet

When an overnight snow storm makes it impossible for Sappho to leave the Smith boarding house for work, she "beg[s] Dora to pass the day with her and play 'company,' like the children" (117). Dora and Sappho take advantage of their enforced isolation to construct an idyllic domestic island:

> By eleven o'clock they had locked the door of Sappho's room to keep out all intruders, had mended the fire until the little stove gave out a delicious warmth, and had drawn the window curtains close to keep out stray currents of air. Sappho's couch was drawn close beside the stove, while Dora's small person was most cosily bestowed in her favorite rocking chair. (117)

Hopkins's description of the scene suggests miniaturization and contraction. The women play "like the children" in a room where the "little stove" suits Dora's "small person." Moreover, phrases like "delicious warmth," "mended," and "cosily bestowed" suggest specifically domestic comfort, while the repetition of "drawn close" suggests an increasing intimacy between the two women. "Locked" in, Dora and Sappho are ironically now "free" to explore their mutual desire in privacy.

Hopkins may not express any actual physical desire between Sappho and Dora (nor does she describe explicitly any physical sexual contact, heterosexual or homosexual, anywhere in the novel), but the scene is loaded with sensuality, albeit of a specifically middle-class "flavor": "A service for two was set out in dainty china dishes, cream and sugar looking doubly tempting as it gleamed and glistened in the delicate ware. One plate was piled with thinly cut slices of bread and butter, another held slices of pink ham" (118). Hopkins's description suggests doubleness, not only through the literal "service for two" and "doubly tempting" cream and sugar, but also through syntax, balancing the alliterative adjectives "gleamed and glistened" and the parallel clauses, "One plate . . . another . . ." (118). Similarly, Sappho herself is described in the same terms as the food. The sweets which "gleamed and glistened" mirror Sappho's body, described later as "all rosy and sparkling."

The scene is overwhelmingly erotic, in a specifically oral way. As the women complete their feast with cream pie and chocolate bonbons, Sappho teases Dora, "And your teeth, your beautiful white teeth, where will they be shortly if you persist in eating a pound of bonbons every day?" (120). Dora teases back, "I'll eat all the bonbons I want in spite of you, Sappho, and if you don't hurry I'll eat your slice of cream pie, too" (120). Hopkins giddily narrates, "At this dire threat there ensued a scramble for the pie, mingled with peals of merry laughter, until all rosy and sparkling, Sappho emerged from the fray with the dish containing her share of the dainty held high in the air" (120). Hopkins's flowery language—"dire," "ensued," "mingled," "peals," "merry," "fray," "dainty"—suggests the lighthearted and inconsequential diction of respectable drawing room conversation. This stilted and feminized language reinforces the specifically bourgeois sensuality of the scene and its fetishization of color, especially pinks and whites: "cream," "sugar," "bread and butter," "pink ham," "cream pie," and "beautiful white teeth."

In this private, safe, and domesticated space, the tea party enacts a displacement of Dora's and Sappho's desire, sensual satisfaction, and veiled sexual aggression. The particular homoerotic significance of this episode is reinforced by the intimate conversation that follows it, a development and extension of the women's oral pleasure. The focus shifts from gastronomic desire to a more direct discussion and simultaneous evasion of the delicate subject of sexual desire. Dora, who at this point is engaged to marry her brother's best friend, asks Sappho earnestly, "Do you ever mean to marry, or are you going to pine in single blessedness on my hands and be a bachelor-maid to the end?" (121). Sappho's reply adds to the ambiguity surrounding her sexuality: "'Well,' replied Sappho, with a comical twist to her face, 'in the words of Unc' Gulliver, "I mote, an' then agin I moten't"'" (121–22). The rest of their conversation reveals Dora's reason for raising the subject:

> "What troubles me is having a man bothering around. . . . I'm wondering if my love could stand the test."
> "That's queer talk for an engaged girl, with a fine, handsome fellow to court her. Why Dora, 'I'm s'prised at yer!'" laughed Sappho gaily.

". . . I dread to think of being tied to John for good and all; I know I'll be sick of him inside of a week. I do despair of ever being like other girls." (121–22)

This exchange reveals a great deal about Dora's and Sappho's understanding of their own sexuality, as well as their relationship. In shaping her novel, Hopkins ostensibly borrowed from nineteenth-century romance conventions, in which the narrative works toward a heterosexual resolution in marriage.[37] Yet this scene presents a potential obstacle to the expected heterosexual coupling; this "queer talk" of "single blessedness" and "bachelor girls" threatens to disrupt the conventional romance narrative. Sappho is not willing to commit herself to any particular desire; her laughing and "comical twist" suggest that a certain anxiety surrounds the subject of heterosexual marriage. Dora's despair stems not from the absence of a potential husband but from her difference from "other girls," for whom heterosexual desire seems effortless and unproblematic. When Sappho recites the traditional maxim of romantic love, "A woman loves one man, and is true to him through all eternity," Dora responds, "That's just what makes me feel so *unsexed*" (122).

Dora's self-diagnosis ripples with anxiety: Because her desire does not correspond to the conventional cultural narrative that culminates in heterosexual marriage, she can define herself only by the negation of desire. By using the word *unsexed,* Dora locates herself in an unspecified space between genders and outside traditional romance.[38] Hopkins's use of *unsexed* also resonates with the developing discourse of female homosexuality. In his 1915 article on "Inversion and Dreams," for example, the American sexologist James Kiernan included a 1910 report of a young woman who had engaged in both homosexual and heterosexual activity and was troubled by dreams and fantasies in which she appeared as both male and female. Kiernan reported that "this the patient regarded as abnormal, believing herself to be what she called unsexed."[39] Like Kiernan's patient, Dora both acknowledges and resists her sexual indifference toward men. Yet in a less self-conscious moment, she readily indulges her desire for Sappho: "Dora gazed at her friend with admiration, and wished that she had a kodak, so that she might catch just the expression that lighted her eyes and glowed in a bright color upon her cheeks" (125–26).

Within the novel, this scene of closeted intimacies has great implications for Dora, who feels here "the sincerity of the love that had taken root in her heart for Sappho" (127). Eventually Dora does abandon her engagement to her initial fiancé, John Langley, but she does not completely abandon marriage. She later marries Doctor Arthur Lewis, a promoter of industrial education who resembles Booker T. Washington. Hopkins makes clear, however, that sexual desire has little to do with their marriage. When Doctor Lewis proposes, Dora rationalizes her decision: "No; she could not remain single; she would marry one whose manliness she could respect, if she did not love him. Love was another thing, with which, she told herself, she was done" (360–61). At the end of the novel, after Dora has married Lewis and had a child, her brother Will assesses her emotional state: "If ever a doubt of Dora's happiness had troubled Will's thoughts, it was dispelled now that he saw her a contented young matron, her own individuality swallowed up in love for her husband and child. She had apparently forgotten that any other love had ever disturbed the peaceful current of her life" (389–90). This description suggests the limits of the heterosexual resolution of Dora's narrative: She trades her "individuality" for the role of respectable matron.[40] Significantly, Dora's voice is also submerged: Her thoughts and feelings are now articulated by her brother. Similarly, by leaving Dora's forgotten "other love" unspecified, Hopkins leaves open the possibility that it is Sappho. Despite the heterosexual resolution of each woman's narrative, Hopkins, however mutedly, suggests that marriage does not necessarily represent complete fulfillment of their sexual or political desires.

Within the context of literary representations of race and sexuality, the scene of Dora and Sappho "locked" pleasurably away has larger implications. The combination of the unspoken acknowledgment and literal marginalization of homoeroticism links *Contending Forces* to the "closet," a literary trope that Eve Kosofsky Sedgwick has identified as "the defining structure for gay oppression in this century."[41] A "skeleton in the closet" is "a private or concealed trouble in one's house or circumstances, ever present, and ever liable to come into view."[42] To be "in the closet" is to be palpably invisible within a structure of visibility, proximity, and knowledge. Although lesbian or gay individuals may desire to be either "in" or "out" of the closet, they can never fully control their status. They must, therefore, constantly renegotiate the boundary between "in" and "out" in a culture that simultaneously seeks out and erases lesbian and gay identity.

It is perhaps no coincidence that this century's defining structure of racial oppression, racial segregation, has been understood in similarly spatial terms. As W. E. B. Du Bois wrote in 1903, "The problem of the Twentieth Century is the problem of the color-line."[43] There are provocative and important connections between the notion of the "homosexual closet" and the novel of passing, which was arguably the most common genre (for both Anglo- and African American authors) for exploring the structures of segregation at the turn of the century. In Charles Chesnutt's words, in the novel of passing "the hidden drop of dark blood" is the "worm in the bud, the skeleton in the closet."[44]

Panic and Passionlessness

When Hopkins voices Dora's momentary fear that "a close intimacy between two of the same sex was more than likely to end disastrously for one or the other," she suggests a sense of sexual danger not confined to the relationship between Dora and Sappho. It returns later, in a scene marked by Sappho's intense ambivalence toward a powerful older woman. In a chapter entitled "The Sewing-Circle," Hopkins presents an all-female scene of instruction in which the elder Mrs. Willis, "the brilliant widow of a bright Negro politician," guides the younger women of the community through moral, political, and cultural questions (143).[45] Significantly, the group's subject for the day is "the place which the virtuous woman occupies in upbuilding a race" (148). During the discussion, Sappho asks, "How can we eliminate passion from our lives, and emerge into the purity which marked the life of Christ?" (154). The question resonates with nineteenth-century racialized constructions of womanhood. As Carby, Tate, and duCille have argued, the question of "virtue" was centrally important in constructing African American womanhood in relation to the "cult of true womanhood."[46] Because African American women were associated with sexual accessibility under slavery while white women were privileged as sexually "pure," it was crucial for African American women to begin to redefine their own sexuality. Nancy Cott has pointed out the potential uses of the ideology that associated passionlessness with virtuous women: "By replacing sexual with moral motives and determinants, the ideology of passionlessness favored women's power and self-respect. . . . To women who wanted means of self-preservation and self-control, this view of female nature may well have appealed."[47] For African American women, passionlessness offered a potential model for transforming negative cultural stereotypes.

Cott also notes that the ideology of passionlessness may have been particularly important for securing a sense of solidarity among women who organized collectively on behalf of women's rights. According to Cott, by placing their love for other women on a higher spiritual plane than heterosexual relationships, "that sense of the angelic or spiritual aspect of female love ennobled the experience of sisterhood which was central to the lives of nineteenth-century women and to the early woman's rights movement."[48] The problematic negotiation of desire and sexuality in the construction of a sisterhood is at the heart of Hopkins's sewing-circle scene. Mrs. Willis, "the pivot about which all the social and intellectual life of the colored people of her section revolved" (148), symbolizes ambivalence about the possibility of women's solidarity. She elicits "the gamut of emotions from strong attraction to repulsion" and seems to have remarkable power over other members of the African American community (144). In responding to Sappho's question about eliminating passion, Mrs. Willis takes a moderate view: "In some degree passion may be beneficial, but we must guard ourselves against a sinful growth of any appetite" (154). This tentative response does not dismiss the possibility of the *usefulness* of passion, a potentially problematic position for women who were attempting to revise the cultural stereotype of excessively passionate African American women.

When the two women continue their conversation in a "secluded corner" (155), Sappho is overwhelmed with conflicting emotions toward Mrs. Willis: "For a moment the flood-gates of suppressed feeling flew open in the girl's heart, and she longed to lean her head on that motherly breast and unburden her sorrows there" (155). Yet this attraction—or "passion"—is immediately tempered by revulsion: "Just as the barriers of Sappho's reserve seemed about to be swept away, there followed, almost instantly, a wave of repulsion toward this woman and her effusiveness, so forced and insincere" (155). Sappho's ambivalence unsettles her: "Sappho was impressed in spite of herself, by the woman's words. . . . There was evidently more in this woman than appeared upon the surface" (157). In this scene, Hopkins raises the possibility of intimacy about sexual secrets between Sappho and Mrs. Willis, only to immediately suppress it. Richard Yarborough suggests that Sappho's ambivalence toward Mrs. Willis reflects Hopkins's own attitude: "Like Sappho, Hopkins never resolves her feelings toward Willis, a powerful figure who captures the author's imagination to a greater extent than her small role in the novel might indicate."[49] Tate has suggested that

Hopkins's discomfort may reflect her awareness of the contempt that her contemporaries probably would have felt for the perceived self-promotion of this ambitious and outspoken female figure.[50]

Sappho's passionate ambivalence may have its source in a powerful identification between these two characters. Just as Sappho elicited Dora's most intimate confessions without "confessing" any details about her own past, so Mrs. Willis extracts facts about other people while withholding information about herself: "Keen in her analysis of human nature, most people realized, after a short acquaintance . . . that she had sifted them thoroughly, while they had gained nothing in return" (144). This scene has an important function in the narrative, as it piques the reader's appetite for the divulgence of Sappho's secret while deferring its exposure. In the tea party scene, Dora, ostensibly out of love for Sappho, "subdued her inquisitiveness, and she gladly accepted [Sappho's] friendship without asking troublesome questions" (127). In the sewing-circle scene Sappho comes dangerously close to divulging her secret: "[Sappho] drew back as from an abyss suddenly beheld stretching before her" (155). Sappho instead veils her own story in terms of an anonymous acquaintance and her hypothetical sin: "I once knew a woman who had sinned. No one in the community in which she lived knew it but herself. She married a man who would have despised her had he known her story; but as it is, she is looked upon as a pattern of virtue for all women. . . . Ought she not to have told her husband before marriage?" (156). Yet Mrs. Willis, like Dora, represses as much as she elicits Sappho's disclosure. To Sappho's question about confessing to a future husband, she answers simply, "I think not," thus preserving the silence that propels the narrative.

Supporting Characters

Mrs. Willis's potential threat is her power to stop the narrative by eliciting Sappho's secret past. Hopkins eventually diminishes this threat by relegating Willis to a minor role. Hopkins sustains the threat of exposure, however, through other female characters, most notably Mrs. Ophelia Davis and Mrs. Sarah Ann White. The narrative of these "two occupants of the basement rooms" (104) of the Smith boarding house almost literally inhabits the space below the main action of the novel. Hopkins tells the story of these "friends of long standing":

They were both born in far-away Louisiana, had been raised on neigh-
boring plantations, and together had sought the blessings of liberty in
the North at the close of the war. . . . As their ideas of life and living
enlarged, and they saw the possibilities of enjoying some comfort in a
home, they began to think of establishing themselves where they could
realize this blessing, and finally hit upon the idea of going into partnership in a laundry. (104)

Significantly, Davis and White do not engage in fantasies based on the romance conventions of finding a husband; they dream instead of "some comfort in a home" and employment in the North, a fantasy that involves a
"partnership" at once affectional and economic—not unlike heterosexual
marriage.

Despite their subordinate narrative and class positions, Davis and White
represent a risk similar to that posed by Mrs. Willis. When they first meet
Sappho, they immediately recognize something extraordinary and uncannily familiar about this beautiful young woman: "'Lord,' said Ophelia Davis
to her friend Sarah Ann, 'I haven't see enything look like thet chile since I
lef' home'" (107). Davis's partner confirms her recognition of the familiarity
of Sappho: "'That's the truth, 'Phelia,' replied Sarah Ann; 'that's somethin'
God made, honey; thar ain't nothin' like thet growed outside o' Loosy-
annie'" (107). This scene flirts with the special kind of paranoid knowledge
that Sedgwick, in her discussion of the mechanisms of the closet, associates
with the phrase, "It takes one to know one."[51] When Sappho confirms her
Louisiana upbringing, White exclaims, "I knowed it. . . . Ol' New Orleans
blood will tell on itself anywhere" (108). The belief that "blood will tell on
itself," which depends on the presumed physical legibility of race, provides
the suspense that structures novels of passing. In 1913, an anonymous writer
summed up the racial logic of "it takes one to know one" in "Adventures of
a Near-White": "I would take a chance with a white man where I would not
dare do so with a colored man. Inevitably a colored man knows but usually
keeps his mouth shut, aided by a generous tip."[52] Sappho attempts to insu-
late herself from recognition among northerners who have no access to her
past, but she risks exposure by those like Davis and White, who are similarly mobile and displaced. Although White's revelation about Sappho is
her Louisiana upbringing, the scene nevertheless raises the possibility that
Sappho's secret past may be revealed at any moment, to or by those who
can decode "a story written on her face" (89).

The significance of the characters Davis and White is that they are not only potentially intimate with Sappho's hidden past but also intimate with each other. Hopkins deftly uses class inflections to neutralize the potential threat of the laundresses' intimacy. Because they are clearly depicted as occupying a social position subordinate to that of the Smiths, they are allowed a wider range of affection (at least until the end of the novel) than Mrs. Willis, who, because of her higher social position, is somehow more threatening in her pursuit of intimacy with Sappho. Hopkins's narrative voice tends to point out and mock Davis's and White's physical and verbal excesses, which run counter to middle-class sensibilities of self-restraint and deference. For instance, Hopkins describes Davis's singing in the parlor in ostensibly comic terms: "With much wheezing and puffing—for the singer was neither slender nor young—and many would-be fascinating jumps and groans, presumed to be trills and runs, she finished, to the relief of the company" (109). Davis and White nevertheless operate as a team throughout the novel, boosting each other with encouragement and taking pride in each other's accomplishments. During Davis's singing in the parlor, "Her friend, Mrs. White, looked at her with great approval" (109). White gives Davis unconditional and enthusiastic praise ("That's out o' sight, 'Phelia!" [109]) and insists on Davis getting recognition *as a woman* for her public accomplishments. When Davis wins a competition at the church fair, Hopkins writes, "And after that the pastor could not forbear saying a few words about how good it was 'to dwell together in brotherly love.' Sister Sarah Ann White said 'the *brothers* had nuthin' to do with it, it was Ophelia Davis an' nobody else'" (218, emphasis in original). By using working-class codes to construct a comic role for Davis and White, Hopkins is also able to voice an ironic critique of the public erasure of women while containing it within an apparently humorous portrayal of minor characters.

Hopkins sustains the relationship between Davis and White almost to the end of the novel, when she quickly and mechanically introduces Davis's romance with a younger man. Richard Yarborough, in a discussion of problematic aspects of *Contending Forces,* writes that "the neat resolution of the intricate plot may not sit well with modern readers weaned on psychological realism."[53] I would argue further that Hopkins recognized that a resolution that left intact a female couple would be a potentially dangerous break in convention. She thus chose to end the novel by reinforcing the narrative limitations she delineated earlier: "A close intimacy between two of the same sex was more than likely to end disastrously for one or the other" (98).

Dismantling the relationship between White and Davis, however, takes substantial narrative energy, an effort that ironically makes salient the intensity of their attachment. When Davis tells Ma Smith about her plans to marry a younger man, she constructs her new fiancé as a rival to her female companion:

> "Sarah Ann an' me'll have to part after I'm married, she's that jealous." . . .
>
> "Now that would be a pity, after you've been together so long," remarked [Ma Smith].
>
> "She's got to drop sayin' ticklish things to me. A 'ooman's got a right to git married, ain't she? . . . Mr. Jeemes says he knows the Lord sent me fer to be a helpmeet to him, an' I dassay he's right. Sarah Ann says my money's the 'helpmeet' he's after, an' somebody to cook good vittals to suit his pellet. But I know better; he's a godly man ef he ain't much to look at." (365–66)

In this conversation, Hopkins uses the voice of the absent White to critique the subordinate role of women in marriage, implicitly contrasting it with the relatively equitable arrangement between the two women. The scene ends with Davis's passion focused on White: "Sarah Ann says I'm a mortalized ol' ijit, an' a insane mannyack, an' Jeemes knows what he's a-fishin' fer. She's insultin', mos' insultin'" (368–69). That Hopkins includes a split, however mechanical, between these two characters is evidence that she gave them an important place in the story. That their "breakup" involves jealousy and protectiveness is also evidence that she wanted in some way to express the passion existing between these women, contrasting it with Davis's feelings about her fiancé, who "ain't much to look at." Like Dora, Davis is compelled by cultural custom to agree to marriage, in spite of her indifference to her fiancé and her passionate attachment to her female companion.

Contending Closets

Despite Hopkins's use of the conventional marriage plot in the conclusion of *Contending Forces,* scenes of female homoeroticism structure the narrative in important ways. Hopkins portrays female couples as potential sites for the expression of desire and identification, at the same time that she contains their threat to the narrative's overall heterosexual trajectory. Hopkins contains these eruptions of homoeroticism within the literally subordinate spaces—the closets—of the novel: the locked room where Dora and Sappho have their tea party, the all-female "sewing-circle" where Mrs. Willis and Sappho negotiate "passion" and secrecy, and the basement apartment where Sarah Ann White and Ophelia Davis make their home and run their business. Although the sexual secret that threatens to destroy Sappho's claim to respectable womanhood is ostensibly her experience of being raped by a white man, it is possible to see anxieties about lesbian desire structuring the passing narrative of *Contending Forces*. In fact, if we understand the rape of Mabelle Beaubean as a symbol of the historical negation of African American women's sexual agency, it could be argued that the figure of Sappho, precisely because of her association with lesbian desire, mediates Hopkins's attempts to imagine a narrative of African American women's sexual agency.

The meaning of marriage, as duCille has shown, differed greatly for African American and white women at the turn of the century. Whereas white women might have begun to question their subordinate role within marriage, for African American women, marriage historically represented one of the civil rights associated with freedom from slavery;[54] it also offered African American women a culturally sanctioned space in which to claim social respectability. In *Contending Forces,* it is possible to see Hopkins negotiating these different meanings of marriage, along with a hesitant engagement with the potential for female homoeroticism and intimacy. For if, in duCille's words, freedom meant "entitlement to desire,"[55] Hopkins's *Contending Forces* suggests that lesbian desire, however frustrated or pathologized, had begun to trouble the relationship between heterosexual marriage and the construction of African American women's erotic entitlements.

Notes

1 Cornelia Condict, letter to the editor, *Colored American Magazine,* March 1903, 398–99.

2 Hopkins published her first short story at the age of forty and was most prolific between the years 1900 and 1904, when she wrote four novels and numerous short stories and biographical articles for the Boston-based *Colored American Magazine.* Between 1900 and 1904, Hopkins not only wrote regularly for the magazine, she also exerted considerable editorial influence. Eventually she was pressured to leave when the magazine was bought out by supporters of Booker T. Washington, who had little interest in furthering the literary efforts of the magazine. After

1904, Hopkins continued to publish her writing, but on a much smaller scale, and she eventually returned to her job as a stenographer at the Massachusetts Institute of Technology, where she worked until her death in 1930. For further discussion of the history of the *Colored American Magazine,* see Hazel Carby, *Reconstructing Womanhood: The Emergence of the Afro-American Woman Novelist* (New York: Oxford University Press, 1987), 121–27; and Ann Allen Shockley, "Pauline Elizabeth Hopkins: A Biographical Excursion into Obscurity," *Phylon* 33 (spring 1972): 22–26.

3 Condict, letter to the editor, 399.

4 Pauline Hopkins, reply to Condict, *Colored American Magazine,* March 1903, 399.

5 Ibid., 399, emphasis in original.

6 For a critique of Hopkins's internalization of racial hierarchies and of the broader imperialist assumptions of ideologies of "racial uplift," see Kevin Gaines, "Black Americans' Racial Uplift Ideology as 'Civilizing Mission': Pauline E. Hopkins on Race and Imperialism," in *Cultures of United States Imperialism,* ed. Amy Kaplan and Donald E. Pease (Durham, N.C.: Duke University Press, 1993), 433–55.

7 See, for instance, Houston A. Baker Jr., *Workings of the Spirit: The Poetics of Afro-American Women's Writing* (Chicago: University of Chicago Press, 1991), 24.

8 Carby, *Reconstructing Womanhood,* 89–90.

9 See, for instance, Michel Foucault, *The History of Sexuality,* vol. 1, trans. Robert Hurley (New York: Vintage, 1980); George Chauncey, "From Sexual Inversion to Homosexuality: Medicine and the Changing Conceptualization of Female Deviance," *Salmagundi* 58–59 (fall–winter 1982): 114–46; Jeffrey Weeks, *Sex, Politics, and Society: The Regulation of Sexuality since 1800* (London: Longman, 1981); and David Halperin, "Is There a History of Sexuality?" in *The Lesbian and Gay Studies Reader,* ed. Henry Abelove, Michèle Aina Barale, and David M. Halperin (New York: Routledge, 1993), 416–31. On the invention of the classification of heterosexuality, see Jonathan Katz, "The Invention of Heterosexuality," *Socialist Review* 20 (1990): 17–34. For a related and intriguing argument that locates the earlier emergence of hierarchies of reproductive over nonreproductive sexual activity, see Henry Abelove, "Some Speculations on the History of 'Sexual Intercourse' during the 'Long Eighteenth Century' in England," *Genders* 6 (1989): 125–30.

More recent work has begun to explore the emergence of gay consciousness, communities, and subcultures in specific historical, cultural, and geographical locations. See, for instance, George Chauncey, *Gay New York: Gender, Urban Culture, and the Making of the Gay Male World, 1890–1940* (New York: Basic Books, 1994).

10 Some scholarship has begun to question this periodization of the emergence of pathologizing models of same-sex desire, particularly as it pertains to lesbians. Rejecting the model of a "pre-sexological" era in which women's "romantic friendships" were seen as innocent, Marylynne Diggs has argued recently

that "the representation of same-sex relations between women as pathological occurred earlier in the nineteenth century than critics have believed and that some writers occasionally resisted them before the turn of the century" ("Romantic Friends or a 'Different Race of Creatures'?: The Representation of Lesbian Pathology in Nineteenth-Century America," *Feminist Studies* 21 [summer 1995]: 336). For a related argument, see Terry Castle, *The Apparitional Lesbian: Female Homosexuality and Modern Culture* (New York: Columbia University Press, 1993).

11 See, for instance, Eric Garber, "A Spectacle in Color: The Lesbian and Gay Subculture of Jazz Age Harlem," in *Hidden from History: Reclaiming the Gay and Lesbian Past,* ed. Martin Duberman, Martha Vicinus, and George Chauncey (New York: Meridian, 1990), 326–31; *Looking for Langston* [film], dir. Isaac Julien, 1989; Thadious Davis, *Nella Larsen, Novelist of the Harlem Renaissance: A Woman's Life Unveiled* (Baton Rouge: Louisiana State University Press, 1994), 325; and Alden Reimonenq, "Historicizing Countee Cullen's Gay Literary Imagination" (paper delivered at the Sixth North American Lesbian, Gay, and Bisexual Studies Conference, 18 November 1994).

I use the designation "Harlem Renaissance" loosely, because it tends to obscure important literary and artistic production during this period in many different geographical areas. Also, black feminist critics have offered important and enabling critiques of how the periodization typically attached to the "Harlem Renaissance" tends to erase women writers who made significant contributions to African American literary production during the first decades of the twentieth century. See, for example, Carby, *Reconstructing Womanhood,* 163–75; and Ann duCille, *The Coupling Convention: Sex, Text, and Tradition in Black Women's Fiction* (New York: Oxford University Press, 1993), 82–85.

12 Henry Louis Gates Jr., "The Black Man's Burden," in *Fear of a Queer Planet: Queer Politics and Social Theory,* ed. Michael Warner (Minneapolis: University of Minnesota Press, 1993), 233.

13 Deborah McDowell, introduction to Nella Larsen, *"Quicksand" and "Passing"* (New Brunswick, N.J.: Rutgers University Press, 1986), ix–xxxv.

14 Pauline E. Hopkins, *Contending Forces: A Romance Illustrative of Negro Life North and South* ([1900] New York: Oxford University Press, 1988). Subsequent references to this edition will be cited parenthetically within the text.

15 Both African American and Euro-American authors wrote novels about passing during the nineteenth century, but they usually had different reasons for exploring this theme. See, for example, Frank Webb, *The Garies and Their Friends* (1857); William Wells Brown, *Clotel* (1853); William Dean Howells, *An Imperative Duty* (1892); Mark Twain, *Pudd'nhead Wilson* (1894); Charles Chesnutt, *The House Behind the Cedars* (1900); and Gertrude Atherton, *Senator North* (1900).

16 Judith Berzon, *Neither White nor Black: The Mulatto Character in American Fiction* (New York: New York University Press, 1978), 74. Berzon also makes a dis-

tinction between white and African American writers' portrayals of mulatta characters; in particular, she notes that in fiction by black novelists written between 1908 and 1920, black women are portrayed as "beautiful (in Caucasian terms), morally upstanding, prim, and wealthy (or at least comfortable)" (62).

17 Mary Dearborn, *Pocahontas's Daughters: Gender and Ethnicity in American Culture* (New York: Oxford University Press, 1986), 139–40, emphasis added. In a recent discussion of the mulatto figure in American race melodrama, Susan Gillman concurs that in the conventions of the tragic mulatto tale, the protagonist is most often a woman. See her "The Mulatto, Tragic or Triumphant? The Nineteenth-Century American Race Melodrama," in *The Culture of Sentiment: Race, Gender, and Sentimentality in Nineteenth-Century America,* ed. Shirley Samuels (New York: Oxford University Press, 1992), 221–43.

18 Werner Sollors, "'Never Was Born': The Mulatto, An American Tragedy?" *Massachusetts Review* 27 (summer 1986): 302.

19 See, for instance, Elizabeth Ammons, *Conflicting Stories: American Women Writers at the Turn into the Twentieth Century* (New York: Oxford University Press, 1991), 80; and Claudia Tate, *Domestic Allegories of Political Desire: The Black Heroine's Text at the Turn of the Century* (New York: Oxford University Press, 1992), 148–49.

20 Baker, *Workings of the Spirit,* 24.

21 Elaine Marks writes that "Sappho and her island Lesbos are omnipresent in literature about women loving women, whatever the gender or sexual preference of the writer and whether or not Sappho and her island are explicitly named" ("Lesbian Intertextuality," in *Homosexualities and French Literature,* ed. George Stambolian and Elaine Marks [Ithaca, N.Y.: Cornell University Press, 1978], 356).

22 Joan DeJean, *Fictions of Sappho, 1546–1937* (Chicago: University of Chicago Press, 1989), 202.

23 Thomas Wentworth Higginson, "Sappho," *Atlantic Monthly,* July 1871, 83. While there is no proof that Hopkins ever saw this article on Sappho, she did draw explicitly on Higginson as a literary influence: The subtitle of her short story "A Dash for Liberty" states that it was "Founded on an article written by Col. T. W. Higginson for the *Atlantic Monthly* June 1861" (*Colored American Magazine,* August 1901, 243).

24 Higginson, "Sappho," 88.

25 According to the *Oxford English Dictionary,* the first English reference to *sapphism* in print occurs in 1890 in the *National Medical Dictionary.* It dates the first appearance of *lesbianism* (as the female equivalent to *sodomy*) to 1870. Nonprint usage probably antedated these instances. DeJean writes that "French usage of 'sapphisme' and 'lesbienne' preceded and probably inspired English terminology, whereas the reverse implantation occurred with the vocabulary of 'homosexual.' . . . Prior to the complex nineteenth-century situation, the dominant French terms were 'tribade,' 'tribadisme'" (*Fictions of Sappho,* 350n.51).

26 Havelock Ellis, *Studies in the Psychology of Sex,* vol. 2, *Sexual Inversion,* 3d ed. (Philadelphia: F. A. Davis, 1915), 197.

27 DeJean, *Fictions of Sappho,* xiv–xv, 200, 280.

28 Susan Gubar, "Sapphistries," *Signs* 10 (autumn 1984): 55. See also Willis Barnstone, *Sappho: Lyrics in the Original Greek* (New York: New York University Press, 1965), xxii–xxiii.

29 John Addington Symonds, quoted in Henry Thornton Wharton, *Sappho: Memoir, Text, Selected Renderings, and a Literal Translation* ([1885] Chicago: A. C. McClurg, 1895), 13. The comment originally appeared in Symonds, *Studies of Greek Poets,* first series (New York: Harper and Brothers, 1880), 127. Symonds played a significant role in articulating emergent models of homosexuality. With Havelock Ellis, he co-wrote *Sexual Inversion,* originally published as the first volume of Ellis's *Studies in the Psychology of Sex.* For a discussion of their collaboration and the eventual erasure of Symonds from the text, see Wayne Koestenbaum, *Double Talk: The Erotics of Male Literary Collaboration* (New York: Routledge, 1989), 43–67.

30 Quoted in Wharton, *Sappho,* 13.

31 That Sappho's poetry fragments were preserved through Egyptian remains could have provided Hopkins with a link to Egypt, an important symbol of ancient African civilization for Hopkins.

Hopkins claimed ancient figures as models for her characters in other works. Her first serialized novel, *Hagar's Daughter, A Story of Southern Caste Prejudice,* took its heroine's name from the Bible. An article on "Hagar and Ishmael," part of a series entitled "Fascinating Bible Stories," appeared in the *Colored American Magazine* one month before the first installment of *Hagar's Daughter;* see Charles Winslow Hall, "Fascinating Bible Stories: IV. Hagar and Ishmael," *Colored American Magazine,* Feb. 1901, 302–6. In this retelling of the story, Hall relates how Hagar, "the stately and passionate Egyptian" and the female slave of Sarah, was chosen to bear a child for Sarah's husband, Abraham (306). Hagar's son, Ishmael, was described as "the son of a Caucasian father and African mother," just as Jewel, the daughter of Hopkins's Hagar, was the daughter of an African American woman and a white man (304). The article presented Ishmael, disowned by Abraham and Sarah, as a hero and forefather who built "a race unconquerable" (306).

Of One Blood; or, The Hidden Self (1902–1903) is Hopkins's most explicit exploration of Ethiopianism; the novel travels back in time to the city of Meroe, the ancient capital of Ethiopia.

32 J[ohn] E. Bruce, "Some Famous Negroes," *Voice of the Negro,* Dec. 1905, 876.

33 Bruce quotes from Alexander Pope's 1712 translation of Ovid's "Sappho to Phaon" in *Ovid's Epistles:* "To me what nature has in charms denied / Is well by wit's more lasting flames supplied, / Though short my stature, yet my name extends / To heaven itself and earth's remotest ends. / Brown as I am an Ethiopian

dame / Inspired young Perseus with a generous flame. / Turtles and doves of different hues unite, / And glossy jet is paired with shining white" (876). According to John Butt in *The Poems of Alexander Pope* (London: Methuen, 1963), the "Ethiopian dame" refers to Andromeda, daughter of Cepheus and Cassiopeia, king and queen of Egypt (30n.41).

I have not found other references to Sappho's African origins, although, as Higginson noted, "Tradition represents her as having been 'little and dark'" ("Sappho," 84).

34 See Carroll Smith-Rosenberg, "The Female World of Love and Ritual: Relations between Women in Nineteenth-Century America," *Signs* 1 (autumn 1975): 1–29.

35 Lillian Faderman, "Lesbian Magazine Fiction in the Early Twentieth Century," *Journal of Popular Culture* 11 (1978): 802.

36 Diggs, "Romantic Friends or a 'Different Race of Creatures'?" 321.

37 For discussions of how Hopkins employs the marriage plot, see duCille, *The Coupling Convention*, 36–43; and Tate, *Domestic Allegories*, 124–25.

38 The *Oxford English Dictionary* defines *unsex* as "to deprive or divest of sex, or of the typical qualities of one or other (esp. the female) sex."

39 James G. Kiernan, "Inversion and Dreams," *Urologic and Cutaneous Review* 19 (June 1915): 352.

40 It also suggests a link to Sappho, who is described elsewhere in identical language. When Sappho sneaks out of the Smith boarding house after she has been blackmailed by John Langley, Hopkins writes, "A form attired in black, closely veiled, . . . was *swallowed up* in the heart of the metropolis" (321–22, emphasis added).

41 Eve Kosofsky Sedgwick, *Epistemology of the Closet* (Berkeley and Los Angeles: University of California Press, 1990), 71.

42 *Oxford English Dictionary*, 2d ed., s.v. "Skeleton in the closet."

43 W. E. B. Du Bois, *The Souls of Black Folk* ([1903] New York: Penguin, 1989), 1.

44 Charles Chesnutt, *The House Behind the Cedars* (Boston: Houghton Mifflin, 1900; Athens: University of Georgia Press, 1988), 192, 75. See, for instance, James Weldon Johnson's *The Autobiography of an Ex-Coloured Man*, one of the best-known novels of racial passing from the early twentieth century. Significantly, a literal closet is the site for the beginning of the narrator's transformation from "black" to "white." At a key point in the novel, the narrator is left penniless and travels to Jacksonville, Florida, in search of employment. He makes this journey as a stowaway, traveling overnight by train in a Pullman porter's closet, the description of which suggests that sexual anxieties are inextricable from his racial transformation.

45 For brief discussions of this scene, see Claudia Tate, "Allegories of Black Female Desire: Or, Rereading Nineteenth-Century Sentimental Narratives of Black Female Authority," in *Changing Our Own Words: Essays on Criticism, Theory, and Writing by Black Women*, ed. Cheryl Wall (New Brunswick, N.J.: Rutgers Univer-

sity Press, 1989), 122–23; and Mary Helen Washington, "Uplifting the Women and the Race," in her *Invented Lives: Narratives of Black Women, 1860–1960* (Garden City, N.Y.: Anchor Press, 1987), 81.

46 See Carby, *Reconstructing Womanhood*, 23–34; duCille, *The Coupling Convention*, 30–47; and Tate, *Domestic Allegories*, 97–98, 152–53.

47 Nancy F. Cott, "Passionlessness: An Interpretation of Victorian Sexual Ideology, 1790–1850," in Nancy F. Cott and Elizabeth H. Pleck, *A Heritage of Her Own: Toward a New Social History of American Women* (New York: Simon and Schuster, 1979), 168–69.

48 Ibid., 173.

49 Richard Yarborough, introduction to Pauline E. Hopkins, *Contending Forces: A Romance Illustrative of Negro Life North and South* ([1900] New York: Oxford University Press, 1988), xl. Yarborough suggests that Willis may have been modeled after Josephine St. Pierre Ruffin, president of the Women's Era Club in Boston during the late nineteenth century.

50 Tate, *Domestic Allegories*, 164.

51 Sedgwick, *Epistemology of the Closet*, 100, 222.

52 "The Adventures of a Near-White," *Independent*, 14 August 1913, 375.

53 Yarborough, introduction to *Contending Forces*, xli.

54 See duCille, *The Coupling Convention*, for a full discussion of the meanings of the marriage plot for African American women writers of this period.

55 duCille, *The Coupling Convention*, 5.

Constructing the Black Masculine:

Frederick Douglass, Booker T. Washington,

and the Sublimits of African American

Autobiography

MAURICE WALLACE

I suspect I must have been born somewhere and at some time.
—Booker T. Washington, *Up from Slavery*

Although Hortense Spillers's seminal essay "Mama's Baby, Papa's Maybe:
An American Grammar Book" aims most directly at advancing an epistemology of black feminism, this particular project of hers would seem to be
useful for, if not essential to, the development of a black masculinist critical theory. "The African-American male," she remarks, "has been touched
by the mother, handled by her in ways that he cannot escape—and in ways
that the white American male is allowed to temporize by a fatherly reprieve.
. . . Legal enslavement removed the African-American male not so much
from sight as from *mimetic* view as a partner in the prevailing social fiction
of the Father's name, the Father's law."[1] Implicitly, Spillers's discourse deconstructs the univocality of black phallocentric literary production to the
same degree that it explicitly pursues a unique line of black feminist inquiry.
Undoubtedly, if there is to be an enduring theory of black male identity
construction in the West, it will be significantly indebted to a careful synthesis of post-Freudian psychoanalysis and the epistemological work of black
feminism, as Spillers's language clearly suggests.[2]

Even if black feminist discourse like that of Spillers proves perfectly
congenial to black masculine identity ("Tell us what it is to be a woman
so we may know what it is to be a man," Toni Morrison recently said),
there are distinct risks one runs by adding psychoanalytic theory to the
project. Some African Americanist scholars hold the systematic application

of Freudian psychoanalysis to African American cultural production in low esteem, dismissing the field of psychoanalysis as "bourgeois and conservative."[3] To impose Freud on the "sable mind," some argue, is to extend European hegemony grievously far. This resistance to the psychoanalytic critique is the inevitable consequence of American conservatism's scandalous (mis)appropriations of psychoanalysis to construct a demeaning narrative of African American historiography.

Like psychocriticism's detractors, I too am cautious about bringing psychoanalysis to bear on black subjectivity.[4] Clinical terms such as *disorder, neurosis,* and *complex* might well represent cultural "contingencies," to use Barbara Herrnstein Smith's apt lexeme, rather than transcendent or universal pathologies that, "warding off [hegemonic notions of] barbarism and the constant apparition of an imminent collapse of standards," the Freudians have used at odd moments to serve their own egoistic fantasies and to "justify the exercise of their own normative authority."[5] Such terms as these, therefore, can be dangerously marginalizing, effecting in their worst ethnocentric formulations cultural xenophobia whenever they are assigned outside the context of contingencies that established them. They ought always to be regarded with healthy suspicion. But to abandon the principles of psychoanalysis categorically is to throw the baby out with the bathwater. Post-Freudian psychoanalysis, eclectically and responsibly deployed, affords black literary criticism a usable polygraph for discerning those persistent, visceral impulses lurking beneath the black subject's ego. In other words, Frantz Fanon's psychoanalytic diagnosis of "the unbearable insularity" of black identity can only be confirmed or rejected in African American letters according to the principles of psychoanalysis that generated it.[6] Moreover, critics and theorists of African American literary production do well to recall, as Arnold Rampersad reminds us,[7] that not a few of the major figures in twentieth-century African American cultural studies—including W. E. B. Du Bois, Richard Wright, and Ralph Ellison—were influenced by the ubiquity of Freudian thought early in the century.[8] It would seem worthwhile, therefore, to begin with the psychoanalytic imperative of black literary theory and criticism by bringing it into dialogic relation with that "literary genre which presumably offers one of the most revealing and 'real' portraits of the self: autobiography."[9]

Despite the repeated claim that autobiography is an inherently dishonest literary genre because of the autobiographer's intense efforts to present for public view a polished portrait of him- or herself, this is precisely the reason black male autobiography, and autobiography generally, lends itself so generously to psychocriticism. Since, as Michael Cooke argues, black autobiography "is the *coordination* of the self as content and the self as *shaped*,"[10] the authorial construction of the autobiographical subject, fully formed and self-conscious, is achieved only at the expense of the exhausting effort required by the author to repress the fragmentary, dueling impulses of a divided consciousness normally kept in the reserve of the unconscious. Psychoanalytically considered, autobiography depends on more than "everything available in memory, perception, understanding, imagination, [and] desire"[11] suitable for public discourse. It rests also on the autobiographer's success in repressing "everything that . . . in some way or other [is] painful . . . alarming or disagreeable or shameful by the standards of the subject's personality."[12] These splits of consciousness unearthed by the psychoanalytic critique of black male autobiography invest the subject with a representational complexity—in this essay, an essential polymorphous libidinality—which makes him marvelously human. To put it another way, from this theoretical vantage point, the black self becomes supremely *text-ured*.

My efforts in this essay are guided by a desire to explore in Frederick Douglass's *Narrative of the Life of Frederick Douglass, an American Slave* and Booker T. Washington's *Up from Slavery* that vast area of repression which the self-conscious autobiographical subject is always skirting, to trespass into "those serpentine caves," as Virginia Woolf said, "where one goes with a candle peering up and down, not knowing where one is stepping."[13] More to the point, this essay is concerned with the early, developmental stage of African American male identity formation characterized in black male autobiography by *preliminal* racial and sexual ambivalence, which I see as corresponding biologically to the pre- and postpubescent stage of boyhood. This developmental stage distinguishes itself from the subsequent stage of *liminal* or self-conscious racial and sexual identification by a nervous panic, a pediatric "neurosis" (Fanon's word) that propels the black manchild headlong into a crucible of identity negotiations.[14]

The line of black masculinist autobiography in which the panic I am describing can be detected begins most notably with Douglass's 1845 *Narrative* and its literary offspring in the tradition, Washington's 1901 *Up from Slavery.* Though both begin with formulaic birth narratives, ironically, neither autobiographer can state precisely the date or the circumstances of his birth.

The problem of racial being and nothingness is perhaps nowhere more poignantly expressed than by Washington in the epigraph to this essay: "I suspect I must have been born somewhere and at some time" (9). Bastard sons of enslaved black mothers and obscure white fathers/masters, Douglass and Washington fashion *non*-Oedipal dramas of slavery in which nuclear relations matter less in the slavocracy than the bourgeois imperatives of ownership, dominance, commodity, and (re)production. Over and above the problems posed by the strained primal configurations immanent in these autobiographical accounts, the bastard/mulatto status of Douglass and Washington figures as a trope of the national illegitimacy felt by both nineteenth- and twentieth-century African American authors.[15] It is a trope that for the black writer, I suspect, has its origins in the biblical themes of bondage, lineage, and inheritance.[16] Metaphorically, the enslaved mulatto is the illegitimate, banished son of the American Abraham and the patriarch's black handmaiden, the American Hagar, casting about for existential determinacy from within the elemental indeterminacy ("born somewhere and at some time") of the slave condition.

Henry Louis Gates's chapter, "Binary Oppositions in Chapter One of *Narrative of the Life of Frederick Douglass, An American Slave Written by Himself*" in his *Figures in Black: Words, Signs, and the "Racial" Self,* proposes a veritable catalog of bipolar identities (nature/culture, beast/human, barbaric/civilized) between which the autobiographical African American manchild is freely and aimlessly conveyed, as through a sublime "oceanic" middle passage of identity formation.[17] Eventually, however, the gentle tide of psychological passage becomes a furious surge and the helpless manchild, surprised by the storm, is tossed ashore onto the strange banks of racial and sexual consciousness. This sudden and violent landing, I affirm, is the moment of identity panic when the distressed pubescent discovers his polymorphism as destitute of cultural relevance or social legitimacy.[18] In short, Gates's catalog of binaries suggests that the most immediate inheritance of the enslaved manchild is a fragile universe of confounded indeterminable identities which recognizes neither temporal nor geographical specificity; neither racial singularity nor familial cohesion; nor, as I hope to prove forthwith, gender differentiation, which, in the interest of culture, was among the first endowments of white children in the antebellum era.

In a stringently Freudian analysis of Douglass's autobiography entitled "'Called into Existence': Gender, Desire and Voice in Douglass's *Narrative* of 1845," George Cunningham argues from this remarkable premise:

"Within the domain of slavery, gender or culturally derived notions of man-and womanhood do not exist [for the enslaved]."[19] Cunningham's hypothesis points plainly to what Eugene Genovese calls "the annihilating implications of chattel slavery."[20] Because the historical American slave belongs primarily to the commercial order of livestock, his or her sex is not the same cultural determinant of power or protection that it is in the society of slaveholders. It is, rather, merely a commercial feature of the slave's being, a convenient accessory for the master. Wholly devoid of cultural import, the slave's gender, insofar as the slaveholder cares, matters only to the extent that it brings value to plantation (re)production. It follows, dialectically, that the slave's struggle for political freedom is also an effort to be freed from the condition of social and cultural nothingness. This struggle is, finally, the crisis of the autobiographical black man-child on *liminality*—that is, on his awakening to sexual consciousness. Symptoms of the impending crisis tend to surface early in the naive impulses of pubescent sexuality that occasionally leap forward indiscriminately in *Narrative* and *Up from Slavery* where neither autobiographer seems to have intended.

In recounting the "most terrible spectacle" of Aunt Hester's rape by Captain Anthony, Douglass seizes, apparently unaware, on his own undifferentiated sexual subjectivity at the time of the incident. He describes Captain Anthony's brutalization of Aunt Hester as Anthony pornographically strips his victim "from neck to waist, leaving her neck, shoulders, and back entirely naked. [Captain Anthony] then told her to cross her hands, calling her at the same time a d——d b——h. After crossing her hands, he tied them with a strong rope, and led her to a stool under a large hook in the joist, put in for the purpose. He made her get upon the stool and tied her hands to the hook. *She now stood fair for his infernal purpose*" (52, emphasis added). With this, and sparing any more horrible details, Douglass turns away from the self-implicating triangularity of the scene, wanting to escape this shameful and painful reality. "Heart rending shrieks from [Hester] and horrid oaths from [Anthony]" serve, by their contrast, to make pronounced the quiet of Douglass's flight from language. That is to say, it is precisely Douglass's silent terror, his inability to "commit to paper," as he says not much later, a fuller disclosure of his feelings while witnessing the "exhibition" that signals an early instance of the kind of repression described above. That Douglass is withholding a more private, unrepresentable reaction to this scene, one that diverges substantially from the decidedly masculine self-portrait sustained throughout the text, is incontrovertible: "I was so terrified and horror-stricken at the sight, that I *hid myself in a closet,* and dared not venture out. . . . *I expected it would be my turn next*" (52, emphasis added).[21] Certainly gay and lesbian studies has made the closet a classic symbol of sexual coverture in a way that is harmonious with the suggestion in the preceding passage of an erotics of slavery which, forsaking gender difference, puts the enslaved biological male and the enslaved biological female equally within reach of the master's wanton hand. In this context, the potential is great for a suppressed/repressed psychosexual voice belying Douglass's fear that he might suffer the same sexualized violence inflicted on Hester. Douglass's introduction in this scene to the barbarous "hell of slavery" (51) is simultaneously his introduction to human sexuality ("I expected it would be my turn next").

I wish to resist the argument advanced by David Van Leer that the youthful Douglass did not understand "the gender specificity of [Aunt Hester's] beating." Van Leer wrongly denies that there are grounds for Douglass's sexual panic:

> [Douglass] rightly labels the scene as one of the horrors of slavery. What he does not understand is that this particular horror is not and never will be his. Not only does the boy's "turn" never come—at least not quite in this way—but the sexual undercurrents in the [Aunt Hester–Captain Anthony] passage clearly indicate the narrator's implicit understanding of the different power dynamics in male and female beatings. His failure to comment more directly on the difference marks his tacit admission that as a male he is shut out from a knowledge of this uniquely female experience.[22]

Van Leer, I contend, gives the slavocracy too much credit. While it is almost certain that homosexual assault was never as prevalent as the heterosexual abuses perpetrated by white male slaveholders, incidents of homoerotic assaults in out-of-the-way places along coffle routes going south and on some plantations are not entirely unheard of.

The problem with Van Leer's conclusion about the gender specificity of plantation rape is twofold. First, it depends on an uncritical, modern conception of rape as a heterosexual violation of women's bodies and fails to comprehend that the slave's rape was motivated not simply by the economic advantage whereby property under force reproduced itself without costs but just as often by antebellum white racialist fantasies about black eros. It is not at all unlikely, therefore, and rather to be expected, that, in light of popular myths about the extraordinary size and potency of the black phallus and slaveholders' absolute control over black bodies, the sexual urges of male slaveholders would seek out now and then black male slaves for their gratification. There is little doubt that same-sex desire was as real in the nineteenth century as the heterosexual impulse.[23]

The second failing of Van Leer's argument is its tacit assumption that the dearth of evidence on this count demonstrates the nonoccurrence of violent homoerotic behavior by white men visited on the bodies of their powerless black male slaves. Admittedly, precious little of the literature of the slave era confesses to homosexuality in general, much less homosexual abuse across the color line. That homoerotic violence could have indeed posed a genuine threat to young Douglass, however, and did in fact occur is corroborated in at least one female-authored slave narrative.

In an obscure and often overlooked passage from Harriet Jacobs's *Incidents in the Life of a Slave Girl* (1861), Jacobs recalls a fugitive friend named Luke whom she meets by chance along the streets of free New York shortly after her own escape. Before his successful flight to freedom, Luke belonged to a young man Jacobs describes as having become "a prey to the vices growing out of the 'patriarchal institution'" (504). The unnamed slaveholder, having been "deprived of the use of his limbs by excess dissipation," shows all of the worst symptoms of sexual deviance according to certain pre-Freudian medical theories current in America from the 1830s until Freud. Dissipation and palsy occurring in otherwise healthy young men were considered by nineteenth-century medical experts to be the consequences of such sexual excesses as onanism and homosexuality, the usual prognosis for which was progressive dementia. Accordingly, Luke's young master, Jacobs says, "took into his head the strangest freaks of despotism" (504). Her indictment of the maniacal slaveholder reflects the popular medical opinion of her day that homoerotic desire was produced by a "strange order of ideas" in the mind.[24] And euphemisms like "vice," "excess," and "dissipation" all signify in nineteenth-century sexual discourse a pathological deviation from the cultural norms of the human sexual economy.[25] In the end, Luke's master takes to bed, "a mere degraded wreck of manhood," brought down in mind and body by sexual excess.

Neither decorum nor literary convention would have permitted Jacobs (or Douglass) to depict blatant homoeroticism. But the image of poor Luke having to "kneel beside the couch . . . [and] *not allowed to wear anything but his shirt*" (504, emphasis added) is amply suggestive. Nevertheless, Jacobs leaves only the simplest conclusions for the prurient reader to draw: "Some of these freaks were of a nature too filthy to be repeated. When I fled from the house of bondage, I left poor Luke *chained to the bedside of this cruel and disgusting wretch*" (505, emphasis added). It is evident that Jacobs's reticence ("too filthy to be repeated") intentionally suppresses details too impolite to name publicly. Her evasion recalls Douglass's vituperation of Captain Anthony in *My Bondage and My Freedom* (1855). In this, Douglass's second autobiography, he denounces Captain Anthony for committing "outrages, deep, dark and nameless."[26] For both Jacobs and Douglass, neither of whom had great difficulty representing miscegenation in their texts, few "perversions" other than onanism and homosexuality remained unrepresentable.

Reflecting on Luke's sexual degradation, Jacobs says somewhat more plainly what Douglass approximates by close association and identification with Aunt Hester: Both male and female enslaved black bodies are vulnerable to the sexual impositions of the master who intends to fulfill his "infernal purpose." One need no longer question *if* sexual subjectivity exists in *Narrative;* one only wonders *how much* primal sexuality is buried in Douglass's rememory of the Aunt Hester–Captain Anthony drama: "It was the first of a long series of such outrages, of which I was doomed to be a witness and a *participant*" (51, emphasis added), Douglass confesses.

Watching the rape from a distance and yet equally vulnerable, the young Douglass turns Freud's Oedipal model on its head by rejecting the role of the entranced child taken in by the coital activity of his oblivious parents. Instead the panic-stricken slaveboy retreats, impotent to injure the primal father as the Oedipal script directs. Identifying with the ravished body of a female, Douglass's fear of also being raped by Captain Anthony instantiates a fluid pubescent libidinality located intermediately between the libidinal masculine and the libidinal feminine.[27] It is within that abstract zone where the space surrounding the one libidinal pole intersects the space of the other in which all boys eventually live. His is a field of both struggle and play, the self-satisfied intersection of dual instincts, a "location in self (*reparge en soi*)," following Cixous, "which doesn't annul [sexual] differences but stirs them up, pursues them, increases their number."[28] But because he has learned from Aunt Hester's beating the primacy of the phallus ("I shall never forget it whilst I remember any thing" [51]), Douglass must hasten, in spite of himself, to extinguish his polymorphic nature, finally and completely, for the sake of gaining "phallic monosexuality"[29] if bodily freedom, political or sexual, is to be his. The psychosocial exigency of the subject's having been prematurely thrust into sexual consciousness is to follow the way of culture by differentiation.

The mature Douglass's preoccupation with the masculine ideal in *Narrative* is coterminous with his fear of the feminine, of being regarded, in other words, as also woman. Perhaps he knows the risk of being classed with the sentimental subject of nineteenth-century white women's writing by virtue of his powerlessness to resist sexual assault. To concede a feminine division of consciousness in the public medium of literature is for Douglass to jeopardize his claim in *Narrative* to the virile perfectibility of black men. It is this phobic posture toward a dynamic sexual identity which, I argue, ultimately provokes Douglass's sudden retaliation against Covey later on, an act punishable by death.

In accord with Fanon's axiomatic faith that "[we] know how much sexuality there is in all cruelties, torture, [and] beatings,"[30] I maintain that Douglass's violent retaliation against Mr. Covey is fundamentally a psychosexual response to the whipping/rape of Hester indelibly inscribed in Douglass's memory as well as to the immediate danger in Mr. Covey's whip.[31] I mean to say that the threat to young Douglass posed by Mr. Covey is the same threat realized by Captain Anthony on Aunt Hester. Viewed this way, the climactic standoff between overseer and slave that transformed Douglass into a man shows that Douglass's achievement of manhood represents much more than a mere physical triumph for the slave. It represents just as profoundly a counterattack of psychosexual virility signifying physiological phallic consciousness. Douglass's age at the moment of his conversion from slave to self-made man—sixteen—places him at the threshold of full biological maturity and marks a critical stage of human sexual development. Douglass's transformation is also, then, his psychic passage from boyhood (and sexual impotency) into phallic manhood (and sexual virility). Thus, what slavery is to freedom, boyhood is to manhood.[32]

Although many critics have paid special attention to Douglass's heroic efforts to achieve mastery and power over Covey in this episode (arguably the narrative's most important), few, if any, seem to have recognized the "interchangeability between power [or force] and sexuality"[33] in the nineteenth century: "The *gratification* afforded by the triumph was full compensation for whatever else might follow, even death itself" (113, emphasis added). Douglass's violent reaction to the threatened beating checks the otherwise unrestrained power of master over slave, including the "deepest, most mysterious, most fearful [power] of all: sexuality."[34]

In a curious footnote, Van Leer remarks: "During the beating that opens the tenth chapter [of *Narrative*] there is some indication of a submerged homosexual threat . . . in Covey's repeated orders—and Douglass's repeated refusals—to strip."[35] Unmistakably, the narrative picture of Covey, enraged by the slave's recalcitrance, ripping the clothes from the slaveboy's body "with the fierceness of a tiger" (102), serves as a graphic reminder of Captain Anthony's brutalization of Aunt Hester. If, as feminist critic Jenny Franchot has argued, "Douglass's narrative construction of [Hester's punishment] privileges it as its originating moment, and thus lodges a memorial urge inside his rhetoric of indictment aimed at exposing slavery's 'foul embrace,'"[36] then the eroticized version of Douglass's punishment that I am positing may be a more tactical maneuver on Douglass's part than a repressed one.

I wish to pursue this line of interpretation in further considering the contest between Douglass and Covey. To do so, it is necessary to cite a substantial portion of the episode.

> As soon as I found what he was up to, I gave a sudden spring, and as I did so, he holding to my legs, I was brought sprawling to the stable floor. Mr. Covey seemed to think he had me, and could do what he pleased; but at this moment—from whence came the spirit I don't know—I resolved to fight; and, suiting my action to the resolution, I seized Covey hard by the throat; and as I did so, I rose. He held on to me and I to him. . . . He trembled like a leaf. This gave me assurance, and I held him uneasy, causing the blood to run where I touched him with the ends of my fingers. Mr. Covey soon called out for help. Hughes came, and while Covey held me, attempted to tie my right hand. (112)

The narrative rehearsal of Covey thinking to "do what he pleased" and Hughes helping to "tie [Douglass's] right hand" recalls and recasts Captain Anthony's binding of Aunt Hester strong and fast to execute his lascivious deeds. Thus framed, Douglass's previous references to Covey as "the snake," simultaneously evoking sex and Satan, seems scarcely coincidental. Undaunted by Covey's determined struggle for corporal dominance, the adolescent strikes back with a virile exhibition of his own, cowing Covey into a physical, even "female," submission reminiscent of the romance. In the second autobiography, Douglass kicks hard at Hughes's groin when Hughes tries to help Covey. The avenging blow to Hughes's groin underscores the sexual threat a whipping (re)presents in Douglass's psychic universe. The rhetorical turn signalled by "I rose" in the passage above, marks, too, a reversal of dialectical positionality for Douglass from defensive sexual object to virile phallic agent. It is by physical confrontation that Douglass is "made a man." Violence is matched with violence and one phallus, as it were, *over-comes* another. The normal plantation relationship of black to white, master to slave, is, in this special moment, inverted. If Douglass, in this scene, is a slave made a man, then Covey is a man made a slave.

The Narrative of the Life of Frederick Douglass is not merely the record of "how a slave was made a man" in the universal sense of "human being"; it also documents how a male slave is *not* made a woman. Douglass's private, preliminary reaction to the violence of the American slave experience subverts the black masculinist pretense of public self-representation. For Covey's insistence in chapter 10 that the slaveboy "strip" off his clothes also signifies the threat to the ex-slave of having his hard-fought identity as an actor in "the prevailing social fiction"—if only marginally—stripped away. Even if Douglass's self-identity is, in the last analysis, not much more than an imitation of the fiction of white masculinity, the broken promise of gaining cultural capital by way of gender leaves the denied victim dispossessed, just as if he were sexually violated, of the privileges of his own body, his own sex. We must believe, therefore, that Douglass's success at resisting Covey was no small victory. By bodily dominating Covey, escaping the tempestuous libidinality engendered by bodily subjugation in a sexually repressed society, Douglass squashes his polymorphism and, desiring to move past the stage of the vulnerable, self-conflicted pubescent, wrests his manhood from Covey as if for his life.

Frederick Douglass's vivid, sometimes painfully enduring anamnesis of the power of slavery in *Narrative* and *My Bondage and My Freedom* differs widely in spirit from the "dim recollections of childhood," as Du Bois once described them, in Booker T. Washington's *Up from Slavery*. Washington's happy version of his passage into liminal adulthood lacks the sense of bitterness evident in Douglass's reflections. This stance on the part of Washington seems to me a function of his social and economic philosophy of accommodationism rather than a manifestation of his anxiety about Douglass's aesthetic influence (as we in literary studies might desire).[37] Not until his third autobiographical effort, *My Larger Education,* does Washington acknowledge the impact of Douglass's life and career on his early development:

> Even before I had learned to read books or newspapers, I remember hearing my mother and other colored people in our part of the country speak about Frederick Douglass' wonderful life. I heard so much about Douglass when I was a boy that one of the reasons I wanted to go to school and learn to read was that I might read for myself what he had written and said. In fact, one of the first books that I remember reading was his own story of his life, which Mr. Douglass published under the title of "My Life and Times." This book made a deep impression upon me and I read it many times. (103)

If David Dudley is right that intergenerational conflict is the key problem in the black male autobiographical tradition, the success of this curiously Oedipal thesis, mapping out as it does hard and fast genealogical lines within the broad tradition of African American literature, depends on our being able to name the Father, intertextually. It is virtually inconsequential that Douglass's and Washington's texts show plainly that "geneological trees do not flourish among slaves . . . [and the role of] father is literally abolished in slave law and practice."[38] In his own oblique manner, Washington, who like Douglass could not name his biological sire with surety, *names* Douglass his literary Father. Just as Douglass "heard whispers" that his father was a white man, Washington remembers "*hearing* [his] mother and other colored people . . . speak about Frederick Douglass' wonderful life," much as most any slaveboy could only *hear* about his paternal lineage.

That Washington, then, removed from Douglass by one generation, misnames the book (the Father's master narrative) he claims to have read and reread lends Dudley support on psychoanalytic grounds. Along these lines, Washington's error bespeaks a breach in the seams of consciousness bursting with the fullness of unconscious repression. Put differently, Washington's confusion about what he claims to remember clearly and what he has mistakenly remembered implies a collision between the conscious and the unconscious in the autobiographical subject. Dudley explains that *My Life and Times* is actually a conflation of the titles of Douglass's second and third autobiographies, *My Bondage and My Freedom* and *Life and Times of Fred-*

erick Douglass. This conflation, however, does not necessarily refute those critics who view *Narrative* as the direct antecedent to *Up from Slavery.* Other than Washington or his scribbling ghostwriter, Max Bennet Thrasher, who can know which of Douglass's two texts was foremost in Washington's mind? The greater concern for this paper raised by the inconsistency between the consciously remembered ("I remember hearing," "I remember reading") and the forgotten (or repressed) is the question of authorial trustworthiness and the superficiality of autobiography, a theoretical issue which interests me much more than determining which Douglass text Washington did or did not remember.

Because Washington's subject is doubly shaped (once by the function of genre, once by signification on Douglass) the critical task of deconstructing Washington's autobiographical pretenses is a peeling away of densely layered ego. Just as Douglass's protective closet conceals his libidinal relation to the feminine (because he identifies with Hester there), Washington's childhood home in the slave quarters ("a poorly built cabin" not larger than "about fourteen by sixteen feet square") joins him to the libidinal feminine insofar as his mother's memory issues from there. Because she was the plantation cook at Hale's Ford and their one-room shanty was both kitchen and bedroom, the narrow cabin with its paradoxical "open" fireplace locates for Washington the domestic center of the text—the architectonic source of origins that appears as equivalent both to Douglass's closet and to Harriet Jacobs's famous garret-space. By contrast, the open space of the fields, the woods—the outdoors—is, in *Up from Slavery,* a distinctively masculine domain. "During the period I spent in slavery," Washington writes,

> I was not large enough to be of much service, still I was occupied most of the time cleaning the yards, carrying water to men in the fields, or going to the mill. . . . The road [from the mill] was a lonely one and often led through dense forests. I was always frightened. The woods were said to be full of soldiers who had deserted the army and I had been told that the first thing a deserter did to a Negro boy when he found him alone was to cut off his ears. (13–14)

The outdoors, full of "men in the fields" and "soldiers who had deserted from the army," names the site where, by surviving its ravages, physical strength, rugged individualism, and mobility validate manliness—a formidable challenge to a small boy, as Washington's example confirms. In his early trials at these masculine rites, Washington's fear of the outdoors, of (men roaming) the woods, overwhelmed him to the point that, often, he quit the effort midway "to wait, sometimes for hours, till a chance passer-by came along" (14) to help him, crying, back to his mother's cabin.

Despite culturally imposed assignments of gender to the indoors and outdoors, to restricted and unrestricted spaces, private and public spheres, Washington belongs exclusively to neither side of this grand division but slips in and out of both discursive universes comfortably and—for the moment—unproblematically. It is only later, when the slaveboy reaches liminality, finally confident that he can manage outdoors, that he is called peremptorily away from his station to domestic work in the "big house." Here gender fixity, suddenly vital to the pubescent, eludes him. In that moment of self-discovery, the subject, aware for the first time of the rigid, extra-gendered white world he is enslaved to, suddenly recognizes his own undifferentiated identity; that is, his sexual formlessness, the "undecideability" (Spillers's term) of his gender. His reaction is a mad dash to satisfy the culturally prescribed role of the masculine prepared for him but denied him in the "big house."

As a structural and discursive universe unto itself, the "big house" contrasts sharply, in its enormity, with the narrowness of the slave cabin. Yet, the comparative expansiveness of the "big house" can in no way match the vastness of the fields, the woods, or the outdoors generally. However sizable or privileged a space it is, the "big house" has in common with the cabin the structural and discursive restrictedness that characterized the writerly postures of nineteenth-century women authors appropriating for themselves, as Jacobs's remarkable phrase goes, "loopholes of retreat" from *their* restricted spaces (i.e., the attic, the pigeon-house, the garret, the parlor). The "big house," then, is also women's space. Accordingly, few men in Washington's account occupy the "big house"; the Civil War, the historical moment of Washington's autobiography, has taken them away. On the rare occasion when (white) men are remembered by Washington to have occupied the "big house," they did so only as disabled soldiers sidelined from a war they promptly returned to after being nursed back to health. Their powerlessness to govern, control, or otherwise dominate the plantation in the manner of a master approximates a bourgeois brand of white male emasculation leaving, by default, the white mistress to oversee the plantation. And yet at Hale's Ford, Washington's mistresses shun the master's sovereignty over the plantation that the privilege of whiteness offers them in his absence, to maintain the privileges of ladyhood (leisure, indulgence, protection) that their white femaleness has provided. By this means of double default (and only this means), the male slaves become pseudo-patriarchs, viceroys of the plantation, with one hope of proving their masculine potential by following the Father in protecting his wife and daughter: "The slave who was selected to sleep in the 'big house' during the absence of the males was considered to have a place of honor. Anyone attempting to harm 'young Mistress' or 'old Mistress' during the night would have had to cross the dead body of the slave to do so" (20). What appears by this time in Washington's discourse about effete soldiers and dauntless slaves as a clever inversion of white male strength/potency and black male powerlessness/impotency, turns out instead to be merely a clever illusion betrayed by the honored slave's eunuchism, the slave being coolly devoted to the protection of the chaste respectabilities of white women while "the males" (the black slave presumably excluded from this gender category) tested and proved their virile selves in the outdoors at war. Strategically, the black male slave, coming indoors, is rendered by Washington a nonthreat in the most dreaded sexual arrangement imaginable in the collective consciousness of the white slaveholding South. In the "big house," male virility—black or white—is nonexistent. Under the conditions of domestication, the maturing, pubescent Washington is confronted squarely by the alarming contradiction of an extragendered free white society and the virtual impossibility of stable gender identity within the slave community. His consequent experience of self-alienation is worthy, if inversely, of the primordial dehiscence which precedes Lacan's mirror stage of identity formation.[39]

In the canon of black male autobiography in which boyhood figures prominently, there is ample evidence of sexual anxiety. The instant of identity panic in which Washington rushes to escape the psychic vertigo characterizing his preliminal stage is not, however, as easy to pinpoint as it is in Douglass's *Narrative*. If there is indeed a single instance of sexual panic to be found in the boyhood chapters of *Up from Slavery,* it lies buried somewhere between the lines of chapter 1 ("A Slave among Slaves"), in the realm of the unspeakable. Because the innocent boy lacks the adult's virtually unlimited access to language, the child's experience of what might be called hegemonically a sexual hysteria is usually unspeakable, as Douglass's case bears out. Like the excitable mute frustrated in his attempt to articulate his delight, the naïf is capable only of sporadic, scarcely intelligible, "ejaculations." Even the mature autobiographer, for whom language poses no impediment, is reticent with respect to the sexual feelings of the naïf—if Douglass's withdrawal into the closet says anything at all about his authorial fears. Since self-conscious black male narrative seems to have observed the traditional constraints of cultural and literary propriety to correct the image of the black male as hypersexual, black male writers (Washington among them), despite their mastery of language, for the greater part eschew anything like a full disclosure of their essential psychosexual constitution.[40]

Regardless of what are either narrative evasions by the mature narrator or punctuated instances of juvenile ineffability, the struggle to manage silences and keep sexuality at bay sometimes fails. There is, for instance, a quietly transgressive je ne sais quoi disrupting the romantic southern idyll in chapter 1 of *Up from Slavery*, which describes "two young [white] mistresses and some lady visitors eating ginger cakes in the yard" (17). The language used by Washington to relate this edenic scene is so suggestive that the readerly tendency Eve Kosofsky Sedgwick describes as "knowing" that the unspeakable is necessarily a codification of erotic meaning (the heuristic "We Know What That Means") becomes entirely irresistible:[41] "[Those] cakes seemed to me to be absolutely the most tempting and desirable things that I had ever seen and I then and there resolved that if I ever got free, the height of my ambition would be reached if I could get to secure and eat ginger-cakes in the way I saw those ladies doing" (17). I am postulating (and pretending to "know" in the Sedgwickian sense) that contrary to what is said, young Washington's hunger/hankering is not for ginger-cakes at all but rather, like that for the forbidden fruit of Eden, the more profound, nameless desire for white women which, as the discussion above suggests, the enslaved man-child cannot articulate, or alternatively, the adult autobiographer dares not confess to. It is revealing that this coded episode lies seductively juxtaposed to Washington's deep sense of his own corporeality, of his own pubescent bodiliness.

Washington's "most trying [childhood] ordeal," he claims, was the acute suffering caused him by a flax shirt worn on his "soft and tender" body "like a dozen or more chestnut burrs or a hundred small pin-points, in contact with his flesh" (18). Even as the slaveboy's "soft and tender" skin recalls the sentimental subject Douglass feared, it further affords the male subject a sensuality typically unacknowledged in conventional models of masculinity. "I had to wear the . . . shirt or none; and had it been left to me to choose, I should have chosen to wear no covering" (19), Washington complains.

One can only speculate about the genuineness of Washington's sexual naïveté when he expresses an unabashed preference for "no covering" to the compulsory flax shirt worn by virtually all enslaved boys who wore anything on the plantation. It is plausible that Washington's innocence here is really authorial subterfuge, the mature autobiographer skillfully throwing his voice in a performance of rhetorical ventriloquism to say what any nineteenth-century adult black male writer knows he cannot acceptably write. This other, provisional image of the boyish servant innocently exposed and indulging the delicate and fanciful Victorian sensibilities of three white maidens is as much a part of the autobiographer's erotic economy, I believe, as his titillating confession of "ginger-cake" reverie.

Contemporary cultural historians and cultural theorists have not failed to explore the intense libidinal anxieties engendered by the proximity of black- and white-skinned people in controlled spaces (the nation, the region, the "big house," the yard). American historian Winthrop Jordan's *White over Black: American Attitudes toward the Negro, 1550–1812* may constitute the most thoughtful documentation of the kind of interracial libidinality produced by the white master/mistress–black slave relation I am interrogating. What Jordan's historiography reveals about the domestic services of "Negro boys" to American Victorians is both instructive, given Washington's experience in that role, and vital to my project of specifying potential moments of gender obfuscation in autobiographies by African American men.

Jordan's discussion of the popular eighteenth-century practice of Negro boys serving at the dinner table in the "big house" and "wearing only a shirt not always long enough to conceal their private parts," is, in connection with Washington's complaints about the flax shirt, telling to say the least.[42] That the complete nudity Washington wishes for might be displaced in his reality only by a semi-nudity Jordan cites as "commonplace" is not a remote possibility: "Until I had grown to be *quite a youth* this single garment was all that I wore" (19, emphasis added). For the domesticated slaveboy, whose education outdoors has been frustrated by his duties indoors, the unremarked exposure of his private parts before a white (women's) audience mocks—indeed negates—the psychophysiology of phallic development. Jordan quotes one traveler observing this domestication of "Negro boys": "I am surprized this [nudity] does not hurt the feelings of the fair Sex to see these young boys of about Fourteen and fifteen years old to Attend them. these whole nakedness Expos'd and i can Assure you It would Surprize a person to see these d——d black boys how well they are hung [*sic*]."⁴³ The irony in this situation is that the slaveboy cannot enter the "big house" until he is of "sufficient size" ("When I had grown to a sufficient size, I was required to go to the 'big house'" [17]), but when, finally, he *is* of "sufficient size" anatomically (double entendre intended), his bodiliness and his developing sex must be treated as invisible by the very persons who would substantiate and authenticate them if they did not fear them.

In black male autobiography from Douglass onward, the problem of paternity and mixed birth complicates for the African American manchild a process that for his white counterpart is usually unproblematic. Since the traditional rites and laws of patrilineal inheritance assume that a masculine code has been or will be transferred from father to son, the panic-stricken white son is met halfway by the willing white father in the son's haste to embrace a culturally meaningful identity. For young male slaves, however, the "mimetic" invisibility of adult African American men as legitimate players in the "prevailing social fiction" of patriarchy and their status as the objects, never the agents, in the patrilineal transfer, cause the black manchild's fateful angst:

> I used to take a great deal of satisfaction in the lives of men who had risen by their own efforts from poverty to success. It is a great thing for a boy to be able to read books of that kind. It not only inspires him with the desire to do something and make something of his life, but it teaches him that success depends upon his ability to do something useful, to perform some kind of service that the world wants.
>
> *The trouble in my case, as in that of other coloured boys of any age, was that the stories we read in school were all concerned with the success and achievements of white boys and men.* Occasionally I spoke to some of my schoolmates in regard to the characters of whom I read, but they invariably reminded me that the stories I had been reading had to do with members of another race. Sometimes I tried to argue the matter with them, saying that what others had done some of us might also be able to do, and that lack of a past in our race was no reason why it should not have a future.
>
> *They replied that our case was entirely different.*⁴⁴

I am arguing that Washington's notion of success is not only materially based but also phallocentric. His ideas about success depend fundamentally on one's demonstrating virility sufficient "to do something" that presumably the impotent (the boy) cannot do. The successful person must, as all phallists worry, "perform." Oddly, though, Washington's schoolmates seem to have known better than he that the "lack of a [patrilineal] past" presented more than a small stumbling block in a black boy's pathway to a mature masculine future. Washington's idealism about the matter in *My Larger Education,* however, is not a feature of the earlier *Up from Slavery.* In fact, Washington's optimistic indifference to having a patrilineal past here is at odds with his initial concern for history that the want of paternal validation represents in *Up from Slavery.* The contrast in sentiment between *My Larger Education* and *Up from Slavery* is striking. In the latter, Washington expresses sore regret about his lack of a past:

> I used to picture myself in the position of a boy or a man with an honoured and distinguished ancestry which I could trace back through a period of hundreds of years, and who had not only inherited a name, but a fortune and a proud family homestead (43). . . . I used to envy the white boy who had no obstacle placed in the way of his becoming a Congressman, Governor, Bishop or President by reason of the accident of his birth or race. I used to picture the way I would act under such circumstances. (45)

Yet it only *seems* that the crisis of illegitimacy felt in the 1901 *Up from Slavery* had been resolved by 1911 when the narrative of *My Larger Education* was completed. Although his envy of "the white boy" in *Up from Slavery* pretends to reflect a fatuous childishness ("I used to picture," "I used to envy"), which the more stolid Washington would later mock good-humoredly, his jealousies are not as fully absent from *My Larger Education* as Washington wants to imply, despite the tone of confidence expressing them ("I used to take . . . satisfaction in"). In the later book, Washington's earlier anxieties do not disappear but are ascribed instead to "other coloured boys," not to his own sensibilities. That Washington abandons the earlier disquieted self of *Up from Slavery* for an air-brushed portrait of childhood that refuses to acknowledge his earlier acute envy suggests a classic case of denial and displacement—Washington straining to kill the memory of longing and envy because it is the memory of dashed hopes. The "lack of a [Fatherly] past" ensures that Washington, whatever his individual material gains, will always lack the capacity to evince traditional manliness and, therefore, self-legitimation.

Because of the slaveholder's practice of trading male slaves more regularly than females, Spillers's idea of the "mimetic" absence of enslaved black males as fathers finds its realization in *Up from Slavery*. Although a slave from another plantation became Washington's stepfather, "he seldom came to the plantation [near Hale's Ford, visiting] . . . perhaps once a year" (31) until Emancipation. (Even following Emancipation, he did not have so much as a surname to bequeath Washington, as the laws of patrilineage require.[45]) And, if it is indeed true that the outdoors constituted the fin-de-siècle proving ground for masculinity, as the American Naturalists urged in their fiction, then the paucity of black male field literature in which boyhood is figured as a fundamental stage of character development means that in the literature of the male "house Negro" like Washington or Douglass, the only acceptable model for masculinity is white and fiercely phallocentric.

Washington's veneration for Hampton College president General Samuel C. Armstrong, "the noblest, rarest human being . . . a perfect [white] man" (59–60), is also a signal that the search for legitimacy has been satisfied by a surrogate. It is General Armstrong, not Washington's stepfather (nor even Douglass, whom Washington revered in his youth), who teaches Washington the principles of the masculine. In the context of General Armstrong's mentorship to him, Washington states: "The older I grow, the more I am convinced that there is no education . . . that is equal to that which can be gotten from *contact* with great men and women. Instead of studying books so constantly, how I wish that our [black] schools and colleges might learn to study men and things" (60, emphasis added). But *contact* in the slavocracy is a relative experience. For the cultural elite, it may signify the patrilinear interface between men and boys as between benefactors and beneficiaries of the great masculinist code. In this vein, the function of contact is to facilitate inheritance. For the slaveboy living outside this culture, contact undergoes semantic dislocation, no longer signifying the prerequisite intimacy of father and son in the patrilineal transfer, as it does for free white boys of wealth and privilege. Rather, it represents a nameless intimacy of another order. Contact, I mean to suggest, "is also the basic schematic type of initiating sexual action (touching, caressing—sexuality),"[46]—which is, as I have argued, Douglass's predicament. That Washington's use of the term *contact* falls into the former denotative category (contact as patrilinear transfer) is hardly a paradox. In the first place, it is consistent with both his early envy of white boys and his post-emancipation adoption of General Armstrong as father figure. In the second place, it seems almost elementary that contact with General Armstrong failed to excite the sexual anxieties of the pubescent/adolescent—as in the case of Douglass facing Covey—because the general, contrary to Washington's portrayal of him as "a perfect man" and despite his wielding absolute power at Hampton, suffered from severe bodily paralysis. Washington's "perfect" white man is a disabled white man—less a model for black masculinity than a reassurance that Washington, in his own socially/politically enforced posture of eunuchism, is not really impotent. Incapable of the sexual aggression played out in *Narrative,* Armstrong, nonetheless, "touched" Washington with the heroism and dogged individualism that have come to signify the masculine ideal in American culture.

Paralysis notwithstanding, General Armstrong's enormous agency over countless bodies of color under his superintendency at Hampton is one of the central ironies of Washington's schoolday reminiscences. "General Armstrong made a personal inspection of the young men in ranks" (65), Washington reports admiringly. Erotic inferences aside, the greater value of Washington's relation to Armstrong, for my purposes, is the correlation between the general's corporeal powerlessness and the impotency of the panic-stricken slaveboy undifferentiated in his self-conscious. Conversely, Armstrong's exceptional fortitude accords with the inevitable triumph of phallic primacy over the last gasps of sexual formlessness in black male self-identity.

However much Washington and black male autobiographers might try to resist white masculinist codes of being and behavior ("In later years, I confess that I do not envy the white boy as I once did" [45]), a good deal of the effort to prove black masculinity in black autobiography has tended not only to be imitative ("what others had done some of us might also be able to do") but sometimes overcompensatory, precisely because the terms *black* and *man* have been historically opposed and therefore mutually combusting units in the lexicography of European anthropology and ethnography. The corollary to this idea suggests that black machismo is the angry effort to overcome the self-combustion of a subaltern identity.

To its credit, black male autobiography has accomplished the notable feat of overcoming black (mis)representation in generations of hegemonic discourse. But I fear that the concomitant strategy of black phallist writers to assert agency through the romanticization of masculinity is a trap. The ends of black male autobiography have been noble and necessary, but occasionally the means have been self-defeating. As black feminist theory and psychoanalytical critiques like Peter Walker's portrait of Douglass have shown us,[47] the glorification of one split of consciousness and the suppression/repression of another do not engender the discursive potency black masculinist production desires for itself. To the contrary, such activity yields little more than the epistemological frigidity of the black male body in bondage.

Notes

1. Hortense J. Spillers, "Mama's Baby, Papa's Maybe: An American Grammar Book," *Diacritics* 17 (1987): 80.

2. Kaja Silverman's recent *Male Subjectivity at the Margins* (New York: Routledge, 1992) skillfully demonstrates some of the psychoanalytic interrogations that might be brought to bear on conventional paradigms of masculinity. Notwithstanding a few important yet regretfully brief exceptions by gay black writers (Marlon Riggs, Essex Hemphill), a work analogous to Silverman's that attempts to answer for the contradictions, deviations, and sudden, extraparadigmatic ruptures presented by black masculinity to the dominant model has yet to emerge.

3. Earle E. Thorpe, "*The Slave Community:* Studies of Slavery Need Freud and Marx," in *Revisiting Blassingame's "The Slave Community": The Scholars Respond,* ed. Al-Tony Gilmore (Westport, Conn.: Greenwood Press, 1978), 56.

4. For a brilliant discussion and demonstration of the limits of psychocriticism vis-à-vis African American literature, see Hortense Spillers, "The Permanent Obliquity of an In(ph)allibly Straight," in *Changing Our Own Words: Essays on Criticism, Theory, and Writing by Black Women,* ed. Cheryl Wall (New Brunswick, N.J.: Rutgers University Press, 1989), 127–49.

5. Barbara Herrnstein Smith, "Contingencies of Value," *Critical Inquiry* 10 (1983): 18.

6. Frantz Fanon, *Black Skins, White Masks,* trans. Charles Lam Markmann (New York: Grove Press, 1967), 50.

7. Arnold Rampersad, "Biography and Afro-American Culture," in *Afro-American Literary Studies in the 1990s,* ed. Houston Baker and Patricia Redmond (Chicago: University of Chicago Press, 1989), 194–230. Also discussed in Rampersad's "Biography, Autobiography, and Afro-American Culture," *Yale Review* 73 (1983): 1–16, and "Psychology and Afro-American Biography," *Yale Review* 78 (1988): 1–18.

8. In the preface to a 1954 edition of his 1896 work, *The Suppression of the African Slave Trade to the United States of America,* Du Bois remarked about the critical reception of his book in 1896, demonstrating how deeply concerned he was about the relevance of psychoanalysis to his own intellectual pursuits, "As a piece of

documented historical research, [the original work] was well done and has in the last half century received very little criticism as to accuracy and completeness. One area of criticism which I have not seen . . . but which disturbs me is my ignorance in the waning 19th c. of the significance of Freud. . . . [The] work of Freud . . . [was] not generally known when I was writing the book, and consequently I did not realize the psychological reasons behind the trends of human action which the African trade involved."

9 Bruce Mazlish, "Autobiography and Psychoanalysis: Between Truth and Self-Deception," *Encounter* 35 (1970): 30.

10 Michael Cooke, "Modern Black Autobiography in the Tradition," in *Romanticism: Vistas, Instances, and Continuities,* ed. David Thornburn and Geoffrey Hartman (Ithaca, N.Y.: Cornell University Press, 1973), 273. Also quoted in Henry Louis Gates Jr.'s *Figures in Black: Words, Signs, and the "Racial" Self* (New York: Oxford University Press, 1987), 95. Emphasis added.

11 Ibid.

12 Mazlish, "Autobiography and Psychoanalysis," 30.

13 Virginia Woolf, *A Room of One's Own* (San Diego, Calif.: Harcourt Brace Jovanovich, 1957), 88.

14 "Preliminal" and "liminal" belong to anthropologist Arnold van Gennep. His study of "life-crisis ceremonies," *Les rites de passage* (1909), taking up among its other discursive streams "the critical problems of becoming male and female" in various societies, accords fruitfully with my own efforts in this essay. Although van Gennep foregrounds the communal or tribal ceremonies (*rites*) that accompany "life-crises" (i.e., death, birth, marriage, adoption, remarriage), rather than the progressions of gender development I am examining, his communal rites, subdivided into preliminal rites (rites of separation), liminal rites (rites of transition), and postliminal rites (rites of incorporation)—the totality of which symbolize the passage of a life cycle—conform very nearly to the stages of gender development I am arguing for as experienced nonceremonially in the individual subjects of *Narrative* and *Up from Slavery*. I deal in this essay only with the first two stages or rites.

15 For example, William Wells Brown's *Clotel* (1853) and Martin Delany's *Blake: or, the Huts of America* (1859) in the nineteenth century, and James Weldon Johnson's *Autobiography of an Ex-Colored Man* (1912) in the twentieth. In each novel, America represents the "strange land" of Old Testament Egypt where Jehovah's chosen nation, Israel, has been forced into bondage. Political freedom for black Americans, these three writings seem to say on one level or another, may not be realizable except abroad.

16 It is no accident that the Bible, the archetypal Western text in some respects, was also the first (if not only) reader for many black Americans before and following Emancipation. Many scholars (Gates, for example) also credit the European picaresque for its typologization of the trope of mixed lineage inherited

by black writers. See Gates, "Binary Oppositions in Chapter One of *Narrative of the Life of Frederick Douglass, An American Slave Written By Himself*" in *Figures in Black: Words, Signs, and the "Racial" Self*. For a history of black literacy and the Bible, refer to Janet Duitsman Cornelius, *When I Can Read My Title Clear: Literacy, Slavery, and Religion* (Columbia: University of South Carolina Press, 1992); Renita Weems, "Reading *Her Way* through the Struggle: African American Women and the Bible"; and David Wimbush, "The Bible and African-Americans: An Outline of an Interpretive History." Weems and Wimbush are collected in *Stony the Road We Trod: African-American Biblical Interpretation*, ed. Cain Hope Felder (Minneapolis, Minn.: Fortress, 1991).

17 I am freely borrowing the notion of "oceanic" identity from Spillers.

18 By "identity (racial and/or sexual) panic," I mean to evoke simultaneously Fanon's discourse of the "neurotic" native and Eve Sedgwick's "homosexual panic." Sedgwick's "homosexual panic" is called, alternately, the subject's "blackmailability." It is much too tempting not to consider the special brand of *racialized* sexual panic which is foregrounded here as the black subject's *blackmaleability*.

19 George Cunningham, "'Called into Existence': Gender, Desire, and Voice in Douglass' *Narrative of 1845*," *differences: A Journal of Feminist Cultural Studies* 1 (1989): 108.

20 Eugene Genovese, *The World the Slaveholders Made* (Middletown, Conn.: Wesleyan University Press, 1988), xvi.

21 In *My Bondage and My Freedom*, the 1855 version of Douglass's autobiography, the slaveboy's hiding place is described as a "little, rough closet, which opened into the kitchen; and through the cracks of its unplaned boards, [Douglass] could distinctly see and hear what was going on, without being seen by old master" (87). The modern equivalent to this architecture would likely be a simple broom closet.

22 David Van Leer, "Reading Slavery: The Anxiety of Ethnicity in Douglass' *Narrative*," in *Frederick Douglass: New Literary and Historical Essays*, ed. Eric Sundquist (New York: Cambridge University Press, 1990), 131.

23 Homosocial, if not homosexual, desire figures noticeably in Douglass's own novella, *The Heroic Slave*. Although ostensibly representing a political alliance, the transracial male bonding between Madison Washington, the "black but comely" slave protagonist whose "appearance betokened Herculean strength," and Mr. Listwell, the white abolitionist sympathizer who "long desired to sound the mysterious depths of the thoughts and feelings of a slave," deserves more critical attention as an early construction of homosocial/homoerotic desire.

24 Robert A. Nye, "Sex Difference and Male Homosexuality," *Bulletin of the History of Medicine* 63 (1989): 41.

25 Ibid.

26 Frederick Douglass, *My Bondage and My Freedom* (New York: Dover, 1969), 79.

27 "Libidinal masculine" and "libidinal feminine" are Hélène Cixous's terms in

"Laugh of the Medusa," collected in *Critical Theory since 1965*, ed. Hazard Adams and Leroy Searle (Tallahassee: Florida State University Press, 1989).

28 Ibid., 314.

29 Ibid.

30 Fanon, *Black Skins*, 159.

31 Earle Thorpe, *The Old South: A Psychohistory* (Durham, N.C.: Seeman, 1972), 127.

32 The most casual reader of Douglass's autobiography cannot fail to recognize Douglass's sense that achieving manhood is inextricable from achieving freedom. That boyhood parallels slavery is somewhat less obvious but not an esoteric connection. "I am but a slave," says Douglass at the midpoint of *Narrative*, "and all boys are bound to someone" (113).

33 Ronald G. Walters, "The Erotic South: Civilization and Sexuality in American Abolitionism," *American Quarterly* 2 (1973): 186.

34 Ibid., 180.

35 Van Leer, "Reading Slavery," n.33.

36 Jenny Franchot, "The Punishment of Ester: Frederick Douglass and the Constitution of the Feminine," in *Frederick Douglass: New Literary and Historical Essays*, 150.

37 Knowing that it is by now a quite common view among African Americanist literary critics that Washington's *Up from Slavery* constitutes a formal revision of Douglass's *Narrative*, one writer has called Washington's text "a corrective rewrite" of Douglass's, viz., David Dudley, *My Father's Shadow: Intergenerational Conflict in African American Men's Autobiography* (Philadelphia: University of Pennsylvania Press, 1991), 41.

38 Washington, *My Bondage and My Freedom*, 34–35.

39 Lacan's mirror stage is precipitated by the fragmentation of the body and its image—"a certain dehiscence . . . a primordial Discord betrayed by the signs of uneasiness and motor uncoordination of the neo-natal months." It is as if both Douglass and Washington experience a second birth into subjectivity, once the dehiscence of race and gender becomes liminal. See Jacques Lacan, "The Mirror Stage as Formative of the Function of the I as Revealed in Psychoanalytic Experience," in *Écrits*, trans. Alan Sheridan (New York: Norton, 1977).

40 For a substantive discussion on this point, see Gloria Naylor, "Love and Sex in the Afro-American Novel," *Yale Review* 78 (1988): 19.

41 Eve Kosofsky Sedgwick, *Epistemology of the Closet* (Berkeley and Los Angeles: University of California Press, 1990), 204.

42 Winthrop Jordan, *White over Black: American Attitudes toward the Negro, 1550–1812* (Baltimore, Md.: Penguin, 1969), 161.

43 Ibid., 159.

44 Booker T. Washington, *My Larger Education* (New York: Doubleday, Page, 1911), 103. Emphasis added.

45 The autobiographer, we recall, adopted the surname Washington years after his

slavery days on the plantation. His adoption of the surname belonging to "America's first great leader" may have inclined Booker T. Washington toward the self-made masculine construction of *Up from Slavery*. This point I owe to Michael Moon.

46 Fanon, *Black Skins*, 56.

47 Peter Walker, *Moral Choices: Memory, Desire, and Imagination in Nineteenth Century Abolition* (Baton Rouge: Louisiana State University Press, 1978).

Native Daughters in the Promised Land:

Gender, Race, and the Question of Separate Spheres

YOU-ME PARK AND GAYLE WALD

On 20 June 1996, the regents of the University of California approved a now infamous resolution mandating that as of 1 January 1997 the university would be forbidden to consider "race, religion, gender, color, ethnicity or national origin" in admitting students.[1] The issue of "race-based preferences"—the deliberately provocative phrase adopted by those opposed to affirmative action—was ultimately put to California voters, who in November 1996 voted to pass Proposition 209 by a margin of 54 to 46 percent. The effect of this initiative, ostensibly designed to boost the percentage of students gaining admission solely on the basis of academic achievement, has been immediate and chilling. A report about admissions to University of California law schools released in the spring of 1997 shows a radical drop in the number of African Americans admitted, down from 104 in 1995 to 21 in 1996. The group that so far has profited most dramatically from the new California policy is Caucasians, despite widely held expectations that Asian Americans would reap the greatest benefits. Ward Connerly, the African American regent who led the effort to promote passage of the resolution, told the *Los Angeles Times* that he "welcomed" such reports. "We are too politically correct to reach the conclusion: they are not as competitive to be lawyers and doctors. If we really want to help those black and Latino kids, we will give them some tough love and get them channeled back into being able to compete."[2]

We begin with these facts, at once familiar and dizzying in their implications, because the complex scenario they point to raises issues that we explore in this essay: access to public institutions; whose interests are represented within the public political sphere; the figuration of race and gender and their pitting against one another (since it often goes unremarked that affirmative action has also benefited white women); media representations that pit socially beleaguered and socially legitimated minority groups against one another; and the privatization of certain interests and needs under a "tough love" policy that has little to do with love and even less to do with justice.

We raise the following questions: How does minority literature represent the boundaries between public and private spheres in the United States? How do these boundaries reinforce and overlap class and gender lines? How does the nation-state participate in dictating how these boundaries are drawn? Rather than assuming that literary texts unproblematically reflect reality, we want to pay close attention to their strategies of representation. We want to ask how the private and public spheres are imagined and figured in these texts, how female subjects negotiate their positions both in and between public and private spheres, and where and how literary texts locate and represent the political and economic power that shapes, inscribes, and sometimes nullifies the hopes, fears, and desires of female subjects.

In what follows, we explore these issues through an analysis of texts by two African American and two Asian American writers: Ann Petry's *The Street* (1946), Gwendolyn Brooks's *Maud Martha* (1953), Cynthia Kadohata's *The Floating World* (1989), and Chang-rae Lee's *Native Speaker* (1995). In looking at these texts, we explore the relation between the public sphere and the simultaneously privatized and publicized subjectivities of black and Asian women. Our choice of these novels is strategic at a number of levels. Most importantly, they enable us to conduct an investigation of how the separate spheres model is constitutive of gender and race discourses, and to do so in terms that insist on the historical specificity of our own endeavor as well as the object of our investigation. Both sets of texts were produced at moments of perceived crisis in the discourses of race, gender, ethnicity, nationality, and labor—crises that subsequently found social expression through the reordering of public and private. It is through the lens of such reorderings that these novels elucidate the particular plights of poor women of color—both "native" populations such as African Americans, who under segregation were explicitly denied citizens' rights within the formal public sphere, and immigrant populations of Japanese and Korean Americans, whose citizenship status has been subject to anxious scrutiny and policing speculation.

The novels by Petry and Brooks, written in the aftermath of World War II, explicitly and implicitly portray the (re)domestication of women workers confronting the return to the nationalized domestic sphere of male citizen-soldiers. Both *The Street* and *Maud Martha* are primarily concerned with the everyday struggles and aspirations of poor African American women. These women are not simply victims of domesticity, and their modes of access to the public sphere are not simple either, sometimes entailing psychological or physical violation. Juxtaposed, respectively, against a romanticized representation of the black masses and the figure of the masculinized soldier-citizen, Petry's and Brooks's protagonists find no easy solutions to the problems posed by their inability to gain meaningful control over the terms of their publicity or privacy.

The novels by Lee and Kadohata address the issues of immigration, nationality, citizenship, and domesticity in the context of the shifting boundaries between internal and external national territories and public spheres. These novels were produced during the late 1980s and early 1990s, another period of crisis, when anti-immigration sentiments were being fueled by collective anxiety about limited resources and job opportunities for "legitimate" subject-citizens. In *Native Speaker,* an acclaimed novel about the formation of a Korean American subjectivity, Chang-rae Lee deftly portrays the way his protagonist, Byongho, is shaped and defined by a sense of secrecy and shame concerning his difference: Asian looks, immigrant parents who don't act like normal parents, and, most importantly, his compromised male sexuality vis-à-vis his white wife, Lelia. The shadowy figures of Korean American women disrupt Lee's narrative, which mostly concerns itself with the legitimation of a male immigrant subject in the public sphere. Tucked away in the hyperfeminized private sphere sanctioned by both traditional Korean ideals of domestic women and the U.S. belief in Asian American self-sufficiency ("they don't ask for social welfare"), these women are denied any meaningful access to the public sphere. In *The Floating World,* Kadohata's protagonist, Olivia, lives through the period immediately following World War II trying to negotiate both a domesticized femininity and a public Japanese identity. During the war the public definition of Japanese Americans as Japanese—and thus the enemy—keeps Olivia and her family from taking root as "Americans." Their position as noncitizens is signified in their failure to gain access to the private sphere.

By juxtaposing these two sets of texts from very different eras in postwar U.S. history, we intend to critique not only the binary logic of separate spheres but also the binary logic of race that persists within the popular imagination even as late-twentieth-century demographic shifts, combined with the emergence of new identity categories such as biracial or multiracial, clearly signal the inadequacy of a black-white model. The juxtaposition of African American and Asian American texts presents particular opportunities for undermining the fetishistic separation of black and white racial spheres without retreating to easy (that is, romanticized) notions of hybridity. As events such as the 1992 Los Angeles uprisings and the murder trial of O. J. Simpson illustrate, even within the most patently hybrid social scenarios, blackness can be made to function as a metaphor for race, not only obscuring the racialization of other U.S. minority populations but keeping public discourse locked within the dominant logic of black and white. At the same time, the representation of bitter antagonisms between different racialized minority populations—another product of the L.A. uprisings, in which conflict between Korean American and African American publics was naturalized as the product of intractable *cultural* differences—has the effect of reinscribing racial polarity by reproducing a rhetoric of whites and others. By focusing on the animosities between Korean Americans and African Americans, public discourse in effect reinforced a binary between the minorities mired in scuffles and whites who look on and regulate. The difficulty of thinking outside a racial binary has important implications for how we organize knowledge in educational institutions—as well as in the public sphere constituted through media representation. For example, in high school and college classrooms, on American literature syllabi, and in anthologies of American literature, African American and Asian American texts are often relegated to and analyzed within separate spheres or lumped together under the potentially trivializing and delegitimizing rubric of minority literature.

Over the course of past decades the notion of separate and distinct spheres of social, cultural, and economic life—a private sphere encompassing domestic life, "symbolic reproduction," and the "modern restricted nuclear family" and a public sphere of "material reproduction, political participation, debate, and opinion formation"[3]—has been subject to rigorous and thoroughgoing critique, so much so that scholars have begun to question the usefulness of such a model. Some of the most trenchant of these recent critiques have come from feminist critical theorists, who have argued that the separate spheres model naturalizes bourgeois male subjectivity even as it seeks to demonstrate that *the* bourgeois subject (understood as male, literate, and landed) is the historical product of complex social changes wrought by European modernity and modernization. Nancy Fraser, for example, has carefully criticized Jürgen Habermas's influential work on the public sphere and on the historical emergence of a public-private distinction in several essays, finding it methodologically and ideologically complicit with women's relegation to the less privileged, or private, side of the binary.[4] Complementing and extending Fraser's work, a number of feminist cultural historians and literary scholars have shown that gender cannot be tidily or consistently mapped onto the separate spheres model, as earlier work had suggested. Contending that the public and the private have never been wholly separate and that women's power cannot be adequately gauged according to the degree of women's exclusion from the public sphere (at least as conventionally defined), these scholars have established that even in the nineteenth century—the era, in the United States, of the publicly celebrated cult of domesticity and true womanhood—women were important social actors within various public arenas, including ladies' antislavery and temperance societies, organizations of working-class women, and popular literary culture.[5]

The relation of such recent feminist work to an orthodox separate spheres model is perhaps best characterized as critically collaborative—attentive to the model's utility (particularly for historicizing and de-universalizing key terms such as *domesticity* and *the family*) and, at the same time, wary of its status as an ideological production largely silent about, and therefore potentially recuperative of, women's subordination within patriarchal gender hierarchies. As Kathy Peiss observes, although the separate spheres model "might seem consigned to the dustbin of historiography," nevertheless it "has retained its salience for feminist cultural historians as an ideology that organizes and gives meaning to social experience, a social construction that is contested and renegotiated over time."[6] In other words, the fact that the separate spheres model is a social construction does not negate the notion that public and private are socially real insofar as they structure the terms of social agency and inclusion, the formation of social identities and subjectivities, and our capacity to imagine alternative or competing narratives of the social. The past few decades of critical analysis point to the emergence of a scholarly consensus about the need to deconstruct the hierarchical binary of an orthodox separate spheres model and to replace it with one that acknowledges that public and private are not stable, unchangeable, or natural polarities. Acknowledging the social pliability of separate spheres demands that we stay alert to how the distinction between public and private has been maintained through legal, cultural, and economic discourses. But it also obliges us to investigate the modes by which various public interests have tacitly or explicitly challenged these discourses, either by constructing alternative publics or by imagining different ways of circulating and distributing power between public and private.

A strict separate spheres analytical framework, with its fetishistic and reductionist separation of *the* public and *the* private, obscures crucial questions about mobility and agency across socially constructed lines of difference. The terms *public* and *private* have born, and continue to bear, the inscription of ongoing struggles around questions of access to social power, where power is a function of one's location within a social geography of separate spheres. Our emphasis on mobility and access here is strategic as well as practical, given the intimate link between social subordination and social immobility. To cite one concrete example: even for the nineteenth-century bourgeois white female subject for whom the notion of a separate and safe private sphere has most relevance, the consequences of a discourse of separate spheres have never only or primarily centered on women's confinement to the private, or on the putatively inverse relation between female domesticity and modes of access to masculine public power.[7] Just as it imagines femininity as a lack of agency, the public-private model imagines masculinity as an ability to access *both* the public and the private. As Fraser puts it, "in both spheres women are subordinated to men."[8] For those who have not enjoyed the privilege of crossing the line or benefited from separate spheres, access to public sites of power is typically accompanied by self-mutilation, sacrifice, or loss.

Alongside the fact that the private sphere has been as exclusionary as the public to the "less deserving," we also need to realize that women's coveted entrance into the public sphere may follow a patriarchal script rather than liberating them from patriarchal restraints. As Doreen Massey argues in *Space, Place, and Gender:*

> Many women have had to *leave* home precisely to forge their own version of their identities, from Victorian Lady Travellers to Minnie Bruce Pratt. Moreover, in certain cultural quarters, the mobility of women does indeed seem to pose a threat to a settled patriarchal order. Whether it be the specific fact of *going out* to work in nineteenth-

century England or the more general difficulty . . . of keeping track of women in the city. The relation to identity is again apparent.[9]

It is certainly true that for some women (especially those with class privilege) leaving home has been liberating. It is also true that an opportunity to become a worker rather than a domestic woman has enabled some working-class women to explore the possibility of defining themselves in a nonsexualized way, on the assumption that by eluding the ruthless sexualizing of their bodies they will become less vulnerable to violation and violence. Yet the possibility of women posing a threat to a patriarchal order when they emerge from the private sphere has been more than anticipated in most modern forms of patriarchy. This threat has been exaggerated and used to justify the confinement of women to the domestic sphere as well as the exploitation and persecution of working women. Hence the efficacy of patriarchy is predicated on its ability to weave in and out of the boundaries between the private and public spheres while maintaining the mirage of separate spheres in which men and women hold their own kinds of power.

Given the centrality of questions of mobility to a discussion of separate spheres, it is surprising that issues of race and ethnicity have figured so infrequently in recent feminist critiques of Habermasian social and cultural theory. It is obvious that the public sphere is implicitly and explicitly racialized as well as gendered—that is, normatively defined as masculine *and* white, and accessed via a privileged relation to patriarchal and white supremacist discourses.[10] Nineteenth-century abolitionist writers were explicitly concerned with elaborating the ways that the boundaries of public and private were constituted by and through discourses of race as well as gender. Eager to debunk the cult of true (white) womanhood, abolitionist authors took great pains to demonstrate that the sexualized violence associated with public rituals such as slave auctions and with the public symbolism of white racial authority (most notably, the cowhide whip) thoroughly permeated the private sphere. In their accounts of domestic bondage, such writers as Harriet Jacobs and Harriet Wilson took great care to portray bourgeois white women not merely as the victims of domestic enslavement but as the powerful overseers of their households, as adept at enforcing the rule of racial and class superiority as the plantation overseers charged with enforcing the will of the slaveholding master. Not only does the conventional bourgeois distinction between public and private fall away in the face of such historical evidence, but it is clear from such examples that the subjective *value* of public and private is radically contingent on gender, race, ethnicity, and citizenship. In short, such examples invalidate the presumption of a necessary or essential coupling between terms like *publicity* and *citizenship, privacy* and *safety*.[11]

Contemporary feminist scholars have elaborated, extended, and amplified these nineteenth-century critiques of the public-private binary and its relation to the racialized and sexualized division of labor, bringing their insights to bear on the experience of twentieth-century immigrant and migrant female workers of color. "Black women's experiences and those of other women of color have never fit [the private-public] model," writes Patricia Hill Collins in *Black Feminist Thought*. "Rather than trying to explain why Black women's work and family patterns deviate from the alleged norm, a more fruitful approach lies in challenging the very constructs of work and family themselves."[12] Angela Davis's *Women, Race, and Class* takes just such an approach, noting that while black women have been able to circumvent many of the conditions of patriarchal domesticity through their outside work, this work has itself been privatized, relegated to the private sphere of white middle-class women's homes. "In 1910, when over half of all Black females were working outside their homes," Davis writes, "one-third of them were employed as domestic workers. By 1920 over one-half were domestic servants, and in 1930 the proportion had risen to three out of five."[13] As Davis demonstrates, the private sphere of middle-class white women's domesticity was constructed through the use of the labor of working women of color, especially black women. Hence white middle-class women's privacy and domestic comfort were dependent on the "outside" labor of women of color, whose public sphere of work was white middle-class women's private sphere.

Asian immigrant women also found it much easier to assume the identity of a worker when they remained within the domestic sphere. Hence their entry into the public sphere of work was compromised from the very beginning, because the moment they began to work as domestics, they were even more thoroughly defined as private beings than when they worked in their own homes; in middle-class white women's private spaces, they were rendered invisible. As Evelyn Nakano Glenn writes:

> For racial-ethnic women, then, employment in domestic service became a long-term proposition, not a temporary expedient. Their concentration in domestic service in turn reinforced their degraded status

in society. They came to be seen as particularly suited for, and only suited for, degraded work. Racial-ethnic status and occupational position became more or less synonymous badges of inferiority. The black cleaning woman, the Mexican maid, the Japanese housecleaner, became stereotyped images that helped to rationalize and justify their subordination.[14]

The public and private spheres are thus not separate for these women laborers but deliberately and persistently superimposed. As a consequence, the identity of racial-ethnic women within the public is compromised by the demand that they maintain their private (that is, degraded) identities even in the public sphere.

When contemporary feminist discourses assume a facile binary logic, their potential to dismantle patriarchal definitions and regulations of women is seriously compromised. Women who don't fit easily into the conventional gender polarities of public and private—for example, women who are not victims in easily recognizable ways because they are not confined to the private sphere, or who are perceived as workers with access to the public—become, in effect, masculinized. That is to say, these women's access to the public becomes a structural alibi for their invisibility *as women*. At the same time, and in a complementary way, feminist critique that works to destabilize the public-private binary by mapping gender onto it in effect renders gender the privileged, and hence public, term of analysis at the expense of issues of race, ethnicity, and nationality. Quite literally, once gender is recuperated from its position of invisibility within the Habermasian paradigm and made part of a public feminist scholarly conversation about separate spheres, terms like *race* and *nation* are rendered invisible and hence privatized. Additive strategies of bringing such terms together within a critique of the separate spheres model inevitably transcribe and reinscribe the binary logic of public and private—the very logic such analyses propose to critique. In effect, the binary logic of public-private becomes the operative principle of such an additive model, in which previously privatized terms are added on to already existing models, leaving the models themselves intact. Instead of producing analyses that make visible the interconnectedness of terms like *race* and *gender,* the binary analytic of public-private initiates a process in which these terms eventually annul one another.

Such theoretical difficulties lend further urgency to the question of whether the distinction between public and private spheres is ultimately another solid thing that will melt into air. Our goal in the following literary explorations is not necessarily to transcend the public-private distinction but to make these categories more historically responsible and more responsive to the needs of subjects who have been marginalized by the separate spheres model. By "marginalized" subjects we mean those who do not have the authority to negotiate the shifting boundaries of public and private and are unable to mobilize the discourse of publicity and privacy to articulate their needs, wishes, and rights. Such authority is necessary if these subjects are to acquire autonomy over the way they are represented within the public sphere. Representation in this context is not mere abstraction; nor is it an issue only within the public sphere. Rather, representation has its own real power; it is in fact the means that those with power use to assert it within both the public and private sphere.

Ann Petry's *The Street* and Chang-rae Lee's *Native Speaker,* despite the half century that separates their publication, both offer opportunities to investigate the fragile boundary between the public and private spheres, a boundary drawn and redrawn according to the alleged needs of privileged social groups. For the female subjects in Petry's and Lee's narratives, the private sphere in which they are trapped is always already inscribed and saturated by the violent racialization and sexualization of their identities, bodies, and labor. In particular, the fascination by and aversion toward the ruthlessly sexualized bodies of these women, exemplified by the real and threatened sexual violence against them in the private, domestic sphere, reinscribes public perceptions and definitions of these women. Furthermore, female subjects of color in both novels are complicit with as well as victimized by the myth of bourgeois respectability and domesticity that prohibits them from reaching out to alternative communities and public spheres. Reading Petry's *The Street* alongside Lee's *Native Speaker* allows us to reevaluate the paradigm of linear historical development in light of women's negotiations with the public sphere. Why does Petry's protagonist in *The Street* share so much of the isolation, despair, hope, and fantasy of Ajuma in Lee's *Native Speaker*?

The Street, Petry's best-selling novel about a poor unmarried black mother living in Harlem in 1944, is primarily concerned with the ways in which racism, poverty, and the patriarchal sexualization of women condition the opportunities and experiences of its protagonist, Lutie Johnson. From its opening description of a blustery November wind to its closing image of snow settling on the "grime," "garbage," and "ugliness" of the New York streets, the novel characterizes Lutie's social and natural environments as assaultive.[15] The opening scenes find Lutie searching for an apartment for herself and her young son, Bub, but it becomes clear that domesticity offers no protection from the social; rather, domestic spaces are those that interiorize the violence of the outside world.

Lutie and Bub's cramped, dark, and suffocating apartment is a far cry from the houses that look to Lutie "like something in the movies" (38). The physical deterioration of the apartment not only mirrors Lutie's emotional deterioration as she worries about her ability to pay the rent and protect Bub (without child care, these two tasks are sometimes mutually exclusive) but also represents the interiorization of "urban decay," the cumulative effect of inadequate urban planning, population migrations, declining infrastructure, and large-scale economic deprivation. "The Street" enters Lutie's home in more than one way, however. Bob Jones, a fellow tenant and supervisor of the building where she lives, embodies the interiorized, domesticated threat of sexual objectification and violation that conditions Lutie's experiences on the outside—at work, in the nightclubs where she occasionally sings, and on the city streets themselves. It would not be overstating the case to say that Lutie's everyday experience is defined as the attempt to avoid rape. Treated as if her body were public property, especially by men, Lutie finds little solace, privacy, or protection from sexual abuse in being able to afford a "room of her own." What privacy Lutie does have, moreover, bears the imprint of her powerlessness; it is a privacy imposed rather than chosen, an isolation Lutie suffers as a result of not having a public of her own, a community that might offer her emotional nurturance and physical protection.

Farah Jasmine Griffin suggests that Lutie could discover such a life-sustaining tonic in the voice of her grandmother and hence, metonymically, in a community of black female kin who are also survivors of racism and patriarchy.[16] Such sources of community are, however, closer to home than Lutie's grandmother. They also lie in the various women—also black and also poor—who occupy Lutie's apartment building, especially Min, the woman who lives with Bob Jones and eventually musters the will to leave him. Petry makes clear that Lutie's desperate attachment to an imagined ideal of bourgeois respectability hinders her ability to connect in meaningful ways with other women (and men). Although *The Street* is typically characterized as a naturalist novel in the tradition of *Native Son* (1940), Petry resists depicting Lutie as a passive victim of environment and circumstance. Ironically, it is Lutie's fidelity to the American dream of meritocratic reward for individual effort—a dream exemplified in U.S. national mythology by Benjamin Franklin—that binds her to the street. Walking home with her groceries one evening, Lutie compares herself to Franklin, insisting—despite the fact that 116th Street in Harlem is not "Philadelphia a pretty long number of years ago"—that "if Ben Franklin could live on a little bit of money and could prosper, then so could she" (64). Insofar as Lutie's American dream enshrines wealth rather than social justice as the privileged object of individual ambition and the measure of civic virtue, *The Street* suggests that Lutie is ideologically trapped, complicit with the social forces that oppress her and whose power lies largely beyond her control. While racism, in Lutie's experience, materializes as an all-but-unavoidable instrument of white social control—"Streets like the one she lived on were no accident. They were the North's lynch mobs" (323)—Lutie is nevertheless responsible for her investment in the ideology of an American dream that professes to be gender- and race-neutral.

Petry's calling the urban milieu a Northern lynch mob is telling because it renders in material form immaterial, invisible ideologies. Indeed, "The Street" of the novel's title refers not to a particular geographical location but to a single, determining environment that makes obsolete conventional distinctions between outside and inside, street and home, sacred and profane. And although black women were frequently the victims of Southern lynchings, Petry's metaphor includes and even centralizes black male subjects within the circle of her analysis. Lynching, as a performative spectacle, is intended to be read as a double-edged threat to masculinized African American subjects: first, as a violation of their physical integrity; and second, as the feminization of their bodies (male or female) so that they can be sexually assaulted and violated. Thus the trope of lynch mobs reveals the moment when Petry herself privileges the masculinized rendering of Lutie's plight and suffering, and privatizes the issue of gender. Lutie's narrative is folded into the larger narrative of racial violence that doesn't read Lutie as a gendered subject. Similarly, when Lutie inspects the name on the mailboxes of her future residence, she envisions herself as one facet of a collective subjectivity—a figure of the black masses:

> She leaned over to look at the names on the mail boxes. Henry Lincoln Johnson lived here, too, just as he did in all the other houses she'd

looked at. Either he or his blood brother. The Johnsons and the Jacksons were mighty prolific. Then she grinned, thinking who am I to talk, for I, too, belong to that great tribe, that mighty mighty tribe of Johnsons. (6–7)

The Street ends on a bitterly ironic note, as Lutie Johnson flees New York, leaving Bub to fend for himself in reform school. Petry's ultimate "solution" to her protagonist's struggle to discover a tolerable means out of poverty is to offer her movement without the promise of mobility, choice without the promise of agency. In a parodic reversal of the slave-narrative trope of emancipatory flight from Southern enslavement to Northern freedom, or of the migration-narrative trope of movement from rural Southern poverty to urban opportunity,[17] Lutie manages to flee domestic entrapment on a Chicago-bound train that "roar[s] into darkness" (436). This is hardly the utopian freedom of the road envisioned a few years later by Jack Kerouac and Neal Cassady, whose novels celebrate and enshrine the fantasy of a masculinized American mobility predicated on the evasion of a domesticating and entrapping feminine and on the assumption of white male entitlement to inhabit the public spaces of others. However dystopian *The Street*'s vision of the road for a penniless and unmarried African American woman in the late 1940s, Lutie's escape from the suffocation of the urban street at the end of the novel nevertheless substitutes for the certainty of imprisonment for the murder of Boots Smith, the egotistical henchman of the powerful slumlord Junto. The specter of imprisonment—the ultimate expression of state power over the individual—hangs heavily over the novel, although its threat never materializes.[18]

In *Native Speaker*, it is not the specter of imprisonment but the realization of confinement that ultimately defeats the immigrant female subject. The male protagonist, Byongho, recollects the arrival of a Korean woman in his domestic space after his mother's death:

> I walked outside. A dim figure of a woman stood unmoving in the darkness next to my father's Chevrolet. . . . Beside her were two small bags and a cardboard box messily bound with the twine. When I got closer to her she lifted both bags and so I picked up the box; it was very heavy, full of glass jars and tins of pickled vegetables and meats. I realized she had transported homemade food thousands of miles, all the way from Korea, and the stench of overripe kimchee shot up through

the cardboard flaps and I nearly dropped the whole thing. . . . This woman, I could see, had deep pockmarks stippling her high, fleshy cheeks, like the scarring from a mistreated bout of chickenpox or small-pox, and she stood much shorter than I first thought, barely five feet in her heeled shoes. Her ankles and wrists were as thick as posts. She waited for me to turn and start for the house before she followed sev-eral steps behind me. I was surprised that my father wasn't waiting in the doorway, to greet her or hold the door, and as I walked up the car-peted steps leading to the kitchen I saw that the food and drink I had prepared had been cleared away.[19]

This woman, who is to replace Byongho's mother, has just arrived from Korea and been transported from the airport. As Byongho's father later ex-plains, she has been imported as part of a plan for the family's "move-up," a plan that includes moving into a "big house and yard" in a ritzy neighbor-hood.

It is not mere coincidence that the acquisition of a private residence, a prominent marker of class mobility for Asian American immigrants in par-ticular, is planned to occur shortly after the arrival of the woman. In both the Korean and American patriarchal imagination, the private sphere will not have been fully attained until the physical domestic space is complemented by always available female labor and sexuality. In the context of the immi-grant domestic sphere, the burden on women can be twofold because they are also required to retrieve and recreate the domestic rituals associated with Korean domesticity. The woman in Lee's text knows only too well what's expected of her: She has risked the scrutiny of customs officers and brought jars of kimchee and pickled meat all the way from Korea. In the name of preserving national culture—a project sometimes touted as patriotism and sometimes evoked as simple nostalgia—Korean immigrants' versions of na-tionalism exact an unreasonable amount of women's labor. Female immi-grants in the Korean American community are thus assigned the role of the preserver of national traditions and spirits *within the private sphere*. Rele-gated to this role and this setting, such immigrant women do not have the mobility that allows access to the public sphere where political, economic, and cultural power are negotiated and distributed. They are also burdened by the shame and self-hatred that Korean immigrants harbor toward the part of their Koreanness that refuses to yield to "real" Americanness. In *Na-tive Speaker,* the woman's pockmarked face, embarrassingly short stature, and ankles and wrists "thick as posts" not only betray Byongho's loathing of her but also anticipate and legitimate her relegation to thorough isolation in her own space until the end of the novel, when she makes her debut in the outside world on a hospital deathbed.

This woman's place even within the domestic sphere is firmly defined at the moment of her arrival. She knows that she won't be greeted by the patriarch and that she doesn't deserve the "food and drink" Byongho would normally serve other male guests. As a symbolic gesture and an economic principle, Byongho shouldn't perform any kind of labor for the woman. The much-touted Asian hospitality, which regulates the privatized yet formal exchange between the public and private spheres, is easily overridden by patriarchal rules concerning labor and class in the domestic sphere.

Once the woman has been established in the domestic sphere, the protagonist understands "that her two rooms, the tiny bathroom adjoining them, and the kitchen and pantry [constitute] the sphere of her influence" (65). Despite Byongho's facile reading of her area of influence according to the separate spheres model, he senses that she doesn't assume authority over her own body, let alone the domestic sphere in which she labors: "Sometimes I thought she was some kind of zombie. When she wasn't cleaning or cooking or folding clothes she was barely present; she never whistled or hummed or made any noise, and it seemed to me as if she only partly possessed her own body, and preferred it that way" (65). Byongho dimly perceives that the woman's body has itself been co-opted and incorporated into the structure of the domestic sphere, so that she cannot assume full authority over it. Rendered identical to her domestic labor, the woman has no access to cultural, political, or "economical" encounters with American society. She doesn't watch television ("she always turned them [soap operas] off after a few minutes") or go shopping by herself (Byongho's father would "take her to the mall and buy her some clothes and shoes"). She is never properly named in the text but remains throughout "Ah-ju-ma," a Korean name for a woman of no significance (similar to "Auntie" in the United States), and is never interpellated by the outside world. Whether it is true that she "preferred it that way" remains unclarified and unclarifiable because the reader never gets a glimpse into her consciousness. Denied interiority, "Ah-ju-ma" occupies a curious (but predictable in representations of domestic workers) mode of hyperprivatized existence in which she has no access to individualized subjectivity.

Thus *Native Speaker*, which is mainly concerned with the Korean American male protagonist's sexual anxiety vis-à-vis his white wife and with his agony over his privatized identity, early on introduces the reader to a Korean woman who leads her entire life within a highly claustrophobic domestic sphere. The issues raised by the main plot of the novel—immigrant subjectivity, cultural interpretation of the American public sphere, and publicity and access to political power—have to be read against the backdrop of the numberless and nameless Ah-ju-mas. During the current period of perceived crisis, when immigrant communities feel beleaguered by anti-immigrant sentiments and legislation, Korean immigrants' negotiations of the boundaries of the public and private spheres in the United States, especially with respect to their needs and rights (to be educated, to work, and so on), tend to be carried out in masculinized terms that persistently make invisible women working in the domestic sphere and ignore their desires and needs.

Unlike both *The Street* and *Native Speaker,* Gwendolyn Brooks's *Maud Martha* focuses explicitly on the protagonist's *gendered* subjectivity in the context of her negotiation of minority status within the U.S. public sphere. Maud Martha's desires and needs are presented to the reader in an unequivocally gendered form, particularly through the interiorized expression of her hopes as a mother and her fantasies as a domestic sexualized woman. The final pages of the novel, which narrates Maud Martha's development from childhood to adulthood (defined through marriage and childbirth), find Maud Martha optimistically contemplating both the end of World War II and her own pregnancy. Not only will U.S. soldiers soon be returning home and life returning to "normal," but "in the meantime, she was going to have another baby."[20] Brooks's juxtaposition of these two events—the one staged within the hypermasculinized public sphere of war, the other within the private sphere of Maud Martha's own body—draws our attention to both the midcentury masculinization of national citizenship and the ways that women were both accorded and denied access to the privileges of such citizenship because of their sexuality. Although black soldiers participated in all American wars, World War II marked the moment when African American men began to organize politically around the war effort to demand their rights as citizens. In early postwar civil rights discourse, full citizenship for black men was (re)imagined as a reward for their wartime contributions, as black civil rights leaders successfully mobilized collective outrage that African Americans who had defended democracy abroad (that is, in the public sphere of war) could not enjoy the fruits of that democracy in their home country. Such slogans were not only effective in rallying people on the battlefield of civil rights, which could now be reinterpreted as the war at home in language that conflated the public and private spheres; these slogans were also instrumental in publicizing black struggles for citizenship as struggles to defend black masculinity. Whereas African Americans had always understood segregation and the various limitations imposed on black enfranchisement as affronts to their constitutionally guaranteed rights as citizens, these outrages were now reconfigured in gendered terms, specifically as insults to black manhood. The modern civil rights movement was thus initiated in the collective imagination, at least in part, through a discourse of the citizen-soldier that conflated issues of race, masculinity, and publicity, while using these issues to foreground the denial of full citizenship to black men.

The end of World War II produced a demand for two parallel reorderings of the public-private divide. On the one hand was a gendered demand that women of all races step aside to allow men to resume their roles as workers and citizens; on the other was a racialized demand that blacks be accorded full citizenship rights in recognition of the wartime contributions of black men. But where were black women's desires for citizenship and mobility within and between the separate spheres being represented? On what imaginary battleground within the newly masculinized discourse of civil rights were black women's civil rights to be fought for? Or, as Maud Martha says to herself at the end of the novel, "What, *what,* am I to do with all of this life?" (178). It is significant that this question, like most of Maud Martha's questions and observations, remains unvoiced to others in Brooks's text. From childhood on, Maud Martha has struggled to access publicity in the socially sanctioned way—by attaining "proper" femininity, like that of the "pale and pompadoured" women displayed as icons of black female "achievement" on the covers of the Negro press, or like that of her sister Helen, who has the requisite "long lashes, the grace, the little ways with the hands and feet" (3). The privatization of Maud Martha's subjectivity—given formal expression in the novel as an unrelenting narrative interiority—operates in at least two ways. Denied entrance into the public sphere as a legitimate worker because of her gender, she is also refused entrance through her sexuality because of her race. As a black woman and "a thing of ordinary allurements"

(20), Maud Martha cannot mobilize normative beauty culture in the interests of her own power, and she thus falls back on reproduction as a way of producing and proliferating her "self."

If we define daily experience in terms of its publicity, then it could be said that very little happens to Maud Martha. She grows up, attends school, goes out on dates, marries, moves with her new husband to an apartment, establishes her identity as a wife, and has her first child.[21] Of course, Maud Martha's experience is more than just a collection of the events that construct women's biographies within the paradigm of marriage and reproduction. *Maud Martha*'s conclusion poses more questions than it answers. In the novel's final line, Maud eagerly anticipates future movement—"the weather was bidding her bon voyage" (180)—yet it is unclear whether she will ever be able to construct the imagined or wished-for mobility that might provide a way out of her kitchenette apartment. The promise of a child may be joyful, but there seems little likelihood that maternity will produce the conditions necessary for an escape from the domestic. Rather, Brooks's novel hints that Maud Martha's subjective interiority will continue to be reflected in her confinement to literal interiors—the word *confinement* resonating at the novel's end with its nineteenth-century associations with childbirth. It seems more likely, in other words, that as in Petry's novel the actual experience of domesticity will continue to have a double effect on Maud Martha's subjectivity, leading her simultaneously to rejoice at the thought of men "back from the wars!" and to domesticate her own ambitions.

Cynthia Kadohata's *The Floating World,* like *Maud Martha,* is situated at the postwar moment when national identity and distinctions between public and private spheres are being reordered.[22] We close this section with Kadohata's novel because it is a contemporary work that looks back at an earlier period of crisis with an eye toward understanding contemporary crises, such as violent anti-immigrant sentiments and policy making. It also provides a means of exploring an alternative model of female subjectivity that reconfigures the relations among work, domesticity, and sexuality. How do we imagine an immigrant woman who is not relegated to the domestic sphere or rendered publicized and vulnerable in the public sphere? When does she assume autonomy over her body and work in both the public and private spheres? How does she achieve the discursive and political authority necessary to negotiate the boundaries of her privacy and publicity? *The Float-*

ing World offers a possible refiguring of the public and private spheres that neither relegates women of color to the private sphere nor makes them vulnerable by publicizing them.

The Floating World's protagonist and narrator, Olivia, grows up in transit, as it were, following her parents as they look for work and social and emotional stability:

> We sometimes traveled in the Pacific states with one or two other young Japanese families, heading for jobs the fathers had heard of. We moved often for three reasons. One was bad luck—the businesses my father worked for happened to go under, or the next job we headed to evaporated while we were in transit. Also, it could be hard even into the fifties and sixties for Japanese to get good jobs. Nothing was ever quite the position my father felt he deserved. The third reason was that my parents were dissatisfied with their marriage, and somehow, moving seemed to give vent to that dissatisfaction. It was hard to leave our homes, but once we started travelling, a part of me loved that life. . . . I remember how fine it was to drive through the passage of light from morning to noon to night. (4)

The perspective of the young Olivia is retained in this passage, which presents the family's predicament as stemming from three disparate causes: inscrutable "bad luck" in keeping jobs, the accident of their Japanese identity, and conflict within the family. The three causes roughly coincide with the difficulties Japanese immigrants had to deal with in postwar America: the economic crisis brought on by slower economic growth, the racializing nationalist discourse that defined Japanese Americans only as Japanese, and the reconfiguring of gender relations within the family. *The Floating World* can be read as a narrative of the process by which the adult Olivia reinterprets these seemingly unrelated factors to reach a deeper understanding of each domain and to attain a holistic view of her own social reality that takes into account how a crisis in the U.S. economy fuels exclusionary nationalist sentiments, how the pressure to assimilate puts strain on the most private and intimate relationships, and how changes in employment patterns in the public sphere and rituals and gender roles in the private sphere influence one another.

The constant traveling of Olivia's family undoubtedly reflects their uprootedness and social instability. Yet the evocation of fine moments when the family drives "through the passage of light from morning to noon to night" suggests that there is more to this recollection than the narrator's nostalgia for her childhood. Learning to make a home out of motels and cars, Olivia also moves flexibly across the imagined boundaries between public and private spheres. Far from idealizing this freedom, however, the text shows us Olivia struggling with a claustrophobic sense of confining family ties. The fact that family members have no stable links to the outside world seems to intensify their interdependency and their sense of estrangement from the larger world. Nevertheless, Olivia's experience and her understanding of the shifting boundaries between public and private empowers her to shape and define her identity as a gendered worker-subject. At a hatchery in a little town in Arkansas, Olivia learns about workers' solidarity as well as their exclusionary politics and their cruelty toward people they perceive as misfits or deviants. In the end, she opts to leave her family and the hatchery to carve out a space where she can draw the boundaries for her privacy and her public existence as a worker.

Traveling to repair and restock the vending machines in the Pacific states where she used to travel with her parents, Olivia reckons with the ghost of her father (Jack) and her own past life, which has been defined by him and what he represents: family legacy, disillusionment, racialized subjecthood, and patriarchy. After she has situated her father as a worker "as young as herself" and has "worked silently together" with him (159), she feels that she can move on: "The dry air smelled faintly of gasoline. I still had another stop, and for a moment I began to worry about my work and forgot about Jack. I tried to calculate from the night sky what time it was, but then I gave up. It didn't matter; it was high time I left" (161). This final paragraph of the novel, despite its inevitably visionary nature, doesn't merely level out the conflicts and contradictions surrounding gendered and racialized subjectivities and the public discourses that represent and regulate them. Olivia's sense of resolution here has more to do with holding her ground as a second-generation immigrant-worker-woman subject than with a facile reconciliation with the outside world. Her achievement of mobility and freedom attains significance only in the context of carefully represented conflicts in both the public and private spheres. It goes without saying that not every immigrant woman can free herself from racial and gender conflicts by becoming a self-employed caretaker of vending machines. Yet through the portrayal of Olivia's struggle to attain autonomy and mobility, the novel allows us to take a critical look at the ways racism, the family, patriarchy, and concepts of immigrants, women, and workers define and shape one another.

Kadohata's *The Floating World* attempts to explore the possibilities available to an Asian American female subject seeking to define herself outside the ruthlessly sexualizing and racializing gaze of the dominant culture. We are not arguing that the liberating potential that the text imagines should be the model for all minority cultures. To do so would be to lapse into the binary logic of whites and minorities that indiscriminately lumps together the varying aspirations and ambitions of different minority publics. Rather, we are interested in performing a consciously limited yet focused reading of a cultural text that addresses the issues surrounding public and private spheres, women's work, and female sexuality. We do so with a view toward finding a piece of the puzzle we need to put together to understand the collective imagination of raced and gendered subjects underlying our legal discourses and daily rituals. Ultimately, the puzzle cannot be completed with only those pieces provided by the stories of African Americans and Asian Americans; pieces from the stories of Hispanic American women, Native American women, and others are also needed.

Nancy Fraser begins her article "What's Critical about Critical Theory? The Case of Habermas and Gender" with Marx's definition of critical theory as "the self-clarification of the struggles and wishes of the age."[23] In her subsequent argument for the need to make the issue of gender central in our understanding of the separate spheres model, she fails to explore the relationships and the possible distinctions between struggles and wishes. What if the concept of struggles implies a privileged relation to the public? And what if the concept of wishes implies privatized desire? How do we link these terms when struggles are waged at the level of wishes, as is the case in the texts discussed here? Wishing well and struggling well must not be relegated to separate spheres but must instead support one another within a dialectical relationship. By looking at the nationalized and masculinized public sphere in the United States from the perspective of women of color who must negotiate a skewed and uneven relationship with it, we have attempted to address questions concerning citizenship, family, labor, mobility, and agency. Although we have attempted to bring these texts into conversation with one another, we are not constructing a linear narrative that follows an optimistic trajectory from Lutie's sense of entrapment to Olivia's departure. Rather, we have attempted to scrutinize the narrativization of *both* the struggles *and* the wishes of African American and Asian American female subjects.

The juxtaposition of these two sets of texts enables us to be historically specific about the ways that immigrant and native minority publics[24] differently negotiate the challenge of gaining power and recognition within and across the public-private binary. Our analysis reveals that the discourse of separate spheres organizes these groups dialectically. African Americans are still the most visible minority group in American society, whereas Asian Americans' presence is often obscured, the product of an imaginative amnesia that derives from the tenacity of the black-white polarity. In media representations, Asian Americans typically earn publicity through sanctioned forms of economic or cultural achievement (including assimilation); by contrast, African American "failure" is relentlessly publicized and spectacularized through media accounts of black crime and poverty (as in Petry's text). Within a culture that fetishizes the mobility of the impoverished but hardworking immigrant (to the disadvantage of African Americans, for whom immigration is less likely to figure as a part of American experience), Asian Americans are widely lauded for taking care of themselves. As *Native Speaker* makes clear, Asian Americans are socially rewarded as the model minority because their problems remain private—in this case, are unloaded onto the backs of economically vulnerable Korean American women. African Americans' problems are, by contrast, revealed in the full glare of the media spotlight, where the most impoverished citizens not only are subject to withering and hostile public scrutiny but are represented as presenting their problems to a weakened and vulnerable welfare state that *they,* in their helplessness and poverty, victimize.[25] Because public institutions have historically been more progressive in allowing black participation, they have been relatively dependable sources of black employment; hence African Americans have traditionally found work as social workers or teachers, in post offices and federal government offices, and in the military. African Americans confront the particular injustice of having labored to build the American nation and yet being relegated to the status of noncitizens, a condition so absurd that W. E. B. DuBois coined the phrase "double-consciousness" to describe it.[26] Automatic linkage of the terms *worker* and *citizen* is similarly denied to Asian Americans, who are on the one hand seen as models of industry contributing to the health of the U.S. economy and on the other perpetually denied recognition as full citizens. Asian Americans have come to occupy model minority status in part because of the belief that they are willing to work without demanding the civic reward for work—recognition as citizen-subjects. One of the supposed merits of Asian

Americans is that they are not interested in running for office and do not vote.

It is significant that while African Americans and Asian Americans are seen as inhabiting, respectively, public and private positions within the U.S. popular imagination of race, *both* groups are feminized (in the sense of being marked under the sign of the feminine). Indeed, it is under the rubric of gender—and, in particular, of women's *labor*—that the relation of these differently racialized publics is best elucidated. Although it is more common for the plights of Latinas and African American women to be linked (perhaps because of Asian Americans' status as the model minority), in fact both Asian American and African American women have served as important sources of U.S. domestic labor, where sexual violence is often a consequence of their domestication and sexualization. It comes as no surprise, therefore, that immigrants (often coded as Asian) and welfare mothers (often coded as black) today define the terrain on which the most recent political assaults on public resources have been waged.

Notes

1 The regents didn't stop with university admissions but extended the resolution to cover decisions in hiring and contracting. Thus what was largely represented in the media as a student issue also directly affects labor.

2 Kenneth R. Weiss, "UC Law Schools' New Rules Cost Minorities Spots," *Los Angeles Times,* 15 May 1997.

3 Nancy Fraser, "What's Critical about Critical Theory?: The Case of Habermas and Gender," in *Unruly Practices: Power, Discourse and Gender in Contemporary Social Theory* (Minneapolis: University of Minnesota Press, 1989), 119.

4 Fraser, "What's Critical about Critical Theory?" and "Rethinking the Public Sphere: A Contribution to the Critique of Actually Existing Democracy," in *The Phantom Public Sphere,* ed. Bruce Robbins (Minneapolis: University of Minnesota Press, 1993), 1–32.

5 See Kathy Peiss, "Going Public: Women in Nineteenth-Century Cultural History," *American Literary History* 3 (winter 1991): 817–28; and Mary P. Ryan, "Gender and Public Access: Women's Politics in Nineteenth-Century America," in *Habermas and the Public Sphere,* ed. Craig Calhoun (Cambridge: MIT Press, 1992), 259–88.

6 Peiss, "Going Public," 817.

7 For an argument that nineteenth-century bourgeois women exercised considerable influence and power despite their relegation to the private, see Ann Douglas, *The Feminization of American Culture* (New York: Knopf, 1977).

8 Fraser, "What's Critical about Critical Theory?" 119.

9 Doreen Massey, *Space, Place, and Gender* (Minneapolis: University of Minnesota Press, 1994), 11.

10 Michael Hanchard makes a similar point about the domain of the public sphere in Brazil in "Black Cinderella?: Race and the Public Sphere in Brazil," in *The Black Public Sphere,* ed. Black Public Sphere Collective (Chicago: University of Chicago Press, 1995), 171.

11 In a provocative reading of the Senate Judiciary Committee's confirmation hearings of then Supreme Court nominee Clarence Thomas, Fraser similarly observes that "categories of privacy and publicity are not simply gendered categories; they are racialized categories as well. Historically blacks have been denied privacy in the sense of domesticity. As a result, black women have been highly vulnerable to sexual harassment at the hands of masters, overseers, bosses, and supervisors. At the same time, they have lacked the public standing to claim state protection against abuse, whether suffered at work or at home" ("Sex, Lies, and the Public Sphere: Some Reflections on the Confirmation of Clarence Thomas," *Critical Inquiry* 18 [spring 1992]: 606). Despite the potential of these insights into the interarticulation of race and gender to complicate the separate spheres model, Fraser is left at the end of the article calling, somewhat defensively and resignedly, for additional work: "In any event," she notes, foreclosing further discussion within her own essay, "we need more work that theorizes the racial subtext of categories of privacy and publicity and its intersection with the gender subtext" (606).

12 Patricia Hill Collins, *Black Feminist Thought: Knowledge, Consciousness, and the Politics of Empowerment* (London: Unwin Hyman, 1990), 47.

13 Angela Y. Davis, *Women, Race, and Class* (New York: Vintage, 1981), 237–38.

14 Evelyn Nakano Glenn, *Issei, Nisei, War Bride* (Philadelphia: Temple University Press, 1986), 5.

15 Ann Petry, *The Street* ([1946] Boston: Houghton Mifflin, 1974), 1–2. Further references to this novel will be given parenthetically in the text. See also Barbara Christian, *Black Women Novelists: The Development of a Tradition, 1892–1976* (Westport, Conn.: Greenwood, 1980).

16 See Farah Jasmine Griffin, *"Who Set You Flowin'?": The African-American Migration Narrative* (New York: Oxford University Press, 1995).

17 Within the African American slave narrative tradition, the trope of the slave's flight to freedom is well known. On images of mobility in black migration narratives, see Griffin, *"Who Set You Flowin'?"*

18 Particularly for African American men, prison is a public institution that bears the traces of a dialectical relation both to the street and to home. In prison, not only individuality but actual citizenship is eviscerated, while the individual is reconstituted through new discourses of punishment and rehabilitation. Moreover, while the disciplinary norms of state prisons demand the radical elimination of individual privacy (in shared cells and bathroom facilities, activities that would

be designated private on the outside are made public and collective), prisons mediate the publicity of African American "deviance."

The threat of imprisonment is prefigured in the text when Lutie, a live-in domestic for the Chandlers, a wealthy white family, is present one Christmas morning when Jonathan Chandler commits suicide in the living room. From this incident Lutie learns not only that violence permeates the private lives of white elites but, more importantly, that wealth and status confer the power to enforce a nominal separation of private and public affairs.

19 Chang-rae Lee, *Native Speaker* (New York: Riverhead, 1995), 62. Further quotations from this novel will be cited parenthetically in the text.

20 Gwendolyn Brooks, *Maud Martha* (Chicago: Third World Press, 1993), 180. Further quotations from this novel will be cited parenthetically in the text.

21 Students reading the novel for the first time in an introductory African American literature course have often complained that they are put off by Brooks's modernist style and are "bored" because "nothing happens" in the plot.

22 Cynthia Kadohata, *The Floating World* (New York: Ballantine, 1989). Further quotations from this novel will be cited parenthetically in the text.

23 Fraser, "What's Critical about Critical Theory?" 2.

24 In "Sex, Lies and the Public Sphere," Nancy Fraser makes an enabling distinction between the word *communities*—which falsely implies consensus and univocality within groups—and *publics*—a term that indicates heterogeneity and retains the implication of unity through struggle (611).

25 See Patricia Williams, *The Alchemy of Race and Rights* (Cambridge: Harvard University Press, 1988). Ironically, Fraser's reading of Clarence Thomas's confirmation hearings overlooks the fact that this and other recent highly mediated juridical spectacles (such as the Rodney King beating and Simi Valley trial, and the murder trial of O. J. Simpson), which have often been falsely touted as facilitating public discourse about race and citizenship, attest to the generally intense public scrutiny that attaches to minority (particularly African American) attainments and failures—especially failures.

26 According to W. E. B. DuBois: "It is a peculiar sensation, this double-consciousness. . . . One ever feels his twoness,—an American, a Negro; two souls, two thoughts, two unreconciled strivings; two warring ideals in one dark body, whose dogged strength alone keeps it from being torn asunder" (*The Souls of Black Folk* [(1903) New York: Penguin, 1989], 5).

★ ★ ★ **PART III**

PUBLIC SENTIMENT

Poor Eliza

LAUREN BERLANT

Sentimentality, the ostentatious parading of excessive and spurious emotion, is the mark of dishonesty, the inability to feel; the wet eyes of the sentimentalist betray his aversion to experience, his fear of life, his arid heart; and it is always, therefore, the signal of secret and violent inhumanity, the mask of cruelty.
—James Baldwin, "Everybody's Protest Novel"

Rodgers and Hammerstein's *The King and I* is a rare instance of classic Americana whose subject is not America. Atypical for its time (1949), the lavish musical is set during a fictive imperial crisis in relations between Britain and Siam that involves the deployment of a variety of military and economic pressures.[1] The arrival of Anna Leonowens in Siam reminds us that Britain also exported a civilizing pedagogy dedicated to undermining corrupt forms of authoritarian rule and immoral modes of intimacy through the education of "native" children away from the worlds of their parents and their nation. Yet to describe *The King and I* this way neglects the sensuous spirit of the play: The spectacle continuously overwhelms the story, displaying the King's visibly smooth and muscular body, the palace's surface of shining metal and richly colored fabric, the women's and children's adorable exoticism, and the intensities of erotic and familial life in the world of the palace. Haunted by the love plot that never develops between the Siamese "King" (Mongut) and the British "I" (Leonowens) whom he imports "for bringing to Siam what is good in Western culture,"[2] the play's story nonetheless uses the tragicomic conventions of "the war between the sexes" to express political and cultural antagonisms that also appear here in stereotypic drag as national tragedy and imperial farce.

The scene of this war is the passing into modernity of Siam, for which the King has prepared by insisting that the elite of his nation develop economic, technological, and rational literacy in the ways of the West. He comes to learn from Leonowens, however, that to be modern requires something more than a cultivated mind—it wants an educated heart. But the King's heart breaks, and he dies when he is unable to follow Siam into the moment in which the nation becomes a state of feeling as opposed to a regime of power. As the play proffers the abjected image of the King's waning virility and pompous philosophizing, it sets up a series of organizing antinomies by which the audience can measure the King's and the nation's progress, including East and West, barbarism and civilization, the vulgar and the refined, the vernacular and the literary, the student and the teacher, the brutish and the feminine. These antinomies are haunted and symbolically resolved by a romance with a constellated third term: sentimentality, intimacy, democracy, America.

This is an essay on the unfinished business of sentimentality. It argues that 1) in the United States a particular form of liberal sentimentality that promotes individual acts of identification based on collective group memberships has been conventionally deployed to bind persons to the nation through a universalist rhetoric not of citizenship per se but of the capacity for suffering and trauma at the citizen's core; 2) that this structure has been deployed mainly by the culturally privileged to humanize those very subjects who are also, and at the same time, reduced to cliché within the reigning regimes of entitlement or value; and that 3) the commodities of "women's culture," the first subaltern-marked mass-cultural discourse, especially represent the paradoxes of liberal sentiment, since they not only locate the desire to build pain alliances from all imaginable positions within U.S. hierarchies of value but render scenes and stories of structural injustice in the terms of a putatively preideological nexus of overwhelming feeling whose threat to the survival of individual lives is said also to exemplify conflicts in national life. "Women's texts" are gendering machines, tracing paths toward survival through plots of feminine feeling that locate the ideality of femininity in fantasies of unconflicted subjectivity in a flowing and intimate world.

The conjuncture of politics and mass norms of affect thereby raises aesthetic questions about the conventions with which exemplary relations have been posited between narratives of the experience and redemptiveness of personal suffering and the collective circumstances in which these plots are inevitably placed. The archive of this essay—*Uncle Tom's Cabin* and a set of related texts, including *The King and I, Dimples, The Bridges of Madison County,* and *Beloved*—inhabits many positions within the domain of the politico-sentimental aesthetic and enables us to understand the ways its conventional forms and ideologies of feeling have influenced the construction and valuation of subjects, types, and publics in the United States since the mid-nineteenth century. Why and how do specific kinds of collective but individually experienced pain get turned into modern forms of entertainment? How do we come to terms with the use of aesthetic conventions of excess (in melodrama, satire, comedy, romance) in processes of national-cultural normativity and critique, insofar as these genres are relied on to express the true suffering and true desires of ordinary persons? How are different types of person and kinds of population hailed by the universalist (but really national) icon of the person who loves, suffers, and desires to survive the obstacles that bind her or him to history? What are the political consequences of the commoditized relation between subjects who are defined not as actors in history but as persons who shop and feel?

Anyone who has seen *The King and I* will know that my title, "Poor Eliza," derives from the scene in which Tuptim, a sexual slave in the King's palace, stages a dramatic adaptation of what she calls *The Small House of Uncle Thomas.* The occasion is a dinner party at which the King is trying to convince the British ambassador of his own and Siam's sophistication, its worthiness to be considered a peer nation in political, economic, and cultural terms. Tuptim's play provides the "native" entertainment. However, she is motivated to perform Stowe's text not to reflect the nation's glory but because this audience is the only sympathetic public she will ever have. The play provides her a licensed opportunity to speak, albeit from a script that she has adapted. Tuptim's complaint is that the King has decreed that she become his currently most favored "wife." She has thereby been denied access to her true love, Lun Tha, and become a prisoner in the King's harem as well as a slave to his sexual will.

Tuptim's hope to build a life around consensual love in a conjugal family rather than the authoritarian rules of royal sexuality crystallizes the play's Cold War–ish espousal of "democratic" individual freedoms in a "modern" capitalist economy. Yet *Uncle Tom's Cabin* is far more than a commercial for U.S.-style democracy in *The King and I.* In the autobiographical text by

Anna Leonowens and its fictionalization by Margaret Landon, there is no royal performance of *Uncle Tom's Cabin*. Its extended acknowledgment here confirms the novel's status as a master sign or supertext, whose reiteration in the twentieth century magnetizes an array of distinct and often conflicting desires about the execution of cultural difference in the global postslavery era. In *The King and I,* the novel's citation touches on the aspect of Stowe's pedagogy that exhorts the nation to embrace the progressive urgencies of a revolutionary historical moment to preserve its ambition to be good as well as great. The citation of *Uncle Tom* here also figures the centrality of the aesthetic to national life. Just as the novel puts forth characters who model virtue for the individual reader, its example is a monument to the fact that inspired art can produce a transformative environment toward which the fallen social world can aspire. The politico-aesthetic tradition of sentimentality associated with the novel is especially animated when a critique of the violently rationalized world is put forth in the name of the authenticity of feeling, especially the feelings of love and suffering, the claims of which stand on the high ground of an ethics beyond politics; sentimental politics are being performed whenever putatively suprapolitical affects or affect-saturated institutions (like the nation and the family) are proposed as universalist solutions to structural racial, sexual, or intercultural antagonism.

It is thus not surprising that very different presumptions about the meaning of the novel's citation are put into play in *The King and I*. For the King, its presence at court is a sign of Siam's modernity: a foreign text translated, an American text appropriated and mastered, a politics consumed that proves the achieved enlightenment of Siamese consciousness. Tuptim's decision to stage the book appears to the King as merely an act equivalent to the other preparations he makes for the event, such as learning Western table manners and adopting Western clothing style to augment the "scientific" knowledge he has cobbled together. Beyond this, however, the King's linkage with *Uncle Tom's Cabin* has already been established through his strong identification with the rationality and wit of "President Lingkong," whom he has been trying to enlist in a plan to bring elephants to the United States to help the North win the Civil War. Lincoln's presence in *The King and I* represents a horizon of possible development for the King, whose voice and body are otherwise staged through a kind of generic Asiatic "bronzeface," his body exposed and his vernacular enjoyed in what a U.S. audience would recognize as minstrel fashion, further highlighting the paradoxical differences and linkages between "their" kind of slavery and "ours." The King's attraction to Lincoln's great and simple wisdom implicitly enables him to imagine saving Siam with similar aplomb at its own time of radical transition. Yet this self-understanding is a joke the play plays on the King. He comprehends the relation between wisdom, greatness, and the abolition of slavery, but he never recognizes the sexual slavery of the harem as relevant to these issues. His speeches about "Lingkong" are staged as funny and stupid, even though the self-misunderstanding he reveals through them has visibly violent effects. But the King's aspiration to be the American president is nowhere quarreled with in the play.

Tuptim's identification with *Uncle Tom's Cabin* also mixes up the personal and the political, but she configures their zones of overlap in distinct and incommensurate ways. "Harriet Beecher Stowa" represents to the slave the unthinkable possibility that a woman can write a book, especially one that challenges the patriarchal national regime that forces her to do sexual hard labor. But Tuptim also identifies with "poor Eliza," whose story inspires her own subsequent flight from the palace. As Lincoln is an emblem for the King, Eliza models for Tuptim the need for the slave's courage to invalidate morally unjust law. Like Eliza, Tuptim breaks the law that has broken itself by escaping to a new space and putting her body on the line to bridge the authoritarian world in which she lives and the emancipated world of freedom and love to which she seeks transport.

Usually the citation of the *Uncle Tom* form involves questions about whether intimacy between and among races is possible in the United States. These questions are frequently played out through love plots in which heterosexual intimacy and gender norms are also deemed fragile. This casts sexual difference and the conventional hierarchies of value associated with it in the United States as vaguely analogous to the scene of racial difference, wherein visible corporeal distinctiveness is explained as something between species and cultural difference. *The King and I* supplements these conventions and reveals their embeddedness in economic and imperial relations by having the King and Tuptim imaginatively enter the War between the States through Lincoln and Stowe. Where they are concerned, the activity of citation marks a desire for identification and translation across nations, lexicons, and systems of hierarchy. It also marks the mobility of categories of privilege and subordination: For example, the King is imperially vulnerable but sexually strong, while Leonowens's lines of privilege are the inverse. For both figures, identification across radically different cultures involves a serious ambition to act courageously, to learn to become something radically different than one is. But the will to appropriate difference to explicate and transform the scene of one's own desire necessarily involves distortion, mistranslation, and misrecognition. In *The King and I,* as in *Uncle Tom's Cabin* and many other texts of sentimental politics, the play between various matrices of "difference" produces comedy amid calamity, making a sort of slapstick of survival. But the desire for vernacularization, the making local of a nonlocal phenomenon, is a serious one as well.[3]

The political tradition of sentimentality ultimately equates the vernacular with the human: In its imaginary, crises of the heart and of the body's dignity produce events that, properly publicized, can topple great nations and other patriarchal institutions if an effective and redemptive linkage can be constructed between the privileged and the socially abject. *Uncle Tom's Cabin* is an archive people come to out of a political optimism that the revolution in mass subjectivity for which it stands might be borrowed for the transformation of other unjust social institutions. The novel's very citation is a sign that an aesthetic work can be powerful enough to move the people who read it into identifying against their own interests. In so doing, the text of sentimental politics figures a radical challenge to the bodies and body politic hailed by it. The artwork is shown to be as potentially powerful as a nation or any world-saturating system: It makes and remakes subjects.

Yet the forces of distortion in the world of feeling politics put into play by the citation of *Uncle Tom* are as likely to justify ongoing forms of domination as to give form and language to impulses toward resistance.[4] In *The King and I,* as in many melodramas, the soundtrack tells this story first, and then the plot follows. Frustrated by the King's imperiousness, Leonowens begins to think of him as a barbarian. But his head wife, Lady Thiang, sings to her: The King "will not always say, / What you would have him say, / But now and then he'll say / Something wonderful."[5] Because he believes in his "dreams" and makes himself vulnerable through that belief, he is, it is suggested, worth loving. He is, in that sense, like a woman, and indeed his patriarchal authoritarianism is revealed as mere bluster. As a result, the King takes on the sacred aura of a sentimental heroine, complete with sacrificial death. This plot turn marks a classic moment of politico-sentimental pedagogy. Although he is a tyrant, the King's story demands sympathy, and then empathy, from the women who surround him. Here they become stand-in figures for the audience, witnessing his death as a process of dramatic de-theatricalization. As the play progresses and the King is "humanized" by feeling and therefore put less on display as a body, the narrative loses focus on the systemic violence of the King's acts. Violence must be taken offstage tactically to produce startling and transformative lines of empathy, but this empathy is mainly directed toward the pain of the privileged for being enslaved by a system of barbarous power in which they were destined, somehow, to be caught.

Can we say something general, then, about the contradictions deliberately or inevitably animated by politically motivated deployments of sentimental rhetoric? Here is a hypothesis: When sentimentality meets politics, it uses personal stories to tell of structural effects, but in so doing it risks thwarting its very attempt to perform rhetorically a scene of pain that must be soothed politically. Because the ideology of true feeling cannot admit the nonuniversality of pain, its cases become all jumbled together and the ethical imperative toward social transformation is replaced by a civic-minded but passive ideal of empathy. The political as a place of acts oriented toward publicness becomes replaced by a world of private thoughts, leanings, and gestures. Suffering, in this personal-public context, becomes answered by survival, which is then recoded as freedom. Meanwhile, we lose the original impulse behind sentimental politics, which is to see the individual effects of mass social violence as *different from* the causes, which are impersonal and depersonalizing.

Thus far, I have focused on the general processes of identification through entextualization that sentimental culture promotes as a way of acknowledging and actually exploiting apparently irreducible social differences to produce a universalism around, especially, modes of suffering or painful feeling. Two other ways of entering the rhetorical conventions of true feeling in the U.S. political sphere also contribute to its symbolic valence: its relation to the feminine and to femininity as a way of living; and its relation to capitalist culture, both at the juncture where abstract relations of value are sublimated into and represented by particular kinds of subaltern bodies and at the place where the magical autonomy of the commodity form (the mirror of the stereotype) is positioned as the disembodied solution to the experience of social negativity or isolation.[6] I will return to the commodity in the next section.

Here let me emphasize the particular place that femininity has played in maintaining optimism around sentimental pedagogy in and about the United States. In Margaret Landon's fictional retelling of Anna Leonowens's books on the court at Siam (Landon's *Anna and the King of Siam* is the source of the musical), a similar domino theory of the *Uncle Tom's*

Cabin effect is put forward: Female authorship leads to female sexual dignity and women's identification across distinctions in racial, class, linguistic, national, and sexual privilege. But in Landon's text the narrative that moves from the end of slavery to the beginning of democratic modernity exists apart from any love plot. In the historical texts it is not Tuptim who resists through Stowe (Tuptim does have illicit love, but she is executed for it).[7] The King's senior wife, Son Klin, brings Stowe into Siam and adopts Stowe as her own epistolary persona.

According to Leonowens and Landon, Son Klin desires not to escape to another man but to identify her way out of her isolation through homosocial sentimentality. Sentimentality is her form of adultery. Son Klin desires to imagine a world where women and kings will violate their privilege, just for a second, to make a fundamental structural shift in the modes of rule that dominate her and her world; she imagines that the sovereign classes might be converted not by principled argument but by being convinced to honor what ought to be their feelings of grief and shame at the scandalous social violences they have been perfectly willing to see as ordinary, or necessary, or hardwired into the system they administer. In this relation to the transformative environment of true feeling about pain, she, too, is a typical sentimental subject. She is not fictional but is transformed by the utopia of fiction into a new kind of person.

Stowe-style sentimentality enables Son Klin to identify against her own privilege with other women in the King's domain. But she can do nothing expressly political about this, apart from learning how powerful affective pedagogy can be. Likewise, in the Rodgers and Hammerstein play, relations of domination are made almost prepolitical, translated into a tactical difference between happy people who know true love and unhappy people who are not civilized enough for it. "Poor Eliza" is placed on spectacular display by Tuptim so that the structural conditions of a genericized subaltern unhappiness might be revealed and empathized with in a way that brings the feeling of a just and happy world into being long before its structural translation in the political sphere has been achieved or concretely imagined. Yet *The King and I*, as it speaks through *The Small House of Uncle Thomas,* marks the space between the real and the fantasy nation by adapting the sentimental rhetoric of sacrifice to its particular locale. In *The Small House of Uncle Thomas* the vehicle for the transformation of the nation into a zone fit for jubilation is neither Christ nor Lincoln but Buddha. Tuptim's Buddha is not identical to the unambiguous Christian savior of Stowe's novel. Feeling virtuous that he has saved Eliza and her baby, the Broadway Buddha actually exacts payment for his deed by sacrificing little Eva (Tuptim): "It is Buddha's wish that Eva come to him and thank him personally for saving of Eliza and baby. And so she die, and go to arms of Buddha."[8]

The King and I thus foregrounds the sacrificial costs to women of critical-sentimental ideology at the same time that it endorses the association of virtuous feeling and proper women as the foundation of a good world.[9] In this, as in so many other ways, the play reproduces conventional sentimental contradictions. Its genres of pain and suffering simultaneously provide pedagogy in proper femininity, valorization of racially and sexually hegemonic normality, and opportunities for critique of the intimate scenes they represent as the experiential real. I have suggested that, historically, the execution of the project of universalizing society through identification with paradigms of pain and love has required much lying about and misrecognition of how to think about relative privilege within the sentimental field of the universal human. In this essay the citation of *Uncle Tom's Cabin* throughout the twentieth century will mark moments in the reappearance of these contradictions as well, which are mainly played out along axes of apparent national nonuniversality—in zones of class, race, and gender. Such citations pose questions central to the story of democratic cultures: What is the relation between the sentimental form of ethical subjectivity and the ideals of liberal culture, which lie about the identity of subjects under the skin, usually in normative terms of feeling? How does the relation between the critical and the universalist tendencies in sentimental discourse produce a confusion between survival and freedom, and between changed minds and changed worlds? Finally, how is this story about race and femininity also a story about the exploitation styles of capitalism and the magical return of value promised by the commodity and the nation form?

The Unfinished Business of Sentimentality

Uncle Tom's Cabin is a much adapted text, one whose moments of comedy and pathos are differently foregrounded in its many recurrences. But the place of "poor Eliza" in this ongoing story is striking: Almost every adaptation of the novel involves an elaborate dramatic staging of the scene where she crosses the Ohio river riding rafts of ice. This event takes less than two pages in the text. Yet it is a powerful scene, electrified by the awesome power of the mother to harness her own sublimity to the sublimity of nature, thus transforming herself into a species of superperson. Even in its syntax the spectacle of Eliza seems to rise out of history and the text, simultaneously flashing into the present tense of the writing and the reading:

> A thousand lives seemed to be concentrated in that one moment to Eliza. Her room opened by a side door to the river. She caught her child, and sprang down the steps towards it. . . . In that dizzy moment her feet to her scarce seemed to touch the ground, and a moment brought her to the water's edge. Right on behind they came; and, nerved with strength such as God gives only to the desperate, with one wild cry and flying leap, she vaulted sheer over the turbid current by the shore, on to the raft of ice beyond. It was a desperate leap—impossible to anything but madness and despair. . . . The huge green fragment of ice on which she alighted pitched and creaked as her weight came on it, but she staid there not a moment. With wild cries and desperate energy she leaped to another and still another cake; stumbling—leaping—slipping—springing upwards again! Her shoes are gone—her stockings cut from her feet—while blood marked every step; but she saw nothing, felt nothing, till dimly, as in a dream, she saw the Ohio side, and a man helping her up the bank.[10]

More than any other scene in the adaptations of *Uncle Tom's Cabin* this one remains unadulterated—elaborated, embellished, naturalized, or made artificial and iconic, but almost never written out of the text, as the death of Uncle Tom frequently is, or reversed, as both Tom's and Eva's deaths sometimes are. This phenomenon recurs even when the story is rendered comic, as in "Felix the Cat in Uncle Tom's Crabbin" (1927), where, as Felix flees Simon Legree by jumping into an ice truck, the intertitle card reads "Felix substitutes for Eliza crossing the ice!"

This one irreverent moment aside, it is worth considering further why the bridge over troubled waters made by Eliza's sublimity survives the continuous transformations of the supertext or semiotic field that *Uncle Tom's Cabin* becomes. In the dramatic texts, this spectacle is often sublimely rendered. Indeed, the dramaturgic and cinematic history shows that if its main purpose is to solicit audience identification with the overwhelming power of the mother's will to survive for her children, the tacit purpose of the adaptations seems often to have been to generate awe at the technological capacities of the play or the film. It makes the spectator merge awe at the woman's power in the face of the danger she endures for freedom, love, and family with the techno-aesthetic power of an entertainment medium to reframe the real, to generate surplus pleasure and surplus pain at the spectacle of the sublime object of sentimentality. Here moral victory and economic survival in plots about vulnerable, desiring, dominated, and powerful women merge with a consumer pedagogy: The act of enraptured consumption becomes inextricable from the moral act of identification.

Additionally, the capacity to experience awe at the bridge sublimely made by Eliza further becomes a sign of personal, cultural, and national modernity, both ideologically and aesthetically speaking. Thus witnessing and identifying with pain, consuming and deriving pleasure and moral self-satisfaction, and imagining these impulses will lead, somehow, to changing the world—this ideological, aesthetic, and capitalist cluster is at the center of the death-driven, pain-saturated, therapy-seeking, and unevenly radical discourse of protest that *Uncle Tom's Cabin* generates. I will turn to two specific later instances of this genealogy; here I want to focus on the way this scene bridges the testifying moral function of suffering—which is the condition that authorizes the reader to imagine changing the world—and the commodified world of aesthetic pleasure, distraction, and instruction that capitalist culture provides. I want to understand how the powerful hunger to know and to adapt the ways other oppressed people survive becomes sutured, with a therapeutic intensity, to acts of consumption; and to know how the virtues of identification with pain have become mediated through plots whose conventions are so formalized that they might as well be things, as though a free gift shimmers inside the tarnished box that promises ever more pleasure.

I have been speaking of conventions, stereotypes, and forms—the diacritics of congealed feeling that characterize the cultural scene of sentimentality. Behind this is a desire to see the sentimental itself as a form, not just a content with scenic themes like those of weeping, sacrifice, and sanctified death. As when a refrigerator is opened by a person hungry for something other than food, the turn to sentimental rhetoric at moments of social anxiety constitutes a generic wish for an unconflicted world, one where structural inequities, not emotions and intimacies, are epiphenomenal.[11] In this imaginary world the sentimental subject is connected to others who share the same feeling. Historically, this involves a fantasy scene of national feeling, which incorporates moments of collective desire, instruction, and identification that persist outside the instability of the everyday. The politico-sentimental therefore exists paradoxically: It seeks out monumental time, the sphere of dreaming and memory, and translates its idealities into an imaginary realm where agency is somehow unconstrained by the normative conventions of the real.

Which is to say that where sentimental ideology is, there will be a drive to separate and compartmentalize fundamental psychically felt social ambivalences in such a way that all the forces in play seem formally equivalent. For example, the critique of patriarchal familialism constantly put forth by sentimental forms can be used to argue against the normativity of the family; yet the sacred discourse of family values within this very domain works to preserve the fantasy of the family as the smallest space of sociability in which flow, intimacy, and identification across difference can bridge life across generations. Likewise, the antisentimental presumption of bourgeois nationalism that proper individual self-management in the everyday will produce nationality in its proper scale has been used to build and to critique identity discourses associated with U.S. subaltern classes,[12] and, on the other hand, sentimental rhetoric is deployed to describe everything from the timeless psychic unity of citizens possessing a national identity to the fragility of normal culture itself when faced with challenges to its unity or continuity.[13] Meanwhile, social progressives have for over a century represented the ordinary effects of structural suffering in tactically sentimental ways—modes of testimony, witnessing, visual documentation—to critique the fallen patriarchal/capitalist world of proper reason; now this same world has assimilated those genres to describe the psychic effects of multiculturalism on those who once felt truly free, nationally speaking.

What conclusions can we reach from this jumble of ambitions to use and refuse sentimentality in the political sphere? In the history of national sentimentality I have elsewhere outlined, we see that at moments of crisis persons violate the zones of privacy that give them privilege and protection to fix something social that feels threatening.[14] They become public on behalf of privacy and imagine that their rupture of individuality by collective action is temporary and will be healed when the national world is once again safe for a return to personal life. Sentimental politics works on behalf of its own eradication. This utopia of autoerasure constitutes the dream work of sentiment and the culture industry that supports it, and in the heritage of sentimentality the nationally supported taxonomies—in particular those involving race, gender, class, and regional hierarchies—still largely govern the horizon of failure and possibility constructed by sentimental authors and readers. Dreaming is both the site of sentimental criticism and the consoling pleasure of its commoditized expression.

By the phrase *unfinished business,* therefore, I mean to designate the specific conjuncture of adaptation, commodification, and affect that distinguishes this modern and nationally inflected modality of expression. I also mean to describe here the way the semiotic substance of sentimentality has been used not only to hardwire the history of slavery into the forms of affect that have long distinguished modes of pain, pleasure, identity, and identification in the American culture industry, but also to see specifically the ways these habits of emotional quotation or affective citation redraw the meanings of American history, in two ways. First, as Jane Tompkins and many after her have demonstrated, sentimentality signifies redefinition, and in the United States the definitions of power, personhood, and consent construe the scene of value in the political public sphere in such a way that any account of sentimentality has to be an account of change and of an ideology of change that explains what gets to count as historic change and what kinds of activities fall out of the dominant definitions. Second, the history of the deployment of sentiment has generated its own archive of gestures, structures, and identities of emotion, prostheses, and modes of commentary that come to signify a metaculture, a place where "adaptation" itself, as a form of domination, fantasy, and necessity, is consented to and worked out. That sentimentality always designates the activity of a transition and an ideology of adaptation to necessity means that the signs of surplus enjoyment, surplus pain, or sublimity itself, made on behalf of the sentimental subject for whom authors reimagine the real world, will link the overwhelming pressures to survive everyday life and overwhelming desires to inhabit an imaginary space of transcendent identity whose mirror of the quotidian allows the utopian and the practical to meet intimately, and in a text you can buy that will give you an experience you cannot, at this time, have elsewhere. We might call this aesthetics of remediation a space of disinterpellation or uncanny self-misrecognition because to benefit from the therapeutic promises of sentimental discourse you must imagine yourself with someone else's stress, pain, or humiliated identity. The possibility that through the identification with alterity you will never be the same remains the radical threat and the great promise of this affective aesthetic.

The Slave's Dimples

The publication of *Uncle Tom's Cabin* immediately generated an entire industry of toys that appeared to turn the fascinating text of pain and survival into new kinds of pedagogical pleasure involving play about slavery. Thomas Gossett reports that "the novel inspired a whole new industry of souvenirs of its leading characters. Enterprising manufacturers hurriedly produced candles, toys, figurines, and games based upon it. One of the games had players compete with one another in reuniting members of slave families."[15] That competition for control of the zeitgeist of national modernity became an after dinner pastime in bourgeois America of the 1850s does not diminish the importance of *Uncle Tom's Cabin* as a figure for the power of a commodity to shock its consumers into a contemporary crisis of knowledge and national power; indeed the novel's capacity to shock has become a continually revived beacon of what the collaboration of capitalism and aesthetics might do to change the course of history, the practices of power, the wounds of identity, or the effects of fantasy. Its referential status as both a hallowed democratic treasure and a bit of banal Americana has everything to do with the way it unsettles the distances and relations between privacy and the public sphere. The toy form of the novel brings politics into the home much as the novel form did, but this time the consciousness it produced must be shared and noncontroversial, requiring a group consensus about what winning would mean, where evil resides, and how to read the moral meaning of different deaths.

The aesthetic and public reverberations of the novel, which helped establish it as the proprietor of a semiotic field of fantasy identifications, were most powerfully registered in the American theater. Here, Stowe's almost Benjaminian concern that the aversive content of contemporary American life be registered in the dramatic spectacle of images that burn feelings into the shocked souls of consenting readers became available to the mediations of embodied spectacle. That is to say, *Uncle Tom's Cabin* and the texts it spawns signify both specific historical crises and the technologies of displacement, achronicity, or catachresis made available by the power to recast and to change the world represented by this tradition of the novel. George Aiken's stage melodrama of 1852 initiated hundreds of popular adaptations; at least six feature films (and many more, if you count partial productions, such as in *Dimples* and *The King and I*) have been made, along with a few cartoons. All shuttle between comic and melodramatic racial representations, and use the codes of slave music and slave death to signify some relation between personal and collective encounters with power.[16] For example, from the 1903 Edwin S. Porter–Thomas Edison adaptation on, slaves are constantly depicted while dancing. But their dance has an elastic meaning, signifying either slave humanity—dance as the only cultural production and site of pleasure the slaves own—or the greatest imaginable abjection to the master culture, as when slaves dance on the auction block or when little Harry dances his way into the slave trader Haley's heart in Pollard's 1927 production.[17]

The centrality of dance, music, and performance to the scene of spectacular identification in the *Uncle Tom* archive became another important bridge between the personal and public narratives of political pain that became an entertainment industry in the years after *Uncle Tom* changed the ways people saw fiction's potential efficacy as evidence for radical thinking. The black/white, slave/free, South/North formulas put into play by the "period" narrative paradoxically provide an achronic image of national taxonomy onto which other forms of cultural domination become mapped. In contrast to gender, whose styles are constantly undergoing transformation, race and nation figure monumentally, in tragic/utopian time, a space of time where meanings are set apart from their circulation in the everyday.

A most spectacular example of the mass-cultural processes by which historical specificity is (mis)translated, via the *Uncle Tom* form, into the unchanging space of sentiment beyond history was produced in 1936, when Shirley Temple, as beautiful as Eva and as comic as Topsy, took on the form in *Dimples*. As in all of Temple's juvenile films, the narrative presumes that personal and public catastrophes have preceded the narrative, which seeks to deliver Temple and her intimates from the bad fate they portend. In the classic mode of the historical romance, the redemption of the heroine would be incomplete if her world were not redeemed with her: *Dimples* is multiply framed by narratives of crisis and cultural struggle that indicate the domain of the metropole, the nation, and Temple's particular audience. The film opens with the following preamble: "Little old New York was neither old nor little in 1850. . . . It was a metropolis of half a million, in which decent folks were beginning to tolerate the theater and young radicals argued against so respectable an institution as slavery."

The theatrical, abolitionist, and youthful rebellion against stale parental proprieties, the sense of an imminently grand national modernity: This constellation of reverberating changes distinguishes the sentimental genealogy of the *Uncle Tom* form. Yet the story *Dimples* mainly tells is of a white child who sells herself to a childless white woman for $5,000. "Dimples" (Temple) does this to keep her con artist grandfather out of jail—not for conning someone but for being conned by men who convince him to "invest" in an ersatz watch thought to have been Napoleon's, a sentimental gift from Josephine. The professor (Frank Morgan) is vulnerable to this con both because he is vulnerable to love and because the "Appleby" family of which he is the surviving patriarch is said to have discriminating tastes. These contradictions make him potentially educable in the terms of sentimental pedagogy. Prior to the con, in the depths of the depression, the professor makes a living by training Dimples and her friends to sing and dance on the street while he picks the pockets of the audience. The film opens amid one of their performances, moving from a close-up of the adorable Temple singing with a mixed-race group of street urchins to the exposure of the professor as a scoundrel and a thief. The loyal Dimples doesn't believe that he could be so venal because he is an "aristocat." Like the King in *The King and I,* she has only a partial, vernacular, and innocent understanding of the social form she so admires. The film further emphasizes the quotation marks it places around the U.S. fetishism of aristocratic taste by having Stepin Fetchit play the professor's "valet," although there is neither money nor food, and although they live in a hovel. Fetchit takes a lot of awful verbal abuse, but the professor, of course, is soundly revealed as the bigger fool.

One might have thought the money the professor invests in Napoleon's watch justly lost had it been acquired in a con. But, in fact, at a time when he had been trying to go straight, he had been entrusted with it during the pre-production days of what the film deems an authentically valuable artwork: the first dramatic production of *Uncle Tom's Cabin,* in which Dimples has been cast as Little Eva. Dimples sells herself to Caroline Drew, the lonely old aristocrat, so that her grandfather can go free and the play can go on.

As with *The King and I, Dimples*'s motives for citing *Uncle Tom* involve a reframing of what, in better times, might have been called "the public and the private." The cinematic image inevitably violates the fantasy of these bounded territories, which hold thematically only when no surprising exchanges take place between the home and the world, which is to say never, or at least mainly offscreen. But in a time of dire financial straits, the aristocratic home is permeable by the streets, while the streets provide a kind of stability the home no longer has; the middle class is imminent and here represents the fulfillment of a national utopian promise. Aristocrats are lonely and nonreproductive, and on the streets everyone knows everyone else's slapstick or tragic story and is happy to do so. Meanwhile, the ascending middle class meets its like at the theater, where it goes for pleasure and instruction. Since the theater stands here for the public sphere, popular culture generally is the space where identifications as middle class can be made by anyone of any social position. The inclusive affects produced by the productive consumption of these commoditized identifications are implicitly foundational for national democracy.

The generic and ideological traces of politico-sentimentality are everywhere in the film. The opening crisis of the genteel professor's economic malfeasance (shades of *The Wide, Wide World*) locates the film in that space between feminism and conservative femininity in which the female complaint resides, but here the complaint is barely audible, as when Dimples says to her future owner, the dowager Caroline Drew, "Sometimes I wonder whether men are worth all the trouble they give us." The film then spends the rest of its time showing that they aren't, but ultimately it doesn't matter, once *Uncle Tom's Cabin* translates the racially, economically, and sexually incommensurate audience into a shared mass of empathetic feeling. These intimacies are mirrored by the way the play of *Uncle Tom's Cabin* is interpellated into the film. In the mirror that the play implicitly claims to provide, the national and domestic divisions of slavery are dissolved by the sacrifice of virtuous citizens of all ranks; meanwhile, the double transformation of history into a novel and the novel into a theatrical commodity brings into being a sentimental way of reading that turns any audience into properly sentimental citizens. In the sentimental mise-en-scène all texts are docudramas, their realism narratively intensified into a kind of soft surrealism that constitutes the really real. In *Dimples,* the play of *Uncle Tom's Cabin* is staged straight, in a way, with a blackface Uncle Tom and Topsy, and Temple ethereal in Little Eva's deathbed scene. But throughout, police are running across the stage, and the professor, disguised as Uncle Tom to hide from them, follows the "real" Uncle Tom on stage, leading to a standard slapstick double-take. Nonetheless, these hilarities and exaggerations provide an even more powerful negative frame for the uninterrupted sentimental auratic of the narrative proper. Crises from every aspect of the entire plot are resolved through these particular tears—except, of course, for the racial and sexual ones.

Thus the critique of value *Dimples* offers is not primarily a sexual or a racial one. As often, the plots of racial and sexual difference provide a pseudo-clarifying ruse for less visible crises of social relation. The film's big questions engage the relative value of a capitalism that sustains aristocratic rankings and mentalities versus one in which class mobility makes plausible the fantasy of everyday democratic experience. The film makes no bones about its democratic affiliation: it is against families and lineages, and for consumer identifications, that is to say, for the middle class, which must reinvent the family. There are no mothers in the film, no Eliza at all, and therefore no one to save the child; nor are there fathers. Each major adult woman is an idiot or an evil, authoritarian, or narrow-minded dominatrix, while men are ineffectual at best. The play disinherits the familial grounding of sentimentality, replacing it with the intimacy of consumers who have had the same moving experiences watching the play.

The argument the film makes for market democracy situates its plot in the difference between two kinds of acting: acting on the legitimate stage, which performs sentimental pedagogy to congeal the passive liberalism of the ascending middle classes, and acting on the street, in which kids simply entertain the mix of people who pass them by, making no pretense to educate or to appeal to higher values. When these two plots mix and produce the dramatic spectacle of Shirley Temple playing Eva, *Dimples* cites *Uncle Tom's Cabin* to link methods of survival on the street and in the parlor to an aesthetic that translates the static status hierarchies of rank, race, and gender into the mobile and labile improvisations of democracy, which the film takes enormous pleasure in at every moment—for example, in the moment after the play when, victorious in making the elite meet the street on behalf of completing the family form broken up by the depression of 1850, the first minstrel show ever performed in the North is supposedly staged in the film's last moments, Dimples fronting a mixed-race chorus of men in blackface singing the song "Miss Dixiana" and dancing like Bill Robinson, as though the South had already, by 1850, been reduced to the region of minor, archaic, and uncanny culture the North has used as its plaything and exteriorized bad conscience ever since.[18]

In addition, as if the representation of this set of different historical stresses weren't entertaining enough, one more contemporary motor for the anachronistic deployment of the "Uncle Tom" form in *Dimples* must not be elided: the Depression. Right after the caption in the opening shot describes the film's location in a radical double movement of modern aesthetics and modern race politics, the camera pans to a sign that says, "Vote Pierce for President! He'll get us out of the depression by 1852!" Charles Eckert has argued that Shirley Temple, along with the industry of commodity like-nesses she generated, was a crucial ideological form for overcoming labor and displacing it from the scene of national fantasy that needed revitaliz-ing after the devastating effects the Depression had had on the modern American ideology of world expansion and political, economic, and cul-tural imperialism.[19] All of the Shirley Temple films of the early 1930s figure her as outside the conventional forms of the family, of bourgeois security, of money; and all place her sympathies and tactical victories squarely on the side of marginal cultures, outside the glamour practices and aspirations of the metropolitan North. She came to represent a mass fantasy of vic-tory over the Depression, helping return a spectacular and ordinary pleasure to thinking about surviving an impossible everyday life where there is no food, no shelter, no future to imagine securing the health and dignity of Americans regardless of their status. Thus the depression of 1850 is a stand-in here, and the story about slavery, poverty, gender domination, and rank—in which only entertainment culture is a healthy enough economic machine to displace the blues, replace the play money with the real thing, and put food on every table and a dimple in every cheek—substitutes for the project a contemporary America should once again desire to undergo.

Here, as elsewhere, the citation of the *Uncle Tom* form displaces the jere-miad, with its political critique made in the language of power; instead, the *Uncle Tom* form aspires to transfigure the public sphere through the force of congealed mass feeling and builds a bridge toward representing new realms of freedom by making a virtue of theater going. As long as the sentimen-tal social problem play is consumed, it implies, virtue will generally prevail. Meanwhile, the painful realities of national, capitalist, and heterosexual cul-ture can be displaced, every once in a while, by a good old Dixie song, sexy dancing and singing, and other kinds of delighted (but not enlightened) consumer distraction. None of this is taken seriously in *Dimples;* the chil-dren's film, a debased genre like the U.S. musical, implies the impossibility of a dignified relation to the state, to politics, and to capital. Personhood is defined by its vulnerability to humiliation, and victories are, at best, per-sonal ones. Consumers can work on the space of diminished agency that individualized worlds of intimacy provide; meanwhile, the moral work of entertainment culture is to work through the scene of national trauma, ex-tracting from it the pleasure and pathos one must have to be moral, but no more.

This Is (Not) a Story to Pass On

In the genealogy we have been tracking, sentimental modes are tactically appropriated to produce political worlds and citizen-subjects who are regulated by the natural justice that is generated by suffering and trauma. But the *Uncle Tom* form has also engendered a parallel universe of textual resistance—to the *Uncle Tom* form itself. First and foremost, this constellation of dissident texts refuses to reproduce the fascinated pleasure-in-violence so spectacularly hardwired into the white and U.S.-identified memory of slavery, even when that memory is used reparatively to express white guilt or national apology. The use of the *Uncle Tom* form against its fundamental claims involves a refusal to elevate the ethic of personal sacrifice, suffering, and mourning over a politically "interested" will to socially transformative action; and it repudiates a tendency to use self-exonerating rhetorical distractions like slapstick, romance, or tragedy to draw a self-critical boundary between an "enlightened" present and an unfortunate past.

An author's or text's refusal to reproduce the sublimation of subaltern struggles into conventions of narrative satisfaction and redemptive fantasy might be called "postsentimentality," a resistant strain of the sentimental domain. Plots in this mode remain saturated by the ideal of a "one people" that can absorb all difference and struggle into a sponge of true feeling. That metacultural ideal of liberal empathy is so embedded in the horizon of ethico-political fantasy that alternative models—for example, those that do not track power in terms of its subjective effects—can seem inhuman, hollow, and irrelevant to the ways people experience optimism and powerlessness in ordinary life. Postsentimental narratives are lacerated by ambivalence: They struggle constantly with their own attachment to the promise of unconflictedness and intimacy with which the U.S. sentimental tradition gifts its politically exhausted and cynically extended citizens. Tableaux of effective domestic pedagogy, moral praxis, and sheer peace dominate narratives that exemplify concepts of justice and freedom in tales of personal destiny. How to deprivatize politics without merely demonizing the fantasy state liberalism proposes?

What distinguishes these critical texts are the startling ways they struggle to encounter the *Uncle Tom* form without reproducing it, declining to pay the inheritance tax. The postsentimental does not involve an aesthetic disruption to the contract sentimentality makes between its texts and readers—that proper reading will lead to better feeling and therefore to a better self.

What changes is the place of repetition in this contract, a crisis frequently thematized in formal aesthetic and generational terms. In its traditional and political modalities, the sentimental promises that in a just world a consensus will already exist about what constitutes uplift, amelioration, and emancipation, those horizons toward which empathy powerfully directs itself. Identification with suffering, the ethical response to the sentimental plot, leads to its repetition in the audience and thus to a generally held view about what transformations would bring the good life into being. This presumption, that the terms of consent are transhistorical once true feeling is shared, explains in part why emotions, especially painful ones, are so central to the world-building aspects of sentimental alliance. Postsentimental texts withdraw from the contract that presumes consent to the conventionally desired outcomes of identification and empathy. The desire for unconflictedness might very well motivate the sacrifice of surprising ideas to the norms of the world against which this rhetoric is being deployed. What, if anything, then, can be built from the very different knowledge/experience of subaltern pain? What can memory do to create conditions for freedom and justice without reconfirming the terms of ordinary subordination? More than a critique of feeling as such, the postsentimental modality also challenges what literature and storytelling have come to stand for in the creation of sentimental national subjects across an almost two-century span.

Three moments in this genealogy, which differ as much from each other as from the credulous citation of *Uncle Tom's Cabin* we saw in *The King and I* and *Dimples,* will mark here some potential within the arsenal that counters the repetitious compulsions of sentimentality. This essay began with a famous passage from James Baldwin's "Everybody's Protest Novel," a much-cited essay about *Uncle Tom's Cabin* that is rarely read in the strong sense because its powerful language of rageful truth-telling would shame in advance any desire to make claims for the tactical efficacy of suffering and mourning in the struggle to transform the United States into a postracist nation. I cited Baldwin's text to open this piece not to endorse its absolute truth but to figure its frustrated opposition to the sentimental optimism that equates the formal achievement of empathy on a mass scale with the general project of democracy.

Baldwin's special contribution to what sentimentality can mean has been lost in the social-problem machinery of mass society, in which the production of tears where anger or nothing might have been became more urgent with the coming to cultural dominance of the Holocaust and trauma as models for having and remembering collective social experience.[20] Currently, as in traditional sentimentality, the authenticity of overwhelming pain that can be textually performed and shared is disseminated as a prophylactic against the reproduction of a shocking and numbing mass violence. Baldwin asserts that the overvaluation of such redemptive feeling is precisely a condition of that violence.

Baldwin's encounter with Stowe in this essay comes amid a general wave of protest novels, social-problem films, and film noir in the United States after World War II: *Gentleman's Agreement, The Postman Always Rings Twice, The Best Years of Our Lives*. Films like these, he says, "emerge for what they are: a mirror of our confusion, dishonesty, panic, trapped and immobilized in the sunlit prison of the American dream." They cut the complexity of human motives and self-understanding "down to size" by preferring "a lie more palatable than the truth" about the social and material effects the liberal pedagogy of optimism has, or doesn't have, on "man's" capacity to produce a world of authentic truth, justice, and freedom.[21]

Indeed, *truth* is the key word for Baldwin. He defines it as "a devotion to the human being, his freedom and fulfillment: freedom which cannot be legislated, fulfillment which cannot be charted."[22] In contrast, Stowe's totalitarian religiosity, her insistence that subjects "bargain" for heavenly redemption with their own physical and spiritual mortification, merely and violently confirms the fundamental abjection of all persons, especially the black ones who wear the dark night of the soul out where all can see it. Additionally, Baldwin argues that *Uncle Tom's Cabin* instantiates a tradition of locating the destiny of the nation in a false model of the individual soul, one imagined as free of ambivalence, aggression, or contradiction. By "human being" Baldwin means to repudiate stock identities as such, arguing that their stark simplicity confirms the very fantasies and institutions against which the sentimental is ostensibly being mobilized. This national-liberal refusal of complexity is what he elsewhere calls "the price of the ticket" for membership in the American dream.[23] As the *Uncle Tom* films suggest, whites need blacks to "dance" for them so that they might continue disavowing the costs or ghosts of whiteness, which involve religious traditions of self-loathing and cultural traditions confusing happiness with analgesia.

The conventional reading of "Everybody's Protest Novel" sees it as a violent rejection of the sentimental.[24] It is associated with the feminine (*Little Women*), with hollow and dishonest capacities of feeling, with an aversion to the real pain that real experience brings. "Causes, as we know, are notoriously bloodthirsty," he writes.[25] The politico-sentimental novel uses suffering vampirically to simplify the subject, thereby making the injunction to empathy safe for the subject.

Of course there is more to the story. Baldwin bewails the sentimentality of Richard Wright's *Native Son* because Bigger Thomas is not the homeopathic Other to Uncle Tom after all, but one of his "children," the heir to his negative legacy.[26] Both Tom and Thomas live in a simple relation to violence and die knowing only slightly more than they did before they were sacrificed to a white ideal of the soul's simple purity, its emptiness. This addiction to the formula of redemption through violent simplification persists with a "terrible power": It confirms that U.S. minorities are constituted as Others even to themselves through attachment to the most hateful, objectified, cartoonlike versions of their identities, and that the shamed subcultures of America really are, in some way, fully expressed by the overpresence of the stereotypical image.

For Baldwin, the pleasure of the stereotype and the narratives of dominant and revolutionary violence waged on its behalf constituted his fundamental experience of the white aesthetic. Yet his narrative of his cultural formation, *The Devil Finds Work,* opens with a stunning revelation about the place of *Uncle Tom's Cabin* in his childhood:

> I had read *Uncle Tom's Cabin* compulsively, the book in one hand, the newest baby on my hipbone. I was trying to find out something, sensing something in the book of some immense import for me: which, however, I knew I did not really understand. My mother got scared. She hid the book. The last time she hid it, she hid it on the highest shelf above the bathtub. I was somewhere around seven or eight. God knows how I did it, but I somehow climbed up and dragged the book down. Then my mother, as she puts it, "didn't hide it anymore," and, indeed, from that moment, though in fear and trembling, began to let me go.[27]

The narrative of self-development Baldwin tells is here linked to familial separation and reading against the grain. Baldwin has the sentimental education he is meant to have (the memory of a mother's protection), and at the same time he distorts it into a course on revolution. *A Tale of Two Cities* joined Stowe's novel in Baldwin's childhood imaginary; the characters were his "friends" and, in many senses, his bridge to another world. First, they constituted a realm of pleasure and beauty outside the family; here the intro-

duction of Baldwin's aesthetic education comes right after a long description of his physical and general repulsiveness to his father, who beat and
taunted him not because they had no genetic relation but either because
he was so ugly or because he was a child and therefore a general "burden."
Second, these novels introduced Baldwin to the language of "revolution"
everywhere saturating his contemporary political world—in Spain and in
U.S. and international workers movements, which included socialist and
labor party activities. But, he says, "I could not see where I fit in this formulation, and I did not see where blacks fit."[28] In short, whatever message
of submission Baldwin sees radiating to U.S. liberals from the *Uncle Tom*
form, he also sees an education in eloquence about pain: how to escape the
negativity of familial inheritance through immersion in the book's imaginary world, how to read history in the body and to identify across genres
and modes of personhood, how to twist what art makes available for fascination into a mode of learning that repudiates the redemptive, normalizing,
and soul-killing demands of properly sentimental personhood.

For Baldwin, the narratives and forms of mass culture provide a schooling in alternative worlds. Its powerful texts do not bind him to his social
negativity but mark the conditions for reading everything as a utopian narrative, provide a map for new conventions of expression and beyond—for
revolution. The revolution in the aesthetic sphere of feeling Baldwin senses
as a positive legacy has recently resurfaced in an uncanny context, with the
publication of Robert Waller's *The Bridges of Madison County*. The novel,
in contrast to the film, has no explicitly racial engagement, traversing the
realm of sexual and national difference in the conventional terms of domestic melodrama and feminine crisis. Frank Rich, writing in the *New York
Times Magazine,* was the first to suggest that the best seller is best understood as the *Uncle Tom's Cabin* of the 1990s, although Waller's novel makes
no internal claim to such a genealogy.[29] But its placement there by Rich
is not fundamentally thematic; it concerns the effects the novel has on its
readers, who read into it a text of liberation from the silences around the
quotidian unpleasantness of heterosexual intimacy, a female complaint. The
imminent social change that citation of the *Uncle Tom* form always heralds
was also accompanied by its other historic legacy, a commodity cluster (a
cookbook, the novel, a CD, a calendar, coffee-table books of photographs
of Madison County, parodies, and other paraphernalia).[30] But Rich's ani-
mation of this genealogy is not merely an instance of the farce wrought by
tragedy's repetition. *The Bridges of Madison County* too resists the sentimen-

tal reiteration whose conventions make it intelligible and marketable, and in a number of ways.

The Bridges of Madison County is *Uncle Tom's Cabin* and *The Key to Uncle Tom's Cabin* rolled into one. A text that can only be described as ersatz—pseudo-novel, -biography, -diary, and so on—it nonetheless uses these variously realist genres to pronounce its authenticity. Like the lovers themselves, the novel claims to be the vanishing point of all that is redeemable in history. The author, Robert James Waller, writes in his framing narrative that he wants to take up the decay and failure of possibility that currently casts history as a record of small and big deaths (of persons, souls, and cultures); he wants to help modern persons be something other than tourists visiting the museums and the unlivable landscapes of their own lives. He wants to represent how to reimagine the sublime encounter between the time and space of the nation and the overwhelming difficulties of everyday life for men and women whose modalities of action, abstraction, violence, and desire within normal life progressively empty them out rather than constitute a well-lived life. But *Bridges* is installed in the genealogy of *Uncle Tom's Cabin* not only because Waller wants to emancipate individuals and nations from the enervating and death-filled present they are generating; he also wants to give his readers the aesthetic tools—through an idiosyncratic model of the photograph—to help them read their lives as evidence for a still shapable future. Like Baldwin's work, this postsentimental text repudiates the compulsion to repeat normative forms of personhood across generations, and refuses to disavow the aggression at the heart of intimacy's institutions. Love is the emancipating vehicle for this new knowledge, but this version of love has a new concept of the archive.

Bridges attempts this by telling of a four-day love affair that started "on a hot dry Monday in August 1965," of the revolution in feeling that followed, and of the archival and autobiographical inheritance the woman, Francesca Johnson, left her children, which we, the readers of the novel, now inherit also and have the responsibility, presumably, to revive as something like a collective project. Robert James Waller has been transformed by the writing of *The Bridges of Madison County,* he tells us, in this particular way:

> Preparing and writing this book has altered my worldview, transformed the way I think, and most of all, reduced my level of cynicism about what is possible in the arena of human relationships. Coming to know Francesca Johnson and Robert Kincaid as I have through my

research, I find the boundaries of such relationships can be extended farther than I previous thought. Perhaps you will have the same experience in reading this story. That will not be easy. In an increasingly callous world, we all exist with our own carapaces of scabbed-over sensibilities. Where great passion leaves off and mawkishness begins, I'm not sure. But our tendency to scoff at the possibility of the former and to label genuine and profound feelings as maudlin makes it difficult to enter the realm of gentleness required to understand the story of Francesca Johnson and Robert Kincaid. I know I had to overcome that tendency initially before I could begin writing.[31]

Now the story of *The Bridges of Madison County* might best be understood, as so many politico-sentimental texts are, as involving the construction of a revolutionary transformation of world and personal history. The text wants to make vital, sensual experience out of the linkage between the person and the world; this involves a wild juxtaposition of incommensurate knowledges, of things that must be represented as crucial to living according to very different scales. For example, *Bridges* involves the telling of world history through an impossible encounter between modernity and two people, brought into what Stowe calls "living dramatic reality" (622) through a vital emblem that shocks or displaces. The male protagonist, Robert Kincaid, is a photographer who travels around finding the lost moments at which nature and human life meet strangely, and so he works for *National Geographic,* allowing with some sadness the magazine to banalize what he thinks is the ordinary sublimity of organic human and natural existence. The female protagonist, Francesca Johnson, is also a world traveler, an Italian woman whose dreams of a lush life become, wrongly it turns out, condensed in what she calls "the sweet promise of America." She marries a soldier after World War II and comes to live in Iowa. But when Kincaid and Johnson meet, they realize that their tourist lives have been not ends but events in the providential path directed toward their meeting. The radical rupture the lovers make makes it possible to reinvent history, as occluded pasts become possible futures, entirely changing the knowledge and desire archives of these persons. From the moment they meet, they historicize, telling the stories of where they have been, reading their meeting as an event produced by all the evolutionary and civilizational activity of the world, making all of their knowledge into memories of love and thereby sanctifying their knowledge, censoring any enigma or uncertainty that might threaten its truth.

They generate immediate artifacts, traces: a note saved, jewelry exchanged, photographs taken; and later, after they part, the *National Geographic* where Kincaid publishes his photographs of Madison County, the cameras he leaves to Francesca on his death, and the few letters they exchange. It is as though they create a commodity cluster about themselves for themselves, just as the sentimental text engenders its own spin-offs in the world. *Bridges* is like a medieval love book, an archive of techniques for performing and commemorating love's elevation of ordinariness to profound and world-historical uniqueness. This process involves not only the exchange of things made radiant by proximity to the lover but also the transformation of love into evidence that can be inherited: an archive of photographs, a diary, and a special box to hold everything close.

Yet when Francesca dies and leaves to her middle-aged children this box and a captioning letter that retells the novel's story, she makes it impossible for her progeny to receive the story as something from *their mother:* The mother they knew is not the woman who writes to them; their inheritance is a disinheritance, for they are now forced to make living up as they go along. The children bring the archive to the novel's narrator and tell him the story again. The narrator, who describes himself as a researcher, is also transformed by the material he finds; he turns the box into a book and leaves it to his readers, hoping that they "will have the same experience in reading this story" that he has had, an experience of entering the archive of love to unlearn what they think they know about love's impossibility and to relinquish their feeling of superiority to its "maudlin," sentimental story. Through this repeated process of autoarchiving, the narrator seeks to teach his audience how to reclaim its neglected desire to be in a living story, which is a story worth telling, a genealogy of love that leads to you, specifies your participation in the world, makes you unique as it makes you collective, and extends you into the future as something unimaginable to you now. This doesn't mean that to live you have to fall in love; it means that you at least have to inherit somebody else's story, be changed by what you unlearn from it, and then pass it on as a goad to someone else's unlearning, in the mode of privatized revolution, a cherry bomb in a can. The experienced disjuncture between personal life and history enables the children to reinvent modernity for themselves, which means to transform radically the affectively distorted and muted body living in a world of violence and shame into a newly unscabbed genealogical body of affect and knowledge that will now inhabit not a death-driven nation or a familial blood-knot but a "realm of gentleness."

This transformation is the inheritance readers must reinvest in their lives. Waller reminds us of the dangers of cynical reason, that realm of "enlightened false consciousness" that trivializes ordinary irrational emotion;[32] he wants to show us how a history of overcoming our learned resistance to nonrepetition will, at least for a moment, revitalize the experience of the intimate, the social, memory, and the nation. It is as though Waller had *Uncle Tom's Cabin* on his lap and answered Stowe's not-Marxist-enough cry, "But, what can any individual do?" not by deploying the saga form that allows personal stories to be told as soap operas or epics, the forms of communal storytelling; rather, he tells it the way Stowe imagines her own novel's destination. What can the individual do? "Of that," Stowe writes, "every individual can judge. There is one thing that every individual can do, —they can see to it that *they feel right*. An atmosphere of sympathetic influence encircles every human being; and the man or woman who *feels* strongly, healthily and justly, on the great interests of humanity, is a constant benefactor to the human race."[33] Individuals are the site of experiment; but to tell the story of sentimental radicalism will be to show how "feeling right"— as opposed to feeling "cynical"—about change has become embedded in textual and political conventions whose contradictory bargains with pain, domination, terror, and exile remain the unfinished business of the post-sentimental, which refuses to confuse survival with freedom. But having said this, the thrilling moment of political, public self-transcendence remains limited by the very evanescence of the weapon—consciousness. The revolution that Waller imagines takes the route of the bridge, not the water; as the countless showers and baths in the novel suggest, it is a revolution that refuses to be dirty, or to stay wet. Francesca makes it impossible for her children to inherit her style of intimacy, empathy, survival, and freedom; but Waller contradicts the gesture he writes for her, insisting that this is a story, after all, to pass on, a story about love's power to transform everything important in the world. His is a revolution that preserves the sublimity of the fantasies that already exist, along with what we might cynically call "business as usual."

My aim so far has been to articulate the two very different kinds of strength the *Uncle Tom* form has provided the entertainment industry that continues to constellate around it: to negotiate, as Stowe's novel negotiates, a radical reimagination of the world through an archive of survival tactics; and to witness critiques of the fraudulent claims to popular consent on which American political culture has based its legitimacy and its claims to have elicited popular consent to its domination of what counts as political. Yet the politics of rage and pain and powerlessness that motors so much of the sentimental complaint and protest industry has also been accompanied by a desire for amelioration at any cost. In a sense, the sentimental bargain has constantly involved substituting for representations of pain and violence representations of its sublime self-overcoming that end up, often perversely, producing pleasure both as a distraction from suffering and also as a figure for the better life that sufferers under the regime of nation, patriarchy, capital, and racism ought to be able to imagine themselves having. Sentimentality, unlike other revolutionary rhetorics, is after all the only vehicle for social change that neither produces more pain nor requires much courage. This ravenous yearning for social change, this hunger for the end of pain, has installed the pleasures of entertainment, of the star system, of the love of children, and of heterosexual romance where a political language about suffering might have been considered appropriate. In these ways the very emphasis on feeling that radicalizes the sentimental critique also muffles the solutions it often imagines or distorts and displaces them from the places toward which they ought to be directed.

Written in 1949, Baldwin's exhortation to refuse to pass on the contradictions of sentimental liberalism might be taken up by Toni Morrison, say. For if *The Bluest Eye* casts Shirley Temple and her ilk among the most vicious lying weapons of whiteness, *Beloved* understands that there is no transcendence anywhere—not through a thrilling or a comforting image. Surely *Beloved* quotes "poor Eliza" in its constant return to Sethe's river crossing. But Morrison's novel shows that when you cross the Ohio, you do not transcend it but take it with you. At any moment a woman who has crossed or who descends from one who has risked the water might be walking through the grass thinking sentimental thoughts about the love and family and peace she might experience when she has the time and money and freedom, when suddenly "she had to lift her skirts, and the water she voided was endless," so that a viewer might "be obliged to see her squatting in front of her own privy making a mudhole too deep to be witnessed without shame";[34] or perhaps she would be overcome by singing, "where the voices of women searched for the right combination, the key, the code, the sound that broke the back of words. Building voice upon voice until they found it, and when they did it was a wave of sound wide enough to sound deep water . . . and she trembled like the baptized in its wash";[35] or perhaps, breaking the water of pregnancy lying flat in a boat, she would remember the middle passage or just think about rain and other kinds of beloved weather. Whatever the case, the desire to disinherit a community from the stories that bind it to weepy repetitions of sublime death and dry, safe local entertainments motivates the novel *Beloved* to show that rather than seeking transcendence of the self who exemplifies the impossibility of existence outside history, and rather than merely repeating the tragedies that seemed long ago to constitute whatever horizon of possibility your identity might aspire to, the postsentimental project would have you refuse to take on the history of the Other as your future, or as the solution to the problem of passing (over) water in the present tense. Sethe's flood poses a challenge to the tears of sentimental culture: to refuse the too-quick gratification after the none-too-brief knowledge of pain. Above all it understands that whatever transformation we might imagine being wrought from the world-making effects of identification must start right here, in the place of corporeal self-knowledge that can neither be alienated into the commodity form nor provide instruction and entertainment to audiences committed to experiencing the same changes over and over again. It asks us to demand of the sentimental project that its protests and complaints be taken seriously in themselves, which involves occupying the present tense with no more time for the big deferrals or fantasies of the always imminent time when the nation and heterosexuality finally pay out fully their parts of the bargain through which they have secured social dominance and ideological hegemony. The old motto of sentimentality might be taken from Fannie Hurst: "Every normal female yearns to be a luminous person."[36] But in the meantime, as we wait for the rapture to take place sometime in the always receding future, we might think about living by an interim slogan—perhaps, as Sethe says, "No more running—from nothing."[37]

Notes

1 The British-Siamese-U.S. triangle is an invention of the play. The story Margaret Landon and Anna Leonowens tell is about French, not British, imperialism in the area. See Margaret Landon, *Anna and the King of Siam* (New York: John Day, 1944), and Anna Leonowens, *The English Governess at the Siamese Court: Being Recollections of Six Years in the Royal Palace at Bangkok* (Boston: Fields, Osgood, 1870).

2 Richard Rodgers and Oscar Hammerstein II, *The King and I,* in *Six Plays by Rodgers and Hammerstein* (New York: Modern Library, 1953), 379.

3 On "vernacularization," see Arjun Appadurai, "Disjuncture and Difference in the Global Cultural Economy," in *Modernity at Large: Cultural Dimensions of Globalization* (Minneapolis: University of Minnesota Press, 1996), 27–47.

4 This general conclusion about the overdetermined political story of *Uncle Tom's Cabin* in *The King and I* has also been reached by Laura Donaldson in *Decolonizing Feminisms: Race, Gender, and Empire-Building* (Chapel Hill: University of North Carolina Press, 1992), 32–51. Donaldson's focus is more on the gendering of colonial relations than the politico-aesthetic formalism of such conjunctures.

5 Rodgers and Hammerstein, *The King and I,* 403.

6 On the intimacy of the stereotype, the commodity form, and normal femininity in the U.S. sentimental tradition, see Lauren Berlant, "The Female Woman: Fanny Fern and the Form of Sentiment," in *The Culture of Sentiment: Race, Gender, and Sentimentality in Nineteenth-Century America,* ed. Shirley Samuels (New York: Oxford University Press, 1992), 265–81.

7 In the Oscar-winning film *Anna and the King of Siam* (dir. John Cromwell, 1946), there is no performance of *The Small House of Uncle Thomas,* and Tuptim is very publicly and visibly executed.

8 Rodgers and Hammerstein, *The King and I,* 429.

9 For an excellent summary of the long critical debate about sentimentality's traditional association of feminine sacrifice and feminine power, see Laura Wexler, "Tender Violence: Literary Eavesdropping, Domestic Fiction, and Educational Reform," in *The Culture of Sentiment,* ed. Samuels, 9–19. See also Amy Schrager Lang, "Slavery and Sentimentalism: The Strange Career of Augustine St. Clare," *Women's Studies* 12 (Feb. 1986): 31–54; and Shirley Samuels, introduction to *The Culture of Sentiment,* 3–8.

10 Harriet Beecher Stowe, *Uncle Tom's Cabin or, Life Among the Lowly,* ed. Ann Douglas ([1852] New York: Penguin, 1981), 117–18.

11 Lauren Berlant, "Intimacy: A Special Issue," *Critical Inquiry* 24 (winter 1998): 286.

12 See Wendy Brown, "Wounded Attachments: Late Modern Oppositional Political Formations," in *The Identity in Question,* ed. John Rajchman (New York: Routledge, 1995), 199–227.

13 See Lauren Berlant, "The Intimate Public Sphere," in *The Queen of America Goes to Washington City: Essays on Sex and Citizenship* (Durham, N.C.: Duke University Press, 1997), 1–22.

14 Ibid., 60.

15 Thomas F. Gossett, Uncle Tom's Cabin *and American Culture* (Dallas, Tex.: Southern Methodist University Press, 1985), 164.

16 Here is the major archive from which I draw my conclusions about the film history of *Uncle Tom's Cabin: Uncle Tom's Cabin,* Thomas A. Edison, 1903; *Uncle*

Tom's Cabin, or, Slavery Days, dir. Robert Daly, 1914; *Topsy and Eva,* dir. Del Lord, 1927; *Uncle Tom's Cabin,* dir. Harry A. Pollard, 1927; "Felix the Cat in Uncle Tom's Crabbin'," E. A. Hammons and Paul Sullivan, 1927; and "Uncle Tom's Cabaña," Tex Avery, 1947. There is also a notable tradition of interpellated scenes from *Uncle Tom's Cabin* in films set in other periods, among which are the Shirley Temple vehicle *Dimples* (dir. William Seiter, 1936); Abbott and Costello, *The Gay Nineties* (n.d.); and *The King and I* (dir. Walter Lang, 1956).

17 For more on the racial soundtrack of sentimental texts in the *Uncle Tom* tradition, see Lauren Berlant, "Pax Americana: The Case of *Show Boat,*" in *Institutions of the Novel,* ed. W. B. Warner and Deidre Lynch (Durham, N.C.: Duke University Press, 1996), 399–422.

18 On *Uncle Tom's Cabin* as a text that ambivalently translates regional, sexual, and racial fractures into the generic utopia of sentimentalism, see Lang, "Slavery and Sentimentalism."

19 Charles Eckert, "Shirley Temple and the House of Rockefeller," in *American Media and Mass Culture: Left Perspectives,* ed. Donald Lazere (Berkeley and Los Angeles: University of California Press, 1987), 164–77.

20 See Lauren Berlant, "The Subject of True Feeling: Pain, Privacy, and Politics," in *Cultural Pluralism, Identity Politics, and the Law,* ed. Austin Sarat (Ann Arbor: University of Michigan Press, 1999); and Brown, "Wounded Attachments."

21 James Baldwin, "Everybody's Protest Novel," in *The Price of the Ticket: Collected Nonfiction, 1948–1985* (New York: St. Martin's, 1985), 31, 29.

22 Ibid., 28.

23 James Baldwin, "The Price of the Ticket," in *The Price of the Ticket,* xx.

24 See, for example, Lynn Wardley's summary in her otherwise wonderful essay, "Relic, Fetish, Femmage: The Aesthetics of Sentiment in the Work of Stowe," in *The Culture of Sentiment,* 206.

25 Baldwin, "Everybody's Protest Novel," 29.

26 *Uncle Tom's Children* ([1938] New York: HarperCollins, 1993) was Richard Wright's first published book.

27 Baldwin, *The Devil Finds Work: An Essay* (New York: Dial, 1976), 565.

28 Ibid., 561, 565.

29 Frank Rich, "One-Week Stand," *New York Times Magazine,* 25 July 1993, 54.

30 Among the related commodities bearing the imprimatur of the novel are the film (dir. Clint Eastwood, 1996), the audio cassette, the CD *Remembering Madison County,* plus a large collection of mugs and T-shirts available on the Web. For a sampling of the related books, see Thomas Garrett, *Building Bridges: The Phenomena and Making of* The Bridges of Madison County (Edmonton, Canada: Commonwealth, 1996); Jane M. Hemminger and Courtney A. Work, *The Recipes of Madison County* (Birmingham, Ala.: Oxmoor House, 1995); Rob Hoskinson, *Bridges in Time: Keepsakes Celebrating the Covered Bridges of Madison County* (Stanchfield, Minn.: Adventure Publications, 1995); Ellen Orleans, *The Butches*

of Madison County (Bala Cynwyd, Pa.: Laugh Lines Press, 1995); Robert James Waller, *The Bridges of Madison County: Memory Book* (New York: Warner, 1995).

31 Robert James Waller, *The Bridges of Madison County* (New York: Warner, 1992), xi–xii.

32 Slavoj Žižek, *The Sublime Object of Ideology* (New York: Verso, 1989), 29.

33 Stowe, *Uncle Tom's Cabin,* 624.

34 Toni Morrison, *Beloved* (New York: Penguin, 1987), 51.

35 Ibid., 261.

36 Fannie Hurst, *Today Is Ladies' Day* (Rochester, N.Y.: Home Institute, 1939), 3.

37 Morrison, *Beloved,* 17.

Representative/Democracy:

Presidents, Democratic Management, and the

Unfinished Business of Male Sentimentalism

DANA D. NELSON

People are not born knowing how to be represented, any more than they are born knowing how to be representative. It's worth insisting that the desire for representivity does not come naturally—for individuals or nations— and then thinking about what political, cultural, and aesthetic practices of representivity mean for the practice of democracy. Habitually accustomed to normative representative practices, we are able to register moments of only the most outrageous instances of representative crisis as such. Citizens finally did become outraged during the weeks of Florida recount in the 2000 presidential election of Democrat Al Gore and Republican George W. Bush, but it's amazing how much it takes for there to be a public registering of people's concern that they're not being represented. For instance, there was no public discussion of representational arrogance during the Clinton impeachment hearings when the Senate and House Republican leadership responded publicly to polls citing a general public unwillingness to proceed with the impeachment by dismissing the American public for its stupidity and lack of morals. Instead, cued by the media, everyone worried about a constitutional crisis, an irrelevant term in the context of a constitutional procedure. However inappropriate, the term's application by the media seemed sentimentally calculated: Invoking a constitutional crisis aims at the singular, representative "heart" of the nation. Its invocation works to blunt citizen politicalness: Everyone should worry that the nation is cracking up and remember that we need to "stick together," and "just get along"—in other words, trust and acquiesce to the better judgment of our leadership, who has, after all, our own best interest at heart. The term's application demonstrated how, in Cathy N. Davidson's words, "sentimental fiction tends to go from politics to metaphor to melodrama"—from (probably healthy) civic disagreement to broken heart to constitutional crisis.[1]

Interestingly, when the media tried reapplying that term—*constitutional crisis*—in the aftermath of the 7 November 2000 election, a chorus of political scientists and legal experts chimed in to correct its misapplication. The problem is not a crisis for the Constitution, they insisted, because there are constitutional remedies for this problem. This expert rejoinder returned media commentators to the thornier, more civically divisive question at hand, about political representation. It remains to be seen whether our legislators have the imagination and will to experiment with remedies for the problems that became so painfully clear in the November 2000 election, problems of equal protection, machinery, ballot design, and underprivileged and underliterate voter access. Political representation is not a settled practice in U.S. history: It's a long problem that begins in the constitutional debates. But because simple access to the vote has had such a heroic history, because so many people have fought so hard to have it, the vote itself has seemed the apogee of the representational struggle: *The vote itself* has been understood as settling the question of political representation, of access to our nation's democracy.

This last election perhaps decisively disproved that theory. Now many realize that neither the "right" to vote nor the actual pull of a lever or punch of a chad guarantees the *count* of the vote. People are now legitimately worried that they don't "count." They wonder whether they can trust the equation of a vote and representation; they are questioning the value of their treasured but amorphously defined representation. And so it's worth returning to the question of representation's problematic coordination with democracy. In the context of current questions about electoral reform, there is little discussion of representation's deeper, problematic history in U.S. democracy. Pundits talk about restructuring the electoral college or uniformatizing state ballots and equipment. But the media is not asking deeper questions about, for instance, citizens' expectations for representation, much less their affective relation to representation, either now or historically, and about what kinds of restructuring might come from such investigations. I think these questions are worth a deeper investigation, and for that purpose, in this essay, I'm concentrating on the early years of the nation. Our national origin narrative has concealed the inchoateness of representivity's logic and desires in the founding years, a period in which norms were locally various, in which there was no national representative identification. This essay traces a consolidating logic for national representivity in an early manifestation.

Although it is a widely regarded patriotic fact that the president "stands for" U.S. democracy as its only generally elected representative, in this essay I argue against that national common sense. I suggest that the president stands in a symbolic space of loss in the democratic imaginary. Presidentialism organizes a strong logic for representative practice that works against democracy, teaching us to desire from representation not politicalness but the strong sensation of unconflicted recognition, and indeed a protection from politicalness.[2] It reorganizes representation into representivity, a model of representation oriented toward spiritualized, virtual "wholeness," an aestheticizing relation where citizens cultivate their subjectivity with regard to the ideal "representative," where the formfulness of representivity is offered *as* the subjectivity of citizenship. This mode for sociopolitical being is aesthetic, formalistic, and compensatory: It depends on the (false) ideal that people's particular *desires* can be satisfied through their identification with (singular) representative desire. I regard the practice of presidentially conditioned representivity as the internalized and privatized state of U.S. "democracy," a state haunted by our disavowed agency in equalitarian self-governance.

In this essay, I begin analyzing the political psychology of presidentially representative democracy in its preliminary consolidation. First, drawing on analyses I began developing in my recent book, *National Manhood,* I outline the competing political practices of democracy in the early nation that presidentially representative constitutionalism seeks to sublate. Then I turn to Weems's 1809 *Life of Washington* to show how Weems sentimentally recognizes and pedagogically organizes the antagonistic energies of representative democracy into a telos of presidential representivity. We've been trained when we hear "sentiment" to look for women. This training does not begin with Herbert Ross Brown and Fred Lewis Patee, or even in the antebellum articulation of the separate spheres. In my analysis of Weems's text, I'll be arguing that we must read sentiment not as a "feminine" but a *nationalist* plot that begins in the constitutional reorganization of government and works hand-in-glove with the universalizing, privatizing logic of constitutional representivity.

A set of theoretical claims and critical concerns background my arguments in the third section of this essay about sentimentalism's political redeployment under the representative organization of nation. Let me briefly outline them here. Female ideologies and practices of sentiment, many have recently argued, interiorize and individuate women. It seems to me that a different kind of claim can be made about male sentimentalisms, which temporarily relieve men of the individualism that capitalist citizenship demands. Attending to these male practices amplifies our understanding of sentimentalism's political and social multivalences and reveals that the long-standing, sweeping association of sentiment and sympathy with middle-class women in the nineteenth century is not just wrong but crucially misleading. This association at once overcalculates women's cultural "power" as it underestimates the effective weight of women's putatively private politics in the public/civic sphere. Even more to my interest here, it effectively hides from our critical view the variety of ways men participated in sentiment and the ways their sentimentalism(s) benefited from sentiment's formal association with women.

Only recently have we begun seriously analyzing antebellum practices of male sentimentalism in male plots and texts like patriotism, fraternalism, corporatism, and professionalism.[3] Our developing understanding of male sentimentalisms are adding to and fundamentally qualifying earlier analyses of sentimentality and our debates over the so-called "feminization of American culture." Expanding our study of sentimentalisms to the broader association I suggest here will allow us to fully develop a political (as opposed to gender) analysis of sentiment, one that will help us better understand its energies and susceptibilities.[4] I offer this essay, which outlines some of the ways that presidentialism's sentimentally representative logic *blocked* (and continues to block) the democratic imaginary, as a preliminary contribution toward rethinking of the national training of sentiment.

Inventing Presidentialism

We commonly understand the post-Revolution Confederation (when we think of it) as a weak precursor to national governance, where the debilities of decentralization led directly to the political crisis and economic dissension that necessitated the formulation of a strong national government. Historians have drawn widely on the jeremiads of contemporaries, who worried about the collapse of the Revolutionary project in the face of growing political discontent. However widespread the register of "crisis" among

Americans in the 1780s may have been, it is an assessment historian Gordon Wood has described as "incongruous":

> On the surface at least the American states appeared remarkably stable and prosperous. . . . Both the Confederation government and the governments of the separate states had done much to stabilize the finances and the economy of the country. The . . . Confederation deficit could not be considered serious. Despite a temporary depression in the middle eighties . . . the period was marked by extraordinary economic growth. In fact . . . it was a period of high expectations, clearly reflected in the rapid rate of population growth.[5]

Wood's observation can point us toward a more useful critical unpacking of the anxieties clustered around the amorphous experience of "national" crisis. It's arguable that the constitutional organization of a centralized nation generates the very national crisis it promises to manage.[6] Constitutional proponents persuasively redescribed local difference as national disorder. "Real" or no, then, the *rhetoric* of crisis trained its register toward real effects as constitutional proponents discursively harnessed inchoate anxieties attending emerging social diversity and intensifying class dissent for a focused political counteroffensive against what John Adams had early labeled "democratic despotism"—local and radical reconceptualizations of democratic practice increasingly present throughout the United States.[7]

Contesting the British principle of virtual representation, citizens of the states had begun more and more to insist on radically conceptualized practices of *actual* representation. This movement was expressed in a range of practices, including new, strict residency requirements for representatives, expanded suffrage definitions framed to ensure structures for electoral consent, and a model of equally weighted electoral districts that reflected the one-state one-vote rule of the Articles of Confederation. Even more pointedly, citizens began showing up at legislative sessions to deliver instructions to their delegates. Certainly the laws enacted by these legislatures may have violated some peoples' sense of right order,[8] but these law-making bodies were, as Wood summarizes, "probably as equally and fairly representative of the people as any legislatures in history."[9]

The citizens of the thirteen states intensified their emphasis on the *local* as the best and most proper venue for democratic practice. Though the ratification battle over the Constitution has conditioned us to see "local" as residing at the state level, it's clear that even the state was under attack as being too distant and abstract for the purposes of emerging practices in democratic self-governance. New Englanders had long insisted that the town was the real center for good government and fair representation, and in the early nation, Virginia counties began acting on similar claims. The prioritization of local democratic involvement, of face-to-face democracy, spread rapidly (though never uniformly) across the country, amplified in the increasing phenomenon of extragovernmental organizations of people, in county assemblies, watchdog committees, radical associations and out-of-doors actions.[10] A clear spillover from revolutionary practice, these organizations of citizenship, now too commonly remembered in (or abjected through) the dystopic rhetoric of vigilantism, riot, and mob, were present in every major city and across the countryside.[11] Political theorists and historians alike have failed to recognize, Hannah Arendt has insisted, the extent to which such councils represented a "new form of government, with a new public space for freedom which was constituted and organized during the course of revolution itself."[12] C. Douglas Lummis takes up Arendt's observation as fundamental evidence for radical democracy's gravitation toward the local: "Again and again, in the phase where revolution was still revolutionary, the polity has broken down naturally into units small enough that the people can confront one another in genuine communities, talk to one another, and choose and act collectively."[13]

It's worth pausing here to clarify my investment in reactivating a historical memory of the local within U.S. democracy. Though there is every reason not to idealize locality as place—for the ways in which communities can constitute themselves through rigid, exclusionary, and antidemocratic practices of political and identity sameness—that in itself is no reason to surrender the value of the local for political *practice*.[14] The value of the local for democracy is that it can work to invest us in our own politicalness; it can teach us a greater ease with political negotiation and disagreement, for the hard and messy dissensual work of self-governance. The local is the only place where we can exercise democratic citizenship in its most robust, demanding, nonsynechdocal, nonvirtual sense. Local exercise is the practice through which we make democracy consciously our own, "mix it with our mental and physical labor, undertake risks on its behalf."[15] The local practices of politicalness that Adams described as "despotism" (figuring citizens as obstacles to democracy) are the very practices that, looked at another way, invest citizens in their democracy—a more unevenly conceptualized practice of a more closely actualized form of self-governance. It is important to insist on the historical existence of these nonuniformatized practices of democracy in the early United States, because it is only in so doing that we can understand the way the Constitution does not generate national identity and its political practices in a void so much as it seeks to subjugate local democratic practices, delegating the "local" to the far more manageable form of the state, and abjecting the local in its more radical instances as disruptive to rather than a rich and challenging venue for developing democracy.[16]

Given the widespread outcroppings of and local enthusiasm for emergent democratic practices in the early nation that I've broadly outlined here,[17] the hard question is: Why didn't the proposed structures of the Constitution—centralizing, abstracting, symbolically if not actually potentially monarchical—incur more organized opposition?[18] Why didn't the revolutionary democratic spirit widely expressed in local, face-to-face practices lead people to reject loudly the virtualization of their growing democracy under the Constitution for the way it displaced the relevance of local and direct self-governance?[19] History of ideas offers no real help at this level for explaining not only cross-sectional support but also local acquiescence to ratification,[20] only because it is more concerned with the organized thinking of men at the center of state and national legislatures than it is with the more far-flung, disorganized, uneven practices of less socially and politically advantaged actors. And though arguments about the strategic fiat of the constitutional framers and supporters offers somewhat more explanatory power on this point, arguments about rushed state conventions, stolen newspapers, and bad roads don't explain broad cross-sectional popular support *after* the Constitution's passage.[21]

I've proposed recently that we look in a different direction from political philosophy's debates over liberalism and republicanism, or the Federalists' economic advantages and political machinations, and turn our attention instead to the way that proponents of the Constitution, most famously "Publius," hold out a reformulated ideal of "national manhood"—purified, vigorous, unified—as a counterphobic ideal for the kinds of social diversity and disruption foregrounded in emergently radical democratic practices.[22] In other words, the conditional disunities and frictions of democratic negotiation entailed both by the more explicitly confraternal model of the Articles and by emergent local political practices is reassuringly covered over by an image of strong national unity, embodied in the National Executive.[23] Thus, the discomfiting actuality of fraternal *dis*agreement—a discomfort that always threatens but is entirely fundamental to the possibilities for deliberative democratic self-governance—disappears in the representatively singular body of the president.[24]

Presidential historian Gary L. Gregg has recently reminded us that, under the Articles of Confederation, there was no single executive officer and that "this lack of a central figure within the government was more important than most commentators and historians have noticed."[25] I'm arguing something a little different, that the transition *to* a governmental system headed by a president, a national union embodied in the single person of the president, is more symbolically important to our practice of democracy than we are in the habit of noticing. John Adams had complained against the title of "president" because he found it too mundane and managerial—not sufficiently grand to inspire the respect he felt was necessary to such an office. Here he clearly misgauged the usefulness and versatility of that title for rerouting democratic energy. The *Oxford English Dictionary* tells us that *president* as a term designating the title of a person who "presides over the proceedings of a financial, commercial or industrial company" is an Americanism (the equivalent British usage is *governor*), and records its earliest usage in 1781, when the U.S. Congress granted a charter to and ordered the organizational structure for the Bank of North America. This idea, to make the national executive somehow equivalent to the designated leader of an economic corporation precociously tapped the energy of corporatism's late-century expansion and economic reordering.[26] Titling the nation's executive "president" made the nation analogous to a corporate body (treated by law as a single individual), it drew on the emergent, rationally entrepreneurial orientation of the corporation for conceptualizing democratic order. Presidentialism arguably anticipates the corporate model of individualism Christopher Newfield has capably described.[27] But more immediately, it reroutes the emergent radical democratic energies I noted earlier into structures of practical, political, and affective containment.

The president stands both as one aspect of, but (even more important) as the symbolic guarantor for the Constitution's scientific system for national politics. The office of the president is designed to transcend individual self-interest, specifically the local and contradictory self-interest of the people. Under the federal plan, the president would reflect a refined and rational version of "the sense of the people." The distance pyramidically installed between the people's general and "disorderly" interests and the president's judicious distillation of their (singular) interest delivers the president to the nation as a purified body. Electoral distance, carefully commissioned electors, term limitations, and the "intermixture" of powers will all combine to provide a presidential entity who has risen above personal passions and factional interest, who will preside democratically by transcending local investments and attending dispassionately to abstracted national interest. This is a structure that promises more representation for "the people": If a House and Senate isn't enough, now "the people" will find an even more concentrated and purified experience of representation in the executive body of the president—the concrete correlative for national manhood.

The constitutional defenders successfully tapped into political tensions and anxieties that *ordinarily* emerge in democratic practice, tied them to a whole range of cultural and economic anxieties, and promised relief for all those anxieties in institutional machinery for national unity, a machinery we've learned to call democratic order.[28] This presidential institutionalization of representative democracy offered a reassuringly hierarchicalized substitute for the messiness of local interaction: a rationally stratified structure, the atomization of factional interests through electoral distance, and (eventually) the ritual release of democratic energy in the form of elections.

Presidentialism provided a strongly uniformizing (and sanitizing) logic for citizens' developing relations to all kinds of political representation in the United States. This form of national political identification came at a substantial cost.[29] It must be clear by now that I think presidentially ordered representivity is bad for democracy. It's bad in the specific sense that it reroutes the radical practice of democracy—the hard work of achieving plussum democratic engagement—for a citizenry that learns from presidentialism to long for self-subordinating civic unity and national "wholeness." It channels democratic energies into nominally democratic, civically and economically stratifying institutions, where patriotic identification arrests questions about local social, political, economic injustices. The presidential incarnation of representative democracy blocks our imagining democracy as the political and cultural processes of multiple and diverse bodies, engaging our disagreements together in self-governance.[30]

The President's Two Bodies

I'm suggesting that the symbolic president cultivates unnecessarily rigid desires for unity, wholeness, and sameness—desires that make us scared of democracy. While presidential representivity has conditioned us to experience the surrender of our own politicalness not as a loss but as a relief,[31] I want to insist that the representative figure of the president has never successfully eliminated our longings for a more heterogeneous engagement, for democratic connectedness. Our abbreviated, contradictory desires split the president into two bodies. The hard body of the president offers us a strong guarantee for national boundaries and self-identity. The soft body holds out for us sensations of democratic recognition for our individuality and of equalitarian exchange. The hard body keeps us hoping for more democratic connectedness than we are taught we can safely have; the soft body of the president delivers only a placebo version of that connectedness and leaves us worrying that he's not adequately protecting our boundaries.[32]

Sociologist Michael Kimmel argues that a hard presidential body has been a key symbolic in presidential elections since 1840. In the race between Van Buren and Harrison, over 80 percent of the eligible white male electorate turned out to vote a manly man into office—who promptly killed himself on the sharp edge of his machismo. Refusing to wear a coat for his oath of office, the Western military hero and Indian killer caught pneumonia on that bitterly cold day and died a month later.[33] Presidential historians argue that the presidential body did not become an essential national symbol until the age of popular presidential elections. But the split symbolic of the president's two bodies was in place much earlier. Indeed, its earlier manifestation clarifies that the ambivalence it represents is less over what kind of president the people wanted once given the chance to vote than it was about a key ambivalence generated within representative democracy.

Presidentialism began consolidating its popular appeal in the aftermath of the fraught politics of the 1790s and early 1800s. This was a period that witnessed the French Revolution, the slave revolt in San Domingue, and an aggressive Federalist crackdown both on political dissent and immigration; it saw an intensification of political anxieties about both sectionalism and "foreign threats" in the Louisiana Purchase. This was a period during which political disagreement was refigured in the terms of nation-threatening violence. It is in this period that we see the developing popular appeal of the presidency as a manager of a national democratic "system."

George Washington died in 1799, just as the national unity he represented as the nation's undisputed first president was breaking down into serious political rancor. Just one year before, President John Adams and his

Federalist colleagues had pushed through the Alien and Sedition Acts in response to rising political dissent—to which the electoral college responded by appointing to the presidency Adams's Republican opponent, Thomas Jefferson. This so-called second American Revolution, the peaceful transfer of power from one party to another, did not consolidate political unity in the United States: For instance, President Jefferson was so fearful of the consequences of Federalist opposition that he enjoined Congress to strict secrecy when he proposed the Lewis and Clark expedition in 1803. So when the itinerant preacher and traveling book salesman Mason Locke Weems began marketing his wildly popular biography of George Washington in the early 1800s, he offered the American public a chance nostalgically and fictionally to recapture a sensation of national unity that could offset their anxieties about ongoing political dissensus.

It seems that then the American public understood that the anecdotal details with which Weems embellished the 1809 revision were to be read as moral embellishment. It wasn't long, though, before moral fiction turned into moral fact, and it perhaps did this *so quickly* because Weems's delivery of a Founding Father with superhero qualities addressed a deeper national logic. Hugh Crawford explains the pedagogical tenor of Weems's biography as addressing the early nation's larger "concern for stabilizing society than [for] glorifying its revolutionary status."[34] I want to suggest something different, that the pedagogical figure of George Washington balances in the fabled body of the national executive deeply countervailing tendencies within the logic of representative democracy.[35] In other words, the biography is less a record of historically progressing political desire than it is of a fundamentally—we could even say ontologically—conflicted institutionalization of national desire.

Recounting Washington's part in the defense of Fort Necessity during the French and Indian War, Weems describes a warrior with a magically armored body:

> By this time . . . Braddock had fallen—his aids and officers, to a man, killed or wounded. . . . Washington alone remained unhurt! Horse after horse had been killed under him. Showers of bullets had touched his locks or pierced his regimentals. But still protected by heaven— still supported by a strength not his own, he had continued to fly . . . where his presence was most needed, sometimes animating his rangers; sometimes striving . . . to rally the regulars.[36]

This same hard-bodied proto-president grew up from a boy with a miraculously soft heart. The childhood that Weems recounts is sprinkled liberally with Washington's tears, as, for instance, when one fall his father chidingly reminds him of his selfish refusal to share an apple with his brothers and sisters the spring before. Then the father only convinced George to do so by promising that God would deliver a bigger apple harvest in exchange for little George's generosity. Confronted with the loaded trees and his father's reminder, "George looked in silence on the wild wilderness of fruit . . . then lifting his eyes, filled with shining moisture . . . he softly said, 'Well, Pa, only forgive me this time; and see if I ever be so stingy any more.'"[37]

Washington's mythical status is so common that we don't often question the symbolic logic of such a story. What *does* it mean for Weems to create a president at once so impermeable and so sentimentally permeable, so hard and yet so soft? It seems to me that Weems presciently reworks the Elizabethan doctrine of the king's two bodies to negotiate the newer tensions of representative democracy. If, as Michael Paul Rogin summarizes, the doctrine worked in two directions, making "the [political] realm independent of the body mortal who governed it" and at the same time allowing the officeholder to "absorb . . . the realm into [his] personal identity,"[38] the two bodies of the president offered a symbolic solution to a central political conundrum facing the constitutionally United States: How do you achieve strong national unity and foster genuine political difference (which is, after all, what democracy depends on)? How do you balance representative abstraction and democratic substance? If, as I've argued elsewhere, the Federalists offered the president as an emblem of national unity that would replace the messiness of democratic politicalness, Weems seems to be insisting that our first president actually delivers on both desires: the desire for seamless patriotic unity *and* the desire for interconnected democratic heterogeneity.

I want to highlight how the charisma we associate with the presidency first develops in relation to a dead/absent president. Living presidents unavoidably remind citizens of political conflict and partiality. But the developing *symbolics* of the representative (dead) president promise to comprehend and manage those many conflicting desires in our place. This reorganization of civic desire toward the dead president registers a mournful loss of public imagination about self-managed democracy — in the sense that the people are always mourning a loss while they sentimentally vest their desires for democracy in the president's singular leadership.

The Unfinished Business of White Male Sentimentalism

Weems's biography of Washington can help us think more about the loaded symbolics of representative presidentialism and its management of radical democratic desires and energies. As my example above (and any anecdotal acquaintance with the biography) evidences, Weems's depiction of Washington appeals strongly to sentiment. Indeed, taking that text with any degree of seriousness means raising some key questions about what it is we think we've come to know *about* sentiment.

The chapter that recounts the "birth and education" of the man Weems denominates our nation's "political father" foregrounds little George's relation to *his* father, the grandfatherly Mr. Washington. Mr. Washington endeavors to give George a liberal education, teaching him to share with his friends, to labor always for generosity and above all, truthfulness. The famous cherry tree anecdote serves to document the successful inculcation of Mr. Washington's long lesson on truthfulness. Describing it to George as the "loveliest quality of youth" "Pa" explains how he "would ride fifty miles . . . to see the little boy whose heart is so honest, and . . . lips so pure, that we may depend on every word he says." By contrast, he offers up "the case with the boy who is so given to lying, that nobody can believe a word he says!"[39] Rather than see his dear George turn into this boy, Mr. Washington avers that "gladly would I assist to nail you up in your little coffin, and follow you to your grave."[40] In a scene of "disciplinary intimacy" I think there is no reason to read as either "feminized" or "feminizing,"[41] Mr. Washington details his own pedagogy to a tearful and anxious George.

> I rejoice in the hope you never will [lie]. At least, you shall never, from me, have cause to be guilty of so shameful a thing. Many parents, indeed, even compel their children to this vile practice, by barbarously beating them for every little fault: hence, on the next offense, the little terrified creature slips out a lie! just to escape the rod. But as to yourself George, you know I have always told you, and now tell you again, that, whenever by accident, you do anything wrong, which must often be the case, as you are but a poor little boy yet, without experience or knowledge, you must never tell a falsehood to conceal it; but come bravely up, my son, like a little man, and tell me of it: and, instead of beating you, George, I will but the more honour and love you for it my dear.[42]

Weems summarizes this episode as "the sowing [of] good seed"—a manly pedagogy with manful results.

Recent scholars of sentiment, like Richard Brodhead, Laura Wexler, and Amy Kaplan, have effectively pointed toward sentiment's use of affect/ desire for pedagogical, and specifically disciplinary purposes in ways that focus attention toward (white middle-class) women's practices. So it's worth dwelling a moment on how this scene elaborates a developing vari- ant of male sentimentalism in the early nation. This is indeed a scene where we can see Mr. Washington deploying the desire for connection—in this in- stance George's intense desires for his father's love—toward a disciplinary aim. In this instance that aim seems to be "truth telling," but subsequent passages emphasize a subtle additional dimension to the lesson. Here and elsewhere, the loving truths rewarded by manly recognition—what Weems denotes the "spirit of a brother"—lead to the "right order" of male self- subordination to a higher authority, the formal "discipline" of fraternity. For instance, in his school years, George's sentimental identification with fatherly male authority lead him often to tattle on his schoolmates for fight- ing among themselves. Weems offers a former classmate reminiscing about how George would upbraid his classmates:

> Angry or not angry, you shall never, boys, have my consent to a prac- tice so shocking! shocking even in *slaves* and *dogs;* then how utterly scandalous in little boys at school, who ought to look at one another as brothers. And what must be the feelings of our tender parents, when, instead of seeing us come home smiling and lovely, as the JOYS OF THEIR HEARTS! they see us creeping in like young *blackguards,* with our heads *bound up, black eyes,* and *bloody clothes*! And what is all this for? Why, that we *may get praise*!! But the truth is, a quarrelsome boy was never sincerely praised![43]

George invokes brotherly sentiment by appealing to the "tender" feelings of their parents. It is by this same logic that George rationalizes hauling in the master to cut off conflict rather than allowing boys to settle their disagreement among themselves.[44] Schoolmate George concisely prefig- ures the work that presidentialism's sentimentally representative logic will do for the disorderly habits of democracy. The president promises to cir- cumvent the messiness entailed by equalitarian negotiation. He reminds "boy"/citizens to preempt disagreement through their unquestioning self- subordination to the higher wisdom of their loving master-teacher-father-president, who has their better interests at heart. The self-governing equalitarian desires of sociopolitical fraternity are representatively routed into the containment device of patriotic/representative sentiment, of loving self-subordination to a hierarchically ordered "fraternity."

Pointing to this outcome should not mean we forget the way presidential sentimentalism registers more radical desires. A recent and illuminating discussion of sentimentalism helps me draw this more complicated approach to the question of sentimentalism generally and presidential sentimentalism in particular. In her tour-de-force essay entitled "Poor Eliza" (in this volume), Lauren Berlant draws on a dense network of *Uncle Tom's Cabin* citations to map what she calls the "unfinished business of sentimentality." By Berlant's measure, sentimentalism's appeal to "true feeling" rightfully invokes a political "desire to build pain alliances."[45] But in its relocation of collective identification to a putatively universal capacity for suffering and trauma at the heart of the liberal individual, and by proposing two "affect-saturated institutions"—the nation and family—as universalistic solutions to a range of nonequivalent antagonisms and oppressions— sentimentalism's equalitarian impulse toward social change is "replaced by a civic-minded but passive ideal of empathy."[46] Sentimentalism at once registers and constrains collective impulses toward radical, democratic change by affectively or psychically reterritorializing political consciousness (the desire for a changed world) as privatized, individualized feeling (the desire for the sensation of a changed heart.[47])

Berlant's analysis points us toward holding sentimentalism's desire for social equalitarianism against its antipolitical nationalist fantasy, the dream-ideal of "one true people." This fantasy misleadingly replaces productive, healthy frictions and antagonisms of democratic processes with (what she terms) a "sponge of true feeling" that promises to eliminate as it absorbs "difference and struggle."[48] Her framework can help us calculate sentimentalism's desires more carefully and specifically (and politically) against its designs. For instance, we might hold the dynamics of sentiment's purifying (or antidissensus) effects over and against its desire for democratic connection, to see *that* radical energy behind or alongside sentimentalism's mistaken (or we might be tempted to say fascist) seizure of "unconflictedness" as the key term for democratic "intimacy."[49]

What is the value of such attempts to locate radical energy behind conservatizing turns? For me the value comes in the way such a move helps us begin to register and calculate the enormous amount of institutional energy that goes into constraining democratic desire, the desire to inhabit fully the space of personal and political freedom. Sentiment—with its emphasis on "civic-minded but passive empathy"—is an institution that works culturally the way majoritarian voting structures work politically to limit, reduce and retrain democracy's equalitarian energies into hierarchicalizing, individual-izing structures of passive submission, to reduce and retrain democracy's vocabulary for political and economic oppression to terms like *freedom* and *equal opportunity*. This kind of analysis underscores how much democratic energy was there and is here, and at the same time how easily that energy can be converted and perverted for countervailing aims. It is a model that underlines the importance of critical reading and critical practice to a demo-cratic project.

I posit my analysis of Weems's text as a way of refocusing our habit of looking to the way women's texts and plots of feminine feeling perform the work of sentiment. Sentiment is not exclusively or pervasively a structure of feminine feeling even if the binary bent of separate spheres from Nathaniel Hawthorne to Carroll Smith-Rosenberg has trained us to see it this way. As critics like Lora Romero help us grasp, we don't have to allow the gen-dering machine of separate spheres to divert us from reading its "other" texts and cultural spaces.[50] From Fireside Poets to secret fraternal lodges, from the formalized excess of eulogy memorials published by men's pro-fessional associations to the monumental excess of the Washington Mall, you can find—if you look—rampant structures of male (public and private) sentimentality throughout the nineteenth century and into our own. And so I'm invoking Berlant's mention of "unfinished business" both to refer-ence the ongoing functionality of a specifically white male sentimentality— what I'm here describing as presidential representivity—and our own in-complete investigation of its implications for understanding antebellum culture and for rethinking men's professional, racial, and national identity formations.

As Berlant helps us see, the turn to sentiment is motored by equalitar-ian—radically democratic—energies. But sentimentalism is geared for the representative management of those energies—it is a machine that turns di-versifying public energies to uniformizing private (dead) ends. There are two key sentimentalist moves in Weems's *Life* that evidence presidential representivity's recodification of democratic impulses, one that directs the sentimental toward a (perverted) representative pedagogy, the other that locates the sentimental in childhood, thereby situating democratic energies in an infantilized and family-arizing past.

As we see when Pa dies, Weems models patriotism as the sentimentally self-subordinating love of a disciplinary and dying father.[51] George's agonized cry on his father's deathbed, "O my father! my father!" denotes him, in Weems's narration, "the happiest youth! Happy in that love, which thus, to its enamoured soul strained an aged, an expiring sire. O! worthiest to be the founder of a just and equal government lasting as thy own deathless name!" This self-subordinating patriotism, Weems insists, is a radically private and privatizing emotion, the premise on which this entire biography is based. Explaining his narrative approach to the biography, Weems insists that "private life is always the real life," that it is the life "behind the curtain" where one discovers the true worth of a patriot and a man.[52] His biography monumentalizes an intensifying reversal in an already conservative political logic of representation. In Weems's lesson, the aim is not to see your own political desires represented in deliberative government but to model your personal desires on those of the representative: "Since it is the private virtues that lay the foundation of all human excellence . . . give us his private virtues! In these, every youth is interested, because in these every youth may become a Washington."[53] This is a pedagogy that insistently substitutes the private for the public—or more correctly redescribes a singular public We as the private "I"—thus relocating radical democracy's desires for a changed world to the liberal-representative containment of a changed (self-disciplined) heart.

Whatever democratic excess cannot be contained by an appeal to the father representative (a signifying chain that slides from God [the "True Father"] to Mr. Washington to George) is corralled in the realm of childhood. We occasionally see a tear in the adult Washington, which inevitably is "a sweet tear of gratitude to [God] who brought him to see this day."[54] But the overwhelming desires for love and approval, the overflowing, copious tears belong to little George, childhood George. If it is this "soft" George that allows readers to rehearse their national desires for democratic connectedness, as I suggested earlier, it is this George that also reminds them those desires must be left behind to grow into representative adulthood. In its very gesture toward the residual radicalness of democratic desire, this move, where Weems locates the more amorphous desires for democratic connection in *childhood,* delineates the double-fistedness of nationally di-

rected male sentimentalism. This sentimentalism keeps moments of democratic affect on a kind of Super-8 reel for us to watch over and again, rehears-
ing in teary-eyed technicolor how sweet we were back then. Repackaging
fresh political feelings as familial nostalgia, Weems's presidential sentimentalism keeps adult male emotion safely oriented toward a self-subordinating
posture, where individual growth within national fraternity is defined by
the pleasurable deferral of self-governance, where brotherly negotiation is
remembered as disgraceful "fighting" and where "big boys" know always
to follow their leader.

This aspect of Weems's biography diagrams the logic of nationalism's
"atavism effect," which David Lloyd explains as the nation-state's ongoing
attempt to caption the continuing force of competing political energies as
"immature," "irrational," or "outdated" affiliations and desires that we have
progressed beyond to move into the fullness and contemporaneity of the
nation space. Analyzing the "double form" by which "nationalism's modernity is posed against the modes it supposedly supersedes," Lloyd describes
how:

> Where the nation-state is assumed as the proper end of historical pro-
> cesses, only one line of development can be seen as the properly his-
> torical in history. Accordingly, movements whose struggles chrono-
> logically precede or coincide with nationalism but are not identical or
> entirely isomorphic with it, can only be seen as *proto*nationalist. . . .
> Popular movements are absorbed into the historically progressive tra-
> jectory of nationalism so that what is significant . . . is the set of traits
> that lend themselves to national ends. Other traits, which may indeed
> be incompatible with nationalism, such as modes of organization and
> communication and certain kinds of spiritualism, are relegated to the
> space of historical contingency . . . [where] they constitute the non-
> sense, the irrepresentable of historiography.[55]

Lloyd's argument helps me elaborate on an argument I began in *National
Manhood,* where I noted the historical correlation between emerging ideologies of Republican motherhood and the consolidation of citizenship in
terms of white manhood. I insisted there on the importance of rethinking the emergence of Republican motherhood at least in part as a way of
locating the historical moment when American men traded in fatherhood as
a social ideal and a political model for a different role in a new white national
fraternity, as economic actors and civic representatives. This new white (or

national) manhood produced and assigned the privacy of the national domestic space to women as guardian-reproducers of its affective purity and
by extension their political virtue. Saying that the structure of male citizenship in the new nation facilitated this space for women is not to deny that
this role enabled women to claim a certain power in the private and public spheres. But taking in this more complicated—and coimplicated—production of gender, race, space, and political representation does allow us to
understand a different political aspect of the separate spheres, the way sentimentalism's public assignment to the private space of women and children
in the early nation corroborates presidential representivity's affective management of radical democracy. In other words, the very desires for democratic negotiation, for the promising if hard-won satisfactions of equalitarian, face-to-face self-governance—expressed, for instance, in the growing
and repeated speculations of political actors in the new nation that economic redistribution would become necessary to assist the growth of political freedom as well as in suggestions that suffrage might need genuinely to
be universalized—these very desires are cast through the relegation of sentiment from the political to the private sphere as a womanish or a childish
excess of feeling that can safely be "protected" in the domestic space but that
would be "impossible" to transport into the nation-space. In just this way
then, Weems's biography both legitimates the people's desire for (more)
democracy and captions them as childish excess—a sweet reminder of our
innocent origins but irrelevant to the self-disciplined and self-subordinating
workaday life of adult, representative nationhood, impossible to bring into
any adult forms of their own.

I want briefly to review my two basic arguments and broadly outline some
directions they suggest for further work in the study of early national literature and culture. First, I've argued that the presidential model of representative democracy influences how we think about democracy, mostly in
antidemocratic ways. If, as Claude Lefort claims, the innovation of democratic society comes in the way that it "is instituted as a society without
a body," presidential representivity teaches something different from that,
something more like the logic Emerson details in *Representative Men*. As he
argues there, when we serve the great Representative, we advance our best
Self: "We need not fear excessive influence. A more generous trust is permitted. Serve the great. Stick at no humiliation. Grudge no office thou canst
render. Be the limb of their body, the breath of their mouth. Compromise

thy egotism. Who cares for that, so thou gain aught wider and nobler?"[56] Rather than saving democratic power's "empty place" as the commons for our diverse freedoms, the presidential model of representivity teaches us to want the president to distill and materialize our freedom.[57] As we have seen in Weems, citizens learn from presidentialism to fill our space with presidential singularity. This has a measurable impact on the democratic imaginary: Presidentialism trains citizens to imagine their share of the work not as their ongoing exercise of self-governance, but as a far more limited exercise in knee-jerk opinion delivery, party affiliation, and "patriotic" self-subordination to "democratic" leadership.

My second argument comes in the analytic pressure I've been bringing to bear on the sentimental aspects of the symbolic president. Sentimentalism, as has been widely argued, normatizes particular structures of class, race, gender, and sexuality. But it does so not simply on behalf of the (good/bad) social and literary agency of white women of the middle classes. More generally, it does so through a kind of *leger-de-gender,* on behalf of a particular, politically privatizing, and arguably masculinizing construction of representative democracy. In other words, by allowing separate spheres logic to endow the political binary I'm locating here, "presidential symbolics/sentimental symbolics," with the self-evidence of gender difference, we have been unable to see a key dynamic developing in the politics of the early nation. Specifically, we have missed seeing the way sentiment is commandeered in the early nation to relegate equalitarian democratic desires to the politically irrelevant, emotionally primitive space of the private (feminine/childlike) individual. This maneuver simultaneously allowed developing male practices of sentiment to coalesce around the pleasures of deferred self-governance in hierarchically ordered fraternity. My preliminary exercise here in rehistoricizing and reconceptualizing one political trajectory for sentiment in the early United States signals the importance of doing more work to understand its flexibly productive relation to representative democracy—an inquiry that will not be complete until we investigate more fully the "unfinished business" of male sentimentalism(s).

Notes

The author would like to thank for their help with or comments on this essay: Liz Barnes, Dale Bauer, Lauren Berlant, Cathy Davidson, and Laurie Shannon. Thanks also to the extraordinarily thought-provoking audience at the 2000 Arizona Quarterly Symposium: You won't find your questions addressed here, but I promise you will in future incarnations of the larger project!

1 Cathy N. Davidson, personal correspondence, 22 December 2000.

2 I'm borrowing the concept of politicalness from Sheldon Wolin: "By political-ness I mean our capacity for developing into beings who know and value what it means to participate in and be responsible for the care and improvement of our common collective life. To be political is not identical with being part of a gov-ernment or being associated with a political party. These are structured roles, and typically they are highly bureaucratized. For these reasons they are opposed to the authentically political" (*The Presence of the Past: Essays on the State and the Constitu-tion* [Baltimore, Md.: Johns Hopkins University Press, 1989], 139). Wolin usefully indexes the constitutionally conditioned disavowal of politicalness for "democ-racy"—a practice that in effect remainders democracy for its so-called citizens. See also Bonnie Honig's illuminating discussion of the strong logic within U.S. theories of democracy that "tend to remove politics from the reach of democratic contest" (*Political Theory and the Displacement of Politics* [Ithaca, N.Y.: Cornell University Press, 1993], 4).

3 Until recently, there were virtually no treatments but Michael Moon's *Dissemi-nating Whitman: Revision and Corporeality in* Leaves of Grass (Cambridge, Har-vard University Press, 1991) and Vincent Bertolini's "Fireside Chastity: The Erot-ics of Sentimental Bachelorhood in the 1850s," *American Literature* 68 (Dec. 1996): 707–37. Recently, there have been several publications that evidence a growing interest in the question of male sentimental practices and texts. See Mary Chapman and Glenn Hendler, eds., *Sentimental Men: Masculinity and the Politics of Affect in American Culture* (Berkeley and Los Angeles: University of Califor-nia Press, 1999), in particular "The Feminization of American Sentimentalism" in their introduction, pp. 2–8. Their new and important collection, which came into print as I was making final revisions to this essay, reprints Bertolini and a small handful of other earlier essays that concern nineteenth-century forms of male sentimentalism and joins them to an exciting new group of essays on this subject. See also Katherine V. Snyder's *Bachelors, Manhood, and the Novel, 1850–1925* (New York: Cambridge University Press, 1999), and Howard Chudacoff's *The Age of the Bachelor: Creating an American Subculture* (Princeton, N.J.: Princeton University Press, 1999).

4 Four recent works offer substantial analyses of some aspect of the interrelation of democracy and sentiment. The first three concentrate on literature in the early na-tion. Elizabeth Barnes's *States of Sympathy: Seduction and Democracy in the Ameri-can Novel* (New York: Columbia University Press, 1997) argues that sympathy was a "building block" for U.S. democracy but also a deeply problematic register in-sofar as it trains citizens to confuse familial and socio-erotic energies. Somewhat differently, Julia Stern's *The Plight of Feeling: Sympathy and Dissent in the Early American Novel* (Chicago: University of Chicago Press, 1997) reads sympathy as

the reactive register of mourning in the wake of revolutionary violence, one that could sufficiently also comprehend and articulate the political exclusions of the developing nation. Bruce Burgett's *Sentimental Bodies: Sex, Gender and Citizenship in the Early Republic* (Princeton, N.J.: Princeton University Press, 1998), argues against the normative opposition between "reason" and "sentiment" in our understandings of political culture and traces out the sentimental construction of the citizen in the early United States. Andrew Burstein's *Sentimental Democracy: The Evolution of America's Romantic Self-Image* (New York: Hill and Wang, 1999) offers a broader historical treatment, one that examines sentiment and sympathy as the "most distinctive emotional force" of democracy in U.S. practice.

5 Gordon S. Wood, *Creation of the American Republic, 1776–1867* (New York: Norton, 1969), 394–95.

6 We can begin to see this if we remember, as historian Paul Gilje reminds us, that for most Anglo Americans of the mid-eighteenth century, out-of-doors political action was a "quasi-legitimate" social practice that worked against tyranny: "Based on an image of society that recognized a single, all-encompassing communal interest, this attitude reflected a belief that the people on the street often (but not always) acted in defense of common, shared values" (6). But soon after the passage of the Constitution, as Gilje details, local anxiety about it increased in coordination with official national policy's reactions against it. See his *The Road to Mobocracy: Popular Disorder in New York City, 1763–1834* (Chapel Hill: University of North Carolina Press, 1987).

7 I want to register here that I'm fully persuaded by Wood's argument that people across the states and across socioeconomic levels were registering the presence of some kind of crisis; I'm also fully persuaded by his move to locate the energy of the "crisis" in emerging political dissensus. Our difference lies in the relative values we attach to the notion of "dissensus," the ideal of "unity" and the constitutional attempt to guarantee national unity. I'm interested here to pressure "fragmentation" as a culturally dystopic framing of what might actually be regarded in the terms of *health:* of human and cultural diversity, of local political variety, of what Christopher J. Newfield has described as the "disunited state of America":

> Our national "disuniting" began with our inception and it's not too soon to get over our regret about this. Our "pluralistic," "consensual" union, however one feels about it, has always rested on a divided, antagonistic multiplicity of cultures whose overlap has been sporadic, conflictual, or incomplete. The burden of providing a unified government has for too long interfered with our ability to understand cultural actuality. . . . Disunity is not a problem—in fact, it is usually preferable to more efficient resolutions. *Disunity* is another word for *democracy.* ("What Was Political Correctness? Race, the Right and Managerial Democracy in the Humanities," *Critical Inquiry* 19, no. 2 [1993]: 336)

8 Laws, for instance, that suspended usual methods for debt-collection and confiscated property. See Wood, *Creation*, 404.

9 Wood, *Creation*, 404.

10 Wood notes that "more such groups sprang up in the dozen years after Independence than in the entire colonial period" (*Creation*, 325). Gilje argues that "throughout most of the eighteenth century, mobs theoretically represented a united community acting to protect agreed-upon morals and customs" and were granted—even by the wealthy elite—a kind of "quasi-legitimacy" (*The Road to Mobocracy*, 5, 118.) Such toleration began to break down beginning in the 1780s, and though Federalists and Republicans continued to support their own out-of-doors actions, Gilje observes that they more and more harshly condemned the actions of their opponents as a national danger (see especially chap. 4, "Political Popular Disturbances").

11 E. James Ferguson points out that conservatives and propertied men reacted with growing alarm: "Tutored in the history of proletarian uprisings in the ancient world and believing themselves to have been the chief sufferers during the late war, they were convinced that from the beginning of the Revolution the propertied classes had been exposed to mob despotism. Three years after the end of the war they were not certain that the Revolution had truly ended" (see *Power of the Purse: A History of American Public Finance* [Chapel Hill: University of North Carolina Press, 1961], 243).

12 Hannah Arendt, *On Revolution* (New York: Viking, 1963), 253.

13 C. Douglas Lummis, *Radical Democracy* (Ithaca, N.Y.: Cornell University Press, 1996), 113. My emphasis on local democracy has nothing to do with an idealistic association of democracy with the local-as-place, and everything to do with rescuing the association of democracy with face-to-face, equalitarian negotation. In this sense, private voting booth democracy contributes unfortunately to the virtualization of democracy, the diminishment and weakening of the public sphere through the abjection of face-to-face political disagreement as being bad for democracy (or "digestion," as our parents told us, schooling us on manners).

14 That, indeed, is the move the Constitution asks "us" to ratify. The superordination of the national over and against the local for the practices of political representation entails not simply a change of venue for politics. It also conditions the local surrender of citizen politicalness. Analyzing politicalness as a civic birthright, Wolin traces how the Constitution "made it possible to contract away our birthright by forgetting its true nature and thereby preparing the way for its being reduced to a negotiable commodity with the result that its disappearance is experienced not as a loss but relief" (*Presence of the Past*, 139).

15 Wolin, *Presence of the Past*, 139–40.

16 Here I want to be clear in my rejection of "Republicanism" as the originary politics of the U.S. political imaginary, where, the story goes, the logic of democracy was a later development. I'm insisting that in colonial localities, and then particu-

larly during the course of revolution itself, Americans developed a variety of even occasionally radical democratic practices and commitments, and that constitutional Republicanism understood itself to be in competition with those democratic logics and practices. As Wolin summarizes of the constitutional debates: "The stakes of the debate were, at bottom, about democracy" (*Presence of the Past,* 96).

17 I'm not trying to present a romanticized tragedy of democratic declension here. I am trying to pay attention to democratic alternatives and to the specific ideological and discursive conditions through which those possibilities were narrowed in the United States.

18 As I was finishing this essay, I discovered Antonio Negri's provocative *Insurgencies: Constituent Power and the Modern State* (Minneapolis: University of Minnesota Press, 1999). His arguments about the Constitution's attack on the self-governing (radically democratic) power of the people parallel and amplify mine. Negri opposes "constituent power" to constitutional power, and argues that the former "is more suffocated than developed by the concept of nation" (3). His chapter on the American Revolution outlines how "constituent power" is translated into a mystical "force of spirit, a strength completely assimilated to the constitution," such that the Constitution absorbs "not only constituent power but the subject of constituent power" (7, 165).

19 I'm using the term *virtualization* to get at a fairly precise point (and one whose implications extend forward from this historical moment) about democracy, which is directed at the way the Constitution promised to "manage" democracy to make it "safe" for the people. To my mind, this constitutes a fundamental restraint on democracy energy and possibility. Constitutional order promises to eradicate the stresses of heterogeneity by distancing people from its "dangerous" expression. As it develops in practice, federal democratic order cleans up the messiness of radical democratic practice by virtualizing it, abstracting its face-to-face negotiations through the managed competition of private voting booths and the symbolically distancing and organizing mechanisms of party politics. Through the developing systematization of constitutional presidentialism and the universalization of white male suffrage, "the people" would come to surrender the idea of locally negotiated, face-to-face democracy for the routine expression of their opinion on ballots, and the embodiment of that "opinion" in the person of various elected officials, especially the president (see Lummis, *Radical Democracy,* 19 for a pithy summary of the relation of "allowing the people to have their say" to democracy). My term, *virtualization,* riffs both on the logic of virtual representation as described by Edmund Burke and rejected by the American colonists (see Wood, *Creation,* 173–81) and on Jean Baudrillard's evocative discussion of the operational simulation of the political economy in *Symbolic Exchange and Death,* trans. Iain Hamilton Grant (London: Sage Publications, 1993). As he notes, the electoral sphere is "the first large-scale institution where social

exchange is reduced to getting a response" (65). Locating the emergence of mass media in the nineteenth-century "universalization" of suffrage (65), he argues that

> "Classical" universal suffrage already implies a certain neutralisation of the political field, in the name of a consensus over the rules of the game. But we can still distinguish the representatives and the represented in this game, on the basis of a real social antagonism in opinions. The neutralisation of this contradictory referential, under the sign of a public opinion which from now on is equal to itself, mediatised and homogenised by means of anticipation (polls), will make possible an alternation, not of parties, but of their "heads," creating a simulated opposition between the two parties, absorbing their respective objectives, and a reversibility of every discourse into any other. (68)

Though it's interesting to see the way Baudrillard traces this logic into twentieth-century political economy, my claims for the purposes of this chapter are more limited and specific, that constitutional order takes away power (removes the impetus and redirects the structures for direct democracy) from the people in order to guarantee national order, all the while promising them recognition (the sovereignty of "The People") *as* (a substitute for) power.

20 Two states (North Carolina and Rhode Island) refused to ratify until after the reconstitution of national governance; votes were close in New Hampshire, New York, Massachusetts, and Virginia; the remainder all showed fairly to very strong Federalist majorities. But the question of the popular vote presents an entirely different picture: Charles Beard calculates that in all likelihood, "not more than one-fourth or one-fifth of the adult white males took part in the election of delegates to the state conventions," and that "not more than 100,000 men favored the adoption of the Constitution at the time it was put into effect—about one in six of the adult [white] males" (*An Economic Interpretation of the Constitution of the United States, 1913* [New York: Free Press, 1986], 250). By state, Jackson Turner Main figures:

> It seems likely that the Antifederalists outnumbered the Federalists by as much as four to one in Rhode Island and South Carolina and by perhaps three to one in New York and North Carolina, and that they were slightly more than a majority in Massachusetts and Virginia. Probably the two sides were nearly equal in New Hampshire in June 1788, although there had been an Antifederal majority earlier. On the other hand, almost all of the citizens in Georgia, New Jersey, and Delaware were Federalists. The situation in the remaining states is uncertain; probably the Federalists had a clear majority in them, though perhaps not as large as the margin of victory in the ratifying conventions suggests. (*The Antifederalists* [Chapel Hill: University of North Carolina Press, 1961], 249)

21 As James Roger Sharp has extensively detailed, the nation saw a continuation of local actions and political dissensions through the 1790s. He insists, though, that whatever support the anti-Federalists had culminated in 1788 and dissipated with ratification. Though political dissension continued, Sharp argues that their very ferocity was generated out of a common commitment to the Constitution, but one they *"failed to recognize* that they *shared"* (*American Politics in the Early Republic: The New Nation in Crisis* [New Haven, Conn.: Yale University Press, 1993], 8; emphasis in original). As he also notes, there was an "abortive plan to call a new national convention to revive the whole question of governance" spearheaded by Virginia and New York (29). Gilje notes some anti-Federalist actions, such as effigy parades, jail rescues, street battles, and demonstrations (*Mobocracy,* 97). Cathy N. Davidson offers a more useful explanation: "Interpreting in radical terms the inherent indeterminacy of the Constitution, many citizens invoked that document as the justification for their political zeal" (*Revolution and the Word: The Rise of the Novel in America* [New York: Oxford University Press, 1986], 157).

22 See Dana D. Nelson, *National Manhood: Capitalist Citizenship and the Imagined Fraternity of White Men* (Durham, N.C.: Duke University Press, 1998), especially the introduction and chap. 1.

23 There was little actual anti-Federalist opposition to the office of the president. As Main notes, significant opposition focused on the issues of re-eligibility and scope of powers, but not on the fact of the office: "Various critics objected to every power that he had been given—his right to make appointments and treaties, his influence over the army, his right to pardon, and most of all his veto. Yet there were many Antifederalists who did not raise any serious criticism whatever, and the amendments that were suggested in the state conventions did not call for radical change" (*The Antifederalists,* 141).

24 Importantly, his unifying energy is representatively routed through/supplied by male citizens in a way that can reassure individual men not only about political discord but about other kinds of cultural and economic dislocations. In the end, what might have most effectively garnered support for—or at least blunted resistance to—the Constitution was the way it convincingly and insistently circuited the ideal of political consensus through the similarly common ideal of a vigorous, strong, undivided manhood. The bribe of national manhood—a manhood that could be claimed through patriotic incorporation (or subordination, as I'll be arguing)—effectively undercut the radicalizing energy of local democratic practices and rerouted the conceptualization of democracy in the new nation, atomizing the idea of participation and fitting citizens out for market competition.

25 Gary L. Gregg, *The Presidential Republic: Executive Representation and Deliberative Democracy* (New York: Rowman and Littlefield, 1997), 23.

26 As Charles Sellers reminds us, under British rule, corporations could only be chartered as nonprofit agencies and only by legislative act. Seven such charters

were organized in the colonial period. But after the revolution, "the number climbed to forty in the first decade . . . and passed three hundred during the commercial boom of the 1790s" (*The Market Revolution: Jacksonian America, 1815–1846* [New York: Oxford University Press, 1991], 44–45). Sellers details how these early corporations soon forged a link between the idea of public good and private profit, effectively convincing courts at least that because corporate entrepreneurship was socially beneficial, large debtors like corporate officers should not be impeded from continuing their entrepreneurial work on behalf of such social good by, say, being imprisoned for debts and bankruptcy (47–90).

27 See especially the chapter "Corporate Individualism" in Christopher Newfield, *The Emerson Effect: Individualism and Submission in America* (Chicago: University of Chicago Press, 1996).

28 This is an argument I detail in chap. 1 ("Purity Control") of *National Manhood*.

29 I'm not making an antinational argument. Rather, I want to insist on alternative national identifications and practices: to point out that our particular form of national identification (triangulated at least partially as I argue here through presidentialism) might not be the most humanly/democratically productive, should not be taken to mean that the nation form can not aspire toward humane democratic productiveness. On this subject, see, for instance, Nikhil Pal Singh, "Culture/Wars: Recoding Empire in an Age of Democracy," *American Quarterly* 50, no. 3 (Sept. 1998): 471–522.

30 For a more concrete map of the way one version of such a process might work, see James S. Fishkin, *The Voice of the People: Public Opinion and Democracy* (New Haven, Conn.: Yale University Press, 1995). He argues for a system he calls "a democracy of civic engagement," which would protect four basic democratic conditions; political equality, deliberation, participation, and nontyranny (63, 64). He notes that this system is grounded in a productive conflict: "Instead of a unified and coherent ideal in which these valued parts fit together in a single clear vision of what we should be striving for, we have conflicting values." His appeal is to "ideals without an ideal," a recognition that there "is not a single ideal vision progressively to be realized. Rather there are conflicting portions of the ideal picture and emphasis on each would take us in a different direction" (63).

31 Wolin, *Presence of the Past*, 139.

32 Both "bodies" do antidemocratic work. The hard body promises to protect us from the fear of democratic difference, and the soft promises to navigate our anxieties about politicalness. In this way, the president's "united" body assists (if it does not actually anchor) the production of what Lauren Berlant has described as the "infantile citizen":

> The infantile citizen of the United States has appeared in political writing about the nation at least since Tocqueville wrote, in *Democracy in America*, that while citizens should be encouraged to love the nation the way they do

their families and their fathers, democracies can also produce a special form of tyranny that makes citizens like children, infantilized, passive, and overdependent on the 'immense and tutelary power' of the state" (*The Queen of America Goes to Washington City: Essays on Sex and Citizenship* [Durham, N.C.: Duke University Press, 1997], 27 and see chap. 1)

Despite the symbolic/representative president's powerful antidemocratic tendencies, there's a value in holding the two "bodies" separately for analytic scrutiny: It's mostly by looking at narratives about the "soft" body that we can find residues of democratic energy and desire that can recall us to radical democracy's potential. As we will see below, the president's "soft" body promises both democratic connection and democratic recognition, the recognition of our individual particularity and difference. This desire for the apprehension and acknowledgment of individual particularity is rerouted by presidential representivity and capitalist citizenship into a prosthetic, uniformatizing and viciously reproductive individualism.

33 See Michael Kimmel, *Manhood in America: A Cultural History* (New York: Free Press, 1996), 38–39. Harrison fought in battles against native peoples in the Northwest Territory before being appointed exofficio superintendent of Indian affairs for Indiana Territory in the early 1800s. As Norma Lois Peterson summarizes, he "was often upset by disregard for Indian rights, yet he negotiated treaties that gained millions of acres for the government." In 1811, he led a force against the organized forces of the Shawnee near Tippecanoe Creek. This engagement soon earned him, notes Peterson, "a commission as brigadier general in the Regular Army and, eventually, full command of the Army of the Northwest" (*The Presidencies of William Henry Harrison and John Tyler* [Lawrence: University Press of Kansas, 1989], p. 18).

34 Hugh Crawford, "Images of Authority, Strategies of Control: Cooper, Weems and George Washington," *South Central Review* 11, no. 1 (spring 1994): 62.

35 I had the pleasure of discovering Burgett's analysis of George Washington's "Farewell Address" in his *Sentimental Bodies* as I was finishing this essay. In "The Patriot's Two Bodies" (chap. 3), Burgett uses Washington's own rhetoric to locate a "paradox" where "Washington's body is called upon both to symbolize national union and to silence national debate" (74–75). As I'll be suggesting in my analysis, I don't think this is a paradox, but part of the (anti)democratic logic of presidential representivity. That minor difference aside, Burgett's analysis shares with mine some substantially similar concerns, including (but not limited to) the way "the democratic synthesis promised by the patriotic [presidential] body remains vulnerable to civil opposition" (70). His essay provides an important corollary to my arguments that the split presidential symbolic became politically plastic in the early nation, carefully showing how Washington himself developed a relation to the contradictory demands of representative/democracy.

36 Mason L. Weems, *The Life of Washington* (Cambridge, Mass.: Belknap Press, 1962), 41.

37 Ibid., 9–10.

38 Michael Paul Rogin, *Ronald Reagan, the Movie and Other Episodes in Political Demonology* (Berkeley and Los Angeles: University of California Press, 1987), 81–82.

39 Weems, *Life of Washington*, 11.

40 Ibid.

41 I'm (I think) obviously referring to Richard Brodhead's influential analysis of "disciplinary intimacy" (his term), where, historicizing Foucault's analysis, Brodhead locates this new family-arizing disciplinarity in an "assumption of the traditionally feminine *affection* as the mode of authority proper for nurture" ("Sparing the Rod: Discipline and Fiction in Antebellum America," *Representations* 21[1988]: 70, 74).

42 Weems, *Life of Washington*, 11.

43 Ibid., 19–20, emphases in original.

44 Shirley Samuels's reading of the revolution fiction of the 1820s and 30s (chap. 4, "Monuments and Hearths" in *Romances of the Republic: Women, the Family and Violence in the Literature of the Early American Nation* [New York: Oxford University Press, 1996]) provides a thought-provoking companion argument to my suggestions here. Particularly in the section "Patriotic Gore" (90–95), Samuels analyzes the bloody, ritualistic scenes that cement the fraternal ties of male citizens as a kind of sexual performance (Samuels calls this "bloody brotherhood"), such that, to combine the terms of our analyses, citizens' energy for democratic disagreement are rerouted, eroticized, and intensified as patriotic opposition to the "foreign enemy."

45 Lauren Berlant, "Poor Eliza," *American Literature* 70, no. 3 (Sept. 1998): 636. Reprinted in this volume.

46 Ibid., 638, 641.

47 Ibid., 644.

48 Ibid., 655.

49 Ibid.

50 See, for instance, Lora Romero's paradigm-shifting analysis of Hawthorne's career, "Homosocial Romance," in *Home Fronts: Domesticity and Its Critics in the Antebellum United States* (Durham, N.C.: Duke University Press, 1997).

51 Weems, *Life of Washington*, 18.

52 Ibid., 2.

53 Ibid., 4.

54 Ibid., 133.

55 David Lloyd, "Nationalisms against the State" in *The Politics of Culture in the Shadow of Capital*, ed. David Lloyd and Lisa Lowe (Durham, N.C.: Duke University Press, 1997), 178.

56   Ralph Waldo Emerson, *Essays and Lectures* (New York: Library of America, 1983),
     629.

57   Claude Lefort, *Democracy and Political Theory* (Minneapolis: University of Min-
     nesota Press, 1988), 17. This is a space structured through the constitutional ma-
     chinery of "separate powers." Lefort elaborates:

> There is no need to dwell on the details of the institutional apparatus. The
> important point is that this apparatus prevents governments from appropri-
> ating power for their own ends, from incorporating it into themselves. The
> exercise of power is subject to the procedures of periodical redistributions. It
> represents the outcome of a controlled contest with permanent rules. This phe-
> nomenon implies an institutionalization of conflict. The locus of power is an
> empty place, it cannot be occupied—it is such that no individual and no group
> can be consubstantial with it—and it cannot be represented.

While Lefort's structuralist argument is compelling in its elegance, my disagreements with it are twofold. I agree with Lefort that the imaginative power of
democracy can be usefully represented in this notion of the "empty place"—a
commons for our diverse freedoms. An "empty place" is certainly structured in
the mechanics of constitutional checks and balances, but, as I'm arguing here,
an important constitutional countersymbol for "democracy" comes in the figure
of the president. Although constitutional power may practically often lie in an
"empty space," it is not that empty space to which Americans habitually turn
for the referential understandings of democratic power. (We might call this the
reader's response objection.) Another way that I would qualify Lefort's optimism about this innovative institutional machinery and its promise to guarantee
democracy is to note that democracy does *not* reside in institutions like the Constitution. Institutions can support and complement the work of democracy, but
they cannot generate it. While the symbolic power of the empty space is eloquent
for how it can speak to the equalitarian distribution of democratic self-managing
agency (if in fact that political state of being exists), this theoretical and institutional abstraction alone does not generate democracy: people do. (We might call
this the *real-politik* objection.)

Fathers, Sons, Sentimentality, and the Color Line:

The Not-Quite-Separate Spheres of W. E. B.
Du Bois and Ralph Waldo Emerson

RYAN SCHNEIDER

This essay is an effort to meaningfully compare texts by two male writers and public intellectuals, Ralph Waldo Emerson and W. E. B. Du Bois, who wrote publicly and in sentimental terms about the losses of their first-born sons: Du Bois in the essay "Of the Passing of the First-Born," included in *The Souls of Black Folk* (1903), and Emerson in the essay "Experience" (1844) and the poem "Threnody" (1847). The fact that such texts exist—that these two men chose to publish sentimental memorials to their children—is additional proof of what a growing body of scholarship already has shown: that women writers were not the only practitioners of sentimentality and that sentimentality itself cannot adequately be addressed using a separate spheres model based on an unqualified gender binary.[1] Such a binary is too exclusive and too rigid to account for sentimentality's power and flexibility—its capacity to appeal, as ideology and cultural practice, to nineteenth-century figures as diverse as Susan Warner, Frances Harper, Mark Twain, and Henry Adams, not to mention Du Bois and Emerson.

Yet studying the sentimentality of male writers suggests that a separate spheres model can be relevant and revealing as a critical frame when it takes as its foundational premise not the belief that women write sentimentally and men do not, but rather that women and men may occupy unique and complicated individual subject positions vis-à-vis the power that sentimentality offers, and that they may arrange their sentimentality in response to what they perceive as its benefits and drawbacks in both a personal and a public sense. Consideration of the personal and public reasons why a particular individual might choose to invoke sentimentality helps expand the separate spheres model by asking us not only to think about how men and women may view sentimentality differently but also to be always cognizant of the reality that not all men—and not all women—deploy sentimentality in the same way. Such a revised notion of the separate spheres does not ignore the reality that one's identification as male or female carries vastly different political and cultural limitations: It acknowledges that women and men historically have not held equal political or economic privileges and that women traditionally have experienced less freedom and greater scrutiny of their actions in the public sphere. But it also allows space for consideration of the multiple ways individual men and women can perceive and react to those limitations—how members of both groups sometimes resist or defy expectations for masculinity and femininity even as they also embrace and affirm them, often within the space of a single text or specific cultural practice.

If we are to productively revise the separate spheres model, our effort cannot be confined to issues of gender. Looking at Du Bois and Emerson shows how texts written in response to similar personal experiences by men in similar professional positions may be shaped in very different ways by an awareness of the need to address the dynamics of race relations.[2] In particular, it shows how a willingness to address the history of political exclusion and disenfranchisement in the United States—a history from which sentimentality derives much of its power—may be more pressing for an African American writer, such as Du Bois, than for a white writer, such as Emerson. The public expression of sentiment clearly holds different personal and public utility—and risks—for each man. Yet it would be a mistake to see Du Bois, because he is African American, as somehow more sentimental, and Emerson, because he is white, as less so. Rather, as I will argue, the goal of comparing their work is to better understand how each of them, as intellectuals and as fathers, perceived the value and liability of writing publicly in a sentimental mode about their personal losses—perceptions that cannot be sufficiently accounted for by distinctions between black and white but that most certainly were inflected by their different understandings of contingencies of race.

In addition to raising new questions about the shape of the separate spheres model, by linking Du Bois and Emerson under the aegis of their shared status as public intellectuals this essay bridges the work of scholars from diverse backgrounds and disciplines that has shown both men to

be key public figures in the development of American thought and letters but has produced few sustained comparative readings of their work.
Regarding Emerson, historian Mary Kupiec Cayton writes, "He was the
first professional intellectual, one of the first media heroes, the first modern American poet and writer."[3] And a host of literary and cultural critics,
ranging from Joel Porte and Barbara Packer to Michael Lopez and Christopher Newfield, recognize Emerson as a thinker whose influence extended
far beyond not only the geographical and cultural limits of New England
but also the chronological boundaries of the nineteenth century.[4] Du Bois
is likewise celebrated. Arnold Rampersad declares, "If the history of ideas
in Afro-America is ever written, Du Bois should occupy the most conspicuous place," and biographer David Levering Lewis asserts, "In a real sense,
Du Bois was seen by hundreds of thousands of Americans, black and white,
as the paramount custodian of the intellect that so many impoverished, deprived, intimidated, and desperately striving African-Americans had either
never developed or found it imperative to conceal."[5] Moreover, critics as
diverse as Anita Haya Patterson, Shamoon Zamir, and Paul Gilroy have
demonstrated, respectively, Du Bois's pivotal role as a political activist, his
engagement with traditions of both American and European philosophy,
and the extent to which his political and intellectual opinions have exerted
a truly transnational influence.[6]

As the parallel commentaries on their intellectual activity and cultural
influence make clear, there is vast potential for comparative study. Yet there
have been relatively few efforts to bring Du Bois and Emerson together in a
sustained fashion that might enrich our understanding of both.[7] That such
a separation exists is proof of the persistence of general habits of segregation
that motivated Du Bois's oft-quoted claim in *The Souls of Black Folk* that "the
problem of the twentieth century is the problem of the color-line." It also
is proof of the need, more specific to habits of scholarly tradition, for critical methodologies that not only put texts by black and white writers side
by side in the same space—whether in a collection of scholarly essays, an
anthology, or an undergraduate syllabus—but also, and even more important, make active use of such space with an eye towards mutually-revealing
comparison.

A comparative reading of Du Bois's and Emerson's texts on the deaths
of their sons reveals both men calling on sentimentality to memorialize
their offspring in similar ways: as martyred innocents—types of sentimental culture's ideal or sacred child—whose deaths signal the cultural degen-

eration of virtue *and* as future intellectuals whose untimely passing marks the loss of a vast potential for public leadership and social change. Both Du Bois and Emerson conceptualize these roles as complementary; indeed, as I will show, each man's status as father and public intellectual necessitates the construction of his son as both sacred child and intellectual heir. For these two figures, arguably among the most influential writers and speakers in the American intellectual tradition, the loss of a son becomes a way to make use of sentimentality's affective charge to enliven possibilities for metaphysical change as well as political and cultural reform. Yet, as I also will show, the use of sentimentality holds different consequences, intellectually and emotionally, for each, in part because of racial contingencies; inscribed within their texts on personal loss are striking indications of how each perceived both the sacrifices and gains of writing publicly in a sentimental mode.

Fathers and Sons

On 20 January 1842, Ralph Waldo Emerson traveled home to Concord, Massachusetts, after completing a two-month lecture series in Boston. Such trips were becoming more frequent in the early 1840s, taking him farther afield as he expanded his efforts as a professional speaker on the lyceum circuit; Emerson came to view the lyceum platform as a new kind of secular pulpit, and, by the middle of the decade, he was as likely to be found speaking to an audience at the Masonic temple in Boston as delivering a sermon to his congregation in Lexington. In short, he had begun to assume the mantle of what today we would call the public intellectual.

Just days after his return from Boston, scarlet fever struck the children of the Emerson household. Daughter Ellen was mildly affected. Baby Edith escaped altogether. But five-year-old Waldo, Emerson's first-born child and his only son, became seriously ill. He deteriorated rapidly and died at 8:15 in the evening on January 27.

Later that same night, Emerson reported the death in a letter to his longtime friend and financial advisor Abel Adams and asked for his help in putting notice of the death in the newspaper:

> My dear friend,
>   My little boy died this evening. He has been ill with scarlatina since Monday night. My darling my darling!

Will you insert in the newspaper that Waldo, son of R Waldo Emerson died on Thursday of scarlatina.

Mrs. A & Abby will grieve for their little favorite.   —R. W. E.[8]

In the letter's left-hand margin, Emerson penned the exact wording of Waldo's death notice as he wished it to appear in print. Published in the *Boston Daily Advertiser* on Saturday, 29 January, it read simply: "In Concord, Ms. on Thursday, of scarlatina, Waldo, son of R. Waldo Emerson, 5 yrs 3 months" (*Letters,* 3:6).

Emerson wrote about Waldo at least forty times in letters and journal entries during the five-year period immediately following the boy's death. Many of the letters are short notes meant to inform family and friends of the sad news; others are much longer, often serving to memorialize Waldo in sentimental detail and speculate on what he might have achieved had not his life been cut short. The journal entries likewise range from brief observations and succinct declarations—"Yesterday night at 15 minutes after eight my little Waldo ended his life"—to page-length records of the boy's adventures and detailed anecdotes meant to illustrate his many virtues and to reiterate that he no doubt would have become an intellectual and cultural leader in his own right.[9] Many of these private letters and journals, in turn, became sources for Emerson's two formal, public references to Waldo's death: the 1844 essay "Experience" and the 1847 poem "Threnody," texts that echo respectively (and uncannily) the terse detachment of the official death notice and the sentimental anguish of the initial letter to Adams.

Like Emerson, W. E. B. Du Bois was just coming into his own as a public intellectual and cultural commentator when he suffered the acutely painful loss of a son. Following the successful publication in 1899 of his sociological study *The Philadelphia Negro,* a comprehensive examination of African American urban life commissioned by the University of Pennsylvania, Du Bois had taken a faculty position at Atlanta University. In the spring of that year, his only child, Burghardt, contracted a severe case of diphtheria. Timely diagnosis and the possibility of treatment were hindered by the fact that Atlanta was home to few African American physicians, and white doctors routinely refused to see black patients. The parents thus remained helpless as their son's fever grew worse and his condition deteriorated. After ten days of struggle, he died at sundown on 24 May; he was little more than two years old.[10]

Less than four years later, Du Bois would write publicly and in highly sentimental terms of his son's brief life and tragic death in an essay from *The Souls of Black Folk* entitled "Of the Passing of the First-Born." Strikingly dissimilar in tone and content from the other essays in *Souls,* this elegiac tribute stands as a singular and complex manifestation of sentimentality (one given relatively little attention by critics) in a book that, more than any other, powered Du Bois's transition from up-and-coming academic to established public intellectual and race leader. Following the sentimental convention of constructing dead or dying children as sacred and ideal, Du Bois characterizes Burghardt as a darling of virtue, a boy with the ability to elicit tenderness and sympathy from the most hardened of hearts and the capacity to draw admiration from all who observed him. Had he lived, the essay contends, his intellectual gifts would have allowed him to inherit his father's newly earned mantle of race man and advance his program of racial uplift. Meanwhile, his physical appearance (light-skinned with fair hair and blue eyes) would have allowed him to reach out to a white audience and expand his father's work of reshaping black-white relations. Burghardt's loss, we are meant to understand, is as much a tragedy for humankind as for his immediate family and, perforce, must serve to rally members of both races to change the conditions of social inequality that allowed it to happen.

Fathers, Sons, and Sentimentality

In the opening pages of "Experience," published in October 1844, Emerson writes publicly for the first time of the death of his son two years earlier, depicting both his son and the personal experience of loss in entirely unsentimental terms:

> In the death of my son, now more than two years ago, I seem to have lost a beautiful estate,—no more. I cannot get it nearer to me. If tomorrow I should be informed of the bankruptcy of my principal debtors, the loss of my property would be a great inconvenience to me, perhaps, for many years; but it would leave me as it found me,—neither better nor worse. So it is with this calamity: it does not touch me: something which I fancied was a part of me, which could not be torn away without tearing me, nor enlarged without enriching me, falls off from me, and leaves no scar.[11]

These brief but oft-quoted remarks on the death of Waldo and Emerson's disconnection from grief give way almost immediately in the essay to a broader discussion of loss in general. The autobiographical, confessional mood is quickly abandoned in favor of a more abstract, universal tone, and the particular experience of Waldo's death is, as numerous critics have remarked, soon subsumed by a series of philosophical observations about the nature of experience. Feelings—or the lack thereof—regarding the boy's passing are presented not as significant in and of themselves but rather as signifiers of the problematic status of all experience: No matter what form it takes, we never perceive it fully.

The fact of Waldo's tragic death in 1842 has become something of a signpost within the field of Emerson studies, a biographical moment that corresponds to what seems to be an increasing tone of skepticism and gloominess in his philosophy. Most critics acknowledge in some fashion that a pessimism of vision beset Emerson in the 1840s and that he seems to see himself as existing in a state of crisis and disconnection that encompasses both life and work.[12] It is not my goal here to offer a psychoanalytic account of the way grief is conceptualized in "Experience," nor is it my intent to explore possible links between a pessimistic sensibility in his intellectual work during the 1840s and 1850s and the losses he experienced in his personal life. These and related topics have been addressed at length in the expansive body of Emerson scholarship. My purpose in noting Emerson's relatively unfeeling, impersonal discussion of his son in "Experience" and his detached analogy of the death with the loss of property is to highlight, by way of contrast, the degree to which the personal and the sentimental are incorporated into "Threnody," Emerson's other piece of public writing about Waldo, and to show how the poem differently envisions both the child's status and the nature of the father-son bond.

"Threnody," which appeared in 1847, three years after "Experience," adds several dimensions to the characterization of Waldo in the essay, all of which humanize and otherwise complicate both its decidedly unsentimental vision of him as a "beautiful estate," and its presentation of his death as no more than a "great inconvenience" that leaves Emerson "neither better nor worse" (*EP,* 473). Before looking more closely at the poem itself—to better apprehend both the shift from emotional detachment to a more intimate mode as well as the various identities and roles Emerson associates with his son in both works—it is enlightening to look at the ways these modes and roles are registered in Du Bois's "Of the Passing of the First-Born," a text in which the father-son relationship is, by turns, intimate and distant, and the child's identity is constructed in multiple ways that speak to the meaning of loss in personal, emotional terms as well as with regard to public, intellectual, and cultural concerns.

That sentimentality is a key element of "First-Born" is evident from the essay's opening lines, which I quote at length as much for the strikingly personal tone they set as for the range of feelings they document:

> "Unto you a child is born," sang the bit of yellow paper that fluttered into my room one brown October morning. Then the fear of fatherhood mingled wildly with the joy of creation; I wondered how it looked and how it felt,—what were its eyes, and how its hair curled and crumpled itself. And I thought in awe of her,—she who had slept with Death to tear a man-child from underneath her heart, while I was unconsciously wandering. I fled to my wife and child, repeating the while to myself half wonderingly, "Wife and child? Wife and child?" . . . Up the stairs I ran to the wan mother and whimpering babe, to the sanctuary on whose altar a life at my bidding had offered itself to win a life, and won. What is this tiny formless thing, this new-born wail from an unknown world—all head and voice? [13]

The scene in which Du Bois learns of his son's birth is among the most dramatic and sentimental moments in "First-Born." The child is understood as possessing a sacred quality—his birthplace is a "sanctuary"—and Du Bois takes care to present him as both his own "creation" and as a being whose origin is somehow outside of or beyond the local family unit. We are meant to understand that he is something more than a son: He comes from an "unknown world" and has ties to something larger. Moreover, I want to point out that the mention of qualities stereotypically associated with an infant— "all head and voice"—is not incidental, nor simply a way to establish the boy's normalcy. References to intellect and speech recur throughout "First-Born," and these opening lines are part of that pattern: Du Bois plays on tropes of head and voice to construct Burghardt as both typical infant and nascent public intellectual, a figure whose identity is defined by the ability to speak in meaningful ways and make his voice heard by those around him.

The sense of wonder and awe that accompanies Du Bois's account of the birth of his son is meant to underscore by way of counterpoint the subsequent tone of alienation and pessimism that will, as in Emerson's "Experience," characterize the description of the child's death. Although Burghardt's arrival is cause for optimism and celebration, the joy of fatherhood will be short-lived. Paternal happiness quickly gives way to a sense of bitterness and anger as Du Bois recounts his son's funeral procession and the racial epithet—"Niggers!"—uttered by whites who passed by (Du Bois, 509). As Du Bois moves from the moment of Burghardt's birth through his sickness, death, and burial, the various dimensions of identity—first-born son, sentimental icon, nascent public intellectual—take on a certain personal utility. On the one hand, they allow him to claim a degree of intimacy with his child, to express fully and in the most sentimental of terms the extent to which he and others are captivated by Burghardt's charms:

> The world loved him; the women kissed his curls, the men looked gravely into his wonderful eyes, and the children hovered and fluttered around him. I can see him now, changing like the sky from sparkling laughter to darkening frowns, and then to wondering thoughtfulness as he watched the world. (Du Bois, 509)

On the other hand, the flexibility of these multiple identities offers Du Bois the chance, later in the essay, to separate himself somewhat from the charms of his offspring and discuss the loss in colder, more objective terms—not unlike those Emerson employs in "Experience." In these moments, Du Bois detaches himself from the sentimental portrait he paints early on and begins to address what the loss might mean in cultural terms. But whereas Emerson distances himself from the loss to construct a more abstract discussion of the meaning of all experience, subsuming the personal within the philosophical, Du Bois detaches himself from his loss not to universalize about experience but to redirect his attention to the conditions of racial prejudice and social segregation that contributed to the boy's death, even going so far as to argue that his son was better off dead than alive given the discrimination he no doubt would have faced as "a Negro and a Negro's son" (Du Bois, 507–8).

Both men dissociate from their losses, but they do so to different degrees and in order to proceed in different directions. Emerson entirely dissolves the father-son bond, characterizing the death of Waldo as inconvenient, and, like the bankruptcy of one's debtors, not permanently debilitating; he does so to show that a particular, personal experience, even the loss of a child, is ultimately no more or no less than a marker for the broader problems of perception humans necessarily encounter in trying to apprehend the meaning of any and all experience.

Du Bois maintains the bond but revises its terms, enlarging his discussion of personal loss to make reference to the broader problem of race. He and Burghardt are not just a father and a son, but "a Negro and a Negro's son." But, unlike Emerson, Du Bois stops short of universalizing the experience of loss and draining it of particular meaning; to treat his son's death as Emerson does would only serve to undermine his goals as a public intellectual by downplaying the significance of the particular racial prejudices that helped bring about the tragedy.

Yet Emerson does not always hold Waldo at such a distance, nor does he maintain such dissociation from the personal, emotional effects of the loss. In "Threnody," he constructs the father-son bond as more intimate than in "Experience," and his use of sentimentality is comparable in revealing ways to that of Du Bois. The poem is a polished collection of a series of verses Emerson began working on almost immediately following Waldo's death—they are referred to as "rude dirges" in an 1844 letter exchange with Margaret Fuller—and many of the lines included in the final published version are lifted verbatim from his letters and journals.[14] Emerson biographer Robert Richardson may be overstating the case when he calls "Threnody" "one of the great elegies in English, and a poem in which Emerson rivals the Milton whose 'Lycidas' he had known by heart for so long," but the poem does possess an epic quality and most certainly affirms the capacity of the individual to overcome the anguish and pain of death.[15] The opening stanza acknowledges, as in "Experience," that a loss has occurred, but there is a distinct longing for the child's return and a sense of melancholy that decidedly contradicts the essay's assertion that the father was not touched by the son's loss:

> The South-wind brings
> Life, sunshine, and desire,
> And on every mount and meadow
> Breathes aromatic fire;
> But over the dead he has no power,
> The lost, the lost, he cannot restore;
> And, looking over the hills, I mourn
> The darling who shall not return. (*EP*, 1167)

Moreover, Waldo is given multiple, vibrant identities in the poem, in contrast to the one-dimensional status of property assigned to him in "Experience." Like Burghardt Du Bois, Waldo Emerson is assigned the roles of sentimental icon and nascent public intellectual, and he is presented as a figure with the capacity to capture and hold the attention of an audience beyond his immediate family. Whereas "Experience" describes him as a "beautiful estate," "Threnody" casts him as a child-prophet who, like Du Bois's son, has a broad-based appeal:

> O eloquent child!
> Whose voice, an equal messenger,
> Conveyed thy meaning mild.
> What though the pains and joys
> Whereof it spoke were toys
> Fitting his age and ken,
> Yet fairest dames and bearded men,
> Who heard the sweet request,
> So gentle, wise, and grave,
> Bended with joy to his behest,
> And let the world's affairs go by,
> Awhile to share his cordial game,
> Or mend his wicker wagon-frame,
> Still plotting how their hungry ear
> That winsome voice again might hear;
> For his lips could well pronounce
> Words that were persuasions. (*EP,* 1168)

As in Du Bois's "First-Born," the tropes of voice and intellect recur throughout "Threnody"; Emerson provides a sentimental portrait of an ideal child who is both typical infant and exceptional future leader: The content of his speech may be appropriate for his "age and ken," but there is no mistaking the maturity of its timbre and its ability to persuade all auditors, women and men, young and old, to heed his message. Emerson ascribes to Waldo the same heightened sense of virtue, precocious charisma, and preternatural wisdom Du Bois associates with Burghardt. And, as "Threnody" unfolds, Waldo is given additional sentimental mantles—"gracious boy," "chieftain" of his playmates, "captain" of the schoolyard, "child of paradise"—all of which serve to expand in striking fashion the one-dimensional view of the child in "Experience."

Most intriguing and telling is not so much the different approaches "Experience" and "Threnody" seem to take with regard to the personal experience of loss—the former dissociating father from son in the coldest of terms and the latter reinscribing that relation with highly sentimental language—but rather what those approaches allow in both a personal and a public sense. The combination of essay and poem permits Emerson to both satisfy the imperatives of his intellectual program—to speak of Waldo's death as evidence of a larger philosophical dilemma regarding the difficulties of perception and self-knowledge—and to construct a more human and intimate memorial to his son.

For Du Bois, Burghardt's multidimensional identity becomes useful from both personal and intellectual standpoints as he begins to consider his child's physical features and the social good that could result from his potential ability to appeal to a white audience (these physical features and the possibility of appealing to or even passing as white are also a source of ambivalence and anxiety, as I discuss in more detail below). The notion that the child is both Du Bois's own creation—his flesh and blood—and something beyond or greater than a biological heir is reiterated in subsequent depictions that refer to Burghardt's intellectual destiny:

> I . . . saw the strength of my own arm stretched onward through the ages through the newer strength of his; saw the dream of my black fathers stagger a step onward in the wild phantasm of the world; heard in his baby voice the voice of the Prophet that was to rise within the Veil. (Du Bois, 507)

Again, we see the tropes of intellectual vision and voice that consistently are associated with Burghardt. Such traits allow the infant boy to be envisioned as a future race man, one who will carry on the dream of his black fathers. Emphasizing that the child is both a biological and an intellectual heir becomes a way to establish the positions of father and son within a distinguished lineage of black male cultural leaders. By linking the child with a history and an intellectual legacy that encompasses even his father's influence, Du Bois shows Burghardt to be both typical and exceptional: typical in that he represents the logical next step in a progression of visionaries and activists, exceptional in that, had he been given the chance to realize his full potential, he not only would have carried on his intellectual ancestors' dream of racial equality but perhaps also achieved it.

The suggestion that Burghardt may have achieved this dream is predicated on the assumption that he can serve as a sentimental icon and an intellectual leader for not only African Americans but also whites. In fact, Du Bois explicitly characterizes the boy's ability to uplift and inspire members of both races: "He loved the white matron, he loved his black nurse; and in his little world walked souls alone, uncolored and unclothed. I—yea, all men—are larger and purer by the infinite breadth of that one little life" (Du Bois, 509). Such transracial appeal is, for Du Bois, the first step toward realizing a vision of society in which black-white distinctions are not automatically problematic. Within Burghardt's sentimentalized world, one in which he offers love without regard to race, where all of humanity benefits from his virtue, and where souls walk "uncolored and unclothed," there exists the possibility that the color line—the problem of the twentieth century in Du Bois's view—may be transcended.

Grounded in sentimentality, this transcendent vision of a world beyond the color line is inextricably bound up with Burghardt's physical appearance and his ability to generate a transracial appeal. Du Bois's discussion of his son's appearance constitutes what is perhaps the most intensely personal moment in the essay. Yet the ambivalent, emotionally charged descriptions of the boy's physical features are given relatively little attention by those few critics who have commented on "First-Born." For them, the tone and subject matter of the essay are fascinating but awkward in relation to *The Souls of Black Folk* as a whole. Appearing in the midst of elegant historicizations of African American culture, powerful polemics on the problems of social inequality, and graceful metaphors for race relations, "Of The Passing of the First-Born" seems almost embarrassingly intimate and clumsy. Shamoon Zamir remarks, "Suddenly, a personal loss that has little to do with the history or politics of racism occupies center stage, and stoic reticence gives way to melodramatic public mourning." [16] In this view, Du Bois's essay on the death of his son seems at once too emotionally fraught and too sentimental—as if he has violated a trust between himself and his audience that permits recollections of the personal, but only in the form of anecdotes from a distant past that eschew pathos in favor of a more rational depiction of racial prejudice or inequality already overcome.

Prior to the essay on Burghardt's painful loss, Du Bois's personal experiences with racism at both an individual and institutional level are presented in *Souls* as obstacles already surmounted, as encounters that, however unjust or improper, helped build his character and increased his capability for leadership. There is the now-famous episode from chapter 1, "Of Our Spiritual Strivings," relating the event of a childhood visiting-card exchange in which "one girl, a tall newcomer" refused Du Bois's card because he was black, an incident that spurred the young boy to excel and prove himself better than both his white and black peers (Du Bois, 364). From that moment on, Du Bois contends, the need to achieve and succeed became a key and permanent feature of his identity, a constant, driving force that shaped his life and career.

And there is the example of chapter 4, "Of the Meaning of Progress," that tells of his efforts while an undergraduate at Fisk University to secure a teaching position at a country school in Tennessee—a common practice among Fisk students seeking to make money during their vacation periods. He describes the prejudices and Jim Crow practices of white school commissioners who invited him for dinner but made him eat separately and alone. In these instances, as with the visiting-card snub, Du Bois uses his experience both to exemplify ill treatment and describe his success in overcoming it. He takes a teaching position despite the insult of being treated as a second-class citizen, and he succeeds in helping his young black charges to learn despite the dilapidated conditions of the school itself. Moreover, he points out how the students and their families—most of which were severely impoverished by segregationist policies—managed to carve out and maintain an existence for themselves even though they enjoyed little opportunity to advance their socioeconomic status (Du Bois, 405–14).

Zamir, along with Arnold Rampersad and Keith E. Byerman, suggest that Du Bois's attempt to articulate the social significance of his son's death is jarring because it differs not just in degree but in kind from the pieces that surround it. In their view, "First-Born" marks a shift in emphasis from rational argument to emotional drama; Du Bois's presentation of Burghardt's passing upsets the carefully constructed balance between personal experience and public argument that exists within and among the other essays. Having established a mode of self-presentation in which incidents from his own history serve in a careful, not-too-personal fashion to elaborate on the problem of racial inequality and to support his argument for social reform, it is as though Du Bois has suddenly gone too far, too fast when he divulges the recent and traumatic loss of his son and exposes experiences and emotions too complex to be articulated or categorized under the rubric of triumph over racial adversity. The discussion of the material and moral particulars of Burghardt's death imparts an acute sense of loss and a new mood of pessimism to the text.

It is not a mistake to identify "First-Born" as different in tone and content from the other essays in *Souls*. Of the fourteen essays that compose the autobiography, only the two described above rely extensively on specific events of Du Bois's life. Despite their origin in personal experience, however, these chapters express little of the sense of immediate and profound loss that characterizes "First-Born." Moreover, they tell us nothing of Du Bois's social or familial relationships, of his roles as son, husband, or father. They portray him as an independent agent, an individual acting alone in the midst of a potentially hostile world without the support of friends or family. In contrast, when Du Bois writes about the death of Burghardt, he presents himself for the first and only time in *Souls* as a figure embedded within a familial framework, as someone with significant emotional connections and close, personal ties to others.

Zamir, Rampersad, and Byerman each call on a particular set of binary oppositions to account for the singularity of "First-Born." Zamir explains its difference from the other essays in terms of oppositions between the political and personal, the rational and irrational. He argues that Du Bois's restrained use of his personal life elsewhere in the autobiography serves as support for political commentary but is itself never made the focal point of examination. And he contends that "First-Born" seems to do just the opposite by allowing an excess of emotion to upset the delicately balanced relationship of autobiography and cultural critique. "First-Born" breaks with the text's overall strategy of personal restraint, according to Zamir, by presenting an element of personal experience that cannot be easily categorized as support for political commentary. He suggests that *Souls* is geared, in general, to control and restrain the personal—to shape it into clear, rational, easily understood anecdotes for the purpose of countering or overcoming racial inequality.

Likewise, Rampersad and Byerman invoke their own oppositions to explain the pattern of generating emotion and formalizing its expression in "First-Born." Both rely on the language of dominance and resistance to describe Du Bois's approach to writing about his son's death. Rampersad sees Du Bois as disrupting the classic conventions of Christian elegy—even to the point of parody—to reveal its inadequacy as a method of expressing the mourning experiences of African Americans.[17] Byerman argues that the complexity of the boy's racial heritage as well as the complexity of the emotional experience of his loss render the elegiac tradition useless as a means of memorial, but sees Du Bois's revisions of that tradition as a highly effective means of subverting racist practices.[18]

Yet as much as Du Bois is invested in the subversive strategies outlined above—in using conventional tools and forms in unconventional ways for purposes of reform—he does not position himself in "First-Born" as over-coming the problems or difficulties raised by his son's death, either from a personal or an intellectual standpoint. He may use Burghardt's loss as evidence of the pressing need for race reform, but he gives no evidence that the essay should be read as a triumph over adversity in the same way the other personal experiences are intended to be read: as proof of his success in overcoming barriers of racism. The multiple dimensions of Burghardt's identity demand a consideration that is less concerned with contextualizing "First-Born" within oppositional frameworks and more focused on revealing the profound ambivalence about the relation of personal experience to public intellectual work on race that exists at the heart of the essay and, by extension, the heart of *Souls*. The point cannot be to identify the essay as an overly personal, sentimental anomaly in Du Bois's larger rational project of conceptualizing race as Zamir does. Nor is it entirely sufficient to view, like Rampersand and Byerman, "First-Born" as evidence of how Du Bois performs the intellectual and literary work of revising received forms or showing them to be inadequate in addressing race-related issues. Rather, the task must be to focus on the subject of the essay itself—Burghardt—and look more closely at the ways in which those concepts of sentimentality and public intellectual status already discussed are further complicated by the dynamics of race, which he literally and figuratively embodies.

The first detailed description of the child's features is admiring of the effects on his looks of a mixed racial heritage:

> How beautiful he was, with his olive-tinted flesh and dark gold ring-lets, his eyes of mingled blue and brown, his perfect little limbs, and the soft voluptuous roll which the blood of Africa had moulded into his features! I held him in my arms, after we had sped far away to our Southern home—held him, and glanced at the hot red soil of Georgia and the breathless city of a hundred hills, and felt a vague unrest. (Du Bois, 507)

This portrait of his son begins with same tone of wonder that defined the essay's opening lines; like the scene of Burghardt's birth, this moment also is intensely personal and highly sentimental. Passages surrounding this one suggest that the child's striking physical beauty corresponds to his height-ened capacity for virtue—we are meant to perceive him as angelic in all senses of the word.

Yet the awe and admiration soon give way to uneasiness and then outright anger at the signifiers of whiteness that appear to have shaped Burghardt's features at least as much, if not more, than the "blood of Africa":

> Why was his hair tinted with gold? An evil omen was golden hair in my life. Why had not the brown of his eyes crushed out and killed the blue?—for brown were his father's eyes, and his father's father's. And thus in the Land of the Color-line I saw, as it fell across my baby, the shadow of the Veil. (Du Bois, 507)

The angry response registers a sense that the boy was doomed from birth to suffer the effects of racial violence, and Du Bois signals his frustration that Burghardt's appearance reflects and reiterates a pattern of racial dominance and oppression whereby whiteness obliterates or limits the possibilities for black expression. By embodying whiteness through his golden hair and blue eyes, he both demonstrates and perpetuates the shadow of the veil. Even beyond the problem of serving as a signifier of white oppression, Burghardt's physical appearance provokes his father's anguish because it may prove to alter or disrupt the generational progression of black male leadership. Whereas Burghardt's transracial appeal is understood elsewhere in the essay as a productive quality, insofar as it will allow him to reach a wider audience and perhaps bridge the divisions between blacks and whites, here the material realities of his whiteness appear to render him unable to stand properly with his black forefathers.

As with Emerson's "Threnody" and "Experience," the contradictory depictions of the child can be viewed in light of the complicated relationship of the personal and the public in Du Bois's work. Sentimentality serves as a means for him to idealize his son's virtue and potential as a leader, and, in the process, invite a sympathetic response to *Souls*'s larger, twofold project of celebrating and uplifting African American culture and restructuring relations between blacks and whites. Yet the status of sentimentality as a link between the private and the political is never entirely secure. In the course of memorializing Burghardt, scenes that invoke the most sentimental of tropes—the joy of the expectant father, the angelic beauty of the newborn son, the sorrow of the child's untimely death—are consistently challenged by other moments when the feelings meant to be signified by these figures and images are seen as misguided or useless. Even more significant are moments when Burghardt's angelic white appearance and capacity to generate sympathy across racial lines are characterized as disturbing, even dangerous to the future integrity of African American culture—scenes in which

Du Bois seems to reject altogether the impulse to memorialize and preserve his son. As I have argued elsewhere, "First-Born" evinces an advance-and-retreat pattern with regard to sentimentality, a pattern that seems to argue for both its potential and its costs as a form for the expression of Du Bois's personal bereavement and a means of advancing his public intellectual visions.[19]

Emerson follows a similar strategy. For him, sentimentality is a way to explore the possibilities and meanings of memorializing his son in the wake of his death. But as many scholars have pointed out, Emerson's memorializations of Waldo, at least in "Experience," do not entirely embrace the need, central to sentimental ideology, to keep and preserve that which is lost. It is a key aspect of Emerson's intellectual project that life and lives can and must constantly be reinvented; following Karen Sanchez-Eppler, it is helpful to acknowledge moments when Emerson appears to reject sentimentalism's belief that cherishing the dead leads to emotional relief. Likewise, it is important to reckon with his insistence that letting go of death creates the opportunity for new beginnings. Rather than foster an impulse to preserve that which is lost, bereavement, in Emerson's view, should encourage a letting go and provide the opportunity and space for remaking to occur.[20]

Yet Emerson's sentimentality is further complicated by the fact that, like Du Bois, he publicly characterizes his son as an intellectual heir who would have inherited his father's role as a secular prophet: an Emersonian man thinking with the power to observe truth and translate it for the good of society as a whole. "Threnody," like the letters and journals, presents a vision of a son who would have carried on his father's project of making his contemporaries more aware of the fundamental unity of individual, society, and nature, a cultural leader who would have provided his audience with the vision and tools to overcome the problems of social fragmentation that Emerson saw as ever more pressing in the 1840s and 1850s.

The sentimentality Du Bois and Emerson invoke is thus inflected, albeit in different ways, by the contingencies of their intellectual programs and, even more importantly, by the fact that the objects of their sentimentality are not only loved ones but also heirs to their cultural visions. The act of writing publicly about the death of a child compelled Emerson and Du Bois to draw on the literary and cultural dimensions of sentimentality as they interpolated personal experiences into their emerging intellectual and political philosophies—an interpolation that proved both useful and troubling in relation to the increasingly active roles each took as leaders and reformers in their not-quite-separate public spheres.

Notes

1 See *Sentimental Men: Masculinity and the Politics of Affect in American Culture*, ed. Mary Chapman and Glenn Hendler (Berkeley and Los Angeles: University of California Press, 1999); *Boys Don't Cry?: Rethinking Narratives of Masculinity and Emotion in America*, ed. Milette Shamir and Jennifer Travis (New York: Columbia University Press, 2002); Dana D. Nelson, *National Manhood: Capitalist Citizenship and the Imagined Fraternity of White Men* (Durham, N.C.: Duke University Press, 1998); Mary Louise Kete, *Sentimental Collaborations: Mourning and Middle-Class Identity in Nineteenth-Century America* (Durham, N.C.: Duke University Press, 2000).

2 It must be noted that although all of the works mentioned above deal primarily with the work of white men, each also includes some discussion of nonwhite figures, whether in direct or indirect terms; *Sentimental Men* and *Boys Don't Cry?* include several essays that address sentimentality and emotion in relation to African Americans and Native Americans, and both Nelson and Kete make references to these issues as well. It is my intent to elaborate on their work by looking even more closely at how sentimental ideology functions with regard to issues of race in the work of an African American writer such as Du Bois and also to study it in relation to the professional status of public intellectual, which Du Bois and Emerson share.

3 Mary Kupiec Cayton, *Emerson's Emergence: Self and Society in the Transformation of New England, 1800–1845* (Chapel Hill: University of North Carolina Press, 1989), 159.

4 See Joel Porte, *Representative Man* (New York: Oxford University Press, 1979); Barbara L. Packer, *Emerson's Fall: A New Interpretation of the Major Essays* (New York: Continuum, 1982); Michael Lopez, *Emerson and Power: Creative Antagonism in the Nineteenth Century* (DeKalb: Northern Illinois University Press, 1996); Christopher Newfield, *The Emerson Effect: Individualism and Submission in America* (Chicago: University of Chicago Press, 1996).

5 Arnold Rampersad, *The Art and Imagination of W. E. B. Du Bois* (New York: Schocken Books, 1990), 292; David Levering Lewis, *W. E. B. Du Bois: Biography of a Race, 1869–1919* (New York: Henry Holt, 1993), 3.

6 See Anita Haya Patterson, *From Emerson to King: Democracy, Race, and the Politics of Protest* (Oxford: Oxford University Press, 1997); Shamoon Zamir, *Dark Voices: W. E. B. Du Bois and American Thought, 1888–1903* (Chicago: University of Chicago Press, 1995); and Paul Gilroy, *The Black Atlantic: Modernity and Double Consciousness* (Cambridge: Harvard University Press, 1993).

7　There have been a few notable exceptions to this pattern. Zamir and Patterson both discuss Emerson and Du Bois in relation to philosophy as well as to literary and sociopolitical issues, but, as the titles of their books indicate, each devotes the bulk of attention to one particular writer. Cornel West also offers some comparative readings of Emerson and Du Bois in his provocative book *The American Evasion of Philosophy: A Genealogy of Pragmatism* (Madison: University of Wisconsin Press, 1989).

8　Ralph Waldo Emerson, *The Letters of Ralph Waldo Emerson,* ed. Ralph L. Rusk (New York: Columbia University Press, 1939), 3: 6. All subsequent references to Emerson's letters will be to these editions unless otherwise noted. They will be cited as *Letters* followed by the volume and page number.

9　Ralph Waldo Emerson, *The Journals and Miscellaneous Notebooks of Ralph Waldo Emerson,* ed. William H. Gilman, Ralph H. Orth, et al. (Cambridge: Belknap Press of Harvard University Press, 1960–1982), 8: 163–65. All subsequent references to Emerson's journals are to these editions and will be cited as *JMN* followed by the volume and page number.

10　Lewis, *W. E. B. Du Bois,* 227.

11　*Ralph Waldo Emerson: Essays and Poems,* ed. Joel Porte (New York: Library of America, 1996), 472–73. All subsequent references to Emerson's essays and poems will be to this edition (unless otherwise indicated) and will be cited in the text as EP followed by the page number.

12　See Porte, *Representative Man;* Packer, *Emerson's Fall;* and Lopez, *Emerson and Power;* see also David M. Robinson, *Emerson and the Conduct of Life: Pragmatism and Ethical Purpose in the Later Work* (Cambridge: Cambridge University Press, 1993). In addition to these critical works, see also Robert D. Richardson Jr.'s biography, *Emerson: The Mind on Fire* (Berkeley and Los Angeles: University of California Press, 1995).

13　*W. E. B. Du Bois, Writings,* ed. Nathan Huggins (New York: Library of America, 1986), 507. All subsequent references to Du Bois's writings are to this edition unless otherwise noted and will be cited parenthetically in the text as *Du Bois* followed by the page number.

14　*JMN,* 8: 56; *Letters,* 3: 7–10.

15　Robert D. Richardson, *Emerson: The Mind on Fire,* 359.

16　Shamoon Zamir, *Dark Voices: W. E. B. Du Bois and American Thought, 1888–1903,* 190.

17　Arnold Rampersad, "Slavery and the Literary Imagination: Du Bois's *The Souls of Black Folk,*" in *Slavery and the Literary Imagination,* ed. Deborah E. McDowell and Arnold Rampersad (Baltimore, Md.: Johns Hopkins University Press, 1989), 120–21.

18　Keith E. Byerman, *Seizing the Word: History, Art, and Self in the Work of W. E. B. Du Bois* (Athens: University of Georgia Press, 1994), 30–31.

19　See "How To Be a (Sentimental) Race Man: Mourning and Passing in W. E. B.

Du Bois's *The Souls of Black Folk*" in *Boys Don't Cry?: Rethinking Narratives of Masculinity and Emotion in America,* ed. Milette Shamir and Jennifer Travis (New York: Columbia University Press, 2002).

20 Karen Sanchez-Eppler, "Then When We Clutch Hardest: On the Death of a Child and the Replication of an Image," in *Sentimental Men: Masculinity and the Politics of Affect in American Culture,* eds. Mary Chapman and Glenn Hendler (Berkeley and Los Angeles: University of California Press, 1999), 76–79.

"Few of Our Seeds Ever Came Up at All":

A Dialogue on Hawthorne, Delany, and the Work

of Affect in Visionary Utopias

CHRISTOPHER NEWFIELD AND MELISSA SOLOMON

This essay began as a series of extended conversations on the positioning of affect within political discourse: the genealogy of anger that Jill Nelson traces in *Volunteer Slavery: My Authentic Negro Experience* in which she documents her agitation for equal treatment in the workplace; the highly contested role of enjoyment (particularly sexual enjoyment) that Jane Gallop defends as an important and hard-won component of her own style of feminist pedagogy, in *Feminist Accused of Sexual Harassment;* and finally, the role of pleasure in the conception and creation of urban living spaces founded on Samuel Delany's politics of cross-class contact. As these conversations grew, it seemed increasingly important to articulate the ways affect gets constituted in and as a result of politics and also to develop new theories about affect itself as an important political field. Here, we hope to share both the music of that dialogue and one particular set of findings we reached about the relation of "pleasure" to self- and community-liberation.

"Pleasure" is not itself an affect, but it is at once the product and sign of what psychologist Silvan Tomkins calls, "the enjoyment affect" and "joy center."[1] Pleasure is the result of drive satisfaction sometimes and of positive affect always.[2] Linked in this way, pleasure and affect say each other's name, and the properties of one have the potential to reveal a great deal about the properties of the other. As we began examining the multiple, politically situated, and often incoherent assumed relations of "pleasure" to utopian self-liberation, we discovered that in our pathway lay the discoveries of what "pleasure" makes visible about (our contemporary cultural conceptions of) affects such as joy and shame. Consequently, this essay is as centrally concerned with affect in general, a "rich phenomenology of emotion,"[3] as it is with pleasure and pleasure-phobia in separate spheres culture. These distinct topics are, at times, nearly impossible to disentangle from each other.

We proceed by untying some of the traditional hermeneutical binds around the concept of "pleasure" to find out which interpretations have limited its domain and as such acted as prohibitions. In what ways might pleasure operate just on or beyond the edge of current critical understanding? Second, we will pause, along the way, for an extended meditation on one particular set of hermeneutics: those originating in and around nineteenth-century separate spheres discourse, in which the separation of private and public spheres and the corresponding gender polarization constrained theories of affect then and now. Because separate spheres discourse focuses on the difficulties of the transition from the private to the public sphere, affects that are encouraged or even lauded in private life come under suspicion and attack in public life, already largely affect-phobic. Any mention of shame, excitement, fear, terror, distress, interest, enjoyment, or anguish in civic discourse swiftly produces a shamed version of that discourse whose central focus is its own reduction, head down and eyes averted.

The two pieces of utopia literature we will here discuss each, in different ways, connect the phenomenology of pleasure to the political project of perfecting the world: Nathaniel Hawthorne's *The Blithedale Romance* (1852), about a utopian community purportedly dissolved by the passions of its individual members, and Samuel Delany's *Times Square Red, Times Square Blue* (1999), in which Delany posits the individual passion of urban residents as the condition for utopian possibility. Both texts generously and richly situate a set of problematics around affect, by generating different and variously bizarre or convincing, interpersonal sets of cause-and-effect relationships between pleasure and the success or failure of attempts to create utopia. Produced under vastly different historical circumstances, these texts are indeed an unlikely pair in a literary essay about affect, but we found, to our surprise, that reading them together, *as if* in dialogue with each other, provided the means or venue for ventriloquizing the ways utopian visions of community-building are received in a (necessarily objectivizing) critical construct, the roots of which tap separate spheres discourse. Together, these texts also give us play space for theorizing some ways out of that objectivist reasoning. One proposition we start with is that reading Delany with and against Hawthorne helps us realize, with a kind of x-ray vision, that the work of affect in Hawthorne criticism remains largely undertheorized, though it is so crucially tangled into the utopian project of Blithedale farm.

A standard reading of *Blithedale,* for instance, understands affect as ruinously one-dimensional: the anomic, unexplored umbrella concept "individual passion" as killing to utopia. Passion wrecks reason.[4] This standard reading makes the work of affect one of the least interesting places one might dwell for a few critical moments: at once a blurry diagnostic target and predictable reagent bringing "ruin" to whichever complex compound it encounters.[5] We wonder to what degree affect-phobia or affect-aversion in criticism germinates in a separate spheres discourse that creates a hierarchy of genders and *in so doing* controls the social potential of affect. Because the work of affect is so little theorized and so largely abjected in literary study, even its barest outlines tend to disappear from view.[6] As such, one formidable challenge is discerning how to bring into discourse something that repeatedly glances off any number of targets and something whose (in)coherence, (ir)relevance, or (in)applicability gets determined by the discourse that reduced it in the first place. Another challenge: tolerating the discomforts of such a paradigm change! Or, if you will, bearing the affects of thinking through affect. Contemporary critics are still less likely to entertain the ways "emotional freedom" functions *against* oppression than they are to fall back on discourses of rights or justice for such leverage. To most commentators, the former doesn't seem to match the weight and gravity of oppression. Passionate freedom is unreliable and irresponsible and can't gain the moral upper hand much less the social power to match the forces of oppression. Emotional freedom, in this view, is little more than narcissism.

One recurring feature of many utopian fantasies is the wholesale unbinding of affect, a counter to Sigmund Freud's link between civilization and repression and between repression and ego stability. Cultures and individuals, in this view, are constituted by defending themselves against drivelike forces from both within and without. The "defensive ego," in other words, is redundant; the ego *consists* of the practices of self-defense. A utopia of liberated affect would be a place where the self would cease to exist—the self's true "no place." We find a particularly valuable alternative in the work of Silvan Tomkins, who devoted much of his professional career to researching affect.[7] Tomkins uncouples drives and affects, which he posits as central to the ordinary metabolism of the organism, part of all conscious and unconscious experience. Hawthorne's America, like Tomkins's and Delany's, generally saw passion as disruptive, but for Tomkins passion is neither inherently alien nor disruptive. Positive affect, especially, is something the organism seeks to maximize.[8] We see Tomkins's work, then, as granting affect a relative autonomy in psychic life. By extension, positive affect is central to individual experience and therefore central to a sustainable, complex society.

We find this supposition profoundly relevant to the work of Samuel Delany, whose theories of "pleasure" and "the pleasant" populate *Times Square Red, Times Square Blue*. His "pleasure" almost always refers to bodily pleasure, whereas "the pleasant" is "pleasure in its most generalized form,"[9] the product and sign of (what Tomkins labels) "enjoyment-joy" and "interest-excitement." Delany's definition of pleasure is never very far away from how pleasure is produced and how it functions. In particular, he believes that maximizing "the pleasant" happens as a direct result of maximizing "interclass contact" in daily life: a supposition that prompts us to examine the clusters of activities which Delany believes maximize this contact and therefore pleasure. He writes, "Life is at its most rewarding, productive, and pleasant when large numbers of people understand, appreciate, and seek out interclass contact and communication conducted in a mode of good will" (111). *Contact* is his term for chance interactions between people, which, unlike networking, are not defined or limited in advance by the type of people engaging in the encounter or an a priori reason for the encounter. Our intent is to use Delany to read out from under the received ideas about the work of affect by opening a dialogue on what besides "ruin" might be said to happen around, through, and because of affective life. His entire book seems organized around this inspiring question: What if life were organized so as to maximize pleasure?

We are motivated to write this essay as an experimental critical dialogue in two voices: Our separate strains meeting for "contact" rather than merged into one unified, married, inseparable unit. For us, it feels materially and theoretically liberating to respect and maintain two distinct voices about a subject ("affect"), which itself contains so many multiplicities. Among these, affect crosses the limits of conscious life, yet is still responsive to external environments (although not in any particularly predictable ways!) Affect is personal and experiential, yet neither exclusively intrasubjective nor exclusively intersubjective. Finally, affect is not untethered from social processes, yet as Hawthorne teaches us, neither is it predictably determined by them. The style in which this piece is written itself performs the asymmetrical relations that are differently punished and cherished yet at the center of both *The Blithedale Romance* and *Times Square Red, Times Square Blue*.

CN: I first read *Blithedale* early in graduate school, around 1983, in a seminar that saw Hawthorne's writings as complex revisions of Puritan intellectual culture. Hawthorne, we learned, was always putting the question of passion to New England's rationalistic theological and political frameworks and finding that passion didn't fit the mold. In this context, *Blithedale*'s Zenobia was an update of *The Scarlet Letter*'s Hester Prynne, and Coverdale was *The Scarlet Letter*'s reborn Dimmesdale. Giving the Puritans their due, we tried to avoid false romanticizations in which passion and "the human" escape repression and overtheologized divinity. We saw no escape in Hawthorne: Those who let passion lead them wound up ashamed and humiliated. They were punished by society, of course, but they were also lain to waste by desire's spontaneous combustion. Hester partially escaped, but only through the Puritan atonement of re-repression. Hawthorne saw affect as irrepressible, but this meant not freedom but a certain doom.

Hawthorne clearly couldn't reject the Puritan rejection of pleasurable freedom. But maybe he was rejecting a more immediate form of regulation which I was learning to call "separate spheres ideology" and "the cult of domesticity." These were bad to the extent that they kept women out of the sphere of politics and economics and stuck them in the sphere of domestic life, where they were to be fulfilled "in marriage and motherhood."[10] Domesticity and separate spheres were bad to the extent that they meant "women's self-renunciation was called upon to remedy men's self-alienation."[11] But at least since the 1970s, feminist scholars had recast the makers and many of the consumers of domestic ideology as shapers of their own destiny who used this patriarchal discourse to do it. Carroll Smith-Rosenberg argued that though "American society was characterized in large part by rigid gender-role differentiation," women (white, middle-class women, that is) "did not form an isolated and oppressed subcategory in male society," for they actively built their world out of their "shared experiences and mutual affection."[12] Other scholars made the even stronger claim that the cult of domesticity meant "not that woman was to be sequestered from the world in her place at home but that everybody was to be placed in the home, and hence home and the world would become one."[13]

Such claims rested on the writing of women like Catharine Beecher and Sophia Hawthorne; the latter, for example, described the home as "the great arena for women" where women "can wield a power which no king or conqueror can cope with."[14]

I chalked up some of the power of this work to rigorous historical and political analysis. I especially liked Carole Pateman's feminist political theory, which exposed the contradiction between liberal ideals of equality in the public sphere and liberal tolerance for subjection in the private, domestic sphere.[15] Domestic tyranny was an enormously important concept for me, and Pateman pointed out the contradictions of trying to raise democratic citizens in despotic homes. But the most important feature of this work, I thought, was the power it granted to affect. Affect was so real on the level of psychic formation and everyday life that it constituted and could alter social power.

I was especially impressed with the work of Jane Tompkins. Tompkins described affect as "sentimental power." Building on other analyses of how and why nineteenth-century proponents of domestic life could feel that emotional states could stand up to superior social forces, she categorically rejected the traditional denigration of "sentiment" as intellectually feeble, naive, morally mediocre, and self-regarding. Sentimental works, she argued, enact "a theory of power in which . . . the very possibility of social action is made dependent on the action taking place in individual hearts." The home could *function* as a kind of already-existing utopian society because it was constituted in part by desires for and ideas about altered states. Tompkins denied that public institutions control the meaning of relationships made from a "spirit of mutual cooperation" and the influence of women's "'loving words,' 'gentle moralities,' and 'motherly loving kindness.'" She embraced feelings usually dismissed in political contexts as regressive and ineffectual claptrap. She then had what I took as the remarkable gall to link this affective world to political economy. "The home, rather than representing a retreat or a refuge from a crass industrial-commercial world, offers an economic alternative to that world," for it is a reflection of the "household economy" which "had supported New England life since its inception" and reflected "the real communitarian practices of village life."[16] Tompkins granted the conservatism of most sentimental writers while insisting on the revolutionary potential of their grasp of the power of affect to make and unmake the larger world. I thought this was wonderful. And very true.

Of course this didn't describe the actually existing families I knew. Nor did it reflect research (feminist or otherwise) on the extent to which the bourgeois family was a site of normalization and social control.[17] It didn't sound like Hawthorne, who wasn't using *Blithedale* to picture the triumph of love. But even if he wasn't finding and celebrating liberating domesticity, I figured, Hawthorne may have been rejecting *repressive* domesticity. Tompkins was valuable in sketching an alternative domesticity, one that no doubt lived in the hopes of many of its ideologues. If this were true, I could read *Blithedale* as tracing the destruction of utopian hopes for "earthly happiness" not to passion as such but to *repressed* passion, passion that lacked a sphere — "domestic" or not — where it could emerge in a relatively safe environment. Hawthorne would then have been criticizing the four main characters for letting their desire for utopian reform regress to a repressed version of the family romance. In Blithedale, they hide inside their complicated family histories.

Still, it's one thing to critique domestic repression, and another to show that reversing repression would make a difference. Repressing affect is bad, but is undoing it any better? Hawthorne never says yes, and his characters stay trapped between repression and desublimation, with no sign of a cure. This ambiguity tortures his critics, who have produced some of the most intelligently undecided readings of his works in American literary criticism. Hawthorne inspires unhappy confessions: At the end of quite a good chapter on *Blithedale*, David Leverenz says, "Hawthorne's [book] makes me feel like Coverdale: bored, annoyed, titillated, and analytically aggressive."[18] In the absence of good theories and examples of un-repression, it was easy to stay close to the frustrated critics.

Leverenz, for example, blasted Coverdale's covertly conventional manhood: "Despite his self-presentation as a patrician aesthete, his voice and behavior express the marketplace masculinity from which he and his 'brothers' try to detach themselves."[19] Another way of putting this is that Coverdale's affective life at Blithedale is ruled by the conventions of the marketplace man at home: passive, entitled, slightly ashamed, and therefore angry. This seemed generally right to me. The novel seemed to provide little basis for another kind of male affective life and pointed toward no undoing of repression. I felt stuck with the transparently fake convention of Coverdale's heteronormative lament: "I was in love with Priscilla."

Thus I shared the critics' irritation with Coverdale. I got a lot of pleasure from *The Blithedale Romance* and yet very little from Coverdale himself. One of *Blithedale*'s biggest problems, I thought, is the presence of people like him. He gets sick from the first ride out to the Blithedale farm and lies in bed during the whole start-up. He lets himself be a businessman's stereotype of the "artist." He's desperate and unreliable. He translates the freedom of the flaneur into voyeurism. Coverdale relentlessly devalues *Blithedale*'s idealism.

It was also easy for critics to read Coverdale as Freud's negative stereotype of the homosexual male. As *Blithedale*'s bachelor dandy, he fails to uphold the regular order of production and reproduction. Hawthorne's culture associated this with what Freud taught us to call narcissism. Coverdale is the kind of Victorian bachelor Freud used to connect narcissism and male homosexuality: These men "proceed from a narcissistic basis and look for a young man who resembles themselves and whom *they* may love as their mother loved *them*."[20] Homosexual love supposedly demands sameness rather than difference and is, under this definition, a regression from complex society to an infantile self-mirroring couple, a paradise for mama's boys.

MS: Queering that (homophobic) reading grid might start with a question like this: Is it possible that the Blithedale "failure" occurs first and foremost as the "failed" relation between Hollingsworth and Coverdale, after which the other "failed" relations seem to pattern themselves?

It's as if Hollingsworth says to each of his fellow reformers, in turn, "Will you support me/my goals?" which each but Coverdale hears/understands as, "I love you. Will you love me?" Hollingsworth treats epistemology—here, the domain or performative range of his idealistic beliefs—*as if* it operates as an affect, and by doing so, he manages to elicit from both Zenobia and Priscilla double returns of love for him and interest-support for his prison reform ideals. This fairly seamless, unarticulated masquerade or substitution of epistemology for affect is key to understanding the failure of utopia at Blithedale farm. To illustrate this dynamic more fully, we could imagine it as a series of repeated conversational substitutions in which Hollingsworth asks each of his three fellow reformers the same question.

1. Hollingsworth: "Will you support me?" (a.k.a. "Do you
   (to Coverdale)   love me? I could love you.")

   Coverdale: "I cannot support you (though I could
       and in fact already do love you)."

Hollingsworth:	"If you don't support my ideals, there is no such thing as love."

---

2. Hollingsworth: (to Zenobia)	"Will you support me?"
Zenobia: (hearing it as "Do you love me?")	"Yes & Yes" (as she writes him a check).
Hollingsworth: (as the check bounces)	"If you don't support my ideals, there is no such thing as love."

---

3. Hollingsworth: (to Priscilla)	"Will you support me?"
Priscilla: (hearing it as "Do you love me?")	"Yes & Yes."
Hollingsworth: (after Zenobia's death and believing himself a criminal who can never be reformed)	"Since my ideals fail, there is no such thing as love."

Neither Hollingsworth nor Coverdale understand epistemology as fully transitive. This results in a permanent break between Hollingsworth and Coverdale, who cares little for Hollingsworth's prison reform philosophies but much for Hollingsworth himself. Under these conditions, the effects of the former are made to poison the latter in a strangely posited cause-effect relation between two elements that cannot actually be illustrated as being *in relation*. Early in the novel, Coverdale registers Hollingsworth's propensity to "befriend" in order to proselytize, but only later experiences the degree to which, in Hollingsworth's universe, affect is ancillary, subservient, yoked to political goals[21] and, as such, emptied of integrity (i.e., definition.) For Hollingsworth, there is a seeming equation at work: Ideals = love, which disables transitivity because it flattens into sameness the two elements whose very differentiation transitivity would require. For Hollingsworth, persons, emotions, situations, goals other than his own (for instance, the project of Blithedale farm!) are either mined for their capacity to advance his own agenda or, in the absence of any such capacity, obliterated.

The "crisis" (as the rupture chapter is named) this creates for those other persons, situations, and goals has many permutations, the sum of which comprise the Blithedale failure. For Coverdale, who loves Hollingsworth and whose labors at Blithedale are made real by such love, Hollingsworth's substitution is nothing short of tyranny, a sign system that makes all others answerable to it. It is the end of relation and the end of his *home* at Blithedale, insofar as he has made his home out of (queer) affective relationships, which are, metaphorically, the very stones he has been digging, hoisting, and building fences with, much more so than with actual earth and mineral formations. Affect *is what is* for Coverdale. It is both the foundation and that which is being erected. For Coverdale, the lack of transitivity between love and knowledge occurs because he puts a brick wall between them: ideals ≠ love.

Zenobia and Priscilla alone treat Hollingsworth's substitution of epistemology for affect as a phenomenon that has transitive potential, though they are no less subject to the punitive results of the brutal disconnect in Hollingsworth himself. Ironically, Hollingsworth creates (as a kind of manipulation for gaining followers) the situation in which both Zenobia and Priscilla can bring together, in bravura moves, the transitivities of love and knowledge, as if the two were connected by mesmeric electricity. Hawthorne's female characters alone seem to understand and occupy transitive spaces as automatically and as effortlessly as breathing. Death for Zenobia is the suffocating realization that her financial support of Hollingsworth was never the bridge between his love for her and his ideals, but rather the mark of love's absence.[22]

The differing shapes and circumstances of Coverdale's, Zenobia's, and Priscilla's love relationships with Hollingsworth, as well as each one's differing response to Hollingsworth's extraordinary inability to recognize affect *as such,* bring into being a confluence of warring and simultaneous (mis)readings of the domain of each one's relation. Each works out of a different epistemology that results in epistemological crisis that results in rupture. In that respect, the Blithedale failure isn't caused by "the individual *passions*" of its members, but instead by their *understandings* of them.

Can you imagine a set of coordinates more prone than these to being graphed by separate spheres discourse? Or a set of coordinates less likely to be recognized as enabling, between them, exchanges that have their own queer motilities, the features of which might never find a way into discussion?

CN: What you're saying is so important—the problem at Blithedale is not that affect runs amok but that it does *not*. The problem is that the characters, especially Hollingsworth and Zenobia, fuse affects with their representations, with their social, epistemological, or romantic ideas. Coverdale sometimes falls into the same trap. For example, he sometimes reduces the affects surrounding his longing to a desire for attachment, bonding, possession, even familial intimacy. He then equates "passion" with desire for the permanent, ego-stabilizing possession of someone else and demands familiar kinds of domestic, selfless compromising as part of the package.

This is the structure of Coverdale's saddest moments. He can't help fixating on the triangle of Hollingsworth, Zenobia, and Priscilla from which he feels excluded.[23] He loses his sense of purpose in coming to Blithedale— pretty much by chapter 8 (of 29) it has been drowned out by thoughts of Hollingsworth, thoughts of Zenobia, thoughts of Priscilla. He knows he's lost himself. He tries to get himself back. He thinks it could be given back to him by one of the others: If Hollingsworth or Zenobia recognized him, he would get himself back again. This quest for Hegelian recognition doesn't work either (see, e.g., 138–39). So he leaves Blithedale, returns to town, and checks into a hotel. The first night, he says, the three others "encroach upon my dreams," and he sees "Hollingsworth and Zenobia, standing on either side of my bed. . . . Bent across it to exchange a kiss of passion" (153). Awakening with an "unreasonable sadness," he pretends to read a book all day while staring from his room into the rear windows of a boardinghouse until, sure enough, two of the three appear in one of its windows. Coverdale renews his sense of having lost himself—his despair that "they should come across me, at the moment when I imagined myself free" (156). This experience of self-loss is the real mesmerism in the book.

Hawthorne shows each desiring character heading toward melancholic isolation. We can try to preserve the domestic paradigm by saying that they all just happen to have a flawed execution of the familiar goal of union. But these characters get melancholia whether they unite or not. When desire fails, it destroys (Zenobia). When it succeeds, it suffocates (Hollingsworth and Priscilla). The novel offers a diagnosis of *inter*subjectivity that anticipates Freud's claim that "the ego is a precipitate of abandoned object-cathexes"—that the ego consists of a series of identifications with lost objects.[24] Thus, romantic desire is a form of melancholia in which the self comes to identify with the always-missing other and to defend itself in vain against the perpetual sense of loss that defines who it is. I think that Hawthorne is suggesting that melancholia is unnecessary.

MS: In reading *Blithedale,* one fears either being (fill in the blank: Coverdale, Hollingsworth, Zenobia, Priscilla) or one fears being one of their victims. This is, in part, because the world of Blithedale is so pleasureless; nobody gets anything. I identify with and fear Coverdale's existence in a world where pleasure is impossible, a world where sentences with triple and quadruple negatives make sense! This likely bears the traces of my own socialization within separate spheres discourse *as a woman:* my panicky recognition of discursive situations in which pleasure, even the *possibility* of pleasure, gets legislated out of existence. At this juncture, theorizing pleasure may merely involve learning how to single it out and recognize its fragilities: at the very least, acknowledging the critical importance of querying its absence.

I think of places in *The Blithedale Romance* where it seems almost futile for Coverdale to test out his friendships with Zenobia, Priscilla, or Hollingsworth: moments when the possibility of communication between Coverdale and anyone else "is certain never to be consummated otherwise than by a failure" (10–11). Coverdale asks Priscilla for one of her purses before he departs Blithedale, but the purse isn't finished. Coverdale, waxing poetic with Hollingsworth as they are "repairing an old stone fence" (129) together, only to hear from Hollingsworth that such musings amount to "nonsense": "You seem," said Hollingsworth, "to be trying how much nonsense you can pour out in a breath" (129). Coverdale tells Zenobia he certainly would have agreed to be her confidante, just at the moment she tells him why she couldn't choose him for that role.

By the time the novel ends, the reader has been well trained in recognizing communication that doesn't communicate, need that doesn't need anything it could have, and other such choreographies for one. Though Priscilla and Coverdale understand and make use of self-pleasure, what we witness is not exactly the refusal of many characters' complex autoerotic worlds to mesh or become other-directed—but more a world in which it is impossible for any one of these four people in any combination to perform for each other anything but resistance, however much they cannot seem to stop looking at each other and looking at each other with hungry intent. Blithedale is a place where no two sets of desires line up symmetrically. Backs are always turned, or in the process of turning, away, and though this gesture isn't performing invitation, it is often nevertheless (almost willfully) read as such.

One thematic that both *Blithedale* and *Times Square Red* illustrate in different ways is the complexity of desire and how desire seldom functions symmetrically: Delany's work because he embraces the lack of symmetricality in sexual experimentation and variation and believes that community life would work best organized to accommodate that, and *Blithedale* because it showcases *resistance* to that lack of symmetricality and the consequences of that resistance, namely, Hollingsworth's insistence that each member think like him in order to couple with him or Coverdale's exile because he both represents and acts on desires that function asymmetrically.

So Coverdale's willfulness may, in part, function to protect the asymmetricalities of his own erotic desire; when lovers turn away from him, instead of following suit, he just eroticizes their backsides. The number of words and phrases for *ass* in his erotic lexicon is formidable! Even (or especially?) from his urban remove in a Boston hotel, ostracized from Blithedale society, Coverdale remarks that there is "vastly greater suggestiveness in the back view of a residence, whether in town or in country, than in its front" (149). Spying on Zenobia and Priscilla from his hotel window, he says, "After several such visits to the window, I found myself getting pretty well acquainted with that little portion of the backside of the universe which it presented to my view" (148). He advances toward the "rear" of the house only when Zenobia has seen him spying and closed the curtain. Though she has forcefully shut him out, Coverdale tells us, "All at once, it occurred to me how very absurd was my behavior, in thus tormenting myself with crazy hypotheses as to what was going on in that drawing room, when it was at my option to be personally present there. . . . In compliance with this sudden impulse, I soon found myself actually within the house, the rear of which, for two days past, I had been so sedulously watching" (162). All of Coverdale's points of conjecture, hope, remove, and alienation (including self-alienation) are connected in the most maddening "knot of dreams" here: Coverdale condemns himself as *absurd* for having *tormented* himself with crazy *hypotheses,* which he (mistakenly) thinks will end by exercising what turns out to be his (mistaken) right to invitation, tried as relief and antidote to his solitary, lonely wondering. This is a person for whom possibility resides where it is least likely and for whom an absurd, mistaken, alienating, and even foreboding circumstance quite often occasions, not retreat or shame, but frontal advance. What's queerest about Coverdale, to me, is precisely this disjunction between his sense of what "to do" in any given situation and the nonaccountability of this sense to alienation, absurdity, and mistake. Those things simply fail "to do" or "to mean" anything predictable. No matter how alienated from or mistaken about others he winds up being, no matter how severed his relationships become, Coverdale never seems to suffer any correlating shame about these circumstances. It is difficult, finally, to separate the filaments of his erotic space from those belonging to his ethical practices at work. Coverdale's style of life is largely shaped by his brave refusal to be shamed by a world in which he finds it difficult to extract sustenance. It seems that absence of pleasure is the circumstance that realizes his ethics of shame refusal.

CN: I love that idea: "the ethics of shame refusal." Is this a "postdomestic" and maybe post-Freudian notion of affect? First of all, I hear you saying that standard "subjection," melancholic heterosexual domestic desire, *does* get disrupted in this book. Subjection gets disrupted in moments of displeasure and not just pleasure. This is such an important thing—we get used to looking for emotional freedom in pleasure when in fact its conditions are laid down in experiences of loss where loss, though painful, goes awry. The lost objects, in these cases, are not incorporated into the individual's identity.

We can see a couple of ways of evading melancholia in the novel. One is to denaturalize melancholia when it acts out. At one point, Coverdale scorns Priscilla's belief that she lives in "a world where everybody is kind to me, and where I love everybody." He insists "my past life has been a tiresome one enough; yet I would rather look backward ten times, than forward once." He asserts that "we may be very sure, for one thing, that the good we aim at will not be attained." Priscilla confronts this melancholic defense by refusing to identify with it. "I don't believe one word of what you say!" she exclaims (75–76).[25] It's easy enough to dismiss Priscilla, but she has already survived enormous deprivation and will continue to do so. There is something about her affective life that can't be bound to Coverdale's. The affective lives of Hawthorne's characters are full of the queer asymmetries you mentioned. Those who survive do so because of them.

The second evasion works through the open grieving of a loss. Coverdale's lamentations are exactly this bringing of sorrow to the surface. He survives quite nicely. Zenobia, for whatever reason, doesn't grieve her loss of Hollingsworth, but denounces him in an exercise of rage she will soon redirect against herself. In contrast, exactly those features that make Coverdale seem weak allow him to survive, for they are symptoms of an open mourning that, experiencing its own processes, evades identification with the lost object. Coverdale's dominant affect is not melancholia but interest.[26]

The sign of Coverdale's avoidance of melancholia is his continuous abundance of *interest* in almost everything, lost and unlost alike. "The function of this very general positive affect," Tomkins wrote, "is to 'interest' the human being in what is *necessary* and in what it is *possible* for him to be interested in."[27] Coverdale keeps his interest ready for all occasions. He is especially remarkable for *maintaining* interest in what rejects him, what does not recognize him, what is supposed to shame him with its asymmetricality yet does not. We might try rereading his voyeurism as a kind of heroic interest. Coverdale's interests show that the ego is not *necessarily* constituted by its lost objects and melancholia. Ties to lost objects may always coexist with interest in current ones—or even with nonmelancholic interest in lost ones.

Postdomestic affective lives manage, then, to maintain a fluid and polyvalent interest that isn't fixed by melancholia. How do they do that? You've already started an answer to the question—shame refusal. Shame targets interest and enjoyment specifically. Interest creates contact and relationships, most of which inspire at least some fear (from social stigma, from unfamiliarity, and so on). Enjoyment implies that the ego need not defend itself against this contact. Where interest and enjoyment, excitement and joy, create contacts and group bonds that reduce the need for ego defense— that *in fact reduce the need for the ego*—shame shuts them down and restores the ego to its usual preeminence. Shame makes the world strange again and fills it up with strangers. It radically narrows the confusing, conflicting, indeterminate, random array of our actual interests and restores the ego's (socially constituted) order. Interest threatens the ego with a sublime variety, with the ego's possible irrelevance to experience.[28] Shame shuts down this matrix of potentially endless affiliation. Shame defends the ego against a utopian intersubjectivity in which the ego might not be necessary. Shame defends the ego against our fragmentary impressions of how this might feel.

We have, then, postdomestic affective life as starting, in *Blithedale,* from interest that exceeds melancholia by keeping shame at bay. What lets this happen? For me, it's Blithedale's apparent failure to manage negative affect.

Anger and shame are felt and mentioned with candid bitterness. Accusations fly at every turn. Blithedale is actually unable to reproduce the domestic paradigm of a group formed of kindred minds, for its differences are open and continuous. What if this isn't Blithedale's failure but its success? It's also somewhat deliberate, since two of the central characters, Zenobia and Coverdale, explicitly repudiate the managerial aspirations of Hollingsworth, the would-be reformer. "Self, self, self!" Zenobia shouts at him toward the end. "You have embodied yourself in a project" (218). Hollingsworth's crime is not simply preferring Priscilla but consolidating the authoritative, preeminent self through the better management of everybody's differences. Coverdale is from beginning to end incapable of that kind of discipline. Coverdale is unprofessional. As a writer, he prefers his own impressions to those of authorities. He's clear about the variation and multitudes of his desires. He's a terrible manager, and that's central to what's good about him. In this sense, art begins where management ends—where shame (at least momentarily) ends. My discomfort with Coverdale owes something to my own professional conditioning, my preference for controlled interests. *Blithedale,* to its credit, escapes *that* kind of domesticity.

Shame domesticates. It works by severing one's interest in others, and hence one's independent, self-generated tie to them, while simultaneously creating a dependence on the source of the shame. Its simplest version is to replace the child's interest in a sibling or friend with obedience to the parent, which destroys the implicit alliance of the siblings against the parent.[29] Shame prevents one from experiencing oneself as independent and one's other affects as valid and real. But there's also the greater half that you describe—Coverdale pursuing enjoyment in a way he can't intellectually assimilate. He notes Priscilla laughing at his law of tiresomeness. She listens to Coverdale's claim that he would "rather look backward ten times, than forward once," and laughs at him, and he moves on with his story. Shame refusal and shame disruption: Blithedale is a stomping ground for both and undermines what so often steers professional middle-class decisions—the cold, desolate, distrustful phantoms that invariably haunt the mind, on the eve of adventurous enterprises, to warn us back within the boundaries of ordinary life (18).

MS: If we play Hawthorne backward, will we hear the sound of Delany? Here's a weird pastoral inversion of (one could say) Delany's politics, a passage from *Blithedale* I picture Delany scratching with the edge of a coin to see what the coating hides: "Many trees mingled their fragrance into a thousandfold odor. Possibly there was a sensual influence in the broad light of noon that lay beneath me. It may have been the cause, in part, that I suddenly found myself possessed by a mood of disbelief in moral beauty or heroism, and a conviction of the folly of attempting to benefit the world" (101).

For Delany, "benefit to the world" occurs as the happy result of "sensual influence"; why, Delany teaches readers to wonder, even bother with the "pretense" of Coverdale's provisional, unconvincing ("possibly" and "may have been the cause") sorts of place holding, nil-result cause-effect sentences, when the thing being theorized (loss of the conviction to benefit the world) bears no probable, provable negative relation to the senses? *Times Square Red, Times Square Blue* is a utopian project that attempts to break down what Delany believes is the false binary between moral beauty/social responsibility and "the untrammeled pursuit of pleasure" (185), something he learns as a child from his socially conservative uncle, a respected judge in the Brooklyn domestic relations court during the 1940s and 1950s: "What homosexuality and prostitution represented for my uncle was the untrammeled pursuit of pleasure; and the untrammeled pursuit of pleasure was the opposite of social responsibility. . . . Pleasure must be socially doled out in minuscule amounts, tied by rigorous contracts to responsibility. Good people were people who accepted this system" (185–86). Delany's vision of social responsibility, in contrast, starts with his challenge for each person to define his or her own ideal sex life and then to organize community life so that it answers to that utopian goal of maximizing pleasure. Community-building will succeed only to the degree that it provides each person all the outlets he or she needs for expansive—instead of "minuscule"—social/sexual interclass "contact," not "contract." His own ideal sex life comprises at least three elements: sex with his committed, central partner; plus casual encounters with a general population of different men; plus "a healthy masturbatory life" (83). Providing this relief map to the varieties of sexual needs he answers to on a daily basis politicizes his disagreement with his uncle's "family values," and not merely because the stories are hot enough to make an uncle blush![30] It also spells out the kind of urban planning an ideal city might include, so that urban residents can maximize their ability to answer, on a daily basis, a variety of their sexual needs.

CN: Yes, it's almost unimaginable, getting contact with the whole range of objects of desire. Imagining it could take the form of social theory, which Delany provides in *Red*. But the more basic starting point for Delany is his literal sex life in porn theaters, which he puts first in the book. We get to watch all this personal and potentially embarrassing stuff *and* watch Delany be utterly unembarrassed. Delany is saying that the prerequisite to thinking of a society of really open interest and desire is refusing the rule of shame—shame that exists to shut interest down. Delany is the great refuser of shame. It's a real joy to watch him do it.

All of the sex Delany describes lacks privacy—anyone in the theater can watch virtually anything that goes on. And then the noted author shows himself to us with his pants down or his mouth on some hard cock *and* refuses the embarrassment. Our embarrassing moments, he says, need not be so embarrassing. He evades the special shame of contact with the "wrong" people, taking as partners the homeless, the disabled, or the schizophrenic. Moving much further down Coverdale's path, Delany finds no one who is outside the zone of his unashamed interest. When we feel less embarrassed, when shame weakens its hold, we can see that his moments of contact are moments of intensity and achieved desire—these are moments where we have gotten what we want. Delany the distinguished author and Delany the blow-job bottom are the same person. In these moments, it's as though we have agency.

What do people want? It's an awkward question to ask in the American context, where virtue means production, efficiency, and delayed gratification. Our common sense tells us that desire seeks "doing as one likes," in Matthew Arnold's phrase, leading to the anarchy of refused subjection. What if desire seeks first and foremost the reduction of shame?

MS: Let's ventriloquize the so-called reasons "why utopia never works." Is it possible to create in dialogue the sound of the violence that meets and polices the attempt to "do as one likes"? We wouldn't have to go back as far as Arnold, either. Contemporary U.S. history provides a near example of the failed utopian ideals of a peace-loving, late 1960s youth generation, resisting U.S. involvement in the Vietnam war with unprecedented, mass antiwar sentiment and social activism. Three decades later, when patriotic service in that same war is used, not to undermine but to buoy the democratic candidacy of the next presidential hopeful, it is depressingly easy to imagine how, in the late 1960s, their LBJ-supporting parents might have "answered" the challenges and revolutionizing hopes of that draft-dodging, hippy, communist, Black Panther– and Homophile League–joining generation with the received notion that "Utopia goes against Human Nature" (whatever *that* is) or by asking, in the spirit of Arnold, "What kind of society would we have if everybody did what they wanted?"

The idea that utopia runs counter to human nature objectifies human nature and operates as a defense against relativism: x can never be y because x is always x. Visions of utopia, which from this angle relativize whatever they touch, thus threaten to violate the (parental, national, sexual, "human") truths they supposedly work against.

CN: Look at Delany outside of the deep Darwinism of market capitalism and what do we see? A person who doesn't want preeminence or control, for these use shame to reduce or block interest even for the winner. For Tomkins, the experience of interest in the outside world enables survival, but it is also the core of enjoyment and joy. This is almost exactly what Delany wants in *Red*. His goal, he says, is "pleasantness," especially across class barriers. Pleasantness is a fundamentally social condition. It expresses a relationship and not a separate state. It involves freedom of interest and contact rather than the power to control interest and control others.

MS: Delany's rhetorical strategy in *Blue* is to argue the merits and benefits of "pleasure" in cruising, and these merits are not presumed in advance to be understood by his reading audience of (assumedly) heterosexual, monogamy-loving, and possibly homophobic interlocutors. Remember this passage, glossing the types of relationships he found at the Capri?

> Despite moments of infatuation on both sides, these were not love relationships. The few hustlers excepted, they were not business relationships. They were encounters whose most important aspect was that mutual pleasure was exchanged—an aspect that, yes, colored all their other aspects, but that did not involve any sort of life commitment. Most were affable but brief because, beyond pleasure, these were people you had little in common with. Yet what greater field and force than pleasure can human beings share? (56)

That last question doesn't feel rhetorical so much as painfully, poignantly necessary when posed against the pleasure-suspecting, pleasure-controlling puritan code of "social responsibility" Delany is trying to pressure. He reminds readers, from a different angle, of Tomkins's theory that affect itself is a "motive . . . , [an] immediately rewarding or punishing experience mediated by receptors activated by the individual's own responses. Motives may or may not externalize themselves in purposes."[31] According to Delany (and Tomkins), pleasure is a force, in and of itself, for what it activates in the individual and need not be yoked to, scaled to, initiated by, or restrained by any mediating "purpose" outside of itself.

CN: True, and yet it's hard to know what autonomous pleasure could mean because it's so readily jerked around by capitalism. Pleasure is still managed by separate spheres discourse: encouraged in a "private" sphere of consumption and intimate relations and tightly controlled in the public world of government and production. Delany argues that capitalist social relations control public pleasure in large part by enforcing class division. Capitalist pressures "perpetually work for the erosion of the social practices through which interclass communication takes place" (111). Lacking everyday familiarity with members of other classes, we perceive them as strangers. As strangers, they carry a potential for threat that we easily exaggerate. Delany is hostile to the new Times Square because it tries to placate "suburban" anxieties about safety by eliminating class mixtures. This maintains fears of class difference rather than offering the experience that might ease these fears and encourage interest in other classes instead. Pleasure becomes dependent on sameness, on a public domesticity. This domesticity keeps tight limits on the range of appropriate affects and relationships.

Delany rejects the domestication of pleasure. He doesn't do it by preferring public over private, or sex communities over suburbanized cities, or pleasure over capitalism. He likes what he calls "contact," but he sees it operating within capitalism and across the public/private divide to ease tensions through interclass communication. It's a relatively modest strategy that tries to build democratic personal lives from existing practices.

Delany contrasts "contact" with "networks": Networks are like professional societies where, for example, a senior member of your field from an important school hears a paper you give at a meeting and helps you get it published. Contact is where you, a struggling writer, start a conversation with the man standing next to you at the remainder table in your local bookstore, start complaining about the treatment your genre receives from reviewers, and he turns out to be a major reviewer who praises your book in his next review. Contact seems accidental, arbitrary, and random—even inherently unjust—and these are potential weaknesses. Networks are organizational—I would say administrative or managerial. They have the advantages of the advanced techniques of management in contemporary society.

But Delany notes some pivotal shortcomings in networks, and the main one is scarcity: "The *amount* of need present in the networking situation is too high for the comparatively few individuals in a position to supply the much needed boons and favors to *distribute them in any equitable manner*" (136, emphasis in original). Networks share the pyramid structure that organizations almost always take on in capitalist life. They sustain the inequality and exclusion that people try to overcome by seeking them out. The result is that networks are spaces of intense competition. Competition increases behaviors of aggression, defeat, shame, and the general channeling of interest into "productive" and self-defensive modes.

One of my favorite things about Delany's idea of contact is that though he wants to mitigate competition, he doesn't link it to the traditional utopian socialist attempt simply to replace competition with cooperation.

MS: He calls network and contact "vector processes rather than fixed positions" (163), a phrase that undoes the binaries "competition or cooperation," and "male or female" by highlighting the changing relational nature of these activities that do not neatly typify gender. "Male-female" gives so much less traction than, say, "stranger-friend": For me, saying the words "stranger-friend" out loud is such an interesting speech act! The hidden or implied verbs inside the phrase "stranger-friend" (finding, recognizing, making, fearing, taming, etc.) suggest that the phrase itself names vector processes or changing relational positions between people. "Stranger-friend" is also such a hopeful pair of words put together, so much less laden, tiresome, reified than "male-female."

CN: Exactly! Delany isn't interested in a utopia of reciprocal feelings among the same, or in cooperation. He wants contact. Without symmetry. He wants lots of things—true love, close friends, many lovers, casual sex, top sex, bottom sex. He wants contact without commitment—nothing lasting, just temporary and passing contact. He wants what Jane Jacobs clearly saw as a great gift of cities: contact without "emotional engulfment."[32] I think of it as a relationship in which pleasure, great in itself, also reduces fear and shame, enabling more open interest, freer interaction, and a reduced need for domination. I think of it as emotional democracy, which is a little too sweet. Pat Califia calls it "whoring in utopia."

Delany's more fundamental contrast is between competition and *complexity*, where complexity means increased information in a differentially structured environment. Tomkins has written that we should define freedom not as the absence of determinism but as the relatively large number of options and pathways opened by the complexity of systems and feedbacks in any organic or social context.[33] Freedom increases as complexity increases. Contact maximizes complexity, and it is thus in contact where most of that freedom begins.[34] Complexity is an indirect factor in Delany's rejection of Times Square–style "renewal." Urban "clean-ups," motivated by a fear of the stranger, unjustly stigmatize many classes of people and should be opposed for that reason. They should also be opposed because they attempt artificially to reduce information and to stigmatize interest in it. Delany simultaneously ties contact to complexity and lessened defenses, which in turn increase the possibility of pleasantness.

Many people associate utopia with moral ideas that unfortunately conflict with selfish, violent human reality. Others associate utopia with a "state of nature" that our necessarily social lives will keep us from finding. Still others see utopia as a symptom of a "repressive desublimation" that reproduces capitalist systems. But utopia also expresses desirable, actually existing everyday feeling and action that has not yet been codified by self-replicating systems. The genius of Jacobs's book on cities was to show the entirely everyday and banal power that people had to make the dangerous safe, the dull interesting, the difficult easy with daily arrangements that included the minor archive of such choices as walking today down West 93rd Street today instead of West 94th. The right urban systems helped—short blocks instead of long, shops next to the park and near their buildings, a mixed population using the sidewalk, strangers intermingled with neighbors or friends. The utopian clearly lives in unashamed experience. This is the realm of the complexity that Raymond Williams defined as the "emergent"—the "specificity of present being, the inalienably physical, within which we may indeed discern and acknowledge institutions, formations, positions, but not always as fixed products, defining products."[35] We could define shame as what "fixes" the emergent by identifying it with visible social formations.

Moments of great capitalist expansion are also moments of great amnesia. In Massachusetts in the 1840s and New York City in the 1990s, complex social systems seemed insignificant next to the wealth of markets. Markets were thought to deliver everything of value, and the market personality was the one that mattered. Productivity dwarfed personal connections, commerce overshadowed the traffic in pleasure, everything queer was cast as a violation. The process of reification that underwrites commodities and markets also denies the complexity of actual interest. Interest produces an utterly polymorphous, "disordered" array of contact where we lead our affective lives. Capitalist norms of social progress, deploying domestic norms for both public and private, would replace the contact-matrix with its reductive dynamics.[36]

In this historical moment, it's utopian simply to remember. It's utopian to remember how much of our pleasure comes from nonmarket webs of association, how much of this we need to live without fear. It's utopian to take in how market competition produces fear, demands fear, lives on it, celebrates it as what makes us produce, as what we produce for. The alternative to the poor market substitute for contact isn't a world of unity and solidarity but a world of complex and unmanageable interest. In envisioning—remembering and realizing—the pleasantness of this, Hawthorne and Delany know how full we all already are of this interest, how it crosses class and sexual orientation and other established boundaries.

Delany, especially, thinks pleasantness is possible when we come to society in a state of plenitude—plenitude in our unashamed interests. The theaters are important not simply for multiplicity but for plenitude. Men are there, they are present in the world, they inhabit the world, the world is full of men. Many of these men are available for contact. But the deeper point is that the world is available. The world is there. We act as though the world is missing when it is not. The world is not missing. The world is present through the constant availability of contact. Delany is saying, "Don't build your cities as though the world were missing." Don't build them as though people were missing. Don't build them as though it's better if they were missing because that helps you control your fear. Above all, don't build them as though *you* are missing—as though the lost object is you, and as though you should live in perpetual mourning for the ego-ideal you have replaced yourself with.[37] It's an interestingly passionate, sex-filled antiromanticism—a profound, Coverdale- and Priscilla-like refusal to take melancholia "seriously," to take it as the truth of the subject.

MS: Delany's own political theories intimately address the ways bodily pleasure is constituted within/as politics: a theory project that can never, for him, be reduced to the space of mere discussion, however politicizing that discussion might be. Actual bodies live within Delany's discourse, and those actual bodies constitute so much of what, for him, *is* political. Remember how objectionable he finds the conversation at "OutWrite," an academic conference focusing on the question, "Why is there homophobia?" ? For him, the academic arguments at that conference existed "largely at the level of discourse," and, as a result, he believes the younger gay activists there found it:

> hard to articulate the greater discursive structure they [were] fighting to dismantle, as do those conservatives today who uphold one part of it or the other without being aware of its overall form. But discourses in such condition tend to remain at their most stable.
>
> In order to dismantle such a discourse, we must begin with the realization that desire is *never* "outside all social constraint." Desire may be outside one set of constraints or another; but social constraints are what engender desire; and, one way or another, even at its most apparently catastrophic, they contour desire's expression. (186)

As much as Delany would bring smart young men out of the porn theaters and into college classrooms (he has, in fact, helped several fill out college applications and edited college-level papers under the bare aisle lights of an otherwise darkened theater) is as much as he would bring smart young men out of college classrooms and into porn theaters for some "lived" queer theory, whose project he defines as the attempt to illustrate "what is wrong with a discourse that places pleasure and the body in fundamental opposition to some notion of a legally constrained social responsibility, rather than a discourse that sees that pleasure and the body are constitutive elements of the social as much as are law and responsibility" (186). For Delany, the real answer to the question, "Why is there hatred and fear of homosexuals (homophobia)?" involves "the systemic relation between pleasure and responsibility in which 'prostitution and perversion' are seen to be caught up" (186).

CN: Delany's utopia is not one of equitably administered justice or a state of personal mastery or pleasure outside of society. It is not the escape from law and form, which Delany thinks is impossible. "Public sex situations," he writes, "are not Dionysian and uncontrolled but are rather some of the most highly socialized and conventionalized behavior human beings can take part in" (158). It is not the escape from order: Delany rejects the right's perennial, influential belief that instinctual gratification destroys order and life, the idea that "the true Eden where all desires are satisfied is red, not green. It is a blood bath of instincts" (185, citing Bruce Benderson). Delany's utopia is instead the ability to reject—at least some of the time and in part—social taboos on contact with others and with the world. Nothing necessarily follows from this contact. It can be good or bad, pleasant or unpleasant, and will proceed without law and without guarantees. All that depends on what we do next. I think Delany's quite right to think a somewhat different world will follow if we think we can build a world that reflects our interest rather than reflects its suppression. The necessity of suppression, of triumphant law, is still a truism among critical theorists. We have yet to escape not so much civilization-as-law as the Freud-like theory of it, the modernist theory of civilization as perpetual sacrifice. The starting point in this escape is not thought but the experience of pleasantness, the experience of one's own unlimited interest.[38]

Finally, I want to consolidate what to me is such a crucial realization about the limit point of separate spheres discourse. Discomfort with a self not founded on defense, on shame about pleasantness, on the usual dichotomy between productivity and indulgence—this is where separate spheres ideology takes its last stand.

MS: I'd like to end with a last look at Hawthorne. I suggested earlier that the *Blithedale* "failure" occurs first and foremost as the "failed" relation between Hollingsworth and Coverdale, after which the other "failed" relations seem to pattern themselves. I want to assert, further, that the framework of Coverdale's erotic love for Hollingsworth is Delany's *avant la lettre*. What Coverdale mourns is the limit space reining in the very things that "move" him about Hollingsworth and his estimation that Delanyesque "contact" rather than Brooklyn domestic relations court "contract" would free them interpersonally and also free up the possibility of real utopia:

> Hollingsworth, at our solicitation, often ascended Eliot's pulpit, and —not exactly preached—but talked to us, his few disciples, in a strain that rose and fell as naturally as the wind's breath among the leaves of the birch-tree. No other speech of man has ever moved me like some

of those discourses. It seemed most pitiful—a positive calamity to the world—that a treasury of golden thoughts should thus be scattered, by the liberal handful, down among us three, when a thousand hearers might have been the richer for them. (119)

It's as if Coverdale has a sudden knowledge of what utopia might look like, listening to Hollingsworth, feeling inspired by him, and picturing that pleasure (of "golden thoughts . . . scattered") radiating out to everybody, "a thousand hearers" habitually. The love and physical delight he feels is pleasure-based (Hollingsworth-based), and his vision of utopia is simply the idea of pleasure shared outwardly with everybody, pleasure's multiplicity and its effects set free in the world: unmistakably metaphorized, here, by an ejaculation shower. But Coverdale understands too well that the way these four associates have, wittingly or not, ordered relations among themselves and with the rest of humanity stands in the way of each receiving all that each could: "a positive calamity to the world."

Notes

Christopher Newfield and Melissa Solomon would like to thank Cathy N. Davidson, Avery Gordon, Jessamyn Hatcher, Ellen Mickiewicz, and Barbara Herrnstein Smith, who each read this essay in various stages of its composition, and offered support, encouragement, and invaluable editorial guidance.

1 Silvan Tomkins, *Affect, Imagery, Consciousness* (New York: Springer, 1962), 1:370.
2 For Tomkins, "the affects constitute the primary motivational system" in humans. They have this primary status "not only because the drives necessarily require amplification from the affects, but because the affects are sufficient motivators in the absence of drives" (*Affect, Imagery, Consciousness,* 1:171). Though Tomkins notes the way that the eight (later nine) primary affects can be hard to distinguish, he stresses the sharp experiential differences between positive and negative affects, which roughly correlate with reward and punishment. The positive affects are enjoyment-joy and interest-excitement; the negative affects are distress-anguish, shame-humiliation, contempt-disgust, anger-rage, and fear-terror. (Tomkins describes *surprise-startle* as a "resetting" affect, and also added *dissmell* to disgust in later volumes.) Positive affects tend to correlate with social bonds. Tomkins conducted decades of empirical studies that linked minute changes in bodily states to affective changes, and his claims about causal connections are complex, too much so to entertain here. The specific sources of enjoyment or terror vary enormously from person to person: Tomkins thought he could always distinguish the physiological and affective changes that belong to a

positive affect like enjoyment from a negative affect like terror; he did not make the same claim about the external activators for each state, since the same stimulus could produce enjoyment in one person and terror in the next. Tomkins's biologism, which we reject, is radically qualified by his pervasive sense of the subject as a profoundly social and cultural being. "One does not understand the human being unless one knows what interests him and what he enjoys and how this came to be" (*Affect, Imagery, and Consciousness,* 1:396).

3 The phrase comes from the Sedgwick/Frank introduction to the Tomkins compendium, *Shame and Its Sisters: A Silvan Tomkins Reader,* ed. Eve Kosofsky Sedgwick and Adam Frank (Durham, N.C.: Duke University Press, 1995), 2.

4 The back-cover copy of the Penguin (1986) edition of *Blithedale* calls the novel "a superb depiction of a utopian community that cannot survive the individual passions of its members." The volume's editor, Annette Kolodny, offers a plausible, commonsense summation of the plot: "The fragile fabric of community that binds the four central characters is gradually rent as, one by one, each plays false to another and, together, they make a mockery of 'the blessed state of brotherhood and sisterhood, at which we aimed'" (xviii). Richard Poirier helped establish an influential opposition between affective and social life such that even when affect has value, it doesn't mix with society: Coverdale, he writes, believes "that participation in society can only thwart the exercise of feelings that are most God-like. This supposition in Hawthorne's Coverdale is made the rationale for a kind of non-sexual voyeurism" (*A World Elsewhere: The Place of Style in American Literature* [(1966) Madison: University of Wisconsin Press, 1985], 121). David Leverenz sees Coverdale's affect as in the service of "marketplace manhood," "translating any intimacy into power relations" (*Manhood and the American Renaissance* [Ithaca, N.Y.: Cornell University Press, 1989], 253. Gillian Brown argues that *Blithedale* repeats the tendency of Hawthorne's other "Gothic Revival romances" to make individuality dependent on "the elimination of work or women. . . . Coverdale's feelings exist largely to screen his ego from the anxiety that work and women cause" (*Domestic Individualism: Imagining Self in Nineteenth-Century America* [Berkeley and Los Angeles: University of California Press, 1990], 131). T. Walter Herbert writes that Coverdale "hungers like Priscilla for vicarious experience, with the difference that he is aware that the impulse serves a desire for psychic domination" (*Dearest Beloved: The Hawthornes and the Making of the Middle-Class Family* [Berkeley and Los Angeles: University of California Press, 1993], 29). These excerpts don't do justice to their authors' subtle readings. They do suggest a nearly continuous theme of positive affect's weakness before the will to domination.

5 American literary history, particularly when grounded in nineteenth-century studies, has tended to link affect to sentimentality. This tradition's landmark criticism appeared in Ann Douglas, *The Feminization of American Culture* ([1977] New York: Anchor, 1993). It received earlier formulations in such works as Her-

bert Ross Brown, *The Sentimental Novel in America* (Durham, N.C.: Duke University Press, 1940), F. O. Matthiessen, *The American Renaissance* (London: Oxford University Press, 1941), Leslie A. Fiedler, *Love and Death in the American Novel* (New York: Criterion, 1966), and became a baseline assumption in strong later readings of Hawthorne that include Joel Porte, *The Romance in America: Studies in Cooper, Poe, Hawthorne, Melville, and James* (Middletown, Conn.: Wesleyan University Press, 1969); Richard H. Brodhead, *Hawthorne, Melville and the Novel* (Chicago: University of Chicago Press, 1976); and Michael Davitt Bell, *The Development of the American Romance* (Chicago: University of Chicago Press, 1980).

6 The feminist defense of domestic feeling seems, in retrospect, to have peaked with Tompkins. Although gendered sentimentality continues to receive widespread attention, and in a long-overdue conjunction with other variables, particularly race, these studies do not accord affect much autonomy or generative force and tend to see it as subordinate to social power. A bellwether moment may have been Hawthorne critic Richard Brodhead's articulation of a Foucauldian functionalism in his 1987 *Representations* essay "Sparing the Rod," in which love was more or less identical with discipline and control. Brodhead's article was incorporated into a book, *Cultures of Letters: Scenes of Reading and Writing in Nineteenth-Century America* (Chicago: University of Chicago Press, 1993). For a fuller treatment of the issues raised by readings that "see through" sentiment, see Christopher Newfield, "Wayward Feelings," *American Quarterly* 50, no. 2 (June 1998): 440–46. For other complex readings of the work of sentimentality, see Hazel V. Carby, *Reconstructing Womanhood* (New York: Oxford University Press, 1987); Lora Romero, *Home Fronts: Domesticity and its Critics in the Antebellum United States* (Durham, N.C.: Duke University Press, 1997); Karen Sánchez-Eppler, *Touching Liberty: Abolition, Feminism, and the Politics of the Body* (Berkeley and Los Angeles: University of California Press, 1993); Harryette Mullen, "Runaway Tongue: Resistant Orality in *Uncle Tom's Cabin, Our Nig, Incidents in the Life of a Slave Girl,* and *Beloved,*" in *The Culture of Sentiment: Race, Gender, and Sentimentality in Nineteenth-Century America,* ed. Shirley Samuels (New York: Oxford University Press, 1992), 244–64, Dana Nelson, *The Word in Black and White* (New York: Oxford University Press, 1993), Saidiya V. Hartman, *Scenes of Subjection* (New York: Oxford University Press, 1997); Elizabeth Barnes, *States of Sympathy: Seduction and Democracy in the American Novel* (New York: Columbia University Press, 1997), Shirley Samuels, *Romances of the Republic* (Oxford: Oxford University Press, 1996), Julia A. Stern, *The Plight of Feeling* (Chicago: University of Chicago Press, 1997), William L. Andrews, *To Tell a Free Story* (Urbana: University of Illinois Press, 1988); Lauren Berlant, *The Anatomy of National Fantasy: Hawthorne, Utopia, and Everyday Life* (Chicago: University of Chicago Press, 1991); Lori D. Ginzberg, *Woman and the Work of Benevolence* (New Haven, Conn.: Yale University Press, 1990); Valerie Smith, *Self-Discovery and Au-*

thority in Afro-American Narrative (Cambridge: Harvard University Press, 1987); and Jean Fagin Yellin, *Women and Sisters* (New Haven, Conn.: Yale University Press, 1989).

7 In contrast, Silvan Tomkins's notion of positive affect emerges from his understanding of "interest": "Psychoanalysis and Behaviorism have regarded interest as a secondary phenomenon, a derivative of the drives, as though one could be interested only in what gave or promised drive satisfaction. We have turned this argument upside down. It is interest or excitement . . . which is primary, and the drives are secondary. . . . Excitement, rather than being a derivative of drives, is the major source of drive amplification" (*Shame and Its Sisters*, 76). This sounds simple enough but is in fact radical; it means that the ego is not essentially or primarily defensive, preoccupied with detecting and diverting whatever seems different from itself—its own strong (drive-like) feelings and other people's feeling in particular. Its default position is interest—interest in itself, interest in the other. Positive affect, then, is associated with uninhibited interest, something like "free interest." As we will see, it is especially associated with shame-free interest. In defining the ego as an effect of interest rather than defense, Tomkins means to be scientific and not political or idealistic. Interest is adaptive, essential to cognitive and physical development. See *Shame and Its Sisters*.

8 According to Tomkins: "positive affect should be maximized; negative affect should be minimized; affect inhibition should be minimized; power to maximize positive affect, to minimize negative affect, to minimize affect inhibition should be maximized" (*Shame and Its Sisters*, 67).

9 Samuel Delany, *Times Square Red, Times Square Blue* (New York: New York University Press, 1999), 121. Hereafter, citations will appear parenthetically in the text.

10 Nina Baym, *Woman's Fiction: A Guide to Novels by and about Women in America, 1820–1870* (Ithaca, N.Y.: Cornell University Press, 1978), 26.

11 Nancy F. Cott, *The Bonds of Womanhood: "Woman's Sphere" in New England, 1780–1835* (New Haven, Conn.: Yale University Press, 1977), 71.

12 Carroll Smith-Rosenberg, *Disorderly Conduct: Visions of Gender in Victorian America* (New York: Oxford University Press, 1985), 60.

13 Baym, *Women's Fiction*, 27. In addition to the other works already mentioned, my thinking was indebted to pioneering work on the role of sentiment and emotions in nineteenth-century private life and gender relations by Mary P. Ryan, *Empire of the Mother: American Writing about Domesticity, 1830–1860* (New York: Institute for Research in History/Haworth Press, 1985), and Christine Stansell, *City of Women: Sex and Class in New York, 1789–1860* (Urban: University of Illinois Press, 1986); and Smith-Rosenberg, *Disorderly Conduct*.

14 Herbert, *Dearest Beloved*, 14. On the problem of "setting up the family as a model for politics" in the period's fiction, see Brown, *Domestic Individualism* and Barnes, *States of Sympathy*, 19.

15 Carole Pateman, *The Disorder of Women* (Stanford, Calif.: Stanford University Press, 1989), 129.

16 Jane Tompkins, *Sensational Designs: The Cultural Work of American Fiction, 1790–1860* (New York: Oxford University Press, 1985), 128, 141, 144.

17 For example, Cott wrote that "the ultimate function of the home was *in* the world" in the sense that "it was to fit men to pursue their worldly aims in a regulated way" (*Bonds of Womanhood*, 98).

18 Leverenz, *Manhood and the American Renaissance*, 258.

19 Ibid., 253.

20 J. Laplanche and J.-B. Pontalis, *The Language of Psycho-Analysis*, trans. Donald Nicholson-Smith (New York: Norton, 1973), 255. Emphasis in original.

21 For more on affect in relation to political life, see Berlant, *Anatomy of National Fantasy*. Berlant posits that "the *political* space of the nation," or "the National Symbolic," harnesses "affect to political life through the production of 'national fantasy'" (5).

22 For a reading of Zenobia's emotions as "typically female," see Brodhead, *Hawthorne, Melville, and the Novel*. Brodhead claims that "Zenobia emotionally submits to Hollingsworth's masculine strength of vision" (95).

23 Nathaniel Hawthorne, *The Blithedale Romance* ([1852] New York: Penguin, 1983), 70. Citations hereafter will appear parenthetically in the text.

24 Sigmund Freud, *The Standard Edition of the Complete Psychological Works of Sigmund Freud*. Trans. James Strachey, with Anna Freud (London: Hogarth Press, 1953–1974), 19:29. Hawthorne anticipates Freud and later theorists such as Judith Butler, who writes that "the lost object continues to haunt and inhabit the ego. . . . The lost object is . . . made coextensive with the ego itself." See Judith Butler, *The Psychic Life of Power* (Stanford, Calif.: Stanford University Press, 1997), 134.

25 A similar process is discussed somewhat differently in Butler, "Melancholy Gender/Refused Identifications," in chapter five of *Psychic Life of Power*.

26 In his response to Butler's reading of melancholia as constitutive both of the ego and its gender, Adam Phillips offers a parallel suggestion: "If, as Butler suggests, 'masculinity' and 'femininity' are formed and consolidated through identifications that are composed in part of disavowed grief, what would it be like to live in a world that acknowledged and sanctioned such grief, that allowed us, as it were, the full course of our bereavement of disowned or renounced gender identities?" (quoted in Butler, *Psychic Life,* 154).

27 Tomkins, *Shame and Its Sisters*, 76.

28 I am thinking of Neil Hertz's notion of the sublime, which he defines as "the moment of blockage, when an indefinite and disarrayed sequence is resolved (at whatever sacrifice) into a one-to-one confrontation, when numerical excess can be converted into that supererogatory identification with the blocking agent that is the guarantor of the self's own integrity as an agent." See *The End of the Line:*

Essays on Psychoanalysis and the Sublime (New York: Columbia University Press, 1985), 53.

29 See Tomkins's example of a fundamental instance of shame as the parent shaming a child in the eyes of a playmate in *Shame and Its Sisters*, 175–76.

30 Delany posits that early porn films helped expand the sexual tastes of American men: "Without intending to be, these movies represented a tremendous sexual education for their working-class audience—in the case of New York City, mostly Hispanic, black, and Catholic white. . . . Generally, I suspect, pornography improved our vision of sex all over the country, making it friendlier, more relaxed, and more playful—qualities of sex that, till then, had been often reserved to a distressingly limited section of the better-read and more imaginative members of the middle classes" (78). Perhaps Delany hopes that, likewise, the frank and explicit cock-worshiping prurience of his own life stories in *Times Square Red, Times Square Blue* will help tutor the next generation of Coverdales.

31 Tomkins, *Shame and Its Sisters*, 45.

32 The phrase is Tom Scheff's, emeritus professor of sociology at the University of California, Santa Barbara, and a theorist of shame. Thanks to Avery Gordon for pointing me to this term.

33 Tomkins writes:

> The conventional concept of causality, which generated the pseudo-problem of the freedom of the will, assumed that the relationship between events was essentially two-valued, either determinate or capricious, and that man's will was therefore either slavishly determined or capriciously free. We feel, however, that this controversy concerns man's degrees of freedom rather than the determinateness of his behavior. The solution to this problem lies in the acceptance of *both* the causality principle and what may be described as the information, complexity, or degrees-of-freedom principle . . . By complexity, we mean . . . the number of independently variable states of a system . . . The freedom of any feedback system, is consequently, a conjoint function of its complexity and the complexity of its surround. (*Shame and Its Sisters*, 35–36)

34 This is not true for all societies, but it is true for our highly organized and administered one.

35 Raymond Williams, *Marxism and Literature* (Oxford: Oxford University Press, 1977), 128.

36 On domesticity's ongoing regulation of public life, see Lauren Berlant, *The Queen of America Goes to Washington City: Essays on Sex and Citizenship* (Durham, N.C.: Duke University Press, 1997).

37 On one's self as the lost object of mourning, see especially Nicholas Abraham and Maria Torok, *The Shell and the Kernel*, ed. Nicholas T. Rand (Chicago: University of Chicago Press, 1994), vol. 1, chap. 6.

38 To our ears this of course sounds simplistic—don't we always show interest? Isn't it largely constituted by society and its laws? What's the difference between conditioned "interest" and "real" interests? Aren't some interests dangerous and destructive? (I should add, for the record, that Delany sharply distinguishes between public sex and the violent, destructive practices common to the Times Square area in the crack era of the mid-1980s, suggesting that anyone who doesn't abhor that terror is a "moral imbecile.") Such questions about interest can't be settled here, and they show the risk of linking a child of empirical psychology like Tomkins to a child of poststructuralism like Delany. But I find their convergence more interesting than my doubts about their epistemologies.

SELECTED BIBLIOGRAPHY

This bibliography contains a selection of contemporary criticism useful in formulating and studying the "separate spheres" debate.

Abelove, Henry. "Some Speculations on the History of 'Sexual Intercourse' during the 'Long Eighteenth Century' in England." *Gender* 6 (1989): 125–30.

Abraham, Nicolas, and Maria Torok. *The Shell and the Kernel,* vol. 1. Ed. Nicholas T. Rand. Chicago: University of Chicago Press, 1994.

Acuña, Rodolfo. *Occupied America: A History of Chicanos.* 3d ed. New York: Harper and Row, 1988.

Ammons, Elizabeth. "Going in Circles: The Female Geography of Jewett's *Country of the Pointed Firs.*" *Studies in the Literary Imagination* 16 (fall 1983): 83–92.

———. *Conflicting Stories: American Women Writers at the Turn into the Twentieth Century.* New York: Oxford University Press, 1991.

Anderson, Benedict. *Imagined Communities: Reflections on the Origin and Spread of Nationalism.* London: Verso, 1983.

Andrews, William L. *To Tell a Free Story.* Urbana: University of Illinois Press, 1988.

Appadurai, Arjun. "Disjuncture and Difference in the Global Cultural Economy." In *Modernity at Large: Cultural Dimensions of Globalization.* Minneapolis: University of Minnesota Press, 1996.

Appiah, Anthony. *In My Father's House: Africa and the Philosophy of Culture.* New York: Oxford University Press, 1992.

Armstrong, Nancy. *Desire and Domestic Fiction: A Political History of the Novel.* New York: Oxford University Press, 1987.

Aron, Cindy Sondik. *Ladies and Gentlemen of the Civil Service: Middle-Class Workers in Victorian America.* New York: Oxford University Press, 1987.

Baker, Houston A., Jr. *Workings of the Spirit: The Poetics of Afro-American Women's Writing.* Chicago: University of Chicago Press, 1991.

Bardes, Barbara, and Suzanne Gossett. *Declarations of Independence.* New Brunswick, N.J.: Rutgers University Press, 1990.

Barnes, Elizabeth. *States of Sympathy: Seduction and Democracy in the American Novel.* New York: Columbia University Press, 1996.

Bausch, Norma. *In the Eyes of the Law: Women, Marriage, and Property in Nineteenth-Century New York.* Ithaca, N.Y.: Cornell University Press, 1982.

Baym, Nina. *Woman's Fiction: A Guide to Novels by and about Women in America, 1820–1870.* Ithaca, N.Y.: Cornell University Press, 1978.

———. "Melodramas of Beset Manhood: How Theories of American Fiction Exclude Women Authors." *American Quarterly* 33 (summer 1981): 123–39.

———. "Onward Christian Women: Sarah J. Hale's History of the World." *New England Quarterly* 63 (June 1990): 249–270.

———. "Reinventing Lydia Sigourney." *American Literature* 62 (September 1990): 385–404.

———. *American Women Writers and the Work of History, 1790–1860.* New Brunswick, N.J.: Rutgers University Press, 1995.

Bell, Michael Davitt. *The Development of the American Romance.* Chicago: University of Chicago Press, 1980.

Bercovitch, Sacvan. *The Rites of Assent: Transformations in the Symbolic Construction of America.* New York: Routledge, 1993.

Berlant, Lauren. *The Anatomy of National Fantasy: Hawthorne, Utopia, and Everyday Life.* Chicago: University of Chicago Press, 1991.

———. "Pax Americana: The Case of *Show Boat.*" In *Institutions of the Novel,* ed. W. B. Warner and Deidre Lynch. Durham, N.C.: Duke University Press, 1996.

———. *The Queen of America Goes to Washington City: Essays on Sex and Citizenship.* Durham, N.C.: Duke University Press, 1997.

———. "Intimacy: A Special Issue." *Critical Inquiry* 24 (winter 1998): 281–88.

———. "The Subject of True Feeling: Pain, Privacy, and Politics." In *Cultural Pluralism, Identity Politics, and the Law,* ed. Austin Sarat. Ann Arbor: University of Michigan Press, 1999.

Bertolini, Vincent. "Fireside Chastity: The Erotics of Sentimental Bachelorhood in the 1850s." *American Literature* 68 (Dec. 1996): 707–37.

Berzon, Judith. *Neither White nor Black: The Mulatto Character in American Fiction.* New York: New York University Press, 1978.

Blanchard, Paula. *Sarah Orne Jewett: Her World and Her Work.* Reading, Mass.: Addison-Wesley, 1994.

Brodhead, Richard. *Hawthorne, Melville, and the Novel.* Chicago: University of Chicago Press, 1976.

———. *Culture of Letters: Scenes of Reading and Writing in Nineteenth-Century America.* Chicago: University of Chicago Press, 1993.

Brooks, Evelyn. "The Problem of Race in Women's History." In *Coming to Terms: Feminism/Theory/Politics,* ed. Elizabeth Weed. New York: Routledge, 1989.

Brown, Gillian. *Domestic Individualism: Imagining the Self in Nineteenth-Century America*. Berkeley and Los Angeles: University of California Press, 1990.

Brown, Herbert Ross. *The Sentimental Novel in America*. Durham, N.C.: Duke University Press, 1940.

Brown, Wendy. "Wounded Attachments: Late Modern Oppositional Political Formations." In *The Identity in Question,* ed. John Rajchman. New York: Routledge, 1995.

Buhle, Mari Jo. *Women and American Socialism, 1870–1920*. Urbana: University of Illinois Press, 1981.

Burgett, Bruce. *Sentimental Bodies: Sex, Gender, and Citizenship in the Early Republic*. Princeton, N.J.: Princeton University Press, 1998.

Burstein, Andrew. *Sentimental Democracy: The Evolution of America's Romantic Self-Image*. New York: Hill and Wang, 1999.

Butler, Judith. *The Psychic Life of Power: Theories in Subjection*. Stanford, Calif.: Stanford University Press, 1997.

Carby, Hazel V. *Reconstructing Womanhood: The Emergence of the Afro-American Woman Novelist*. New York: Oxford University Press, 1987.

Castiglia, Christopher. "In Praise of Extra-vagant Women: *Hope Leslie* and the Captivity Romance." *Legacy* 6 (fall 1989): 3–16.

Castle, Terry. *The Apparitional Lesbian: Female Homosexuality and Modern Culture*. New York: Columbia University Press, 1993.

Cayton, Mary Kupiec. *Emerson's Emergence: Self and Society in the Transformation of New England, 1800–1845*. Chapel Hill: University of North Carolina Press, 1989.

Chapman, Mary, and Glenn Hendler, eds. *Sentimental Men: Masculinity and the Politics of Affect in American Culture*. Berkeley and Los Angeles: University of California Press, 1999.

Chauncey, George. "From Sexual Inversion to Homosexuality: Medicine and the Changing Conceptualization of Female Deviance." *Salmagundi* 58–59 (fall–winter 1982): 114–46.

———. *Gay New York: Gender, Urban Culture, and the Making of the Gay Male World, 1890–1940*. New York: Basic Books, 1994.

Chudacoff, Howard. *The Age of the Bachelor: Creating an American Subculture*. Princeton, N.J.: Princeton University Press, 1999.

Cixous, Hélène. "Laugh of the Medusa." In *Critical Theory since 1965,* ed. Hazard Adams and Leroy Searle. Tallahassee: Florida State University Press, 1989.

Collins, Patricia Hill. *Black Feminist Thought: Knowledge, Consciousness, and the Politics of Empowerment*. New York: Routledge, 1990.

Cook, Blance Wiesen. "Female Support Networks and Political Activism: Lillian Wald, Chrystal Eastman, Emma Goldman." *Chrysalis* 3 (1977): 43–61.

Cooke, Michael. "Modern Black Autobiography in the Tradition." In *Romanticism: Vistas, Instances, and Continuities,* ed. David Thornburn and Geoffrey Hartman. Ithaca, N.Y.: Cornell University Press, 1973.

Cornelius, Janet Duitsman. *When I Can Read My Title Clear: Literacy, Slavery, and Religion*. Columbia: University of South Carolina Press, 1992.

Cott, Nancy F. *The Bonds of Womanhood: "Woman's Sphere" in New England, 1780–1835*. New Haven, Conn.: Yale University Press, 1977.

———. "Passionlessness: An Interpretation of Victorian Sexual Ideology, 1790–1850." *Signs* 4 (winter 1978): 219–36.

Cott, Nancy F., and Elizabeth H. Pleck. *A Heritage of Her Own: Toward a New Social History of American Women*. New York: Simon and Schuster, 1979.

Cowan, Ruth Schwartz. *More Work for Mother: The Ironies of Household Technology from the Open Hearth to the Microwave*. New York: Basic Books, 1983.

Cunningham, George. "'Called into Existence': Gender, Desire, and Voice in Douglass' *Narrative of 1845*." *differences: A Journal of Feminist Cultural Studies* 1 (1989): 108–36.

Davidson, Cathy N. *Revolution and the Word: The Rise of the Novel in America*. New York: Oxford University Press, 1986.

———., ed. *Reading in America: Literary and Social History*. Baltimore, Md.: Johns Hopkins University Press, 1989.

Davis, Angela Y. *Women, Race, and Class*. New York: Vintage, 1981.

Davis, Thadious. *Nella Larsen, Novelist of the Harlem Renaissance: A Woman's Life Unveiled*. Baton Rouge: Louisiana State University Press, 1994.

Dearborn, Mary. *Pocahontas's Daughters: Gender and Ethnicity in American Culture*. New York: Oxford University Press, 1986.

Degler, Carl N. *At Odds: Women and the Family in America from the Revolution to the Present*. New York: Oxford University Press, 1980.

DeJean, Joan. *Fictions of Sappho, 1546–1937*. Chicago: University of Chicago Press, 1989.

Diggs, Marylynne. "Romantic Friends or a 'Different Race of Creatures'?: The Representation of Lesbian Pathology in Nineteenth-Century America." *Feminist Studies* 21 (summer 1995): 317–40.

Donaldson, Laura. *Decolonizing Feminisms: Race, Gender, and Empire-Building*. Chapel Hill: University of North Carolina Press, 1992.

Donovan, Josephine. *Sarah Orne Jewett*. New York: Frederick Ungar, 1980.

Douglas, Ann. *The Feminization of American Culture*. New York: Anchor, 1993 [1977].

Dublin, Thomas, ed. *From Farm to Factory: Women's Letters, 1830–1860*. New York: Columbia University Press, 1981.

Du Bois, Ellen, Mari Jo Buhle, Temma Kaplan, Gerda Lerner, and Carroll Smith-Rosenberg. "Politics and Culture in Women's History: A Symposium." *Feminist Studies* 6 (spring 1980): 26–64.

duCille, Ann. *The Coupling Convention: Sex, Text, and Tradition in Black Women's Fiction*. New York: Oxford University Press, 1993.

Dudden, Faye E. *Serving Women: Household Service in Nineteenth-Century America*. Middletown: Wesleyan University Press, 1983.

Dudley, David. *My Father's Shadow: Intergenerational Conflict in African American Men's Autobiography.* Philadelphia: University of Pennsylvania Press, 1991.

Dye, Nancy Schrom. *As Equals and as Sisters: Feminism, the Labor Movement, and the Women's Trade Union League of New American Feminism.* New York: Columbia University Press, 1980.

Elshtain, Jean Bethke. *Public Man, Private Woman: Woman in Social and Political Thought.* Princeton, N.J.: Princeton University Press, 1981.

Engels, Friedrich. *The Origin of the Family, Private Property, and the State.* Ed. Eleanor Burke Leacock. New York: International Publishers, 1972.

Epstein, Barbara. *The Politics of Domesticity: Women, Evangelism, and Temperance in Nineteenth-Century America.* Middletown, Conn.: Wesleyan University Press, 1981.

Erickson, Erik H. "Inner and Outer Space: Reflections on Womanhood." In *The Woman in America,* ed. Robert Jay Lifton. Boston: Houghton Mifflin, 1965.

Faderman, Lillian. "Lesbian Magazine Fiction in the Early Twentieth Century." *Journal of Popular Culture* 11 (1978): 800–817.

———. *Surpassing the Love of Men: Romantic Friendship and Love Between Women From the Renaissance to the Present.* New York: William Morrow, 1981.

Fanon, Frantz. *Black Skins, White Masks.* Trans. Charles Lam Markmann. New York: Grove Press, 1967.

Fetterley, Judith. "Reading *Deephaven* as a Lesbian Text." In *Sexual Practice/Textual Theory: Lesbian Cultural Criticism,* ed. Susan J. Wolfe and Julia Penelope. Cambridge, Mass.: Basil Blackwell, 1993.

———. "Nineteenth-Century American Women Writers and the Politics of Recovery." *American Literary History* 6 (fall 1994): 385.

Fetterley, Judith, and Marjorie Pryse, eds. *American Women Regionalists 1850–1910: A Norton Anthology.* New York: Norton, 1992.

Fiedler, Leslie A. *Love and Death in the American Novel.* New York: Criterion, 1960.

Fisher, Philip. "American Literary and Cultural Studies since the Civil War." In *Redrawing the Boundaries: The Transformation of English and American Literary Studies,* ed. Stephen Greenblatt and Giles Gunn. New York: Modern Language Association, 1992.

Fishkin, James S. *The Voice of the People: Public Opinion and Democracy.* New Haven, Conn.: Yale University Press, 1995.

Foucault, Michel. *The History of Sexuality: An Introduction,* vol. 1. Trans. Robert Hurley. New York: Vintage, 1980.

Fox-Genovese, Elizabeth. "Placing Women's History in History." *New Left Review* (May–June 1982): 5–29.

———. *Within the Plantation Household: Black and White Women of the Old South.* Chapel Hill: University of North Carolina Press, 1988.

Fraser, Nancy. *Unruly Practices: Power, Discourse, and Gender in Contemporary Social Theory.* Minneapolis: University of Minnesota Press, 1989.

———. "Sex, Lies, and the Public Sphere: Some Reflections on the Confirmation of Clarence Thomas. *Critical Inquiry* 18 (spring 1992): 595–612.

———. "Rethinking the Public Sphere: A Contribution to the Critique of Actually Existing Democracy." In *The Phantom Public Sphere,* ed. Bruce Robbins. Minneapolis: University of Minnesota Press, 1993.

Freedman, Estelle. "Separatism as Strategy: Female Institution Building and American Feminism, 1870–1930." *Feminist Studies* 5 (fall 1979): 512–29.

Freud, Sigmund. *Three Essays on the Theory of Sexuality.* Trans. James Strachey. New York: Basic Books, 1962 [1905].

Friedan, Betty. *The Feminine Mystique.* New York: Norton, 1963.

Garber, Eric. "A Spectacle of Color: The Lesbian and Gay Subculture of Jazz Age Harlem." In *Hidden from History: Reclaiming the Gay and Lesbian Past,* ed. Martin Duberman, Martha Vicinus, and George Chauncey. New York: Meridian, 1990.

Garber, Marjorie. *Vested Interests: Cross Dressing and Cultural Anxiety.* New York: HarperCollins, 1992.

Gates, Henry Louis, Jr., ed. *Reading Black, Reading Feminist: A Critical Anthology.* New York: Meridian, 1990.

———. *Figures in Black: Words, Signs, and the "Racial" Self.* New York: Oxford University Press, 1997.

Gilroy, Paul. *The Black Atlantic: Modernity and Double Consciousness.* Cambridge: Harvard University Press, 1993.

Glenn, Evelyn Nakano. *Issei, Nisei, War Bride.* Philadelphia: Temple University Press, 1986.

Gonzales-Berry, Erlinda, and Chuck Tatum, eds. *Recovering the U.S. Hispanic Literary Heritage,* vol. 2. Houston, Tex.: Arte Público Press, 1996.

González, John M. "Romancing Hegemony: Constructing Racialized Citizenship in María Amparo Ruiz de Burton's *The Squatter and the Don.*" In *Recovering the U.S. Hispanic Literary Heritage,* vol. 2, ed. Erlinda Gonzales-Berry and Chuck Tatum.

Gordon, Linda. *Heroes of Their Own Lives: The Politics and History of Family Violence in Boston, 1880–1960.* New York: Viking, 1988.

Gossett, Thomas F. Uncle Tom's Cabin *and American Culture.* Dallas, Tex.: Southern Methodist University Press, 1985.

Gould, Philip. "Catharine Sedgwick's 'Recital' of the Pequot War." *American Literature* 66 (Dec. 1994): 641–62.

Gregg, Gary L. *The Presidential Republic: Executive Representation and Deliberative Democracy.* New York: Rowman and Littlefield, 1997.

Grewal, Inderpal. *Home and Harem: Nation, Gender, Empire, and the Cultures of Travel.* Durham, N.C.: Duke University Press, 1996.

Grewal, Inderpal, and Caren Kaplan. "Warrior Marks: Global Womanism's Neo-Colonial Discourse in a Multicultural Context." *Camera Obscura* 39 (Sept. 1996): 5–33.

Griffin, Farah Jasmine. *"Who Set You Flowin'?": The African-American Migration Narrative*. New York: Oxford University Press, 1995.

Grimshaw, Patricia. *Paths of Duty: American Missionary Wives in Nineteenth-Century Hawaii*. Honolulu: University of Hawaii Press, 1989.

Gubar, Susan. "Sapphistries." *Signs* 10 (autumn 1984): 43–62.

Haas, Lisbeth. *Conquests and Historical Identities in California, 1769–1938*. Berkeley and Los Angeles: University of California Press, 1995.

Halperin, David. "Is There a History of Sexuality?" In *The Lesbian and Gay Studies Reader*, ed. Henry Abelove, Michèle Aina Barala, and David M. Halperin. New York: Routledge, 1993.

Hanchard, Michael. "Black Cinderella?: Race and the Public Sphere Collective." In *The Black Public Sphere*, ed. Black Public Sphere Collective. Chicago: University of Chicago Press, 1995.

Hansen, Karen, ed. *African Encounters with Domesticity*. New Brunswick, N.J.: Rutgers University Press, 1992.

Hartman, Saidiya H. *Scenes of Subjection*. New York: Oxford University Press, 1997.

Hayden, Dolores. *The Grand Domestic Revolution: A History of Feminist Designs for American Homes, Neighborhoods, and Cities*. Cambridge: Harvard University Press, 1981.

Herbert, T. Walter. *Dearest Beloved: The Hawthornes and the Making of the Middle-Class Family*. Berkeley and Los Angeles: University of California Press, 1993.

Hertz, Neil. *The End of the Line: Essays on Psychoanalysis and the Sublime*. New York: Columbia University Press, 1985.

Holloway, Karla F. C. *Moorings and Metaphors: Figures of Culture and Gender in Black Women's Literature*. New Brunswick, N.J.: Rutgers University Press, 1992.

Honig, Bonnie. *Political Theory and the Displacement of Politics*. Ithaca, N.Y.: Cornell University Press, 1993.

hooks, bell. *Feminist Theory: Thinking Feminist, Thinking Black*. Boston: South End Press, 1989.

Horsman, Reginald. *Race and Manifest Destiny: The Origins of American Racial Anglo-Saxonism*. Cambridge: Harvard University Press, 1981.

Horton, James Oliver, and Lois E. Horton. *Black Bostonians: Family Life and Community Struggle in the Antebellum North*. New York: Holmes and Meier, 1979.

Howard, June. "Unraveling Regions, Unsettling Periods: Sarah Orne Jewett and American Literary History." *American Literature* 68 (June 1996): 365–84.

———. ed. *New Essays on* The Country of the Pointed Firs. New York: Cambridge University Press, 1994.

Hull, Gloria T., Patricia Scott Bell, and Barbara Smith. *All the Women Are White, All the Blacks Are Men, But Some of Us Are Brave*. Old Westbury, N.Y.: Feminist Press, 1982.

Jones, Jacqueline. *Labor of Love, Labor of Sorrow: Black Women, Work, and the Family from Slavery to the Present*. New York: Basic Books, 1985.

Jordan, Winthrop. *White over Black: American Attitudes toward the Negro, 1550–1812.* Baltimore, Md.: Penguin, 1969.

Kaplan, Amy. *The Social Construction of American Realism.* Chicago: University of Chicago Press, 1989.

———. "Nation, Region, and Empire." In *The Columbia History of the American Novel,* ed. Emory Elliot. New York: Columbia University Press, 1991.

Kaplan, Amy, and Donald E. Pease, eds. *Cultures of United States Imperialism.* Durham, N.C.: Duke University Press, 1993.

Kaplan, Caren. *Questions of Travel: Postmodern Discourses of Displacement.* Durham, N.C.: Duke University Press, 1996.

Kaplan, Carla. *The Erotics of Talk: Women's Writing and Feminist Paradigms.* New York: Oxford University Press, 1996.

Katz, Jonathan. "The Invention of Heterosexuality." *Socialist Review* 20 (1990): 17–34.

Kelley, Mary. *Private Woman, Public Stage: Literary Domesticity in Nineteenth-Century America.* New York: Oxford University Press, 1984.

Kelley, Mary, ed. *The Power of Her Sympathy: The Autobiography and Journals of Catharine Maria Sedgwick.* Boston: Massachusetts Historical Association, 1993.

Kerber, Linda K. "The Republican Mother: Women and the Enlightenment—An American Perspective." *American Quarterly* 28 (summer 1976): 187–205.

———. *Women of the Republic: Intellect and Ideology in Revolutionary America.* Chapel Hill: University of North Carolina Press, 1980.

———. "Separate Spheres, Female Worlds, Woman's Place: The Rhetoric of Women's History." Lecture given at University of Richmond. 92 min. 1984. Videocassette.

———. *Toward an Intellectual History of Women.* Chapel Hill: University of North Carolina, 1997.

Kerber, Linda K., Nancy F. Cott, Robert Gross, Lynn Hunt, Carroll Smith-Rosenberg, and Christine M. Stansell. "Beyond Roles, Beyond Spheres: Thinking about Gender in the Early Republic." *William and Mary Quarterly* 46 (July 1989): 565–85.

Kessler-Harris, Alice. *Out to Work: A History of Wage-Earning Women in the United States.* New York: Oxford University Press, 1982.

Kilcup, Karen, ed. *Soft Canons: American Women Writers and Masculine Tradition.* Iowa City: University of Iowa Press, 1999.

Kolodny, Annette. *Lay of the Land: Metaphor as Experience and History in American Life and Letters.* Chapel Hill: University of North Carolina Press, 1975.

———. *The Land before Her: Fantasy and Experience in the American Frontiers, 1630–1860.* Chapel Hill: University of North Carolina Press, 1984.

Koppelman, Susan. *Two Friends.* New York: Meridian-Penguin, 1994.

Kostenbaum, Wayne. *Double Talk: The Erotics of Male Literary Collaboration.* New York: Routledge, 1989.

Kraditor, Aileen S., ed. *Up from the Pedestal: Selected Writings in the History of American Feminism.* Chicago: Quadrangle Books, 1968.

Lacan, Jacques. *Écrits.* Trans. Alan Sheridan. New York: Norton, 1977.

Lang, Amy Scrager. *Prophetic Woman: Anne Hutchinson and the Problem of Dissent in the Literature of New England.* Berkeley and Los Angeles: University of California Press, 1987.

———. "Slavery and Sentimentalism: The Strange Career of Augustine St. Clare." *Women's Studies* 12 (Feb. 1996): 31–54.

Lerner, Gerda. "The Lady and the Mill Girl: Changes in the Status of Women in the Age of Jackson." *Midcontinent American Studies Journal* 10 (spring 1969): 5–15.

———. *The Creation of Patriarchy.* New York: Oxford University Press, 1986.

Leverenz, David. *Manhood and the American Renaissance.* Ithaca, N.Y.: Cornell University Press, 1989.

Lewis, David Levering. *W. E. B. Du Bois: Biography of a Race, 1869–1919.* New York: Henry Holt, 1993.

Lewis, Jan. "The Republican Wife: Virtue and Seduction in the Early Republic." *William and Mary Quarterly* 44 (Oct. 1987): 689–721.

Lloyd, David, and Lisa Lowe, eds. *The Politics of Culture in the Shadow of Capital.* Durham, N.C.: Duke University Press, 1997.

Lott, Eric. *Love and Theft: Blackface Minstrelsy and the American Working Class.* New York: Oxford University Press, 1993.

Lummis, C. Douglas. *Radical Democracy.* Ithaca, N.Y.: Cornell University Press, 1996.

Lurie, Susan. *Unsettled Subjects: Restoring Feminist Politics to Poststructuralist Critique.* Durham, N.C.: Duke University Press, 1997.

McKendrick, Neil. "Home Demand and Economic Growth." In *Historical Perspectives: Studies in English Thought and Society in Honour of J. H. Plumb,* ed. Neil McKendrick. London: Europa, 1974.

Marks, Elaine. "Lesbian Intertextuality." In *Homosexualities and French Literature,* ed. George Stambolian and Elaine Marks. Ithaca, N.Y.: Cornell University Press, 1978.

Massey, Doreen. *Space, Place, and Gender.* Minneapolis: University of Minnesota Press, 1984.

Matthiessen, F. O. *The American Renaissance.* London: Oxford University Press, 1941.

McClintock, Anne. *Imperial Leather: Race, Gender, and Sexuality in the Colonial Contest.* New York: Routledge, 1995.

McDowell, Deborah E. *"The Changing Same": Black Women's Literature, Criticism, and Theory.* Bloomington: Indiana University Press, 1995.

McGaw, Judith A. "No Passive Victims, No Separate Spheres: A Feminist Perspective on Technology's History." In *In Context: History and the History of Technology: Essays in Honor of Mel Kranzberg,* ed. Stephen Cutcliffe and Robert C. Post. Bethlehem, Pa.: Lehigh University Press, 1989.

Merish, Lori. "'The Hand of Refined Taste' in the Frontier Landscape: Caroline Kirkland's *A New Home, Who'll Follow?* and the Feminization of American Consumerism." *American Quarterly* 45 (Dec. 1993): 485–523.

Michaels, Walter Benn. *The Gold Standard and the Logic of Naturalism: American Literature at the Turn of the Century.* Berkeley and Los Angeles: University of California Press, 1987.

Mitchell, Juliet. *Woman's Estate.* New York: Pantheon, 1971.

Mobley, Marilyn. *Folk Roots and Mythic Wings in Sarah Orne Jewett and Toni Morrison.* Baton Rouge: Louisiana State University Press, 1991.

Moon, Michael. *Disseminating Whitman: Revision and Corporeality in* Leaves of Grass. Cambridge: Harvard University Press, 1991.

———. *A Small Boy and Others: Imitation and Initiation in American Culture from Henry James to Andy Warhol.* Durham, N.C.: Duke University Press, 1997.

Morrison, Toni. *Playing in the Dark: Whiteness and the Literary Imagination.* Cambridge: Harvard University Press, 1992.

Naylor, Gloria. "Love and Sex in the Afro-American Novel." *Yale Review* 78 (1988): 19–31.

Nelson, Dana. *The Word in Black and White.* New York: Oxford University Press, 1993.

———. *National Manhood: Capitalist Citizenship and the Imagined Fraternity of White Men.* Durham, N.C.: Duke University Press, 1998.

Newfield, Christopher. "What Was Political Correctness? Race, the Right and Managerial Democracy in the Humanities." *Critical Inquiry* 19, no. 2 (1993): 308–36.

———. *The Emerson Effect: Individualism and Submission in America.* Chicago: University of Chicago Press, 1996.

———. "Wayward Feelings." *American Quarterly* 50, no. 2 (June 1998): 440–46.

Norton, Mary Beth. *Liberty's Daughters: The Revolutionary Experience of American Women, 1750–1800.* Boston: Little, Brown, 1980.

Padilla, Genaro M. *My History, Not Yours: The Formation of Mexican American Autobiography.* Madison: University of Wisconsin Press, 1993.

Pateman, Carole. *The Disorder of Women.* Stanford, Calif.: Stanford University Press, 1989.

Patterson, Anita Haya. *From Emerson to King: Democracy, Race, and the Politics of Protest.* Oxford: Oxford University Press, 1997.

Peiss, Kathy. "Going Public: Women in Nineteenth-Century Cultural History." *American Literary History* 3 (winter 1991): 817–28.

Pérez-Torres, Rafael. *Movements in Chicano Poetry: Against Myths, Against Margins.* New York: Cambridge University Press, 1995.

Person, Leland. "The American Eve: Miscegenation and a Feminist Frontier Fiction." *American Quarterly* 37 (winter 1985): 668–85.

Pryse, Marjorie. "Archives of Female Friendship and the 'Way' Jewett Wrote." *New England Quarterly* 66 (March 1993): 47–66.

————. "'Distilling Essences': Regionalism and 'Women's Culture.'" *American Literary Realism* 25 (winter 1993): 1–15.

————. "Reading Regionalism and the 'Difference' It Makes." In *Regionalism Reconsidered: New Approaches to the Field*, ed. David Jordan. New York: Garland, 1994.

Pryse, Marjorie, and Hortense Spillers, ed. *Conjuring: Black Women, Fiction, and Literary Tradition*. Bloomington: Indiana University Press, 1985.

Rafael, Vicente L. "Colonial Domesticity: White Women and United States Rule in the Phillipines." *American Literature* 67 (Dec. 1996): 639–66.

Rampersad, Arnold. "Slavery and the Literary Imagination: Du Bois's *The Souls of Black Folk*." In *Slavery and the Literary Imagination*, ed. Deborah E. McDowell and Arnold Rampersad. Baltimore, Md.: Johns Hopkins University Press, 1989.

Rebelledo, Tey Diana. *Women Singing in the Snow: A Cultural Analysis of Chicana Literature*. Tuscon: University of Arizona Press, 1995.

Renza, Louis. *"A White Heron" and the Question of Minor Literature*. Madison: University of Wisconsin Press, 1984.

Rich, Adrienne. *On Lies, Secrets, and Silence*. New York: Norton, 1979.

Richardson, Robert D., Jr. *Emerson: The Mind on Fire*. Berkeley and Los Angeles: University of California Press, 1995.

Robinson, Lillian. "Treason in Our Text: Feminist Challenges to the Literary Canon." *Tulsa Studies in Women's Literature* 2 (spring 1983): 83–98.

Rodríguez, Manuel M. Marítin. "Textual and Land Reclamations: The Critical Reception of Early Chicana/o Literature." In *Recovering the U.S. Hispanic Literary Heritage*, vol. 2, ed. Erlinda Gonzales-Berry and Chuck Tatum. Houston, Tex.: Arte Público Press, 1996.

Roman, Margaret. *Sarah Orne Jewett: Reconstructing Gender*. Tuscaloosa: University of Alabama Press, 1992.

Romero, Lora. "Vanishing Americans: Gender, Empire, and New Historicism." *American Literature* 63 (Sept. 1991): 385–404.

————. *Home Fronts: Domesticity and Its Critics in the Antebellum United States*. Durham, N.C.: Duke University Press, 1997.

Rosenberg, Rosalind. *Beyond Separate Spheres: Intellectual Roots of Modern Feminism*. New Haven, Conn.: Yale University Press, 1982.

Ryan, Mary P. *Cradle of the Middle Class: The Family in Oneida County, New York, 1790–1865*. Cambridge: Cambridge University Press, 1981.

————. *Empire of Mother: American Writing about Domesticity, 1830–1860*. New York: Institute for Research in History/Haworth Press, 1982.

————. "Gender and Public Access." In *Habermas and the Public Sphere*, ed. Craig Calhoun. Cambridge: MIT Press, 1992.

Salvídar, José David. *Border Matters: Remapping American Cultural Studies*. Berkeley and Los Angeles: University of California Press, 1997.

Samuels, Shirley, ed. *The Culture of Sentiment: Race, Gender, and Sentimentality in Nineteenth-Century America*. New York: Oxford University Press, 1992.

Sánchez-Eppler, Karen. *Touching Liberty: Abolition, Feminism, and the Politics of the Body.* Berkeley and Los Angeles: University of California Press, 1993.

———. "Raising Empires like Children: Race, Nation, and Religious Education." *American Literary History* 8 (fall 1996): 399–425.

Sánchez, Rosaura. *Telling Identities: The Californio Testimonios.* Minneapolis: University of Minnesota Press, 1995.

Sánchez, Rosaura, and Beatrice Pita, eds. Introduction to *The Squatter and the Don,* by María Amparo Ruiz de Burton. Houston, Tex.: Arte Público Press, 1992.

———. Introduction to *Who Would Have Thought It?*, by María Amparo Ruiz de Burton. Houston, Tex.: Arte Público Press, 1995.

Scott, Joan W. "Gender: A Useful Category of Historical Analysis." *American Historical Review* 91 (Dec. 1986): 1053–72.

———. *Only Paradoxes to Offer: French Feminists and the Rights of Man.* Cambridge: Harvard University Press, 1996.

Sedgwick, Eve Kosofsky. *Between Men: English Literature and Male Homosocial Desire.* New York: Columbia University Press, 1985.

———. *Epistemology of the Closet.* Berkeley and Los Angeles: University of California Press, 1990.

Sedgwick, Eve Kosofsky, and Adam Frank, eds. Introduction to *Shame and Its Sisters: A Silvan Tomkins Reader,* by Silvan Tomkins. Durham, N.C.: Duke University Press, 1995.

Sellers, Charles. *The Market Revolution: Jacksonian America, 1815–1846.* New York: Oxford University Press, 1991.

Sharp, James Roger. *American Politics in the Early Republic: The New Nation in Crisis.* New Haven, Conn.: Yale University Press, 1993.

Sherman, Sarah Way. *Sarah Orne Jewett: An American Persephone.* Hanover, N.H.: University Press of New England, 1989.

Sicherman, Barbara, et al. *Recent United States Scholarship on the History of Women.* Washington, D.C.: American Historical Association, 1980.

Silverman, Kaja. *Male Subjectivity at the Margins.* New York: Routledge, 1992.

Sklar, Katherine Kish. *Catharine Beecher: A Study in American Domesticity.* New Haven, Conn.: Yale University Press, 1973.

Smith, Daniel Scott. "Family Limitation, Sexual Control, and Domestic Feminism in Victorian America." In *Clio's Consciousness Raised,* ed. Mary S. Hartman and Lois W. Banner. New York: Octagon, 1974.

Smith, Valerie. *Self-Discovery and Authority in Afro-American Narrative.* Cambridge: Harvard University Press, 1987.

Smith-Rosenberg, Carroll. "The Female World of Love and Ritual: Relations between Women in Nineteenth-Century America." *Signs* 1 (autumn 1975): 1–29. Rpt. in Smith-Rosenberg, *Disorderly Conduct: Visions of Gender in Victorian America.* New York: Oxford University Press, 1985.

Snyder, Katherine V. *Bachelors, Manhood, and the Novel, 1850–1925*. New York: Cambridge University Press, 1999.

Spillers, Hortense J. "Mama's Baby, Papa's Maybe: An American Grammar Book." *Diacritics* 17 (1987): 65–81.

———. "The Permanent Obliquity of an In(ph)allibly Straight." In *Changing Our Own Words: Essays on Criticism, Theory, and Writing by Black Women*, ed. Cheryl Wall. New Brunswick, N.J.: Rutgers University Press, 1989.

———, ed. *Comparative American Identities: Race, Sex, and Nationality in the Modern Text*. New York: Routledge, 1991.

Stansell, Christine. *City of Women: Sex and Class in New York, 1789–1860*. Urbana: University of Illinois Press, 1986.

Sterling, Dorothy, ed. *We Are Your Sisters: Black Women in the Nineteenth Century*. New York: Norton, 1984.

Stern, Julia A. *The Plight of Feeling: Sympathy and Dissent in the Early American Novel*. Chicago: University of Chicago Press, 1997.

Stoler, Ann. *Race and the Education of Desire: Foucault's* History of Sexuality *and the Colonial Order of Things*. Durham, N.C.: Duke University Press, 1995.

Strasser, Susan. *Never Done: A History of American Housework*. New York: Pantheon, 1982.

Sundquist, Eric J. *To Wake the Nations: Race in the Marking of American Literature*. Cambridge: Harvard University Press, 1993.

Tate, Claudia. "Allegories of Black Female Desire: Or, Rereading Nineteenth-Century Sentimental Narratives of Black Female Authority." In *Changing Our Own Words: Essays on Criticism, Theory, and Writing by Black Women*, ed. Cheryl Wall. New Brunswick, N.J.: Rutgers University Press, 1989.

———. *Domestic Allegories of Political Desire: The Black Heroine's Text at the Turn of the Century*. New York: Oxford University Press, 1992.

Tennenhouse, Leonard, and Philip Gould, eds. "America the Feminine," a special issue of *differences: A Journal of Feminist Cultural Studies* 11, no. 3 (1999/2000).

Tentler, Leslie Woodcock. *Wage-Earning Women: Industrial Work and Family Life in the United States, 1900–1930*. New York: Oxford University Press, 1979.

Thomson, Rosemarie Garland. "Benevolent Maternalism and Physically Disabled Figures: Dilemmas of Female Embodiment in Stowe, Davis, and Phelps." *American Literature* 68 (Sept. 1996): 555–86.

Tichi, Cecilia. "Women Writers and the New Woman." In *Columbia Literary History of the United States*, ed. Emory Elliott. New York: Columbia University Press, 1988.

Tobias, Shiela, and Ruth Milkman. *Gender at Work: The Dynamics of Job Segregation by Sex during World War II*. Urbana: University of Illinois, 1987.

Tompkins, Jane. *Sensational Designs: The Cultural Work of American Fiction, 1790–1860*. New York: Oxford University Press, 1985.

Ulrich, Laurel Thatcher. *Good Wives: Image and Reality in the Lives of Women in Northern New England, 1650–1750.* New York: Random House, 1982.

Van Leer, David. "Reading Slavery: The Anxiety of Ethnicity in Douglass's *Narrative.*" In *Frederick Douglass: New Literary and Historical Essays,* ed. Eric Sundquist. New York: Cambridge University Press, 1990.

Walker, Peter. *Moral Choices: Memory, Desire, and Imagination in Nineteenth-Century Abolition.* Baton Rouge: Louisiana State University Press, 1978.

Warner, Michael. *The Letters of the Republic: Publication and the Public Sphere in Eighteenth-Century America.* Cambridge: Harvard University Press, 1990.

———, ed. *Fear of a Queer Planet: Queer Politics and Social Theory.* Minneapolis: University of Minneapolis Press, 1993.

Washington, Mary Helen. *Invented Lives: Narratives of Black Women, 1860–1960.* Garden City, N.J.: Anchor Press, 1987.

Welter, Barbara. "The Cult of True Womanhood: 1820–1860." *American Quarterly* 18 (summer 1966): 151–74.

———. *Dimity Convictions: The American Woman in the Nineteenth Century.* Athens: Ohio University Press, 1976.

White, Deborah Gray. *Ar'n't I a Woman? Female Slaves in the Plantation South.* New York: Norton, 1985.

Wiegman, Robyn. *American Anatomies: Theorizing Race and Gender.* Durham, N.C.: Duke University Press, 1995.

Williams, Patricia. *The Alchemy of Race and Rights.* Cambridge: Harvard University Press, 1988.

Williams, Raymond. *Marxism and Literature.* Oxford: Oxford University Press, 1977.

Yellin, Jean Fagin. *Women and Sisters: The Antislavery Feminists in American Culture.* New Haven, Conn.: Yale University Press, 1989.

CONTRIBUTORS

José F. Aranda Jr. is Associate Professor of Chicano/a and American Literature in the English Department of Rice University. He is the author of numerous articles on early U.S. criticism, nineteenth-century Mexican American literature, and the future of Chicano/a studies, as well as the book *When We Arrive: Literature, Colonial History, and the Politics of a Chicano Nation* (2001). He has begun work on a book tentatively entitled "Why I Dreamed of Jeannie But Became a Chicano Instead," as well as a long-term project writing the cultural biography of nineteenth-century Californio writer María Amparo Ruiz de Burton.

Lauren Berlant is Professor of English at the University of Chicago and coeditor of *Critical Inquiry.* She is the author of *The Anatomy of National Fantasy: Hawthorne, Utopia, and Everyday Life* (1991) and *The Queen of America Goes to Washington City: Essays on Sex and Citizenship* (Duke University Press, 1997). Her edited works include *Intimacy* (2000); with Laura Letinsky, *Venus Inferred* (2000); and with Lisa Duggan, *Our Monica, Ourselves: Clinton and the Affairs of State* (2001). Her essay in this volume is from the forthcoming *The Female Complaint: The Unfinished Business of Sentimentality in American Culture.*

Cathy N. Davidson is Ruth F. DeVarney Professor of English, Vice-Provost for Interdisciplinary Studies, the founding co-director of the John Hope Franklin Institute at Duke University, and the general editor of the Oxford University Press Early American Women Writers Series. She has published numerous books, including *Revolution and the Word: The Rise of the Novel in America* (1986), *Reading in America: Literature and Social History* (1989), *The Book of Love: Writers and Their Love Letters* (1992), *Thirty-Six Views of Mount Fuji: On Finding Myself in Japan* (1993), and with Linda Wagner-Martin, *The Oxford Companion to Women's Writing* *in the United States* (1995) and *The Oxford Book of Women's Writing in the United States* (1995). In collaboration with photographer Bill Bamberger, her most recent book is *Closing: The Life and Death of an American Factory* (1998).

Judith Fetterley is Professor of English and Women's Studies and Associate Dean of Undergraduate Studies at the University of Albany, State University of New York. She is the author of *The Resisting Reader* (1978) and of *Provisions: A Reader from Nineteenth-Century American Women Regionalists, 1850–1910* (1992). With Jo-anne Dobson and Elaine Showalter, she founded the Rutgers University Press American Women Writers series. Most recently, she has completed, with Marjorie Pryse, a forthcoming critical study of nineteenth-century American women regionalists, titled *Locating Regionalism: History, Theory, and the Reading of Nineteenth-Century American Women Writers.*

Jessamyn Hatcher is a Ph.D. candidate in the department of English at Duke University. She is writing a dissertation called "Psychoanalysis and Everyday Life: The Popularization of Psychoanalysis in the United States, 1909–1935."

Amy Kaplan is Professor of English and American Studies at Mount Holyoke College. She is the author of *The Social Construction of American Realism* (1988), as well as the forthcoming *The Anarchy of Empire in American Culture,* and coeditor of *Cultures of United States Imperialism.*

Linda K. Kerber is the May Brodbeck Professor in the Liberal Arts and Sciences and Professor of History at the University of Iowa. She is the author of the prize-winning *No Constitutional Right to Be Ladies: Women and the Obligations of Citizenship* (1998). Her other books include *Federalists in Dissent: Imagery and Ideology in Jeffersonian America* (1970), *Women of the Republic: Intellect and Ideology in Revolutionary America* (1980), and *Toward an Intellectual History of Women* (1997). She is coeditor of *U.S. History as Women's History* (1995), and of the anthology *Women's America: Refocusing the Past* (2000). She is the advisory editor to the Gender and American Culture series of the University of North Carolina Press.

Dana D. Nelson is Professor of English and Social Theory at the University of Kentucky. Author of *The Word in Black and White: Reading Race in American Literature, 1638–1862* (1992), *National Manhood: Capitalist Citizenship and the Imagined Fraternity of White Men* (Duke University Press, 1998) and coeditor, with Russ Castronovo, of *Materializing Democracy* (Duke University Press, forthcoming), she is currently working on a book-length project from which her essay in this volume is drawn, "Representative/Democracy."

Christopher Newfield is Professor of English at the University of California, Santa Barbara. He is the author of *Criticism, Inc.: The Humanities and Modern Manage-*

ment (Duke University Press, forthcoming) and *The Emerson Effect: Individualism and Submission in America* (1996). He coedited *After Political Correctness: The Humanities and Society in the 1990s* (1995) and *Mapping Multiculturalism* (1996).

You-me Park teaches in the Justice and Peace program at Georgetown University. She has written on the areas of gender, labor, and sexuality for a wide range of international journals including *Interventions* and *Positions*.

Marjorie Pryse is Professor of English and Chair of the Department of Women's Studies at the University of Albany, State University of New York. She and Judith Fetterley, who edited together *American Women Regionalists, 1850–1910* (1992), have also coauthored *Locating Regionalism: History, Theory, and the Reading of Nineteenth-Century American Women Writers* (forthcoming).

Elizabeth Renker, Associate Professor at Ohio State University, is the author of *Strike Through the Mask: Herman Melville and the Scene of Writing* (1996). She is currently writing a cultural history of American literature as a field of study in the United States from 1865–1950.

Ryan Schneider is Assistant Professor of English and Comparative Literature at San Diego State University. His essay in this volume, "How to Be a (Sentimental) Race Man: Mourning and Passing in W. E. B. Du Bois's *The Souls of Black Folk*," also appears in the collection *Boys Don't Cry?: Rethinking Narratives of Masculinity and Emotion in America* (2002).

Melissa Solomon is a Ph.D. candidate in the Department of English at Duke University. She has previously published an essay on Henry James in *Novel Gazing: Queer Readings in Fiction* edited by Eve Kosofsky Sedgwick (Duke University Press, 1997) and is the author of "Flaming Iguanas, Dalai Pandas, and Other Lesbian Bardos," an essay in the forthcoming *Regarding Sedgwick: Essays on Queer Culture and Critical Theory*. She is writing a dissertation titled "Queer American Ladies and Friends" on lesbian allegory and affect in turn-of-the-century American literature.

Siobhan B. Somerville is Associate Professor of English and Women's Studies at Purdue University, where she also teaches in the American Studies Program. She is the author of *Queering the Color Line: Race and the Invention of Homosexuality in American Culture* (Duke University Press, 2000). She has also published work in *American Literature, Journal of the History of Sexuality,* and *Concerns*.

Gayle Wald is author of *Crossing the Line: Racial Passing in Twentieth-Century U.S. Literature and Culture* (Duke University Press, 2000). She is currently Assistant Professor of English at George Washington University.

Maurice O. Wallace is Professor of English and African American Studies at Duke University. He is the author of *Constructing the Black Masculine: Identity and Ideality in African American Men's Literature and Culture, 1775–1996* (forthcoming, Duke University Press). He is currently at work on a book called *Hostile Witness: James Baldwin as Artist and Outlaw.*

Autobiography (*continued*)
Douglass, Frederick; *Narrative of the Life of Frederick Douglass* (Frederick Douglass); *Up from Slavery* (Booker T. Washington); Psychoanalysis

"An Autumn Holiday" (Sarah Orne Jewett): "category crisis" in, 165; class and, 162; gender and, 161–162, 164; listening in, 165; marriage and, 163–164, 166; narrative structure of, 162, 164; sexuality and, 162; transvestitism in, 160–164, 165. *See also* Jewett, Sarah Orne

Baldwin, James: *The Devil Finds Work*, 313; on mass culture, 314; and revolution, 314. *See also* "Everybody's Protest Novel" (James Baldwin)

Beecher, Catharine: imperialism and, 185, 187–193. *See also* Separate spheres; *A Treatise on Domestic Economy* (Catharine Beecher)

Beloved (Toni Morrison): as post-sentimental text, 319–320; *Uncle Tom's Cabin* and, 219–320

Black feminism. *See* Separate spheres: black feminists' critiques of

Black women: subjectivities of, 264, 278–279. *See also* African American literature; African American women writers; *individual authors and works*

Blithedale Romance (Nathaniel Hawthorne): affect, undertheorized in critical readings of, 379, 403 n.4; asymmetrical desire in, 388–391; Coverdale, 383–394, 401–402; epistemology in, 386; Sigmund Freud and, 387, 390; interest (affect of), 391; David Leverenz on, 383; loss and, 390–391; love in, 385–386, 389; melancholia, 387–391; passion in, 378–379, 381, 386–388; post-domestic in, 390–

392; professionalism, 392; queerness in, 384–387, 390, 401–402; repression and, 383; separate spheres and, 381, 383, 386; shame and, 391–392; transitivity, 385–386; utopia in, 378, 383–384, 401

The Bridges of Madison County (Robert James Waller): archival, 317; critique of heterosexuality in, 314; love in, 316–317; as post-sentimental text, 314–318; *Uncle Tom's Cabin* and, 314, 318

Brodhead, Richard, 13. *See also* Jewett, Sarah Orne: Richard Brodhead on

Canon, the literary: and the politics of recovery, 68, 122; feminist transformation of, 17; New Criticism and, 68; relationship to separate spheres, 15–18; and women's exclusion from, 15. *See also* Chicano/a Studies: conferring canonical status in; Feminism: and the literary canon

Capitalism: amnesia and, 399; interest (affect of) and, 399; relationship to separate spheres, 41–42, 45, 48, 399. *See also* Pleasure: capitalism and; Sentimentality: capitalism and; *Uncle Tom's Cabin* (Harriet Beecher Stowe): capitalism and; *Who Would Have Thought It?* (María Ruiz de Burton): United States as model of nation, democracy, and capitalism in

Carby, Hazel, 210–212, 223

Chicano/a Studies: conferring canonical status in, 137; postcolonial theory and, 141, 148 n.36; Recovering the U.S. Hispanic Literary Heritage Project, 123; resistance theory and, 122–124, 141; María Ruiz de Burton, place in, 122–125, 132, 140–141

Citizenship: African Americans and,

Democracy (*continued*)
(Mason L. Weems): radical democracy vs. presidential representivity and; President: containment of radical democracy through; *Who Would Have Thought It?* (María Ruiz de Burton): United States as model of nation, democracy, and capitalism in

Diggs, Marylynne, 218

Dimples (Williams Seiter, dir.): class and, 306–308; democracy and, 307–308; the Depression in, 308, 309; gender and, 307–309; history and, 305, 307–308; politico-sentimental in, 307; sentimental pedagogy in, 306, 308; public/private in, 306; race and, 307–308; slavery and, 305, 307, 309; Shirley Temple in, 305–309; *Uncle Tom's Cabin* and, 305–309

Domestic fiction, 201–203; relationships between interiors and exteriors in, 201. *See also* Domestic(ity)

Domestic(ity): borders of, 184–185, 187–189, 193–194, 201; and race, 185–186, 270; relationship to "foreign," 183–203; and tyranny, 382, 396; and U.S. imperialism, 183–204; women's influence in, 188–203; World War II and, 265, 277. See also *Blithedale Romance* (Nathaniel Hawthorne): postdomestic in; Domestic fiction; *The Floating World* (Cynthia Kadohata): domesticity in; Hale, Sarah Josepha: and "imperial domesticity"; Imperialism, U.S.; *Maud Martha* (Gwendolyn Brooks): domesticity in; Separate spheres: domesticity and; *A Treatise on Domestic Economy* (Catharine Beecher): and "imperial domesticity"

Douglas, Ann, 16

Douglass, Frederick: *My Bondage and My Freedom,* 244. See also *Narrative of the Life of Frederick Douglass* (Frederick Douglass); Slavery: Frederick Douglass on; *Up from Slavery* (Booker T. Washington): influence on Frederick Douglass

DuBois, W. E. B.: comparisons with Ralph Waldo Emerson, 356–372; death of son, 357–360, 362–363, 368, 371–372; *The Philadelphia Negro,* 359; public intellectualism and, 356–360, 362–364, 366, 370, 372; and race, 356, 359, 363–364, 366–371; sentimentality and, 356–358, 360, 362–363, 367, 371–372; son and social change, 360, 366; son as sacred and intellectual heir, 358, 360, 362, 366, 370–371. *See also* Color line, the: W. E. B. DuBois on; Emerson, Ralph Waldo: comparisons with W. E. B. DuBois; "Of the Passing of the First Born" (W. E. B. DuBois)

DuCille, Ann, 212, 229

Dunn, Mary Maples, 50

Ellis, Havelock, 159

Emerson, Ralph Waldo: comparisons with W. E. B. DuBois, 356–372; death of son, 257–261, 264–265, 372; public intellectualism and, 356–358, 364–365, 372; race and, 356; sentimentality and, 356–358, 365, 372; son as intellectual heir, 358–359, 364, 372. *See also* DuBois, W. E. B.: comparisons with Ralph Emerson Waldo; "Experience" (Ralph Waldo Emerson); "Thernody" (Ralph Waldo Emerson)

"Experience" (Ralph Waldo Emerson): compared to "Thernody"; detachment in, 359–360; loss in, 361, 365–366, 372; philosophy of, 363; as unsentimental, 360. *See also* Emerson, Ralph Waldo; "Thernody" (Ralph Waldo Emerson)

"Everybody's Protest Novel" (James

Baldwin): on *Native Son,* 312–133; as post-sentimental text, 311–313; truth, 312; on *Uncle Tom's Cabin,* 311–313. *See also* Baldwin, James

Faderman, Lillian, 158–159, 218
Fanon, Franz, 238–239, 245
Feminism: backlash against, 13; and generational conflict, 3, 5; and the literary canon, 17; moralism within, 185; race, class, and, 154, 155, 176 n.24. *See also* Canon, the literary: feminist transformation of; Marxism: feminist critiques of; Separate spheres: black feminist critiques of; Separate spheres: feminist historians' and literary critics' use of
The Floating World (Cynthia Kadohata): autonomy in, 280–282; domesticity in, 265, 280; family in, 281–282; mobility in, 281–282; private sphere in, 264, 280–282; public sphere in, 264, 280–282; subjectivity in, 264, 280–283; work in, 282
Fraser, Nancy, 25, 267, 283, 286 n.11
Freedom: confused with survival, 299; Silvan Tomkins on, 398. *See also* Pleasure: freedom and
Freeman, Estelle, 50–51

Garber, Marjorie, 160–161, 163, 172
Gates, Henry Louis Jr., 211, 240
Gender: as a category of analysis, 11, 21–23, 150; relationship to term "woman," 10–13. *See also* Affect: and gender; Affirmative Action: race and gender pitted against one another in; Autobiography, black male: gender formation in; Nation: gender relations in; Public sphere: gender and; Slavery: gender formation and; *individual authors and works*

Genovese-Fox, Elizabeth, 58 n.16
Glenn, Evelyn Nakano, 270

Hale, Sarah Josepha: Anglo-Saxonism and, 198–199; colonization of Africa and, 195–198, 202; female medical missionaries, 199–200; *Godey's Lady's Book,* 187, 193, 199; and "imperial domesticity," 185, 193–203; *Liberia,* 195–196; *Northwood,* 194–195; policing of "foreign" and, 194–197, 201; race and, 193, 195–199, 201; Thanksgiving Day and, 193–194, 198; views on slavery, 193, 195. *See also* Imperialism, U.S.; Separate spheres
Harlem Renaissance, 231 n.11; homosexuality and, 211–212
Hayden, Dolores, 51
Hertz, Neil, 406 n.28
Hietala, Thomas, 186
Hope Leslie (Catharine Sedgwick): as an anti-romantic text, 70, 74, 85; argument for gender equality in, 73, 78, 82, 84; and challenges to authority, 75; challenges to ideology of separate spheres in, 70–72; contradictory nature of, 77–88; critique of Charlotte Temple in, 70; and difference, 81–82; Hope Leslie as representative American in, 73, 76; imagining America in, 71, 80; relationship of gender to class and race in, 81, 83–84, 86, 88; representations of Anne Hutchinson in, 87–88; representations of Native Americans in, 79–84, 88; and "republican sisterhood," 71–74; and "reverence of the self," 75, 78; rhetorical complexity of, 78–79, 82–84; role of epistolary in, 72; significance of brother-sister relationships in, 72–74, 78, 83–84; significance of New Critical methodologies to, 68; significance of

Kessler-Harris, Alice, 48

The King and I (Rodgers and Hammerstein): body of the King in, 292, 294, 296; democracy and, 292–293; feeling in, 292, 298; female authorship, role in, 295, 298; identification and, 295; imperialism and, 291–292, 295; gender and, 293–294, 296; Abraham Lincoln and, 294–295; modernity in, 293–294; politico-sentimental in, 294, 296, 298–299; sexual slavery in, 293–295; soundtrack of, 296; *Uncle's Tom Cabin* in, 293–296, 298–299; violence in, 298

Lebsock, Suzanne, 44

Lerner, Gerda, 32–33, 38–39, 47 n.6

Life of Washington (Mason L. Weems), 335; body of Washington in, 335–336, 352 n.35; childhood in, 336–338, 341, 343; Hugh Crawford on, 335; paternal/fraternal in, 338–399, 341–342, 350 n.24; presidential representivity in, 327, 335, 338; private sphere in, 341; radical democracy vs. presidential representivity and, 332–333, 336, 338, 340, 342; sentimental pedagogy in, 327, 335–338, 340–341. *See also* Constitutionalism; President; Representation

Literature, minority: public and private in, 264; teaching of, 266. *See also* African American literature; African American women writers; Autobiography, black male; *individual authors and works*

Lloyd, David, 342

Marxism: feminist critiques of, 48; separate spheres and, 33–34. *See also* Separate spheres: Marxism and

Masculinity. See *Narrative of the Life of Frederick Douglass* (Frederick Douglass): masculinity in; President: and masculinity; *Up from Slavery* (Booker T. Washington): masculinity in

Matthiessen, F. O., 15

Maud Martha (Gwendolyn Brooks): African American soldiers in, 278–279; black women's subjectivity in, 264, 278–280; domesticity in, 265, 278, 280; mobility in, 280; private sphere in, 264; public sphere in, 264–265, 279

Melville, Herman: association between writing and women, 102–111, 118 n.62; *The Confidence-Man*, 101; and documentation of wife-beating, 94–96; and failure, 101; "Fragments from a Writing Desk," 104–105; *Mardi*, 108, 110, 111; "The Paradise of Bachelors and the Tartarus of Maids," 106–108; physical struggles with writing, 102; *Pierre*, 100–101, 110; relationship to readers in "Hawthorne and His Mosses," 101, 105; scholars' response to documentation of wife-beating, 93, 99; secrecy about writing and, 109; wife and daughters as copyists for, 108–110; violence and writing, 102, 104, 110–111; and "womanless fiction," 93, 111, 144 n.23

Mexican American(s): debate about heterogeneity of culture, 123; participation in hegemonic discourses, 124; "proletarian character" of, 123, 135; relations to left-activist politics, 123; role in American literary history, 124, 140

Mendívil, Tornel y: analysis of U.S. domination of Mexico, 121–122, 139–40; use of "the nation" concept, 121

Michaels, Walter Benn, 13

Miscegenation, 212

Mitchell, Juliet, 33–34

Morrison, Toni, 237. See also *Beloved* (Toni Morrison)

Motz, Marilyn, 42–43

Mulattas/mulattoes: Judith Berzon on, 214, 232 n.16; symbol for conflicts and tensions, 215; "tragic," 214, 232 n.17

Narrative of the Life of Frederick Douglass (Frederick Douglass): birth and, 239–240; George Cunningham on, 240; gender formation in, 244–246; masculinity in, 245–247; Oedipal model in, 244; panic in, 239; rape in, 241–242, 244–247; sexual subjectivity in, 241–246; David Van Leer on, 242–243, 246. *See also* Autobiography, black male; Douglass, Frederick; Slavery: Frederick Douglass on

Nation: gender relations in, 184

Nationalism. *See* Imperialism, U.S.: nationalism and; Jewett, Sarah Orne: nationalism, imperialism, and; *Native Speaker* (Chang-rae Lee): nationalism and; Separate spheres: nationalism and

Native Americans, 186. See also *Hope Leslie* (Catharine Sedgwick): representations of Native Americans in; Separate spheres: and Native Americans

Native Speaker (Chang-rae Lee): domesticity in, 265, 275–277; female labor in, 276–277; immigration in, 265, 275–277; Korean American patriarchy, 276–277; mobility, 276; nationalism and, 276; private sphere in, 264, 272, 275–277; public sphere in, 264, 272, 277, 279; sexuality and, 265, 272; subjectivities in, 264–265, 272, 275, 277; violence in, 272; white

women in, 265, 277; women's bodies, 272

"Of the Passing of the First-Born" (W. E. B. DuBois) appearance of son, 366–367, 370–371; critical reception of, 362, 368–370; loss, 362–363, 367–368; personal and public in, 368–371; place in *The Souls of Black Folk,* 360, 367–370; sentimentality and, 360, 362–363, 367–368, 370, 372. *See also* DuBois, W. E. B.

Passing: literary genre of, 213–124, 231 n.15, 234 n.44; and social construction of race, 223, 226. See also *Contending Forces* (Pauline E. Hopkins): passing in

Pateman, Carole, 382

Pedagogy, 21–22. See also *Dimples* (Williams Seiter, dir.): sentimental pedagogy in; *Life of Washington* (Mason L. Weems): sentimental pedagogy in; Literature, minority: teaching of; Sentimentality: and pedagogy; *Uncle Tom's Cabin* (Harriet Beecher Stowe): pedagogy and

Peiss, Kathy, 267

Pleasure, 377–378; capitalism and, 396, 399; freedom and, 378, 398; separate spheres and, 278, 396; utopia and, 378. *See also* Affect: relationship to pleasure; Separate spheres: pleasure/pleasure-phobia and; *Times Square Red, Times Square Blue* (Samuel Delany): and pleasure; Utopia: pleasure and

Post-sentimentality: definition of, 310–311; memory and, 311. See also *Beloved* (Toni Morrison): as postsentimental text; *The Bridges of Madison County* (Robert James Waller): as post-sentimental text; "Everybody's Protest Novel" (James Baldwin): as post-sentimental text; Sentimentality

President: containment of radical democracy through, 332–333, 338, 344; hard and soft bodies of, 333–334, 341, 351–352 n.32; history of, 331–334; loss and, 327, 334, 336; and masculinity, 333; and sentimentalism, 328; wholeness and, 333. *See also* Democracy: the president and; *Life of Washington* (Mason L. Weems); Sentimentality: presidentialism and

Private sphere: African American women's labor and, 270–272; Asian American women's labor and, 270–272; and immigration, 265; Japanese identity and, 265; Korean American women and, 265, 270; power and, 268; reordering of, 264, 277, 280; representations in minority literature, 264; social reality of, 264, 267–268; violence in, 269, 272. *See also* Asian American women: and the private sphere; *Contending Forces* (Pauline E. Hopkins): private space in; *Dimples* (Williams Seiter, dir.): public/private in; *The Floating World* (Cynthia Kadohata): the private sphere in; *Life of Washington* (Mason L. Weems): private sphere in; *Maud Martha* (Gwendolyn Brooks): private sphere in; *Native Speaker* (Chang-rae Lee): private sphere in; Sentimentality: public and private in; Separate spheres; *The Street* (Ann Petry): private sphere in; *Times Square Red, Times Square Blue* (Samuel Delany): public and private in; *Uncle Tom's Cabin* (Harriet Beecher Stowe): public and private in

Prop 187, 143

Psychoanalysis: and black male autobiography, 239; black subjectivity and, 238, 244, 258 n.2; influence on W. E. B. DuBois, Richard Wright, and Ralph Ellison, 238, 258 n.8

Public sphere: access to, 283; gender and, 269–271; interests represented in, 264; race and, 269–271; women's entrance into, 268, 280; women's labor and, 268–271. *See also Dimples* (Williams Seiter, dir.): public/private in; *The Floating World* (Cynthia Kadohata): public sphere in; Literature, minority: public and private in; *Maud Martha* (Gwendolyn Brooks): public sphere in; *Native Speaker* (Chang-rae Lee): public sphere in; "Of the Passing of the First-Born" (W. E. B. DuBois): personal and public in; Sentimentality: public and private in; Separate spheres; *The Street* (Ann Petry): public sphere in; *Times Square Red, Times Square Blue* (Samuel Delany): public and private in; *Uncle Tom's Cabin* (Harriet Beecher Stowe): public and private in

Race: black and white model of, 266; hybridity and, 266. *See also* Affirmative action: race and gender pitted against one another in debates about; Citizenship: and race; *Dimples* (Williams Seiter, dir.): race and; Domestic(ity): and race; DuBois, W. E. B.: and race; Emerson, Ralph Waldo: race and; Feminism: race, class, and; Hale, Sarah Josepha: race and; *Hope Leslie* (Catharine Sedgwick): relationship of gender to class and race in; Jewett, Sarah Orne: race and; Passing: and social construction of race; Public sphere: race and; Sentimentality: race and; Separate spheres: race and; *Uncle*

Race (*continued*)
Tom's Cabin (Harriet Beecher Stowe):
race and
Rampersad, Arnold, 238
Regionalism: as alternative cultural
vision, 149–150, 172, 179 n.56. See also
The Country of the Pointed Firs (Sarah
Orne Jewett); Jewett, Sarah Orne
Representation: citizens' affective relationship to, 326; citizens' expectations
of, 326; logic of constitutional, 327–
328, 333; normative practices of, 325;
presidentialism and, 327–328, 332–
333; U.S. history of, 326, 328–331. *See
also* Constitutionalism; Democracy:
representation and; *Life of Washington* (Mason L. Weems): presidential
representivity in; *Life of Washington*
(Mason L. Weems): radical democracy
vs. presidential representivity and
Resistance theory. *See* Chicano/a
Studies; *Who Would Have Thought
It?* (María Ruiz de Burton): status as
"resistance literature"
Rogin, Michael Paul, 336
Romero, Lora, 13, 84
Rosaldo, Michelle Zimbalist, 54
Ruiz de Burton, María: access to Anglo
cultural authority, 127, 130–133; biography of, 122, 125–32, 142; Californio
identity of, 124–126, 128–131, 138, 142;
Lisbeth Haas on, 128–129; as part of
white educated elite, 124–125, 128,
132, 135, 137–138, 142; relationship to
Jefferson Davis, 132–133; relationship
to Varina Davis, 132–133; relationship
to hegemonic discourses, 132–133;
relationship to Abraham Lincoln,
130–131; Rosaura and Beatrice Pita
Sánchez on, 124–128; *The Squatter and
the Don,* 127–129; status as "subaltern,"
123–124, 128, 130–132, 137, 142, 145

n.22, 148 n.37. *See also* Chicano/a
Studies; *Who Would Have Thought It?*
(María Ruiz de Burton)
Ryan, Mary P., 44–45, 188

Saldívar, José David, 142
Sappho: discovery of papyrus manu-
scripts of, 216, 233 n.31; Pauline E.
Hopkins and knowledge of, 216, 232
n.23; nineteenth-century narratives of,
215–216; racial identity of, 216–217.
See also *Contending Forces* (Pauline E.
Hopkins): use of the name "Sappho"
Scott, Joan, 69, 78
Sedgwick, Catharine: importance of,
67. See also *Hope Leslie* (Catharine
Sedgwick)
Sedgwick, Eve Kosofsky, 14, 157, 252.
See also Closet: Eve Kosofsky Sedgwick on
Sentimentality: James Baldwin on, 291;
and capitalism, 292, 297, 299, 301–304,
320; and citizenship, 292, 302; critique
of patriarchy and, 302; democracy
and, 345 n.4; and desire for social
equality, 301, 303, 339–440; and "difference," 295–297; and feeling and,
291, 201, 307, 310–311; as a form, 301;
femininity: 297, 299, 327–328, 340,
343–344; and history, 292, 303, 305;
identification and, 297, 299, 301, 303,
311, 320; male, 328, 338, 340, 345 n.3,
355; nation and, 299, 301–305, 327–
328, 339, 343–344; pain, suffering, and,
292–319; and pedagogy, 297–299,
304; politics of, 292, 294, 296–297,
299, 301–302, 319, 328, 340; power
and, 14, 328, 355, 382, 404 n.6; presidentialism and, 328, 336–337; public
and private in, 302, 304, 328, 340, 343–
344, 355; race and, 291, 356, 373 n.2;
slavery and, 303–305, 310; subalterns

Uncle Tom's Cabin (Harriet Beecher Stowe): capitalism and, 304; comics of, 300, 304; dance and, 304–305; Eliza and, 299–301; feeling and, 296, 301, 309; film versions of, 304–305, 309; gender and, 295; geography in, 201–202; heterosexuality and, 295; history and, 304; pedagogy and, 304; politics of, 296; public and private in, 304; race and, 295, 304; resistance to, 310; social change and, 296; slavery and, 304, 310; substitute for jeremiad, 309; theatrical productions of, 305; toy forms of, 303–304. See also *Beloved* (Toni Morrison): *Uncle Tom's Cabin* and; *The Bridges of Madison County* (Robert James Waller): *Uncle Tom's Cabin* and; *Dimples* (Williams Seiter, dir.): *Uncle Tom's Cabin* and; "Everybody's Protest Novel" (James Baldwin); *The King and I* (Rodgers and Hammerstein): *Uncle Tom's Cabin* and; Post-sentimentality; Sentimentality

Up from Slavery (Booker T. Washington): autobiographical genre and, 249; birth and, 239–240; fathers and, 239–240, 248, 254–257; gender formation in, 250; identity formation and, 247–253; influence on Frederick Douglass, 248, 261 n.37; masculinity in, 249–256; mothers in, 249; nudity and, 253; panic in, 239; physical space in, 249–250, 256; separate spheres and, 250; sexuality and, 241, 252, 253; white women in, 250–253. *See also* Autobiography, black male

Utopia, 394–395, 398; interest and, 399;

memory and, 399; pleasure and, 394. See also *Blithedale Romance* (Nathaniel Hawthorne): utopia in; *Time Square Red, Times Square Blue* (Samuel Delany): utopia and

Warner, Susan: *The Wide, Wide, World,* 201–202

Washington, Booker T. See *Up from Slavery* (Booker T. Washington)

Welter, Barbara, 31–33

Who Would Have Thought It? (María Ruiz de Burton): critiques of gender inequality and racism in, 133–135, 140; imagined intervention in U.S. domination of North America in, 122, 132, 142; importance to Chicano/a and American studies, 125, 140–141; Mexican-Spanish colonialism in, 141–142; postcolonial theory and, 141; representations of Mexico in, 132, 136, 138–139; Rosaura and Beatrice Pita Sánchez on, 134–137, 139, 141–142; satire of the United States in, 133–134; status as "resistance literature," 134–135, 141–142; support of constitutional monarchy in, 136–137; United States as model of nation, democracy, and capitalism in, 139–143. See also Chicano/a Studies; Colonialism; Ruiz de Burton, María

Williams, Raymond, 398

World War II: African American soldiers, citizenship and, 278; Japanese Americans and, 265, 281; women workers and, 265, 277. See also *Maud Martha* (Gwendolyn Brooks)

Library of Congress Cataloging-in-Publication Data
No more separate spheres! : A next wave American
studies reader / edited by Cathy N. Davidson
and Jessamyn Hatcher.
p. cm. — (Next wave)
Includes bibliographical references and index.
ISBN 0–8223–2878–X (cloth : alk. paper)
ISBN 0–8223–2893–3 (pbk. : alk. paper)
1. American literature—19th century—History and
criticism.   2. Women and literature—United States—
History—19th century.   3. Feminism and literature—
United States.   4. Sex role in literature.   I. Davidson,
Cathy N.   II. Hatcher, Jessamyn.   III. Next wave.
PS217.W64 N6   2002
810.9′003—dc21   2001054481